American Dreams

Book 2
A Family Born in the
Land of Promise Trilogy

BY

GWEN KARELLA MATHIS

Dedicated to Antonia Nemec Karella

If not for her courage, hard work, and faith in her Bohemian Dream, her descendants would never have been able to live their American Dreams.

Imagination Ex-Press

Preface

America at the Dawn of the 1920s

Post-World War I in America is an era of change and growth. As the 1920s begin, America becomes a world power, but there is a growing division between the rich and the working classes. For American farming, it is the beginning of a radical decline in profitability, production, and farm ownership.

However, industrialists like the Rockefellers and Copper King Clark are rapidly building fortunes through business trade monopolies. Railroad tycoons—like Vanderbilt with transcontinental railroad systems—control the price and profit of goods and services as they supply transit and freight systems linking the East and West Coasts of America. For them, business is booming. These new-money millionaires become the elite class, America's equivalent to European nobility.

With dwindling fortunes and the decline of European power in the aftermath of World War I, most of Europe's aristocracy is struggling to protect their inherited assets while they attempt to rebuild their decimated economies.

The 1920s also becomes a decade of learning and exploration, hailed by amazing invention and innovation in medicine, science, flight, communication technology, and mechanical farming mechanization.

This time period is accompanied by radical political and economic changes that come with the implementation of prohibition, women gaining the right to vote, and the crash of the US Stock Market.

In contrast to the rapid transformations happening in the world and the cities of America, the farming community of Madison, Nebraska, remains seemingly unchanged from when the Karella family first moves to the area over forty years earlier. Vaclav and Antonia Karella's children grow up, get married, and begin giving their parents grandchildren.

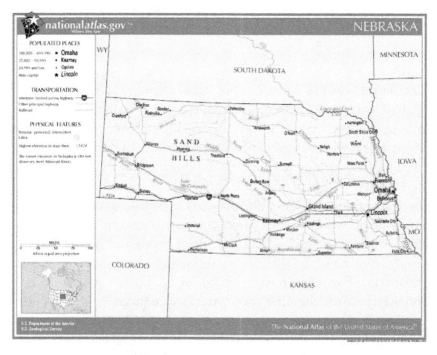

National Atlas Map of Nebraska—Free Media Wikimedia Commons

Real change is felt by the Karellas beginning with the loss of their matriarch, Antonia Karella, in 1900. Then, as 1921 arrives, grain prices drastically plunge, and the future begins to feel ominous. The following spring in April 1922, Anton Karella's wife, Anastasia, dies. This story picks up the Karella family history at the funeral wake held for Anastasia in May 1922.

CHART A
A CUMULATIVE TOTAL FOR THE DISPOSITION
OF NEBRASKA'S 49,031,680[a] ACRES OF LAND SURFACE

Years	Total acres encumbered—all classes of entries[b]	Total acres vacant and not appropriated	Improved Real Estate (acres)	Unimproved Real Estate (acres)	Original Homestead Entries (acres)	Final Homestead Entries (acres)	Original Timber Culture entries (acres)	Final Timber Culture entries (acres)
1870	5,342,237	39,766,357	647,031	1,426,750	1,921,516	104,357	————	————
1880	13,632,604	30,678,899	5,504,702	4,440,124	7,296,607	3,085,854	1,799,329	————
1890	35,103,185	11,226,584	15,247,705	6,345,739	16,587,534	6,575,763	8,681,428	363,712
1900	39,765,561	9,796,638	18,432,595	11,479,184	19,820,601	9,560,399	8,879,809	2,364,913
1910	56,511,282	1,379,486	24,382,777	14,239,454	34,614,710	11,862,568	8,876,351	2,546,698

[a] Territorial Nebraska had an estimated size of 219,160,320 acres.

[b] Railroad land grants from the United States to corporations in Nebraska totaled 7,641,755.78 acres and from the State (using internal improvement lands) 531,103 acres for a total of 8,172,859 acres. Grants to the State for common schools, public buildings, saline lands, land grant college and state university totaled 3,025,779 acres. The figures in the total acres encumbered column reflect railroad and state selections, generally in the decade in which this land was patented, or transferred to the State, and they show the repeated entries, under preemption, homestead and timber-culture laws on the same land. Federal reserved land was a small amount at this time.

Useful in compiling the figures on this chart were the *Annual Reports of the General Land Office*, the published U.S. Census returns and the land figures compiled by Addison E. Sheldon, James C. Olson, and Leslie E. Decker and used by them in their books.

LAND DISPOSAL IN NEBRASKA 1854–1906

287

Chart from Nebraska State History on Land Allocation for Land Grants and Land Disposal 1870–1910

[11] Addison E. Sheldon, *Land Systems and Land Policies in Nebraska*, (1936), pp. 59-60. Sheldon reported that land warrants in 1858 were selling at prices ranging from 75c to $1.00 an acre in New York and as much as $1.75 on a credit plan in Nebraska. Basic statistics are drawn from the United States Census Reports as well as the annual reports of the Nebraska State Board of Agriculture. The 1860 federal census reported 2,473 farms in Nebraska Territory, whereas a revised figure in the 1900 census was 2,789. Averages given were 203 and 226 acres respectively.

[12] *Nebraska Farmer*, June 1861. An enumeration of these expenses was:

A house	$250.
Breaking 40 acres	120.
500 walnut fence posts	25.
500 holes for posts	5.
Lumber for fence	125.
Nails	6.37
	$531.37

References from Nebraska State History—Nebraska Farmers Report Development Costs 1858–1861

Important History Notes about the Karella Farm

Anton J. Karella—Journal Entry

When I hit a difficult patch in my life, I think of what my parents, especially my mother, did for me and my brothers and sister. Immigrating to America and working our farm in Nebraska was the hardest and best thing our parents ever did. I know why we have thrived here. It is because of the farm. Working together to make the farm productive created security for our family. Our land is "A Quarter Section Homestead" and equals 100 acres of rolling open land and 60 acres of trees.

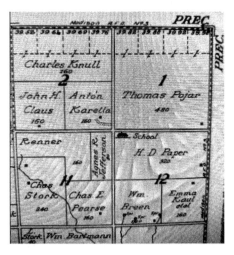

Stanislaus and I didn't know anything about farming when Papa moved us all to the homestead, but we were willing to learn. Fortunately, we had a good neighbor one mile from our home by the name of Thomas Pojar.

Image of Historical Madison land plat of Karella and Pojar Land locations, supplied by Rob Pfeifer

Thomas and his grandson, Rudy, taught Stanislaus and me most of what we had to know to get the farm producing grain. Our first undertaking was cultivating 20 acres of wheat in 1880, which yielded approximately 1,000 bushels and sold at approximately $1.17 per bushel, a net income of about $850.00. Each year, we plant a little more of the original 100 acres.

The crops we planted over the years have produced good yields, and by the 1900s, we now have several acres of corn-producing fields in addition to our wheat production, and the grain goes to market by train. The train depot is in Madison, making it a short haul to ship the grain after harvest.

Most of the farm chores we do by hand. In our community, children feed the small animals and gather eggs from chicken coops, mothers travel to town by horse and wagon, the men clean the outhouses, women handwash clothing and hang it outside on a line to dry in the yard, and children walk to school regardless of the weather.

Our lives are linked to the changing of the seasons. Time is measured by the work we need to get done between sunup to sundown, and we strive to keep Sundays reserved as a day of worship and for picnic gatherings.

The whole family works. We use our wits and talents as a team to help the family prosper. Papa and Mama taught us how to manage our money carefully and to spend what we need wisely.

Anton J. Karella—Journal Entry

All the local farmers and ranchers need lumber to build with. I put a plan together to build a sawmill, and I presented my sawmill idea to Papa. He liked it. We will cut down local trees, mill it into lumber, and sell it. Stanislaus has an idea too. He wants to buy the threshing machines we need for harvest, and then he wants to rent them when he is not using them on the farm. Papa has approved both of our ideas, and we are very excited about our new projects. It will mean more hard work, but we are excited about the future.

Image of historical advertisement of Karella businesses,
located and supplied by Rob Pfeifer

The Nebraska Karella Family Tree

Photographs of Firstborn Sons of Three Generations with Their Wives

Married from 1863–1900

- Wenceslaus Vaclav Karella 1839–1922
- Antonia Nemec Karella 1839–1900

Married from 1895–1922

- Anton Karella 1868–1934
- Anastasia Holy Karella 1877–1922

Married from 1926–1972

- Ambrose Jerome (Rusty) Karella 1898–1972
- Delora Lucy Holt Karella 1910–2004

Three-Generation Chart

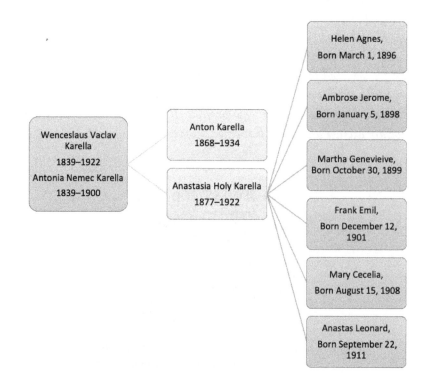

Wenceslaus Vaclav Karella
1839–1922
Antonia Nemec Karella
1839–1900

Anton Karella
1868–1934

Anastasia Holy Karella
1877–1922

Helen Agnes,
Born March 1, 1896

Ambrose Jerome,
Born January 5, 1898

Martha Genevieive,
Born October 30, 1899

Frank Emil,
Born December 12, 1901

Mary Cecelia,
Born August 15, 1908

Anastas Leonard,
Born September 22, 1911

CHAPTER 1

Forty Years after the Karellas Move to Madison, Nebraska

Shock of Loss and Remembered Love

The Scarlet fever came on swiftly, and its severity ended Anastasia Karella's life within a week on April 16, 1922.

Deluged with problems that needed immediate attention, a month passed before the Karella family gathered for a wake in May. Joined in prayer, they celebrated experiences, thoughts, and feelings about the woman who had been loved as a wife, mother, sister, daughter-in-law, and friend. After the ceremony, the family sat in small groups talking quietly. Tears and sadness mingled with smiles and laughter over memories they had made with Anastasia.

Anastasia Holy Karella with her son, Ambrose Jerome Karella, Family Photograph

Vaclav felt his age more than usual today as he remembered his young daughter-in-law who had passed away. He would turn 83 on September 1 and guessed it was only natural he should feel old. He moved off to sit by himself and waved Uncle Ed over. "Ed, will you sit with me for a private talk? I have some important family business to discuss with you." Ed nodded and pulled up a chair, sitting close so he and Vaclav could speak softly.

Vaclav's eldest son, Anton, sat alone in a room crowded with family, feeling crushed by the loss of his wife. He could barely comprehend how to take the next step. Anastasia had been his rock and soulmate. The memories he had made with Anastasia were the only ones worth remembering in that moment. *How,* he wondered, *do I face the future without her?*

Anton Karella
Family Photograph

Stanislaus stood to one side of the room, still reeling from a bit of breathtaking news. Vaclav had come to the farm before anyone else began to arrive for the wake and requested a family meeting with him and Anton. As the second son, Stanislaus had always known Anton would inherit the family assets when their parents were both gone. But their father discarded old-world tradition in revolutionary style. He divulged his plan to divide the family assets up between his three sons, though Emil John would not be told of his good fortune until he came home on his own.

Right after receiving this news, they all went downstairs to greet the family and friends arriving for his sister-in-law's wake. Stanislaus could not help feeling overwhelmed with emotion as he held his wife's hand during the family prayer. His mind began to ponder possibilities that had never entered his imagination. He never expected to receive an inheritance, which made him cautious about getting married. He had to be frugal to be sure he could save what he needed to take care of a family once he committed himself. But now, his father set him free by saying, "Boys, I want each of you to be independent and able to follow your own dreams, and your inheritance will be yours to control and do with as you see fit."

Once the family broke up into little groups after the ceremony, Stanislaus pulled his Anna aside and told her the news. She slipped her hand through his arm, and he laid his hand on top of hers. As they looked into each other's eyes, the moment was bittersweet because they would both miss Anastasia, yet they could smile because they had choices and a bright future ahead.

Frank Emil sat in a chair with his elbows on his knees, looking at the floor lost in thought. He knew he had to go. Not just because it would be exciting to travel with his friends and see an exotic place he could hardly imagine. Though that was true, the most urgent reason for this need to flee from Madison sat across the room. Frank stared at his father. He had never seen him like this. His father had always been a tower of strength, always rock-sure of what to do and when to do it . . . now, he looked . . . lost.

Frank was having a hard enough time dealing with his own feelings. It felt like he was in a cage, and he had to get out. With determination, he stood up and walked over to his uncle Stanislaus and his wife, Anna. Low and urgently, he said, "Uncle Stanislaus, I've got to go. I can't miss my train. I don't know how to tell Papa I'm leaving." He looked at his uncle, hoping he would volunteer to convey this bitter news to his father.

Anna watched the exchange and remained silent with her arm curled around her husband's. His fingers took comfort and courage from his touch on her hand.

Stanislaus began to slowly shake his head and replied solemnly, "I am sorry, nephew. I cannot burden my brother with anymore upsetting news this day. You must tell your father you are still going to South America as you had planned before your mother took ill."

Stepping away from Anna, he hugged Frank and whispered in his ear, "God be with you on your journey, nephew. I understand your need to go. Eventually, your father will understand too. Be safe on your adventures and come back to us. Always remember that we love you and that this is your home."

Stanislaus stepped back to his wife's side, watching his nephew walk away. Anna took hold of his arm again and whispered, "You have done the right thing, Stanislaus. It is his choice. He must face his father with his own decision."

Stanislaus looked into her sweet eyes and replied, "You are right, my love, but they are both in such pain right now. I pray this does not make it worse."

Frank straightened his shoulders and walked slowly across the room to stand in front of his father. "Papa, can I talk with you a minute?" he whispered.

Anton shook himself out of his melancholy thoughts and saw his second son, Frank, standing before him. "Yes, of course, sit down, son," Anton replied.

"Papa, I have to go," Frank said.

"Of course, I'll see you at home later," he replied.

"No, Papa. I am not going home; I am leaving for South America. The boys and I are catching the afternoon train. I am sorry, but I cannot . . . I just . . . have to go . . ." His voice trailed off as he turned away. He turned back for a moment and whispered, "I am so sorry." Then Frank walked swiftly out of the house.

Vaclav Karella had been standing with his granddaughter Martha and her husband, Rudy Pojar. As his one-year-old great-grandson, Charles Anthony, slept on his shoulder, Vaclav watched the exchange between his son Anton and Anton's son Frank. Though he could not hear what was being said, their body language and expressions said enough to know it had left hurt and sadness in both of them. Seeing Frank walking toward the door of the house, Vaclav gently handed the baby boy over to his father, Rudy. Then he said softly, "I think I should go and sit with Anton for a spell."

Vaclav settled in the chair beside his first-born son and whispered, "There are many things in life that are hard to understand."

Anton looked at his father, saying, "Frank is gone. I don't know when or if he will come back."

Vaclav nodded and did not respond immediately. After a moment, he said, "My son, I am proud of the man you have become. You know many things, but you cannot know everything. You were always responsible, faced every situation that came up with courage and fortitude. You won all your battles by sheer willpower, even when you were only a little boy. But, Anton, you will never have all the answers to every question. I can tell you from 82 years of experience, that is not an easy truth to accept for one who prides himself for always being in control of the situation."

Anton nodded his head but did not speak. Vaclav was relieved to see his son was listening and went on to say, "We have many things in common. As fathers, we have children we often do not understand. We have had remarkable women for wives. We now face the challenge of not becoming discouraged and giving up on life as we face the rest of our life journey without them by our sides. But there are gifts that balance those losses. We have love. We have family and a faith community surrounding us with support and comfort. We are not alone, even though you might feel that way right now. Because your son needs time alone to sort out his feelings does not mean he does not love you or this family.

"We each have choices we must make, just as we each have a unique purpose. For you and me, it is recognizing we have the means to make a living with our hands that puts food on our tables and takes care of our family. We have the choice to live the life before us and cherish this life despite the changes that have reshaped our worlds.

"But most importantly, son, if you truly believe that our souls do not die, then your Anastasia and my Antonia are still very much alive where it counts the most."

Anton looked at his father and asked, "Where is that, Papa?"

"In our hearts. In our hopes. In our memories and our dreams. If you look as I do, you will see them in the faces of our family, taste their joy in the food we eat, and hear them in the laughter of our children, grandchildren, and in our nieces and nephews. They are all around us. I have seen my Antonia in you and your brothers and sister over and over again in the last 22 years since my Antonia has been gone. Just as I see your Anastasia in my grandchildren."

Tears filled Anton's eyes, and he asked, "Papa, is that why you talk out loud to Mama?"

"Yes, I know she is close. I can feel her presence, and it comforts me to speak with her about all of you."

Anton whispered his next question, "Does she answer you?"

"God gives me the answers I need when I ask but not in your mother's voice . . . it is like she touches my heart and my thoughts, letting me know things will be all right. That is how God works, but you must learn to quiet your spirit and open your heart by leaving the pain and sorrow behind. Then you will feel peace in the answers you receive. Anton, you are strong. We all love you, and there is still much to do with the time that you have been given. Accept the healing that comes from love and start letting all the rest of it go. Worry adds nothing to your life." Then Vaclav suggested, "Just live each day as it comes. That will be enough for now."

"Papa, thank you; I love you so much and thank you for your guidance all my life."

Vaclav smiled and placed his hand on his son's shoulder, saying, "I will always love you."

As the rest of the family was leaving to go home, Stanislaus walked up to his father and said softly, "Papa." Vaclav looked up at his son waiting. "If you would like me to, I will record this event in the family Bible."

His father looked relieved and nodded as he replied, "Please do. Thank you, Stanislaus."

Late That Night

In the quiet with only the snap of the fire to break the silence, Stanislaus sat holding the family Bible. Always a deep thinker, Stanislaus researched his ideas and only told people about them after his decisions and plans were in place. Yet, he trusted Anton. They had grown up with a profound respect for one another. His older brother made him feel secure. As firstborn and undisputed leader, Anton had always possessed a clear vision of what to do and when. But Anton had also given Stanislaus room to be himself and supported his ideas.

Looking back over the years, he and his Anna had hoped to have children, but apparently, that was not part of God's plan. When it came to children, again Anton had been sensitive to their feelings of being childless. *Perhaps God's plan for Anna and me is to be free of other responsibilities now when Anton and his children need our help, support, encouragement, and guidance the most,* he thought.

This time, he and his Anna would be the strength and comfort that Anton and his family needed. Anna felt as he did, and by taking on the duty of recording this sad event, he would take the first step toward building a bond between him and his older brother as equals. *It is a great life purpose that only Anna and I can fulfill,* Stanislaus thought as he opened the Bible to the family section. On a blank page, he wrote in beautiful flowing lines:

In the spring of 1922, our family suffered the unexpected loss of Anton's wife, Anastasia Holy Karella. At the time of her death, she was survived by her husband, Anton, who is 54, and six children; Ambrose is 24, and Frank Emil is 21. They are still unwed and living at home. Anastasia's two youngest children: Mary Cecelia is 14, and Anastas Leonard is 11 years old.

Antonia's eldest daughter, Helen, is 26, has two children—a son, Francis; a daughter, Margaret Mary—and is due to deliver her new baby in May. They are living in their tractor house with Helen's husband, Alvin Bean, and travel to his construction jobs around Nebraska.

Martha Genevieve is 22 and is married to Rudy Pojar, and they have one son, Charles Anthony, and live in Madison.

Anastasia is also survived by Anton's father, Wenceslaus Vaclav, who is 82 years old, living in the Madison house. Stanislaus is 51 and is still living with his wife, Anna, and Uncle Ed on the farm. The youngest Karella son, Emil John, is 42 and moved to Chicago, Illinois, ten years prior and is now married to Emily Karella of the Chicago Karellas, and they have one son named Raymond. The only daughter of Antonia and Wenceslaus Vaclav, Anna Karella Kratochvil, is now 49 and living with her husband, Anton Kratochvil, in California with their nine children: Luis, Joseph, Anton, Katherine, Rose, Emil, Edmund, Raymond, and Mary. Antonia was a God-fearing woman, a good wife, and an excellent mother and sister. She will be sorely missed.

Martha Karella Pojar and Husband, Rudolph Pojar, Married Feb 10, 1919

Frank Emil Karella, born December 12, 1901

Stanislaus closed the Bible and returned it to the shelf. Walking silently into the bedroom, he was surprised to find his Anna was still awake. "Are you alright, Stanislaus?" she asked sweetly.

"Yes, my love. I am happy to find you are awake. I have an important idea I would like to discuss with you."

Alone on a June Evening

The mantel clock read 10:00 p.m., and his three children had already gone to bed exhausted. Anton sat before the fire, warming himself and drinking a cup of coffee. Deep in thought, he looked at Anastasia's favorite pictures sitting on the mantel. His eyes came to rest on a wedding photograph dated February 10, 1919. *That was quite a year, wasn't it, Anastasia? That was the spring our beautiful daughter, Martha Genevieve, married Rudolph James Pojar.* Smiling, his eyes moved on to a baby picture sitting next to it, and he remembered the last time he and Anastasia had talked about that photograph. *You and I had been looking at this picture shortly after Frank turned 19 years old.* He let the memory fill his mind, reliving the moment he had asked, "Do you even remember when our Frank Emil was a cooperative sweet baby, instead of the quarlsom 19-year-old boy he has become? A boy who cannot wait to join the Army Air Corps?"

Anastasia had laughed in response and replied, "Lately? I'd say only when he is sleeping."

As Frank's birthday passed and his departure for the Army Air Corps grew close, Anton remembered hoping that day would arrive sooner than later. His son and his wife had been butting heads over everything, and that morning, it was about breakfast. Anton recalled hearing his son Frank stomping down the stairs after his mother had yelled at him to come down to breakfast for the third time.

Frank had come into the kitchen in a huff. When he saw Anton sitting at the table, he made sure to speak to his mother carefully. "I turned 19 years old this month, Mama! I'm not a high school kid anymore. You don't need to yell at me about breakfast!"

Listening to his son's rather selfish attitude, he decided to step into the conversation before another battle between mother and son developed and said, "Apparently, she does, Frank. As you don't seem to remember that breakfast is served at precisely 7:30 a.m. so the rest of the world can get to work on time." Frank had frowned but wisely chose not to say another word. He sat down, said a quick prayer, and ate his breakfast, staring at the tabletop lost in thought. His friend Mark had come over just as Frank was finishing his food, and they sat at the table whispering. Nevertheless, Anton heard almost all of what his son said as he sat quietly behind his newspaper.

"I need some adventure . . . a few more weeks . . . no one telling me what to do anymore . . . did I tell you about the Army Air Corps AAC recruiter . . . I'll be stationed at Head Quarter Operations in Fort Worth, Texas. He said so . . . yes, I'll fly . . . after bootcamp."

Anton remembered shaking his head and deciding not to explain how wrong his son was about some of his assumptions. Those lessons were best learned personally.

Smiling, he looked at another photograph. This one was of his eldest son, Ambrose. He and Anastasia had often wondered how their firstborn son, Ambrose, and his younger brother, Frank, could be so different. They were only three years apart. Ambrose had always been creative, helpful, a natural leader, responsible, hardworking, practical, and goal-oriented. Frank often described his older brother as "all work and no play." When Frank was in a talkative mood, he would add, "I have bigger dreams than that." But Frank could never explain what he meant by that statement except to say, "Papa, I want something different than the life you and Ambrose have chosen." Anton did not understand, but he hoped his son would find what he wanted in the Army Air Corps.

Ambrose Jerome Karella, 23, eldest son of Anton and Anastasia Karella, GMK family photograph

Anton's eyes settled on his favorite picture of his younger brother, Stanislaus. *What a good man and brother he has always been*, Anton thought. He recalled visiting with Stanislaus on a day during the fall of 1919 after Frank had left for bootcamp. They had been celebrating because the farm had just had a record-breaking year in crop sales. He remembered he had taken Anastasia over to the Schoolcraft district in Battle Creek to visit her relatives that morning, then went to see Stanislaus at the homestead. They had talked about the family businesses. Closing his eyes, he could hear the conversation in his mind. "What a great year we have had! Congratulations, Stanislaus! You made the right choices."

"Now, to be honest, this year's success was due to group decisions made by you, me, and Ed. But thank you for trusting my opinions regarding the farm business. I am also pleased with the progress we are making with the tractor. It is so much easier than using a team of horses. Remember what it was like when it was just you and me and two horses doing all the work?" his brother asked. "And how much better it was after Ed came to live with us?"

Anton remembered replying, "I certainly do!"

His mind jumped to another memory about Uncle Ed. He had been talking to Ed and said, "Stanislaus and I find it amazing that your visit that was only expected to last a few months turned into years. We can't tell you how thankful we are that you decided to stay and be Uncle Ed to the whole Karella family. I wonder," Anton had reflected, "if anyone besides us even remembers that your last name is not *Karella.*"

Stanislaus Karella
family Photos

Ed had smiled at his comment, but Stanislaus replied, "Ha, you'd have a hard time convincing Mary Cecilia and Anastas Leonard that he's not a Karella. Have you ever heard that gypsy Karella girl story they tell, the one about how Ed here became their Uncle Ed?"

Ed grinned, knowing exactly which story Stanislaus was talking about. The three men had smiled at each other, and Ed replied, "We are brothers of the heart. No matter how distant our blood relationship is, I'll always gladly be Uncle Ed to this family, and that's all that matters to me."

About that time, Anton remembered Anastasia had walked into the kitchen. She had surprised him by being at the farm when he left her with her family. It was like she could read his thoughts and said, "My father brought me out here. He is picking out a few new laying hens and will come in to pay Stanislaus for them after they are caged. Would you like some coffee before I go and collect some eggs to take home?"

Anastasia knew he would never turn down coffee, and after filling their cups, she opened the basket she had brought with her. It was filled with fresh-baked berry kolaches. Closing his eyes, thinking of that pastry, he could taste the delicious flavor on his tongue. Smiling, he thought, *Anastasia, you were always that way—thoughtful and planning ahead. Darling, I never realized how many wonderful memories I made or how many important conversations I had while drinking coffee and eating your rohlikys or kolache until now.*

Opening his eyes, Anton looked around the room. He noted the clock said 1:00 a.m., his coffee was cold, and the fire was out. *Now, that is odd,* he thought. *I did not feel time passing or the coldness in the room until I opened my eyes.*

Regretting the loss of the warmth he left in his memories, Anton stood up slowly, turned down the lamp, and began to climb the stairs. "Anastasia," he said softly, "please help me get some sleep tonight." Suddenly, he stopped on the stairs as a thought struck him. For some reason, the letters his father used to write to his mother after she passed away came to his mind. He vividly remembered reading one when his father had been sleeping in his chair by the fireplace. *I could write down my thoughts to you, Anastasia. What do you think . . . talk to you in my journal? I think I will start tonight, right now.* Entering his room, Anton sat down at Anastasia's old dressing table with his journal and began to write.

Anton J. Karella—Journal Entry

My dear Anastasia, when you came to our family, we always remembered to thank God for giving us strength when we asked for it and for the friendships and faith community God gave us because we needed them. My parents knew you were God's gift to me. You opened my heart and gave my world meaning outside my work. I found the order and execution of a well laid out plan more interesting than talking about something as ambiguous as love until I met you. You taught me so many things about life. How could I know you were a gift I would not be able to keep?

You always said I was born understanding business but nothing of the heart, while you were born understanding everything about love, laughter, and emotions. We were so perfect for each other you said we were two sides of one coin.

I am sorry for the years I was totally obsessed with just providing the money and security we needed. Our arrangement made life easy for me, leaving the emotional things to you that I was not very comfortable with.

Darling, it never crossed my mind there would ever be a time when you would not be at home waiting for me. You made me want to understand things that were important to you. You made me understand what love felt like and what it meant . . . now, I feel empty. I am not sure how to fix that without you. I am getting by at work, but I am not doing well with the children. Lord knows I could use your guidance, especially with Mary Cecilia. She is still friends with Agnes Moore, and they have grown much closer since that fateful week we lost you. Ed is watching out for Anastas, so I don't worry too much about him. Helen wrote to me, heartsick that she could not come home. She will have our new grandchild soon, and I told her it is better to focus on herself and the health of the baby right now.

Frank left for South America. I have no idea when he will come back.

Ambrose is strong but works all the time. I fear he is too much like me in that regard. He is also like me in that he does not talk much about his feelings. Having Martha, Rudy, and their baby nearby helps me remember your advice about letting people see how I feel. Martha asked if I needed help going through your things. I said yes, and she is coming over tomorrow. Our sweet girl will be able to do what I have not had the courage to do myself. She will help me sort through your treasures and make sure each of our children is given a keepsake from you.

I don't know what we will do without you, Anastasia. I still have Papa to help me see the way, though he cannot replace you. I have always trusted his counsel. He and Mama loved you right from the beginning. They knew I was in love with you long before I realized it myself. I think you did too. Now, I feel an emptiness in my heart that only you can fill. Perhaps God will let you fill it back up at least in my dreams, my dearest one. Goodnight for now, my love.

Anton laid down his pen, closed the journal, and turned down the lamp. As he lay down on the bed, his head sunk gently into his feather pillow. Closing his eyes and pulling the covers over his shoulders, he realized the expression of his emotions on those pages had left him exhausted and quickly fell into a deep sleep.

CHAPTER 2

Memories and Moving On

Children Change

Anton watched the serious face of his daughter Mary Cecilia as she prepared breakfast. Gobbling down her food, she hurried to clean up the dishes and the kitchen before leaving to visit her friend, Agnes. Suddenly, Anton wanted to see her smile and said, "Mary, don't worry about the dishes. I'll take care of them. Get going. Go see your friend." Dropping the worried woman look, Mary's expression changed into a young girl's radiant smile. She hugged him with enthusiasm, then ran out the door. His son Anastas volunteered to clean up when his sister left.

Anton saw Uncle Ed walking up to the house through the kitchen window. He shook his head at Anastas and replied, "Thank you, son, but don't worry about the dishes. Your Uncle Ed is on the porch. Open the door so I can say good morning and then go enjoy your day." After they exchanged quick hellos and goodbyes, Ed and Anastas left.

As Anton cleaned up the kitchen, the housework eased his mind. He reflected on how his children had changed. *They seem to have grown up and become adults in little bodies. I believe I have let too much time slip away unnoticed, Anastasia. I promise I will do better. I will pay more attention to them and everything else too. Help me be strong, my love.*

Martha Karella Pojar

Martha served her family breakfast, and after cleaning up, she told her husband, Rudy, she planned to spend the day with her father. Rudy gave her a quick kiss and a hug, saying, "Tell Papa we love him." Nodding, she hurried through her tasks, left the house, and arrived at her father's home around 9:30. Martha set the covered basket she carried on the kitchen counter, then father and daughter greeted each other warmly.

Both Anton and Martha were well aware of the two months that had slipped by. It was time to sort out what should be done with Anastasia's personal things. Martha and her father had always had an uncanny mental connection and often understood each other without speaking. Father and daughter headed for the stairs, climbing to the second floor to the bedroom where Anastasia's things sat undisturbed. As Anton walked next to his daughter, he stopped at the door lost in a memory of Martha as a younger girl. It was the day she first met their neighbor's grandson.

He smiled and thought, *Anastasia, remember when Martha took a shine to Thomas Pojar's grandson? We instantly liked the boy and encouraged their friendship. Remember how overjoyed we were when Rudy proposed and that Martha had found a love match?*

As Martha walked into the room, her mind was filled with conflicting feelings. She walked directly over to the beautiful wooden chest placed to the right of her mother's dressing table. Sitting down on the floor next to it, she felt ready to help go through her mother's things. It would have been too hard for her papa to do alone. But now as she ran her hand lovingly over the smooth wood of her mama's hope chest, she trembled with emotion. Martha closed her eyes as her mind filled with the past. A sad, fond smile turned up the corners of her mouth as she spoke softly, "Papa, did you know Mama called this her magic box?"

Martha's words pulled Anton back to the present. Walking toward his daughter, he looked at the chest, and a poignant whisper slipped from his lips, "I gave it to her on our wedding day. What else did your mama say about it?"

Her eyes seemed to look inward as she replied, "I remember one day I was sitting wide-eyed, waiting breathlessly. Mama was going to let me take a peek inside. I asked Mama what made her box magic, and she replied, 'Because it saves and protects precious things from the ravages of time.' Her answer sounded so mysterious. I didn't understand it, but I didn't have to. It was the way Mama said the words that made me believe it was magic.

"I certainly believed it was magic when Mama pulled a beautiful doll from this box. It was the prettiest thing I had ever seen. She had a beautiful face, glass eyes that looked real, and wore an emerald-green dress with a matching bonnet on her head. Mama held her close to me so I could see her and told me the doll's name was *Little Miss Holly.* 'Martha, if you are a good girl, I will let you play with her. You must be gentle when you play with Miss Holly. She is delicate.'

"I loved that doll, and I was always careful when I was allowed to play with her." Looking up at her father, Martha said softly, "Mama gave Little Miss Holly to me as a wedding gift when I got married."

Tiny tears slipped down her face as she stood up for her father's hug. She hid her face in his shoulder, and in a muffled voice, she said, "I miss her, Papa."

She could hear his heartbeat and whispered words at the same time. "I do, too, sweet girl." But in his thoughts, he said, *I always will.*

Knowing he had to change the mood they were in, he gave Martha a final squeezy hug, saying as cheerful as possible, "Now, my dear, dry those tears and let's take a look inside your mother's magic box." Martha nodded, then knelt down to undo the latch, and Anton lifted the lid. The smell of cedar drifted into the room.

Glancing inside, they saw her mother's jewelry box and on top of it was a beautiful hair comb next to Anastasia's brush. There were three sets of gloves and a lovely wool winter scarf partially covering several small, neatly stacked boxes. Curious, Martha opened one and found what she believed were her brother Ambrose's baby booties. The next box she opened had her name on it with a note that read, "*Year-1*" and was delighted to find her own baby slippers. Deciding to open one more, she saw that it contained a set of her eldest sister's miniature shoes.

Anton whispered, "Your grandfather made those for her as soon as Helen started to walk."

"She will be happy to see them again, don't you think, Papa?"

Anton nodded, unable to speak. Seeing those tiny shoes and slippers reminded him of the wonderful years he had with his Anastasia.

After putting the scarf on the floor, two things caught her eye.

First was a bundle of letters. Picking them up, she could see they were from her brother, Frank. The return address said Fort Worth, Texas. "Papa, would you mind if I read some of these letters from Frank?" She held them up.

Anton looked at the letters and replied, "Yes, you can read a couple of them if you want. I remember most of them as though they had come yesterday."

He pulled a photograph out from under the envelopes and said, "Martha, look. Here is a picture of your brother in his uniform.

Frank Emil Karella served in the Army Air Corps 1920–1922

"Is that about the time frame when Father Clemens talked to his priest friend in Chile about Frank going to South America?" Martha asked wistfully.

"Close. Father Clemens made those arrangements the following spring after Frank got out of the AAC and came back to Madison. But that is a very long story. Are you sure you want to hear it?"

Holding the bundle of letters in her lap, she replied, "I do, Papa."

"Then we'd better go down to the kitchen and get some coffee. But before we get sidetracked," Anton replied, "let's have a look at what else is in the bottom of the chest."

Anton figured if they went downstairs, they would not return to this room, and he would have to finish going through Anastasia's things alone, and he didn't want to do that.

Nodding in agreement, Martha set down the letters by the scarf on the floor and pulled a stack of her mother's fancy shawls from the chest. Suddenly, she saw a book spine and gasped. "Papa! Look! I see a book you used to read to us when we were young children and still living at the farm!" She gently pulled *The Blue Fairy Book* from the chest and handed it to her father. Smiling softly, he leafed through it and found the picture of the maiden and fairy sprite, Rumpelstiltskin.

Anton had learned as a young boy that the world was not a safe place for an emotional man. Men had to be smart and strong, make precise logical decisions, and earn a good living to protect their families just like his father did.

When he had been a young boy in Bohemia and his aunties, Masynda and Julienka, made up plays and told stories with their marionettes—or Papa read from the *Book of Bohemian Fables*—only then did he let his imagination and emotional spirit fly free in safety.

Maiden and the mischievous fairy sprite Rumpelstiltskin from the *Blue Fairy Book*, illustrated by Henry J. Ford

His papa would read a few chapters to them at night before they fell asleep. After they moved to New York, his father began to collect books and started a tradition of reading aloud to them on Sundays after dinner.

Anton found his father's old books when he was moving his parents from the farm to the Madison house. His papa had given them to him, saying, "Son, you should share them with your children as we used to do when you were just a boy."

After that, on many cold winter evenings at the farm, the whole family gathered by lamplight, and he would read aloud, sharing those magical worlds with his family. Anastasia had loved to listen to his voice and bought him a new book each Christmas to add to his collection.

By removing a few more things from the chest, Martha revealed a whole row of book spines with neatly printed titles. Anton leaned over Martha's shoulder to look at the colored bindings and knew it was the collection of Andrew Lang's *Coloured Fairy Books*. There were twelve of them, and each book was bound in a different color. Lang's fairy tales were not gruesome like those the Grimm Brothers wrote. Lang's books were imaginative and a little mischievous, but they were wonderful stories. He loved them all and so had his children. Lang was also a good poet, and one of the last gifts Anastasia gave him was *Lang's Blue Poetry* book to add to his collection.

"Martha, please move the rest of those boxes and see what else is there." Lining the bottom of the chest were three books by Charles Dickens: *Nicholas Nickleby, Oliver Twist*, and *Great Expectations*. Next to them were Robert Luis Stevenson's *Kidnapped, Treasure Island*, and *The Strange Case of Dr. Jekyll and Mr. Hyde*. Next was Sir Walter Scott's *Rob Roy* and Jane Austen's *Pride and Prejudice* and *Sense and Sensibility*. His eyes watered a bit as he realized his wife had thought of his books as so precious. She kept them safe in her hope chest, and he thought, *Thank you, Anastasia.*

Ready for a break, Martha picked up Frank's letters in one hand, stood up, slipped her other arm through her father's, and said, "I'd love to hear Frank's whole story now. Let's go get that coffee and a few kolaches."

Anton put on a pitifully hungry look and replied, "I don't have any kolaches, Martha."

With a tinkling laugh, she replied, "Then it is a good thing I brought some with me, isn't it, Papa? They are in the kitchen."

Setting the *Blue Fairy Book* back in the chest and closing the lid, he pulled Martha quickly to the door of the room and replied, "Then what are we waiting for? Let's go! This has been hungry work!" Laughing, they walked down the stairs arm in arm. Anton felt comforted sharing all these memories with his daughter. Now, he was actually looking forward to telling her Frank's story.

After filling their coffee cups, Martha set a selection of Bohemian sweet rolls between them on a plate. Anton popped a whole one into his mouth and washed it down with coffee. Seeing her father do such an undignified thing made her giggle.

Anton cleared his mouth and said, "In my defense, I had to eat at least one of them now. You might eat them all before I finish talking."

Martha shook her head, smiling at his silliness, which she liked a great deal more than his quiet sadness. Grinning at him, she opened the first letter from Frank.

Newsy Letter from AAC Airman Frank Karella

Dear Mama and Papa,   *February 1919, AAC Bootcamp*

This is just a short note to let you know me and the guys start our eight weeks of bootcamp tomorrow. I won't have much personal time now, but I'll write more when I get to my post in Fort Worth, Texas. Can't tell you how excited I am to finally be here. Some of the guys I met said they heard the training regimen is brutal because we have to be really fit to fly and parachute from the aircraft. Maybe I'll have bigger muscles than Uncle Stanislaus by the time I get back! That would be something to brag about. Hope everyone at home is doing well, and that's all I have to say for now.

Your son and soon-to-be airman, Frank Karella

Dear Mama and Papa,   *November 1920, Fort Worth, Texas*

I must humbly confess I didn't know much about what I was signing up for when I joined the Army Air Corps. I foolishly thought when I left home, I would have no one telling me what to do anymore. I can laugh at myself now looking back over the past year.

Mama, the drill sergeants at AAC bootcamp made me realize just how good I had it at home with you. Thank you for not kicking me in the seat of my pants as I deserved.

Papa, thank you for letting me go and not trying to warn me about my misconceptions.

I'll admit I have learned my lessons the hard way and can appreciate, in hindsight, your patience and all you have done for me.

By the way, please tell Ambrose I am sorry for all the grief I gave him over his junk lying around the house. I am really glad he gave me one of those old Brownie Cameras he fixed up. The ones I complained so much about. I am enclosing some of the photographs I took with it. I hope that makes him smile.

Now that I am settled into my AAC career, I am proud to say I did learn to fly Model 75 Boeing Stearman biplanes. Flying is scary and exhilarating. Learning to parachute from the planes in the case of an emergency was not what I imagined it would be, and it took a lot of nerve and concentration.

Frank's Texas Jackrabbit auto and clarinets

I am pleased to tell you that I also learned to play the clarinet. In fact, I am so good at playing the clarinet the AAC moved me out of the flight cadets and into the Air Corp Army Band full time. I suppose that means I am a much better musician than I was a pilot.

As I think about it, I believe music turned out to be a better deal for me. The extra money I made playing in the band at private parties in the evenings and at the officer's club enabled me to buy a used Model T Ford from the company commander. I named it Texas Jackrabbit after one of my buddies in the motor pool gave it a special tune-up! It is really fast on the road now, and the guys and I are planning to drive it to Galveston on our next long weekend pass.

Gosh, it is getting late. Sorry this letter is going to be a short one. We get up real early. Mama, I have learned to appreciate and miss the breakfasts you cooked for me. Nobody here cares if I miss breakfast. Papa, you were also right about not being late for work. They are pretty tough around here on a guy who does not get to work on time.

I love you both very much,
Airman Frank E. Karella

"I remember laughing at the way Frank wrote about getting out of the AAC. His letter said, 'Papa, I confess that after two uneventful years in military service, not counting learning to fly an airplane, discovering my passion for the clarinet and playing band music, I am ready to be discharged in January. Look for me after New Year's 1921 because I am coming home. I have missed the green rolling hills and fields of Nebraska.'

Seawall Specialty Co: Fort Worth Texas WPD

"Your brother came to see us as soon as he got to town. Frank told me that when he climbed into his Texas Jackrabbit and pointed its nose toward home, he figured he would probably experience more adventure driving from Texas to Nebraska than he had in his two years in the service.

Fort Worth Texas airfield, Hicks, 1920 military photograph

He also said he learned a new appreciation for the Nebraska landscape and the color green.

Frank Karella—AAC Cadets

"Martha, in that stack of notes and letters, you will also find a postcard picture of downtown Fort Worth. It looked like a sizable modern town to me. Frank said he did some sightseeing there but didn't have much to say about it. He also told us his airfield was pretty much sitting by itself in the desert. Your brother made Texas sound pretty colorless and tame.

"Personally, I think Frank imagined it would be like the old Wild West with outlaws, Indians, and cowboys chasing each other over the landscape. Like in those penny pamphlet westerns he adored as a little boy.

"Keep looking, Martha. I believe there is a postcard from a trip he took with some friends to see Galveston on the Gulf of Mexico and a picture from the seashore.

"Your mother and I enjoyed our talk with Frank when he got home. He was so relaxed and happy that we spent most of the day catching up on everything.

Hotel Galvez, Seawall Specialty Co: Galveston WPD

"That was the afternoon I asked if Frank wanted to move back into his old room. Before he could say anything, your Mama decided to give him a push and said, 'I think it is a good idea, Frank, since you are still unmarried.'"

Anton shook his head, smiling, and said, "It was a good thing that Frank developed a sense of humor while he was away."

Martha laughingly replied, "I didn't hear about that. Mama didn't really say that to Frank, did she?"

Grinning, Anton nodded his head and replied, "Oh yes, she did, and you should have seen Frank roll his eyes at the dig about marriage. He didn't take the bait, though. He just smiled at your mother. It was clear to me that your brother grew up a lot during his time in the service. Anyway, after Frank got settled in his room, I suggested he take a drive out to the farm to see his uncles. I knew they had a business proposal they wanted to talk over with him.

"When Frank went out to the farm the next day, they offered him the management and delivery concession for the homestead's poultry, meat, and egg business. He had worked that business before, but now since he had his own automobile, they told him he could set his own schedule. They would

Seashore in Galveston, Tichnor Bros. Inc
Galveston WPD

pay for gas used for delivery runs and give him a weekly salary. Frank told me he happily shook hands on that deal.

"Your mother and I wondered how long Frank would remain happy here in Madison.

"Frank kept himself busy working five days a week and played his clarinet in the church band at St. Leonard's on Sundays. On Saturday nights, he and three of his friends practiced the new jazz and band music being played on the radio. As a group, they volunteered to play their music regularly for the young people's social held by the church. Father Clemens told me the church dances got very crowded when the boys played."

Anton swallowed another sip of coffee, then began the story by saying, "Father Clemens explained how the idea for Frank and his friends got started. Our first conversation about Frank happened on a Sunday in January of 1922. The rest of the congregation had already left the church when your mother and I waved at Father Clemens.

He was headed for the vestibule of the church to change out of his mass vestments, but he stopped and waited when he saw us wave. As we approached him, he asked, 'What can I help you with today?'

"'Father, we'd like to talk to you about Frank. How is he doing? It's been a year since Frank got home, and what I mean is . . . does he seem happy to you? He has seemed restless to us when we see him at the family gatherings, but he does not talk much about anything. We were hoping maybe he might have said something to you about what he wants to do in the future.'

"Father Clemens replied, 'I have noticed Frank likes to keep busy. He loves to play music and is very talented. I am thankful he and his friends volunteer so much here at the church. Tell you what, I'll keep an eye on him and let you know if during our conversations anything comes up that is a worry.'

"Father Clemens stopped us after Mass the following week, saying he had been thinking a lot about ways to help Frank and his three friends. He could easily see that Frank was not cut out for farming. Outside of his love for his family, Madison would never be able to hold his interest for long. Modern music vs. old fashioned music had been the topic of many conversations Father Clemens had overheard at church since the boys began to play for the dances. It was the impression the boy's music had on the young adults of the parish that gave him an idea.

"He did not want to lose them to the world they would find in the big cities. They might gain money and fame with their music, but they could mess up their lives in the process. 'Frank and his friends are good boys. Perhaps I can introduce them to adventure without too many risks through a friend. I need to write a letter, and I'll let you know when I have more information.'

"That is when he wrote to his friend Father Jose de Flores in Santiago, Chile, in February of 1922. He wrote about wanting to help four young men of his parish. They were very accomplished musicians, and farming was not enough to keep these boys interested. What they needed was an adventure for a good purpose. Father Clemens explained about prohibition, that the new jazz and dance clubs opening up around the country were reported to be fronts for selling illegal alcohol, and about the gangster Charles Luciano's organized crime syndicate. That all the places the boys might get a job in the big cities to play their music might get them mixed up with a bad crowd.

"Now, I'll read you the letter Father Clemens gave to me from Father Flores about Frank."

Dear Father Clemens,   *Metropolitan Cathedral, Santiago, Chile*

How happy I was to see the letter from you, my friend, sitting on my desk. I recently took on all the duties as pastor. Now, the church pays for a secretary who collects the mail and handles small projects for me around the church.

As I read your words, I remembered my visit to see you in Madison before I transferred to my first parish in Mexico. I recall that Madison was a quiet community with somber, hardworking, good-hearted people. Maybe reserved is a better word for those dear people, but they were somber compared to my family and community I grew up in.

Remember how I reciprocated the favor? You came for a visit to my hometown, and my family showed you what it is like to be part of the Latin culture. Remember the singing and how everyone played an instrument of some kind? Gosh, there were several kinds of horns and many variations of guitar and stringed instruments. Remember the mariachi? They sang and played music until everyone had fallen asleep, including us, and we were the guests of honor. As I told you, a person can always find music, laughter, fantastic food, and dancing at the Flores home, and our festival celebrations flow right into the streets, and the whole neighborhood gets involved.

OK, the reason I brought up those old memories was because they gave me an idea. As I thought about our past experiences, I vividly remember how you reacted to the music, food, and camaraderie in my home.

A little exposure to that culture might just work the same way for the young performers you mentioned. I could invite the boys to come here and tour the churches in Santiago as guest musicians. They could "donate their talent" by giving fundraising performances for a few of our church's projects. Yes, my friend, that might be just what the Lord wants from us and them. What do you think about this idea?

Anton put down the letter and said, "Father Clemens thought the idea sounded terrific and would be a perfect solution. It would challenge and reward the young men, so he stopped Frank after Mass on the following Sunday and asked him to come to the rectory. He told Frank about an opportunity that included travel, adventure, and a mission that would also put him and his friends in good favor with God.

"Frank told me he smiled calmly when Father Clemens told him about the idea, but inside, he was thrilled. Frank could not believe his good fortune. Nor could he believe he was going to travel to South America *and* play music! Laughing, he said, 'And I thought seeing the Gulf of Mexico, ocean beaches, and pretty girls was terrific. But it is nothing compared to this!' I told him I thought it was an amazing opportunity.

"Frank went and talked with the guys immediately after we finished our conversation. Of course, his friends agreed. Frank went back to Father Clemens the following Monday."

Martha had been totally focused on the story. She absently filled her father's cup as he spoke. Now, she waited for him to take a drink, and before he even set down the cup again, she asked, "Then what happened, Papa?"

"March 1922, Father Clemens came to see your mother and I and shared his and Father Flores's plan for the boys. After Anastasia and I gave our support for the plan, Father Clemens went to see the parents of the other boys. With the parental consent, the two priests proceeded to make all the arrangements.

"Anticipating travel dates, your brother began spending a lot of time at the library reading about South America. By the end of

March, Frank's four-member band had tickets to leave Madison on the 15th of May by train to California and then by ship to Chile as visiting entertainers. They would stay at the rectory of the Catholic Metropolitan Cathedral in Santiago as guests of Father José de Flores. In exchange for room and board, the boys would donate their time and musical talent to help raise money for several charities of the Catholic Churches in Santiago."

"How wonderful that must have been," Martha said.

"Frank and the boys stayed away from anyone who had the sniffles that spring. None of them wanted to be sick in two weeks when they started out on their fantastic adventure. That is why he was out at the homestead the night your mother took ill . . ." Anton's voice trailed off to silence.

Abruptly, the lighthearted banter disintegrated. Martha regretted asking her father to tell Frank's story. She just didn't think . . . and chided herself for her thoughtlessness and for the sadness that returned to her father's face.

Left to right: Helen Agnes Karella, Jenny Pojar (Rudy Pojar's sister), Martha Genevieve Karella, Grandpa Wenceslaus Vaclav, and Ambrose Jerome Karella. Photo taken at Grandpa Wenceslaus Vaclav's home in Madison, Nebraska. Family photograph.

She realized too late that this story ended at her mother's wake That was when Frank left for South America. "I'm sorry, Papa. I should not have brought any of this up."

Anton shook his head, saying, "Loss is part of life, sweetheart. We can't run away from it. Your grandfather says the ones we love never really leave us; they live on in our hearts. Let's just be happy you and I shared this day and had a wonderful time together. We can do that, can't we, sweetheart?"

Martha hugged her father and replied, "Yes, of course we can. I love you, Papa."

"Good," he replied with forced levity. "Now, I think it is time you headed home to your family. I am sure they are missing you. Don't worry about me. Stanislaus will be here soon to go over the business ledgers, and those discussions take hours."

Family Chart:

Rudolph Pojar and Martha Genevieve Karella Pojar

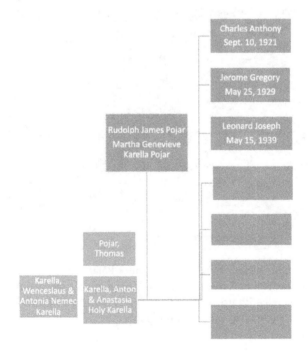

Anton J. Karella—Journal Entry

Business is starting to be a worry. The changes we are seeing in the agricultural world of grain products traded on the commodity markets is not good. Stanislaus and I were worried about the rapid farming expansion during the war and consequently the overproduction of grain since the war ended. There is just too much American grain hitting the market, and now grain prices have begun to tumble.

We just received more distressing news. Our government has cut off international subsidies to European countries, and they can't afford to buy our grain, so our European grain sales have fallen to practically nothing. Seed prices and our normal bills are just as high as they ever were or higher. The banks have raised interest rates. Cultivating more land to make up sales in volume production is not going to work. We will look into buying a second tractor instead. We calculate that reducing labor costs will realize better profit from the land we currently have under cultivation.

If grain values keep falling by the mid- to late-1920s, despite living in a simple cost-effective way, we predict many farmers will go bankrupt. Those who do plant and harvest might not be able to sell their grain because of the glut of low-priced grain already in storage. Stanislaus and I are afraid many farmers we know might fall deeply into debt and might not be able to pay their loans. Others might even lose their homesteads due to foreclosure for unpaid taxes. Part of the reason we have flourished on the homestead is timing. Receiving our land in 1879, we had more time, and there were less farmers to compete for our grain sales. Because of that dynamic, the market paid more money to people like us who grew grain.

Our land always had a greater meaning than just dirt to be plowed. Owning land fulfilled the greatest desire of Mama's and Papa's hearts. It meant security for our family, and it was always the plan to make this land an inheritance that would be passed down from one generation to the next.

Life has never been easy for us. Farming is hard work. But as a family, we agree it is worth the toil put into it. The wheat and corn we plant not only produces a product to sell, but it also feeds our livestock and supports our families. In addition to working the farmland, Mama and Papa had trade skills and continued to use those talents to offset costs even after we moved to the farm.

As Stanislaus and I have grown older, we still pool our money with the family business money. Stanislaus and I have worked side by side for years to make the farm produce an income. We constantly look for new opportunities that will put meat on the table and extra money in the bank. Papa made sure we were educated and trained us to manage our money wisely. We will continue to watch the market closely and spend prudently.

Ambrose Jerome Karella with
McCormick steam engine
on the Karella homestead farm,
family photograph

Anton J. Karella—Journal Entry

We voted to buy a 15-year-old Cyrus McCormick tractor. There were older ones that would have been cheaper. Some models have been in use since 1832. Papa said those older machines are not going to be reliable. Ambrose is familiar with the McCormick engine, so he will be able to keep it running for us.

We will plow and seed all the fields with the tractors, which will replace our horse-drawn farming equipment. That process is too slow, and the extra labor required for plowing and planting is eating up profit. The second bigger tractor was an expensive investment. But we've calculated that it will allow us to cultivate our existing fields faster using less labor, and with quicker and earlier planting, we might get two crops in one growing season from some of our fields. Everything we do from now on must be planned with even more care.

CHAPTER 3

Leadership of the Next Generation

Mid-October 1922

After five months, Anton felt like he had begun to adjust to life without his wife. As he said to his daughter, Martha: life goes on. Planning Grandpa Vaclav's birthday party would be a fun diversion. As enthusiastic as the grandchildren, Anton and his siblings wanted to celebrate their father's 83rd birthday on September 1 in grand fashion.

As celebrations go, it was the best party the Karellas had thrown in years. Holys, Kuchars, Beans, Pojars, and Karellas gathered in the church hall with parish friends. Each family group brought a special dish of food from their childhoods.

The list of delicious victuals included dill and sour cream cucumbers, pickled beets and onions, roast pork with caraway gravy, homemade sauerkraut, shredded potato cakes, and thick beef goulash stew. These Bohemian dishes were seasoned with onion, chili peppers, paprika, thyme, cumin, and marjoram. The au gratin dumplings were made with crushed garlic, cottage cheese, and ham. The desserts included baked apple strudel, berry and fruit preserves, sweet butter, and a choice of more types of Bohemian breads than anyone could have imagined.

A technique to create a browned crust topping for a Bohemian potato and pork casserole:

- *Ingredients for main dish: boiled with salt, thinly sliced potato and onions layered with diced pork sausage mixed in small curd cottage cheese. Lightly sprinkle with layers with salt and black pepper in and bake in a shallow baking dish for 40 minutes on 350. Cover generously with gratin mix and finish baking until crust is golden brown at 350 degrees.*

- *To make the gratin crust: use your favorite breadcrumbs, grated cheese, egg, and a little butter.*

A gratin style dishes are baked or cooked with overhead heat to form a golden crust and is served in its baking dish.

Father Clemens volunteered to run the phonograph and played all the records he had in the church library. The atmosphere of laughter, fun, and dancing lifted everyone's spirits and brought back feelings of happier times and better years. Vaclav and Father Clemens sat together and let people seek them out. Each person would sit a spell visiting, then move away to socialize with someone else in the room.

The camaraderie and joyful celebration went on and on, and no one wanted it to end. Around midnight, Father Clemens began to circulate around the room, subtly urging people to think about heading home. As the evening was coming to a close, Vaclav sat quietly observing his wonderful family and Karella kin.

There was so much of Antonia's strength in his boys it made him proud, and he thought, *Antonia, My Heart, it's all done now. The things that we hoped and dreamed about, the things we planned and worked so hard to achieve. Just look at them! What a family we made . . . and what a life we had. Thank you for your courage. I am not sure that I could have done so well if I had been in your shoes. To come so far alone on such a quest and live with so much uncertainty hanging over my head each day. Just the thought of what you did for us inspired me to keep going all these years . . . but then I have never been alone. You have always been here with me.*

Suddenly jolted out of his thoughts, he realized someone was talking to him. "Vaclav," said Father Clemens as he touched him on the shoulder, "Anton is waiting to take you home. Are you ready to go?" He nodded, and the old friends walked side by side to where Anton waited.

Wenceslaus Vaclav, 83 years old

Time to Go Home

Twenty-seven days later on September 28, 1922, Grandpa Vaclav Karella sat in front of his fireplace watching the flames dance. He had been thinking about his remarkable birthday celebration and the question Father Clemens had asked him that night. Though he knew Father Clemens had been talking about a ride home with Anton, it had sounded entirely like something else to him. Since hearing those words, "Vaclav, are you ready to go?" they had been echoing constantly in his mind. Now sitting comfortably before the warm fire, Vaclav whispered, "I am ready to go." Closing his eyes, he finished by saying, "Antonia, my sweet angels, I hope to see you in my dreams." Relaxing with a smile on his lips, he quietly passed away.

Numb and Overwhelmed

The loss of his father shattered the fragile peace Anton had rebuilt in the past five months since losing his wife. He sat behind his desk at the lumbermill unaware of his surroundings. Part of his mind thought, *I must go on . . . things to do . . . responsibilities . . .* then his conscious thoughts would go blank. Every once in a while, it would feel like he woke up, but then he would think, *I do not need to worry. They are capable of taking care of everything. I just need a little more time. I must sort things out.* Then his mind would wander away, dipping into one memory after another . . . as he disappeared into times gone by . . . and hours evaporated uncounted.

Uncle Ed and Uncle Stanislaus Discuss a Promise

Uncle Ed sought out Stanislaus to talk about a promise he had made to Stanislaus's father, Vaclav. "Stanislaus, you seem at peace with your papa's passing. How is Anton doing these days?"

"He is struggling. Anton didn't have much time to completely adjust to losing Anastasia. Papa was his rock and mentor. Unlike the rest of us, Papa went through everything Anton was experiencing. Papa's words and advice helped Anton. Now, that calming voice is gone. But my brother is stronger than he realizes. When he is ready to listen and talk, I will be there."

Ed nodded, then brought up the subject he wanted to discuss. "Though the relationship between me and your papa was technically uncle and distant nephew, over the years, he treated me more like one of his sons. I want to tell you about a conversation we had at Anastasia's wake. Vaclav asked me to remain here in Madison to help you, Anton, and Emil for as long as you needed assistance."

"Ed, I know about this conversation. Papa told me about it because he felt a pressing need to complete his plans and insisted on getting his affairs legally settled as soon as possible after Anastasia passed. Right after we transferred the titles for the Karella land and businesses, he told me he asked you to stay on the farm. You see, the Karella homestead and farm business will go to Emil when he is ready. What concerned Papa is that Emil has never run the farm or a business like it. You have helped me with the farm and the homestead for years. That makes you the best person to train Emil now that Anton has inherited the lumbermill, and I have inherited Papa's place in town.

"Eventually, my wife, Anna, and I will want to move into the Madison house. It was important to Papa and also to us to be sure

36

that you would stay on the farm and help Emil when I move." Stanislaus stayed quiet for a moment, then went on to say, "There is one other thing we need to discuss. Papa also told me one day, you would want to travel back to France to visit your family. In exchange for your agreement to help out here first, he promised the Karella businesses would pay for your travel to France and back if that is what you want to do."

Ed nodded his head in agreement and replied, "Yes, that is what he asked of me, and I agreed to always be here for this family as long as you need me."

Stanislaus smiled. "Ed, I want you to know you are an important part of this family. I don't know what I would have done without all your help over the years. Thank you for making this commitment to Papa and to us. And though I understand that someday you will go to visit your family in France, we will insist on another promise from you when you do."

Uncle Ed smiled and asked, "And what would this new promise be?"

Stanislaus replied, "That you will come back to us and never forget we love you and that you will always be part of our family."

An Unexpected Surprise

Stanislaus prepared to make a big change because of his brother Emil. Emil had come home for their father's funeral, then decided not to go back to Chicago right away. He asked permission to go on living at the homestead for a while. Emil confided in Stanislaus, telling him he and his family wanted to be part of the Karella family in Nebraska again.

That change of heart had fulfilled the condition in his father's will; Emil had to come home on his own and chose to stay in Madison before he could learn about his inheritance. Now, Stanislaus could complete his father's wishes regarding the family land. At the end of supper prayers, Stanislaus whispered softly to his father in heaven, "I'll talk to Emil in the morning, Papa." That evening, Stanislaus asked, "Emil, would you please meet me down in the kitchen at 6:00 a.m. tomorrow morning for a private talk?"

Us Kids (the Beans)
with Raymond Karella
Charles Pojar

Margaret Mary Bean, Francis Bean, Jerome Howard Bean Raymond Karella, Joseph Gerald-Bean & Charles Anthony Pojar
Family Photo

Emil nodded in agreement immediately. Quickly lost in reflection, Emil still felt ashamed for staying away so long. He had missed so much. There would never be a chance to tell his papa he was sorry or how much he loved him. Emil believed his brothers were giving him another chance to be part of the family, and he wanted to please Stanislaus.

Stanislaus cleared his throat, and the sound brought Emil back to the present. "In the morning, then. Goodnight, little brother." Suddenly, Stanislaus stopped on the stairs and looked back at Emil, saying, "Sorry, Emil. It's just habit—the little brother thing—please don't take it wrong. We realize you are a grown man with a family of your own. But Anton and I have missed our little brother."

Emil shook his head and replied, "Thank you, Stanislaus, for your thoughtfulness. I promise I will never take offense to that endearment again. I now understand the love behind the words. It's comforting to hear them once again."

Watching as his older brother nodded and continued up the stairs, Emil smiled. As Stanislaus disappeared from sight, Emil thought, *How blessed am I? Even after I ran away! When I came back, my brothers greeted me and my family with open arms and affection. They've treated me with respect and have forgiven me for my selfishness. I will not mess up my chance to make amends. I have missed the love and closeness of my family for too long!*

Alone in his room with Emily, Emil told her about his plan. His wife confirmed he was doing the right thing, saying, "Darling, I am happy to hear about your change of heart. I have known for years you regretted being estranged from your family. I would not have been able to endure such separation from mine. This reunion commemorating an ending can also be a new beginning for you and us. I am as excited as Raymond to be here. We love getting the chance to know our family here in Nebraska."

A Momentous Morning

Emil had coffee brewing by the time Stanislaus walked into the kitchen.

Stanislaus gave Emil a quick hug of appreciation, saying, "Good morning, little brother," grinning at the reference to their conversation of the previous evening. "Thank you for meeting me so early. Mornings were not your favorite time of day, as I recall."

Emil smiled. "And good morning to you, big brother. You are right about me and mornings. But that had to change when I became a station clerk in the city and even more so when I became a husband and a father. I'm very familiar with early mornings and long days now. It took extremely early mornings just to get my work done and have a little time to spend with Emily!"

"We have all been down that road, Emil, and know the routine well," replied Stanislaus with laughter in his voice. After pouring two cups of coffee, Stanislaus motioned to the table. Both men fondly remembered sitting together at this same table as younger boys.

After the brothers took a few sips of coffee, appreciating its warmth and savoring its flavor, Stanislaus got right to the point. "Emil, this meeting is about family matters.

"Anton is troubled. Anna and I are going to move to Papa's old house in town to be near him. He has little desire to run his business since his Anastasia passed away, and with Papa gone as well, Anton's mind and heart are nearly broken. I can see he has lost his direction and needs my help. Since his eldest son, Ambrose, has no interest in managing the sawmill and Anton's second son, Frank, has left the country, I am going to help Anton take care of the sawmill operation. My Anna will help guide Anton's youngest two children, Mary and Anastas, who are still living at home. Now, about the farm. Uncle Ed knows everything about running the homestead and our farm businesses. He will continue to live here and help you with all of that."

Emil John Karella with wife Emily, family photograph

Stanislaus could see the confusion all over Emil's face. Perhaps he was even a little angry his older brother assumed Emil would be willing to run the homestead. Holding up his hand to stop Emil's outburst, Stanislaus handed his younger brother a large envelope. Emil stared at the envelope with even more confusion. Then Stanislaus said softly, "Papa had this prepared for you. Anton and I have known about this since before Papa died."

Frowning, Emil had no idea what his brother was talking about. He had taken the envelope automatically when Stanislaus held it out to him. But he was totally at a loss to understand what any of this meant. The one thing that stuck in Emil's head and kept repeating itself was that Stanislaus said he was moving away from the farm! Emil kept thinking and asking himself, *How is that possible?*

Calm as ever, Stanislaus continued to speak while Emil's mind could make no sense of what he was hearing. "Be at peace, brother. Anton and I agree with Papa on this matter. Now, it is time for me to leave. I am meeting Anton at the sawmill. Anna, Mary Cecilia, and Anastas will be packing up all of our things starting tomorrow. We want to get moved into Madison by the week's end. We will see you out here on Saturdays for the family gatherings and picnics. That is, if you choose to continue those family traditions."

With that odd comment, Stanislaus stood up from the table and walked to the door. Perplexed, Emil jumped up and followed him as Stanislaus left the house and climbed onto the wagon sitting in the yard. Emil called after him from the porch, "Stanislaus! I don't understand!"

"Open the packet I gave you!" yelled Stanislaus with a grin. "Then you'll understand." Snapping the reins across the horse's rump, the wagon rolled away.

In a daze, Emil returned to the kitchen table to take a closer look at the packet. As he sat down, he recognized the handwriting and thought, *This packet belonged to Papa, and he wrote my name on it. Oh, Papa, I am sorry for staying away so long.*

With shaking hands, Emil opened the seal and pulled the contents out onto the tabletop. Under the ribbon that tied the papers together was another envelope addressed to him also in his father's handwriting. Taking a deep breath to calm himself, he opened the envelope and unfolded the letter. A flood of tears ran down his face even as his heart began to pound with exhilaration while he read the words.

"I, Wenceslaus Vaclav Karella, due hereby record this deed of transfer of my 160-acre Nebraska homestead in the name of my son. I bequeath this 160-acre homestead to Emil John Karella for the sum of $1.00 and with much love and affection. Wenceslaus Vaclav Karella."

Handwritten research notes by Florence Karella Roggenbach about the note she saw that Vaclav had written on the land documents

Emil could scarcely breathe or believe what the document said. Suddenly, he was a little boy again crying like a baby, but they were tears of joy. Not only had his wonderful father forgiven him, but he had also bequeathed to him a totally unexpected and unbelievably generous inheritance. His father had given him the homestead!

Closing his eyes, he thought, *Oh, Papa, I should have come home sooner. I should have written to you and told you I never meant to hurt you. I ran away to Chicago to get what I wanted. I did not want to admit I was hurting you and the family by running away from home. Now, I realize I could have had the life I wanted and my family here too. Please forgive me.*

Anton and Stanislaus are far more deserving of this gift. Yet, they agreed to this.

My brothers want me to have the homestead—something I can call my own. I am my own man now. Not just a boy living off the gracious-ness of his older brothers. Papa, I promise to make you proud of me. Thank you! Opening his eyes, he walked to the staircase, and with more excitement than he had felt in a long time, he yelled, "Emily! Raymond! Wake up! Come down here! I have something extraordinary to share with you!"

Karella Homestead, Moving Day

"Ed, will you tell Emil that was the last trunk?" said Stanislaus. "I have a few more of Anna's boxes in the kitchen, but I'm ready for a break. Do you two want to sit down and have a cup of coffee with me before I load these boxes and head to town?" Stanislaus asked.

"Sounds great!" Emil and Ed replied in unison.

"Besides, there are a few things we wanted to discuss before you go," Emil said.

Emily was in the kitchen baking and had just removed a pan of rohlikys and set them on the counter to cool. As Emil poured the coffee, he kept eyeing the rohlikys, as did Stanislaus and Uncle Ed. Emily pretended not to see them as she brushed the hot rolls with butter and sprinkled them with black poppy seeds. As she finished, she glanced at the men and burst out laughing. "I have never seen more pitiful looks! You may have these," Emily said as she set the baker's pan of rohlikys on a hot pad in front of the men.

"Thank you," they replied as one.

She raised an eyebrow, which was her no-nonsense look, as she gave them the pot of sweet butter and replied, "Enjoy this batch. The rest are for dinner!" Nodding in agreement, the men greedily ate every Bohemian crescent roll within their reach.

While enjoying their treat, Emil said, "Stanislaus, Ed and I have been talking, and we think installing a telephone out here on the farm would be a good investment. What do you think?"

Stanislaus replied, "Anton and I did talk about needing a telephone out here a while back. It would be an advantage having fast, reliable contact with the farm, but with grain revenues taking such a hard hit last year, we need to have a meeting about it. Grain prices are half of what they were two years ago. It might not be the best use of money right now. I'll let Anton know we talked about it, though, and let's plan to meet at the sawmill next week to make a final decision. In the

Early 1920s Telephone—can be seen at Madison County Historical Museum, Photo by GKM

meantime, could you find out what the costs of the equipment and installation would be?"

"Sure, we can do that," Ed replied. Then he added, "Sorry to cut our talk short, Stanislaus, but Emil and I have some work to finish before we head over to the train depot. I need to show Emil where we deliver our grain for shipment and pick up the new freight schedule."

"Yes, of course. Ed is right," Emil said as they headed to the door. "We will also stop by the Northwestern Exchange to get the telephone information while we are in town. The only other thing I'd like to get a price on is a radio for the farm. *The Daily News* in Norfolk published information about additional radio stations that will reach our area. It would be nice to have more news and weather sources out here."

Stanislaus nodded and replied, "I understand, but considering costs, it might have to be one or the other of these items. Let's talk about both options when you bring the information about the telephone next week."

1920s telephone service operator switchboard-can be seen at the Madison County Historical Museum, Photo by GKM

1923, Late January

Ambrose went out to the farm looking for his papa's brother Stanislaus. As he walked up to the house, his uncles Ed and Emil were walking toward the barn, and Ambrose waved and asked, "Is Uncle Stanislaus here?"

"Yes, we just left him in the kitchen," replied Emil. "If you hurry, you will catch him before he leaves. It's his last load of household items for the Madison house, and the girls are waiting for him in town."

"Thank you, Uncle Emil. Uncle Ed, I'll see you both later," Ambrose replied, then knocked on the door.

"Good morning, Uncle Stanislaus, Aunt Emily," Ambrose said politely. "Uncle Stanislaus, I need to talk to you. Do you have some time right now?"

"Good morning, Ambrose," replied Emily. Then she said, "Please excuse me. I am excited about going to town with Emil and Ed. I am sending a telegram to my parents, asking them to pack my household goods and my piano and put them on a train to Madison. I'll see you both later."

Stanislaus waved at Emily as he asked, "Ambrose, would you like to have some coffee while we talk?"

Ambrose nodded, and once they were both sitting down, he said, "I am very worried about Papa. As head of the Karella family, Papa has always held with the tradition of having the main holiday family celebrations at our house. He surprised everyone this year when he asked Martha if she wanted to host a joint Pojar and Karella Thanksgiving dinner. Then he asked Uncle Emil to host the family's Christmas gathering."

"Ambrose, I don't think that is anything to worry over. I am sure Martha enjoyed hosting the holiday gathering this year just as Emil and Emily did," Stanislaus replied.

"That may be, but since the holidays ended, Papa has become so sad and distant he will not talk to me about anything. He is going to the lumbermill every day, but the foreman says he just sits in his office. I'm gone several days during the week working in Norfolk, and that leaves my little sister and brother pretty much on their own. Papa has not been giving them direction, and I don't know what to do."

Stanislaus could see the distress on Ambrose's face and hear it in his voice. This behavior was so unlike his brother. It made him worry about Anton even more than he already was. He did not share that observation with his nephew but thought, *I should give Ambrose something to do to keep him busy. Then I can think about what I should do about Anton.*

"Ambrose, why don't you write to your older sister, Helen? Let her know what is going on and see what she thinks. In the meantime, I will stop by and see your father. Oh, and Ambrose, please come by Grandpa Vaclav's old house next week. Anna and I will be completely moved in by then, and I have something else I need to talk to you about. There is no rush, though. What I have to say can wait until then."

"Yes, I will come by the house after you get settled in town. Thank you for the talk today and your advice, Uncle Stanislaus," Ambrose replied in relief. "I'm sure Papa will listen to you. And I'll write Helen tonight."

Ambrose's Letter to His Sister Helen

Dear Helen,   *January 1923*

I am sorry to write to you about this and worry you. I need your advice and your help with Papa. First, let me tell you what is going on. Since the holidays ended, the foreman says Papa is not interested in the mill or his work. Did you know Grandpa Vaclav gave the homestead to Uncle Emil? Now, Uncle Emil and his wife, Aunt Emily, and their son, Raymond, are not going back to Chicago.

Grandpa Vaclav gave his house to Uncle Stanislaus. Since Uncle Ed and Uncle Emil are running the homestead, they don't need his help. Now, Uncle Stanislaus and Aunt Anna are moving into town. Uncle Stanislaus said he is going to help Papa run the lumbermill. Aunt Anna is going to do what she can to help Martha with the housework and with Mary Cecilia. You know how difficult our little sister can be. Mary argues with Martha over nearly everything. Stanislaus hopes Mary will respond better to Auntie Anna's directions.

Mary does have a close friendship with her old schoolteacher, Agnes Moore. Agnes just married one of the Pojar boys, and that makes her family now. I am hoping Mary Cecilia will continue to follow Agnes's advice without quarreling.

I am doing what I can to watch out for Anastas, but I am gone several days during the week, and I worry. I am hoping Uncle Ed will take charge of him. I wanted to know what else you think I should do. I hope to hear from you soon,

Your brother,
Love, Ambrose

Later the Same Week

A loud knock on the door brought Mary Cecilia running to see who it was. "Uncle Stanislaus! I'm so glad to see you!" she said in relief. "Maybe you can get Papa to eat. I have had breakfast sitting on the table for an hour. He has not come down yet, and it's time that Anastas and I left for school."

Stanislaus hugged his niece and said, "Don't fret, Mary Cecilia. Go with your brother and get yourselves off to school." Seeing the food on the table, he said, "I'll see your father eats that delicious-looking breakfast you made. Now, off with the two of you." He watched the two youngsters dash out the door, then headed for the stairs to the upper level of the house.

"Brother! I'm coming in!" Stanislaus announced as he opened the door. His brother still lay in bed with his head buried under a pillow. "Anton, get out of bed!" Stanislaus commanded.

Anton's head jerked out from under the pillow and looked in the direction the order had come from. He could have sworn it was his papa's voice that had ordered him to get out of bed. But as his eyes cleared, he could see Stanislaus standing in his bedroom.

"Stanislaus," he said groggily, "for a minute, I thought you were Papa."

"Anton, if it had been Papa, he might have dumped a bucket of cold water on your head for catching you in bed this late in the day.

We have a lot to talk about, so get up and come down to breakfast. Or I might do as Papa would have done."

Stanislaus ate a piece of bacon thoughtfully and drank coffee while he watched Anton eat. He got up and refilled both their coffee cups, then sat down across from his brother. Stanislaus knew he had to be blunt and to the point and said, "Anton, you have got to snap out of this depression."

Anton felt exhausted even though all he seemed to do lately was sleep. He looked up from his food and said, "Don't you think I have tried? I can't seem to figure out what to do or find my direction. I always knew my direction before . . ." He trailed off.

"Since when did you have to do anything by yourself, brother? You have family! We all care! I CARE! We are going to get through this together. You and me, just like we used to do when we were boys. We are the men of the family now, and you don't have the luxury of quitting or giving up!"

Anton frowned. "Who said I'm quitting?" he replied with more vigor than Stanislaus had expected.

Anton's reaction was a good sign. Stanislaus decided to use the same tactic again. "Well, let me see . . . why would anyone believe you are a quitter? Maybe because you are not eating, not managing your business, not talking to anyone . . . including your children! You are scaring them and me with this behavior! You need to change what you are doing.

"Our parents brought us to this great country, and we have built good solid businesses and lives that we must take care of. We are going to do this together! I will be here every morning. We are going to eat breakfast, and then I am going to go to work with you every day. If you are worried—talk to me—and we will figure it out. We are going to start enjoying our families. God has given us a good life, Anton. Our parents were an inspiration, and they taught us how to be strong and work hard. They showed us what it takes to be happy with the gifts we have been given, so let's decide to be happy and live our lives! Do you remember what Papa used to say after Mama died?"

Anton replied softly, "No one is guaranteed a tomorrow."

Stanislaus's voice softened when he replied, "That's right. So, get up and start living, and I'll help you."

The Following Week

When Ambrose heard Grandpa Vaclav had deeded his house in town to his second son upon his death, he worried about what would happen to his grandfather's tools and the workshop. Ambrose found himself immensely relieved when his uncle Stanislaus asked him to come over for a visit.

The following week as Ambrose headed over to his grandpa's old house to see Stanislaus, he hoped to have a chance to find out what was going to happen with the workshop and tools.

"Thank you for coming to see me and for explaining your concerns, Ambrose," his uncle said. "You have no need to worry anymore. I am aware that your grandpa Vaclav gave his tools to you. Now, I can also tell you that the workshop will be yours for as long as you want it."

Relieved to hear the tools were still his, Ambrose was overwhelmed with gratitude to discover the workshop was his as well. Just knowing it would be there for him was a great comfort. Nevertheless, Ambrose believed it would take a while before he could work in that space without being overcome with grief. It was their special place—the place where he and his grandfather shared so much over the years, and he missed the man deeply.

Anton Karella Reaches Out to His Eldest Daughter

Shortly after receiving her brother's disturbing letter, Helen received another letter. This one was from her father, Anton, and as she read it, her eyes stung as she held back her tears. Her father had asked her to come home for a while. Stanislaus was helping him at work, but he needed her help at home.

Helen set the letter aside, thinking while her children slept. She had felt terrible not being able to go home when her mother passed away. Nor had it been possible for her to go home when her grandfather passed. In her heart, she knew she needed to be with her father and her brothers and sisters as much as they needed her. Determined to ask her husband to let her go to them, she waited for him to get home from work.

As soon as he stepped through the door, Helen asked, "Alvin, will you sit with me a moment, please?" He responded to the seriousness in her voice and sat down beside her. She handed him a letter, and he felt relieved to see it was from Anton. After reading the message from his father-in-law, Alvin knew what Helen wanted. His wife had grieved after the deaths in her family, and it had been hard on her to be away from them. Alvin put down the letter and took hold of her hand.

"Please, let me and the children go and stay with Papa for a while. I am sure I can help him. Losing Mama and then Grandpapa in the same year has just been too much all at once. My brothers and sisters don't know what to do. They are also hurting with the loss of Mama. Since it is Papa asking me to come home, I think he will listen to me.

"Francis will be old enough to go to school next year. It's a good time to put down roots in Madison. I know it is sooner than you would like for us to stop traveling with you. But since we are having another child—"with that comment, Helen put her hand on her slightly protruding stomach for emphasis, then went on to say—"I would have had to move back to Madison in a couple of months anyway. If the children and I go now, I could be helping Papa and be near the doctor when it is time to deliver our baby. Since that will not be until the end of September, I could really help everyone right now."

Alvin held his wife in a warm embrace and whispered into her hair, "You are right, Helen. I will not worry about you or our children or the new baby with your papa to watch over you. Besides, when have I ever been able to say *no* to you? Yes, my sweet wife, we will do this for Anton and for our family."

The Makings of a Bedtime Story

That evening when Helen tucked her two-year-old daughter, Margaret Mary, and her three-year-old son, Francis, into bed, she said, "I want to tell you a story. Years ago, when your papa and I got married, he worked for a road construction company, and his job took him away from home for long periods of time. This was before and also after you and your brother, Francis, were born. One day, he got so lonely for us that he built a house on an old tractor frame. Your papa created a house on wheels so he could pull it just like a work wagon. After that, he took us with him in the rolling house wherever his work was! Wasn't that clever of him?"

She paused, and the children responded by clapping their hands and saying ,"Oh yes, Mama! Papa is very clever!"

"Now, while we were on the road with your papa, Grandma Anastasia got sick and passed away, and then your great-grandpa Vaclav passed away too."

"That made Grandpa Anton real sad two times, right, Mama?" little Francis asked.

"Yes, it did," she replied, "and that is why Grandpa Anton sent your papa and me a letter. In it, he wrote, *'Please come home, Helen. This sadness is too great, and we need one another.'* Your papa is a kind and generous person, and God helped him understand what to do. That is why he is taking us to live with your grandpa for a while. When we get there, it will be our job to help Grandpa Anton not be so lonely and help him forget about being sad. Just like it is your papa's job to continue going back to his construction job to work. He will miss us, but he knows we will be safe and well taken care of because we are living with your grandpa Anton."

"Is Papa sad that we are going to live with Grandpa and not with him?" her daughter asked.

"Yes, but he decided that your grandpa was sadder. Your papa will come to see us whenever he gets a few days off. So, my darlings, that is why we are going to live at Grandpa Anton's house in Madison."

Good News

Anton sat quietly after reading the letter from Helen. He closed his eyes in relief and thought, *Stanislaus was right. I am so glad I wrote to Helen. Thank You, Lord, for answering my prayers and helping Alvin understand. Thank You for bringing my dear daughter home.* Anton went in search of his other children to give them the good news and to begin preparing for Helen and his grandchildren's arrival.

Ambrose had the largest bedroom in the house, and it would easily fit two beds for his sister and the two older children. The third child, Jerome Howard, born May 11, 1922, was just a year old and only needed a cradle. Volunteering to give up his room, Ambrose assured his father he didn't mind doing this for Helen and the kids. "Papa, I travel so much for my blacksmith work that I'm not home often enough to need that much space. I'll move my things into Martha's old room. I know it is the smallest bedroom in the house, but it will do fine when I need a place to sleep."

Alvin and Helen Karella Bean

When Alvin dropped his family off at Anton Karella's home in Madison, true to his loving and creative nature, he suddenly brightened up and said, "My dear children, don't look so sad! I am the luckiest papa in the world! I still get to see my wife and family at the end of each job, and so I will see you all again soon." After hugging them and kissing each of them on the forehead, he said, "Please be good and help your mama and your grandpa."

Helen had been standing next to her husband when he made that statement. She felt so proud of him. No words could explain how thankful she was for this kindness he had bestowed on her father. Helen would make sure the children understood how kind their papa was, thinking, *I will make this into a regular bedtime story so they will never forget how wonderful their papa is and how and why they came to live with their grandpa Anton.*

Helen Karella Bean held her baby son, Jerome Howard, Margaret Mary stood on one side of their grandpa Anton, while her brother

Francis stood close to their Grandpa's other side. From the doorway, everyone waved goodbye to Alvin. Margaret Mary reached up and took hold of her grandpa's hand, and sounding very grown up, she said, "Grandpa, my papa is very kind, isn't he?"

Anton was astonished by his tiny granddaughter's observation and replied, "Yes, he is."

Two Weeks Later at Anton Karella's Home

Within weeks of Helen and the children's arrival, everything had changed for the better. Ambrose sighed in relief. The whole family had begun to revive with the excitement of having a baby and the laughter of children in the house again. Grandpa Anton smiled regularly, and it eased Ambrose Jerome's heart to watch his father taking charge of the older children. It didn't matter if Grandpa Anton was being marshaled by little Margaret Mary on how to set the breakfast table or reading books to young Francis; he clearly enjoyed it all. Seeing the improvement in his father lifted a huge amount of stress from Ambrose's mind, and he began coming home more often from Norfolk. He found that he loved entertaining his older niece and nephew on the few evenings he had with them.

As spring faded into the warmth of summer, Alvin visited his family in Madison between construction jobs. Late in May, Alvin came home to celebrate Jerome Howard's second birthday. During the family dinner, he and Helen made an announcement, telling everyone they were going to have another baby. The new baby would be born sometime around the middle to the end of September. Grandpa Anton immediately voiced his concern, wondering if they had enough space in Helen's room for another bed.

"Papa, do not worry," Helen said. "We don't need another regular-sized bed yet. We only need a cradle, and that will not take up much room. Baby Jerome will need his small bed for a while yet. We can just put a second cradle right next to his."

Madison County Fairgrounds, 2021—Photo taken by GKM

Five Months Later

The heat of the Madison summer had been particularly hard to bear during Helen's pregnancy. September had not cooled off yet, and her fourth child was due in a few weeks. She desperately needed a break from the chaos created by her three rambunctious toddlers.

Helen had been invited to join the group going to the Madison County Fair, but she had convinced her family to take the children and let her stay home. All she wanted at the moment was some heavenly peace and quiet.

Seeing her need for a little rest, Anton, Stanislaus, and his wife, Anna, volunteered to take Francis, Margaret Mary, and little Howard to the fair. The children were so excited Auntie Anna only had to ask them to put on their shoes once. Anton and Stanislaus laughed to see the children lined up by the door waiting for Auntie Anna to tell them it was time to go.

Helen napped on and off the entire afternoon and did not hear the family return until the kitchen door opened around sunset. She waddled into the kitchen right in time to see Anton, Stanislaus, and Anna each carrying a sleeping child. Helen grinned, thinking, *Thank heaven there were three adults keeping track of the children. All three grownups look ready to drop from exhaustion at any moment.*

After Anton, Stanislaus, and Anna returned to the kitchen from putting the children to bed, Anna said, "Helen, it took all three of us to keep up with the children—how on earth do you do this alone?"

Helen hugged Anna as she thanked them for the restful afternoon they had given her. Grinning at Anna's question, clearly surprised at how much effort it took to keep track of the children, she laughingly replied, "After so many years of doing it every day, mothers just get used to it."

CHAPTER 4

Meaningful Beginnings

Commitment to Live

Francis Bean, eldest son of Helen Karella Bean & husband, Alvin

The sound of children's laughter penetrated his conscious thought. The sweetness chased away a coldness clouding his mind. The remnant of a nightmare . . . *he had been lost and alone . . . running. Then, as he followed that joyful sound, he escaped from the darkness!*

Opening his eyes, his breathing slowed as Anton realized what he had felt was only a bad dream.

Swinging his feet out of bed, he stood up and walked to the pitcher and basin sitting on Anastasia's dressing table. Splashing cold water on his face, he looked at his reflection in the mirror. The troubling fragments of his dark dream made him ask himself, *Who has a perfect life? Who never experiences loss? The answer is nobody, Anton! Let go of that old pain and remember the love. That is what Papa advised you to do.*

Right as he thought the word love, once again, laughter rang through the walls along with a bumping sound. It made Anton smile knowing little Margaret Mary and Francis were thumping down the stairs. *They are probably hungry,* he thought, sure his grandchildren were headed to the kitchen looking for breakfast.

Refocusing his eyes, he thought, *We are born, and we die— everything else is subject to change based on what we do with our choices.* "Get busy living, old man," he said to himself in a whisper, "or you will drive everyone you love away."

Right then, infectious laughter bubbled up the stairs once more, and Anton promised himself in a hushed voice, "From today on, you will live each moment. You will not judge those moments as good or bad—you will only seek the good despite what happens! You will do this for yourself and your family." Then, closing his eyes, he whispered, "Anastasia, I promise to do this for you too. You tried to show me how much I have in this life and all the love I have to live for. Stanislaus has been trying to do the same, and now I can finally see it for myself . . . thank you."

Drying the water off his face, Anton dressed quickly and hurried down to the kitchen.

When the children saw him, they squealed with delight, yelling in their excitement, "Grandpa! We are hungry! Can we have breakfast, please?"

Scooping them up into his arms for a hug, he wiggled his mustache against their cheeks and necks and made them giggle because his whiskers tickled. "Yes!" Anton replied with enthusiasm as he set them down on the floor. "Shall we have pancakes?" The children eagerly nodded yes, and Anton replied, "Alright then, pancakes it is!"

The Arrival

The whole Karella family sat together in church on Sunday, September 30, 1923, feeling excited but at the same time a little worried and wondering the same question. *When is Helen going to have her baby?*

Doc Linden said the baby would arrive at the end of September, and here it was . . . the end of September and no baby.

Margaret Mary Bean, only daughter of Helen Karella Bean & husband, Alvin

Secretly, Anton felt relieved the baby had not arrived yet because he and Stanislaus had just completed their surprise project for Helen, and they had not brought it home yet.

Even though they still sat in church, Anton whispered to his brother, "Stanislaus, let's bring the present over to the house this afternoon. Tell everyone to come over after lunch around 4:00 p.m. Then we can give Helen her surprise."

Stanislaus nodded and whispered to Ambrose . . . he nodded and whispered to Martha . . . she ignored the frowns she received from the people sitting in the pews behind them and whispered to her husband, Rudy, and asked him to pass the information on to Mary Cecilia. Eventually, everyone at church knew the secret. That was, all except Margaret Mary and Francis who didn't know how to keep a secret yet.

Helen waited at home having felt too uncomfortable to go to Mass with the family. She said she felt huge and would have taken up too much space in the pew. But honestly, she didn't want to run the risk of going into labor and having the baby in church.

She felt thoroughly pleased to see Stanislaus's wife, Anna, at her kitchen door about an hour later. *Mass must be over,* she thought.

As her aunt Anna walked into the house, she asked, "Helen, how are you feeling?"

Helen grimaced and replied sourly, "As big as our wagon horse!"

Anna's tinkling laughter lightened Helen's mood. "Now, Helen, you will forget all of this discomfort once the baby is born. You sit down and put your feet up. Mary Cecilia and I will make lunch for Ambrose, Anastas, Margaret Mary and Francis, and little Howard.

Grandpa Anton and Stanislaus will be here in a bit. They had to stop by the sawmill, and then they were coming right home."

The brothers set the gift down on the porch, then Stanislaus knocked on the door, and Anna opened it. The men carried the gift in, and the family sitting around the table turned to look at Helen and suddenly yelled, "SURPRISE!"

Taking hold of Helen's hand, Anna said, "It's for the baby."

Then Stanislaus added, "I want everyone to know the baby's grandpa made this little cradle himself at the sawmill."

Helen's eyes teared up with happiness, and she smiled as she got slowly to her feet so she could examine the beautiful wooden cradle. "It's perfect, Papa!" she exclaimed.

Stanislaus smiled at the happiness he saw in his niece's eyes and said, "Your papa and I learned how to make many lovely things out of wood from your grandfather Vaclav when we were young men."

Helen had been standing between her father and her uncle as she reached out to touch the cradle, and her smile turned into a strained look. She suddenly felt . . . a change. Putting one hand on her belly, she grabbed her father's arm tightly and whispered tensely, "Now, Papa, stay calm and don't be alarmed . . . but I need you and Anna to help me to my room. I need Uncle Stanislaus to go get the doctor . . . and I need Ambrose to take charge of all of the children and keep them down here in the living room."

Everyone in the room simultaneously felt happy, nervous, and anxious, and they were laughing and even felt a little scared as they stood frozen in place with the realization: *The baby is coming!*

Then Anton said, "Get moving! Quickly now! Do as you were asked and hurry." Supporting Helen between himself and Anna, the three of them climbed the short flight of stairs and got Helen back to her bed without any issues.

Doctor Linden and his nurse arrived within 20 minutes, and they left Stanislaus in the kitchen with orders to boil water and get a stack of fresh linens ready. Then they went up to see Helen and check on her progress.

Anna and Anton joined Stanislaus in the kitchen and helped Stanislaus prepare everything the doctor asked for.

Many Long Hours Later

All the children lay wrapped in their blankets, snoozing on the floor in front of the fireplace. The sleepy-eyed adults in the kitchen drank coffee to try to stay awake. It was obvious the children were far more comfortable than the grown-ups who had been awake and waiting all night for news. When it came, everyone thanked God it was good news!

After a long labor, Helen happily held her new son, Joseph Gerald Bean, who stubbornly refused to be born in September. Instead, he arrived in the early morning hours of October 1, 1923.

Holiday Tradition

The gatherings at Anton Karella's home for a holiday feast usually had the house filled by the whole family. Anton decided it was time to start some new traditions, or everyone would just feel sad. It was only the second Thanksgiving without *them*. Anton shook his head, thinking, *Anastasia and Papa would want us to be happy!*

Knowing he had to begin somewhere, Anton gave Mary Cecelia permission to accept the invitation to attend the Voborny Thanksgiving celebration with her boyfriend, Stanley. Then he telephoned his daughter Martha Genevieve and encouraged her to take their son, Jerome Gregory, with her husband, Rudy, and spend Thanksgiving at the Pojar family's celebration.

Martha had been so surprised and pleased with his consideration of her husband and the Pojar family's feelings that she immediately promised they would spend Christmas with him. That reaction had been unexpected, but it made Anton very happy.

Anton's youngest son, Anastas, would enjoy the Thanksgiving celebration as long as Uncle Ed came to dinner and shared more stories about Europe. Stanislaus and Anna had already said they planned to attend.

Next, Anton called the farm and talked to Emil. "Don't cook anything, Papa, and tell Helen not to worry either. Em, Raymond and I will bring all the dinner fixings."

"Thank you, brother," replied Anton. "Helen will be extremely pleased to hear that! The children keep her running constantly. See you all on Thursday." As Anton hung up the telephone, he thought, *I've made a good start on making some new traditions.* There was only one moment of sadness, and it concerned his son Frank. *I think Frank would like my idea about starting new traditions. He is definitely making new ones of his own somewhere in South America. I hope he is happy.*

Thanksgiving Day, 1923

Anton was the only one awake in the house. Enjoying his second cup of coffee, he read the newspaper with the radio playing softly in the background. Unexpectedly, a loud knocking began on the kitchen door. Opening it, Anton was surprised to see Uncle Ed, Stanislaus, his wife, Anna, Emil and his wife, Emily, and Anton's nephew, Raymond, on his porch. They laughed and yelled, "Morning! Happy Thanksgiving!" Anton could see their arms full of evergreen boughs. He could smell they had been freshly cut, and as the group made their way through the house, the aroma of pine sap filled each room. The scent made the house feel festive and filled his head with wonderful memories of past holidays.

Suddenly, giggling and high-pitched laughter came from the living room as Margaret Mary and Francis came bouncing down the stairs. Helen followed yawning. She held baby Joseph in one arm while toddling Howard clung to her other hand, insisting on walking on his stubby legs.

Everyone dressed for cold weather emptied their arms, then went out to the wagon for another load. This time, Raymond brought in branches of holly with redberries to add to the evergreens. The rest of the arrivals brought in the makings of the feast they would have later. Anton's sister-in-law, Emily, said, "Helen, we've decided that this Thanksgiving, we are going to make a pork roast instead of a turkey! It was time to butcher that old, spotted porker at the farm before he got too big to handle. Stanislaus suggested it would make a good-sized tasty meal for today."

Anton smiled and replied, "I think that is a wonderful idea. Pork roast sounds scrumptious." Then he looked at his brothers and said, "Why don't we take charge of the baby boys? Everyone else seems to have the rest of the preparations under control."

As Helen worked beside Anna in the kitchen preparing the pork roast for the oven, she hummed a familiar a tune. Suddenly, Anna laughed and said, "I recognized that tune you are humming! It's that *We Have No Bananas* song from the radio . . . but who is the singer?"

Anna tried to remember, but Emily replied before she could. "It is Billy Jones."

"I can never remember all the silly words to the song, but the tune is stuck in my head," replied Helen.

"Oh goodness," Emily said, "I know what you mean! Catchy tunes like that can drive me crazy until I learn to play them. By the way, talking about music, I don't think I've told either of you about my wonderful news!" Helen and Anna shook their heads, and Emily said, "I just got a letter from my parents. They have shipped my piano along with our household items from Chicago."

"How wonderful that there will be more music at the farm!" replied Helen.

"It is nothing fancy, just a small upright-style piano that has good tone. I can't wait to play it for our family gatherings. We can sing Christmas carols," Emily said excitedly.

"Maybe you could help us practice the hymns for church," suggested Anna.

Emily nodded and added, "I could even host a regular choir practice!"

The three women bustled about the kitchen singing happily while they prepared the rest of the food. Glancing up periodically, Helen, Emily, and Anna found it delightful to watch the three elderly Karella brothers sitting at the table keeping the baby boys busy.

Anton listened to the wonderful sound of the women's voices coming from the kitchen and felt peace in his heart as he sat with his brothers and played with his grandsons.

In the other room, Ambrose and Anastas oversaw replenishing the firewood bin and keeping the living room fireplace going. They stoked the fire with pieces of wood and chunks of coal, and it gave off enough heat to keep both the living room and dining area warm. Their other job was to keep the phonograph playing or find holiday music on the radio for everyone to enjoy.

Emily left Anna and Helen in the kitchen to supervise the other decorating. She enlisted her son, Raymond, Francis, and Margaret Mary. As they made a Christmas advent wreath with some of the pretty holly, three pink candles, and one purple candle, Emily explained to the little ones that the candles represented the four weeks before Christmas Day. She placed it on the fireplace mantel high enough so curious toddler hands could not reach it.

After that, the group made small evergreen wreaths with pretty ribbons and the rest of the holly and berries to set around the candles on the dinner table. The pure excitement and joy shown by the children surpassed any lingering sadness regarding missing family members.

Delectable foods filled the dinner table, and they called the family to take their seats. Anton held out his hands, and one by one, each person took hold of the hand on either side of themselves. When they completed the circle, Anton began the Thanksgiving prayer. "Dear Lord, we thank you for this bounty on our table, for the people that have gathered to praise Your name, and for all the blessings You have bestowed on our family. Watch over our loved ones near and far who cannot be with us . . . and those that sit at Your Thanksgiving feast in heaven . . . in Your Holy Name, may this food bless our bodies . . . make us strong—"

Suddenly, a loud whisper came from one end of the table. "Is prayers over yet?" asked four-year-old Francis.

"I don't think so. Grandpa didn't say Amen yet," replied three-year-old Margaret Mary.

All the adults looked at the two children whispering to each other, grinning quietly.

"I'm hungry . . . do you think Grandpa will say Amen soon?" whispered Francis.

"Be patient. Grandpa will say it when he's good and ready," Margaret Mary whispered back, sounding exactly like her mother.

Grandpa Anton couldn't help himself. He let out a laugh and loudly said, "AMEN! Let's eat! I'm hungry! Who else is hungry?"

"I am!" Francis yelled.

"Me too!" yelled little Margaret Mary.

This playful situation brought back beautiful memories from Anton's childhood. Something very similar had happened between him, Stanislaus, and their father, Wenceslaus Vaclav, when they had been young boys in Kutna Hora, Bohemia.

Glancing at Stanislaus, Anton could see he remembered that long ago moment too. How extraordinary to see the parallel between generations, though he was now the father, and these were his grand-children. It occurred to him they had just made a precious memory to add to that legacy of loving playfulness. That thought made him truly happy. It had been a while since he felt so alive. His heart was healing. He felt peace flooding his entire being as he watched his wonderful family laughing and teasing one another as they eagerly filled their plates.

The family feasted on roast pork, baked apples, mashed potatoes, gravy, and corn on the cob saved from this year's harvest, hot and dripping with sweet butter. The final treat that followed this magnificent meal was pumpkin pie with whipped cream.

When Anton left the dinner table, he felt so stuffed he barely made it to his chair in the living room. Clearly, everyone else felt the same way as they sat around the fire with satisfied smiles on their faces. Closing his eyes for a minute, Anton thought, *Papa, Mama, and Anastasia, I know you were here today. I could feel you in the warmth of the laughter and appreciate the cooking skills you taught our children through the delicious flavors in the food . . . and in the love we shared today. Thank you for helping us find reasons to be grateful and putting joy in our hearts. Now, I know this Christmas is going to be a wonderful celebration!*

Almost Christmas

Helen had put the babies to bed, and now she noted her son, Francis, had fallen to sleep on the floor by the fire. Talking quietly with her brother Ambrose, she also noticed Margaret Mary was still wide awake. Deciding she should get up and take care of Francis, Ambrose thought of it first and waved at her to stay where she was. Helen watched as her brother gently picked up his nephew and carried him up to bed.

Sitting in the quiet with her daughter, Margaret Mary snuggled close to Helen's side and wrapped her tiny arm around her mother's, then whispered, "Mama, will Papa be home for Christmas?"

"Yes, my sweet girl. Are you getting excited?"

"Oh yes, Mama, I am!" she replied.

"Me too!" her mama whispered back.

Helen Karella Bean and
husband Alvin Bean

CHAPTER 5

Ambrose Jerome Karella: Son, Grandson, and Brother

1924, Time Moves Forward

At 26 years old, Ambrose admitted he had always felt the need to be responsible. Even four years ago, he had taken being the eldest son of his generation seriously. He made every effort to lead by example, though at times, that was close to an impossible task.

Reflecting on Memories

Ambrose had always been inspired by his father and grandfather's accomplishments. He dreamed that one day, he would have his own blacksmith and repair shop in his hometown of Madison. Ambrose never rushed into things. He took time to think wisely before taking a big step. Therefore, he decided to work for a blacksmith in the nearby town of Norfolk first before opening his own business.

He believed working for the Karella family businesses was not the same as working for an established businessman in the trade. His Norfolk job would put all the training Ambrose had acquired over the years into practical use, and his work would get noticed by potential customers he wanted to attract for his future business.

Early in his blacksmithing career, Ambrose brought projects to his grandfather's workshop as often as possible. He did this in hopes of enticing his elderly mentor to keep working with him.

Years ago, his grandpa Vaclav had encouraged him not to wait any longer. As his teacher, Vaclav had told him he was ready to open his own blacksmithing business in Madison. But then his mother suddenly passed away, and Ambrose found it hard to deal with that loss. He put off making any changes in his career. Five months after that, he suffered another huge shock when his grandfather Vaclav also passed away.

Putting his future on hold, Ambrose found it far easier to continue working mindlessly for the smith in Norfolk. The work kept his hands and body too busy to give into his pain and sorrow.

This time also gave him endless hours to think about what he had learned from the people who influenced him the most. Courage and patience, he learned from his mother, Anastasia, and his grandmother Antonia. He thanked God regularly he had been blessed to have such strong and inspiring women in his life.

His father, Anton, and grandfather Vaclav had taught him to have a solid work ethic and told him he could do anything he set his mind to. They selflessly dedicated their lives to making sure their children received an education. As teachers, they were excellent role models of success, demonstrating how to build businesses and how to secure a future for a man's wife and children in a new land.

These two men proved to Ambrose that with education and applying what he learned, nothing was impossible. Once he set his mind to the task—and with enough time—he could accomplish his goals.

When his older sister, Helen, and her family moved back into their papa's house in January of 1923, he had been relieved. Ambrose immediately turned over the worries he had regarding his little brother and sister to Helen.

Returning his focus to his work kept him away from home a good deal during the remaining cold months of the year. During this time, once he did not have to worry about his brothers, sisters, or father, he discovered he had not dealt with his own feelings of loss. Ambrose still found it hard to think about the future, missing his grandfather's guidance deeply.

Family Concerns

The family worried a little about Ambrose. Having been a rather private person all his life, the Karella family understood Ambrose mourned the loss of his mother and his grandfather in his own way. They were forced to see that as an explanation for why he had become so reserved with everyone, except Uncle Stanislaus and Helen's older children. Ambrose only spoke when he had to, even with those who lived in the same house. Helen mentioned how quiet and distant Ambrose had become to her father.

Anton replied, "Ambrose is not running away like Frank did. He is dealing with his feelings. The quietness is unconsciously done. Please don't pester him. In time, he will come around. I am sure of it."

A Nickname Solves a Problem

Ambrose's clients in Norfolk started calling him Rusty. It might have been because of his fair skin, faint freckles, and shock of curly red hair. Or it could have been because he quit introducing himself. His unusual name made people ask questions. Either way, the change served his purpose. Rusty's customers quit asking personal questions and kept the conversation centered on business, and he continued to use the nickname at work.

When he started using the nickname with family, no one argued against it. They quickly discovered he responded better when they called him Rusty. He was talking to them again. That was all that mattered to the family, and the nickname stuck.

Rusty felt his confidence growing as his reputation as a skilled smith and leather worker became more known. When customers mentioned he made leather or iron work look effortless, Rusty just smiled. He remembered feeling the same way as a boy when he watched his grandfather work. Those comments always reminded Rusty just how much he had learned about skill and creativity from his grandfather. That knowledge usually made him feel proud. Once in a while, it still made him sad, though his bouts of sadness came with less and less frequency as time passed.

With such a creative mind, it was not long before Rusty suggested adding electrical or mechanical repairs as a service to his boss in the Norfolk smith shop. The man thought it was a good idea and decided to promote the repair service through the remainder of the winter. Once the service center opened at the smith's shop, the new work kept Rusty far too busy to dwell on sadness. Before he knew it, the weather warmed up, and he looked forward to spring.

An Old Workshop Filled with Wonderful Memories

Winter was finally over, and the first warm weekend in May, Rusty stopped by to see his uncle Stanislaus. After his visit was over, Rusty found himself drawn to the old workshop.

The large barn door creaked with disuse. Suddenly, a vivid memory filled his mind. He was a schoolboy again and excited about becoming his grandfather's apprentice. Rusty spent every afternoon after school with his grandfather in this place for five years. Such thrilling times full of invention and new ideas, and they had shared it all.

Light and fresh air poured in as Rusty squinted, and his eyes adjusted to the darkness. Unused to anyone's presence, the pigeons roosting in the rafters burst into flight. Rapidly flapping wings broke the silence with wind whistling through their flight feathers. As suddenly as the flurry began, it was over. The air above him went silent as the frightened birds exited the building through the single window above the hayloft.

Walking along the dusty benches and looking at the tools on the wall, Rusty remembered the thrill he had always felt in this place. His grandfather would say, "Ambrose, it is going to be an era filled with stimulating innovation and marvelous inventions." Smiling softly, he could hear his grandfather's voice during those many conversations about the new conveniences being introduced into American cities.

Grandpa Vaclav would say, "Of course, Ambrose, you can't expect that these inventions will reach our small farming town any time soon. No matter how common electricity, indoor plumbing, and refrigerators become to big-city dwellers, I believe they will always seem almost miraculous to simple farmers like us."

Rusty remembered nodding knowing his grandfather was right. He had been taught that the only way a person made life better was by working hard in a trade or building a successful business. His grandfather had shown him that one way or another, everything had a cost. Nothing was completely free.

Even as a young man, he believed success in life was a matter of perspective. By the time he graduated high school, he had mastered many crafts and possessed an innovative mind, which he felt ensured he would never be without an income or a job. Each discipline and craft he learned could yield a good living. Yet, Ambrose's first choice was working with metal and leather, which were his grandfather's favorite skills.

Now, this dusty place brought back fond memories and good feelings of being praised by his grandfather. After a long lesson, Vaclav would say, "Ambrose, the skills you have mastered make me proud, and the quality of your work is excellent. I am also reassured by your common sense. I have great confidence in you and your ability to build a solid future for yourself."

As Rusty looked around the old workshop, he felt blessed to have such vivid memories of the man who taught him so much. Smiling, he realized how much he missed this place. Deciding to do some cleaning, he took off his jacket and hung it on the peg near the door. Dusting off the bench, he said, "Gosh, it will be nice to work in here again." Then he softly added, "Grandpa, I'm back. I feel your presence in this place, and that makes me very happy."

Anastas Leonard Karella

Helen frowned a little and said, "I would like this summer to be a happy one, Rusty. Once Anastas is out of school, I want him to take on a few chores around here. Could you talk to him? He is not listening to me, and I need help."

"Helen, I don't think I can do anything about this problem. These days, Anastas does not listen to anyone except Uncle Ed. I love Anastas too! But I don't know what to do with him, and neither does Papa."

No Answers to an Issue

Rusty was frustrated because he didn't understand Anastas's thinking. He had grown up understanding a person had to work hard to get what they wanted out of life. It made sense to focus on being productive, knowing it was the only logical method that allowed a man to accomplish his goals.

Achieving goals took serious discipline and dedication. It wasn't fun and games. His youngest brother was clueless about what Rusty believed it took to be successful. He had tried many times to get his little brother to understand his thinking was flawed, without success.

Though they shared a close bond of love and friendship, the contrast between their thought processes was completely opposite. Granted, Anastas was only 13, but still, he seemed immature for that age and somewhat irresponsible and impulsive on top of his lack of perception.

The boy did not want to work in the shop with him. Nor did he have an interest in working at the family's lumber mill and only worked out at the homestead to please Uncle Ed. All Anastas talked about was getting out of Nebraska and seeing America. He even daydreamed about seeing Europe.

On numerous occasions when Rusty had had enough of Anastas's attitude, he would sarcastically ask, "And just how are you going to afford to travel, Anastas? You are not interested in any kind of work that will make money."

Anastas would laugh and reply, "I'll figure it out. I will find a way."

Most of the time, Rusty would shake his head, irritated at such a ridiculous answer, but kept silent. Once in a while, he let his annoyance show and would reply, "You are a dreamer. Trust me. You will have to get a job and make some money before you can travel. You might try sparing that truth some thought."

Anastas would usually reply with something like, "You are a real sourpuss, Rusty. Don't underestimate me. I'll figure out how to see the world. Just see if I don't."

Helen cleared her throat and asked, "Rusty, have you thought of any ideas that will help?"

Shaking his head to get rid of his old frustrations, he thought about Helen's current dilemma and suggested, "Helen, why don't you call Uncle Ed out at the farm? I'm sure he will know the best way to influence Anastas."

Rusty made sure to word his suggestions carefully. Though Helen had been less emotional after her son, Joseph Jerald, was born, she would still cry if she got frustrated, and he never knew what to do when that happened. Helen took Rusty's advice and confided in Uncle Ed. After Ed stepped in to help with her baby brother, Helen calmed down, and so did Rusty. In fact, things improved around the house so much Rusty enjoyed coming back to the cheery atmosphere created by Helen and her four children.

Rusty looked forward to the times when his brother-in-law came home for a visit between road construction jobs. Alvin would hold his infant son while Helen spent time with her toddler and Grandpa Anton entertained his two oldest grandchildren. It worked out nicely, and Rusty and Alvin would spend hours talking softly about the changes taking place in Nebraska and around the world.

Anton was not the only one to change for the better after Helen moved back home. Everyone benefited from the new arrangement. Celebrating birthdays in February, March, May, and October were always fun and exciting now because of the children's reactions. Having holiday gatherings at Thanksgiving and Christmas with all the children's giggles and laughter helped their grandfather Anton rediscover his joy in life. At the same time, the children's irrepressible happiness helped their uncle Rusty find a special kind of peace as well.

Rusty had grown fond of his visits with Francis and little Margaret Mary, and he loved teaching them gardening. Sometimes, he also took them to the shop with him, and they would make small toys out of pieces of leather, just as his grandfather had taught him to do as a young child. These activities helped keep his grandfather's memory alive within the next generation of children, and that made Rusty happy too.

The Men Gather to Discuss the News

The Karella men took turns hosting a gathering to discuss and debate the current news. In September of 1923, it was Stanislaus's turn, and family members gathered in his kitchen. Anton, Uncle Ed, and Rusty sat at the table covered with newspapers as Stanislaus poured the coffee. Everyone enjoyed discussing the news as they used to do every morning at the farm.

"Who would have thought Harding would die while he was president?" Stanislaus asked no one in particular.

Uncle Ed replied, "I think it was all those corruption scandals involving Attorney General Daugherty and that Ohio gang the press has been writing about. Harding tried to hide out in San Francisco after the bad news broke in the newspapers. Didn't help, though. All the worry gave him a heart attack anyway! Couldn't bear to have all that sinfulness uncovered. That's what I think."

"That might be true. But now that Coolidge has taken over, do you think he will be any better?" Stanislaus asked the group.

"Well, he has been talking about cleaning up the government and restoring good old-fashioned values. Coolidge has always been a conservative, and he says government should not interfere when it comes to business and industry. He also supports tax cuts for businesses. Though, I'm not sure he means farming businesses like ours. But more important to me is that I have read he is advocating isolationism in foreign policy," Uncle Ed said.

"I guess we don't have much choice but to wait and see if it is all talk or if he is really going to put his words into action," Rusty said. Then he added, "By the way, I have some news to tell you." That announcement got everyone's attention, and Rusty smiled before saying, "I'm ready to open my own blacksmith, leather, and mechanical repair shop in Madison come next spring!" His news was met with solid approval and encouragement by the older men of the family.

Summer 1924: Peace, Hope, and New Beginnings

At a family picnic on the homestead, Anton listened to Rusty talk about how his business was steadily growing. Anton held up a hand, and his son looked at him and asked, "Did you have something you wanted to say, Papa?"

"Yes. Perhaps it is time to expand your business."

"How so, Papa?" Rusty asked.

"I was thinking you could include design and construction of specialized harnesses, bridles, and other leather gear for horses. Like the ones your grandpa Vaclav taught me and you to make," Anton replied.

"That is actually a great idea. Would you have time to come to Grandpa's old workshop and help me draw up some designs?" Rusty asked.

"I would enjoy that very much, son," Anton replied.

This congenial moment began a deeper connection between them as men. Father and son agreed to work together in Grandpa Vaclav's workshop. Rusty discussed each project with Anton, and before long, they had a regular schedule for the work to be done and spent many hours together in the workshop they both loved. It comforted them to feel the spirit of Vaclav guiding their hands as they collaborated on the new leather designs Rusty would sell in his shop.

Though every day at his shop kept him busy, at least once a month, Rusty made time to meet up with his uncle Stanislaus, uncle Emil, uncle Ed, and his father if he wasn't busy with the grandchildren. They would share a pot of coffee and some rohliky while they discussed the news.

Rusty had been thinking a lot about the idea of prohibition and all the trouble caused by it and said, "I am very glad we don't live in a big city. There is so much crime and violence connected with bootlegging. I also have a problem with the whole idea of making alcoholic beverages illegal. We've been making our own fermented beverages for generations! Grandfather taught us all how to make cordials, beer, and wine. We've always made it for personal use. It's been a natural part of our family celebrations and feasts. I don't think the government has the right to say that what we made for years and for our own use is now illegal."

"You make a good point," said Uncle Emil. "It's true—our home brew is nothing like the moonshine whiskey being made in hide-a-way stills in the backwoods countryside around Chicago. Nor is it like the bathtub gin crazy people are making in the cities." Uncle Emil held up a newspaper from Chicago and went on to say, "Based on these articles, most of that stuff being bootlegged is not much better than poison. I'd say what we make and what they are making are very different, and I don't think what we make should be considered illegal. Though, I would suggest we keep that notion to ourselves."

Nodding in agreement with that statement, Uncle Stanislaus took over the conversation. "The stories from the newspapers I get from New York City have me concerned about a closely related problem, and that is the criminal aspect connected with bootlegging. I've been reading about the five big crime families that run the violent gangs in the cities. There is some kind of association between them, and according to the articles, these gangs control everything illegal going on across the whole United States."

After a little more discussion, Anton called for a vote. The men agreed to continue making home brew in secret for personal use, which ended the talk about the family's fermented spirits.

Uncle Ed changed the subject. "As you all know, I still receive letters from relatives living in France, and I track the news reports about Europe. I'm worried about the growing influence of this prejudiced, radical German named Adolf Hitler and his Nazi party. According to what I've learned, Hitler and his Nazis tried to seize control of power in Munich in recent months. The German government squashed his rebellion, arrested him, and threw him into prison!"

Anton spoke up, saying, "Ed, aren't you glad you live with us in America now? With what is going on over there politically in the aftermath of World War I, are you still considering making a trip back there to see your kin?"

Ed looked at Anton and replied, "Anton, it's family, and I feel I must go back at least once to visit them. That will not be for a while yet. I'm sure things will settle down with Hitler in prison, and there will be nothing to worry about," replied Ed.

The idea of Uncle Ed going to Europe and possibly putting himself into danger made everyone a little anxious. Rusty liked to think he added a brighter side to these conversations. This seemed like a good time to bring up the positive things he had read about. "Say, has anyone else been reading about the latest inventions and recent discoveries?" Rusty asked the group. "I think that the new traffic light Garrett Morgan invented is a great idea because it will reduce accidents between horse drawn vehicles and automobiles on the streets in the cities. Then there is Clarence Birdseye, who just introduced a new process to freeze perishable foods like vegetables and berries. He says with his process, those kinds of foods can be made to last through the winter without spoiling. Of course, my favorite is John Harwood's latest invention, a self-winding watch!" Rusty said.

Anton and Stanislaus smiled broadly at Rusty's bright-eyed enthusiastic talk. Anton replied, saying, "Son, you have always found innovation inspirational, just like your grandfather."

"That's true, Papa. I do admire many of the new inventions and amenities I have been reading about. But at the same time, I think I have developed a more creative mind by growing up without the use of many modern amenities. An easy life can distract a person from inventing new solutions."

Stanislaus laughed, saying, "Rusty, you sound just like your grandpa. After telling us we could not buy a new tool, I remember he was fond of saying, 'Doing without makes a more creative mind, which is your greatest asset.'"

Rusty started to bristle up, thinking they were making fun of him.

"Now, don't get your hackles up, Rusty," said his father, Anton. "You know we are just teasing you. Your grandpa was right about a lot of the new inventions."

Then Stanislaus added, "Pamper me, please! I would love to have one of those indoor toilets—that's better than having to use an outhouse any day of the week!" Everyone laughed knowing that statement was true, especially during the cold of winter!

A Well-Deserved Business Reputation and Its Rewards

By the summer season of 1924, Rusty turned 26 years old and had achieved several milestones. On a professional level, his reputation as an excellent smith was the best in the region, and he had a strong and steady business to prove it. On a personal level, he had re-established a wonderful rapport with his father. Within a year, their collaborative leather designs for horse tack had brought in more customers than ever.

Unbeknownst to Rusty, it was some of these original harness designs that caught the eye of an important horseman by the name of James Holt from the Madison Downs' racetrack. The high quality of Rusty's work captured Mr. Holt's attention immediately. Holt was well known in the area for his racehorses and slightly radical ideas about creating a new jockey saddle. Holt believed Karella's unique designs in saddlery reflected some of his own ideas. That was why James Holt began to keep track of the leather products Rusty Karella made and took note of colleagues who mentioned the man's work and bought his products.

1924, Weekend of September 11th, a Birthday Celebration

The fall season generated great excitement among the nieces and nephews. The new school year had begun, and that meant there would be a big birthday party held at the Karella homestead. Friday evening, September 11, the party started on time, celebrating Anastas Karella's 14th birthday.

The whole family attended the party. This would be a day none of the family would ever forget. Not because it had been an exceptionally fun gathering, which it had been, but because it was the night before Anastas Karella vanished.

The following day, everyone had exhausted all possibilities, and no one could find Anastas. On Sunday, an alert went out to all townsfolk, the church congregation, and around the farming community of Madison. Anyone who had any information about Anastas's absence was asked to come forward. No one wanted to call it a disappearance—not yet—but no one could find him either.

The Karellas asked every neighbor and person they knew to help search for the missing boy. But when Monday came and went with no news, Anton asked Father Clemens from St. Leonard's to help. Father

called Anastas's friends together, hoping one of them might know something they had not revealed yet. When Anton walked into the pastor's office, Father Clemens had five boys standing in a row looking nervous and staring at the floor. "Boys, this is a serious matter. I have called you here because all five of you have been regularly seen with Anastas Karella. He is missing, and I think one or more of you might know something about where he is. If that is the case, you had better confess what you know *now* because the next person you will be talking to is the county sheriff." Father paused, then

Anastas (Shorty) Karella at
14, Madison, Nebraska

continued, "This will become a much more serious matter once we file a missing person's report."

One boy seemed more uncomfortable than the rest and shifted from foot to foot. Father Clemens asked Michael Collins to step forward. "Do you know where Anastas is?" The boy still looked at the floor when he shook his head. Father kept watching him, then asked, "Do you know anything about where Anastas went or what he might be doing?"

This time, Michael's ears turned red, and Father Clemens kept asking more questions. "I believe you have knowledge about Anastas, and by withholding that information, it is as bad as lying. God would hold you accountable if anything bad happens to Anastas because you did not help us find him."

Finally, Michael looked up in great distress and said, "He made me swear not to tell."

Father Clemens excused the other boys, and when it was only Michael, Anton, and himself, he turned back to the boy with a stern face. Anton had relaxed a little, but Father Clemens did not. "Young man," Father said firmly, "this oath you made was wrong. Now, it is time for you to make it right by telling Anastas's father where he is or exactly what you know."

The boy looked at Anton and said, "Sir, he went to join the Army."

Both older men started firing questions at the boy. "What Army?"

"I don't know," the boy replied.

"Where is this Army?"

"I don't know," the boy replied again.

"When did he leave?"

This time, the boy said, "That night, after his birthday party."

"How did he leave town?"

"I saw him jump on the train, and then I threw him his bag full of stuff, and that's all I know. He's my best friend, and I'm worried about him too. But that's all I know. God as my witness, I'm not lying."

At that point, Father Clemens allowed Michael to go home, then sat down with Anton. "My friend, there is not much you can do. We will pray that Anastas is all right and that he will contact us when he gets settled. Once we know where Anastas is, perhaps we can talk to the Army about this, but for now, we have no place to start."

Father Clemens could see how this latest blow had hurt Anton. After the last two years of pain, Anton seemed to finally be reviving from his grief. This new loss would be hard on him. "Let me call

Rusty to come pick you up." Anton nodded in silence and sat staring out the window.

St. Leonard's Parish Community

Starting the last Sunday in September, the whole parish of St Leonard's joined in a prayer every week for Anastas's safety. They also added a prayer that the boy would write home and tell his family where he was.

Anton's Decision

The Karella's Thanksgiving celebrations of 1924 were overshadowed by the disappearance of Anton's youngest son, Anastas. Though the family attended morning Mass together, this Thanksgiving Day, each family had decided to have their own dinner at home.

Waiting until the rest of his family had left, Anton sat by himself in the church, thinking, *I can change nothing by worrying. Nor can I change the outcome of decisions other people make. All I do is lose precious time with those I have with me, and I have no guarantee that I will even be here tomorrow! I refuse to waste any more of the time I have regretting the past.*

Closing his eyes and kneeling, he made the sign of the cross and began: *Dear Lord, help me live with joy each day and appreciation for what I do have. If it is Your will, Lord, my boys, Frank and Anastas, will return. I will rejoice if and when they do. I will be brave and tell them all the things in my heart. Until then, I will live as my courageous mother, wife, and father did. I will remember the gifts I do have. I will be loving and live for the family that surrounds me. I promise to bring Your joy and love with me in all things I do. With Your blessings and strength, I can do all this and more. The rest I give into Your hands. In Your Holy Name, I pray. Amen.*

1924, a Joyful Advent Season

Helen had been thrilled the previous summer when Alvin promised to quit road construction and find work in Madison. Today, she received a letter from Alvin saying he would be home for Christmas!

"Papa, Papa, where are you?" Helen called as she waddled down the stairs as best she could being a little over six months pregnant. "I have wonderful news!"

Anton came trotting to the stairs to give her a steady arm and smiled at the pure joy on his eldest daughter's face as she showed him the letter. He had only begun to read it when she started devising ways to make this Christmas extra special.

She has always been my happy child, thought Anton. Then he said, "Helen, let me help you with the plans!"

"Oh, Papa! I would love to plan our Christmas celebrations with you. Where shall we start?"

Anton grinned at her enthusiasm and replied, "Well, I think we should start with a Christmas tree hunting party! What do you say, my dear daughter? Do you want to go on a sleigh ride with me? We can use the harness with the bells. Our wagon horses love the sound they make!"

"Papa! Let's get everyone to go!" Helen exclaimed excitedly.

"Great idea," he replied. "We can take both of the big sleighs and hook up the sleds behind them to haul the trees we cut."

"We'll need at least three trees or maybe four. One for us, one for Uncle Stanislaus and Aunt Anna, and one for the farm. Maybe Martha and Rudy Pojar would want to go too! That way, we can take turns having a decorating party at each other's homes. What do you think, Papa?"

"I think we better start making some telephone calls to set the date for our sleigh ride tree-hunting party," Anton replied with a warm smile.

Christmas Tree Hunting

The December temperatures ran between -1 and -10 degrees, and they had plenty of snow on the ground to use the big sleighs. Everyone agreed to meet early at the farm. By 10:00 a.m., both the big sleighs were hitched to double teams of horses and carried extra blankets, axes, and saws.

Stanislaus drove the first sleigh with Anna, baby Joseph, little Howard, and Helen, who insisted she would be just fine in her pregnant condition if she stayed in the sleigh. On the tree sled tied behind it rode Ambrose, Margaret Mary, Anton, and Francis.

Uncle Ed drove the second sleigh with Emily, Martha, Stanley Voborny, and Mary Cecilia inside. Behind it on the sled rode Emil, Raymond and Rudy Pojar, and his son, Charles Anthony.

The adults and children finished arranging themselves securely on the sleds, laughing and excited, then yelled, "READY!" Stanislaus and Uncle Ed snapped the reins across the horse's rumps. The horse teams lunged forward. Their movement made the harness bells jingle merrily while eight sets of horse hooves kicked up clouds of frozen white dust that flew under and around the sleighs and pelted the sled riders with miniature snowballs. Looking back to check on the children, their mothers saw red cheeks and heard lots of belly laughter. Those jolly sounds mingled with loud squeals of delight and excitement as the sleds bounced up and down and slid side to side on the ice and snow behind the sleighs.

Within 20 minutes, they reached the wooded acres on the homestead. The horses slowed with the slight pull on the reigns, then stopped with their snorting breath turning into plumes of white clouds in the frosty air.

The children's eyes shimmered with delight in the aftermath of their sled ride. The men put the children in the sleighs. The little ones giggled as Helen, Emily, Anna, Martha, and Mary Cecilia snuggled close to them under thick blankets. "Brrrr! Your noses and cheeks are frozen! Let's stay warm while your uncles and papas tromp through the wet snow and find us four perfect Christmas trees. Or . . . do you want to go with them?" Aunt Anna asked.

"Noooo," the children replied immediately as they snuggled deeper into the soft blankets, "we want to stay with you where it's warm!"

Christmas Decorating Party at the Farm

With two large trees strapped to each sled, everyone piled back into the sleighs. Sitting close and on top of each other as they were, every person stayed warm. The children held the blankets up to their faces on the ride home to keep their cheeks and noses warm too.

Back at the farm, the men set up one of the trees in the living room using one of Grandpa Vaclav's inventions: a tree stand that held water. As the tree thawed out and soaked up the water, the tree would release fresh pine sap, which smelled heavenly. By continuing to water the tree, it would stay fresh and keep its needles throughout the 12 days of Christmas.

"Emily," Emil called to his wife, "the tree is set up in the living room and ready for decorating. But can we have a break before we bring in the decorations?

"Yes, you may have a short break," Emily replied. "Would you please play some music on the phonograph while we pass out the hot apple cider that I put on the stove before we left for the tree hunting?" Emil nodded, agreeing that he would do as she requested as she left the room.

Martha immediately jumped up, saying, "Helen, you stay put. Anna and I will help Emily." Soon, everyone sipped delicious hot, mulled apple cider.

"We made this with the apples we harvested this fall. Stanislaus, do you remember when Papa planted the sapling apple trees back in 1916?" Emil asked.

Stanislaus smiled and replied, "Yes, I remember he got them from the seed and feed store in April during the Arbor Day celebration that year. They grew really fast but did not bear fruit for three or four years. Papa was disappointed and then in about . . . what . . . Anton . . . maybe 1920 . . . we couldn't begin to eat all the apples those trees produced."

"As I recall, they were little green Lodi apples and a few red McIntosh," replied Anton. Grinning, he went on to say, "I believe that was the first year Papa taught us how to make hard cider, wasn't it, brother?"

Stanislaus nodded with a grin, remembering the taste of that original batch of hard cider very well. It was the first time he and Anton had gotten tipsy together.

The women and older children sat at the table with several bowls of popcorn and dried bright-red cranberries. With needles and thread, they made long, festive strings of popcorn accented with the berries that they could drape around the Christmas tree.

The men had an assignment too. They each had a sack of peppermint candies and two large stacks of Christmas bows made of brightly colored fabrics. This was a Karella family tradition from the old days in New York. Aunt Anna had learned how to make the cloth bows from her mother-in-law, Antonia, when she and Stanislaus first got married. Helen had learned the tradition from her Aunt Anna. Stanislaus, Anton, and Emil showed the younger men how to tie a piece of peppermint to each bow, then tie each bow to a tree bough.

The last thing to be done was attaching the Christmas candles to the tree branches, but they did not light them. Uncle Emil, Aunt Emily, Raymond, and Uncle Ed would only light the tree candles on Christmas Eve when it was time to say the Christmas prayer.

By the time the tree decorating was finished, everyone was exhausted and had eaten too much popcorn and drank too much cider to be interested in eating dinner. Deciding to head home while it was still light out, the women got themselves and the children into their cold weather clothing. "Remember, Rudy, your tree will stay fresh until tomorrow if you keep it outside and frozen. Just bring it in a little before you are ready to decorate it and stand it in water," Anton told him as they loaded the tree on the small sleigh.

"It's getting late. Don't wait for us, Rudy. We will see you all tomorrow," Stanislaus added. Martha and little Charles waved goodbye as their sleigh disappeared down the lane.

Anton checked to be sure the trees were still securely tied to the sled behind the biggest sleigh. Stanislaus and Ambrose settled the children between adults or sat them on a grownup's lap. After everyone was covered with warm blankets, Stanislaus climbed into the driver's seat, saying, "Anton, I will drop you and the family and your tree off at your house before Anna and I go home. That way, Anna and I won't have to carry anything tomorrow, and we can just walk over to your house if the weather is still fair. We are looking forward to the rest of the decorating parties," Stanislaus said as he snapped the reigns across the horse's rumps.

"I agree with you," said Anton. "Decorating at the farm this afternoon brought back a lot of great memories."

When everything went quiet, the brothers knew everyone else had fallen asleep. They smiled and enjoyed the ride without talking while they listened to the sweet jingling of the sleigh bells all the way home.

1924, an Unforgettable Christmas

Alvin surprised everyone by coming home two weeks early for Christmas, then announced he was home to stay. "Oh, darling, thank you! That is the best Christmas gift you have ever given me," replied Helen when she hugged him.

Alvin could feel the baby between them kick him from inside his wife. Laughing, he said, "This is the first one of our children that I have felt kick me. Does he do that a lot?"

Helen grinned and replied, "Well, your first-born son, Francis, was the worst for kicking. This one is just letting me know things are getting a little cramped inside this space," she replied. Their fifth child was due to be born at the end of February, and Alvin was indescribably happy that he would be home for that wonderful event.

Suddenly, Alvin released his wife and turned away as he tried to suppress a coughing spell.

Concerned, Helen asked, "Alvin, are you alright?"

In a bit, he turned back to her and replied, "Oh, darling, don't worry. It's just a little something I'm getting over. I could not feel better being surrounded by my delightful wife and children. Tell me what we are going to do for Christmas."

"I am going to plan the most spectacular Christmas feast we have ever had! It will be a wonderful gathering with so much family celebrating together!"

Helen's plan came together perfectly, and remembering it was almost as good as being there all over again. For dinner, Emil and Uncle Ed had brought in the biggest turkey they had at the farm. She slow cooked it with a special stuffing of apples, onions, carrots, and cinnamon soaked in chicken broth. As it baked, delicious aromas wafted through the whole house every time the oven door was opened.

Each of the wives brought a side dish for the feast: rohlikys covered in black poppyseeds, mashed potatoes, thick brown gravy, green beans in creamed onion and pecan sauce, candied carrots, and cranberry sauce to serve with the turkey.

Her mouth began to water just thinking about that delicious dinner. She giggled as she remembered the desserts. Going a little crazy with the baking, she had filled the whole dinner table full of Great-Grandma Antonia's kolaches and houska bread and half a dozen fruit pies and several dozen cookies.

Martha and Mary strung popcorn and cranberries to drape over the fresh pine boughs the boys brought in to decorate the fireplace. Those fragrant evergreens smelled heavenly, reminding Helen of her childhood Christmases. Grandpa Anton kept music playing on the phonograph during the day, and after playing all the records he owned, he found some orchestra music on the radio for everyone to listen to.

By 10:00 p.m., the children had fallen asleep by the fireplace . . . that was when Rusty went down to the basement and brought up several old bottles of Great-Grandpa's homemade mulberry cordial. Going around the room, each adult made a toast and thanked God for all the good fortune the family had been blessed with. It had been the best Christmas ever!

Helen felt everything in her world falling into place. It was the first time in years her husband and children had been able to share the whole Christmas holiday together with her father.

Rusty worked at his blacksmith and repair business in town and only went to Norfolk occasionally and enjoyed being home with the family again. Uncle Emil and his family were happy about inheriting the farm and would not be going back to Chicago. Uncle Ed enjoyed working with Emil, and they were doing a good job running the farm businesses. Her sister, Martha, and Martha's husband, Rudy, were content with their life in Madison and loved living nearby with their son, Charles Anthony.

Her baby sister's attitude had improved greatly since Mary Cecelia got engaged, and she and Stanley Voborny had set their wedding date for right after Mary's graduation in the spring.

Her papa was completely involved in his work at the lumber-mill again and thrilled Uncle Stanislaus was working with him. But best of all, she loved watching her father laugh and play with his grandchildren.

Helen was grateful the only stress the family felt during the holidays of 1924 was that they didn't know much about what Frank was doing nor had they heard anything from Anastas. But Helen Karella Bean had always been an optimist and still believed the summer of 1925 was going to be a summer to look forward to!

CHAPTER 6

1925, an Unpredictable Year

Living with Change

Anton had spent quite a bit of time during the holidays thinking about the changes that would come to his household in January 1925. Helen and Alvin would move into their own place. Certainly, this was a good thing for them as a family. But Anton would no longer have his marvelous grandchildren underfoot to distract him and use as an excuse to put off what he knew he should do.

Anton J. Karella—Journal Entry

After three years, my common sense has finally asserted itself. I can admit now that uncertainty and change in life is normal. I have come to recognize that the only things I can control are the choices I make. Running from life and hiding in the past with my deceased wife and father's memories is not good for anyone. I choose to release the hurt of loss and allow the love I shared with Anastasia and Papa to be stowed away in my heart. I will continue to talk to them as friends, but I will not forget the value of the day before me. All the rest of my todays are for living and growing. I will redirect my energy into building my relationships, improving my work, and celebrating each day I have with my family and friends!

Smiling, Anton felt relieved with his decision as he set down his pen. Somehow seeing the words of his resolution on the page in front of him helped. Reading his words once more, he nodded his head, confirming the truth he saw there, and closed his journal.

The Bean Family's Future

Excited to move into their own home, Alvin Bean, his wife, Helen, and their children were happy to know they would live right down the street from Grandpa Anton's place.

The month of January turned cold and icy. Madison had a lot of snow on the ground, which always made things difficult, especially for Helen in her advanced stage of pregnancy. Yet. she would let nothing dampen the excitement her family felt about living together in their own home again. Soon, the new baby would be born, and she knew they were going to have a wonderful summer.

All the snow and ice had melted by the second week in February. The weather was still cold enough to make Alvin cough, though he thought he might finally be getting over the worst part of his illness. At least it seemed better than it had been, so he refused to let a little discomfort spoil his surprise.

Alvin woke early on February 14th. Quietly, he bundled up the children and took them to Grandpa Anton's house before Helen woke up. He left her a note about the children and that he would be back by 10:00 a.m. so they could have breakfast together.

As Anton and Alvin helped the children out of their cold-weather coats, Anton noticed Alvin still had that nagging cough he had at Christmas. "Alvin, have you seen the doctor about that cough of yours?"

Alvin shook his head and replied, "No, but I have been feeling better now that the weather has begun to warm up."

Anton looked at him as he held baby Joseph and said softly, "I'm glad you are not ignoring it. You have 5.5 wonderful reasons to make sure you are healthy and strong."

Valentine's Day at the Bean Home

Alvin walked into the kitchen right at 10:00 a.m. He smiled, noting that Helen had the table set for breakfast, and the food on the stove smelled delicious. "Happy Valentine's Day, darling," he said, then handed Helen the card he had bought for her.

With a radiant smile, she opened the card. After reading it, her eyes twinkled with delight as she leaned up to kiss him, saying, "It's beautiful! Thank you! I'm sorry . . . I did not get one for you."

Alvin grinned and took her into his arms and replied, "That is all right, wife. All I need to feel appreciated is to spend the afternoon with you and have you all to myself! Your father said he would keep the children for the whole day. Let's sit by the fire and tell each other all the stories we have never had time to share. I'll tell you about working on the highways, and you can tell me about everything you and the children did while you lived with your father while I was away working."

Valentine's Day card,
Public Domain

Everything about the day had been a delightful surprise. They ate a quiet breakfast and lunch together . . . alone, which they had not done since the first year of their marriage in 1918. Then they shared all the stories and memories they had made separately during their seven years together. Both Helen and Alvin enjoyed Valentine's Day immensely.

While they laughed and bonded over the stories they shared, Helen watched the bright daylight shining through the kitchen windows play across her husband's face. Normally, they only saw each other in the dim light of candles, firelight, or gas lamps, so she had not realized her Alvin was not well. In this bright light, she could see it in his face: *That cough. He has had that cough since he got home and has not been able to get rid of it. He also mentioned many times how tired he has been since he got home. This health problem started way before Christmas*, she thought, *and now he keeps saying he should find work. But I am going to insist that he recovers from this illness before he does anything else. We have enough savings put away, and it will last until he feels better. What he needs is my tender loving care, and he will be better in no time!*

Helen smiled as she listened to another of Alvin's stories. The sun's warmth coming through the window was not only helping Alvin, but it was also energizing Helen. Having Alvin home so she could take care of him reenforced her belief that 1925 was going to be a great year!

A Child Is Lost

Doctor Linden held the tiny baby who did not cry after he was born, and that worried him. Then they discovered the child would not suckle. Nothing anyone did could change the fact that newborn Bernard Sebastian Bean was growing weaker.

Before the night of February 26th was over, Doc Linden was forced to deliver the sad news. The baby's parents grieved for the loss of their newborn son. The other four children of Alvin and Helen Karella Bean stayed with their grandfather all the next day while everyone else went to the church.

At St. Leonard's, Father Clemens blessed the little coffin, and as the prayers for the faithfully departed were being said by everyone gathered there, Helen sadly decided she had been wrong about the summer of 1925. Eventually, she would be able to appreciate all that was still good and right with the world. But at this moment, it was just too much to ask.

A Child Is Found

Sunday March 29th, there was cause for celebration throughout the community of Madison. The Karella boy had been found! Anastas Leonard Karella had finally written to his family. Today, the entire congregation of St. Leonard's Church gathered to hear Father Clemens read the boy's letter of apology during his homily.

Father explained that it was appropriate to share this wonderful news at this time during the Lenten season. This would be a time of repentance and reconciliation for the people of God as they waited for the miraculous resurrection of the Lord Jesus on Easter. The church was filled with excitement. Everyone was anxious to hear the boy's letter.

Father Clemens stood up in front of the church and began, "My dearest parish community of Saint Leonard's Catholic Church: Today, we have an early Easter blessing. An answer to all our prayers for the past six months of worry that we have shared since the disappearance of Anastas Karella last October. Let us rejoice that the boy has been found and is unharmed. With the permission of his family, I will now read the letter that Ambrose and his family received from Anastas."

Dear Ambrose,   *France, 1925*

I am healthy and safe. Actually, better than safe, though what I am going to tell you may come as a bit of a shock. I am a cook in the French Foreign Legion, and we are in France.

I cannot tell you how glad I am Papa insisted all of us brothers learn to cook as well as our sisters. Please tell Father Clemens I will not be part of the infantry. I will be feeding soldiers, keeping our men healthy with food. I think he and Papa will like that idea very much.

Ambrose, I am so sorry for scaring everyone, but I am not sorry I left. I want you to understand. I felt I needed to go. I knew the family would stop me if they found out. I would never ask you to lie for me. That is why I purposely kept my secret from everyone.

Depiction of
Legionaries from the
French Foreign Legion

I hope you will forgive me. Please tell Papa and the family I love them and that I'm sorry I worried them too. I promise to keep in touch. Please tell Uncle Ed I have been using the skills he taught me. Please write me about the family. I have enclosed an enlistment picture of our uniforms. They look dashing, at least that's what Uncle Ed used to tell me about them when he wore the uniform. Please tell him I agree with him.

Your brother always,
Legionnaire Anastas Karella

A murmur of surprise ran through the congregation. Clearly, everyone was curious and had many questions they wanted to ask. The obvious one was how on earth did a Nebraska boy end up in the French Foreign Legion? But for now, they settled on a round of applause for such good news. Father held up his hands for silence and said, "Thank you, Anton and Ambrose, for allowing us to share in this wonderful news. A magnificent affirmation that God has answered all our prayers for Anastas's safety. Now, let us pray."

After receiving that first letter from Anastas, Rusty wrote to his little brother explaining how the church congregation had prayed for him and asked about him often. He also made sure Anastas knew that the whole family looked forward to hearing his letters at the family picnics and gatherings. Praise God, Anastas wrote regularly to his father and siblings describing his experiences in France.

Uncle Ed made a special visit to see Anton. He worried that Anton would be angry about how his stories had influenced Anton's youngest son.

"Ed, Anastas's choices are not your fault. He has a mind of his own," Anton replied, "and as we found out, he has no trouble making decisions. All we can do is wait and hope that in time, God will bring him home."

Springtime, Household of Alvin Bean

May was half over the day Helen heard Alvin having a very bad coughing fit in the kitchen. She hurried to see if he was alright, but he was gone when she walked through the door. His coat was missing from the peg, then she noticed his handkerchief on the floor. Thinking it must have dropped out of his pocket when he put on his coat, she picked it up. She found fresh blood on it.

Waiting until after supper when the children were in bed, Helen came into the living room.

Alvin was sitting by the fire and said, "Helen, I am tired and think I will go to bed early tonight."

Helen nodded at him. It was time they talked about his condition, so she followed him to their room. She waited quietly until he changed into his nightshirt. As Alvin climbed into bed, she said, "Alvin, you must go to the doctor." She held the handkerchief behind her back but did not show him. She would, though, if Alvin refused to be reasonable.

He looked up at her. She thought he looked like he was going to argue against her suggestion, but then he nodded and replied, "You are right. I'll go see Doc Linden tomorrow."

She sat down on the bed next to him and kissed him and said, "Good! Now, sleep well, darling. I am going with you tomorrow."

Arriving at the doctor's office, Alvin asked Helen to sit in the waiting room while he talked to the doctor alone. When Alvin came out of Doctor Linden's office, he took Helen by the arm. Politely saying good day to the woman at the desk, they left the building without talking.

The chilly breeze brought on a fit of coughing. Alvin quickly covered his mouth with a fresh handkerchief. He did so before the coughing got bad, then quickly folded it and returned it to his pocket when the coughing let up. It wasn't a long walk to get home. As soon as they were through the kitchen door, Helen turned to him and asked, "Alvin, what did Doctor Linden say?"

Alvin took off his coat and walked over to the fireplace to get warm. He regretted so many things . . . wished he had more time . . . but time was up. It was unavoidable; he had to tell her the truth.

Kneeling down to stoke the fire, he replied, "Doc Linden says I have diabetes. He gave me a list of food I cannot eat any more like potatoes, bread, and no more desserts or anything with sugar in it. He says that is why I have been so tired. You might have seen blood on my clothing recently. I have been getting cuts and bruises that don't heal. He said that is from the diabetes, too, and that is also why my vision gets blurred once in a while.

"The doc gave me a new medicine called insulin. Apparently, it was developed in 1921 and has been used successfully in conditions like mine since 1922. He told me I should start feeling better if I watch what I eat."

Helen had been watching Alvin closely as he explained his condition. He had not said anything about the coughing or the kind of blood she had seen. Instinctively, she knew there was more to this condition than what he had told her. "Alvin, what else did the doctor say?"

He finally looked up at her, and her breath caught in her throat. "I am so sorry," Alvin whispered softly as he opened his arms to her.

Helen crossed the room quickly and leaned into his chest. Putting her arms around his waist, she asked softly, "How much time do we have?"

"We still have a little . . . but . . . it is . . .

Bean Children—Howard, Gerald, Margaret Mary and Francis

tuberculosis . . . and there is not much he can do for me. Doc says I won't cough as much once the weather warms up."

She caught the sob before it left her throat. Even so, her shoulders shook with her silent grief. She had to ask, so she whispered, "There is nothing he can do?"

Alvin tipped her head up to look into her eyes as he shook his head. Then he held her close again and whispered, "Helen, he thinks maybe I have six months to a year. I think we should keep this to ourselves for now. Please don't say anything to anyone until I talk to your father." He felt Helen nod her head in agreement as she clung to him.

With her head on his chest, Helen could hear the raggedness of Alvin's breathing. Holding on to him tightly, she understood what that sound meant.

Alvin lay his cheek on her hair and whispered, "Now is the time to be strong, my dear wife. I think we should try and be happy while we still have time together and enjoy this time with our children." He gently lifted her chin again with his fingers so he could see her beautiful eyes and asked, "Why not leave the sadness for later? Do you think you can help me do that, darling?"

Helen blinked away her tears as she looked into her husband's eyes and nodded.

At a Point of No Return

Anton sat quietly without interruption as Alvin whispered his confession. No words could express the sorrow and sympathy he felt for the man, the husband, and father who sat before him. The younger man diligently prepared for the protection of his family, even as he prepared for his own death. Anton would keep their secret and gave his word to take care of the family his son-in-law would leave in his care. When Anton hugged Alvin, it was full of compassion, and the younger man nearly crushed him in his need for that compassion. In their exchange, he had received respect and love and even shared the fear Alvin was not able to show anyone else.

Alvin knew he could trust Anton and knew Anton understood what it was like to feel helpless to stop death and the pain it would cause the people he loved. As he headed home, anxious to see Helen, Alvin's heart found the beginnings of peace.

Anton watched Alvin walk away and felt the dark weight that had been transferred unintentionally to his heart. He knew how to deal with that darkness now. Shaking off the shadows, he began to list the important things he needed to get done to live up to his promise to Alvin.

First Karella Family Picnic of the Summer

As the weather got warmer at the end of May 1925, the whole Karella family was excited except Helen. Rusty, Uncle Ed, and Stanislaus found that unusual. Helen was always the happiest person they knew. When everyone stopped to chat after Mass, she left the church on her own. However, the family that remained decided if the temperature got up into the 80s by the following week, then Emil and Emily would host the first Karella picnic of the summer at the farm on Sunday, June 7th after Mass.

Rusty, Uncle Ed, and Stanislaus mentioned Helen's odd behavior to Anton when he joined them outside the church. "Listen," Anton said, "Helen just told me that Alvin has advanced diabetes. Though Doctor Linden gave Alvin that new medicine called insulin, Alvin is really disappointed that he can no longer eat her wonderful desserts."

All three men were disturbed by this news, though Anton made it sound like everything was under control.

Suddenly, a new thought made Rusty laugh, and he said comically, "Gosh, we know Helen. With Doc saying *no sweets*, she will never let Alvin eat sugar again. That is tragic! Helen makes the best desserts in Madison."

Grandpa Anton's Bean Children—Howard, Gerald, Margaret Mary, and Francis

"That kind of treatment would make anyone down in the mouth!" Uncle Ed added dramatically.

Stanislaus grinned, saying playfully, "Not being able to eat any more of her wonderful desserts would be a sentence worse than death."

Though Anton smiled at their silly banter, no one noticed that the smile did not reach his eyes. *Let them have their fun,* he thought. *It is not the time for the truth right now—there will be time enough for that later.*

Middle of June: a Weary Traveler Heads to Nebraska

The slow release of steam hissed, and the rattling clank of the train car couplings warned Frank Emil Karella to get ready. With legs pumping and chest heaving, the young man lunged. His fingers clutched the metal rung near the freight door and pulled his feet up to the doorframe—right in time.

Steel wheels clacked on the tracks. The steam engine chugged along faster and faster as he hung onto the side of the freight car. Shoving hard on the door, it slid open just enough for him to tumble inside.

Frank lay on the floor, relieved he could catch his breath. Each gulp of air felt gritty with dust, and he could smell he had not had a bath in too many days. His father, Anton, would find it hard to believe his son was illegally jumping on a freight train.

Old box train cars Frank Karella rode when he hopped trains coming back through New York from South America

The car suddenly darkened, and the engine whistle blew, echoing as it passed through a narrow break in the rocks and into the tunnel. Scooting up and leaning up against the wall, he thought, *Keep it together,*

Frank. Not that much farther to go. Only a few days more, and you'll be home. As the clackity-clack of the wheels on the track reassured his mind with its monotony, he relaxed and slept.

After years of being on the road, Frank's body had learned to sense change. Even in his sleep, his unconscious awareness woke him suddenly. Sitting up alert, Frank took in his surroundings, then felt the train slowing down. Time to get ready to jump off before the train pulls into the yard in Sioux City, Iowa. He'd been lucky so far. Frank hadn't been caught by any of the brutal train yard guards called bulls, and he'd been hopping trains all the way from New York.

Frank landed on his feet. Settling his duffle bag more comfortably on his shoulder, he thought, *Now, what was the name of the priest here in Sioux City?* Frank walked around town, found the Catholic Church, and then the pastor. Soon, he was cleaned up and sharing a meal with the priest and telling him about the last two years he'd spent in Santiago, Chile; Lima, Peru; and Panama.

The Train Schedule to Madison

Father Mac held out a piece of paper, saying, "Frank, this is the Omaha train schedule you asked for. Once you get to Omaha, you'll need to find the train going to Colfax and then Madison. I will pray you arrive home safely. Give Father Clemens my regards when you get there. If you feel like volunteering in the future and want to help me with some fundraisers, like you did Father de Flores, I'd be happy for your help and talent."

Frank smiled and replied, "I'll be sure to give Father Clemens your regards and let him know how you helped me." Frank waved as he headed toward the train station and said, "Father Mac, thank you again for letting me clean up and for the great meal."

Train to Madison, Nebraska

With the familiar chugging of the steam engine in his ears, Frank sat by the open freight door and looked into the night. *That should be Omaha up ahead,* he thought as he watched the lights getting closer in the distance. The darkness made him wait for the train to slow down more than usual. He wanted to get closer to the lights so he could check the landscape forward and backward. It looked clear. Holding on to his duffle tightly, he jumped, stumbled, and almost fell. He caught his balance, though, and managed to stay on his feet.

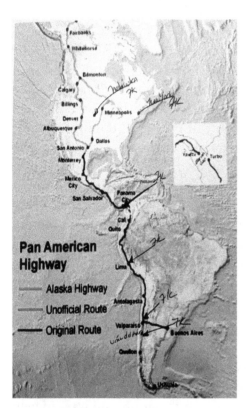

Pan American Highway

Alaska Highway

Unofficial Route

Original Route

Map of Frank's travels in South America

Suddenly, out of the darkness came a shout from behind. A big hand grabbed his neck as he heard a deep angry voice ask, "Where do you think you're going, boy?"

Outnumbered three to one, Frank stood still, did not struggle, and wisely told the truth. "I'm going home to Madison, Nebraska." The two men standing on either side of the big man who still had a grip on him held lanterns at face level as they watched and waited.

The big bull who held onto the boy with a tight grip recognized the army duffle bag he held and asked gruffly, "You a soldier?"

Frank nodded and replied respectfully, "Yes, sir, I served at Fort Worth, Texas, U. S. Army Air Corps."

The big man nodded, replying, "My brother, too—he's about your age. So, tell me what you are doing here jumping trains!"

Again, Frank replied honestly, "Sir, I don't have much money. I want to get home, and I was using the money I had to buy food along the way."

The bull nodded his head again and seemed a little more understanding when he replied, "Look here, boy. You buy a riding train ticket from Omaha to Madison right now while I'm watching you, and I'll let you be on your way."

Frank replied immediately, "Yes, sir. Right away, sir." The three train bulls walked Frank to the station clerk window. They made sure he purchased the correct train ticket, then wished him well as they left him on the train platform.

Shaking with relief, Frank was glad the bulls had not thrown him in jail. Having lost his appetite in the ruckus, Frank sat quietly on the bench until the next morning.

As he waited for the train, he felt like it was a perfect time to thank God he had gotten this close to home before his luck ran out. Dozing off and on through the night, Frank woke immediately when he heard the whistle of the early morning train pulling into the Omaha Station right on time.

Boarding and finding his seat, Frank stowed his duffle in the overhead shelf, sat down, and his mind, began to relax. *If I go to sleep*, he thought, *I might be able to forget how hungry I am.* Closing his eyes, the sway of the train lulled his mind, but the part that was still awake examined the odd feelings that had been driving him so hard. Now that he was so close to Madison, Frank finally realized it was homesickness. He admitted he longed to see all the familiar faces he loved and visit all the places he knew. Frank could hardly wait to get back to his hometown.

July: Frank Emil Karella Arrives Back Home

It could have been minutes or hours that Frank had been dreaming on that comfortable seat gently rocked by the train car. Waking feeling homesick, Frank discovered it was the rumble and growling of his empty stomach that actually woke him. He looked out the window, and right as he recognized the landscape, the conductor walked through the car announcing the on-time arrival. He could see the Madison train station up ahead. Frank stood up, stretched, then retrieved his duffle bag from the shelf. Chuckling, he thought, *I have never thought of this train depot as beautiful, but at this moment, I don't remember seeing a more beautiful sight.*

It had been close to three years since he left this station headed to a destination in South America. Heaving his duffle to his shoulder and moving toward the door, he whispered, "Thank You, Lord! It feels good to be back home!"

Madison Railroad Depot, 1925. Photograph courtesy of the Madison County Historical Museum of Nebraska

CHAPTER 7

Frank Emil Karella

Home in Madison

F rank walked away from the train station headed toward the sawmill house where he had grown up. He couldn't wait to see the
astonishment his appearance would cause in town.

*I have missed Papa, my siblings, and all the rest of my family so
much,* he thought as he walked down the street. *Being away from
them has made me realize how precious every single one of them are.* As
Frank walked along lost in memories, he vividly recalled not wanting to come home. *I guess some of the traveling I have done in the last
year was to put off dealing with my real feelings, but now I am sorry I
wasted so much time.*

Almost Three Years Earlier

After Frank and his friends fulfilled their musical obligation to Father
Flores in Santiago, Frank realized he was not ready to go home.
His confession had been spontaneous as he sat with the priest one
evening at the rectory. "Father, it happened so fast I could not comprehend it. My departure date for this trip was only a month away.
All I thought about was my upcoming adventure. I stayed out at the
homestead when Mama said she felt unwell. I never once thought
her illness might be serious. Then she was gone! But then, while we

were here, my grandfather passed away too!" he remembered telling Father Flores. "I just can't go home yet!"

Father Flores had understood. Being both kind and sympathetic, the priest gave Frank the space and time he needed to sort out his feelings.

To help Frank and the boys afford to extend their stay, Father Flores made some inquiries and facilitated a few introductions to prominent Chilean businessmen. Because of Father Flores's recommendation, he and the boys got hired to play several music venues around Santiago. One introduction led to another, and soon they stayed so busy playing music and sightseeing that time just disappeared. They also enjoyed a lot more travel than they had originally planned on.

Looking back, Frank could see that agreeing to such an aggressive entertainment schedule made it easier to ignore the real reasons why he felt compelled to keep moving. Though it took a while, he eventually figured out he was not running toward adventure as much as he was hiding the truth from himself. He was doing a great job of running away from the pain in his past.

Lost in Thought as Frank Walked through Madison

Frank smiled inwardly, thinking, *I am not sorry I went.* Then he laughed as he remembered the first day he arrived in Chile, wide eyed and so amazed by the size of that modern city. *Not to mention being stunned by the beautiful classical structures like the church we were going to live in. I told Father Flores how surprised I was. I certainly felt like an idiot when he informed me the City of Santiago was founded in 1541 and that his city was world famous for its neoclassical architecture. For heaven's sake, the City of Santiago was already 235 years older than the whole country of America! The construction on the grand cathedral we were going to live in was completed in 1775!*

Stopping to look both ways before he crossed the street near the post office, Frank heard someone yell his name. He looked around and saw his brother-in-law, Rudy Pojar, waving at him. "Frank!"

Rudy yelled again. "I thought that was you! When did you get back to town?"

Frank grinned and returned the greeting and said, "Actually, Rudy, I just got off the train. But, look, no one knows I'm here yet because I want to surprise Papa. Keep my secret, ok? At least for a few hours. I'm headed to Papa's house now."

"Sure thing, Frank. Won't tell anyone but your sister. Martha would kill me if she found out I had seen her brother in town and didn't tell her. I'll let her know you want to keep it a secret until after supper. How'd that be?" Rudy asked.

"That will work. Thanks, brother," Frank replied. "Now, I've got to get home before anyone else sees me and Papa hears I'm back over the radio before I get home."

That comment made Rudy laugh, and he replied, "In this town, that's not too far from the truth. You never know who's watching and might see you. That's hot news everyone is going to want to hear!"

"Ok, enough jokes. See ya later," Frank said jauntily as he started down the street again.

Lost in Memories Once More

Thinking about the radio as he continued to walk down the street, Frank remembered putting his foot in his mouth when he told Father Flores he couldn't believe he was hearing Al Jolson on the Chilean radio singing "Toot Toot Tootsie Goodbye."

"I don't know why that should surprise you, Frank," Father had said. "Radio reached as far as Argentina by 1920 and arrived here in Chile long before you did."

That information sure set me on my ear! I learned quickly to ask more questions and find out about history before I opened my big mouth to give my opinions. I also learned to be more perceptive about other people's feelings and learned to respect their customs and cultures. I am proud to admit my travels around South America taught me a lot.

Suddenly, Frank came out of his personal reflections. He realized he had found his way to his old street without even thinking about it. Turning the corner, Frank saw the house he had grown up in and began to feel a little nervous.

He told himself he had made a decent effort to send his sister Helen at least a postcard or a short letter from each country he had worked in. Nothing of any length. Usually only a few words to let her know he and the boys were alright and a little about what they were doing since they left home.

Now that the house was in sight, he realized it had been a very long time since he left. Not that the house had changed, but he knew he had. He hadn't thought this through. Frank overlooked the possibility that his family might still be upset with him about the way he left town after his mother's death. He never considered this surprise might backfire. Now, he wished he had warned Helen or his brother he was coming back. But, mostly, he hoped just showing up at his father's door unannounced would be received as a welcome surprise.

Madison, Home of Anton J. Karella

Anton sat listening to the music on the radio, sipping on a cup of hot coffee. He enjoyed the George Gershwin orchestra music program the station played in the mornings. Anton couldn't help thinking that both his mother and his wife would have liked the tune playing, "Rhapsody in Blue."

In truth, he was running a little behind schedule this morning. Normally, his eldest daughter, Helen, would have made breakfast for him and done these chores around the house. But she and her family had moved into their own home several months ago, and he was still not used to her being gone.

Anton kept reminding himself he should have been at the sawmill already. He expected his brother Stanislaus to be calling to check up on him any minute. Right as he finished that thought, Anton heard someone knocking on his front door.

Stanislaus? He wondered, then thought, *No, it couldn't be Stanislaus because my brother would have already walked into the house shouting my name.* Curious, Anton headed to the front door.

A Father and Son Reunion

With his scruffy army duffle bag over his shoulder, Frank walked up to his old home and knocked firmly on the door. He hoped his father was still at home. When Anton opened the door, all doubt and hesitation left Frank. He dropped his duffle bag, and both men instantly grabbed each other in a bear hug and cried happy tears, unable to speak.

After the initial surprise and their emotional greeting was spent standing in the doorway, Anton said, "Please come in, son. Let's sit down in the kitchen and catch up."

Frank picked up his duffle from where he had dropped it carelessly, only then worrying he might have damaged his clarinets. *I'll check them later*, he thought as he followed his father through the house and into the kitchen he knew so well.

"Do you want some coffee, son?"

"Yes, please," Frank answered with a tired sigh. "I need it this morning." Anton listened as he pulled a second cup from a cupboard and began pouring coffee, and Frank continued talking. "I caught the early train out of Omaha, and it stopped in Colfax before coming to Madison. I've been traveling for over a week to get here. I started out in New York! However, my travel stories can wait. I have something else I need to say to you first."

It was the serious tone in Frank's voice that drew Anton's complete attention. He turned to look at his son, even though Frank had gone silent for a moment. "I'm sorry, Papa," Frank said softly. "It was terrible of me. Running off like I did right after Mama died, and I regret not being here when Grandpa died. All I can figure out is that I was trying to run away from the pain I felt at losing Mama. It happened so fast. I just couldn't face it. It is still hard to push away the guilt I have felt over not being here when Grandpa passed away."

Anton's face drained of color, and his eyes stung with tears. He sat down heavily on the chair across from his son, setting the coffee cups on the table. With his throat aching and threatening to close off his words, he began to speak slowly "Son, I ran from pain for a long time too. It is time to put all that behind us. Let's be thankful we have the love of our family, we have food on the table, and more than enough work to keep us all busy. Let's concentrate on the future and on what we have."

Texas Longhorn steer, Nebraska, GKM 2018

Frank nodded his head, saying, "Papa, you are so right! I am so happy to be home."

Smiling, Anton spoke encouragingly, "Let's start fresh! Tell me about the most fantastic thing you've seen on your travels."

Frank grinned, then asked, "From any trip or place?"

"Sure, any trip, place, or time," replied Anton.

Frank started digging through his duffle and pulled out a cigar box. With a smile, he opened it and searched through his pictures and found the two he was looking for. "Ok, I am choosing the very first fantastic thing I saw when I was 19 in flight cadet school in Fort Worth." Showing him the picture, Frank said, "They are Texas Longhorns! Did you ever imagine cows could have horns that long? I swear I don't know how they pick up their heads. I was told that the breed was nearly extinct in 1920. But then some Texas cattle breeders began to show an interest in saving the species while I was still at Fort Worth. I was told that their horns can be six to ten feet wide. This one, they said, had short horns for a Longhorn."

Anton laughed in surprise. "I never expected you to be impressed by an animal as common as a steer. I admit this is something I have never seen before either," he said, delighted.

"There is another fantastic thing that is high on my list," said Frank. "It was something I learned in Chile while I was learning to speak Spanish. I remember I found it odd at first that Spanish-speaking people were singing American songs with English words. Yet they only spoke Spanish. Then I personally experienced the reverse when I heard the traditional Latin ballad 'Besame Mucho.' I knew it was a love song by its tone, yet after learning that it meant 'Kiss Me a Lot' in English, I realized I preferred to hear it sung in Spanish. It sounded and felt more romantic that way. Gosh, did we love listening to Father's radio. The boys and I picked up many Spanish words from listening to the radio announcers. It was the best way to learn new American songs too. By playing them as part of our repertoire for the church fundraisers, we discovered just how popular American music was in Latin America, long before we started playing in supper clubs around Santiago."

As Frank finished talking, the telephone rang, interrupting their conversation. Anton answered it and heard the concerned voice of his brother Stanislaus on the other end of the receiver. "I am so sorry I worried you, Stanislaus. Frank surprised me before I could leave. Yes, Frank, my son Frank. Yes, Frank Emil is home. I don't know. He just walked up to the door. I had no idea he was coming home. I know! He completely surprised me too. Would you mind if I stayed here a while longer with him? Thank you. Oh, sure, that would be great! We would love to see you and Anna here at the house for supper. Say around six? Yes, that would be fine." Then Anton said goodbye and hung up the receiver.

"Sorry, Frank, seeing you at the door made me completely forget that your uncle Stanislaus was waiting for me at the sawmill. They will come over for dinner, so I hope you have not made any plans yet."

Frank shook his head and replied, "All I really planned was to show up here and surprise you!"

"Well, son, you certainly accomplished that goal! What a wonderful surprise it was," Anton said as he sat down at the table again.

"I'm thrilled that it made you as happy as it made me, Papa!"

Catching up on the Happenings in Madison

"Ok, Papa, now it's your turn to talk for a while. Tell me what has been happening around here with all the family."

"Son, that question has a lot of answers," Anton replied with a smile.

Frank smiled back and said, "I have the time if you do."

Anton nodded and resettled himself in his chair, trying to get more comfortable and began by saying, "So much has happened while you have been gone. You have become an uncle several times over. Helen had two more children: Jerome Howard was born in May of 1922 just after you left, and Joseph Gerald was born in October of 1923.

"You remember your sister Martha and Rudy Pojar had their son Charles Anthony in September of 1921? You will not believe how much he has grown since you've been gone. She and Rudy have not had any more children, but they are all well and are still living here in Madison.

"Your sister Mary is getting ready to finish high school, and she is now engaged to Stanley Voborny. Mary's best friend, Agnes Moore, married one of Rudy Pojar's cousins. I'm happy Agnes is part of our family now. The young woman has felt and acted like a daughter to me since your mama passed. Oh yes, and your brother Anastas is now serving in France with the French Foreign Legion."

"What did you say?" sputtered Frank. "He just turned . . . what . . . 14 this last September?"

"That's right," replied Anton, "I'm pleased you remember his birthday, and that is also when Anastas disappeared. However, that is a longer story than I care to talk about right now. Suffice to say, Anastas has been writing to us. At least now we know where he is."

Frank was still reeling in shock over the disappeared remark and the fact that his 14-year-old brother was a Legionnaire in France! He decided he would have to corner his brother Ambrose as soon as possible to get the full story about this.

Anton continued talking and said, "Now, you might remember your older brother, Ambrose, apprenticed to a blacksmith in Norfolk just before you went into the Air Corps. You gave him permission to drive your Texas Jackrabbit while you were gone. Ambrose drove it to Norfolk to work on Mondays and came home on Fridays until eight months ago. That is when he opened his own business here in Madison. Oh yes, we all call him Rusty now. That is all I'm going to say about the name. You'll have to get the reason for the nickname from him. The point I intended to make is, your Jackrabbit is now parked in the barn next to my automobile. Rusty keeps both autos in good running condition, and the key for yours is hanging by the front door."

"Any girls in his life yet?" Frank asked.

Anton lifted his brow in surprise and replied, "Interesting question. Tell me . . . are there any girls in *your* life, Frank?"

Frank laughed at his father's evasive reaction to his question and replied, "Ok, I guess I deserved that. I surmise by your reply Ambrose is still all work and no play, just like when we were boys growing up together?"

Anton cleared his throat and said, "You mean Rusty, don't you?"

"Got it. *Rusty*," replied Frank, grinning. "That is going to take some getting used to."

Anton nodded in agreement and replied, "In answer to your question, you are correct. Your brother *Rusty* is very serious about the world and his work. If there is a special girl or girlfriend in his life, he has not mentioned her to me.

"He does make a marvelous uncle, though. Rusty grew very attached to Helen's children and spent every moment of his free time at home with them when they lived here with us. I think he would make a great father."

Both men had gone quiet as they finished their coffee. "Frank," Anton said, "if you want to, I'd love to have you move back into the house. There is plenty of room."

The smile his words caused in Frank's eyes meant the world to Anton, but his son's reply meant even more. "That would be great. I have missed you, Papa, and the rest of the family too. It will be good to be here again."

Anton's eyes got a little teary, and he nodded his head quickly to cover his emotions and replied, "Good! Let's get you settled in that big room at the top of the stairs."

Frank was surprised and asked, "Isn't that Ambrose's . . . I mean . . . Rusty's room?"

"I know—it's hard to get used to calling him that, but I'm working on it too. And to answer your question, Rusty moved into Martha's old room. He gave the big bedroom to Helen and the kids when they came to live with us. Now that they have moved out, the big room is empty. It's yours if you want it."

"I'll be happy to move into it. Thank you, Papa," Frank replied.

A Late-Night Chat Between Brothers

Frank sat up late after his father had gone to bed. He enjoyed being back in the house he had grown up in. As Frank meticulously cleaned his clarinets, he tried to understand the feeling of being the same and, at the same time, very different. Suddenly, he thought he heard footsteps on the stairs.

Rusty made an effort to be quiet until he saw the lamplight shining through the door of his old bedroom. He stopped and said, "Hello, Frank, it's good to see you."

The smile of welcome on Rusty's face was unmistakable. Frank put down the clarinet and got up to hug his older brother and replied deliberately, "It's good to see you, too, *Rusty*."

With a chuckle of appreciation, Rusty replied, "So you heard about that, did you?"

Smiling, Frank nodded and said, "I certainly did. I was also told I'd have to ask you why. I'd love to hear about that and a whole lot more! I am curious why you are coming home so late tonight? Or is this a regular coming home hour for a working man that owns and operates a blacksmith and repair business?"

Rusty shrugged his shoulders and replied, "Sometimes . . . well, maybe most of the time lately. Now that you are here, I'll try to get home a little earlier in the evenings. It's been strange since Helen and the kids moved out. I guess I got used to their noise and laughter, and now it seems too quiet here. That is why I stay late at the shop, but I do get a lot of extra work done. I also stop by Helen's house to see the children a couple of evenings a week, and those always turn into late nights.

"I did mean to get home earlier today. I can't tell you how many people came by to tell me they saw you. Or to tell me they heard you were back. Martha and Rudy called me at the shop about 6:00 p.m. They told me Emil and Emily are planning a big shindig to celebrate your return. They are holding it out at the homestead tomorrow. I will try to get out there in the afternoon, but I have some rush orders that need finishing before I can leave the shop. Say, are you up for some coffee right now? Maybe catch up a bit between just the two of us?"

Frank smiled and replied, "Thought you'd never ask. But coffee? At this hour? How about one of Grandpa's home brews instead? Or maybe I should ask if there are any left."

Rusty grinned and nodded his head that there were and replied, "Do you remember where Dad keeps it in the basement?"

"Of course," Frank replied with a boyish grin of his own. "Do you want to split one, or are you up for a whole one tonight?"

"Gosh, I think we ought to really celebrate, don't you?" Laughing, he suggested, "Let's have a couple."

As Frank pulled off the cap on a bottle of home-brew, he said, "This bottle of beer reminds me of a place I went to in Fort Worth, Texas, called Hells Half Acre. Do you remember those old western stories about Butch Cassidy and the Wild Bunch Outlaw Gang?"

Rusty nodded.

Front left to right: Sundance Kid, Tall Texan, Butch Cassidy. Standing: News Carver and Kid Curry. Fort Worth, Texas, 1900, Hells Half Acre. Public Domain.

"Well, some of us cadets from the airbase went drinking in a saloon where that gang of outlaws hung out in 1900. It's the area where all the cheap saloons and bawdy houses were. The outlaw gang snuck into town on the Fort Worth & Denver City Railway. Even the lawmen didn't recognize them for outlaws—they were so far into southern Texas. I saw a picture of them on the wall. They must have been feeling pretty safe to dress up and have their picture taken all together. Nobody knows why.

"This area in Fort Worth was pretty wild. It's hard to believe all that crazy Wild West stuff was going on down there when Mama and Papa first met here in Madison. I went there just before the enactment of prohibition shut down the saloons, but I never told the folks that I went there."

"That was wise of you, Frank," his brother replied with a grin. "What else did you do that you did not tell the folks about?" Rusty asked quietly.

"Since you asked, big brother, move a little closer, and I'll tell you," replied Frank in a husky whisper only loud enough for his brother to hear.

Fourth of July, Welcome-Home Picnic, Karella Homestead

"Holy Moses, it's good to be back at the homestead!" Frank exclaimed as he hugged Uncle Ed. "Papa tells me you are going to take a vacation and go visit your family in France."

Ed nodded.

"Then I am really happy I got home in time to see you before you left," Frank replied.

"I am happy to see you again too! We'll have time for a chat later," replied Uncle Ed as he nodded toward the group of people headed their way.

Frank received hugs, handshakes, and welcome-home wishes from an army of Karellas, Holys, Beans, Pojars, Vobornys, and Kuchars, as well as a few close friends and neighbors who joined the picnic gathering because they heard Frank had come home.

Suddenly seeing a person Frank had messages for, he made his way through the well-wishers to the priest's side, saying, "Father Clemens! How good it is to see you. I have a couple of messages for you. First, Father Mac in Sioux City, Iowa, sends his best regards. He let me get cleaned up and fed me lunch when my train dropped me off there." Father Clemens smiled, and Frank went on to say, "And I am also supposed to tell you Father Jose de Flores sends his warmest regards. I cannot thank you enough for your introduction to him and the arrangements you two made for us."

"You are welcome, Frank," Father Clemens replied. "And thank you for delivering those messages from my friends. I did receive a letter from Father Flores, though. He wrote that the concerts you gave on behalf of his cathedral projects were well attended successes. The parishioners loved your music."

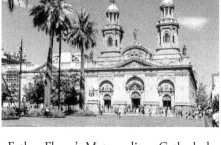

Father Flores's Metropolitan Cathedral, Santiago, Chile

"That's great to hear! I don't know if Father Flores told you," said Frank, "but he landed us our first big gig at the Richmond in Santiago. That is after we finished performing for his fundraisers. I've got to say I was very impressed; Father Flores knows a lot of important people!"

Postcard from Frank Karella, Santiago, Chile

Father Clemens laughed and nodded in agreement. He remembered his time in the seminary with Flores. He had learned Flores not only possessed a charismatic personality, but Flores could also make friends with anyone he met. However, above and beyond that, his family connections throughout South America were very impressive.

Frank went on to say, "It was a friend of one of Flores's friends that introduced us to another guy by the name of Señor Raphael Mendoza. He owns a vineyard halfway between Santiago and the coast. He was recommended to come and see us perform at the Richmond. Mendoza said a friend of his needed a group for his place in Vina Del Mar, which is a town on the coast of Chile."

1922, Richmond in
Santiago, Chile

Frank was so excited to relate this story to the priest he did not realize a group of avid listeners had surrounded him within minutes. They all wanted to hear his stories.

Anton noticed the crowd and made his way to his son's side. Tapping Frank on the shoulder, Anton said, "Son, why don't we all go over to the tables so you can sit down and relax, and that way, everyone will be able to hear about your travels."

All the relatives and friends standing around murmured their agreement with that suggestion. Frank nodded at his father, then followed Father Clemens to the tables and chairs. Someone handed Frank a cold beer before he started talking again. He took a sip and closed his eyes in appreciation. "Delicious! Granddad's recipe, right?" Frank asked enthusiastically. Everyone nodded, and he replied, "Gosh, he sure knew how to make good home brew!" Everyone smiled at his reaction and nodded in agreement.

Before Frank had a chance to get back to what he had been saying, a child's voice asked, "I was wondering, Uncle Frank, what instrument did you play in your band?" Frank turned to his left and saw Helen's little girl, Margaret Mary, looking up at him.

Delighted with the little girl's question, Frank replied, "Well, hello, Margaret Mary! Would you like to sit with me while I tell everyone about my clarinets? That is the instrument I play, and I learned to play two kinds of clarinets when I was in the Army Band."

"Oh yes, I would," Margaret Mary replied as she climbed up on his lap. "Mama showed us your picture with your Army airplane at Fort Worth. Thank you for the pecans you sent in the big bag at Christmas. We put them in cookies. Mama also said you were working in a place called chili. I'm wondering, Uncle Frank, why would someone name the place they live in after bean soup?" That silly idea made Margaret Mary quit talking for a minute, and then she scrunched up her shoulders and giggled.

Before the little girl could start chatting again, Frank replied, "You are very welcome, Margaret Mary. Would you like to hear about my adventures in South America?" She nodded her head. Then Frank asked sweetly, "Good! Can you also be quiet so I can

Castillo Wulff, Vina del Mar, Chile

tell the rest of the family about my travels in South America too?" Margaret Mary nodded once again and sat quietly watching him.

Father Clemens approved of the gentle way Frank talked with his little niece. Then he cleared his throat and said, "Now then, Frank, you were talking about Mendoza, who had the vineyard outside Santiago, and a friend who lived on the coast in the town of Vina del Mar."

"Yes," he replied as he hugged Margaret Mary and went on to say, "that is exactly where I was in my story. So, Mendoza made the introduction to a man by the name of Wulff, and we were hired to play at a castle named Castillo Wulff.

"The castle was built right on the ocean in 1906 by Gustavo Adolfo Wulff Mowle. The man was a German-born coal trader who had been to Chile on business many times and then decided to settle there years ago."

Frank saw the question in everyone's eyes and answered it by saying, "I can see you are wondering if it is the same Wulff I met. The answer is yes. After he built the castle, he liked to share it with lots of friends and used part of it each summer as guestrooms. Mr. Wulff hired us to play the whole summer season at his castle while he had company in residence. It was Gustavo Wulff who introduced us to another guy from Lima, Peru, Xavier Chavez, one of his guests at the castle. Chavez promoted entertainment venues in Lima, Peru, and also booked entertainment for Panama City in the country of Panama.

"Chavez promised he would get us a job in Lima after we finished the summer season for Gustavo. Chavez made good on his promise,

Lima, Peru, Av. De Mayo

and we were performing in Lima for the holiday season leading up to last Christmas. We worked right through New Years and then got laid off. The boys and I made enough money to do a little sightseeing, and we were glad to have some free time. One night, we met a captain in a dinner club who owned a big sailboat. He offered to take us to the Galapagos Islands to see giant man-size prehistoric lizards, but it was 500 miles away. We had to turn down that offer because we didn't have that much time or the money to get us there and back.

"Our band could only afford to go without working for about ten days. Chavez said we should take a train trip along the Andes Mountains and back. He recommended the Callao, Lima & Oroya Railway. It is the second-highest railway in the world. The highest one is in Tibet. On our route, the train worked its way up into the Andes Mountains on a switchback path that climbed to 15,692 feet at the Galera Summit. We passed through about 60 tunnels and rolled over many steel bridges. At the highest point on our trip, we were at 15,807 feet above sea level. On that train ride, we did get to see a lot of scenery and lots and lots of llamas."

As Frank looked at the faces staring at him with incredulous looks, he realized his adventures seemed pretty unbelievable. It all happened to be true and was exactly what happened, so he said, "I know you might wonder if you should believe everything, I'm telling you. But I do have some pictures with me if you want to see them."

"Can't wait to see those pictures," said a male voice from the back of the crowd. It sounded like Rudy Pojar and was followed by a feminine giggle that sounded like his sister Martha. Then his heckler went on to say, "Frank, finish your story first! We can always see the pictures later!"

Sightseeing on train in Peru and llamas by the train track

Frank smiled and continued his recital. "When we got back from our trip and walked into the hotel in Lima, the desk clerk gave us a letter that had arrived from Chavez.

"It said he booked an opening night for us in Panama and wanted us packed up and ready to catch The Ocean Pearl, docked in the harbor. It was headed for Panama.

"When we found the boat, we were surprised to discover the captain was going to drop us off without charging us for the trip.

Turns out he owed Chavez a favor, which was lucky for us. Our band was nearly broke by the time we landed in Panama.

Panama City—1924 FK

"We were all excited to perform in Panama City and pleased to discover it was a very nice dinner club. The boys and I spent most of this last year in Panama, and I'm sad to say the wages were not as good as they had been in Peru.

"Chavez also gave us a contact for a guy in Panama that could act as our interpreter, guide, and cab driver and would work for a cut-rate price if we let him play music with us.

"Sammy was born and raised in Panama City and also happened to be a good acoustical guitar player. He played with us and gave us pointers on Sunday nights when we practiced our Latin music. We would get together after we were done performing at the dinner clubs, and that was always late so it didn't interfere with his regular job.

Panamá Canal, Panamá, PD prior to 1924

"Sammy would also meet up with us on our days off and took us to see the Panama Canal for the first time. It's hard to believe, but the builders literally cut a canal system through a strip of land that is 50 miles wide and is the only land that separates the Atlantic and Pacific oceans. That strip of land in Panama also joins the North American and South American continents. I saw a ship bigger than any building you've ever seen start traveling through that canal system. We watched from a hill much higher than the canal, and it seemed to take forever for the water between the flood gates to rise enough to let the ship pass to the next section of the canal. Ships from all over the world use the Panama Canal on a regular basis, but it takes a long time to make the entire passage. Yet, it still takes less time and is safer using the canal system to go between the Pacific and Atlantic oceans than it is to sail around the South American continent.

"We soon realized the Panamanian gigs were never going to pay well, and it was getting hard to meet our rent and have enough to eat. The guys and I had been on the road nearly three years when the money finally ran out. It turned out to be a good thing that we ran out of money while we were in Panama.

Mapa de Panamá Canal, https://creativecommons.org/lincenses/ by-sa/2.0/deed .en

"Sammy introduced us to his beautiful girlfriend, Chef Erika, who had contracts with several ships whenever they docked in Panama or were waiting to make the passage through the canal. Erika supplied local cuisine specialties that the ship's chef put on the menus when they were in port.

"Erika called in a favor and got us an interview with a steward on a Dutch ocean liner waiting to go through the Panama Canal. The ship would be making a stop in New York before heading to Europe. That steward knew we were flat broke and would only hire us for the cost of a bed and food, and we still had to work full time and perform as musicians while we were on board the ship. In exchange, the captain would drop us off in New York.

"I was assigned to housekeeping, and I cleaned staterooms when our band was not performing. The rest of the guys got stuck in the kitchen. They had to split up the work from two lunch shifts washing dishes and then play in the band for the two dinner shifts. I'm thankful my job was making beds and not doing dishes!" Everyone laughed at Frank's expression. Frank went on talking right up until the dinner bell rang. Then everyone headed for the food.

Frank Seeks out His Sister Helen

Before it got too late, Frank found a moment to spend alone with Helen. No one disturbed them when they saw brother and sister with their heads close together and tears in Helen's eyes. "I'm sorry about the baby, Helen," he whispered softly.

His sister smiled through her tears and nodded. She looked like she wanted to say something but only replied, "Thank you, Frankie." Seeing Mary Cecilia headed their way, she said, "I think it's time I looked for Alvin and my children."

Helen walked away as his youngest sister, Mary Cecelia, came up to him, pulling her boyfriend, Stanley Voborny, by the hand. She gave her brother a hug of welcome and kept him from walking away by saying, "Excuse me, Frank. Can Stanley and I see your pictures, please?" Nodding his head, he walked with them over to the picnic table and handed his sister a stack of photographs, and he heard her whisper, "See, Stanley, I told you he wasn't fibbing!" Smiling, Frank kept walking. He thought it was a good time to look for Uncle Emil.

As the picnic was winding down, Frank and Uncle Emil sat talking about their mutual love of adventure and, of course, music.

"You know, Frank, your dad and I love music too. It was one of the most precious connections I had with Anton, even though he was many years older than me. You and I share more than a name and love of music. We share a desire to see new places and experience adventure, though the ones I had going to and from Chicago seem pretty tame in comparison to yours."

Right then, Rusty walked up carrying a plate of food and sat down as he said," Hello there! Can I join you two?"

"Glad to see you made it out here before the victuals were all gone, brother. Please go ahead and eat. I was just telling Uncle Emil that Papa has always seen a similarity between Uncle Emil and me. I think that is why Papa seemed so happy for me when Father Clemens first proposed the trip to visit Father Flores in Santiago. I would never have guessed where learning to play the clarinet would take me. I am gratified that my music paid my way and allowed me to travel to other countries.

Anastasia Holy Karella's cousins—the four sons of Katharina Koryta and Joseph Kuchar, also Frank Karella's cousins

"Do you know I think the last two weeks were the hardest of my three years of traveling? Would you believe I was hopping on freight trains to get out of New York so I could get back to Nebraska?"

Emil's eyes went wide. He also sounded impressed when he asked, "Do you mean to say you hopped on freight trains like a vagrant? You did not pay to ride?"

Grinning, Frank shook his head. Then he indicated he wanted his uncle to speak a little more quietly. Motioning to Emil and Rusty in a conspiratorial fashion, he wanted them to move closer, then whispered, "I didn't have the money to pay. I needed to save what I had to buy food. I hopped on empty freight cars at each stop out of New York and across the country. I didn't run into any bulls until I crossed into Nebraska."

Frank could see the questions in Emil's eyes and explained, "Bulls are a kind of train police. They stand watch in the railroad stations, and they are the guys that patrol the train yards to stop guys like me from hopping on the trains without paying. I didn't run into any of them until I reached the outskirts of Omaha. I only got caught once, and it was scary. When that big guy grabbed hold of my neck, I thought he looked ready to break me in half. There were two other guys with him as well.

"I made sure I spoke respectfully and told them I was headed home. One of them recognized my military duffle bag and asked if I had served in the Army. When I said I had, they told me they would let me off if I promised to buy a ticket from Omaha to Madison. I used the last of my money to buy that ticket and didn't have anything to eat that day until I got to Dad's house here in Madison."

Uncle Emil grinned and replied, "I will keep your secret about that part of your adventure to myself." Rusty nodded he would too.

Even though Emil felt compelled to dissuade that kind of behavior in Frank for his own safety, at the same time, he was proud of his young nephew's resourcefulness. Emil could not wait to tell his wife, Emily, about Frank's secret adventures—ones he could have wished he had experienced himself.

End of July, an Encounter with Destiny

The Madison summer was turning out to be a warm one. Frank rolled down the windows of his Texas Jackrabbit and let the air blow through as he drove down the road. He didn't like running behind schedule, but having a flat tire on the way to Norfolk was not his fault. He hoped there would be no delays at his scheduled stops. Just maybe he could make up the time and still get home and change out of his work clothing to get to band practice without being late.

The deliveries went smoothly until the last stop. When he got to McFarland's Meat Shop, Frank found the delivery door blocked with boxes. Parking in the shade, Frank ran around the corner to the front of the store and literally ran into a lovely woman coming out the door. "Pardon me, miss," he said as he caught his balance and hers before they fell to the ground. Frank couldn't help but stare. Then, pouring on the charm, he extended his other hand and said,

"I am so sorry. I did not mean to run you over. My name is Frank Karella, and who have I had the pleasure of running into?"

The woman grinned as she stared back boldly. *Cheeky fellow*, she thought, and then decided to catch the handsome charmer off guard.

Extending her hand, she shook his firmly and replied, "Helen Craven."

Frank Emil Karella, Helen Craven Karella, 1925, near music school, Norfolk, Nebraska

Wow, Frank thought, *she is icy.* Totally impressed by her cool demeanor, he asked, "So is it *MISS* Helen Craven?"

Withdrawing her hand, she replied, "Yes. It is *Miss* Craven."

Frank smiled with confidence and asked, "So, Miss Craven, what do you do when you are not bumping into young men at the market?"

She enjoyed the game they were playing. Not many men had the courage to face her down when she was so direct. She decided to play this game a little longer. "I own and operate the Music Conservatory of Norfolk," she replied in a sophisticated tone.

Single, beautiful, and she loves music? How perfect! Frank thought, smiling at her.

"And you, Mr. Karella? What do you do when you are not running into defenseless women at the market?"

Chuckling, Frank replied, "The pleasure of bumping into beautiful women aside, what I do during the day is manage a poultry and egg business for my family's farm. But at night, I play music in a local band." He noticed when he said he played music, she slightly raised her brows and caught the flicker of interest in her eyes. Feeling even more confident, Frank thought, *I have surprised her, and now I'm going to surprise her again.* "Miss Craven, could I interest you in coming to hear my band play some music?"

She was tempted and replied, "When would this band be playing?"

"After I finish this delivery, I'll be heading back to Madison, and the guys will be meeting me right after dinner. I'd be delighted if you would join me for dinner and then for some music. What do you say, Miss Helen Craven? Are you up for a little adventure?"

Laughing out loud, she suddenly felt reckless and replied, "Pick me up in an hour," as she wrote down her address and handed it to him, adding, "and don't be late, Mr. Frank Karella. I detest tardiness."

Tipping his hat to her, Frank replied, "Your wish is my command. An hour it shall be."

Helen Craven smiled, turned, and walked down the street.

Frank dashed through the door of the market and shouted, "Bobby! I need to get my load delivered. Right now! Please!"

Bobby came from behind the butcher's counter and asked, "What's the big hurry, Frank?"

"Bobby, I have a date, and I can't be late!" Frank replied, laughing with excitement.

The Beginning of Forever

Mesmerized during dinner, Frank found himself listening to Helen talk about music. It was such a switch in positions. He was usually the one who could talk about nothing else, but here sat a beautiful woman who was as much in love with music as he was.

"So, Frank, what do you call your sound?" Helen asked as they ate dinner.

"That's a good question. Perhaps my immediate response might not actually be the answer to your question."

Helen could not help being impressed. This man was very perceptive. She decided to wait before replying to his observation and just smiled at him.

As Frank looked into her eyes, he wondered if this was some kind of test and if he was passing or failing. Seeing she was not going to make this easy on him, he asked, "I would love to hear what you really mean by your question, Helen."

Helen grinned and replied, "In the old days, I believe the only self-expression and real freedom people had was found through classic music or art. Those mediums allowed every person to escape the cage of their station in life. Be it life in the gilded cage of royalty to running from rats in the streets, music and art allowed everyone to escape into dreams.

Family photo collage of Helen Craven's brothers and parents kept on her desk at the school

"My students at the conservatory often debate on how the sound of music that identifies a style was developed."

"Such as?" asked Frank, leaning over the table and resting his chin on his fist, fascinated by the woman and the words coming out of her mouth.

Keeping her composure was becoming a little difficult for Helen with the way Frank stared into her eyes. Somehow, she felt like he was beating her at her own game, so she launched into some descriptions of music she thought would shake him up. "Oh, let me see. The dusky grind and earthy slide of pain and hope *is the blues*. The spunky sexy rhythms of tango, mambo, cha-cha, and merengue *is Latin*. The romantic waltzing glide and sensuous swirl of orchestra, piano, and symphony *is classical*. Of course, America has its own sound too. The first type was naturally cultivated by immigrants coming to America as a way to remember the stories of their life and roots. It is sung, generally, in a sing-song manner and is accompanied mostly by a fiddle, which is called *hillbilly*. The second type is completely unique. Lyrically, this music is based on thoughts about life, lost love, longing, loneliness of empty wide-open spaces, life of cattle ranching, or following the herds, and that is *cowboy or American country music.*

"I have a friend who knows one of the founders of the National Life and Accident Insurance Company in Tennessee. He said they are going to launch their own radio station with a live broadcasting studio in Nashville. WSM Radio Station will go live this October, and one of their programs is going to be called the *Grand Ole Opry*, which is going to feature the hillbilly and cowboy sound. Their broadcasting slogan is going to be 'the home of country music.'" Helen paused, waiting for Frank's reaction to what she said.

Smiling confidently, he replied, "A brilliant assessment of music, but you didn't mention my sound." As he said this, he didn't break a smile as he caught her reaction. Her eyes went wide, and he could almost see her mind scrambling to figure out what type of music she had forgotten.

Laughing, Helen realized it was no use. Flustered now, she could think of nothing except the handsome man sitting across from her giving her his undivided attention. "I give up! What did I forget?"

"Jazz. Which, I think, is a seductive, sensually fun combination of the first three kinds of music you described. However, I would love to learn more about the last two groups if you will be my guide," he murmured softly.

"I would be delighted," she replied with a sexy smile of her own.

Wow, she is stunning, thought Frank. *The local boys I play music with these days are pretty good. Though not as good as the boys that went to South America with me. I can't wait for her to meet them when they come back from Chicago!* "Say, we'd better get moving. We don't want to be late for our jam session," Frank said as he helped her with her coat.

With Helen's knowledge of all types of music, she inspired the musicians to play much longer than usual. This made it very late by the time Frank parked the Jackrabbit in front of Helen's house. When Frank took her hand to help her out of the automobile, he did not let go. Lacing his fingers through hers, they strolled slowly toward the house. The biggest hit song of the year kept rolling through his mind as he looked at her. *Yes, sir, that's my baby. No, sir, I don't mean maybe. Yes, sir, that's my baby now! Ace Brigode and His Virginians got the words right in that song,* Frank thought. *It feels like they wrote it for me and Helen.*

As they reached her front door, Helen started to pull her hand away. Frank hung on and then gently pulled her into his arms. He hesitated only a moment to see if she would resist or give in to the temptation to let him kiss her. When she smiled and stared sweetly up into his eyes, he melted like butter, and the kiss they shared set off an explosion in his senses like a firecracker on the Fourth of July.

Breathless and startled by the intensity of the reaction they had to one another, they stepped apart and nervously laughed, and both their faces flushed. Then Frank and Helen both started to talk at the same time, which made them start laughing again.

Feeling a bit shy, which was an unusual experience for Frank with a woman he was attracted to, he took hold of her fingers slowly and quietly asked, "Can we do this again, Miss Craven?"

Helen had been just as overpowered by her reaction to Frank as he was by her. Yet her quirky sense of humor came bubbling out and asked impishly, "Do what, Mr. Frank Karella? Kiss again, have another date, have dinner, listen to music, or . . .?"

Chuckling at what she was saying, Frank cut off her words as he kissed her again. Then, looking into her eyes, he whispered, "Miss Craven, how about all of the above?"

Their last lingering kiss goodnight had Frank's body humming as he jauntily hopped into the Jackrabbit. He started singing the tune "Yes Sir, That's My Baby" and sang it over and over again all the way back to Madison, feeling thrilled by the truth in the words.

CHAPTER 8

Endings and Beginnings

First Week, September 1925

Alvin Bean knocked on the door, hoping Anton would be alone on this Friday morning. The door opened, and his father-in-law said, "Hello, Alvin, please come in. Would you like some coffee? I just made a fresh pot." Alvin nodded and sat down at the kitchen table. "Thank you, Papa. I wondered if I could have a private word with you."

"Of course," Anton replied as he poured the coffee and brought it to the table. Sitting down, he thought, *Alvin looks so tired. He seems to have aged years since he got the diagnosis, but it has only been five months.*

Alvin took a sip of coffee and got right to the point of his visit. "Papa, you know everything that is going on with my health already. That is why I can talk to you openly man to man. I'm going to ask you for a favor." Looking his father-in-law in the eyes, he went on to say, "When it's time, will you let Helen and the children move back in with you?"

Anton nodded solemnly. He saw and felt the pain in the younger man's eyes.

Alvin looked away from the compassion he saw in Anton's face. Letting his eyes drift around the kitchen, he let them settle on the tabletop as he imagined his children happily eating breakfast where he sat. Speaking softly, he said, "My family has had happy times here with you, and I thank you for that. As for what is coming, I have made many arrangements." He paused to clear his throat, then went on to say, "Helen will have the savings we have in the bank, and I'm also selling the tractor house.

"A few weeks ago, I placed a for sale ad for it in the *Teiglach Omaha Tribune* and *The Omaha Morning Bee*. I just received a letter from Frank Taylor's Circus. They wrote saying their circus will be wintering in Omaha this year. They are interested in buying the tractor house, and I'm towing it to Omaha next week to make the deal. While I am in the city, I will see Doctor Chapman at the Creighton University Medical Center-Bergan Mercy Hospital. Doc Linden thought they might have a treatment or something I can take that will give me . . . a little more time." Anton nodded solemnly just listening, letting Alvin work out the worries in his mind.

End of September

Helen pleaded, "Alvin, please let me go with you to Omaha. I am sure Papa will watch the children for us."

Alvin lovingly brushed the hair from Helen's face and kissed her. "Darling, think about that. The four of them would be too much for him alone."

Helen shook her head, wanting to change his mind, but then she realized her husband was correct. Trying to think of an alternative, she thought, *If I ask Martha or even Mary to help, they will want to know what Alvin and I are going to do in Omaha. We don't need pity or the rest of the family getting upset right now about something that can't be changed.* Helen was forced to admit

Joseph Alvin Bean, born December 16, 1889, died October 6, 1925, buried October 8, 1925, at St. Leonard's Cemetery, 36 years old.

Alvin was right. Without someone to help him, Papa could not handle the children alone. Alvin reclaimed his wife's attention by taking her into his arms and held her close as he lay his cheek on her hair. *I love the scent of it,* he thought, then kissed her long and slow on the lips. "Now, my beautiful wife, I must be off."

Preparations and Passing

An envelope arrived for Helen Bean with a money order for the sale of the tractor house and with it were instructions. "Please see your father with this, darling. He'll help you with everything at the bank regarding this money and the rest of our assets." With this was another piece of folded paper, which had her name on it. Helen unfolded it with trembling hands.

My Dearest Helen,   *October 1, 1925*

I got a good price for the tractor house. With that money added to what we have in the bank, you should have money for anything you might need. I have asked your papa to bring you and the children home to live with him when the time comes. Please do this for me. It will be good for him. It will be good for you, too, and especially for the children.

My darling, you have been an amazing wife, mother, and the best woman I have ever known. I love you so much. I must confess to you that I should have gone to the doctor a long time ago. I am so sorry I didn't.

As for what I have found out at the hospital, Doctor Chapman says my conditions are in the advanced stages. He has put me in his clinic, and there are a few treatments I can try for free. Though they have not said it out loud, they don't think I have much time. I can tell by what they say when they don't think I can hear them. Most of them think the treatments might have worked if I was not already so sick. My sorrow is compounded knowing this now, when it is too late to make better choices.

I needed to tell you what is on my mind while I still have time. My passing here will be better for you and the children. Darling, I did not want the last memory you or our children have of me as being lifeless in our bed or being taken away from our home in a coffin. Let them remember me as just going off to work. Let them feel excited for the future when we had more hellos, hugs, and kisses to look forward to upon being reunited.

I am sorry I will not be with you to help raise our children and that I am leaving you alone. Forgive me for my thoughtlessness and for the time I have wasted. I regret that we spent so much time apart during our marriage and that I focused so much on the future. Now, I am leaving you alone in that future, and it breaks my heart. I am consoled knowing your papa will take care of all that is most precious to me.

My dear Helen, my wonderful wife, be strong and brave. I know it is in your nature to take care of everyone else. But I'm asking you to do better than I did. Please take care of yourself too. Our family will need you more than ever.

God bless and keep you and our children always,
With all my heart and love,
Alvin

A Sad Meeting, Madison Train Station

One after another in each Karella clan home, the phone rang. When they hung up the receiver, each person who had spoken with Anton was filled with shock and dismay. Father Clemens, Stanislaus, Martha, Rudy, Emil John, and Uncle Ed promised to meet Anton and Helen at the train station to pick up Alvin's body. It would arrive on the early morning train from Omaha. The group would escort it to the church and then to St. Leonard's Cemetery, where they would hold a private family burial service. They mutually agreed the children did not need to know that their father had passed away, which was part of Alvin's last requests. They were too young to comprehend it. The family would find the right time in the future to help them understand.

A New Bedtime Story at Grandpa Anton's House

Mary Cecelia had put the toddlers and Francis to bed on the other side of the bedroom, then went to bed herself. Helen sat quietly next to Margaret Mary on the edge of her bed. "Would you like me to tell you a story?" her mother whispered softly.

Ringling Bros. Circus poster—promotional poster for Ringling Brothers by the Coach Lithographic Co., Buffalo, New York, ca. 1899. Public Domain Wikipedia Commons

Margaret Mary whispered back, asking a very insightful question. "Will it be about how we first came to live with Grandpa Anton or this time?"

"Margaret Mary, do you know why we came to live with Grandpa Anton again?"

"Yes, Mama, I do."

Helen did not know how to react to what her daughter said. She and Alvin had been so careful about talking in front of the children, and she and her papa had decided they were too young to know the facts.

Helen was silent so long, then Margaret Mary asked, "Are you still going to tell me a story, Mama?"

"Yes, sweetheart. But first, could you please tell me why you think we came to live with Grandpa this new time?"

"Mama, I know I should not have listened. I heard Daddy say something about the circus to you. You were both whispering, so I know it was supposed to be a secret.

"Then I started remembering Uncle Emil and Grandpa talked about going to the circus a long time ago too. I got really excited when I saw Daddy hooking up the tractor house to the truck. I thought he was going to take all of us to the circus to see the animals and the pretty people from the posters that you showed me. But then he left without us. That is when I figured out the secret you were talking about."

"Sweetheart, exactly what did you figure out?"

"Daddy said he was going to get a new job and not go back to his old job. That's how I figured out the secret. Daddy took our tractor house and is gone because he got his new job with the circus! That's why he will be away for a long time. Because the circus travels all over the place.

Jerome, Gerald, Helen, Margaret Mary, Francis—Bean family

"It's just like before when he would leave with the tractor house to go back to his road construction job. That is why we live with Grandpa again. Because Daddy knows we will be safe living with Grandpa while he is gone."

Helen's eyes were tearing up, though she smiled and whispered, "Margaret Mary, I am so proud of you, and I love you so much!" As she hugged Margaret Mary, her daughter giggled, pleased by the praise her mother had given her.

What harm could her dreams do, at least for a while? Let her keep that sweet image in her head, Helen thought as she hugged her daughter. *I prefer to hear her laughter and giggles than soothing her heartaches and drying her tears.* Tucking the covers around Margaret Mary, she leaned over and set her lips on her daughter's forehead in a lingering kiss while she closed her eyes and prayed. *Lord, please grant my children a little more innocent happiness sheltered by loving kindness. Eventually, they will feel the pain of loss and learn to endure this separation. I know You will help them understand we will see Alvin again when we return to our home in heaven, where we will all be together again with You.* Standing up and turning down the lamp, darkness filled the room, and she whispered, "Goodnight, sweetheart. Mama loves you very much."

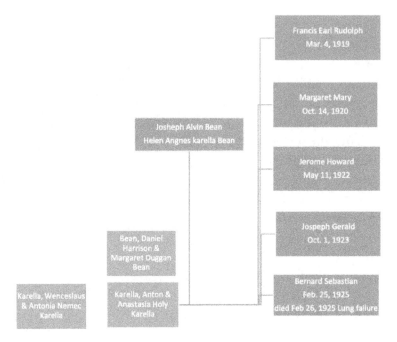

Bean family chart

New Year's 1926, Late Night Visit Between Brothers

Mary Cecilia helped Helen put the four children to bed hours ago, and then they went to bed themselves. Their papa had just said good night and went upstairs. Rusty and Frank sat at the kitchen table. "Feel like sharing another one of Grandfather's home brews?" Frank asked. Rusty nodded, and Frank went to the basement and returned with two bottles.

"What's got you smiling like that?" Rusty asked.

"A woman. What else?" Frank replied.

"Is it that beautiful Craven girl you brought to our picnics all last summer?"

Frank nodded as he popped the caps off the bottles and handed one to his brother and replied, "Her name is Helen, and I love her."

"Are you going to marry her?" asked Rusty. Then he said, "You haven't known her very long."

Frank took a sip of beer, then nodded his head up and down. "I'm thinking seriously about it. We have so much in common. I don't think it takes that long to be ready to marry when your relationship feels right. In answer to your question, yes, I believe I am. I just haven't decided when and where I should ask her to marry me yet. Speaking of women, what about you? You work all the time. Do you make any room in your life for the opposite sex?" Rusty grimaced at his brother's question, and Frank went on to say, "Rusty, I'm not criticizing you. I am concerned that you are not leaving any room in your life for love. I can vouch for it—being in love is wonderful!"

Rusty quit frowning and replied, "I'll keep that in mind, Frank. But, no, right now, there are no women in my life except our sisters, my nieces, and our aunties, and I have had more than enough advice from them about looking for girls, making time for girls, and being introduced to girls they thought would be a good match!"

"Listen, Rusty, I get the point you are making! I do. And I know the women in our family can be a pain in the backside when they are trying to do things *for your own good!* Gosh, I can't tell you how often I heard them say that to me. We put up with them because we love them, and they keep interfering in our lives because they love us. But, Rusty, are you happy just working all the time and being alone?"

Rusty took a sip from his beer bottle before he replied softly, "Frank, I'll keep my eyes open. When the right girl comes along, I promise I will let myself fall in love, not fight it."

The brothers smiled at each other and clinked their beer bottles in a salute as Frank said, "Here's to the girl that finds you, brother, and helps you fall in love."

1926 Springtime Wedding Plans

Frank wrote his old traveling band buddies, Becket, Harold, and Mathew, who were playing a gig in Chicago. He let them know he would not be joining them to play music. That had been their plan when the four of them got off the Dutch cruise ship from Panama in New York. Frank told the guys he planned to head home to Nebraska first, and that was when they went their separate ways. His buddies decided to try their luck at the jazz clubs in Chicago before they went back to Madison for a visit. Knowing it would shock them, he wrote, *Sorry, boys, I'm getting married.* He would love to have seen their faces when they read his letter.

June Bride at the Sacred Heart Church in Norfolk

Frank and Helen were married in the Sacred Heart Catholic Church in Norfolk. It was a small gathering because they were leaving for their honeymoon trip right after the ceremony, and the family reception would be postponed until after their return.

After Frank and Helen left on their honeymoon, Frank's three friends contacted Anton to find out when the family would be holding the homecoming party for the newlyweds. "Mr. Karella, we plan to make a trip to Madison to see our folks. We would like to coordinate our visit so we could play the music for Frank and Helen's reception at the homestead. Make it kind of a wedding gift for the lovebirds when they get back to town. Would that be ok with you?"

1926, Summer Weddings and Old Stories

The Karella family and nearly the whole town of Madison turned out for the wedding picnic held to celebrate the union of Frank Karella and his new bride, Helen Craven Karella of Norfolk, upon their return from their honeymoon in June of 1926.

Anton had intended to keep the entertainment a secret from everyone except Father Clemens. He wanted to surprise the whole family. However, he soon discovered that was not going to happen. Anton realized he needed help from the family to make all the arrangements. The Karellas were part of a close community, so it wasn't long before the whole town of Madison knew about the surprise.

Each person who heard about it was just as excited as Anton to share in the fun and wanted to help greet the newlyweds. Some people volunteered to bring food or refreshments. Some volunteered their musical talent and instruments and said they would take a shift playing music at the gathering. There were quite a few singers in their group who also wanted to accompany the musicians. What started out as a family reception was turning into a county shindig! Delighted with all the volunteers, Anton realized they would have continuous music, singing, and dancing all night long.

The Arrival

Raymond Karella came running across the farmyard and up to his uncle Anton and his parents, yelling, "They're coming! The Texas Jackrabbit is driving up the lane!"

"Ok, everyone! To your places," Emil said, pointing at the musicians. "And, the rest of you, get out of sight until the music starts!"

Everything was set up, and everyone was ready. Becket borrowed a clarinet from Father Clemens. It sat next to his stool along with his saxophone. Harold played percussion, and his drums were the first thing they set up when they arrived at the farm. Father Clemens, Uncle Stanislaus, and Uncle Emil brought Emily's piano out on the porch for Mathew, and he was ready to strike the opening notes to start the music.

Frank parked the Jackrabbit below the house. Hurrying around to Helen's door, he opened it and helped her out of the automobile. At that moment, the band started playing the tune "Baby Face" by Jan Garber. Frank's head jerked up, searching for the music. He could not believe his eyes! HIS BOYS WERE BACK!

A huge crowd of people came into sight from behind the house clapping. Well-wishers and laughter surrounded Frank and Helen as they walked up to the large wooden porch. Becket, Harold, and Mathew finished the tune and sat waiting with the instruments, hoping for a chance to hug and kiss Frank's pretty new wife and tease their old friend.

After hugs and introductions were made, everyone got settled at the tables, and Frank joined his boys for one set of songs, which included "When the Red, Red Robin" by Al Jolson, "See See Rider Blues" by Ma Rainey, "Bye Bye Blackbird" by Gene Austin, and, finally, "California, Here I Come" by Al Jolson. Everyone cheered the great singing and live music.

The children had plenty of room and were told to go play and enjoy themselves. The women had brought enough food to feed an army, and the weather was perfect.

With the children safely occupied, the adults took advantage of the opportunity to chat. The wonderful music encouraged wives to pull their husbands to dance on the grass, joining teenagers thrilled to be dancing outside a church function. Anton noticed his daughter Mary and her fiancé, Stanley Voborny, were having a splendid time.

Little Margaret Mary Bean

During the long reception party, six-year-old Margaret Mary had lots of cousins to play with. She gathered up a small group, and they all sat beneath the shade tree on a blanket just like her great-grandpa Vaclav used to do. Leaning against the tree, she said, "I want to tell you a story." Adults listening to her would often comment that little Margaret Mary sounded exactly like her mother, Helen.

Seeing her daughter under the shade tree with some of her cousins made Helen smile. She remembered sitting under that same tree with Grandpa Vaclav, listening to his stories. It made her happy to

Frank Karella, son of Anton and Anastasia, while in the Army, stationed in Fort Worth, Texas

know this tradition had come down from him to her. Now, she had passed it on to Vaclav's great-granddaughter as well. At a gathering like today, Helen enjoyed taking a bit of time to sit on the blanket with the other children, watching their faces as her daughter told her stories.

Margaret Mary asked, "Did I ever tell you what I know about our uncle Frank?" The children shook their heads. Smiling, she said, "When Uncle Frank joined up to fly Army airplanes, Grandpa Anton told me he was stationed at Fort Worth, Texas! At Christmastime, Uncle Frank would send us a big bag of pecans. Mama and I shelled em, chopped em up, and put em in cookies."

Helen left the children walking back to the porch where the music was playing, and the tables were being refilled with food and refreshments. Several other musicians from the church took turns giving Frank's friends a break, and everyone was thrilled that the music never stopped. Just after her mother walked away, Margaret Mary whispered in a conspiratorial fashion, "Do you want me to tell you about Aunt Mary Cecilia when she didn't want to finish high school?" The children all nodded their heads yes.

Above: Stanley Voborny, 23 years; below: Mary Cecilia Karella, 18 years

"Uncle Rusty told me Mama and Aunt Martha were having an argument with Aunt Mary. He heard them yelling and sneaked down the stairs so he could find out what was happening. Just as he got near the kitchen, he heard Mama shout, 'Mary Cecilia! You Will Not!'" Margaret Mary shouted those words just as her mother had, and that made the children jump.

Margaret Mary quickly put a shushing finger to her lips and motioned for the children to come closer before she went on with her story. "That's

when Uncle Rusty peeked around the wall. The door to the kitchen was open, and that's where his sisters were fighting." The children gasped, and Margaret Mary put her finger to her lips, shushing them again. With big eyes glued to their storyteller, her audience quieted down immediately.

Uncle Stanislaus overheard the last part of what Margaret Mary had whispered and curiously moved closer just as the children did so he could listen in. He thought Margaret Mary had a mischievous look on her face as she dramatically explained the fight between the three sisters. "Mama and Aunt Martha were telling Aunt Mary she *could not* quit school! Aunt Mary yelled back, 'I don't need any more schooling because I am going to be a housewife just like my mama!' That's when Mama and Aunt Martha put their hands on their hips and shook their heads and pounced on Aunt Mary, asking, 'Is that good-for-nothing Stanley Voborny pressuring you to get married again?'"

At that comment, Uncle Stanislaus nearly laughed out loud, but he controlled it. His little niece had thoroughly captured his interest, and he wanted to know what happened next. Margaret Mary did not notice her great-uncle watching as she went on with her story. "Uncle Rusty had just got a look at Mary's shocked expression when Mama noticed he was watching them, and that's when Mama stormed over and slammed the door shut right in his face!"

The children inhaled sharply with a frightened sound and whispered that they thought Uncle Rusty was very brave! If their mamas had slammed a door in their faces, they would have been very scared.

The six-year-old storyteller shook her head and boasted, "Uncle Rusty wasn't afraid! Cause my mama is his sister, and he would never be afraid of his sister! But he still wanted to know what was happening in the kitchen. So, do you want to know what he did next?"

Everyone in her audience nodded and whispered, "What did he do, Margaret Mary?"

"Uncle Rusty leaned his ear on the wood so he could listen to them through the door!"

The children gasped hearing about that sin!

Margaret Mary continued in a slightly louder whisper, "Uncle Rusty said he knew it was a little sinful to listen through the door, but he wanted to know what Mama and Aunt Martha were going to do to make Aunt Mary behave!"

Stanislaus chuckled softly, not wanting to alert Helen who stood nearby. She would surely interrupt this remarkable storytime if she knew what was being said. He wanted to hear what happened just as the children did.

Margaret Mary went on quickly, "When Uncle Rusty put his ear on the door, he could hear everything they were saying. Mama yelled her question about Stanley Voborny at Aunt Mary for a second time, and Aunt Mary squeaked in surprise asking, 'How do you know about Stanley and me?'

"Uncle Rusty said my mama sounded disgusted when she shouted, 'For heaven's sake, Mary, do you think Martha and I are light in the head?' Then Aunt Martha said, 'Of course, we know you are sweet on Stanley.' But then they threatened Aunt Mary, 'But if you don't promise to finish high school before you get married, we will tell Papa about you and what we think of Stanley trying to get you to quit school!'

"Uncle Rusty said that the fight wasn't over yet! Aunt Mary yelled at Mama, 'That wasn't Stanley's idea! It was mine!" But my mama had the last word!"

Uncle Stanislaus could see Margaret Mary was wearing her mama's no-nonsense look for this part of her story. Little Margaret went on to say, "My mama got right in Aunt Mary's face and said, 'Mary Cecilia, I guarantee it won't matter to Papa whose idea it was! You'd better promise you'll finish high school right now or else we will take it all to Papa!'"

Impressed, Stanislaus grinned, recognizing the glare Margaret Mary wore on her face. She had her mother's actions and looks down perfectly!

About that time, Helen noticed her uncle Stanislaus's expression from across the yard. Touched he was paying such close attention to her daughter, Helen walked back over to the group right in time to hear Margaret Mary mimicking her voice perfectly. The shock of what she heard registered on her face right as her daughter repeated the threat Helen and Martha had made to her sister Mary. Helen inhaled sharply and said loudly and sternly, "Margaret Mary!"

All the children jumped when they heard those loud words. It was Aunt Helen! Margaret Mary stopped talking mid-sentence. The rest of the children turned toward their aunt Helen with guilty looks on their faces.

Chuckling and wearing a wicked grin, Great-Uncle Stanislaus pleaded, "Oh, Helen, please let her finish the story! She was just getting to the best part!"

Helen pursed her lips to suppress a smile and gave both of the rascals a warning look. Shaking her head, looking directly at her daughter, she said in her no-nonsense tone, "*Margaret Mary*, I think it's time for you to come help me in the kitchen—*right now, young lady!*"

Nearly breathless with laughter, Stanislaus had a great time retelling the whole incident to Uncle Ed and his brother Anton. Anton grinned, asking, "Do you want to hear the rest of the story?" Both Ed and Stanislaus nodded.

Uncle Rudy pulling the children in the grain wagon

"Helen had already warned me about the issue developing with Mary Cecilia and Stanley Voborny. I liked Stanley, so I chose not to interfere as long as Mary stayed in school. Stanley's folks sharecropped on the Warrick place. When I talked with Stanley, he said he planned to sharecrop first to save up and then own his own farmland. I advised him to stick to his goals and that he could achieve them with enough time and hard work."

Stanislaus and Ed were nodding in agreement when Ed noticed Emily, then Emil waving at him from across the yard. "Excuse me,"

Ed said, "I see Emily and Emil are waving at me, and I'm going to find out what they need."

With the unexpected moment of privacy, Anton caught his brother's eye and said, "Stanislaus, I don't think I ever thanked you for all you have done for me, especially after Anastasia and then Papa passed away."

Stanislaus smiled warmly at his older brother and replied, "You don't need to, Anton. That is what family does, and we do it gladly for each other. Now, quit stalling and finish this tale!" he said as he crossed his arms over his chest just like Margaret Mary had done, making Anton grin.

Anton knew it was Stanislaus's way to change the subject when the conversation became too personal to talk about. The love they shared was deeply understood, so Anton replied with a smile, "Ok. Back to the story. I had noted my sixteen-year-old daughter, Mary, was pouting regularly when being ordered around by her eldest sister. I believe Mary only did as she was told because she feared Helen would make good on her threat, convincing me that the match was not a good one. Luckily, her sister's ruse worked. Though Mary Cecilia did just finish high school in May, she also set her wedding date for next month. I think she would have set it on her graduation day if she thought she could have gotten away with that bit of rebellion."

Frank and Helen Karella Live in Norfolk

The mood of the celebration was as magical as the music, and the dancing lifted everyone's spirits. No one wanted to leave. Frank and Helen made their way around the party, sitting down to chat with as many guests and family as possible. Exhausted after spending hours circulating, in need of food, Helen and Frank were happy to sit down with Anton. After filling their plates, they took the time to tell him they were going to make their home near Helen's school. "Papa, you know Helen still owns and operates the Norfolk Conservatory of Music. I decided to interview with the hospital before our wedding. When we got back, I had a letter notifying me that I got the job I wanted. I am really excited; I am going to be the band director and manager of the recreational grounds for the Regional Hospital in Norfolk."

It took Frank and Helen nearly the whole night to thank everyone who had helped create such a wonderful party for them. The celebration ran so late that when it was time to leave, parents were searching for children in the dark who had fallen to sleep on the ground. Mothers had just covered them with blankets and let them dream on while the adults chatted.

The newlyweds overnighted at the Karella Farm and woke up early but not early enough to catch Emil in bed. Looking at the clock, Frank knew Emil was already out doing chores. They heard Emily busy making breakfast in the kitchen as they walked down the stairs and entered the bright room. Emily smiled at them and told them to sit down at the table. Then she rang the bell on the porch, and soon, a smiling father and son entered the kitchen, saying, "Well, good morning, sleepyheads!"

Emily shooed her husband and son to the sink to wash up as Raymond asked, "Uncle Frank, did you and Aunt Helen sleep well? I made sure to put an extra blanket on your bed like Mama said."

Frank's eyes twinkled, and he grinned at his nephew when he replied, "Yes, Raymond, we were comfortable and toasty warm."

Helen blushed a little and instantly took over the conversation before Frank said something embarrassing. "Yes, thank you, Raymond! We were delightfully comfortable. It was very considerate of you!" Helen added as she took the cup of coffee Emily handed to her.

"What are you plans now?" Emil asked as he sat down at the table in front of his food.

The two couples chatted until ten that morning about the pros and cons of living in Madison or Norfolk. Eventually, Frank stated that Norfolk was where they both had jobs, and it was not that far from the family. They promised to continue to come back for family gatherings if they were given enough warning so they could plan those events into their schedules.

Finally, Frank said, "It is getting late, and we still have to stop at Dad's place." He first hugged Emil, then Emily, and finally Raymond. As they drove away from the farm, Frank said, "Helen, Uncle Stanislaus will probably be at Dad's house when we get there. They are going to want to hear about our long-term plans, and that's going to make it late in the day before I can pack up the rest of my things I've got stored there and put them into the car. We probably will not get home to Norfolk until later this evening. Will you be ok with that?"

She smiled and replied, "Frank, I love your family and especially your father. It will be nice for you to sit with him and his brother and talk for a while."

Frank grinned happy with her answer and nodded, thinking, *Late or not, I'm still looking forward to carrying my bride across the threshold of our new home, no matter when we get back to Norfolk!*

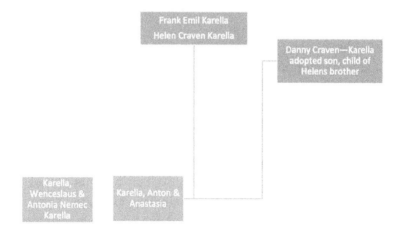

Frank Karella family chart

The Karella Brothers Review Businesses

With spring planting completed, it was time to review the books and look at expenses. Stanislaus had his own office at the sawmill and walked around the corner and sat down in front of Anton's desk, asking, "Anton, how does your schedule look today?"

Anton shrugged and replied, "Nothing that can't be done later. What do you need?"

"It's time to review the family business ledgers," Stanislaus replied.

Business Costs and Falling Grain Prices

Anton and Stanislaus's father had taught them to understand making profit through multiple trades, pooling revenues to produce a sustainable income, and managing costs constantly. Emil John didn't have their experience. When he had taken over his inheritance and began managing the homestead businesses, Stanislaus continued to manage the business books and kept a close eye on what was happening in the grain markets.

The family's best year ever had been the sale of their harvests from 1919 and 1920. Yet, grain revenues had been falling steadily for the last four years. He wanted to review the ledgers one last time with Anton because it was time to turn over the responsibilities for the farm books to Emil John.

Stanislaus pointed out that they took a huge revenue drop in 1922, and then it plunged again—nearly 50%—for the harvest after Emil John took over in 1923. When grain prices only fell slightly in 1924, they hoped the prices had hit the bottom of that trend.

July and August of 1925 showed a slight increase in sale price. It was the first time grain prices had been over 1.00 per bushel in four years. Stanislaus wanted to believe this would be a solid trend.

The farm's grain revenues were only half of what it had been in 1920, and though they had been watching expenses, he was still concerned. The farm income was the family's major source of income, and after that was the sawmill, then the last was the poultry business.

Stanislaus showed Anton the expense ledger, saying, "The tractor and steam engine for the threshing machines were good investments. I'm glad we made those purchases during our better years, and we still make money on those rentals each harvest, which has helped compensate for lower grain revenues. The only large expense we face at the moment is Uncle Ed's round trip passage to Paris."

Looking at the books for the meat and egg business showed it was still a solid source of income. Though it had never been a huge money maker, it paid for itself and offset family costs of buying chicken and eggs. So far, it was still a good business.

Anton pulled out the records for the sawmill, and the brothers reviewed them too.

Overall, the combined businesses showed a profit, and they could still add a little to savings each month but nowhere near the volume they used to add each year.

	Wheat	Corn	Oats	Rye	Barley
Average 1909–1913	88.8	62.9	39.6	72.1	61.1
1918–19	207.8	152.1	69.4	152.0	95.9
1919–20	222.3	150.6	78.5	142.9	123.8
1920–21	184.5	64.1	53.8	143.6	79.1
1921–22	102.9	52.2	33.5	81.5	46.1
1922–23	98.3	75.6	38.5	67.8	52.1
1924					
January 15	96.7	73.6	43.4	63.5	56.5
February 15	98.0	76.5	45.4	64.5	58.0
March 15	98.8	77.2	46.2	62.8	60.0
April 15	95.8	78.2	46.5	60.4	61.0
May 15	96.8	78.6	46.3	60.1	60.0
June 15	98.5	80.8	46.8	61.6	61.9
July 15	105.8	98.3	49.4	68.8	68.8
August 15	116.8	107.4	49.1	79.8	75.7

Average yearly price of the principal grains at the farm for the four years preceding the war and years 1919 to 1920 and the average monthly price from January to August 1924

During the upcoming harvest, Uncle Ed would be gone. With the equipment they had, Stanislaus believed the family could handle the harvest without hiring anyone to replace him. Between himself, Anton, Emil John, and Rusty, they should be able to do most of the work. If need be, they could get some of their relatives from the Pojar clan to help. The Pojars were mostly ranchers and always had a few spare cowhands to lend them during harvest.

The brothers were satisfied with their plan and were ready to show Emil John. After running the farm for three seasons, they believed Emil was ready to be in charge of everything regarding the homestead businesses.

"Stanislaus, would you please set up a meeting with Emil for the beginning of next week? Then we can go over everything with him when we give him the ledgers for the farm. At that time, we can let Emil know the three of us will still consult on major changes and what is funded by family savings."

Stanislaus nodded his head as he closed the books and picked them up. Then he said, "I am going to suggest a crop change to Emil at that meeting. We should only plant enough oats to feed our livestock. We need to replace the rest of those acres with soybeans. The stock market reports on corn and soybean prices seemed to be holding steady at about $1.08 per bushel.

"I agree with you, Stanislaus. That's a good idea," replied Anton as Stanislaus left his office.

A Second Wedding in 1926 at St. Leonard's Catholic Church—Madison, Nebraska

Nervous and not quite eighteen, Mary Cecilia Karella looked into the mirror, thinking, *My wedding day is finally here! I've waited so long for this moment; I can hardly believe it's really happening!*

Standing behind her baby sister, Martha checked the closures on Mary's dress and adjusted her wedding veil. Helen handed Mary her wedding bouquet and whispered, "You look lovely, Mary. Stanley is a very lucky man."

Martha walked around Mary one last time to be sure she was ready and nodded with satisfaction, then said, "Honey, it's time to go to the church."

Arriving with her sisters in their father's automobile and driven by their uncle Stanislaus, Anton met them. Opening the car door for the bride and extending his other hand to help her, he asked, "Are you ready?" Mary Cecilia nodded, putting her hand in his. "I am proud of you, sweetheart," Anton whispered as he put her hand through his arm and waited for her sisters to adjust her dress. Father and daughter walked through the church doors and paced slowly up the aisle to meet the handsome, young Stanley Voborny waiting with the priest by the altar. Anton whispered, "I love you very much, Mary."

Though she smiled sweetly up at him, her attention had been captured by the dashing young groom standing beside her.

The gentle voice of their pastor broke the silence, saying, "Who gives this woman in marriage?"

"I do," replied Anton, placing Mary's hand in Stanley's and then went to sit in the front row of the church next to his eldest daughter. He took hold of Helen's hand and gave it a squeeze. She looked up at her father and knew he understood how sweet and bitter this moment was for her.

Stanley J. Voborny and Mary Cecilia Karella Voborny wedding picture, July 20, 1926, by David Voborny

Memories of a day similar to this floated into the minds of both father and daughter as they watched the young couple become man and wife.

Anton rejoiced that his daughter had found love. Watching his child glow with happiness, Anton felt fulfilled as a parent and very proud of the young woman Mary had grown into.

Anton J. Karella—Journal Entry

My dear Anastasia,

You would have been so proud of our little Mary Cecilia today. She is all grown up and in love with a man who has made her his wife. Thank you for being such a wonderful wife and mother. Your faith gave our daughters a beautiful example to emulate.

Because you taught them about what is important in life, each of our girls recognized love when they found it. I rejoice in the Karella tradition

of finding love matches just like you and I had, and through faith, our life was filled with God's blessings.

As parents, I know we always saw eye to eye on this. Being married, raising a family, and making a living is hard but worth it when a family is supported by love. You showed me that love makes living each day worth the toil and trouble a couple may encounter. Your love always made me feel that if I worked hard enough, we could build a better tomorrow for our family, and we did do that, my love . . . together.

Our Helen found love, as did Martha. Frank told me he knew he found the love of his life before he got married. What more could we hope for? Only love can see us through the hard times. Helen and I have both discovered it is love that leads us through sorrow too. Love has the power to bring us back to life, as it happened for me.

My darling, though we cannot know what the future will bring, right now, Mary Cecilia and Stanley are filled with hope and happiness. God willing, they will live a long and fruitful life together. Goodnight, my dear Anastasia.

Anton set down his pen and turned down the lamp. As he got comfortable in bed, he closed his eyes and thought, *It was a wonderful day* and fell into a peaceful sleep.

First St. Leonard's Church and School, Madison, Nebraska, 1902

CHAPTER 9

Rusty Karella, An Unexpected Project, 1926

Rusty had been thinking a lot about what his brother Frank had said about love. But, honestly, he had no extra time in his life to invest in the notion of love. He had set big goals for himself. Rusty needed to focus on his work and reputation now that he was self-employed. With the hours he reserved for customer projects, he had even less time to meet girls, let alone find a woman he wanted to make his wife.

Still, seeing the happiness at the recent weddings of his brother and sister had given him a reason to at least think about the subject. Observing Frank and his Helen and then his sister Mary Cecilia with her Stanley made him aware that love did have its rewards. Seeing the sweetness between them had touched his heart in a strange way he did not quite understand.

Maybe there was an emptiness inside him, one he had not recognized before. But admitting he had a place that needed filling and figuring out how to fill it were two very different things. Just considering such things made his head hurt.

In his experience, the women he admired were too old for him or were related to him. Most of the pretty girls he had met he found intimidating and demanding. He reacted to most single females in varying degrees of resistance because he felt they pushed and crowded him into a corner he did not want to be in. The longer he thought about it, the jumpier it made him. So, once again, he pushed away thoughts of girls and falling in love. Allowing his mind to retreat into more familiar territory, he concentrated on finishing the work in front of him. After a few more hours, Rusty put his tools away and checked the letter box as he locked the shop, ready to head home for dinner.

A Surprising Letter

When Rusty got home, he sorted through his mail and found a letter from a man named James Holt. Inside, he found an invitation to meet at Mr. Holt's residence in Madison. The letter included a telephone number and Holt's address. It also outlined the reason for the appointment, but it did not go into detail about the work or the time frame for the project to be completed for his racing stable. Putting down the letter, Rusty found himself instantly intrigued.

Anton had just walked into the kitchen to say hello when Rusty glanced up at him and said, "Papa, look at this letter I received from Mr. James Holt." He handed the letter to his father.

"Is this the same Madison horseman from the grudge match in the paper last summer?" Anton asked.

Rusty Karella, 28 years old, Madison, Nebraska

"Yes, it is," replied Rusty. "I am going to call him in the morning to find out when we can meet."

A Morning Telephone Call

1920s telephone

"Operator, please connect me with MA1055, the James Holt residence. Yes. I'll hold. Thank you."

"Hello, am I speaking to Mr. James Holt? This is Rusty Karella. Yes, sir, I did receive your letter. Yes, I would be interested in meeting with you and hearing more about your ideas for the horse gear you mentioned. Next week? On Tuesday? Yes, that would work for me as well. Thank you. I will see you then."

The Holt Residence

On Tuesday, Rusty arrived promptly at 10:30 a.m. sharp. He rang the doorbell, and within seconds, a rather disheveled youngster in a nice dress opened the door. Rusty introduced himself, explaining he had an appointment with Mr. Holt.

"That is my father," the skinny bit of a girl replied. "I was told to bring you to his study when you arrived. Please follow me," she said politely, and Rusty did as he was bid.

Madison Downs racetrack and winning horse and jockey, preserved by Madison County Historical Museum

Possibly in his early 40s, lean, and well-dressed, Holt was younger than Rusty had expected him to be. The man must have heard them coming because he stood by an open door in the hall ahead. Out of the corner of his eye, Rusty noticed several photographs of racehorses at Madison Downs hanging on the walls. He only got a glance at them before the man extended his hand, saying, "Jim Holt."

Extending his own in return, he replied, "Rusty Karella," as they shook with a firm grip.

Mr. Holt looked at his daughter and said, "Thank you, Delora. You may go and check on your mother now."

Rusty observed the scruffy girl did as she was told immediately. *How refreshing,* he thought. *She does what she is told without argument.* Looking at his host, Rusty said, "I thought your note said your name was James."

"That is my given name, but everyone calls me Jim." Rusty nodded his head in understanding while Jim motioned him through the door. Pointing to a seat, he continued to talk, saying, "Please sit down, Mr. Karella. May I call you by your first name?"

"My given name is Ambrose, but everyone calls me Rusty. First names will be fine with me," he replied.

"Thank you, Rusty. Now that we have the formalities out of the way, let's talk. I have been admiring your leatherwork for over a year now. I must say your reputation precedes you, and the quality of your work is excellent."

"Thank you. It is good to hear horseman of your caliber have noticed."

Jim nodded his head in acceptance of the compliment Rusty had given him. Then he went on to say, "I have already outlined a bit about my ideas for improving the riding equipment we are using. I'd like to get right down to business and tell you what I hope to gain by this project. Then I would like to hear some of your thoughts."

Receiving Rusty's nod of agreement, Jim proceeded to lay out his ideas and the results he wanted to get from the changes he proposed to make. Rusty got excited as he listened, then threw in a few of his thoughts regarding stripping down the weight and shape of the standard saddles and paying close attention to stirrup length.

Madison Downs racetrack, race in progress and grandstand in the distance,
preserved by Madison County Historical Museum

Once Jim could see Rusty's enthusiasm for the project and design work, Jim simply said "Rusty, I can tell you and I will work well together. I'm going to be open about this. You are the man I want to do this project; do you want the job?"

Looking around the room, Rusty saw several pictures of famous jockeys as well as more racehorses at Madison Downs and thought, *This would certainly be an intriguing project. It would take an interesting mix of my talents to design the hardware, harnesses, and the custom leather saddles he wants.*

Pleased to see the younger man taking his proposal seriously, Jim was gratified when the younger man finally gave a nod and replied, "Yes, Jim, I am interested."

Having taken each other's measure during the past hour and agreeing they wanted to work together, both men relaxed. They began to smile, knowing it was time to begin the horse-traders haggle over the cost of the project.

"Rusty, after my horse won the grudge match in 1925, I set that money aside to use for racing gear improvements. That match purse was unexpected income, and I feel justified investing some of that extra cash in changes that will help all my horses win more races.

I am pleased you want to work on this project. You were my first choice for this job. Your skills are remarkable for being such a young man. I can tell from your knowledge during our discussion of horse tack you have earned your excellent reputation through firsthand experience with horses."

"Thank you. I grew up with many types of horses, and I was apprenticed to my grandfather. He taught me nearly everything I know about leather and metal work."

"Does that mean your family is from Madison?" Jim asked.

"My grandparents moved to Madison in 1878. We have been working our homestead since 1880."

"My goodness, it seems that your people and mine moved into this town very close to the same time. Do you have a big family?" Jim asked.

"Yes, sir. I have three uncles and one aunt on my father's side and many more on my mother's side of the family. I have six siblings, many cousins, and now I have nieces and nephews as well," Rusty replied.

"That's good to hear! I like working with dedicated family men. In my experience, they understand teamwork, know how to set priorities, and stay committed to goals. Rusty, let's get started as soon as possible. When can you have an estimated cost assembled for me so we can set a budget for this project?"

"I'll need to take an inventory of the different equipment you have, then review and list the measurements of the four horses I am to fit. Once I have those numbers, I can estimate the kind and quantity of materials I will need to order. Then I will outline the leather and metal work that I will need to design and manufacture. I should be able to assemble cost estimates in two weeks. Once the ordered items are received, I can estimate how long it will take to design and manufacture the other items needed to complete your project," Rusty replied.

"Wonderful. Can you come by tomorrow? I have meetings all day at Madison Downs, but my daughter Delora will be here and knows where everything is and will be able to show you around. How does that sound?"

Rusty stood up and extended his hand, saying, "Sounds good to me. I do have some work to finish up. How does the day after tomorrow sound, say 10:00 a.m., for me to drop by?"

Jim shook Rusty's hand as he replied, "That will be just fine. I will let my daughter know she can expect you in two days."

Delora Lucy Holt

Delora did not actually leave the hall after her father had dismissed her. She merely stayed out of sight, then tiptoed back to the closed door and eavesdropped, hoping to find out more about her father's visitor. After listening to the fascinating talk through the wooden door, Delora experienced a thrill knowing this young man would be back in two days.

Alerted by the sound of the men walking across the room, Delora turned and dashed silently down the hall and around the corner into the kitchen out of sight. Keeping quiet, she could hear them talking as they walked toward the front door.

Listening from the kitchen, she heard her father say goodbye and close the door. Wanting her father to think she had been in the kitchen the whole time, she hastily set up the trays and began preparing lunch for her father and mother. *Just maybe,* she thought, *when father comes to check on lunch, I might be able to learn a little more about Mr. Karella.*

The trays were almost ready when her father stepped into the kitchen and said, "Oh, there you are, Delora." He took in the fact that Delora was busy preparing food and said, "I am pleased to see you are getting lunch ready. I think I shall eat with your mother today. Please bring the tray up in 45 minutes. I have a few things to finish up in my office first. Delora, why don't you join us for lunch? You might enjoy what I have to tell your mother about my new project."

Delora smiled brightly and replied, "Yes, father, I'd like that."

The Library and Study

Jim walked back to his study pleased with his daughter's attitude. He hadn't seen her eyes so bright and smiling like that in years. Certainly not like when she was five years old and would keep him company for hours while he worked in his study before she started school. *No, the real problems with her started two years ago when he took her out of school,* he thought, *but that could not be helped.*

Jim selected several items from on top of his desk and created a new file and wrote a label for it in bold letters—***Karella Project***—then put it away in his file drawer.

He happened to glance at one of his favorite pictures of his daughter Delora on his desk. She was sitting on the coffee table in the living room when it was taken. He remembered that day in 1915 clearly.

A Past Memory from the Summer of 1915

Jim remembered he and little Delora had just come out of his study to have lunch with Margaret, when Delora's eldest brother, Oscar, came running into the house with a new Kodak Brownie camera. His son was very proud having purchased it with money he saved from his summer job at Madison Downs. Oscar scooped up his little sister and swung her around in circles, making her giggle. Then he set her on the coffee table and told her to pose pretty, and he snapped her picture. Jim shook his head. Those sweet memories hurt sometimes. He missed those easy days with his daughter.

The memories he had surrounding that picture of Delora brought back another memory as well. In the early years of his marriage, he often

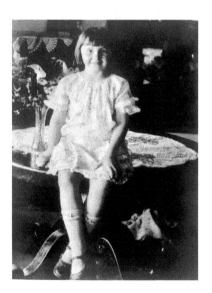

Delora Lucy Holt, born 1910

used his study in the house as his primary office and held meetings there with people who were not affiliated with the racehorse business at Madison Downs. Using his study in such a manner made it easy to begin a tradition of having lunch together with his family when he worked at home. Jim and his wife, Margaret, and their young brood of children would meet every day at noon to eat together.

By the time Delora was five years old, her older brothers were busy with their own plans when it came to eating lunch. Jim missed them when they were off with their friends, but at the same time, it was delightful to spend the afternoons surrounded by just his girls.

On this particular day after lunch, Margaret planned to go shopping and take the girls with her. Violet wanted to go, but little Delora wanted to stay with her papa. When Margaret and Violet left the kitchen, Delora had taken hold of his hand and asked, "What shall we do now, Papa?"

"My dear young lady, your papa has paperwork to do. But you may come back to the study and look at books while I work." She had smiled and nodded.

Even at five years old, Delora could sit happily for hours looking through his library of books. When he asked her what she liked about them, she replied, "I like the way they smell, Papa, and this leather sofa is warm and soft." He had nodded, thinking he agreed with her. She learned to read very young; he was proud of the fact he taught her himself.

Lost in the Past with a Holt Family Secret

Jim recalled he had turned his mind to his work as he set out the breeding history on the new horse he had purchased and began looking over the delivery documents.

Delora went to the bookshelves and picked up a cigar box he kept on one of the lower shelves that contained old family photographs. Looking through them, she stopped on one particular picture that caught her attention. Holding it up, she asked, "Excuse me, Papa, who is this?"

He looked up and replied, "That would be your great-great-grandfather and great-great-grandmother Kilgore on your mother's side of the family."

"Was Mama's great-great-grandmother an Indian?"

He got up from his desk and went to sit by her on the sofa. Taking the picture from her, he looked at it for a minute. Impressed at how observant and intelligent Delora was, Jim felt pleased she was curious about the photograph.

Margaret Kilgore Holt's great-great-grandmother had indeed been a Canadian First Nation woman. Even the age of the photograph could not disguise the woman had been a dark-haired beauty. Quite striking really, with an Indian bone structure that made her eyes, nose, and cheekbones very distinctive. The ceremonial dress she wore only confirmed that heritage. He smiled and, catching Delora's eye, nodded his head as he answered her question, "Yes, Delora, she was of Canadian Indian heritage."

After getting the answer to that puzzle about the lady in the picture, Delora moved on to her next question, "Why is Great-Great-Grandfather Kilgore wearing that strange hat?"

The photograph of the Kilgore ancestors preserved the image of a youthful man wearing a mustache, lambchop sideburns, and an extremely tall stovepipe top hat. The picture itself was a remarkable heirloom. The story it told was even more compelling. "Delora, people came to Canada and America from all over the world, and they had very different customs and clothing than we have here in Nebraska.

"Your great-great-grandfather Kilgore's family lived in Kilgour near Falkland in County Fife, Scotland. His

A female Kilgore descendant, Great-Grandmother Delora Lucy Ballou. This woman was Margaret Kilgore Holt's grandmother.

people came from Scotland through Ireland and then to Canada. When he was a young man, the clothing styles were very different. I would say that kind of hat was from the English influence on world fashion from the late 1790s. Canada was part of the British Empire in your ancestor Kilgore's time, just as it is to this day. My guess is that your great-great-grandparents were *wearing* the best clothing they owned to have their photograph taken on their wedding day.

"Even our own President Lincoln was famous for wearing a stovepipe hat like your ancestor Kilgore did. Did you know that our President Lincoln was six-feet-four-inches tall?" he whispered.

Delora shook her head.

1861–1865, President Abraham Lincoln in stovepipe silk hat center at Antietam, 1862—Public Domain. Silk top hats came into being in 1797—created by English haberdasher John Hetherington.

Then he told Delora, "President Lincoln's head would have almost touched our ceiling without his hat, but with his hat, he was another eight inches taller. That made him about seven feet tall. Can you imagine it? He was as tall as the ceiling here in my study!"

He remembered Delora looked up to the ceiling as her eyes went round, and he could tell she was imagining a man tall enough to touch it with the hat on his head. Even remembering her innocent reactions to his story could still made him smile.

Back to the Present—1926

Shaking his head, Jim realized he had been so absorbed with old memories that the whole morning was gone. He decided it was too late to start another project. Suddenly, there was a knock on his study door.

"Father, lunch is ready. I am taking the tray up to Mother now. Shall I tell her you are coming?"

He walked over and opened the door, replying, "Yes, Delora. Here, let me carry the tray, and we will go up to see your mother together."

His wife, Margaret, had been as good as bedridden for the last two years. She had been so vibrant only three years earlier. Now, she barely had the strength to go to the washroom with assistance and rarely got out of bed for any other reason.

As he and Delora walked into the room, Margaret was sitting up in bed, and she made room for Jim to sit next to her. He asked, "How are you feeling this afternoon, dear? Would you like to get up? I'll help you walk around the room. Did you notice that the boys brought your pretty coffee table and two chairs in here? Now, we can sit at the table and share our lunch."

His wife shook her head and replied, "Thank you, Jim. When did they do that?"

"When Delora was helping you with your bath. We wanted to surprise you. Are you ready to get up and have lunch?"

"It was so kind and thoughtful, but I don't think I'm ready to get up again. Can't you just sit with me? I'll eat my sandwich and potato salad here with you, then I'll need my medicine and a nap. After that, I'm sure I'll be ready to get up and sit at the table for dinner."

Jim nodded his head in resignation, replying, "Alright, Margaret, we will try at dinner."

Later That Day

Jim came back to his and Margaret's room at dinnertime, intending to insist that his wife allow him to help her get out of bed. They would sit at the table tonight and eat together. He had just stepped into the washroom to rinse his hands as Delora brought in the tray of food and began setting it on the little table.

When Delora looked at her mother, her mama looked glassy eyed. But then she smiled and held out her hand. Delora crossed the room and took hold of it and asked, "Are you alright, Mama?"

Margaret leaned her head back on her pillows and closed her eyes, then whispered, "What did you ask me?" Then she opened her eyes and asked, "How was school today? Did Oscar bring home the eggs like I asked? JW was going to bring me a magazine. Did the boys get back from the market yet? Please go get your grandpa Kilgore. I heard his voice in the hall earlier, and he didn't even come in to say hello." Then Margaret leaned back into her pillow and closed her eyes again.

While her mother had been talking, her father came up behind Delora. Now, she turned to look at her father, and he stepped to her side. Delora didn't know what to do. Her mama had been saying the oddest things.

"My girl, please answer me," her mother said.

Delora began to explain, "Mama, Grandpa Kilgore died in 1908, the year JW was born. Oscar and JW are at work right now, and I have not been to school in two years."

Margaret opened her eyes and lifted her head to look at Delora and scolded her, saying, "Why have you quit going to school? Jim, why have you let her quit school?" Out of energy, Margaret leaned her head back on the pillow, closing her eyes, and whispered, "Education is very important . . . I will have to speak to your . . . grandfather . . . about . . . this." Margaret fell asleep.

Jim noticed his daughter had begun to cry. He motioned for Delora to leave the room and followed her into the hall and whispered, "Delora, the young man I hired two days ago. Do you remember him? His name was Rusty Karella?" Delora nodded as she wiped her eyes. "Good. He will come by in two days in the morning around 10:00 a.m. I'd like you to show him to the stables out back when he arrives to take inventory of the tack. Can you do that for me, my girl?"

Delora smiled a little and nodded again.

"That's my good girl! Very good indeed. Rusty will be out there for a while. He will be taking measurements for our project. Please answer any questions he has and show him where to park at the side of the house. I want him to be able to come and go without needing to walk through the house each time he has to come check on something.

"Now, I'm going back to sit with your mother. Off to bed with you. I've got meetings at the track that will keep me busy all week, and I am glad I can leave Rusty and my project with you. Thank you, Delora."

Jim walked back into the room. It was early, but he decided he would go to bed anyway. After changing out of his clothing and putting on his nightshirt, he got into bed. Margaret rolled up next to him, and he pulled her into his arms.

She snuggled on his shoulder, and he lay his cheek on her hair. "Oh, Margaret," he whispered. "Where have you gone? What has happened to you? I miss you, darling. I keep hoping you'll start improving, but you must try, darling. You must help me. I don't understand this or how to help you. The doctor said you would improve with rest, but it's not working, and I don't know what else to do."

Margaret opened her eyes and resettled herself next to her husband. She thought she had heard his voice, but it sounded so far away, and she just felt so tired and so confused. After a while, she whispered, half asleep, "What . . . did you say, Jim dear?"

Hugging her, he whispered back, "Nothing, darling, go back to sleep. We will talk in the morning."

The Karella Go to the Madison County Fair, September 1926

Madison County Fair Grounds 2021—Photo taken by GKM

"Are you sure Rusty won't go with us to the county fair, Papa? There is going to be a musical review with lots of pretty girls! I would think he would want to go and at least look," Helen said.

Anton shrugged his shoulders and replied, "He has a mind of his own, and right now, it is focused on his work. Rusty just agreed to a new contract job with a horseman from Madison Downs named Holt."

Helen frowned. "Rusty is always working on some job these days. We hardly ever see him. When is he ever going to meet a girl with the kind of work schedule he keeps?"

This father-daughter conversation came to an abrupt halt when Helen's oldest son, Francis, shouted at his sister, "Hurry up, Margaret Mary! Everyone is waiting! We are going to miss the buggy races!"

CHAPTER 10

Unforeseen Friendship Forms in 1926

Sweet Dreams

Delora let the disturbing issues with her mother fade as she allowed excitement to fill her completely. Mr. Rusty Karella would come back to her house in two days! It was so exciting! Her father told her he wanted her to show the man around, talk to him, and help him. Delora didn't think she would be able to sleep she was so thrilled about the idea. Despite her excitement, it had been a long workday. Exhaustion soon won out over the tingle of exhilaration, falling asleep almost as soon as her head hit the pillow.

Delora woke early as she usually did. But unlike most of her mornings, today, she felt energized and hurried through her morning duties. After lunch, she straightened up the kitchen, then walked out to the stables to look at everything. She wanted to know exactly where the items were her father said Mr. Karella would need.

That evening, she washed her hair, then sat in front of the mirror as she tied it up in curling rags. Patting her head to be sure she had not missed any hair, she smiled and thought, *When it's dry, I'll have very nice waves.*

Forgetting everything else except the thought that she would see the handsome Mr. Karella tomorrow, Delora twirled around in her floor-length nightgown. Then she whirled her way slowly across the room toward her bed and plopped down on it. Grinning, she couldn't help wondering what Mr. Karella would think of her when she answered the door tomorrow. She wanted to surprise him. Last time he came, she had no warning, and she had looked awful. This time, she was going to look very different.

Letting out a sigh and a short tinkling giggle, she snuggled into her pillow and blankets. Closing her eyes, she thought, *I hope Rusty Karella thinks I look pretty.*

In the morning, Delora chose her clothing carefully and made sure to be down in the kitchen when her father walked into the room. "Good morning, Delora," he said, eyeing her approvingly.

James Holt home,
Madison, Nebraska

"Good morning, Papa," she replied as she put his dry toast on a plate. "I've already got Mama settled. She's had her breakfast and tonic and is relaxing." Picking up the plate and cup, she walked to the table and said, "Here is your coffee and toast. I must go check to see if the laundry is dry on the line and get it into the house before Mr. Karella arrives."

Delighted with his daughter's attitude, he smiled at her and said, "Thank you, my dear." Jim noticed her clothing was clean and tidy. Even her hair looked like it had been washed and curled. He nodded his head in approval, thinking, *Yes, that's much better.* He finished his breakfast as he watched Delora taking down the laundry from the line in the back yard. Feeling very pleased with her improved behavior, Jim walked out into the yard to say goodbye before he left. "Delora, have a nice day. I have a late meeting today, so I won't see you until suppertime." His daughter waved and smiled at him in response, and Jim left his home in a very good mood.

The First Visit

When Rusty arrived at the Holt home to conduct his inventory, he was greeted once again at the front door by . . . well, he was not sure it was the same girl he met on his first visit. This young lady looked more grown up, so he asked, "Pardon me, miss, are you the same young lady I met two days ago?"

Delora smiled, happy she had achieved such a change in her appearance that he was not sure if she was the same person. Just knowing she had succeeded improved her confidence tremendously. Which, in turn, made it much easier for her to talk to the handsome young man.

"Yes, Mr. Karella, I am," she replied. "I also know all about why you are here and where everything is that you will need to see. Now, if you will follow me, I'll show you." As they walked, she added, "I will check on you throughout the day so you can ask me where to find anything else you might think of that you don't see."

Rusty was impressed with the girl's behavior. "You can call me Rusty," he said as he followed her.

"Thank you, Rusty. Please call me Delora," she replied over her shoulder.

Unable to disguise his surprise, he thought, *Where did that shy, gawky little girl go that I remember? The one who guided me to her father's office and disappeared without a peep?* Shrugging his shoulders, Rusty followed Delora out the kitchen door to the back yard and then to the stables and tack shack.

Jim was right. Delora knew the answers to every question he had. The young woman also showed Rusty where to park near the stable area behind the house. He unloaded a few measuring tools, his notebooks, and writing materials. Not one to waste time, he took off his coat and got to work.

First, Rusty set up a makeshift work bench, then pulled a few of the saddles and harnesses from the tack shack for close inspection. Completely captivated by his work, Rusty was oblivious to the fact the Holt girl did not go back to the house immediately. However, he did notice she would silently disappear and then reappear throughout the day to ask if he needed anything.

After Delora's initial conversation with Rusty, her bravery faded. So, she sat quietly in the yard just watching him work. During that first workday, she checked on him periodically to see if he needed anything but did not stay long enough to say much else.

Second and Third Visit

The next day when Rusty returned, Delora found the courage to talk to him in brief spurts. He did very little talking back. By his third visit, she made a point of having everything done in the house. That way, she could stay out in the stables the entire time he was there except for lunch when she went in to take care of her mother.

While watching Rusty, Delora could see how meticulous he was about his work. She found his quiet intensity comforting, and she didn't feel as though he was purposely ignoring her. That fact encouraged her natural curiosity, and as the hours went by, she inched closer and closer to his workstation. Eventually, Delora was sitting right next to Rusty. As she watched what he was doing, she calmly and softly began to ask him questions.

A Friendship Forms on the Fourth Visit, Late Fall of 1926

The Holt girl was generally so silent Rusty didn't really notice her comings and goings at first unless she said something to him. During his second and third visit to the Holt stables, his workday started out basically the same. The Holt girl showed up like a shadow. She sat quietly nearby, and she politely and promptly helped him when he requested her assistance. Then he would forget she was there.

In the afternoon of the fourth day, Delora surprised him. She found a second stool and managed to sit beside him, without him even being aware she was there. Delora actually startled him when she spoke, asking, "Do you mind me watching you work? I think it is interesting!"

Having turned to look at her, he found himself responding to the gentleness in her voice. Uncharacteristically, he spoke without thinking and replied, "No, I don't mind. You are not disturbing me or my work."

After a brief silence, she asked, "Where did you grow up, Rusty?"

For some unfathomable reason, Rusty told Delora a bit about himself and quite unexpectedly enjoyed talking about his life. "When we first came to town, my whole family lived on my grandfather's homestead here in Madison County. When my grandmother got sick, my grandfather moved her into a house in Madison. As my father and his siblings married and had children, they moved from the farm to their own homes. My parents moved our family closer to our family's lumber sawmill, but I know we mainly moved there to be near Grandpa, who was alone after Grandma died."

"Where do you live now? Do you have any brothers and sisters?" she asked.

"I still live with my father. It is a family custom that unmarried children remain living under their parent's roof. My two younger sisters are married and live around Madison." Almost to himself, he said quietly, "I do miss Ani, though; we were very close."

Catching the sad tone in Rusty's voice, Delora asked, "Who is Annie—is she your sister too?"

"No, actually, what I said was A-N-I, and that is my nickname for my baby brother, Anastas. He is a soldier in the French Foreign Legion now, so I suppose he has outgrown that nickname. My other brother, Frank, just got married this spring and lives in Norfolk. My older sister, Helen, lost her husband last fall, and now she and her children live with Papa and me. It is hard to believe so many family members are gone already. I still miss them very much."

"Oh, Rusty, that is so sad. I am sorry to hear that your grandma as well as your mother *and* your sister's husband have all died."

Rusty looked over at Delora for a moment. He could tell she was sincerely moved by what he had told her and thanked her for her kindness. Yet, Rusty wanted to move the attention away from himself and said, "What about your family?" Rusty asked, "Why don't you tell me about them?"

"Rusty, it is kind of a sad story. Are you sure you want to hear it?"

She had replied so quietly he had to lean close to hear what she said. Wrinkling his brow in reaction to her crestfallen look, he replied firmly, "Yes, of course I want to hear it. You can talk while I work," he suggested.

Delora Reveals Unexpected Circumstances

"Alright," she replied, taking a deep breath, and began, "I suppose the problems started just before my little sister, Marcella, was born when I was twelve. Mama would get depressed occasionally back then. But our home life still felt normal, and we enjoyed being a family and spending time together. Then Mama discovered she was going to have another baby, and she was always happy—at least at first.

Years Earlier, Delora Eavesdrops on Conversations in September 1922

Delora sat listening to her papa on the telephone with the doctor, "I don't understand it, Doctor. She has fallen into a depression again, even with Marcella Juanita to look after. Margaret also caught a flu that the boys brought home from school. She is having a hard time breathing and is restless and can't sleep." Her papa went silent for a time, then replied, "Yes, of course, I'll stay here until you get here. Thank you, Doctor, I appreciate you coming over to see her so quickly."

When the doctor arrived, Delora remained within hearing distance as they talked about her mother. "Jim, I have given Margaret a tonic that will help her sleep and another that will help with her depression.

She should take a dose of each in the morning just before she has her breakfast." Her father nodded as he received these instructions, then the two men walked out of hearing range as her father led the doctor back downstairs and to the front door.

Her mother did seem happier for a time. But things began to change, then when she stopped nursing Marcella at 12 months, her mother's depression came back worse than before. Her mama had been plagued with continuous ailments, too, and her papa took her to the doctor many times.

The doctor prescribed stronger sleeping drafts and stronger tonics as her mother's condition dragged on. He assured her papa that these medicines would help with the ailment as well as help alleviate Margaret's mood changes. Then he also promised the new medicine would allow her mama to relax and sleep more.

Delora vividly remembered Doctor Linden telling her papa that all Margaret needed was rest. That news filled Delora with hope and happiness. She missed the mother she knew as a little girl. The doctor also told her papa that her mama could not have any more babies. Then, putting his hand on her papa's arm, he added, "Jim, you and Margaret already have five children. That is more than enough to keep any mother and father busy and happy. However, right now, you and the children must take care of all the chores and home responsibilities until Margaret feels better."

Delora came back out of her memories for a moment when Rusty said, "Delora, I agree with that doctor. I mean, what he recommended to your father. It was good for your family and sensible."

"But, Rusty, Papa told us that with the doctor's help and the medicine he prescribed for Mama, the illnesses would pass. That everything would return to normal at home . . . but . . . nothing worked out that way," she finished sadly.

"Ok then, tell me what did happen," Rusty said as he concentrated on his work.

"Mama's legs just grew weaker. Eventually, she was not stable on her feet anymore. Sometimes, when Papa used to talk to Mama in the mornings, I could hear them through the wall. That was when

Mama's mind was still clear, and Papa could talk to her about her health and what they needed to do to help her get better.

More of Delora's Memories from Years Past

Delora remembered standing outside her parent's bedroom door holding little Marcella in her arms. The baby had started to walk, and as soon as school was out, her father put her in charge of watching Marcella. Delora spent most of her time at home keeping track of her sister.

This evening as she stood listening at her parents' door, she was filled with sadness. Many times, she had heard her Papa say, "'Margaret, can't you try? Maybe if you walked a little each day, you would get stronger. I'll help you.'" But her mama didn't want to do what Papa asked.

She would refuse and say, "Jim, I'm not sure enough on my feet anymore to get out of bed alone. I can't do it. Maybe all I need is a little more rest. I have been taking my medicines, Jim. They do give me relief from my nerves, and I have been sleeping better these days. Don't you think so too?"

At that point, Delora had peeked through the bedroom door, and her papa nodded, then asked, "Margaret, what do you expect me to do? You cannot keep track of our toddler from that bed! Marcella has been crawling, and now she toddles everywhere within seconds of taking eyes off her! Oscar, JW, Delora, and Violet are all in school. I have work to do and can't always be at home taking care of the baby. If you don't think you can get up, maybe I should ask one of my sisters or one of yours to come in and help."

Delora didn't understand it, but her mama was adamant when she told Jim she did not want anyone but him and her children to know how sick she was. She got very agitated about the subject until Papa gave in, saying, "Fine, I won't ask any of the family to help. But then what are we going to do about this problem?"

Back to the present, sitting on the ground by Rusty, Delora stopped talking. After several moments of silence, Rusty looked at her. When she continued to stare at the ground with her mouth shut, he asked gently, "What happened next, Delora?"

"It was decided that I should stay home from school to help out. You see, I already knew how to cook breakfast, as I had inherited that chore before Marcella was born. I also knew how to take care of the baby and did quite a few other chores around the house already. I didn't know it then, but apparently, Mama promised my father this would be a temporary arrangement. Just until she felt a little better and a little stronger, and then I'd be able to go back to school.

"I had no idea it was Mama who decided it should be me that stayed home to take care of her and Marcella. I had thought it was Papa's idea, and I had a hard time believing he would really make me stay home from school. When he first told me, I tried to talk him out of it, and it hurt when he would not listen or change his decision."

Remembering a Life-Changing Moment

Delora vividly remembered running up to her mama's room for help, yelling, "Mama, can I come in?"

"Yes, Delora, come in. What is wrong? Sit on the bed next to me and tell me what has made you so upset."

"I poured my heart out to her, saying, 'Papa said I must quit going to school. That I must stay home to take care of you and Marcella. I know you have been sick. But, Mama, the doctor gave you medicine, and you said you would get better.'"

"Delora," her mother had replied, "that is what we hoped would happen. I'm not better . . . yet. Your father asked me what I thought would help me get better. I told him having you here to help me and look after Marcella would be the best thing for all of us right now."

The memory faded as Delora said, "Rusty, I didn't want to do what they asked, but I loved my mama, and when she took hold of my hand and asked, 'Can you do this for me, Delora? Marcella and I need you. Please, just until I feel a little stronger?' I could not say no. It was really hard wanting to help but also wanting what I wanted at the same time."

Rusty thought about what he had just heard. He had not been in the exact situation Delora found herself in, yet he understood what she said. *Wanting what you want and choosing to do what you must do is very confusing and difficult,* he thought. "Delora, you did do the right thing. Don't you think so too?"

"Most of the time, I believe I did. Yet, by agreeing to take care of Mama and Marcella, my whole life changed, and my new duties started the very next morning. After Father finished his toast and coffee, he left the house early, saying he would be at Madison Downs if I needed anything. Then I made breakfast for my two brothers and my sister Violet and made sure they left for school on time. After that, I got Marcella up and dressed and took her to Mama's room to play until I finished making breakfast for the three of us and brought the tray up. We would eat in Mama's room, and then I would give Mama her medicines. After that, she would give me a list of other duties and chores to get done during the morning before it was time to make lunch. That was how it started, and that is still what I do today even though Mama promised it would only be for a little while."

"That was good of you, Delora. I'm sure it turned out better than you thought," Rusty replied.

Suddenly, Delora's voice got a little shaky as she replied, "No, it didn't, Rusty. I stayed home just like they wanted me to do. I've taken care of everything! All the while hoping Mama would get better, and Papa would let me go back to school. But the situation did not end. What I just described to you is exactly what my life still is today.

"I love them, but lots of times, I feel like my life is over, and that just makes me want to cry. Looking at Rusty and hoping he would not think badly of her, she asked, "Can I tell you what I did? Promise you will not think bad of me?"

Rusty nodded and replied, "Go ahead, tell me what you did."

Involuntarily, Rusty Becomes Protective

Delora thought back for a moment, then began, "The next evening after I agreed to do as they asked, I listened at Mama and Papa's door. I wanted to know if Papa and Mama changed their minds, hoping they would let me go back to school. But then I heard Papa say he went to my school and talked to Principal Blackpepper.

"He told Mama he withdrew me from school indefinitely. He said he told Mr. Blackpepper his wife was bedridden with an ailment and that he had a young toddler as well and that they could not be left alone. Mr. Blackpepper agreed with Papa—that I was needed at home—and said Papa's decision was completely understandable. I cried myself to sleep that night and many nights after that. A week had gone by when my oldest brother, Oscar, finally asked Papa about why he was keeping me home from school.

"I overheard Papa tell him that someone had to take care of Mama and the baby, and Mark Blackpepper said he made the right choice. Papa told Oscar that even Delora's principal understood that he was doing what was best for his family."

"Was that all that happened?" Rusty asked.

"I suppose so. That was when I realized I would never get to go back. At first, though, on school days, I got up very early. After everyone left the house, I would put Mama's food and medicine by her bed, and then I'd take Marcella for a walk down the street and around the corner. I'd go to see my friend Sally Martin. My birthday and Sally's are only two days apart, and we used to have sleepovers and celebrate them together.

"Anyway, we would visit until she had to leave for school. I missed her and all my friends. I even told her I was jealous she had homework. As wintertime grew colder, I quit going to see Sally and quit looking out the window at neighborhood kids walking to school. After that, I quit getting up extra early because it hurt too much to see them having fun as they walked by my house when I had to stay home."

Rusty felt confused by these odd details in her story and asked, "Delora, how long has your mama been like this?"

Delora replied sadly, "Going on two years."

"And how old are you?"

Delora whispered her reply, "Going on sixteen."

"So, your papa had you quit going to school when you were 14? To—?"

Delora finished the sentence for him: "To cook and clean for everyone in the house and take care of Mama and my baby sister."

As Rusty asked his questions, he put his tools away for the day. Then he sat listening quietly, waiting for Delora to finish her story. She finally went silent, sitting slump-shouldered, staring at the ground. He spoke softly, "Delora, sometimes harsh things happen in real life."

She looked up at him with a fragileness that made him want to protect her. Abruptly, Rusty changed the subject, saying, "Delora, I have finished my work for today. I need to get going." Then she looked so dejected that before he walked away, he also said, "I think you are a brave girl." Then he patted her on the shoulder and added, "I also think you are doing a wonderful job of taking care of your responsibilities."

Driving away from the Holt house that day, Rusty did not know what to make of this situation he found himself in. He had begun to feel very protective of Delora. Of course, that was natural given what she had told him. But against who? Her mother? Her father, the man who also happened to be his employer? This whole situation was becoming very complicated. But no matter how hard he tried, he just couldn't let it go or stop thinking about all the things Delora had told him.

Shaking his head, he thought, *When Delora first started telling me her story, I had not expected to hear so much about what was going on in my employer's life. It feels awkward and maybe even a little improper. But I don't know how to stop what began so innocently just as talk. If I make Delora quit talking to me now, she may feel like I am turning my back on her. I don't want to hurt her feelings or make her sadder than she already is.* His mind went still for a moment, then he thought, *I guess it won't hurt—letting her talk about it to me. Maybe I am helping her cope with her problems.*

Arriving back at his workshop, Rusty made a stronger effort to dislodge those uncomfortable thoughts and feelings from his mind by turning his attention back to his work.

Rusty actually had all the information he needed to complete Holt's budget assessment. Sitting down at his desk, he finished his proposal and decided to deliver it to Jim at the racetrack in the morning. As Rusty readied himself for bed, he realized the things Delora had told him kept floating around in his thoughts and filled his mind with concern. Just before slipping off to sleep, he thought, *Perhaps it would be smarter to stay away from the Holt house for a while.*

Pricing and Contracts

Rusty called Jim Holt, and after a brief chat, Rusty said, "Jim, I have finished the pricing assessment you asked for."

Rusty heard a pleasant chuckle on the other end of the telephone before Jim replied, "That was fast work, and I am very pleased to hear it, Rusty."

"Would you like me to meet you at the track to go over it this week?" Rusty prompted.

"Actually, would you mind dropping it off at the house? You can leave it with Delora. By the way, I hope my daughter has been helpful. Now, regarding your question. If you don't mind, I'd like to look over the numbers a bit first, and then we can set a meeting for next week."

"That is fine with me, Jim. I'll drop it by your house today," Rusty replied.

City Press   September, 1925

DAILY HAROLD NEWS

Madison Downs Grudge Match

"May The Best Horse Win!"

says rancher J.B. Thornton of Omaha and owner of Red Cyclone who challenged Madison's Midnight Express to a one-on-one match race. The 2 yr old studs have been going head to head all summer. This is the last race of the season for these 2 yr. olds. The race will be held at

Madison Downs on Midnight Express's own turf says James Holt, long time Madison horseman and owner of the stud. Holt says "Madison Downs is a top-notch racetrack and a great place to spend a Saturday afternoon. Come get some fresh air and see the magnificent horses Nebraskans breed. The track has excellent ballpark seating so everyone watching can see the whole race and our jockeys are happy to sign autographs. I bet you will have fun and who doesn't like to cheer for a winning horse."

There they go! September 10 through September 28 at Madison Downs, Madison, Nebraska. Post time 3 P.M., Saturday 2:30. No racing Sunday or Monday. Special bus leaves Omaha 11:30 A.M. Tuesday through Friday, Saturday 11:00 A.M. Go!!!!!

Jim Holt, horseracing news by GKM 2021

An hour later, Rusty knocked on the door, and Delora answered it. Surprised, she asked, "Why did you use the front door today?"

"I'm not working. I just need to drop this packet off for your father's review. Do you want to put it in his office for me?"

"No," she said, smiling demurely. "I'd rather you walk with me to my father's study. You can put it on his desk yourself, and then I can show you the library."

They walked through the house to the room where he first met Jim. Rusty placed the packet on Jim's desk, and then Delora began to tell him about the family pictures on the walls and let him look at the framed newspaper article about the grudge match horserace.

Rusty took his time looking around. He smiled, thinking that many of the famous horses and jockeys in the photographs he was looking at would soon be using gear and horse tack that he designed, and that knowledge made him glow with pride.

Several Days Later

Rusty deliberately spent several days at his shop, catching up on other orders, keeping himself too busy to think about anything else. He needed a break from Delora's innocent questions that dredged up so many unsettling feelings.

After several intense days of uninterrupted work, Rusty felt in control of himself again. With his thoughts firmly in check, he was eager to resume his project preparation at the Holt stable. However, when he arrived at Holt's house, he found Delora waiting for him by the tack shack. Rusty's newfound determination to keep away from Delora and sensitive subjects was quickly forgotten. He couldn't help smiling at her; she was such a pretty sight.

Delora had been watching at the window for Rusty every day. When she spotted his car coming down the street, she made a mad dash down the stairs and out to the stables so she could be there when he walked into the back yard. Delora smiled with delight at seeing him and said softly, "I've missed you, Rusty."

Seeing her sincere smile snatched his breath away, and his heart skipped a beat. *Now, these are some odd feelings,* he thought. But what he said was, "Delora, I missed you too."

Rusty startled himself with that truthful and automatic reply. Though his hands were busy pulling tools from his canvas carrier, his thoughts raced. That instant, honest reply had taken him by surprise. As hard as he tried, he couldn't stop the reflections that followed. *She's so sweet, quiet, genuine. I actually do enjoy her company and I did miss her.* Shaking his head to dislodge such reckless thoughts, Rusty redirected his attention to his work.

Pulling his stool up to the saddle bench, he set one of the stripped-down saddle trees from his shop next to one of Holt's saddles. Ignoring Delora, Rusty began assessing the modifications he needed to make.

Familiar with Rusty's intense concentration, Delora did not realize he was trying to ignore her. She simply grabbed her own stool and set it next to his, leaning into his side to watch him work. After a short silence, feeling gratified that he had missed her, too, she asked, "I was wondering, do you like living at home?"

Refusing to look at her and concentrating on the saddle in front of him, Rusty decided her question was harmless enough and replied, "I suppose so. I used to spend most of my week in Norfolk. Now, I have my own business here in Madison. My work still takes me away from home for days at a time, so I'm only home a few nights a week. I do like living with my father, my sister, and her children. We are a very close-knit family.

"It was my father that taught me how to ride and shoe horses. I learned how to tend farm crops and livestock from my father's brother Stanislaus. But most of what I know about everything else, I learned from my grandfather Vaclav.

"Grandpa taught me to forge metal, work with leather, and invent tools and other useful things." Rusty's hands stopped moving as he remembered those long-ago moments, then said softly, "I guess I could say we also learned to repair machines and motors together too."

"Your grandpa sounds wonderful. Do you still see a lot of him?" After a moment, Delora began to worry because Rusty had stopped talking and continued to work on in silence. She was about to leave when he quietly spoke.

"I don't see him anymore because he died too."

The sadness in Rusty's voice touched her heart, and she whispered, "I am very sorry to hear that. I feel sad for you. It must be very hard to have lost so many people that you love."

Rusty shrugged his shoulders. Unexpectedly, this conversation began making his eyes fill with tears. He needed Delora to leave and replied, "I'll be fine, but I think you should go back into your house now. I have a lot of work to do and no more time to talk."

Delora got up from her stool and stood behind Rusty for a moment. She didn't know what to do, realizing she had somehow upset him but had no idea how to fix what she had done. Delora felt like he had shut her out. She waited a bit, thinking he might say something else. He didn't, so with a pensive look on her face, Delora turned and walked slowly back to her house.

Rusty had felt Delora standing behind him waiting, and he kept wishing she would go away. Only after he knew she had disappeared into her house did he let out a shuddering breath. He had never spoken to anyone like this about his grandfather. In doing so, he realized that death still hurt too much to talk about with anyone except his father.

As Rusty continued to work on in solitude, he admitted that deep inside, he had felt comforted by Delora's reaction to his pain. She had shown compassion for his loss. He also realized he felt safe showing her his feelings. Instinctively, he knew Delora did not think of him as weak or pitiful for showing his emotions.

Third Week of the Project

Just the thought of Rusty's visits made Delora giddy with happiness, and she wanted to look and act her best whenever he was around. She started spending a great deal of time fixing her hair and wore her prettiest clothes.

When Rusty came to her house to work, he told Delora about many things that were part of his world. Sometimes he told her about cities and places he had seen, and other times he told her about ideas he had for tools that he would invent to make his work easier. Delora loved hearing anything Rusty wanted to tell her. He also asked how she liked the work he was doing for her father. He listened carefully when she spoke to him and made her feel important. Delora missed him terribly on the days that he worked at his shop or went to the Downs to see her father.

It did not take Rusty long to realize Delora knew a lot about the horse business. She also understood her father's goals behind winning races and commented, "My father used to tell me the more our horses win races, the more their babies are worth."

Because of Delora's keen interest in her father's business, Rusty began to explain the theory behind the sleek lines of the saddle—why he used very supple leather that conformed to the horse's girth for comfort. And why he wanted to reduce the weight and extra leather that might impede the animal's full stride but would still keep the jockey securely in control.

If she did not understand what he told her, she asked astute questions, and he took the time to explain it better. Delora's questions stimulated his imagination and thoughts. Some of the things she said even gave him a few fresh ideas, so Rusty looked forward to her company while he worked.

Best Intentions

Delora glanced out the kitchen windows toward the stable and saw Rusty. Flushed with excitement, she hurried to finish taking care of her mother, then dashed to her room to change her clothes and fix her hair. She glanced in the mirror and nodded, then took off down the back stairs and out the kitchen door.

"Hello, Rusty," she said with a tinge of breathlessness. "I have missed seeing you this week!"

Rusty looked up and felt a tingle of excitement at her words. He could see she was honestly happy to see him. It showed clearly in her expression, and that truth made him happy too. "And a good morning to you, Miss Holt," Rusty replied in a teasing tone accompanied by a warm smile.

Delora had been thinking about Rusty's offer to teach her how to work leather if she was interested. Today, she would tell him she wanted to learn. That would give her a chance to spend a lot more time with him. *Plus,* she thought, *logically, if he is teaching me about his work, he won't stay away several days during the week.*

Delora spoke up sweetly, reminding Rusty of this promise.

"You are sure you want to learn about this?" he asked. She nodded vigorously. "Ok then," he replied, "pay close attention."

Delora nearly glued herself to his side instantly. As she sat there listening and watching, her whole body tingled with happiness. This side-by-side learning technique gave them both a feeling of comfort. It was a special kind of contact they both craved. Rusty also looked forward to Delora's thoughtful questions and appreciated how well she retained the information he explained to her. In return, Delora found it exciting that Rusty took her questions seriously and answered them quickly.

Being naturally observant during their time together, Delora noticed when the work got intense, Rusty often stopped to rub his neck.

Thinking about it, she compared Rusty's actions to the times her mother complained of aches and pains in her neck and shoulders. Delora had learned to rub them to ease her mother's discomfort. Seeing the way Rusty acted, she guessed his neck and shoulders hurt him too.

Rusty stopped to rub his neck again, thinking, *I don't understand this tension I'm feeling. I'm totally relaxed when I work with leather in my shop, but when I work here in the Holt stable, it almost feels like my nerves are on edge.*

There also seemed to be an odd tension on the right side of his body he had never felt before. Rusty rubbed his neck again and moved his shoulders periodically to make the odd sensation go away. He did not connect the fact that it was the same side where Delora sat most days.

Delora's Innocent Gesture

The next time Delora saw him rub his neck, she stepped up behind him. He sat on his short barn stool, concentrating on making notch marks on the cinch straps with a tool he called a leather punch. When she began to rub his neck, he stiffened up at first, but he did not stop her, and eventually, his neck muscles began to relax. His reaction made her more confident, and she began to rub his shoulders, working on the knots she detected with her fingers. Delora liked the idea that she was making him feel better. It was nice to do something for Rusty since he made her feel good too.

Delora leaned on Rusty's back so she could continue watching what he was doing while she worked on his strong muscles and resumed asking questions. As usual, he answered her promptly, but she also noticed his ears had turned red. After she finished rubbing his shoulders and sat back down next to him, she could see his ears turn back to their normal color.

The next time she rubbed his neck and shoulders, Rusty's ears showed the same reaction. Suddenly, a thought occurred to her, *Maybe his ears turning red means he likes how it feels when I rub his neck and shoulders, and maybe he likes me too!* That eye-opening possibility made Delora smile, and her body prickled with exhilaration at such a prospect.

Ignoring Warning Bells

Rusty could sense something in his situation was changing, but he could not quite identify it. What he felt seemed a little dangerous edged with excitement. The sensation seemed to be all around him. He felt drawn to it, yet he could not explain where it was or what it was. None of it made any sense, and every time he tried to put his finger on the problem, the connection between the details disappeared.

Making an effort to figure it out logically, he went through his life in detail, thinking, *I know it is not my project for Holt; everything is on track, and I am making great progress. I've spread out my time between the shop and the Holt stable to make sure none of my other client orders fall behind, so these crazy feelings are not being caused by any of my responsibilities. Could it be my health?* He wondered. After only a moment, he shook off that idea. *No, that doesn't track because I've never felt better or happier in my life. I just don't know what is niggling at my brain!* Rusty would never have guessed his current feelings that switched between excitement and anxiety or satisfaction and wellbeing were being caused by the Holt girl.

Rusty's sense of propriety would only allow him to acknowledge that Delora was a lovely person, sweet, and shy. At the same time, he found her very intelligent and not the least bit self-centered, silly, or spoiled like most girls her age he had met. He also respected her, particularly regarding how she coped with her difficult situation at home. When it came to their friendship, he found it easy to understand why she felt moody and emotional some mornings. Yet she possessed good self-discipline and would settle into an even frame of mind quickly as they worked together demonstrating her strong character, which he greatly admired.

Though Rusty generally steered away from thoughts about his feelings, he could not deny it felt good to see Delora come running, excited to see him each time he arrived at the stables. She enjoyed being out of doors and never got tired of watching him work. And the girl asked good questions! Delora consistently showed an honest interest in his designs and listened to what he had to tell her. She also took his advice to heart. Just recently, he discovered Delora had a funny sense of humor and a charming, tinkling little laugh. The thought of just that sound could make him smile. Yes, overall, he found Delora's company refreshing. She seemed to be far superior in many ways to any other girls he had known.

James Holt and Margaret Ballou
Kilgore Holt, wedding

Suddenly, Rusty wondered if his judgment might be faulty. Truthfully, he'd never spent much time around teenaged girls or even older girls to actually judge whether or not Delora was really that different from other girls.

Like this train of thought always did, it began to make his brain hurt. Rusty had to admit he didn't really know much about girls of any age. The only thing he knew to be true lately was that he looked forward to seeing her, and he found Delora Holt's company very pleasant.

Left to right: Oscar Samuel, Delora Lucy, and James Winfield, the first three Holt children of James (Jim) and Margaret Kilgore Holt

James Holt, Family Man of Madison County

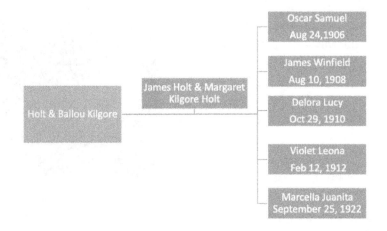

CHAPTER 11

Projects and Decisions

Project Meeting, Early September 1926

Jim Holt stood up to shake his visitor's hand, saying, "Rusty, how good to see you again." Sitting back down at his desk at the Downs, he continued talking, "When I reviewed the pricing you left for me with Delora, I was pleased to see you had already ordered the supplies we need. I'm satisfied with your estimates for the work and the hourly labor listed for the project too. Here is the budget I promised. Sorry it took me a week to get it ready. Since we already have three weeks on the books, how much longer will you need to get the work done?"

"I estimate one week per saddle, barring any unforeseen issues once I receive that last order of leather. I'd say you can safely plan to break in the new equipment by the first week of October," Rusty replied. Then, glancing down at the budget, he looked up and added, "Jim, I feel confident we can complete the project according to this pricing. However, if I hit any issues, I will let you know before we spend more than is allocated."

"Agreed," Jim replied.

"Now, since I've ordered the special leather already, it might take a week before it arrives. But I have already started on the other parts I am designing. In addition, I have begun to cut and shave

191

the wood for the customized saddle trees while I'm waiting for that leather delivery."

"Excellent! Rusty, you have my permission to work here at the Downs, at my stables, or at your shop. You can also leave notes for me with Delora about anything you need. Don't wait for a meeting to give me updates. I'll look for your notes each evening at home. Thank you for your professionalism. I am excited to get this project completed."

Shaking hands once more, Rusty left Holt's office at the Downs. Halfway to his shop, Rusty changed direction, deciding to go see his father and talk to him about the meeting he just had.

"Son, I can't tell you how proud I am of you," Anton said as Rusty concluded his review of his meeting with Holt and showed his father the budget. Anton stared at his son, thinking, *Something is bothering Rusty,* then asked, "Son, is there something you want to talk to me about? Is something worrying you?"

Rusty nearly said yes, then thought, *What is there to tell him? I can't even figure out what is wrong, so how can I explain this uneasiness I feel?* After a moment, Rusty shook his head, saying, "No, Papa, it's nothing to concern yourself over."

A Personal Dilemma

At first, 28-year-old Rusty Karella thought of 15-year-old Delora Holt as a little girl, much like one of his younger sister's friends. He enjoyed her quiet curiosity, and they were friendly and comfortable together. Charmed by her sincere interest, he began sharing more personal thoughts in addition to discussing the work he was doing for her father.

Subconsciously, he began to spend more time on his design work at the Holt stable than he did at his shop or at Madison Downs.

By nature, Rusty took his life and work very seriously, even during his early apprenticeship with his grandfather. That tendency only increased as he got his job in Norfolk and increased again running his business in Madison.

His demanding life had left him unprepared and inexperienced when it came to understanding women or the feelings love can produce. Rusty could not imagine the recent changes in his perception might be caused by a girl's attention, and he would not have guessed his feelings involved Delora. He had never thought of his life as lonely. Nor did he realize that it actually was. Discovering that fact led Rusty to an unexpected turn of events.

Now, all Rusty knew for sure was that something had changed. He felt exhilarated every morning and could not wait to get back to his project each day. Of course, this new test of his professional skills was both challenging and refreshing. Certainly, this creative innovation mode he was in explained the stimulation he felt all day and even at night when he returned home exhausted from his workday.

Delora Lucy Holt

The more time Delora spent around Rusty, the more she looked forward to seeing him. Just thinking about him made her work in the house easier, and before she knew it, all her tasks were completed. In the mornings after she got her mother settled for the day, Marcella played in her mother's room for the next couple of hours.

After everyone had lunch, her mother took a nap, and so did Marcella. Delora brought out blankets and set them under the shade tree, and Marcella took her long naps in the yard, not far from where she spent her time with Rusty. If Marcella woke up, she played with her toys in the yard within sight of the workbench in the stables.

After weeks of spending time with Rusty, Delora noticed she could fluster him a bit when she teased him. What a revelation that had been, and Delora had been amazed to discover this handsome man could not ignore her. That knowledge made her feel wonderful and powerful for the first time in her life.

Thinking about it produced a new tingling sense of excitement and anticipation. After making that remarkable discovery, teenage Delora liked experimenting with her new power. Once she started teasing Rusty and got the first reaction, she found it hard to stop teasing him. Seeing him respond to her thrilled her and made her heartbeat faster. At times, she giggled just because of the giddy feelings that ran through her. Delora also learned to recognize when Rusty grew tired of her silliness because he was quick to say, "I'm too busy for this, Delora. Please take your little sister and leave."

Rusty didn't always work at their stable. It was those times when he stayed away that Delora made another discovery. She felt so lonely she could hardly deal with the anxiety she felt when she did not see him or talk to him. Rusty's visits were important! She never stopped to question why his visits were so vital to her; she just knew they were. Each time he returned to her, the anxiety fled, and she felt happier than ever before. In her daydreams, she imagined this wonderful friendship going on forever.

Being only 15 and inexperienced with the world outside her home, she noticed that time moved slowly for her. Days felt like weeks, and weeks felt like months. Thinking of time in this manner, it came as a complete shock the day Rusty told her he would finish the job for her father in two short weeks.

Rude Awakenings

Collecting and sorting his tools at the Holt stable, Rusty took half of them to the trunk of his car. Delora came out of the house when she saw him and joined him by the saddle rack and workbench. "What are you doing, Rusty?" she asked.

"I am almost finished with my work here, so I am putting away the tools I will not be needing anymore." As he looked at her, Delora reacted to his news in the strangest manner. She stared at him as her face went blank, her eyes went wide in shock, and then she stiffened up. The peculiar set of her jaw made him think she looked almost angry, but that made no sense.

Rusty's news made Delora feel like she had a rock in her stomach. The very thought that he would not be coming to see her anymore frightened her. She could not imagine her life without him in it. Then she could feel her eyes filling with tears. Delora clenched her teeth and her fists. She tried desperately to keep her tears from falling. When that didn't work, she ran into the house to hide the fact that he had made her cry.

He had no experience dealing with such baffling female reactions. When Delora ran off to the house, Rusty shrugged his shoulders. After refocusing his attention on his work, he wondered, *Who knows what goes on in the mind of a woman?*

Delora hid in her room and cried for an hour, feeling desperate. She hated feeling like this and thought, *I haven't felt this way since . . . since . . .* Suddenly, Delora sat up as a revelation occurred to her: *I haven't felt like this since Rusty came. He has changed the way I feel just by being here. I cannot lose him or his friendship. I refuse to allow my life to go back to what it was. Not again!*

As she sat there, one thought led to another until she remembered something her brother Oscar had said: "Someday you will get married, and then you will have a life of your own."

Yes, Oscar was right, she thought. Delora decided then and there she wanted Rusty to be more than just her friend. Quite suddenly, everything made sense. She had to keep Rusty for her own. If she kept Rusty, that meant she would marry him and become his wife. If Rusty made her his wife, that meant he would take her away, and they would make a new life together. *How wonderful that would be,* she thought.

Smiling at this newfound wisdom, she wiped away her tears, thinking, *I could leave this house for good! I could have a family of my own—how wonderfully exciting that will be!* All sadness was forgotten as she began daydreaming of the adventures she would have with her Rusty when she was free from her mother and father.

Hurrying downstairs, Delora ran out the back door, intending to talk over her revelations with Rusty. Abruptly, she stopped on the back porch because another thought struck her: *I can't let Rusty leave today without admitting he loves me!*

Thinking rapidly, she walked slowly from the porch to the stable. Her mind hummed with another idea and said softly, "Rusty." He turned to look at her. "I'm sorry I ran off like that. You are my friend.

I was upset to think that soon I wouldn't be seeing you anymore." The truth of her confession made Delora honestly feel like crying again.

As Rusty listened to Delora and watched her face, he thought, *Oh, for goodness sakes! Is she going to cry?* Trying to sooth the girl and keep her from crying, he said, "Delora, I'll still be coming here for two more weeks. I'll see you until then. Don't worry so much. Are you alright now?" Despite her watery eyes, she nodded her head and gave him a weak smile. *Now, that's an improvement,* Rusty thought. *At least she is not crying.*

That Evening

Sitting alone in her room, Delora's mind moved quickly from tears to despair, then back to hope as she remembered Rusty's words. "I'll be back to see you for two more weeks." Rusty could not know how literally she took those words.

Just as her father did when watching a horse, Delora's mental stopwatch clicked on, and she knew her time with Rusty was ticking away. She had only two weeks to convince him that he loved her. Much like her father, Delora could be very determined when she set her mind to a task, especially when it was so important.

How am I going to get his attention? she wondered. Thinking about Rusty, she realized every time she had been upset, he had been very kind and tried to make her feel better. *Maybe if I did cry, he would be kind, and I could tell him I didn't want him to go away. Then, maybe, I can tell him I love him, and he will tell me he loves me.*

The next day Rusty came to work at the stable, Delora was cordial and talkative. Pleased and relieved he did not have to deal with feminine emotions, Rusty relaxed in her presence. Delora waited for her chance. When Rusty sat down on the stool to sort through his tools, she decided to try and get his attention. She let the notion of his leaving fill her, and she started to cry. Then she leaned against his back and said, "I don't want you to stop coming to my house to see me."

As a rule, Rusty did not overreact to things people said or did. Unknowingly, he had become very sensitive to Delora's moods, actions, and words. Now, at this moment, her actions and words made Rusty's back stiffen immediately. Probably reading more into what she said than what she actually meant, he wondered, *Did she just scandalously imply I have not been honest in my agreement with her father? That I have not been coming to this stable for legitimate work reasons?*

Quite agitated, Rusty replied firmly with logic, saying, "Delora, I come here because of the contract I have with your father." Something inside him would not let him add, *I do not come here to see you.* Instead, he finished by saying, "It is only natural that when my job is finished, I'll stop coming here."

His words had been firm and true. Yet, as he said the words, he felt confused by his own feelings of dismay. He had not thought about not seeing her again, and now that he did, he did not like that idea at all. Rusty was shaken by the odd feelings bubbling up inside him and wondered, *What exactly is going on here?*

His response made Delora cry harder. Now, she really was scared he would stop coming over.

Exasperated and moved by her distress, Rusty turned halfway around to put his arm around Delora's shoulder to comfort her. He patted her on the back gently, and when she did not stop crying, he turned to fully face her but remained sitting on the stool.

Delora instantly moved closer and placed both of her arms around his neck and put her head on his shoulder. Innocently, Rusty continued patting Delora on the back, asking her not to cry.

His soft voice was comforting. Delora lifted her head to look into his eyes. They were so full of concern as he spoke softly to her that it brought on more tears. At the same time, his look made her tingle inside.

Time seemed to slow down, and she could not help staring at his mouth as he talked to her. She didn't even hear what he said. Without thinking, she leaned over and kissed him on the lips.

An electric shock passed between Delora and Rusty through the touch of their lips and sent shockwaves of feelings tumbling through each of them.

Delora could see her actions took Rusty by surprise. Her bold move had surprised her as well. Instantly feeling embarrassed, Delora quickly hugged Rusty hard around the neck. She felt hot in the face, and she could feel he had stiffened up again. Interpreting that reaction, Delora feared he was upset, that he might push her away, and she was unsure of what to do next and just hung on to him tightly.

Rusty's breath caught in his throat, and it took a moment for the shock of that kiss to dissipate, even as a thrill continued to move through him.

He told himself he had to control this situation but never expected to have to fight his reactions to do it. Taking a deep calming breath, Rusty quietly asked Delora to look at him. Judging by her stranglehold on his neck, he could tell she had shocked herself too. He did not push her away but insisted she look at him.

Delora did as he asked, moving slightly away from his chest far enough to look at him. As she did so, her face grew hot all over again as he stared into her eyes.

His body was talking—not his mind—and the exploding feelings inside him were nearly overwhelming. Blood felt like it was pounding in his ears, his heartbeat raced, and every impulse he had was to take her into his arms and kiss her again.

Clenching his jaw and breathing out slowly, he asked in a confused whisper, "Delora, why did you kiss me?"

"Because I love you," Delora whispered back. She could see doubt in his eyes, and that made her feel a little desperate again. Trying once more to convince him of the truth, her tears began to flow and choked her whispered speech. "I do. I really do love you, and I do not want you to go away. I do not want you to leave me behind."

This lovely woman's first four words sent another stream of fire through his veins as he leaned close to understand the rest of her muffled speech. Rusty gently placed his finger under her chin and lifted it slowly and said softly, "Please look at me." Knowing what he had to say and saying it was the hardest thing he ever had to do, but it had to be done. He said, "Now, listen to me. You do not love me. Delora, I am too old for you."

Hearing Rusty's words made all those lonely feelings begin flooding back into her heart, and she feared they would drown her. In desperation, she argued back, "Yes, I do love you! Don't you love me too?"

Once again, his voice was gentle but insistent and a little sad when he replied softly, "It is not that simple."

She stared at him and felt true fear and did not try to check the flow of her tears when she asked desperately, "Why can't it be simple? Why can't it be true?"

"Because it is not possible, Delora." Rusty ran one hand through his hair in frustration as he searched for the right way to say what had to be said. "We are talking about a commitment that will last for the rest of our lives. This is no place for a schoolhouse infatuation. I'm a grown man, and you're still a schoolgirl. You're too young to know what you want."

Delora instantly and adamantly denied his statement shouting, "No, I am not!"

Confused, Rusty replied, "Not what?"

"I am not a schoolgirl! Not for two whole years! Don't you remember? I told you that my days turned into years with no change. I didn't know what to do! All I ever wanted was for Mama to get better, but she didn't. She's worse, and until you came, I believed that was going to be the sum of my future. My brother Oscar would come by and visit with me from time to time. When I asked him what I should do, he would say, 'I don't know. Papa will figure it out, so cheer up. You won't have to do this forever. You will get married someday and have a home and a life of your own.'

"I wanted to believe him, but I could only stand my thoughts chasing themselves around in circles for so long before I started resenting Papa for expecting me to take over being a mother to my sisters, the housekeeper, and a nursemaid for my mother! Then I started feeling mad at my mother for not getting better!"

Rusty watched fascinated as Delora's face flushed as more and more of her deep feelings about her life poured out. Suddenly, right before his eyes, the frightened girl disappeared, and an angry woman stood in her place.

"After two years of things just getting worse, I felt lonelier than I ever had. Rusty, every evening before I crawled into bed, I prayed. I promised God I would keep helping Mama, take care of my sisters, and to think kindly of my brothers, even though they didn't help me at home. I asked God to forgive me for being mad at my parents at times. I promised to do better. I promised to have faith that God would send me something to hope for and maybe a little happiness too. He did answer my prayers, Rusty! God sent me you!"

Rusty leaned back in disbelief. Delora had actually yelled those words with fire in her eyes. He had expected her to calm down and accept his explanation. But hearing how bewildering and sad she had felt about her life, and her revelation of how she felt about him, made him feel anxious, alarmed, and possessively protective.

Infuriated by his silence, Delora yelled at him again. "I do love you, Rusty!" And then, in a soft voice, she pleaded, "Don't you love me too?"

Perplexed and feeling protective at the same time, he wondered, *How am I to respond to this? What does she want from me? Does she expect an answer?* Rusty continued to sit there feeling completely disconcerted.

Into that silence, Delora desperately raved that she had no friends or anything to look forward to. "You should not tell me I don't know what I want because I do!

For Rusty, Delora truly transformed in that moment. It was a woman delivering this impassioned and desperate speech. Though Delora continued to cry, it was more frustration and anger than a little girl's fear of losing a playmate.

Rusty suddenly felt compelled to calm the woman in front of him. He wanted to comfort her as he'd seen his father do when his mother had gone into a rage over something he'd said or done. Giving into the subconscious and ardent feelings that had been developing in him, he groaned, struck by the realization of what was happening to him. "Lord help me!" Pulling her back against his chest, he admitted to her "I am in love with you too. Now, stop crying. Please!"

Delora stopped crying instantly but not because he asked her to. She did so because he had hugged her to his chest with his strong arms, and she felt warm and safe. When she leaned back to look at him, she could see that he meant what he said. That was when he kissed her. The sensations coursing through her felt marvelous, and she eagerly returned his kiss, which led to more kisses.

Abruptly, he made Delora back away from him. As Rusty held her by the arms, he thought she appeared dazed, almost as dazed as he felt looking at her. He could not let things get any further out of hand. He needed to think about what was happening and consider their situation.

Delora stared at Rusty's red face and clenched jaw. Observing those reactions kept her from resisting being set at arm's length.

"Delora, I need some space between us," he whispered. Rusty worked to calm his breathing, then confessed, "I cannot think when you are so close to me. Please go back to the house." Delora looked frightened and crushed after he ordered her to go inside. He perceived that she thought she had done something wrong and displayed those hurt feelings on her face.

Rusty quickly reassured her, saying, "Do not look at me that way, or I may never let you leave this stable. I will be back in two days. We will talk then. Will that be alright with you?"

The fear in Delora's eyes was instantly replaced with warmth. What she heard was his promise to come back and spend more time with her. Beaming sweetly at him, she nodded, indicating she would do as he asked. "I will not forget. You have promised to come back to me in two days. I will be waiting for you," she said as she danced across the yard, picked up her little sister, then twirled around making the child giggle. She smiled back at Rusty and happily waved before she disappeared through the door of her house.

Amazing Turn of Events

Rusty was caught up in a whirlwind as his blood ran hot then cold alongside Delora's emotions as they ranged from anger to tears, revealing her feelings about what she had been through over the last two years. Then he soared to an unimaginable height with her profession of love for him. This was a revelation that knocked him to his knees. Then it seemed within seconds, he was being transformed by her mesmerizing laughter and playfulness. How could so much emotion be contained by such an itty-bitty woman? He could hardly breathe because he was caught up in a stampede of exciting possibilities rampaging through his mind and heart. Almost desperately, he told himself he needed time to think clearly, to sort out what he had learned.

Rusty put his tools and materials away quickly and left the Holt house. As he drove away in his automobile, he felt like he had just survived a tornado.

When Rusty returned to the Holt's stable two days later, Delora found it much easier to get him to kiss her. She only resorted to crying when he ordered her to go to the house. Confident now that he cared, she made him promise to come back to her before she would do as he requested.

Rusty sat at his shop in a state of confused frustration. Yet, beneath those feelings, he felt a spark of excitement he had never experienced before. He didn't need to go back to the Holts to finish this project. In fact, it would be far easier on many levels if he stayed away and finished the work at his shop. Logic be damned, though; he could not bring himself to stay away. Time was almost up. Next week, he would make his last trip to the Holts' stable. He would not have another opportunity to alter the course of his or Delora's future. It was now or never.

When Rusty arrived at the Holt's, he parked the car on the street and walked around the house to the stables as he had been doing for the past month. Delora had been watching for him and ran out the back door to greet him. Her excitement mirrored the way he felt at seeing her again, and his pulse quickened. She slid her arms around his waist and lay her head on his chest, declaring, "Rusty, I cannot live without you."

When Rusty's arms tightened around her, she looked up into his face for a kiss, and the look he read there jolted him. He only hesitated a moment, then he kissed her. This kiss was very different from the other kisses they had shared.

It jolted Delora in return. They could not stop the emotional storm roaring through their bodies. A physical need pushed them into a state of euphoria so exhilarating and powerful Rusty could not tell her to go back to the house. There would be no stopping what they both wanted—not this time.

A Realization

If he were being honest with himself, Rusty would have recognized that part of the thrill the two of them experienced came from doing something they knew they should not be doing. Yet, none of the logic trying to creep into his mind made a difference, and it was far too late for that kind of observation.

Kisses easily turned into an explosive passion that felt overwhelming. The experience Rusty and Delora shared in each other's arms profoundly changed both of them and filled them with completeness, filling an emptiness inside they didn't know they had.

Later, as Rusty held Delora and smoothed her hair back from her sleeping face, he thought, *I have been falling in love with this little bitty woman, I guess, since that first day she talked to me out here. But, now, I am completely and helplessly under her spell. Rusty,* he thought to himself, *you know your heart is hers now and forever, so what are you going to do about it?* As Rusty lay his cheek on Delora's hair, he said softly as if it were a prayer, "Mama, neither the Bible stories about love that you read to us as children nor the fairy tales about love that Papa read to us prepared me for the love I feel for this wonderful woman. What am I going to do now? I cannot let her go."

Foremost in Rusty's mind was the fact that he had to protect Delora and make this right. He was old enough and wise enough to know their troubles had only begun, yet his heart would not allow him to turn away from the decision floating in his mind. The thought had occurred to him long before this moment, and he knew exactly what had to be done as soon as possible, and now he found the courage to say it out loud.

Gently shaking Delora awake, he said, "My Bitty girl, I am going to ask your father for your hand in marriage."

Delora's eyes flashed open instantly. Her body filled with panic, and she shouted, "No, you cannot!"

Rusty reacted immediately. He shifted to look at her sitting beside him, and with a slightly angry tone, he asked, "Why can't I do the honorable thing by you?" When Delora did not answer him, he stood up in agitation, staring at her while he waited. When she still didn't respond to his question, he became confused and hurt but continued to wait, not knowing what else to do.

Delora did not look at Rusty as she sat silently, thinking, *I already know what my father will say, and it will be no! That is why we have to keep this all a secret! We need to get away first, then get married so my father can't stop us.*

In reaction to Delora's silence, Rusty began to pace. Then, returning to stand in front of Delora, he set his hands around her arms and stood her on her feet. Looking into her eyes, he said, "Answer me! Why can't I go to your father and make this right?" She still was not answering him. Rusty had no idea how to explain his most pressing concern delicately. Living on the farm, he learned that when they introduced a bull in the cow's pasture, it often took only one mating to set a calf growing in their bellies.

He and Delora dared not wait to set things right between them—her reputation and much more could be at risk. Determined, he made another attempt to convince her to let him go to her father, saying, "When I go and talk to Jim, I will insist on a short engagement in the off chance that we—well, that you—might be . . . pregnant."

Into that intense silence, Delora stubbornly replied, "My father will not allow our marriage because of our age difference and because I am the one who takes care of my mother. He will never let me get married!"

"Delora, I believe I can change his mind if I explain why," Rusty replied. Such circumstances were the last thing he wished to explain to his employer, who also happened to be her father. But he saw no other way to convince Jim Holt to let him marry Delora immediately.

Shaking her head at Rusty, Delora said, "I know what we have to do. We need to keep our relationship secret, run away together, and then get married."

Once again, Delora completely shocked Rusty, incredulous she would even suggest such a thing. Even after he told her he was willing to walk through hell to do this right and explain to her father that there was no choice. That alternative was far less appealing than what Delora suggested, and while Delora's suggestion was unorthodox, the excitement the idea caused in him was undeniable.

Making her his wife forever without any opposition made this impulsive decision far easier to make. Only moments passed before he replied in a secretive tone, "You are right, and I agree with you. For now, I have to go, but on Friday, let's discuss our ideas and make a plan."

Delora flew into his arms, hugging him with joyful enthusiasm. "Ok," she whispered.

Ambrose Jerome (Rusty) Karella and Delora Lucy Holt, courting, 1926

CHAPTER 12

Plans

Friday

Delora felt like she was sitting on pins and needles all week while she waited to see Rusty. This would be his final visit to her house. They had to decide today what to do about their future wedding.

Delora watched for him from the top floor window facing the street, and when she saw his automobile, she ran down the stairs and out to the stables to wait for him. The way they greeted one another left no doubts about the way they felt about each other. After several feverish and breathless kisses, Rusty deliberately made Delora back away from him so he could think, and they could talk.

First, they agreed to keep their relationship secret, so they arranged their first clandestine date away from the house for that weekend. Rusty left the final project report for Jim in the study and said, "Delora, I will finish up my business with your father at Madison Downs." Then, just before he left, he promised, "Delora, I'll be waiting for you tomorrow night around the corner, one block from your house—just like we agreed. Meet me at 11:00 p.m."

The Following Day

Delora was a bit jumpy all morning, but no one took notice. After she cleaned up the dinner dishes, she went to her room, claiming she felt tired. Truthfully, she was afraid her building excitement was beginning to show and did not want anyone asking about it.

This would be the first time she had ever done such a thing, and Delora enjoyed the thrill of sneaking out that night even though it was scary. Once she found Rusty waiting for her in the dark, they both enjoyed themselves immensely.

During their date, they discussed plans to continue their clandestine outings and developed a few strategies to avoid discovery. Two and three times per week, Delora carefully readied herself for another date. After putting her mother to bed with her tonic, Delora would wait for her father to say he was going to bed.

Once everyone had gone to their rooms, Delora went to her room and sat as quietly as possible in the dark, waiting for all her siblings to settle down for the night and for silence to reign in the house. She watched the clock as the minutes slowly ticked by.

At 10:45 p.m., she'd sneak quietly down the hall and the stairs, carrying her shoes, then tiptoe through the kitchen. Once she stepped through the back door, she closed it silently and put on her shoes, then dashed away into the darkness.

Four Weeks Later

Their physical relationship had been going on for a little over a month. During that time, Rusty kept pleading with Delora to let him go to her father. He felt desperate about making their relationship an honest one. Delora refused. She was determined to elope, saying, "No, don't you understand? I want to start my new life as soon as possible."

"But, Delora," Rusty would argue, "don't you want to have a nice wedding with all the family around you?" Wistfully, he hoped to change his sweetheart's mind about her radical idea.

Delora acted as though she hadn't heard a word he said. "All we need is to escape from my parents' house with a plan that will give us time to get far enough away to get married without anyone coming after us too soon."

Rusty had never participated in such deviant behavior in his whole life, and it went against his grain to do it now, particularly with such an important outcome depending on the success of such behavior. Somewhere in the night, which seemed ages ago, this fifteen-year-old girl had turned into a formidable woman. Yet, he felt compelled to remind her the law was on her father's side. She was still only fifteen and would need her father's consent to get married until she was eighteen.

Delora corrected Rusty instantly, "I'm almost sixteen!"

"My apologies, Delora. Alright, so you are almost sixteen. That does not change the issue we have," Rusty pointed out.

Delora's frown suddenly turned into a radiant smile, which did not improve Rusty's humor. Trying to change his mind with her pretty smile did not alter the predicament they were in.

As Delora's eyes lit up, she announced, "Rusty, don't you see? *That's it!*"

Baffled with her statement, Rusty asked, "What? What is it?"

"How long have we been seeing each other?" Delora asked.

Bewildered, Rusty thought, *Now, what is that supposed to mean?* Delora's response to his question convinced him he would never understand the workings of a woman's mind. "Do you mean how long have we been intimate? Is that what you mean?" he asked, a little frustrated with the guessing game going on. Then he replied, "Almost a month," uneasy with that truth.

"Rusty, don't you see? My sixteenth birthday is only a week away, and that's what has inspired my great plan! I have a friend who lives a couple of blocks down the street from my house. Her birthday is only one day apart from mine. When we were younger and I still went to school, sometimes we celebrated our birthdays together." She stopped and looked at him as though what she had said explained everything.

Rusty shook his head and replied, "I don't see how this has any bearing on our problem."

Delora rolled her eyes. "What if I go to my father and say that Sally asked if I could come for the weekend to celebrate our birthdays together like we used to?"

Rusty began to nod his head in understanding, thinking, *Now, that might work if Delora pretends to go to Sally's, but instead, we drive to* . . . his mind was working fast while he ran his fingers through his hair trying to think of where they could go. Suddenly, he exclaimed out loud, "Sioux City, Iowa!" Excited, Rusty went on to explain, "Delora, it's only a couple of hours drive from here. We could be there, get married before a justice of the peace, and have at least two days together before anyone started looking for you."

Delora could not be more pleased with her Rusty; the man had caught on to the idea and provided the next pieces of their plan. He knew where to go, how to get there, and who to see so they could get married!

Delora Sets the Plan in Motion

One day before her birthday, Delora initiated the first step in their getaway plan. After settling her mother for her nap in the late afternoon and cleaning up the kitchen, Delora found herself staring at her feet, standing in front of her father's office door. She tried to breathe in the courage she needed. Calming herself, she knocked firmly on the door.

"Come in."

Hearing her father's voice through the wooden door, Delora quickly turned the knob and entered. Standing in front of her father's desk, she asked about spending her birthday weekend over at Sally's.

Always a stickler about a person's responsibilities, her papa asked, "Who will take care of your mother if you are gone?"

Delora wanted to scream at him. Instead, she quietly and sweetly suggested a solution to her temporary absence. "Perhaps Violet could do it. She is fourteen now, the same age I was when I started taking care of Mother *and* Marcella. Now, since it's only Mother, couldn't Violet take care of her as a birthday present to me for just one weekend?"

Her father was quiet so long Delora was afraid he was going to say no. She didn't realize she was holding her breath until her father nodded his consent. Then he said, "Since Marcella started school in September and will not be a distraction, I believe Violet will be capable of taking care of your mother by herself for a few days."

Delora released her breath slowly and replied sweetly, "Thank you, Papa." Turning to leave the study, her father spoke again before she reached the door.

"Delora, when Violet and JW get home, please have them come see me."

"Yes, Papa," she replied demurely and hurried from the room.

Right after Violet, Marcella, and JW walked into the house, Delora sent Marcella to the kitchen, then told her brother and sister to go see their father. Jim Holt expected the knock on his office door and told his children to come in. "Violet, since it is your sister's birthday and she will be away this weekend, you will stay home from school tomorrow and take care of your mother. JW, you will see to it that Marcella gets to her classroom tomorrow. Please be sure she gets home safely too." JW nodded in agreement.

"Now, Violet, Delora will instruct you on what you need to do to take care of your mother. If you have any concerns, I will work at home tomorrow, too, and you can come to me for help if you need it."

Violet replied, "Yes, Papa."

The Next Step

Now that Delora had her father's permission to be away from home, the first step of her getaway plan was in motion. Still, she had to be very careful not to give herself away by her actions. With that in mind, she decided she could only take a small valise filled with a few of her favorite things to keep from looking suspicious. Delora carefully chose what she wanted to take with her and packed her little suitcase before going to bed.

When Delora opened her eyes in the morning, she felt wonderfully excited and not a bit scared, thinking, *Today is going to be the best birthday of my life.* She dressed carefully and took time with her hair. Pleased with what she saw in her looking glass, she went to wake Violet. After going over all her sister needed to know about her mother's food and medicines, Delora took her small suitcase downstairs and left it by the front door.

Delora deliberately waited until 10:00 a.m. when her father was usually occupied reviewing racing statistics for his breeding studs and mares. It would be a perfect time to say goodbye to him and set the second step of her plan into place.

Jim Holt sat at his desk piled with notebooks. He looked up from them when Delora entered and said, "Papa, I've come to say I'm leaving."

Her father beckoned for Delora to come to him. She walked up to his chair, and he stood to give her a brief hug and kissed her forehead, saying, "Happy birthday, Delora. Do have fun with your friend Sally. Please convey our family's best wishes for her birthday too."

"Yes, Papa," Delora replied, then reminded her father that Sally lived close enough for her to walk by herself.

Jim sat down behind his desk again and nodded, pleased he did not have to interrupt the work he was doing to take Delora over to Sally's. "Have fun, Delora," he said as he turned his attention back to his notebooks and stacks of papers.

"Yes, Papa," she whispered, turning away from him. A secret smile spread across her face as she left his study. Without hesitating, Delora picked up her little suitcase in the hall and walked out of the house. It was the last time she walked through that door as a Holt.

An Unforgettable Birthday

Exhilaration coursed through Delora's veins, and she had to force herself not to run. "Stick to the plan and don't draw attention," she whispered encouragingly to herself.

Rusty had agreed to wait for her two blocks away, right out of sight of Sally's house. By doing so, if anyone who knew her family saw her walking on Friday morning, they would report having seen her walking in the direction she should have been going to reach Sally's place.

Making the turn onto Sally's street, she immediately saw Rusty's auto parked in the shade and him standing beside it. Delora hurried over, and he took her suitcase, dropped it in the trunk, then opened the passenger door so she could get in. On Delora's seat lay a rose and a box of candy.

As Rusty slid in behind the steering wheel, he turned to smile at her, saying, "Happy Birthday, Bitty!"

Overjoyed, she smelled the rose for a minute, then set it aside to open the box of candy. *This is the best birthday I've ever had,* she thought. *I'm sixteen, truly free, and I'm on my way to get married!*

Stuffing the first luscious piece of chocolate in her mouth, she offered the second piece to Rusty. He popped the chocolate into his mouth, enjoying the rich flavor as he drove the car. Licking the melted chocolate off her fingertips, she giggled and said, "Thank you for the rose and the chocolates."

He nodded and smiled in response. Now that it was actually happening, Rusty wondered if Delora might be a little afraid of what they were doing. "Do you still want to do this, Bitty?" Rusty asked softly before he started the engine.

Delora, bubbling with happiness, smiled brightly and replied, "I certainly do, Rusty! Let's get going before someone sees us!"

Though Rusty had been afraid Delora might change her mind when the reality of what they were doing hit her, the opposite was true. Relieved to hear she still wanted to go through with their plan, he drove casually away from the Holt's neighborhood. He handed Delora a road map and said, "Bitty, find Sioux City. It's near the border of Nebraska and Iowa on this map. Ok?"

Delora grinned and took the map. She had no intention of changing her mind and began to search the print for their destination as they drove out of Madison. Her Rusty was a man of the world at

28 and had promised to take care of her and keep her safe. Thrilled over their grand adventure, Delora periodically let out giggles of excitement. She had complete confidence in Rusty and absolute faith he could do what he promised.

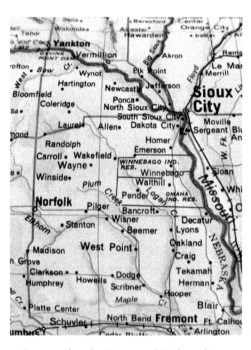

Route taken by Rusty and Delora from Madison to Sioux City, Iowa, to get married

Delora remembered all during the month before her birthday, Rusty kept reminding her that it bothered him, the sneaking around they were doing behind her parents backs. He said, "It feels wrong and disloyal. Not to mention, it is a deceitful way to treat my future father-in-law whom I respect." But now that they were headed for Sioux City, she could feel that Rusty had calmed down and felt in control of their situation again. He had given her what she wanted. Therefore, his stern expression didn't dampen Delora's happiness, and she grinned as she ate another piece of chocolate.

With a serious look on his face, Rusty broke the silence, saying, "Delora, we need to review our plan for when we reach Sioux City. Let's say we have two nights and three days before anyone starts looking for you or asking questions. The drive into the city will take us about two hours. I have done quite a bit of work in Sioux City and know a lot of people there. I don't want to run the risk of anyone recognizing me before we are married, so I have made arrangements with a justice of the peace to marry us this afternoon right after we get into town. I picked a hotel close to the judge's office, and that will make it easy for us to stay out of sight."

Delora vaguely paid attention to what Rusty was saying, happy to leave all the rest of the arrangements to him. The only part of their plan she had been concerned about was leaving Madison. But now as they drove, Rusty insisted Delora practice what she was to say when they went before the justice of the peace.

"Bitty, you will have to lie, and I regret that. But it cannot be helped, as you are not legally old enough to get married without parental consent."

Delora nodded only half-listening as she watched the landscape whiz by. Eventually, Rusty became a little cross. "Bitty, are you listening? This is important!" he said with more frustration than he intended to use. Modulating his tone, he went on to say, "Please pay attention to what I'm telling you. When the judge asks for your date of birth, you must remember to say you were born October 29, 1908."

Delora grinned and looked at him with her brilliant blue eyes, and he lost his train of thought. Then she brought him back to the moment when she replied sweetly, "Yes, of course, Rusty. I can do that. Being born in 1908 makes me eighteen instead of sixteen."

Relieved, Rusty nodded at her encouragingly and said, "Yes, Bitty girl, that's exactly right! You will be wonderful. You will do just fine. I know it."

Pleased with his praise, she snuggled close to Rusty's side, watching the road in comfortable silence, then fell asleep. Delora woke as Rusty parked by the hotel where he had made a reservation for two nights. Getting out, he walked around the auto and opened her door. After getting out of the auto, she brushed the wrinkles from her dress. Then, holding on to Rusty's arm, she let Rusty guide her quickly down the block to the justice's office.

They were expected and greeted at the door, "Mr. Karella, Miss Holt?" asked the woman in a suit sitting at a desk. Rusty nodded, and she responded, "Welcome. I am the justice's clerk. Please have a seat." They spent ten minutes filling out the document, which the two of them would sign as husband and wife. As they finished, another couple walked in and took a seat in the lobby, waiting for their turn.

Delora had been steady as a stone throughout their whole adventurous relationship up to this point. She hadn't made one bobble with her mother or father or around her sisters and older brothers. But as they walked into the justice's private office, Delora finally began to feel a little nervous.

In her mind, she recited her answers flawlessly in preparation for the wedding ceremony. Yet, when the time came to answer the question about her birthdate, she stuttered so badly over the information it was a miracle no one got suspicious.

Luckily, everyone in the judge's office chuckled kindly and congratulated her, saying, "Oh, how sweet. She has got the nervous jitters because she is so excited about getting married!"

Fortunately for the newlyweds, the judge nor his clerk who acted as witness caught on. After a round of congratulations were said, the court clerk asked the newly married couple to follow her and had them sign the document that would be registered with the state of Iowa on November 2, 1929.

The clerk told Rusty and Delora they would get the official stamped, state document in the mail from the recorder's office. Rusty was given a receipt on October 29th for the recording fee, stating his official marriage certificate would arrive within a week.

After politely accepting their congratulations, Mr. and Mrs. Ambrose Jerome Karella left the justice's office. Walking arm in arm, they strolled back to the hotel. Bitty stood on her tiptoes to watch Rusty sign the hotel register—Mr. and Mrs. Ambrose Jerome Karella.

When they asked about food, the hotel manager directed them to the restaurant next to the hotel. He smiled as he watched the young couple walk into the street holding hands. The newly married Karellas spent their wedding night, Friday, October 29, 1926, and the following night at this same hotel.

Come Sunday morning, Rusty felt edgy. Now that he was legally Delora's husband, he did not wish to worry Delora's father any more than necessary. Nor did he want to stay away so long that his new father-in-law mounted a search for his daughter. Over breakfast, Rusty explained, "The two nights we've spent together here registered as husband and wife with the desk clerk as a witness will be sufficient to prove our marriage has been consummated. We also have the file receipt for our marriage certificate, so there will be no grounds for an annulment. With those protections in place, we must return to Madison today."

As Rusty and Delora drove back to Madison, he thought about what needed to be done. There would be no time to waste about delivering proof of their legal marriage. Rusty wanted Delora's father to understand all the ramifications quickly. By doing so, Jim would not try to petition for an annulment on the grounds that his daughter lied about her age.

During the trip back to Madison, the enormity of what she and Rusty had done began to sink in, and Delora began to experience a little honest fear over it. Rusty was glad she was beginning to understand the magnitude of their choices and what they would face at home. Yet, upon seeing her fear, Rusty immediately reassured her, "Don't you worry about a thing, little Bitty. I'll take care of you just as I'll take care of everything else." After that, Delora relaxed until Rusty pulled the car up in front of a house she did not recognize.

To protect his new wife, Rusty took Delora over to his sister's house. Martha Pojar answered the door and said, "Rusty, how good to see you!" Her eyes traveled immediately to the lovely young girl holding on to her brother's arm. Without preamble, Rusty

1926, newly married Delora Lucy Holt Karella heading back to Madison, Nebraska, with husband, Rusty Karella

217

introduced his wife. "Delora, this is Martha Pojar, my sister. Martha, this is my wife, Delora. May we come in?"

Stunned by her brother's news, Martha stood frozen in place in momentary silence. Coming to her senses, she replied, "Oh, my goodness! Yes! Yes, please come in. I'm sorry for keeping you standing on the stoop."

Once they were seated in the living room, Martha wanted to pepper her brother with questions and intended to. That was until she noticed Rusty's very-young wife looked a little frightened. Deciding her questions could wait, she immediately smiled at Delora and hugged her warmly. "Welcome to the family, Delora. Would you like a cup of tea or coffee? Maybe something to eat?" Martha's kindness melted Delora's budding fear immediately.

Rusty could see his Bitty relaxing with his sister, which allowed him to relax for a moment as well. Extremely happy Martha refrained from asking hundreds of questions that surely were whizzing around in her head, he asked to use her telephone.

Before leaving the room to make his call, he asked, "Would it be alright for Delora to stay here with you for a while? I must go and see Papa. Then he and I must go and see Delora's father."

Once again, Martha refrained from asking questions and replied, "Of course, I'd be happy to have my new sister visit for as long a time as you need. Would you like that, Delora?" In answer to her question, Rusty's wife nodded sweetly.

Relieved knowing he could leave his wife in his sister's care, he knew it would be one less worry to deal with while he faced his father and then hers. "Bitty, I should be back for supper." Then, looking at Martha, he went on to say, "That is if it's alright with you and Rudy. Are we invited?"

"You surely are," Martha replied. Then she added, "You know you did not need to ask."

"Thank you, Martha," he replied. Then Rusty turned to Bitty, saying, "I'll be back as soon as I can."

Delora had never thought of herself as a timid person scared of her own shadow. But she had to admit the relief she felt not having to confront her father at this moment lifted a great weight of fear from her shoulders. Delora found herself so relaxed with Martha that before she realized it, she was talking about private matters only she and Rusty had talked about on the way back to Madison.

"Martha, Rusty warned me he planned to address this issue of our marriage as soon as we got back. He's got many good reasons to face down our parents today. First, there is his business in town and his reputation we need to protect. Secondly, we also want to live in Madison and raise our children around both of our families."

"I should think so!" Martha replied. It pleased her to hear some of what was going on. "Bitty, I hope you realize my brother is trying to protect your reputation too. He has always been an honest man, and he wants to win the acceptance of both our family and yours. Oh, do you mind me calling you Bitty? I heard Rusty called you Delora first. What do you want me to call you?"

"Bitty is the nickname Rusty gave me. He used to say I was a little bitty thing when we first met, and I guess it just stuck. You can call me Bitty; I don't mind."

"Alright, Bitty it is. Now, you keep talking, and I'll start preparing dinner while I listen. How would that be?"

"That would be wonderful," Delora replied sweetly, then began to talk again about her and Rusty's ideas for living in Madison. "Rusty said that by going immediately to my father, he hoped to neutralize at least some of the hostility he expects. My husband is proud to have me for his wife and wants to make both our families proud of our union too. But first, we must undo some of the hurt we caused by sneaking off."

There it is, thought Martha, though she did not interrupt in hopes Delora would keep talking. *That's why I knew nothing about her.* When Bitty stopped talking, Martha said, "Sneaking off, you say?" She let the words hang in the air like a question without asking one directly.

Delora smiled, thinking about the past weekend, and looking at Martha, she replied, "I suppose it would not hurt to tell you a little about us."

Anton Karella's Home

Rusty arrived at his father's home within minutes of leaving Martha's place and went to find his papa. Feeling like an errant schoolboy, Rusty gave his father Anton the short version of falling in love with his employer's daughter and eloping with her. Then he asked, "Papa, will you accompany me and act as mediator with Mr. Holt, my new father-in-law?"

"Mediator?" replied Anton, raising his brow. Rusty only nodded gravely in response.

His father nodded, indicating he would do as requested but said very little. *What could he say? What is done is done*, he thought. "Son, I know my parent's dreams were not my dreams. I know the dreams I had for my life are not your dreams. But will this marriage make you happy? Is this part of your dream? How long have you known this girl?" Anton asked bluntly.

"Papa, it does not matter how long we have known each other. We have spent many hours day after day getting to know one another for almost two months. I know that does not sound like very long to you. But I love her, Papa, and she loves me. I did not know how empty that part of my life was until Delora filled it. She is part of my life's dream now and the family we are going to have together."

Anton heard Rusty's message loud and clear. "So, you believe your wife could already be pregnant?" Anton asked in a direct no-nonsense manner.

Rusty looked embarrassed for a moment but nodded yes. "Papa, I refuse to be ashamed of me or my wife in this situation, especially now that we are married. I admit I would have preferred to be married before I knew that a baby might have been conceived, but our love was honest and took us both by surprise. Papa, I cannot imagine my life without her now."

"Then we had best go and see your father-in-law and make the situation clear," Anton replied.

"Thank you, Papa," Rusty whispered wholeheartedly.

The Holt Home

It was Sunday evening, October 31ˢᵗ, and Jim had expected Delora to be home after lunch. Mr. Holt always got into a bit of an agitation when things did not run smoothly in his household.

Violet had been complaining about her mother. His wife had been complaining about Violet. Little Marcella was crying and asking where Delora was. His two sons had run off with their friends, leaving their poor papa to deal with all of the disruption and chaos by himself.

When Jim heard the knock on the door, he thought, *Finally! There she is! Delora probably brought her friend home as a buffer, knowing I am not going to be happy with her tardiness.* Jim answered the door, looking confused and thinking, *What on earth is Rusty doing here, and who is the man with him standing on my porch, unannounced and unexpected?*

Red faced, Rusty stood silently on the porch and let his father do the talking. "Excuse me, please. James Holt, I'm Anton Karella, Rusty's father. May we come in? We have information about your daughter and my son that we need to discuss."

Jim's eyes narrowed as he stood taking in what had just been said. He did not like the sound of it, and with a clenched jaw, he nodded curtly and indicated the two men should follow him.

Sitting in Mr. Holt's office between his father and Delora's father was the most intimidating hour Rusty ever lived through in his life. The bones of the facts were laid out when Rusty said he had fallen in love with Delora and she with him, then he explained how the rest had happened.

Rusty ended his explanation by sliding the receipt for their certificate of marriage across the desk. Mr. Holt glanced at the document, then turned his steely gaze back on Rusty. "Our official wedding certificate is coming from the registrar's office on November 2nd through the mail," Rusty finished quietly.

Wisely, Rusty left out *how* this falling in love happened, and Mr. Holt stuck to the questions he *needed* to know, such as what kind of a husband and provider he would be to his daughter and what kind of father he would be to Holt's grandchildren. During that hour in the Holt study, it was made clear that Rusty believed Delora was pregnant. He assured Mr. Holt that he and Delora would live in Madison. And yes, Rusty would let his wife come and visit with her father.

After everyone had said their piece, Mr. Holt asked if Rusty had anything to say about his behavior.

Rusty responded by saying, "Sir, our relationship took us both by surprise. I honestly did fall in love with her as she did with me. We married to prove my intentions were honorable toward your daughter. We both love our families. We want to live here in Madison and raise our children here and share our lives with our families."

The expression on Mr. Holt's face as he listened to Rusty was cold and stony and remained so when he said, "Honorable? Is that what you call what you've done?" The rest of the conversation was directed at Mr. Anton Karella.

When the Karella men left Holt's house, Rusty carried a sealed envelope containing a letter from her father to Delora. Rusty also had the man's word that he would forgive his daughter for being led astray by an older man who should have known better. At the same time, it was made clear that in James Holt's eyes, Rusty would remain the man who had betrayed his trust and stolen his daughter.

A Father's Compassion

On the drive back to Anton's house, Rusty stayed very quiet. Anton broke the silence first, saying, "Son, you've taken an important step toward digging yourself out of the hole you dug."

Rusty looked at him and said, "Papa, I told you I had no choice!"

"Son, please do not misunderstand what I am saying. Right or wrong, your choice is made, and I am not judging you. It is obvious you have a lot of work ahead of you to set everything right with the family. But, son, I am proud of the honorable man that you are.

"I will admit this whole situation came as quite a shock." Grinning at Rusty to take the sting out of what he just said, he added, "I am not unhappy with you. You found what you wanted. You fought for what you wanted by seizing the only option you thought you had. Now, you must mend your family ties."

Rusty nodded but did not say anything.

"Rusty, I would like you and your wife to come live with me, Helen, and the children, at least until you two are ready to have your own place. It is an honored Karella family tradition, and it would make me very happy to have a chance to get to know my daughter-in-law."

More relieved and grateful than he knew how to express, Rusty quietly accepted his father's gracious offer, saying, "Papa, thank you for coming with me to see Jim and for not judging me. I humbly accept your offer. Delora and I will come live with you, and I know you are going to love my Delora."

As Rusty finished talking, they pulled up in front of Anton's home. "Papa, I will go pick up Delora from Martha's house, and then we will be back. I can't wait to introduce you to my lovely wife."

Anton waved as Rusty drove away and headed into the house. Helen was waiting for him, and as soon as he was through the door, she asked, "Papa, tell me! What has happened?"

"Helen, your brother proved you wrong. Rusty had no problem finding a girl all by himself. Sit down. I have a lot to tell you, and I'd rather you hear it from me than from Martha. She only has part of the story, which I am sure she has been able to wheedle out of Rusty's unsuspecting wife." The conversation between father and daughter went on until they heard Rusty's car pull into the driveway.

Rusty set down Delora's little suitcase and introduced his wife. "Delora, this is my father, Anton, and this is my eldest sister, Helen."

Delora instantly took hold of Helen's hands, saying, "Helen, I am so sorry. Rusty told me about the tragic loss of your husband. I am glad to have you for my sister."

The sincerity of Delora's words moved Helen, and she hugged Delora, saying, "Welcome, Delora. I am very happy we will be living together, at least for a while."

Then Delora looked up into Anton's eyes. "May I call you Papa?" she asked softly.

Anton smiled and replied just as softly, "I would be honored to have you call me Papa. Welcome to my home that is now your home too. It will be wonderful to have my son and his lovely wife living here with us, and we want you to be happy about that too."

"I am, Papa—I mean, *we* are," she replied as she took hold of Rusty's hand.

"Have you eaten yet?" Helen asked.

"Yes, at Martha's," Rusty replied.

"Then I think it is time to get you two settled. Just follow me," said Helen. "By the way, I should tell you that the news about you two travels fast. The telephone has been ringing constantly. Apparently, most of the husbands and wives in the family are coming over for dinner this coming Friday night. Everyone is excited to welcome you to the family, Delora." Rusty smiled seeing Delora so relaxed with his big sister. His Bitty girl was going to fit in just fine with the Karellas.

End of November 1926

While they sat in the automobile outside the Holt house, Delora looked at her husband and said softly, "It has been a month, Rusty. I need to talk to him—alone.

"In Papa's letter, he asked. Please. Papa requested a private talk with me. He did not demand or order me to come to him. I am ready to see him now. I feel safe because I know you will be waiting for me."

"Bitty, it goes against my nature to let you go into a situation alone where you will feel vulnerable."

"Oh, Rusty, I'm not in danger of being vulnerable anymore. You made me safe when you married me. You protected me when we first returned to Madison. You did not make me face my father then. This is different. I am Mrs. Rusty Karella now, and I need this visit with my father—for us, our baby, and the whole family. I miss my brothers and sisters, too, and this estrangement has cut me off from all of them."

Nodding his head in acceptance, Rusty leaned over, kissed her, and said, "Call me at Martha's when you are ready for me to pick you up."

"Yes, I will. I love you, Rusty, and thank you for understanding," she replied as she got out of the auto and stood on the curb.

Delora sat in her father's study on the sofa she had always loved as a child. As she looked around the room, Delora remembered the good times she had shared here with her father. Those days had been filled with love. The same love that she could now see in his eyes, just as she also detected pain. Delora took pity on her father and made the first move by saying, "Papa, I am sorry I caused these hurt feelings between us. But I need you to know this was my choice. I love Rusty, and he loves me."

Jim dropped his head to his chest and closed his eyes against the tears he felt as he listened while his daughter spoke to the heart of the issue. Hearing her voice again in his study and seeing her sitting on that sofa brought back so many memories—good memories—and the emptiness when she was gone. Taking a deep breath, he replied, "My daughter, I am the one who is sorry. Delora, I am sorry you felt you needed to run away with a stranger."

Delora held up her hand and said, "Papa, that is not what happened."

"But, Delora, you knew him less than two months! How can you say he was not a stranger?"

"Because we talked more in those two months than you and I had in two years. We talked about what mattered to me. He cared about what was happening to me. He felt he was protecting me."

Jim flushed as he heard the words "protecting me," and the flush turned a shade darker with his angry thoughts. *Just who did he think he was protecting her from? Her family, the ones who loved her? It was my job to protect my daughter, not his! That man wormed his way into my confidence and stole my child.*

Prudently, Jim did not share those thoughts. What he said to Delora was, "You could have told me how you felt. We would have had a big family wedding, and I could have given you to him as a father has a right to do."

Delora shook her head at her father, "No, Papa, that would not have happened. You might think it would have now, but I knew it would not happen—not then.

"I also want you to know that eloping was my idea all along. Rusty wanted to come to you properly and ask you for my hand. He wanted to do the honorable thing right from the beginning, and he continued to ask me to change my mind right up until we ran away on my birthday.

"I was the one. I told him you would say no because that is what I was afraid you would say. Once you were aware of what we wanted to do, you would do everything you could to stop us. I wanted to go, Papa. I needed to go. I decided not to give you a chance to stop us, and I did not give Rusty a choice about it either."

"He is the man. He should have known better," grumbled Jim, not ready to let Rusty off the hook for his actions so easily.

"Papa, if you persist, I will have to leave. I will not let you say anything bad about my husband or his actions that were nothing but good! Rusty has wanted this reconciliation from the beginning, and now I hope you will allow a healing to begin between my new family and my old family. Can you do that for me, Papa?" Delora pleaded softly. "I want Rusty's and my baby to have a Grandpa Holt and a Grandpa Karella. I don't want our child to choose between the two of you. I want to introduce my new family to my old family at celebrations and gatherings, and I want to laugh with my brothers and sisters again."

Jim nodded silently, then said, "For you, I will try." Delora decided that was a good start and figured it was time to talk about other family matters. "Papa, how is Mama?"

During the next several hours, father and daughter cried, asked forgiveness, and received the blessings of being reunited in love. With a warm embrace, they said goodbye to each other as Rusty pulled up to the curb outside, and Delora promised to come and see her father again soon.

Family Gatherings

Since the Holts were not Catholic and the Karellas were, the families did not see each other at church on Sundays. However, as the holidays approached, the Karellas invited the Holts to an advent party at the homestead and a family dinner at Anton's home in Madison.

At those functions, Mr. Holt greeted his daughter with warm hugs and a kiss on the forehead whenever they saw each other and took time for long visits. Holt also talked at length with Anton, clearing the air between them so they could become friends.

Unfortunately, Mr. Holt remained frosty toward Rusty. Under the circumstances, all his father-in-law could do to show his displeasure for past sins was to act cold toward Rusty whenever they met.

Holiday Season 1926

A week before Christmas, Delora began to get very emotional about how her papa was treating her husband. Even though she barely showed her condition, Delora would cry easily, and it made Rusty worry for his wife and the baby. Rusty suspected the emotions were brought on by two reasons. He went over to Martha's home to talk to her about it.

A Sister's Advice

"Rusty, I'm glad to see you. You sounded upset on the telephone. How can I help?"

He explained how emotional Delora was getting and that he was worried about it and was not sure what to do to fix it.

"Rusty, I need to ask: was Delora close to her mother and father?"

"Delora has told me several stories. But from what I can tell, she was close to her mother prior to 1922 before her mother got sick. However, she adored her father when she was young and spent a great deal of time with him growing up."

"Alright, good to know," Martha said. "First, you need to understand that women get super sensitive when they are pregnant! Second,

I think part of Delora's problem is that she misses her father as well as her siblings. To complicate matters, at the same time, she feels protective of her husband too. In my opinion, Delora feels caught in the middle, and that is adding to the stressfulness of being pregnant. "So, brother, what are you going to do about this?" Martha asked.

"I don't know. That is why I'm here asking what you think I should do. All I know is that I want Delora to be happy, and I don't want her to feel she has to choose between her father and me. Do you have any words of wisdom or any ideas about what I should do to fix this situation?" he asked hopefully.

"Since you asked me, I think you should take her to see him together, then ask for your father-in-law's blessing," Martha recommended.

Rusty looked shocked at first until he realized she was right about James Holt loving his daughter. He would never refuse to bless his child. If, as husband and wife, they managed to mend this wound and heal the hurt between the Holts and the Karellas, they could finally be a happy family. When Rusty returned home all he said was he wanted Delora to take a drive with him. She had no idea what he planned to do.

Rusty Puts His Faith, Love, and Hope into Actions

Delora felt apprehensive standing beside Rusty as he knocked on the door. Violet answered it, and instantly, she threw herself at Delora, hugging her and saying, "Oh, Delora, I'm happy to see you." Stepping back and inviting them into the house, Violet looked at Rusty, smiling, then whispered a little nervously, "Papa's in his study."

Rusty had not warned his father-in-law they were coming. When they entered the study without knocking or announcing themselves, they took Jim totally by surprise. Rusty hurried to say, "Please do not get up, Jim. We would like to sit and talk with you for a moment." After making sure Delora was comfortably seated, Rusty turned back to her father, saying, "Father Holt, we are here to ask for your blessing."

James Holt looked as astonished at Rusty's words as Delora did. But at least her papa was listening. "We," Rusty said as he took hold of Delora's hand and then continued, "realize it is late to be asking this."

James Holt huffed at that understatement but did not interrupt.

Rusty kept talking, hoping Papa Holt would continue to listen and believe what he was saying. "Please, sir, we are all family now. I love your daughter, and she loves both you and me. I don't want any bad feelings to come between us. I am proud to have a Holt daughter for my wife and proud to be your son-in-law. I would like you to accept me. Delora and I will be even more proud when we make you a grandfather."

Delora could see that her papa melted on the spot. Rusty had laid his heart on the table, and her father felt the honesty and respect in his request. Looking at Delora and then at Rusty, he said, "From this day forward, I will call you *son*, and I ask that you call me *Dad*."

Delora's eyes filled with happy tears, and she replied, "Thank you, Papa. We love you very much!"

A Telephone Call Sets Curiosity in Motion

Frank called from Norfolk to Madison to wish Rudy and Martha Pojar Merry Christmas. He talked to his brother-in-law first, extending his and his wife's best wishes. The shock came when his sister Martha got on the telephone. "Oh, Frankie, I suppose you heard the news," Martha said excitedly.

"What news?" Frank replied.

Martha couldn't help herself. She didn't think she was betraying a confidence since everyone would know soon anyway. "Rusty and Delora just found out they are going to have a baby!"

"What? Rusty and who?" Frank grumped. "Martha, I am in no mood for jokes right now."

Suddenly, Martha thought, *Frank must not be keeping up on Madison news. Apparently, no one thought to tell him about Rusty, so he doesn't know anything about our brother getting married.* The telephone line remained silent while Martha went on thinking about what she should say.

Helen Craven Karella, Madison, Nebraska, Frank Karella, Madison, Nebraska, Karella homestead picnic

"Are you still there, Martha?" Frank barked into the telephone.

"Yes, brother, I am. Listen, all I'm going to say is that Rusty got married to a girl named Delora Holt about two months ago. She just told me they are going to have a baby. That is all I am going to say. The rest of the story you'll have to get from Rusty."

Frank sputtered in disbelief. He was having a hard time taking in what his sister had just told him about Rusty getting married *and* having a baby. And on top of that, Martha had just hung up on him! Frank immediately decided to make a few more telephone calls and find out what the heck was going on.

Mr. & Mrs. Ambrose Jerome Karella Look Forward to the Holidays

Delora could not have been happier with her husband and father. She felt so relieved to know there would be no more tension between her family members. This Christmas would now be filled with real excitement and joy.

Snuggled together one evening, Delora said, "I am so proud of you, Rusty. Thank you for thinking about Papa's feelings and helping him make peace. I love both of you so much. It has been wonderful since we visited Papa. I am excited that we will spend Christmas Eve with him.

"I am also looking forward to Christmas Day here with your papa, Helen, and the children. Rusty, I loved going Christmas present shopping and helping Helen pick out something special for each of the youngsters, and do you know what else I've been thinking?"

Chuckling, he asked, "What have you been thinking, wife?"

"That I can't wait until next Christmas," Delora replied with tinkling laughter. She knew just how to bait Rusty and hoped he'd fall into her trap.

"Why next Christmas and not this one?" Rusty asked with a grin.

"Because our baby will not be born until July, and I'll have to wait six whole months before I can buy our baby Christmas presents!"

Her sweet way of thinking made him laugh. Delora was good at teasing him and knew how to make him stop being too serious. He was just happy that the anxiety between the Karellas and Holts had been resolved. He could ask for no better Christmas gift, except being able to keep his wife and have a healthy child. Hugging his happy wife and kissing the top of her head, he said, "My sweet Bitty, I am delighted that you are finding joy in Christmas now, and when our baby comes, we will have even more cause to celebrate all over again."

"Yes, we will," mumbled Delora as she let out a huge yawn. "I'm very tired . . . need to sleep." Delora went silent, and Rusty shifted her to a more comfortable position on his shoulder.

He thought, *These days, Delora can fall asleep faster than she can finish a sentence.* Then he fell asleep too.

Holt family left to right, standing: James, Oscar, Delora Lucy, and Violet; sitting: father James (Jim) Holt, daughter Marcella, mother Margaret Kilgore Holt

CHAPTER 13

Life-Changing Events

March of 1927

Rusty found it hard to find enough time in the day for everything he wanted to do or had to do. Five months had gone by in a blur since he and Delora got married. They hardly spent any time with the family, outside of his Papa, Helen, and her children.

Though they still lived with his father, his business picked up enough that he felt they could afford to move into their own home. That was why he told Delora about the sign for rent he saw in the window of Helen's old place, which was just down the street. Rusty planned to talk to his father about it after dinner. His papa knew the owners of the property and would have no problem finding out how much they wanted for rent.

A Month Later

Helen had just gotten off the phone with her sisters, Martha and Mary. Everyone was excited about Rusty and Delora having a housewarming party. Helen couldn't be happier about the newlyweds moving into her old house down the street. That made planning for what Delora might need easy since she knew the house so well.

May of 1927

Rusty and Delora enjoyed the quiet in the house. The painting and renovations Rusty did, based on what Delora wanted, made the house feel like it had always been theirs. Delora found it thrilling to manage her own home, and with their first child due in two months, she felt very content as a married woman.

Family Matters

Delora puttered around her kitchen working on a pie recipe as she listened to her husband reading a letter out loud from his brother Anastas. She pursed her lips as she cut the edges off the dough hanging over her pie tin. What was left inside the tin would become a flaky golden-brown crust after she baked it.

However, she was not pursing her lips in annoyance because of her pie. It was the contents of the letter her husband was reading that irritated her, and she said, "Honestly, Rusty, I find it difficult to believe even half of the stuff he writes."

Wanting to humor his pregnant wife but also feeling he should defend his brother, Rusty patiently replied, "I know you feel that way now. You don't know him yet. But in time, you will see he is a remarkable person and one that does not lie."

Thinking about her own past, Delora blushed a little. She knew she was capable of telling a lie when necessary and found it difficult Anastas would not do the same thing. She said, "Oh come on, not even a little white lie to achieve something wonderful?"

Rusty laughed at what his wife said, instantly thinking of their get-a-way plan that allowed them to get married. He walked over to hug his wife and replied, "I was not making a comment about us. I was merely trying to make a point about my brother. I don't regret the white lies we told because it got me the most wonderful wife in the world," he said as he kissed her sweet nose.

"All I meant is that Anastas did not lie when he was growing up. In my experience, rather than lie, Anastas always chose not to say anything. Please wait to meet him before you judge him.

"He disappeared before I met you and your father. Anastas is a year younger than you and was only fourteen when he went missing. I can still recall how worried we were. The family discovered that he ran away to join the Army, but when we didn't get any news of him, we believed Anastas was dead. I cannot express how overjoyed we were to discover he wasn't. But that didn't happen until he wrote to us after reaching Europe. The whole family was so relieved that he was alive we realized it did no good to be angry. Anastas made his choice, and the family learned to be patient and wait for his letters. Thankfully, news has come often while he has been posted in Europe.

"That will change once his regiment is deployed to the battlefield in Morocco. After that, there is no telling when we will hear from him again. We can only pray he comes home from the Legion. When he does, I hope he will tell us his story. I would really like to hear the whole of it from him."

That evening after Delora had fallen asleep, Rusty thought, *I can now sympathize with Anastas. He felt relentlessly drawn toward something he wanted with all his heart despite the dangers.*

In a way, my own recent hair-raising adventures with Delora are proof enough for me. What the heart wants is not always easy. Desires of the heart can overcome many obstacles. Meeting and marrying Delora is nothing in comparison to the crazy adventure my brother is on. Yet, those scary and thrilling feelings I felt during my adventures with Delora were just as intoxicating for me as Anastas's are for him. I know I wouldn't turn back now even if I could. How exhilarating it must be for my baby brother, Rusty thought, *to achieve his dreams of seeing the world and how incredible to live those adventures as part of the French Foreign Legion!*

Rusty discovered a new kind of gratification when confiding in his brother through their letters. He even told Anastas about his Holt family misadventures right up to the story of how he and Delora ran away to get married. Rusty closed his last letter to his youngest brother with the announcement that he and Delora were expecting a baby.

Rusty looked for a specific letter he had saved from Anastas. Finding the right envelope in the stack of letters, he opened it.

Searching the flowing script, Rusty found the part he loved most and wanted to reread.

"Brother, I am impressed; it was amazingly brave of you to leap into an unknown future as you did. I'm proud of you and think that maybe you and I are a lot more alike than I used to think. I am so happy that it all worked out so well for you and Delora. I am excited and truly looking forward to you making me an uncle!"

After he finished reading and before Rusty fell asleep, he reflected on the fact that he and Anastas had always had a close bond as brothers. Now, it was a true pleasure developing a friendship with him as grown men.

Dear Ambrose,   *Morocco, 1927*

By the time I can mail this letter, I will be at my new post. I can hardly believe it. I will be in Morocco tomorrow. Since I exceeded the expectations of my sergeant as the troop cook, he has recommended me for my own mess tent. I will work directly for the senior sergeant.

I needed to experience the world. Being part of the Legion is a dream come true for me. I hope since Papa admires you so much, he will come to understand me a little better too. I know Uncle Ed understands. I am comforted by the fact that you have told me you also understand. Thank you for telling me.

I must go for now. I promise to write when I can.

P.S.

I almost forgot to tell you. I have a new nickname, and I like it. The soldiers have

1926, depiction of Legionnaire in Morocco

stopped calling me cook or hey kid and have started calling me Shorty. I have built up a reputation for making really good food, and I have been told that the enlisted men fight over who gets to eat in "Shorty's" mess tent. Of course, space is getting limited; most of the officers eat in my mess tent already.

Really must run now,
your loving brother always,
Ani

It had been over thirteen months since Anastas ran off to join the French Foreign Legion. All the old resentments had been replaced by admiration for the man his little brother had become. Ani was the nickname Rusty had called his baby brother from childhood, a private endearment they used only between themselves and never with anyone else. Seeing him sign one of his letters this way reminded Rusty of how close they had been and was glad that closeness remained.

In a similar fashion, Rusty's admiration for his wife had grown as well. She was such a tiny bit of a thing, yet there was nothing small about Bitty's fearlessness or the joy she found in life. It was an attitude that often reminded him of Anastas's love for life, not to mention that the two of them were nearly the same age.

Rusty sat quietly looking at his beautiful young wife, knowing his child was growing inside her. His child would come into the world soon, and that knowledge gave Rusty a profound sense of peace. His thoughts went out to his little brother like a prayer. *Ani, if what you are finding on your journeys in faraway lands is anything like the contentment I feel with my Delora, then I can only be happy for you, little brother.*

Uncle Ed

The whole family loved Uncle Ed and missed him. When he left for France to visit his family, no one considered he would never come back. The last thing the family expected was to hear that Uncle Ed passed away while traveling in Europe.

When the family gathered to talk about him and celebrate his life, Rusty stood up and said, "Papa, Uncle Stanislaus, and I talked about what we wanted to say about Uncle Ed. First, we found it hard to remember when Edmund Shoe was a complete stranger to us. That was over 16 years ago. Uncle Ed simply arrived in Madison and introduced himself as our distant relative. At 12 years old, I remember listening to Ed and Papa talk." Looking at his father, Anton, he nodded and went on to say, "They took an instant shine to one another and became the best of friends nearly from the first moment they met. I know we all loved him dearly and will miss him terribly."

Sitting with his papa, Rusty said, "I hope you do not feel betrayed by our beloved and departed Uncle Ed for his influence on Anastas's choices."

Anton shook his head and replied, "No, my son, I don't. Anastas may have loved Ed's stories, but the choices he made were his own. He is like Frank; they were both determined to follow their own dreams.

"That freedom is all my parents wanted for me. The ability and opportunity to pursue a dream of my own, not theirs. I don't see how I could refuse to give my son's the same gift. All of you are now pursuing your own American dreams, and it fills me with pride to see each of my children finding happiness in their choices."

Rusty took on the duty to write to Anastas about Uncle Ed. The whole family knew how hard Ed's death was going to be on the youngest Karella son. When Anastas wrote back, he said, *"Brother, my heart tells me this is part of life. My only wish, if I had the ability to change anything, is that Uncle Ed could have seen me living my own adventures just like he told me to do. Thank you for writing to me about this. It will take time to get used to him being gone, especially when I think of home. However, I know his spirit is close to me, and every time I speak in French, I still hear his voice."*

An Accident in Madison

In the spring of 1927, only months before Delora's first child was due to be born, Delora's younger sister, Violet, was involved in a serious car accident. Sadly, Doctor Linden determined Violet would be confined to a wheelchair for the rest of her life. Delora had been crushed by that news and went to see her sister at the hospital as often as her condition allowed. Once Violet's condition stabilized, the doctor sent her home.

Right before the accident, a young man name Dr. Martin Smith started working for the Holt's family doctor. The timing was fortunate. When Violet was sent home to recuperate, Dr. Smith took over her case. Shortly after that, old Doctor Linden passed away suddenly, leaving his entire practice in the hands of the younger man.

The new doctor started making house calls to the Holt residence to check on Violet's progress. Upon finishing with one such visit, Jim Holt asked him to come to his study for a talk. "I'm glad to hear you have decided to stay on in Madison. Now that old Dr. Linden has passed away, this town needs you more than ever. I want to thank you personally for all you are doing to help Violet."

Doctor Martin Smith accepted the compliment with a gracious nod and replied, "I'm sorry I don't have better news about Violet's condition."

Jim slowly shook his head, saying, "I am happy she lived through the accident; now, we will deal with the rest of her health issues day by day. However, I do have another concern I'd like to talk to you about." When Dr. Smith nodded for him to proceed, Jim said, "It concerns the health of my wife, Margaret."

Dr. Smith nodded again and said, "I was given a stack of files for several of Dr. Linden's patients just before he died. I confess I have not had time to review them or talk to him about them before it was too late. Your wife's file was among them, and I put it with Violet's information."

Jim looked at the floor a minute, then looked at the younger man and asked, "Could you perform a new examination? Could you see if you can determine what is wrong with Margaret and if anything can be done?"

"Exactly how long has she had this condition?" Dr. Smith asked. "Did Dr. Linden ever explain what he thought was wrong?"

James started to shake his head. Then he became lost in uncomfortable reflections about his wife's condition. Slowly, almost to himself, he began to talk about his fears. "I permitted this to go on—for years. I should have asked questions. This is my fault. I expected her to get better after Dr. Linden had given her medicine to calm her nerves and to combat some temporary depression and sleeplessness while she was ill.

"The illness did seem to pass, and she began to show lucid periods throughout the day. Yet, after taking her medicine, she became increasingly lethargic and could hardly get out of bed on her own. Eventually, she grew weaker, and her relapses into illness became normal, almost expected. I was busy with work, and I had my eldest daughter stay home from school to help take care of her. I just didn't question the doctor."

Violet Holt in wheelchair with toddler, nephew Newell Holt

Sitting in silence, Dr. Smith listened, watching Mr. Holt as he sat behind his desk deeply lost in his own memories. Jim Holt was still talking, so Doctor Smith kept listening.

"Margaret would be sleeping when I got up in the morning and would generally be sleeping when I came to bed in the evenings. Time got away from me. I lost track of her condition—how long it had been going on. Nor did I realized how bad things had gotten until Margaret could no longer get out of bed on her own.

"But even after I had Delora quit school to take care of her, I was distracted, worrying about running the horse business. I admit I've made a terrible mistake in ignoring Margaret's problem. I made things worse by ignoring it.

"After my daughter and I had our heart-to-heart talk, I realized I was largely to blame. I know a great deal of the reason she felt she needed to run away and get married was because I had turned a blind eye to this situation with Margaret."

Dr. Smith had been watching Jim Holt wrestling with his thoughts for quite a while before he cleared his throat to gain Jim's attention. He was about to ask Jim if he was all right when Jim looked at him and said, "I'm sorry. You did not need to hear all that. To answer your question, Doctor Linden did not specify what was wrong with Margaret. I do fear that somehow the condition she is in now is my fault. I believe it has something to do with the medicines she has been taking for years."

Dr. Smith blinked with surprise at Jim's confession, not exactly sure what he could or should say. Instead, he stuck to what his professional training taught him to do in any medical situation. He promised to have a look at Margaret's file before his next appointment with Violet. "At that time," said the doctor, "I will perform a new examination. Then, based on the facts of her case, I will assess her condition."

After reading Mrs. Holt's history and making a thorough examination of Margaret's condition, Dr. Smith took her off all existing tonics and medications. Then he prescribed copious water consumption to rinse her system. He went on to explain she would go through a series of serious symptoms. "At first, she will experience headaches, chills, tempers, and shakes, but this part of the therapy is necessary to affect a complete recovery."

Seeing the alarmed look on Mr. Holt's face, the doctor hurried on to say, "However, once these *passing* afflictions subside, you must be sure Margaret gets out of bed. She must walk around the room with assistance at least three times a day to recondition the muscles in her legs. Over time, she will be able to take longer walks inside with less assistance and eventually outside the house as well. Soon, she will need no assistance walking at all."

The only explanation the doctor gave was to say, "Mrs. Holt's condition did not require the extended use of tonics, which were in part keeping her bedridden." Based on his medical knowledge and experience, he felt sure that once her system had been thoroughly flushed with water and she received no more medicines, her body would begin to respond to good food and exercise. She would be able to regain her full strength and mental awareness.

That news was all Jim needed to hear to set about instituting the changes the doctor prescribed. Mr. Holt's beloved wife, Margaret, recovered her strength and never took another tonic as long as she lived. Her family celebrated the unexpected miracle of regaining the wife and mother whom they had thought was gone forever.

Margaret thanked God for her life and thanked her family for not giving up on her.

Though she could never reclaim the years she had lost, she felt blessed and glad to have the years ahead. Margaret's timely recovery allowed her a few years to be with Violet before complications from the car accident claimed the young girl's life.

Margaret also worked diligently to repair the rift between herself and her eldest daughter, Delora. With Rusty and Jim's help and support, the two women mended the injury the years of illness had caused. Mother and daughter became closer than they had ever been, and Margaret could not wait to hold Delora's baby.

In loving memory of James (Jim) Holt and wife, Margaret Kilgore Holt

CHAPTER 14

Unexpected Emotions

Norfolk Home of Frank and Helen Craven Karella

Frank rushed into Helen's office at the Music Conservatory, asking, "Darling, can you please clear your schedule for the first week in July? I'll do the same at the hospital."

Helen looked up and asked, "What's going on?"

Delora Lucy Holt Karella

"My sister Martha just called and told me there is a big Fourth of July party being planned out at the homestead in Madison. We haven't been to a big family gathering since our wedding reception, and I really want to go."

Helen Craven Karella smiled, knowing her husband was champing at the bit to talk to his brother Rusty face to face. The Karella party did sound like fun, so she replied, "Let me look at the schedule, Frank. I'm sure with this much lead time, I can change my appointments around so we can go."

Frank walked around the desk and pulled her to her feet. Giving her a kiss that left her quite breathless, he whispered, "Thank you, darling. Now, I'll let you get back to work." Then, with a rakish smile, he added, "I'll see you later," winking at her.

Madison, Home of Rusty and Delora Holt Karella

At a gathering at Anton Karella's home, Rusty and Delora announced to the family they were going to have their first child. Rusty's youngest sister, Mary Cecilia Voborny, was sitting next to him at the table and beamed with happiness.

"That is so perfectly exciting," she said to her brother. "Stanley and I are going to have a baby too! Just think of it, Rusty. Our children are going to be the same age."

A Son Is Born

Delora bore her baby on the first day of July 1927. "Rusty, I am very happy to report that both Delora and the baby are doing fine," Dr. Smith told him with a satisfied smile. "Your young wife had no trouble with the delivery, so you can take your wife and baby home this afternoon when she wakes up."

"Doctor, do you think Delora and the baby will be fit to go to a family picnic in three days?" Rusty asked.

Nodding his head in response, Doctor Smith replied, "Just make sure the two of them rest between now and then, and she should have no issues attending a family gathering. I only have one restriction for her: she should not lift anything yet, not even food baskets."

Nodding, Rusty replied, "I'll make sure she does not lift anything until you say she can, Doctor."

Ambrose James (Andy, AJ, Jr.) Karella, born July 1, 1927

Two Days Later

Sun shone through the bedroom window, and the song "My Blue Heaven" played softly on the radio in the other room. Rusty watched his sleeping wife and infant son who slumbered between them. *My son's name, Ambrose James, will always have great significance,* Rusty thought as he proudly touched the tiny hand tenderly.

His son would share his initials—AJK—and would be the third generation of Karella men to do so. The name Ambrose honored his father and the Karella family's Bohemian heritage. His second name, James, honored his wife's father on the Holt side of the family. The choice of names achieved a delicate balance between history and personal honor. Making peace with James Holt before last Christmas had been the wisest thing he had ever done.

"Grandpa," Rusty whispered softly, "our Bohemian legacy will live on through this little child. He is the first-born son of the fourth generation of American Karella men. I only wish that you could have held him. He is so beautiful." Rusty's throat grew too tight to speak anymore, and his heart was so full of love his chest could barely contain it.

Madison Family Gathering

When his sisters had proposed a family gathering be held at the homestead on the Fourth of July, everyone hoped they would be celebrating a birthday of a child along with the independence of their nation. God must have agreed because Rusty's son had arrived with perfect timing.

When Rusty drove up to the farmhouse with Delora and the baby, the celebration was already in full swing. Holts, Holys, Karellas, Vobornys, Beans, Pojars, Kuchars, and many friends from church along with Father Clemens had come out to the farm for the party. Uncle Emil had the radio playing out on the porch, and several couples danced on the grass to the tune "Me and My Shadow."

Karella clan gathering—Madison, Nebraska, 1927

Each of the families attending had brought their favorite foods to share. The women who were not dancing set up the picnic tables as their men uncovered dish after dish of luscious-looking food. The tabletops held creamed corn, fried chicken, potato salad, and home-made pickles; home brewed beer and cordial; every kind of fruit pie; and, of course, rohlikys, Houska breads, and berry kolaches. In fact, there was so much food the women had to set up an extra station for the dishes, silverware, and napkins so everyone could serve themselves.

Rusty smiled as he and his family walked up to the house, acknowledging the roar of congratulations that erupted when they were recognized. Many of the guests at the picnic had not met Rusty's wife yet and were anxious to see the baby too. Taking Delora's arm, he said, "Welcome to my family, Bitty. They sure do know how to throw a great party, and they are going to love you!"

Frank and Rusty Talk

"There you are!" said a familiar voice. Grabbing Rusty by the arm, Frank pulled his brother off to sit by themselves so they could talk for a bit in private. Frank couldn't wait to hear the whole story, saying, "Ok, Rusty, spill it! I want to hear it all."

Rusty stared at his brother with a blank look like he didn't know what he was talking about.

"Oh, come on, Rusty! I want to hear the details: when, where, and how did this happen? And so fast!"

Rusty knew Frank would never let it go until he knew at least a little of what had taken place between him and Delora. Relenting, he said, "I met her while I was doing some contract work for her father. We fell in love and didn't want to wait for a formal wedding and all the time that would take, so we eloped, and now we have a baby."

Frank looked disappointed and shook his head. "That's it? That's all you have to say?" Rusty nodded his head, and Frank frowned. "So, I take it, this is going to be a guessing game." Then he continued with his questions, "Alright, you said you two eloped. Does that mean it would have been a shotgun wedding if you had waited?"

Rusty went red in the face, but this was not embarrassment. It was instant and straightforward anger. With a clenched jaw, Rusty replied in a stilted tone, "Because you are my brother, I will not call you out for slandering my wife's honor with that question."

Frank took a step back and said in an apologetic tone, "Rusty, I'm sorry. I would never besmirch your wife's name or her honor. I can see that you love her deeply. I can also tell your protective instincts are just about to remove my head! Peace, brother, I am happy for you.

"It was just a shock to hear you went from *no girl* in your life the last time we talked when I got home from South America to *not only being married* but that your *baby would be born* before I saw you again."

Rusty nodded, unused to the hostile feelings he had just experience because he wanted to protect Delora. "I'm sorry, Frank. I love her, and yes, it all happened rather quickly. Please let it go at that. It took us a while to get the family past the hurt feelings that we caused by our rash actions, and now all we want is to be happy."

Frank smiled and replied, "I get it, big brother! I must say, though, I'm impressed. I thought Helen and I moved fast to the marriage stage when we realized we were in love. But you sure beat our record! It only took two months—that's what I heard. Is that right?" Rusty only nodded, and Frank went on to say, "Gosh, even Anastas would be impressed at how quickly you made up your mind about what you wanted."

Rusty finally laughed and admitted, "You are right, Frank. Anastas said much the same thing in one of his letters after I told him what Bitty and I had done."

"Ok, enough talk. I'm hungry," said Frank, changing the subject, knowing Rusty would not provide any more details. *I'll have to see what Martha knows,* he thought to himself. Then, clapping his brother on the back, he added, "Let's go get some of that Bohemian houska bread that Mary Cecelia made with Great-Grandma Antonia's old recipe."

Relieved Frank quit asking questions, Rusty replied, "And a couple of beers to go with that bread!"

As the brothers headed toward the food, Frank replied, "Now, that's an even better idea!"

Baby Gifts

After the ladies had eaten, they gathered around Delora, the baby, and Mary Cecilia. Mary's first child was due sometime in August, which was only two months away. Because her due date was so close, the women of the family decided to celebrate the two events together.

Delora sat next to Mary, feeling like she truly belonged to a sisterhood within the Karella clan. Both mothers received handwoven cradle blankets, precious baby booties, and miniature clothing the women of the family made or had from their own babies.

"Delora, these nightgowns belong to my Charles Anthony," said Martha Karella Pojar. "They are like new because he grew out of them within months. You will soon see that for yourself. Our big sister, Helen, had enough children that she just kept her baby clothing, and all three of her boys shared them at one time or another."

"I suspect your little Ambrose will only wear these things for a short while before he outgrows them too. Then you can pass them on at the next baby party," Martha suggested.

Delora held the infant gowns up, nodding, and said, "What a wonderful tradition, Martha. Thank you."

Home of Stanley and Mary Cecilia Voborny, Two Months Later

It was Mary Cecilia's birthday, but there would be no party this year. Mary was overdue, and Doctor Martin Smith had gotten a frantic call from Stanley Voborny at 1:00 a.m. After questioning Stanley, Doctor Smith figured Mary had finally started her contractions. Getting dressed quickly, he went over to the Voborny home to check on the expectant mother.

Stanley heard a knock on the door and rushed to answer it. "Doctor, I thought you said the baby would come days ago! Mary is agitated and groaning," Stanley said worriedly.

"Stanley, please calm down. Let me go in and check on Mary, then I can give you a better answer. The first baby a woman has tends to be the most unpredictable." Doctor Smith opened the bedroom door and disappeared within. A few minutes later, he opened the door, stating his request hurriedly, "Stanley, please call this phone number. It is my nurse. Tell her I need her to come here right away! It looks like your child is going to be born right here at home and very soon."

Stanley Joseph Ervin Voborny came into the world on his mother's 19th birthday, August 15, 1927, announcing his arrival with a loud cry.

Toddler Ambrose James Karella at one year and cousin Ervin Voborny, both born in 1927

As the child's papa held his first-born son, his exhausted mother smiled, saying, "Stanley, to save confusion, why don't we call our son Ervin?" Stanley grinned and nodded in agreement. As he rocked his baby son in his arms, Stanley looked at his wife and whispered, "Thank you, Mary, for this wonderful gift."

Later That Morning

Delora called Helen Karella Bean and asked, "Have you had any news yet from Mary or Stanley? Mary told me her baby is due this month, and Martha and I wanted to bring some food by the house so she didn't have to cook. We were going over today."

"Good heavens, you have great timing, Delora. Mary just had her baby early this morning. It's a boy, and they named him Ervin, and he and Mary are doing fine," Helen said. "No one will be awake over there yet, but Papa and I were delighted to hear everything was fine at 2:00 a.m. when they called us."

"That's great news! Go back to sleep, Helen," said Delora. "I'll call out to the farm and let Emily know, then I'll talk to Martha and Aunt Anna. We'll make sure to take the food over around lunchtime, and it will be enough to last through the week."

Four Months Later, December 1927, Holt Home

Margaret closed her eyes, listening to the beautiful voices singing "What Child Is This" as the lilting strains of the music floated over the congregation. Sitting quietly in church, she thought, *Thank you, Lord, for bringing clarity back to my mind. It's been the first Christmas season—in years—that I can remember.*

The nativity scene brought tears to her eyes. The statue of Mother Mary holding baby Jesus made her keenly aware of being alive. She hugged her daughter Marcella sitting by her side. Then she thought, *Though my babies are all grown up, I feel blessed, Mother Mary, to be back in the loving arms of my husband and children. I know the joy you felt holding your baby. I have reclaimed that joy too. Thanks be to God!*

Closing her eyes, she began to pray silently, *Thank you, Lord, for the time you have given me. Thank you for opening my mind and my heart. Thank you for restoring health to my mind and body, which has allowed me to come back to the world and my family. Thank you for giving me the courage to build a new relationship with my daughter. Thank you for helping Delora and her husband forgive me and for the gift of my grandson, Ambrose.*

I am thrilled they are going to spend Christmas Day with us this year. I promise not to waste this second chance. I will cherish each day and all that comes with living each day.

"Margaret, Marcella," whispered Jim Holt, "Are you ready to go? The car is warm now. Oscar and JW will meet us at home. Delora, Rusty, and the baby are already at the house with Violet."

Margaret smiled, taking hold of Marcella's hand, and replied, "Yes, darling." Then, also taking hold of her husband's hand as she stood up in the pew, she said, "We are ready to go."

James Holt family, back row: JW, Oscar, Delora, Violet;
front row: Jim Holt, Marcella, Margaret Holt

Home of Anton Karella, Nearly a Year Later

Dear Papa,   *England, August 1928*

I have spent three very busy years in the service using the skills you insisted we boys learn when I was but a child. I will be forever grateful for that advice and direction. Being able to cook has served me well, and it has also kept me safe.

Papa, I had little free time to see all the places Uncle Ed told me so much about. I really must see those places for myself now while I am so close to those cities and countries. Don't worry, though. I saved most of my pay, and the Legion gave me pre-paid travel papers back to New York, which I have safely tucked away.

Please feel no anxiety over this. I have made friends who wish to travel with me, and I have grown quite capable of conversing in local languages over the years.

I want you to know I hope to be back for my 18th birthday in September. If not by then, at the very latest, I promise I'll be home for Christmas. Please pass on this news to Ambrose and the rest of the family. I look forward to the day I am with you all again.

With love always, your son,
Anastas

Autumn in Nebraska

The 1928 harvest season was over in Madison, and everyone began to settle into their winter routines. Rusty's repair business workload had slowed dramatically as the farmers were putting most of their machinery away for the winter. He loved this time of year when he got to sleep in and could spend mornings with his wife and son.

Rusty got up before Delora and sat at the kitchen table reading the newspaper in the early morning quiet.

It wasn't long before Bitty came into the room with Ambrose. After sitting him in his chair, she walked past Rusty, giving him a quick kiss and said, "Morning" as she went to the refrigerator for milk, then to the stove to make the baby's porridge.

Rusty smiled and replied, "Morning, honey. Morning, Ambrose." Ambrose responded to his daddy's voice and let out a happy gurgle.

Delora sat down next to the baby's chair, and Ambrose began to pump his arms up and down excitedly as he saw the spoonful of food headed toward his mouth. Delora grinned at her baby's bright-eyed enthusiasm for breakfast.

Charles Lindbergh with his airplane, Spirit of St. Louis, Public Domain

"Bitty, can you believe this headline? Charles Lindbergh has made the first non-stop transatlantic flight in his airplane, the Spirit of St. Louis. Look, here is his picture standing next to the airplane."

It seemed like the baby just spit up everything Bitty had gotten him to eat. As she held Ambrose by the sink trying to clean him up, she replied in frustration, "Rusty, I know invention and science, airplanes and all kinds of machines get you excited. But I must tell you, some of those things don't seem very practical to me." Glancing over at her husband, she could see he looked disappointed with her observation. Sitting back down at the table with the baby in her lap, she clarified, "What I mean is that some of the things you get excited about don't affect our life here in Madison. Those are the things that seem like a waste of time to me. Of course, I don't feel that way about things like the telephone or the radio."

Jiggling her son up and down on her knee, Ambrose let out a gurgling laugh. Delora's heart melted as she smiled at her son, and she went on to say, "I love listening to the radio with you and using the telephone. Those things have changed our lives in a good way. Oh, speaking of the telephone! I forgot to tell you that your dad called while you were at work yesterday. He said he got a letter from his sister, Little Anna, in California and wants you to come over and read it."

Delora had been patting Ambrose on the back, and he let out a loud burp, then giggled again, and this time, he was making silly bubbles with his mouth. The tender feelings flowing through Delora helped her decide it was time to give her husband some wonderful news, news he couldn't read in the newspaper or get over the telephone.

"Rusty," she said sweetly. Her tone of voice had his instant attention. "I have another message for you," she said as she nestled Ambrose against her shoulder.

Rusty sat waiting as she smiled at him. With curiosity driving him crazy, he took the bait and asked, "Bitty, are you going to tell me? What is the message?"

"I thought you might like to know—you are going to be a daddy again sometime around Christmas."

Rusty got up immediately and sat next to her at the kitchen table. With his heart in his eyes, he whispered, "Are you sure?"

Bitty grinned at him radiantly, pleased that she had her husband's total attention. With sparkling eyes, she nodded her head yes.

Rusty held her face gently and kissed her while baby Ambrose snuggled close to his mama's neck and fell asleep. "That is wonderful news, my Bitty girl," he whispered softly.

October 1928, Rusty and Delora Ask for a Blessing

"Will you marry me?" Rusty asked softly.

Delora blushed. It was in her character to be practical. She might have stated the obvious under other circumstances. After all, they had been married for nearly two years, had one child already, and another one on the way. Instead, her heart fluttered, and she smiled shyly up at her Rusty and said, "Yes, I will marry you."

Martha Karella Pojar and her husband, Rudy, were not only family but had been their closest friends since that incredible night when she and Rusty had returned to Madison from their elopement to Sioux City.

Mr. Ambrose Jerome (Rusty) Karella and wife Mrs. Delora Lucy (Bitty) Holt Karella

Delora could not be happier to learn that Rudy and Martha would be their witnesses as they said their vows before God in Church. Father Adam Brass, the new pastor of St. Leonard's Catholic Church, would bless their civil marriage.

Martha had helped Delora make a new dress for the event, and now she helped Delora do her makeup.

Delora could not believe how nervous she was as she walked up the aisle of the church holding Rusty's hand.

Father Brass was a close family friend, and he was pleased Rusty had come to him and asked for his help with this important ceremony. He smiled warmly at the young couple as they approached the sanctuary of the church, asking, "Welcome, Rusty and Delora, what do you wish of the church on this beautiful day?"

"To have our marriage blessed in the sight of God," said Rusty and Delora in unison.

After saying their vows to each other, Father Brass said, "Now, your union of love will be stronger than ever, as you have made a commitment to each other before God. Congratulations to you both, and I look forward to baptizing your children."

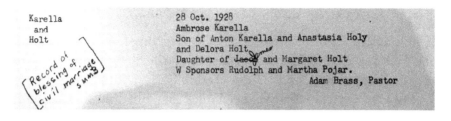

Karella
and
Holt

Record of blessing of civil marriage sums

28 Oct. 1928
Ambrose Karella
Son of Anton Karella and Anastasia Holy
and Delora Holt,
Daughter of Jacob and Margaret Holt
W Sponsors Rudolph and Martha Pojar.
                              Adam Brass, Pastor

St. Leonard's Church register listing showing
Karella/Holt civil marriage, blessed October 28, 1929

End of October 1928, a Holiday Trip

It had been six years since Emily Karella had seen her family in Chicago. Sitting down with Emil John after the fall harvest, she asked if they could afford to go to Chicago for the Thanksgiving holiday and spend it with her family.

Emil didn't want to disappoint his wife, but the farm finances were far from healthy. The grain yield had been good, but the grain prices were so low they had barely cleared enough money to pay the property taxes.

What was left had to last through the winter, and they would still need part of that money to buy seed in the spring. Then he looked at the meat and eggs sales, which had improved dramatically in the past few months. After adding those sales to their total income, he looked at his wife and said, "Em, we can afford one round trip train ticket to Chicago. I want you to go and spend Thanksgiving with your folks.

"You won't need to worry about me or Raymond. You know how my family is here in Madison. Raymond and I will have plenty of company and more than enough food while you are gone. Of course, we will miss you, but we know how much you miss your family too. So, go and have fun!"

Emily was torn. She didn't want to leave her son and husband alone for the holiday, but she missed her parents so much that she finally gave in to the wonderful idea. Hugging her husband, she whispered, "Thank you, Emil. I promise to return home before Christmas." Then, giggling with excitement, she added, "I'm going to call my folks and tell them the good news!"

Thanksgiving Celebration, Madison, Nebraska

Anton hosted a glorious traditional Thanksgiving feast. After leading the Thanksgiving prayer and pronouncing the blessed food ready to eat, the happy chaos and clamor created by 14 adults, six children, and two babies was nearly silenced once they filled their plates with food. After that, the only sounds heard around Anton's dinner table were softly spoken requests, please pass me this, or please pass me that, whispered thank yous, and sighs of satisfaction. The loud ring of the telephone was easily heard above those contented murmurs. Emil John jumped up, excited to answer the telephone, knowing it was his Emily calling from Chicago.

"Yes, operator, this is Emil Karella. I will accept the call."

The family sitting around the table quieted down instantly and waited patiently to hear what Emily had to say as they finished their dinner.

When Emil hung up the receiver, he announced, "Em is having as wonderful a time with her family, as Raymond and I are having with all of you. The best news she gave me is that she is coming home the 13th of December! Praise the Lord, I can't wait!"

Everyone cheered this news with joy, saying, "We are glad she will be home for Christmas."

Emil John had planned a beautiful weekend for himself and Emily in Norfolk upon her return from Chicago. Preparing for the trip to meet her train, he waited in the telegraph office for a telegram from his father-in-law confirming Emily's arrival time in Norfolk.

"Your telegram is here, Emil," said the clerk at the counter.

Emil walked to the window, reaching for the message and said, "Thank you, Pete." He took the telegram and saw it was from his father-in-law, but as he read it, the color drained from Emil's face as he shook with shock.

The telegraph clerk was shouting for help. Emil Karella looked like he was going to pass out even as he stood at the counter window. A stranger grabbed Emil by the arm and guided him to a bench by the wall. "Are you all right?" the concern gentlemen asked.

Emil shook his head. "No, I'm not alright. My—my wife . . . it says my wife is dead."

The stranger looked at the clerk, and Pete said, "I'm calling Emil's brother."

The Family Pulls Together

Stanislaus arrived at the telegraph office and sat down with Emil. He retrieved the telegram crumpled in his brother's hand and read it. It said that Emily had died suddenly due to complications from pneumonia. Stanislaus took a deep breath and let it out slowly. "Emil, come on. I will take you home."

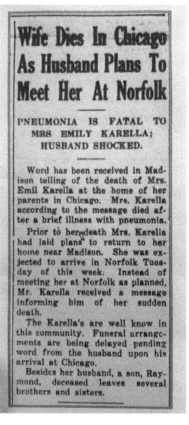

Just as he said this, Anton came through the door. Quickly taking in Emil's condition, he turned to Stanislaus, who shook his head and handed him the telegram. It only took Anton a minute to read the short, terse message.

Stanislaus broke the silence, saying, "Anton, help me take Emil home."

Nodding, Anton opened the door and let Stanislaus and Emil walk out first, then closed the door behind him as he followed them.

Newspaper clipping
RE: Emily Karella dies, 1928

Shocking Newspaper Editorial Found in the Madison Star Mail for December 13, 1928

The Karella clans of Nebraska and Chicago were shocked and devastated by a sudden death in the family.

The Following Day

The family sat silently around Anton's table as he explained the situation, "Stanislaus and Anna are moving out to the farm today. They are going to take care of Raymond and the farm while Emil goes to Chicago to attend his family there and make final arrangements for Emily."

Emil looked over at his brother and said, "Thank you, Stanislaus. I don't want Raymond to only remember his mama's funeral, nor do I want him to remember his family in Chicago with such sadness. It's better for him to stay here right now and let me take care of this."

Stanislaus replied, "Take as long as you need, brother, and don't worry about anything here."

Anton looked at Emil and said softly, "Raymond will stay with Stanislaus and Anna tonight and will return to the farm with them tomorrow. You are going to stay with me tonight, and I will take you to the train station tomorrow." Emil nodded in agreement but said nothing.

The next morning, Anton waited with Emil at the depot until the train for Chicago was ready to depart from Madison. While they waited, Anton said, "My dear brother, I am so sorry for the terrible loss you have suffered. Emily was such a wonderful person. We all loved her very much. I understand the sorrow that fills you all too well. I also know it is hard to think about this right now, but I must ask. Have you decided what you are going to do about the funeral and where she will be laid to rest? The only reason I'm asking is that people who love you and Emily are going to want to know what they can do."

Emil John was still reeling from the tragic truth that his Emily was gone. His voice choked with tears as he replied, "No, Anton, I have not been able to think about that. Not yet," he finished in a whisper. Staring at his brother, but not really seeing him, Emil spoke up, feeling lost and wondering, "How could this happen, Anton? I still can't believe she is gone. I keep feeling I will wake and find this is just a bad dream." Emil's eyes cleared, and seeing the look in

Anton's eyes, he shook his head, saying, "I know. You don't have to say it, Anton. I am not lying to myself; I know she is truly gone." Anton nodded, relieved to hear his brother say it.

In his grief, Emil muttered, "I have a hard decision to make. Emily's parents telephoned. They're asking me to let her be laid to rest in their family plot in Chicago. I just don't know what to say to them."

The train whistle signaled its arrival, which effectively changed the subject before Anton could respond to what Emil had just said. "It's time for me to go," Emil stated in a sad, quiet voice as he picked up his suitcase.

"Emil," Anton replied softly, "whatever you decide to do, we will be here to help. God bless you, brother; we will be praying for you."

Emil hugged his eldest brother, whispering, "Anton, I had no idea what you went through when you lost your Anastasia. Now, I am beginning to understand, and I'm sorry I was not here for you." As the brothers held on to one another a moment longer, their shoulders shook in silent grief.

Then Emil was gone.

1928, Christmas, Madison, Nebraska

Shorty, now 18 years old, looked out the window of the train car and saw his hometown of Madison getting closer by the minute. Today, the town seemed much bigger than it had when he left this place four years earlier. *Of course,* he thought, *I had been a frightened little boy in the dark that night, so naturally things would look quite different now.* Then he smiled, coming back to the present and thinking, *I did promise Papa I'd be home for Christmas, and today is the 23rd. Papa will probably think I cut it a bit close to the mark, but I made it, and that's what counts!*

Anton Karella

Thank you, Lord, thought Anton as he waited for Anastas at the train depot. *I have so much to be grateful for. How poignant this homecoming makes Christmas this year. Somehow, it seems appropriate Anastas is returning now. Four Christmases ago, we all thought he was dead. My son's return is like a rebirth, and what an extraordinary Christmas gift it is!*

"Papa!" yelled Shorty as he threw his arms around his father.

"Anastas!" Anton replied in a choked-up whisper. "It is so good to have a chance to hug you again!"

Both men started laughing and were a little red-faced as they backed away from the hug and the emotion they both felt.

Grinning, his father looked him up and down, declaring, "Shorty, you look like a man now."

He smiled and replied, "Thank you, Papa. I feel like one, too," noting with pleasure that his father had used the nickname given to him by the Legionnaires.

"We have a lot of news to share, and I can't wait to hear all about your travels. Let's go home and get you settled, then we can talk," suggested Anton. Then he asked, "How does that sound?"

"It sounds great! Let's go!" Shorty replied as he picked up his duffle bag.

When Shorty hefted it to his shoulder, Anton saw his son had proudly attached his Legionnaire patch to a spot where it could be seen all the time.

Paris, France, GKM 2016

Home of Anton Karella

Shorty sat across from his father in the kitchen as Anton explained what happened to his aunt Emily. And that the celebration of life for Emily was held five days before he got home.

Shorty had left town as a 14-year-old boy, and by that time, Uncle Emil had lived in Chicago for many years. He had known very little about his uncle back then and nothing about his uncle's wife.

Nevertheless, Shorty could now feel the heartache in his family who had known her, and in that way, he shared in their sorrow.

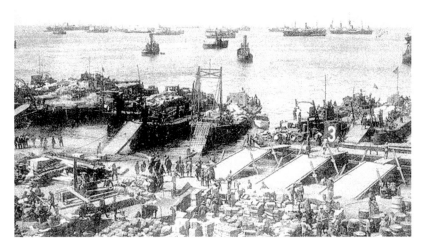

Depiction of Franco/Rif conflict landing, Alhucemas Bay, 1925

Christmas Eve, Stanislaus and Anton sat before the fire in the living room. The Karella clan desperately needed some relief from the sadness of losing Emil John's wife. As the brothers sat watching him, they could see Shorty's presence gave everyone a good reason to rejoice in the holy season, a season celebrating the arrival of another precious boy. The return of Shorty gave the whole family something happy to focus on. Grateful to have a cheerful diversion, the listeners sat spellbound as Shorty talked about his time in the French Foreign Legion.

"At first, the guys and I were billeted in France, and that gave me an opportunity to see some of the country on our free days. After our troop received deployment orders, we shipped out to different posts scattered around Morocco. The Legionnaires I was with had been loaned to the Spanish Army. You see, it was the Spanish who were in a territorial battle with Riffian rebels."

One of Shorty's brothers-in-law, Stanley Voborny, spoke up and asked, "Who are these Riffians you mentioned?"

"The Riffians were Berber-speaking tribesmen who lived in the Rif region along the northern edge of Morocco, close to the border with Northern Africa. Technically, our superiors referred to this war as the Franco/Rif conflict."

1926 Travel poster for the Orient route and fares for Paris to Constantinople, Turkey—Public domain

"But why were you in Morocco?" asked Rudy Pojar.

"Well, let me explain. When this conflict broke out in 1920, it was between the army of Spanish Morocco and the Rifian tribes rebelling against Spanish and French rule in Morocco. In 1921, the Spanish Army in northeastern Morocco collapsed. That defeat pushed the Spanish Army backward during the following five years, but they only fought occasional battles. To break the stalemate, the Spanish military began to beef up their ranks with soldiers from the French Foreign Legion. That is how, and why, I found myself cooking for the Legion in May of 1924 in Morocco.

"I know some of you are wondering why I go by the name Shorty. Believe it or not, the nickname was given to me as a compliment from the guys in my unit. Most of the other cooks were just cooks, and the guys didn't know one from another, except when it came to me. The guys would say, 'I want to eat the food that short kid makes or the short cook makes.' Eventually, everyone just called me *Shorty*. Whenever new guys wanted to know about the food, the guys would say, 'Shorty makes the best grub at the outpost.'"

Anton spoke up, saying, "Yes, Shorty wrote to Rusty and I explaining how his cooking talents had paid off well when he was in the Legion."

"Yes, I did, and I will always thank you for teaching me how to cook, Papa," replied Shorty. Then he went on to say, "I could not write about our location while the war was going on. But now, I can tell you that I was posted in a location north of the Oureghla River—a fair distance from the fighting.

"But on April 13, 1925, about 8,000 Rifs attacked the frontline camps. In barely two weeks, 39 of our 66 French outposts had been stormed, overrun, or abandoned."

Shorty's audience gasped.

"Don't worry," he said. "We had a steady stream of new Legionnaires arriving weekly to beef up the Spanish Army.

ROME, Italy, Al Karella, 1928, GKM

That provided us a superior force and the equipment to turn the course of the war in favor of France and Spain. The tribes eventually surrendered to our French authority, and in 1926, Spanish Morocco was officially retaken.

"With the end of that war, the Legion began the process of reducing military personnel. It was not surprising to discover they no longer needed me as a field cook. Funny thing—when the Legion let me enlist, no one had a problem with my age. When the war was over, they decided I was too young to stay in the Legion and released me from service.

"When I received word that I was going to be discharged, they also told me the Legion would pay my passage home. After I collected my remaining pay and travel papers, I wrote to Papa. I told him of my plans to see more of Europe with two friends before I came home.

"My travel companion's names were Jacque, from Paris, and Ayaz, from Istanbul, Turkey. They had both ridden the Orient Express train from Paris to Istanbul and back. Using their travel knowledge of the route, we planned to see as much of Europe as we could between those two points. We bought tickets that allowed us to get off and on the train along the route of the Orient Express, and we took our time reaching Istanbul at the end of the line.

Athens, Greece, Al Karella, 1928, GKM

Constantinople (Istanbul), Turkey, Al Karella, 1928, GKM

Ephesus, Turkey, Al Karella, 1928, GKM

"My adventures traveling across Europe fulfilled one of my childhood dreams. I bought a camera and took pictures of the places we visited so I would remember all the things I saw and places I visited."

"Can you tell us about the places you went?" his sister Martha asked wistfully.

"Sure. We started in Paris, France, and got off and on the train as we traveled through different countries.

"The places we spent the most time were Rome, Italy; Athens, Greece; and Istanbul. Ayaz explained that when he was a boy, his city was called Constantinople. Learning about his historic city was fascinating.

"We also took a day trip by boat across the Black Sea to Ephesus, Turkey. That's where the apostle John took Jesus's mother, Mary, after Jesus died on the cross. The temple where he wrote his gospels, the ones we hear them read in church, *the gospel according to St. John*—well, my feet stood in the remains of the temple where he wrote them in Ephesus."

Martha, Helen, and Mary sighed as Shorty handed them a picture of temple ruins in Ephesus. Looking at the photograph, Helen said, "How incredible that you stood where St. John did."

"I did find it humbling to think of that as I stood in that place. I will never forget it," replied Shorty softly. Shaking off the solemn mood, Shorty wanted to finish his story and said, "By the time my friends and I arrived in Istanbul, I knew I had to start making my travel arrangements back to America. Particularly if I wanted to make it home by Christmas, as I promised Papa, and now, here I am," he said with a nod to his father.

"Yes, Shorty, we were all thankful that you let us know what was going on and that you were safe," Rusty added.

"We were all praying for you, son," his father said.

"It must have worked, Papa," a grinning and unrepentant Shorty replied. "I am here without a scratch."

"Yes, you are and thank heaven for that!" Helen said. His sister's comment took the strain out of the moment and made everyone laugh.

Rusty and Delora's New Baby Arrives

Delora had been wrong when she said that her new baby would arrive before Christmas 1928. Her second son decided he wasn't ready to be born until January 24, 1929. The whole family in Madison had been worried about the baby being overdue. But young Charles Dale was born healthy and had no problem

Collection of travel items, Al Karella, 1928, GKM composition

announcing his arrival with a strong set of lungs once he finally decided to be born.

Shorty Can't Sit Still

Spending Christmas and New Years with the family and visiting with his aging father had been wonderful. But during the anxious wait for Rusty and Delora's son to be born, Shorty started getting restless again. Rusty could see it and tried to provide a distraction. He asked his brother to spend time at the house with his nephew Ambrose while he and Delora were getting used to having a tiny baby and a toddler in the house at the same time. Bored, Shorty's fascination with his toddling nephew wore off quickly.

Even after spending so much time in Europe and time away from the family, Shorty still found himself plagued with a desire to travel. Within six months of returning to Nebraska, Shorty set out to see more of America and chose to spend quite a bit of his time in the mountains of Idaho on the Snake River. This time when he left, the family knew where he was going. They did not have to guess what he was doing, either, as Shorty wrote regularly to his papa and his brother Rusty about his travels.

Dear Rusty and Delora,   *April 1929*

This land here in Idaho is amazing. The ground is fertile, and though there are great stands of forest, there is also lots of open rolling hills and plenty of space for grazing cattle. You would not believe the variety of fruiting trees that grow here as well.

I know the thoughts running through my mind caught me by surprise. But honestly, when I look at this land, it makes me think that someday I'd like to be a farmer. Can you believe I'm saying such a thing? Though I believe this to be true for my future, it's still a long time from now, when I'm at least as old as you are, Rusty. Did I get your goat with that one, big brother? The part about being old? Ha, I bet I did.

All kidding aside, I have been missing the family again, and I think I even miss Nebraska.

I have loved living in Idaho, but I'm ready to head back to Madison soon. I might even get there before it snows.

Be seeing you soon,
Your loving brother always,
Ani

Rusty laid the letter down, smiling. His brother had used their secret name to close his letter. Since he went exclusively by the name Shorty, it made this letter even more precious to him.

Amazing News

The most momentous surprise after Charles Dale being born was the announcement that Rudy and Martha Pojar, after nine years, were going to have a baby in the spring. It was only their second child, and he was born on May 25, 1929, and they named him Jerome Gregory.

"Congratulations, Grandpa," said Martha with a grin as she handed Jerome Gregory to her papa, Anton. "I think he looks a lot like you," she whispered happily.

Changes That Impact Every American

Collage of newspapers about Black Tuesday, 1929—library research—2021, GKM

Though Shorty had intended to be in Madison by winter, his plans changed radically on October 24, 1929. The headlines in the newspapers called it Black Tuesday, the day the U.S. Stock Market crashed.

From that date on, everyone in America had to rethink his or her plans. People began to take precautions, canceling all extra expenses, and everyone adopted a *let's wait and see* attitude as they worried about what was going to happen to the banks.

CHAPTER 15

Terrible Times for Nebraska and America

Anton J. Karella—Journal Entry

My Dear Anastasia,

It is 1929, and I find it hard to comprehend you have been gone for seven years. Helen and the children are doing fine, and I am glad they are here with me. But, truthfully, we could all use some of your wise guidance, calm faith, and unwavering hope in the face of so much change. Not only in what is affecting our children and their families but all of America it would seem.

Since the death of Emil John's wife, Emily, last Christmas, his heart has not been able to focus on the operation of the homestead. Stanislaus has taken over supervising the farm businesses again and counsels Emil's son, Raymond, the best he can. We all hope and pray Emil John finds his balance soon.

There was enough money to plant the fields this spring, and the crops are growing well. By all indications, we will get a good grain yield, and hopefully, the market price will hold, and the sales will be enough to pay the yearly taxes and buy seed in the fall. The lumber business has fallen off as well. Money is in such short supply the only time we cut any wood is for special orders or when our backstock is depleted. The businesses are barely breaking even. But we are thinking ahead and have begun searching for ways to cut unnecessary expenses and to stretch every dollar. Being the patriarch of the family is a heavy burden to carry without you, my darling.

Anton J. Karella—Journal Entry

My Dear Anastasia,

As winter descends on us, the anxiety and stress I'm feeling about the future is very hard to deal with. For most of the past nine years of the 1920s, our Nebraska community experienced an immigration boom like that of the 1880s just after our people settled on the farm. Stanislaus and I believe these new people moving into the area helped our local economy and bolstered our lumber and poultry businesses. Thankfully, we made sure to put savings away, just like Mama and Papa taught us to do.

The homestead has produced a good grain harvest each year since we began to farm the land in 1879. As time went on, the grain sold for better and better prices. Our businesses grew stronger, and we were able to invest in improvements, diversify, and save even more.

I am disturbed to write that in the latter part of the 1920s, our forward momentum abruptly halted for several reasons. Government subsidies have been cut off, and grain prices have been very low, but after the Stock Market crashed, now the banks are struggling too. President Hoover and our government are saying this is a temporary situation, but Stanislaus and I are not so sure that is true.

Winter of 1930: Karella Family Meeting

Gathering at the home of Anton Karella, the heads of the Karella families knew it was time to face some hard facts. Anton sat at the head of the table, Stanislaus sat next to Emil John, and Rusty sat across from his two uncles. Helen, Anna, and Delora poured coffee, then took the seats at the end of the table.

Anton stood, holding up his hands for quiet as he called the meeting to order and said, "It is time everyone understands everything that is going on and how the economy has affected the family finances. Stanislaus, will you please give your update first?" When Stanislaus nodded, Anton sat down.

Anton's brother stood and began, "The grain yield suffered because of the lack of rain this past growing season. We are familiar with drought conditions and expect that kind of impact to reduce the amount of product we sell. What we did not account for is the market price for grain falling 25% lower than last year. We barely cleared enough to pay the tax on the farm. To pay the farm's operating expenses this winter and buy seed for spring planting will require tapping into the family savings. We must plant, then hope and pray we can grow and sell enough grain to pay the taxes. If we don't plant, we will not be able to pay next year's taxes." Then, with a worried look, Stanislaus sat down.

Anton stood and spoke next. "The mill only cuts new lumber for prepaid orders now. The plan is to sell off the last of the pre-cut stock in the lumberyard. Once it is gone, there will be no revenue to pay the workforce at the sawmill, and I will have to lay off the operators."

When Anton sat down, Rusty stood and spoke next, "Right now, everyone is trying to keep their farms going. About half of my customers can pay their bills for machinery repairs or smith work. Though I am still doing the work, I have no choice but to let those customers I know well pay what they can when they can. Consequently, while my accounts receivables are growing, my cash intake is getting very low. For now, Delora, the kids, and I are still doing alright without asking for help. But it's hard to say how long that will be true if the economy does not turn around."

Emil John finally spoke up, though he remained seated when Rusty sat down. "I'm sorry," Emil began quietly. "I know I have not been much help during the last year, but I still read the newspapers. Even President Hoover says to be patient. That the banks will rebound, and the markets will firm up."

Rusty spoke up, asking, "Uncle Emil, do you really think they are telling us the truth? God knows, I want to believe them. But everything seems to be getting worse, not better. I say we must be careful with every cent we spend from now on. Plan and be ready for it to get worse. I am very worried. I don't have any idea what to do accept to keep working and pray things will at least hold where they are."

Anton stood again, saying, "Rusty is right—we must plan that it will get worse. I suggest from now on, we try to barter for what we need before we spend cash for anything. Next, we spend cash money only for what is necessary. Stanislaus and I can make furniture or do home and building repairs with the wood we have at the lumbermill for barter trades with the mercantile or the doctor." Those ideas inspired each family to come up with more ideas.

Helen and Delora volunteered to plant and manage a vegetable garden throughout the coming summer and supervise getting the berries and fruit harvested with the help of local children. They would make preserves, can, and store as much eatable food as possible. Stanislaus, Emil, and Raymond said that in addition to managing the crops, they would expand the root cellars at the farm and in the two houses in town. The girls would need the extra room to store all the apples and canned items they made. Emil said he had stacks of empty burlap seed bags in the barn. He would be sure they were ready to use when the apples were ready to pick. Rusty said he would keep all the equipment operating, asking that he be notified of any problems so he could take care of those issues immediately. Aunt Anna and Anton volunteered to watch all the children once they got out of school for the summer when their mothers were busy in the garden or cooking in the kitchen.

Once everyone had added their thoughts, Anton spoke up again. "Since Stanislaus and I have been thinking about the state of things for a while, I also went by and had a talk with the Pojars and the Vobornys. They are making similar preparations. We have agreed that if the farm supplies the grain for livestock feed, some chicken meat, and fresh eggs, they will supply beef and pork at slaughter time. From now on, I suggest we set regular monthly meetings to discuss our progress unless something drastic happens."

Home of Rusty Karella

It had been three years since Rusty got married, and in that time, he and Delora had two growing sons, the Stock Market crashed, banks were failing, Nebraska was suffering from a drought, and now all the family businesses had come to a standstill. The family had laid out as many contingency plans as possible, hoping they could outlast this bad economic and weather trend.

Rusty, along with the other men in the family, could not say they found comfort in what they discussed or read about in the newspapers or heard on the radio. Nevertheless, it was better to be aware than not knowing what was being predicted or what was happening. Each week, they met to decipher the truth from what they had learned, separating fact from fiction.

Broadcast News Items the Karellas Believed

Prior to 1930, banks had been engaged in unsafe, unmonitored business practices. Loans made against customer deposits to businesses and individuals were often unsecured. Banks only kept a certain percentage of the deposits on hand as liquid cash, and the rest they invested in different ways through loans.

During President Hoover's administration, the Senate and the Congress worked to create bank operation policy reforms and a monetary buffer for the banks until things could stabilize, but no one knew how long that would take.

Calvin Coolidge stands next to radio equipment used on automobiles during the presidential campaign in 1924, Public Domain

After six months of legislative battles, the collective government committees produced the Smoot-Hawley tariff bill in June 1930. The bill raised rates on both agricultural and industrial products to historic levels and provided for a commission to subsidize farmers who had lost money by selling their grain below cost. Ultimately, all the government's political measures and strategies failed. Now, the newspapers were telling Americans to expect that harder times were coming. No one knew how long the issues with the banks and the economy would last nor how bad things would get.

The Karellas were relieved they had already begun to prepare for the worst, ensuring what money they had in savings would last as long as possible.

The Effect of Newspapers and Radio

Newsmen understood exactly how to use American's *need to know* to their advantage. When news was bad, the American population glued themselves first to the printed newspapers and magazines, and then part of that audience began to follow the radio. The Karellas were like every other American: they read the newspapers and listened to the radio every day because they needed to know what was happening across their state and country.

Radio had been making an impact since 1902. At first, it was just another novelty of invention, then it became a popular form of entertainment with pre-recorded programming.

The first live radio broadcast in America was made by KDKA in Pittsburgh, Pennsylvania, as they aired the 1920 Calvin Coolidge presidential election results during its inaugural show. However, daily broadcasting did not commence until 1921, which was why Frank Karella heard American music on the radio when he and his friends were in South America.

The purpose of radio and radio programming evolved rapidly. By 1930, 12 million Americans owned radios. That kind of audience gave real power to those who controlled what people heard. Its shear potential inspired inventors, entertainers, and businessmen alike to invest in the medium. All radio advocates had their own ideas on how to tap into such power. As a result, huge advancements were made in live broadcasting, and radio nearly wiped out phonographic entertainment as an industry.

Readership of newspapers and radio popularity were two business segments that grew while every other sector of business failed across the United States. The subjects that made those news mediums indispensable to the American people were their reports on the continued bank closures, job losses, and company failures. Every single American reading or listening to the news felt the bite of fear from those predictions. They felt the results of those predictions as they became realities that spread across the nation heralding a debilitating economic depression.

A Third Karella Son and a Voborny Cousin Are Born

Despite threats of economic and political disaster that hung over everyone's head, the Karellas refused to relinquish the dreams they had worked so hard for. Yes, the economy in Madison continued to falter, and yes, the drought persisted across Nebraska, yet day-to-day life still went on.

Fathers did what they could to make a living. Mothers bore children and took care of their homes. Family groups pulled together and used all their talents to make ends meet each day and found comfort and hope in their faith. They also found joy in each other's love and in the new lives they brought into the world. Tiny souls who needed protection and love drove and inspired parents to work hard and use their imaginations to find ways to make things better.

Despite the dry and desperate days of 1930, Rusty and Delora welcomed a third son into their family on the 26th of July. They named that little soul Lloyd Elliott.

As Rusty played with his older sons, Delora listened to the jazzy tune "Puttin' on the Ritz" while she dressed the baby in warm clothing so they could go visit Stanley and Mary Karella Voborny. Mary had delivered their second child, whom they named Bernard Charles, and the Karellas helped celebrate the birth of a new cousin.

The Karella clan had much to celebrate. Gathering at the family farm, everyone smiled when they heard the hit song on the radio "Happy Days Are Here Again" as they toasted the health of Delora and Mary and their new babies.

Home of Rusty Karella

Ambrose James Karella,
three years old

Rusty and Delora's baby Lloyd was small, almost frail, nothing like his two older brothers had been at the same age. Through the providence of God, Lloyd eventually put on weight. The baby took a lot of care, and doctors cost money. Rusty had been struggling to make a living and provide food for his family all year, and there was no work coming in.

In January of 1931, only five months after Delora gave birth to Lloyd, she came to Rusty crying. He instantly stopped what he was doing and asked, "Delora, what is wrong? Please tell me!"

She had finally gotten Lloyd to sleep, and Ambrose and Charles were sitting in front of the radio, listening to the "Lone

Ranger." Delora needed to talk to Rusty and now hugged him in desperation.

As Rusty put his arms around her, he could feel her trembling. "Bitty, please, tell me what is wrong. We can fix anything if we stick together."

"There is nothing to fix, Rusty," she sobbed. "I'm going to have another baby."

Rusty marshaled his feelings of fear and said, "Bitty, that is wonderful news."

His wife loosened her hold and stepped back from his chest to look into his eyes and asked, "How can you say that with all the troubles we are having taking care of the three children we already have?"

Rusty responded with the conviction she needed to hear, "Our children are a blessing, Bitty. God has seen us through before. He'll give me new inspiration, and He'll see us through this too! Don't you worry—I'll work out a plan." His Bitty stopped crying, and now she smiled up at him with trust in her eyes. She believed in him and what he told her.

Rusty had been racking his brain; his anxiety felt as heavy as the anvil in his workshop. *Dear God*, he prayed, *You and I need to come to an understanding. There must be a way to make more money. Please, I need a solution!*

Quite suddenly, it was almost as if his grandfather was standing next to him, as he had done when teaching Rusty about invention, and would say, "You must work the problem backward to find a solution to the issue."

Rusty's mind stopped churning for a moment, then slowly, he began to do as his grandfather had taught him and started asking the right questions.

What do people need or continue to want most, even when they have no money? What will people find money for during times like these? Rusty had been thinking so long and so hard he said out loud to himself, "I need a break and a drink."

That was when he headed down to the basement to get one of the few bottles of his grandfather's homebrew left. Suddenly, Rusty stopped mid-stride on the stairs—an idea was forming.

Wait a minute, he thought. *I do have a skill, one that Papa and Grandpa taught me. In fact, the Karellas are famous for it around Madison! With it, I can make something people will find the money to pay for or barter for. I don't care which way they pay as long as it puts food on the table and buys milk for the baby! Yes, I know exactly what I'm going to do!*

With a feeling of relief, Rusty opened a bottle of homebrew and sent up a toast to his grandfather, saying, "Tell the Almighty thank You for the inspiration! I will put your lessons to good use, Grandpa!"

When Rusty returned to the kitchen, he had a real smile on his face as he went through the details of his plans.

CHAPTER 16

Rusty's Plan

Prohibition, a Cornfield, and Good Old Bohemian Knowhow

Rusty had prayed for an idea, and the inspiration came. Now, he had to get creative about turning that idea into a living. Depression or not, bogus laws or not, Rusty figured out a way to make more cash. He exhausted every talent he had and every trade he'd been trained in.

The only choice he had left was to take a chance and put his old brewing skills to good use. Making his scheme work was going to be tricky because the United States had a nationwide ban on the production, importation, transportation, and sale of alcoholic beverages, and this law had been instituted back in the early 1920s. Nevertheless, Rusty had a family to take care of, and he had a plan on how to do just that.

For generations, his people had made their own fermented beverages, and this tradition was part of their

Prohibition Blues, 1920,
America Goes Dry

family stories and history all the way back to Bohemia. It was considered another food item, and those Bohemian recipes had come to America with his grandparents Vaclav and Antonia.

As a young boy, his father had taught him how to cook, and his grandfather taught him to make beer. In fact, brewing beer was his first fermentation lesson. Then he learned to make liquors from different kinds of grain that grew on the homestead, and in time, he made excellent cordials from berries and fruit. Over the years, those homemade beverages came in handy when he and his brothers wanted to sweeten a barter deal around town. With such a value-added item, the Karellas always came out ahead in those deals. The clan's fermented beverages made a popular gift at holiday celebrations, and that was what people always asked for when a Karella wanted to thank a neighbor for help.

Memories like these led Rusty from one idea to another, and eventually, he realized men always wanted alcoholic beverages and seemed to have money for it be it legal or not.

Scratching his chin, he thought, *Taking care of my family outweighs the potential risks. But, since I know what I am considering is illegal and could have consequences, I've got to be sure Delora agrees we should do this. If she does, then we will need Papa and Stanislaus's help. We'll just have to be very careful. I'll finish laying out my plan, and then it will be time to talk to Delora.*

January 1931, the Agreement

"Bitty, what do you think?" Rusty asked. She had an intense look on her face, and that pleased Rusty, knowing she understood the seriousness of his proposal.

Finally, Bitty replied, "What choice do we have? This may be a way to feed our family, and that is all that matters to me. But you must promise me to be very careful."

Nodding his head in agreement, he replied, "Alright then. As a precaution, we will not discuss this again. What you do not know cannot be held against you. Now, I will talk to Papa and Uncle Stanislaus."

A Clandestine Meeting

There was a long silence after Rusty finished his explanation, then he added, "The only other person who knows any of this is Delora, and she supports it."

Stanislaus and Anton looked at each other with concern, then their faces cleared of all emotion. "Rusty," Anton said, "this could be the solution we need to save the farm from the tax collectors. Tell us only what we must know."

Stanislaus nodded and added, "Yes, I'm in too. What do you need from us?"

"First, I would like permission to begin making inquiries to certain people who have grown accustomed to our beverages over the years. I need inventory to get started, and I am asking to use what is left of Grandpa's home brew, the mulberry cordials, and some of that applejack we made last year.

"In addition, I plan to make corn whiskey in the summer as long as there is corn growing in the field. But I will not make whiskey on homestead land. We can brew beer pretty much any time of year as we have always done. I could use your help making a lot more beer.

"In the fall, we boost our production of mulberry cordial and applejack when the berries and fruit are ready to pick. That will give us enough product to sell year-round.

"Only what we have traditionally made at the farm should be stored out there. But I'll transport it to different locations for delivery as the orders come in. It will be easy for me to move around a lot as I do so much work for all the farmers in the area. Everyone knows I travel to different work locations all the time.

"We cannot allow odd comings and goings that might draw attention to our property at the homestead. Nor should any of what we make be stored in the family's Madison houses except a few bottles for personal use. In case something goes wrong, we don't want this business to be tracked back or connected to the Karella clan in any way."

Both men facing Rusty nodded and murmured agreement and gave Rusty the permission he asked for.

"Alright then," he replied, nodding his head, "since we agree, I will proceed with preparations and will give you an update next week."

A Select Clientele

Practically every farmer in the area had been a customer of Rusty's and currently owed him money for blacksmith work. Many of them would become clients.

However, there was one specific customer on the list who owned a small corn farm and a small herd of dairy cows that was located only a couple of miles from his workshop. Rusty planned to approach the man with a unique proposition.

This customer could be trusted, but still, Rusty gave the man as little information about his reasons for his proposal as possible while adding an enticement that was sure to clinch the deal. "Jackson, I'd like to come to an understanding with you. If we can agree to a deal, I'll throw away the blacksmith debt you owe me, plus I'll become your daytime handyman around the farm. Are you interested in hearing more?"

Jackson nodded immediately, and Rusty went on, "My compensation would be your permission to let me use your cornfield and some of the corn you've got growing. Plus, one two-gallon can of milk each week from your dairy cows and a flock of those goslings I saw out there in your yard that look like they just hatched. But no questions. I just need a yes or a no."

Jackson replied, "Yes" and held out his hand to shake Rusty's. He was curious, though, and thought, *Rusty's got little kids, so the milk makes sense. The geese have a lot of purposes, but for the life of me, I don't know what he wants with the field or the corn,* but Jackson didn't ask. He was too relieved and happy to be rid of the debt he owed Rusty. Besides that, he needed a man of Rusty's talents to rebuild his barn and repair his grain silo, both of which were in desperate need of fixing.

What the two men did discuss was what should be said to neighbors or the townspeople. As far as everyone was concerned, around Madison, Rusty had become Jackson's part-time handyman to do some needed repairs on his buildings and his equipment in barter for a flock of geese and milk from his dairy cows.

Several days a week, Rusty worked around the farm. After sunset, the small cornfield became the perfect camouflage for hiding his fermenter and still. It was impossible to see through the standing stalks, and Rusty could go there without anyone wondering what he was doing.

First, Rusty needed to dig a pit big enough to work in, and he used ratty old boards from around the farm to reinforce the dirt walls. Then he made a frame at the top of the pit for a trap door, which he covered with cornstalks and dirt to disguise it. After that, he was ready to build his fermenter and still.

He made several trips to his barn and shop in town for the metal, tools, and other apparatus he needed. Manufacturing the still took about another week. His final test was making sure the tubes for escaping heat and steam blew out flat along the ground rather than rising in a shaft straight into the air.

Rusty also dug a root cellar underneath the storage shed at the back of his blacksmith shop in town. He hauled the dirt from his excavation out to the farm wagon-by-wagon and expanded the vegetable garden with it.

This new root cellar would hold his secret stash. Since he stored his wagon at the back of his shop, it would be easy to move product from the root cellar to the wagon without being seen.

Finally, Rusty felt ready to start fermenting cracked corn and barley mash and distilling whiskey. Now, he had to figure out a code name, something to call his product that would keep him and Bitty from ever using the word whiskey in conversation around the kids or in passing to anyone!

Walking through the kitchen at home, Rusty noticed Delora's canning supplies and jelly jars sitting on the counter. She and Helen had been doing an inventory for what they would need to purchase before summer. He stopped, staring at the jelly jars. Suddenly, he realized they were perfect to use for bottling his product.

"We'll have lots to eat this winter, won't we Mother?"

Grow your own
Can your own

WWII victory poster—grow and can your own food

Picking one up and looking at it critically, he nodded his head, thinking, *Yes, these jars will fit nicely into the postholes! Good code name for my product too. I could say, "Hey, Joe, when do you want your jelly jars delivered? Do you want corn relish, apple jelly, mulberry jelly, or brewed jelly?"* he thought, smiling.

Rusty had worked for most of the local farmers and townspeople over the years and already knew who liked to have a sip or two. Using that knowledge, it was fairly easy to establish a select list of steady clients who would be interested in his *jelly jars*.

The trickiest part of his business was delivery, but Rusty already had a clever plan for that too. During the day as he went about repairing the farm fences, he dug slightly deeper holes under specific posts in the fence that lined the roadside by the farmer's property. Rusty and his client would choose a location of a certain fence post, set a date for delivery, and agree on the payment. The extra-deep hole beneath the fence post made enough space for him to stash a round *jelly jar* of product.

Planting the *jar* under the post made that post a little higher than the one on either side of it. This was a sign easily deciphered by his customer, proof the merchandise had been delivered. The client would come at night and pull up the post, take the *jar*, and leave the *coin* in the same place under the replanted post. Rusty could easily ascertain when a *jar* had been picked up, as the post would then be a little lower than the other posts beside it. Once he saw that, he'd go at night to *collect the coins*. Rusty created fenceposts delivery spots along many roads in different areas around Madison. His work was going splendidly, and the jelly was well received.

At Rusty Karella's Home

Holding his wife tenderly, he thought, *With the jelly business going so steadily, Delora will never have to fear that her children will ever go hungry*. Then he kissed her and started to get up. Delora pulled him back into her arms and said softly, "Rusty, I've been thinking. All my children have been baptized Catholic, you are Catholic, your whole family is Catholic, and I want to be a Catholic too."

Thrilled about Bitty's decision, Rusty replied, "That is marvelous to hear, wife. You've made me very happy!" Then he hugged her close and kissed her sweetly on the lips. "I'll make the arrangements for private lessons right away. How about once a week here at the house? Would you like that?"

Delora smile and replied, "Thank you. I would love it. That would be perfect."

As it happened, Rusty had one jelly jar client who could come right to his house in broad daylight, which made it easy for him to arrange private convert lessons every Thursday at their house. Their family priest would now have a legitimate reason to come to the Karella's home each week. Once Delora received her Catholic conversion lesson for the day, Father could carry his compensation home with his books.

As the elderly priest put a small jelly jar in his bag, he said, "Please don't think poorly of me, Delora. A little of this helps me sleep at night when my arthritis flares up. My knees get so painful that it's hard to kneel to say my rosary, especially right now while the weather is so cold."

Delora smiled understandingly and replied, "Thank you for my lesson today. By the way, my husband's father also suffers from terrible arthritis. I'm glad it helps you sleep. Just be careful and watch your step. It's slippery out there today. I'll see you next week, Father."

The Loss of a Little Soul

Delora had no more than told the priest to be careful about falling when she slipped on the porch stairs and fell hard down two steps. When she tried to get up, she felt a searing pain and grabbed her stomach. The priest tried to help her get up, but Delora screamed. The priest ran down to Anton's house on the same street, shouting for help.

Anton left the house without a coat, running up the street. He could see Delora still laying on the ground. While he helped her into the house, he told the priest to call Dr. Smith. The doctor arrived at the house within 15 minutes. During that time, Anton called Rusty, then went to get his automobile. Delora was in terrible pain, and Dr. Smith insisted they transport her to his office.

Rusty and Anton waited, and when Dr. Smith came out of the examination room, he shook his head. Rusty jumped up and nearly shouted, "Delora?"

"No, Rusty, Delora will be fine, but she lost the baby." Rusty was both relieved and heartbroken at the news. The doctor watched Rusty's face and explained, "The fourth and fifth month of pregnancy is very delicate. This fall was too hard and caused hemorrhaging. Once there is too much blood loss, the fetus cannot survive, and it is natural for the body to abort what is left in the womb. I am sorry."

After her miscarriage, Delora became fiercely protective of her boys. She had never thought of herself or her children as fragile. Nor had she ever considered the possibility that she could lose one of them until after she lost one. But that knowledge didn't make her angry, not with herself or with God. It only made her love her husband and her boys even more.

Work Helps

Within six months, the volume of the jelly jar business exceeded Rusty's expectations and kept him so busy he could barely think of anything else, especially the baby they had lost. He was relieved Delora did not become depressed after her miscarriage. In fact, she was positive, energetic, and more determined than ever to make the pie business a success. *My wife's a marvel,* he thought.

Money Well Spent

It had almost been a year since they started the jelly business, and it created enough revenue that the whole clan profited in subtle ways. Money was banked as payments for special lumber orders, or for meat and egg deliveries to Norfolk, and of course compensation for bakery items to the mercantile.

As a result of those deposits, in October of 1931, they paid for the taxes and seed for the farm and purchased fabric in Norfolk for the women to sew clothing for the children. Baking supplies were purchased locally for Delora and Helen who made desserts and Bohemian pastries for the family. In fact, their bakery goods were so delicious Mr. Cray at the mercantile said he'd buy whatever they wanted to sell, and there was always milk for the babies in the clan. All these expenditures were made carefully and by all the women in the family so the shopping didn't draw attention to the quantity of goods being purchased.

A Fly in the Ointment

The only thing the clan did not consider was that some of their jelly customers were purchasing more than they consumed themselves and were sharing their jelly with family members in Norfolk and selling some of it in other towns.

Though the U.S. Government did have laws prohibiting alcohol, they never truly financed a department to investigate those types of crimes. There were a limited number of revenue agents who worked in conjunction with local police, and those agents normally worked cases that went after major bootlegging operations in the big cities.

It was just plain bad luck that a team of revenuers had been sent to Norfolk because of a lead they had got wind of in Omaha. They were having lunch at a local café and happened to overhear a conversation at the next table, and two comments caught both men's attention.

"It's the best jelly around, and it goes down fast!" the man had said rather loudly, "But I have to drive all the way to Madison to get more—that's why it's pricey."

After a bit of additional surveillance and a few more comments too suspicious to mistake for a breakfast spread you put on toast, the suits watched the man exchange a jar for money, and before long, the team of revenuers showed up in Madison and started poking around.

A Near Disaster

The two men were strangers in town and had been sitting in their automobile watching people all day. Eventually, one of them walked into the mercantile and casually asked to see the jelly section. The store owner, Mr. Cray, pointed to a shelf where the preserves were kept, and the man in the suit and hat looked at what was there but did not buy anything.

Delora Karella happened to be in the mercantile later that week to drop off pastries to Mr. Cray and pick up more sugar. She observed a man dressed in a suit and hat and asked the clerk if they had gotten a new jelly shipment in yet. It sounded like a very odd question to her, and it sent shivers of worry up Delora's spine. *Could this man know anything?* she wondered. Delora went home immediately and waited for Rusty.

When he walked through the door, Delora pulled him into their bedroom and whispering urgently. She told him what had happened at the store. "Rusty, I don't like the way that man looked. He is not from around here, and he was acting odd and asked strange questions. He asked about jelly!"

Rusty nodded and replied, "That is peculiar. I just repaired Mr. Cray's radio today, and he was telling me about a strange character that came into his store at the beginning of the week. He asked to see the jelly section—that is why it struck Mr. Cray as odd. You might be right, Delora; it does sound suspicious. I'll be watching for anything unusual and thank you for telling me."

The team of revenuers spent a few days in and around Madison but found nothing and returned to Norfolk. They watched the café, waiting for the man they had seen to return. Once they spotted him in Norfolk, they shadowed him, suspecting he was a middleman for a bootlegging operation and possibly connected to the one they were investigating in Omaha. Finally, their stakeout paid off. The revenuers caught the man at a delivery spot with a box of jelly jars filled with liquor and arrested him.

What the revenuers really wanted was the still and the operator, so the suits cut a deal with their prisoner. The three of them drove to Madison, and their prisoner led them to a blacksmith who was delivering a piece of farm equipment in a wagon. Rusty was fingered as the contact who delivered the liquor outside of town and picked up his payment.

Fortunately, Rusty was kind of prepared because of what Delora and Mr. Cray had told him. That is why he remained calm when the men in the suits and hats approached him, holding up their badges, and took him into custody. Rusty had never admitted to anyone he was the one making the *jelly*, nor did anyone know where the jelly came from. To the entire list of clients, Rusty was just the jelly jar delivery guy. They would leave a note in a feed bag hanging by his shop door with what they wanted. If they wanted one or two jars, he used a posthole delivery system and got the payment that way. If it was an order for a larger quantity, there were a few different delivery locations he used, and the money had to be left in the bag with the note in advance. Those deliveries Rusty made using his wagon so he didn't draw any attention.

The *suits* believed they could squeeze a simple delivery guy into revealing who the moonshiner was and arrested Rusty in Madison and took him to Norfolk. During the questioning, Rusty only admitted to delivering a few bottles because the *suits* said they had an eyewitness. The revenuers were not ready to quit yet and had Rusty taken before a Norfolk judge to scare him into talking. The charge against him was bootlegging.

The bailiff stood and said, "Your Honor, this man before you is charged with the crime of transporting and selling illegal alcoholic beverages."

The judge silently reviewed the folder sitting on his bench containing the statements supplied by the revenuers and the one eyewitness. The agents had not witnessed this man in the act of selling or transporting alcohol. What they had against this man all seemed very sketchy, and the judge frowned.

Finally, the judge looked directly at the people in his courtroom, and though it was time for him to sentence the man standing in front of his bench, he stopped for a moment and asked, "Mr. Karella, do you have anything to say for yourself before I pronounce my judgment?"

"Your Honor, the only reason I turned to bootlegging a few bottles of whiskey was to buy medicine for my littlest boy and food for the other kids and for my wife. If I am sent away to jail, the city and state will have my wife and three kids to feed if I'm not there to do it." Rusty trembled, really scared for the first time in his life, not for himself but for his family.

"You have been arrested for the crime of supplying an illegal substance for payment. It is now my duty to pronounce sentence on you. I hereby decree that if I ever see you before my bench again for this crime, I will throw the book at you! *If there is a next time,* you will go to prison!

"Today, I release you under the conditions I have stipulated in this warning. Do you understand the judgment I have just rendered upon you?" the judge asked crisply.

Rusty hung his head in relief for a moment, then looked up at the judge, and said, "Yes, Your Honor, I understand what you have said, and I thank you for what you have done for my family." Rusty shook like a leaf as he left the courtroom. The officers gave him back his belongings and sent him on his way.

He walked to a café down the street from the courthouse and had a cup of coffee, hoping to calm his nerves. "Do you have a telephone I can use?" he politely asked the waitress.

On her way past him to take another food order, she replied, "Sure, use the phone on the wall by the end of the counter."

Rusty called his brother Frank at the hospital where he worked. "Frank, this is Rusty. Can you drive me back to Madison?"

"Are you in Norfolk?"

"Yes, I am, but I can't go into that right now. I'll catch a ride over to the hospital, and then we can talk." Rusty was relieved that Frank asked no questions but said he'd drive Rusty home. "Thanks, Frank, I really appreciate it."

The hour drive back to Madison in the Texas Jackrabbit was an eyeopener for Frank. He thought, *Good Lord, I've done some crazy stuff in the past but nothing like this.* Then he asked," Rusty, you are going to stay out of this from now on, right? Promise me you won't get involved with those bootleggers again.

1920s wall-mounted telephone

You don't know how lucky it was that you were only a delivery boy and that the judge let you go! It scares me just to think of what could have happened to you today." Frank shuddered at the thought and added, "Can you imagine what Papa would do if he found out?"

Rusty hung his head and prayed God would forgive him for the lies he had told his brother, but he could not afford to let anyone know the truth. "Frank, you can't tell anyone about this. Not even Helen," he pleaded. Then he said, "Papa never needs to know, right?"

"Don't worry. I won't tell a soul about this," Frank replied right as he pulled up to Rusty's shop. "I'm driving back to the hospital right now. If Helen doesn't know I came down here, she will not ask questions that I'll have to fib about. I love you, brother! Please be safe and go home!"

Rusty and Delora's Decision

Ambrose, Charles, and Lloyd slept as Rusty sat down with Delora at their kitchen table. They needed to decide what to do. Rusty couldn't shake the fear he'd felt as he was being led before the judge. It was the thought of what might have happened to Bitty and his boys. What would they have done without him? He had not stopped thanking God for his reprieve, nor would he for some time to come.

There was still a decision to be made and a dire warning hanging over his head. "We are trapped in a dilemma without options. If I no longer make and sell jelly jars, where will the money come from that has been keeping the farm safe and feeding our family?"

Bitty reached across the table and took hold of her husband's hand. "I know there's no work, and that's saying a lot, considering everything you can do. I don't see that we have any choice. You and I will not allow our children to go hungry as long as there is a way to put food on the table. As for what happened today, we can't tell anyone about it. Especially your Papa. I don't think his heart could stand the strain."

Rusty nodded at his wife, but he also thought, *If the situation was not so desperate, I would not even consider going back into business. It's going to be a while before it's safe to start up again anyway. I'll go work every other day at Jackson's place in the mornings and work at my shop in the afternoons, staying in plain sight. I know the revenuers will keep watching me for a while. I can get my friends around town to help me watch for the strangers in the hats hanging around and asking questions. They'll let me know when the hats finally go back to Norfolk for good.*

Delora took hold of Rusty's hands, refocusing his attention on her and said, "I have an idea. Helen and I are going to make a lot more pies. Mr. Cray at the mercantile said he would buy all the pastries we want to sell because he turns them as fast as we bring them in.

"Thankfully, I kept that flock of geese you got from Jackson. They are laying eggs now, and the rest of the ingredients I need to make cream pies will only cost a few pennies. Helen and I can sell every one we make. It's a good cover for the extra things we buy, and it will keep some spending money coming in until you can start making jelly again," Delora said pointedly. "We must take this risk, Rusty, and be darned careful while we are doing it."

Helen was thrilled with Delora's idea, and they started baking after taking a few days to collect the ingredients they needed: flour, sugar, butter, cornstarch, salt, fresh goat cheese from Jeff Potts, and lemons from Mable Brown's tree. Mable and Jeff both expected a pie in barter for supplying the fruit and cheese, and Delora quickly shook hands, sealing that deal.

Rusty kept busy and waited, while his buddies watched the revenuers. Those men were certainly keeping tabs on Rusty as they continued to snoop around town, forcing Rusty to keep his operation shut down.

He remained visibly busy repairing anything he could find to work on. Periodically during the day, Rusty's friends would stop by his shop with a radio or a roll of wire or some horse harness. Looking like customers gave them a chance to visit with Rusty and tell him what the hats were doing. This was also the way Rusty heard the *hats* had finally left the area.

The revenuers found the people of Madison to be a closed-mouthed group. It was clear the farmers did not like them, nor did they trust strangers who went snooping around their community. The suited men never found any information leading to any kind of illegal activities.

Revenue agents were in limited supply, and when they reported they had come up empty-handed with the lead in Norfolk, their boss told them to quit wasting time in a little farming town. "Get back to Omaha on the double," the chief said. "That's where you are needed."

Rusty waited two more weeks to be sure the *hats* weren't laying a trap. The stockpile of jelly jars in his root cellar remained ready for him to cautiously resume making deliveries once he was sure it was safe.

CHAPTER 17

1931–1933 the World Continues to Change

Moving Ahead

Part of Rusty's security measures included Delora not being aware that Uncle Stanislaus and his father were both involved with the jelly business. Although he did keep the client and shipment activities secret, Stanislaus and Anton played an instrumental role in handling all the revenue except what Rusty put away for himself and his family.

What took place with the *hats* was something they had to know, and Rusty met privately with his uncle and father to explain exactly what had taken place and why the jelly operation had to shut down for a while. They agreed, and the three of them waited a month. By that time, they were all convinced it was safe for Rusty to restart the jelly business.

The timing could not have been better. Rusty sent out the word that *jelly* was ready, and revenue poured in all through November and December of 1931. Stanislaus and Anton banked the jelly funds, making it possible to pay the property tax on the homestead, and the family's most important asset was still safe for another year.

As far as the family holidays went, Thanksgiving 1931 was a particularly sweet celebration.

Uncle Stanislaus and his Anna had helped Grandpa Anton host the traditional Thanksgiving celebration, and all his children and their families came. Frank and Helen drove in from Norfolk. From around Madison, there were five family groups that joined the fun: Rudy and Martha Pojar and their two children, Mary and Stanley Voborny and their two children, Helen Bean and her four kids, Uncle Emil and Raymond, and Delora, Rusty, and their three boys. The group created quite a merry chaos filled with indulgent laughter as uncles, aunties, parents, and grandparents encouraged the children's rambunctious antics. Before everyone went home that night, Stanislaus and Anna led everyone in a prayer of thanks to God for the support and love they shared and for the family's continued safety despite the economic depression and the continuing drought in Nebraska.

In December, the Karella clan gathered at church and celebrated Christmas Mass together. Afterward, they had lunch at Rusty and Delora's home. It had been crowded but so fun. Everyone went home by three o'clock in the afternoon to prepare for their own family celebrations. Those celebrations would include music and storytelling, a homemade supper, and finally an exchange of simple handmade gifts, which had taken time and effort to create and were more precious than any item bought in a store.

Rusty and Delora enjoyed hosting their first Christmas lunch for the family. Their boys had been so excited to have all their cousins come over to play. Then they got to eat special treats at dinner and tore open their presents with gusto. Despite the fact it had been a very long day without naps, it took both Rusty and Delora hours to get the boys settled and put to bed. The children had fallen fast asleep when their parents slipped out the door and went to the kitchen for a cup of jelly, and then they had a Christmas celebration of their own.

1932, Home of Rusty Karella

Delora divided her considerable energy between her work with Helen building their pie business and taking care of her three sons who were now four, two, and one.

Helen's children were all older, but they still got along well with her boys and kept themselves busy when their moms baked.

New Years was busy as the family planned another group meeting to review family finances. She and Helen were excited to talk about their contributions from the pie business. Humming to herself as she got ready, Delora unexpectedly started craving dill pickles. Suddenly, she put her hand to her belly, and she knew! *I'm pregnant*, she thought, ecstatic with joy.

Anastas Shorty Karella, Rupert, Idaho, Minidoka County

Rusty's little brother stayed in Rupert, Idaho, for two years after the Stock Market crashed. In the summer of 1931, Shorty wrote to his eldest brother, saying he was coming back to see the family in Madison and would look for work in Nebraska.

Time slipped away, and Shorty had not made travel plans yet when he received a letter from Rusty. The letter explained about Delora's fall and how Anton and old Father Clemens had been the ones to rescue her and took her to the doctor.

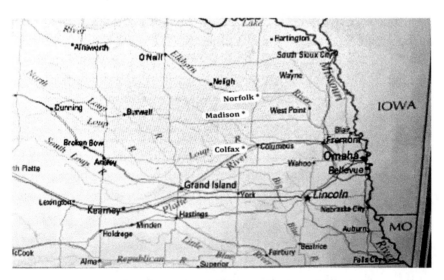

Transportation railroad map showing locations of Norfolk, Madison, and Colfax—made by GKM

Rusty went on to write that Delora recovered from losing the baby, but the whole incident had seriously affected Anton. Ever since Delora's fall, he started experiencing shortness of breath and chest pains. After receiving this last letter from Rusty, Shorty started worrying about his papa's health and thought, *I've been gone for most of the last seven years. Now, Papa has been complaining of pain in his chest and has lost much of his vitality and body strength. How old is Papa? Oh my word, that can't be right! Can Papa really be 63 years old?* Suddenly, Shorty felt an urgent need to go home.

A Doctor's Prognosis

It took some pushing from Stanislaus and badgering from Rusty to convince his 63-year-old father to see the family doctor, and it was a good thing he did. According to Dr. Smith, the strain of the last few years had weakened Anton's heart. Dr. Smith prescribed no stress and a lot more rest if Anton wanted to stave off a heart attack.

Dinner Guests, Home of Rusty Karella

Delora had been sparkling with happiness since she figured out she was pregnant but had not told Rusty yet. She decided to have a special dinner and invite two people who had helped her so much when she fell and suffered the loss of the other baby. It was time to put that incident behind them and celebrate this new life.

"Rusty, please ask Father Clemens to plan on staying for dinner after my lesson on Thursday, and I want Anton to join us for dinner too."

Overjoyed to see the smile back in Delora's blue eyes, Rusty quickly promised to do as she asked and thought, *Dinner would be a nice way to thank Father Clemens. Though he has retired as pastor of our church, Father Clemens graciously consented to continue as Delora's teacher. Besides that, the dinner sounds wonderful, and I look forward to a relaxing evening with my dad and one of his oldest friends.*

Home of Anton Karella

Delora had asked Helen to watch the boys for her on Thursday, and Helen volunteered to keep them all night. Helen missed having babies around the house. Her own children were growing up so fast that she missed how a tiny child can make a mother feel needed.

Helen also decided it was a nice time to invite her sisters Martha and Mary over for a visit. Calling them up, she said, "Dad's gone to dinner at Rusty and Delora's place. I am watching all the kids and could use some company. Come over, and we can visit and play some cards—and bring your children."

Martha and Mary did come over, but they decided to leave their children with their husbands, happy to have a little free time with their eldest sister.

The five older boy cousins ran upstairs to play in Francis's room. Margaret Mary, being the only girl cousin, preferred to play with two-year-old Charles while her mother held one-year-old Lloyd as she drank tea and talked with her sisters. Eventually, Margaret Mary found herself entertaining both little boys while her mother played a game of cards with her aunties.

A Wonderful Surprise

After a pleasant dinner and before Delora served one of her scrumptious cream pies for dessert, she stood at her place and said, "Rusty, Papa, Father Clemens, I am very happy to have you at this dinner table tonight. I have a surprise I want to share with each of you before anyone else knows."

She could see she had captured each man's curiosity, wondering what she wanted to tell them. "Rusty, you and I are going to have another baby around the middle of July." Delora basked in their approval and enjoyed the happiness she caused by telling them her marvelous news. Delighted with their reaction, Delora said, "Now, it's time for dessert!"

Rusty helped Delora clear the table of food, then helped her in the kitchen. Meanwhile, Anton and Father Clemens sat by the fire talking. "You know, old friend," said Anton thoughtfully, "when Delora lost the baby, I was afraid God was punishing me for my part in helping Rusty make jelly."

"No, Anton, God does not work that way. Jelly consumption is a personal choice, and that is not something you can control even if Rusty wasn't making the jelly," replied the priest. Then he added another thought, "No, what happened to Delora was an accident plain and simple, tragic though it was. But now, you can see that God holds no grudges and has seen fit to bless our Delora and Rusty with another child."

Anton nodded, then Father Clemens added, "Did you know our girl will be getting baptized at Easter Sunday Mass this year? Delora is an excellent student and has finished her conversion lessons. She is such a delight to teach, and she embraces her faith wholeheartedly."

Anton looked at Father Clemens and replied with tears in his eyes, "My Anastasia would have been so proud of her son and his wife."

"What do you mean would have been?" replied Father Clemens, looking at Anton with a knowing smile that only faith can put in your voice and heart. "She *is* proud of them, and she has been helping them every step of the way, and you, too, my old friend."

Rusty Writes Shorty

Dear Anastas,   *February 1932*

Money is tight, and business is bad, but the family is still doing alright. Shorty, I think it is a good time for you to be here at home. I encourage you to come as soon as you can. Papa isn't getting any younger, and I am eager to hear about your travels. I can't wait for my boys to meet their world-traveling uncle, and they are going to love your stories as much as I do.

Your nephews are growing like weeds. Ambrose will be five years old the first of July; Charles will be three, and Lloyd will be two this year.

I have more great news. Delora and I are going to have another baby, and it will come mid to late July.

We have all missed you, little brother, and cannot wait to see you again!

Travel safe, with all our love,
Rusty and Delora

The Wanderer Finds Roots

By mid-June, Shorty left Idaho, making his way back to Nebraska. He had turned 21 and felt old. Traveling across Nebraska to reach Madison County, he worried about the number of dried-up farm fields and empty farmhouses he saw along the way.

Upon arriving in his hometown, Shorty focused on catching up on the last couple of years while spending a good deal of time with his brothers, uncles, his eldest sister, Helen, and their aging father.

After a couple of weeks, Shorty made a trip to Norfolk to visit his brother Frank and Frank's wife, Helen. When he returned to Madison, he divided his time between the Vobornys and the Pojars. He had always had a good relationship with his sisters' husbands, Stanley and Rudy. The three of them liked to hunt and fish, and he looked forward to doing a little of both with them.

While Shorty was with his sister Martha and Rudy Pojar, he received a request from his uncle Joe Pojar to come for a visit. Uncle Joe owned the Valley Ranch in Elgin, Nebraska.

Uncle Joe's place was in the beautiful wild grasslands of northeastern Nebraska, and it had survived the drought so far. Joe was still doing good raising grazing cattle, and he offered Shorty a job as a cow-punching ranch hand. The two men struck a deal, and Shorty went to work right away. When he called his father to give him the news, he said, "I love the freedom of riding horses over the rolling hills of northeastern Nebraska. Papa, I don't know exactly how to describe what I am feeling. All I can say is that something here feels right for the first time in my life."

Anton smiled, knowing that this was the first time he had heard such a sound in his son's voice, and replied, "I think what you are feeling is contentment, Shorty."

Anton J. Karella—Journal Entry

Dear Anastasia,

Stanislaus found a forecasted commodity product chart in one of the newspapers Emil John gets from Chicago and New York. We had hoped the price on grain was going to stabilize, but it's not. According to the chart he showed me, the worst is yet to come. It is already bad, but next year could be the most severe all-time low ever.

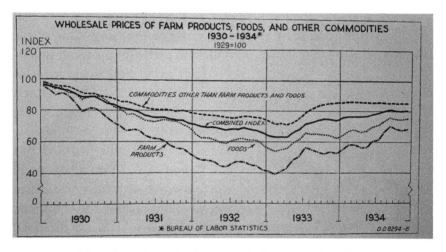

Chart from the Federal Reserve Bulletin, October 1924

All of us have read about the warehouses all over the country packed with surplus grain and manufactured goods of all types they cannot sell because no one has any money to buy it. Stanislaus and I agree we cannot afford to sell the grain we grow and only earn pennies against each dollar it costs for production. But there is little chance of us selling anything in this market.

Since we know we are not going to be able to sell our normal crops, we have planted a lot of the farm with livestock grasses that can be baled and grains that make the best animal fodder for cows, pigs, goats, and sheep. We'll use it for barter with cattle ranchers.

This year, through Rusty's resourcefulness, we have a way to pay the taxes and protect the farm. We are raising chickens, grain, and vegetables out there to feed our families, and we barter the hay and grains with the Pojars and the Vobornys for meat. There is nothing else we can do.

June 1932, Elgin, Nebraska

The supper bell rang, and Shorty headed into the ranch house to wash up. As the food was served, Uncle Joe spoke to Shorty about the work schedule for the next day. "I'll need you to bring in that breeding bull from the outer pasture in the morning. One of the hands from the T-Bar Ranch is coming to pick him up about noon."

Discharged Legionnaire becomes a Nebraska cowhand

Joe's prize bull made a lot of money for the ranch. Shorty's uncle rented the Angus to neighboring farmers with dairy cows in season. If a milk cow did not give birth to a calf periodically, its milk bags dried up. Now, when a farmer did not intend to increase the size of his milk herd, they would breed for meat calves. That was when the farmers used Joe's bull to produce heavier and more muscular calves. Once they were weaned, the hefty calves were worth more when it came time to sell them.

A Runaway Bull

At dawn, Shorty saddled one of the quarter horses, intending to fetch the bull from the south pasture. Riding the fence line with the morning sun warming his back, he easily spotted the break in the wire as he approached the bull's pasture.

Black Angus bull

The animal was nowhere to be seen, but he would not waste his time running down the bull until he fixed the hole in the fence.

Every good ranch hand carries an extra spool of wire and a wire-stretching tool in his saddlebags, which was why Shorty could quickly repair the fence. Afterward, he rode off in search of the escaped bull.

Reaching the neighboring spread in about 20 minutes, Shorty stopped at the ranch house. The only person in sight was a young girl sitting on the porch, so he dismounted and tipped his hat to her as he introduced himself.

He explained he had come from Joe Pojar's ranch right over the hill and was searching for a very large Black Angus bull that had escaped from its pasture. With his explanation finished, Shorty asked the young lady if she or any of her father's stock hands had reported seeing the animal.

The Rancher's Daughter

The shy ten-year-old, Flossie Mary Owens, had been staring quietly at the handsome young rider during his whole explanation. Now, the young man stood silently waiting for her reply. "Nice to meet you, Shorty. My name is Mary. I heard Jack tell Daddy that there was a bull he did not recognize wandering around down by the creek. Daddy told him not to fret; he was sure someone would come looking for the animal soon enough." Mary pointed in the direction she thought he should go and said, "If you ride toward that large tree off in the distance, you will probably find your bull."

Shorty smiled, somehow recognizing something special about the girl. Then he shook off the silly thought and said, "Thank you, Miss Mary" as he politely tipped his hat again. Setting it snuggly back on his head, he mounted his horse and gigged the gelding into a trot. As the horse's gait changed into a smooth canter, Shorty thought, *What a sweet and intelligent young girl. She sure is different than my sister Mary was at that age! There was something about that girl . . . her quiet politeness and the way she listened. If I had a daughter, that is what I hope she would be like.* Shorty would never forget meeting Mary Owens.

Madison, Nebraska: Girl Cousins Are Born

Rusty proudly held his first daughter in his arms. He had taken his three sons over to their grandpa Holt to spend the day when Bitty went into labor. On July 23, 1932, a healthy baby girl came into the world, and Rusty and his wife named her Florence Delora Karella.

He rocked the baby and hummed a tune playing on the radio, "Goodnight Sweetheart Goodnight." Tiny Florence seemed to like the vibration his chest made when he hummed. Soon, he noticed both his ladies were sound asleep. The beautiful sight made him smile as his heart filled with a profound protectiveness and love.

The next day, he called over to Mary and Stanley Voborny's and asked, "Hey, baby sister, are you ready to celebrate the arrival of our girls with the Karella clan?"

On the other end of the telephone, Rusty's sister Mary teased him right back. "Tell Delora she took long enough to have that baby. We've been waiting for five months for this call." Then, giggling, she added, "We can't wait for the big party this weekend."

Stanley and Mary's first daughter, Eleanor Francis, had been born in March when it was only 50 degrees out. Rusty and Stanley learned, as new fathers, not to expose young babies to cold temperatures. That was why the clan waited for the weather to get warm to hold the baby parties at one time. Up till now, these fathers had five sons between them. Now, they were delighted that they each had a little girl to spoil. In fact, the whole clan could not wait to see the babies. They were the first girl cousins to be born in Madison since Helen Bean's daughter Margaret Mary was born 12 years earlier in 1920.

Business and Protection

Though Rusty's jelly jar business was as good as it had been before the hats nabbed him, this time, the family was even more careful to hide the origins of the money they banked.

Rusty and Delora hid as much of the jelly cash as possible. To avoid causing suspicion, they spent only enough coin to help family members and themselves keep food on the table or for the supplies Bitty needed to operate her pie business.

Bitty had gained quite a reputation for her cream pies. Everyone wanted to know how she made the pies taste so creamy. Delora knew better than to tell and kept her recipe a secret. *Afterall,* she thought, *that is why people are willing to pay me to make them.*

Her secret ingredient was goose eggs, and occasionally, they were not available. Delora had to experiment with substitutions and discovered she could use a combination of duck eggs and goat cheese, which worked out well. Everyone seemed to find the new combination as delicious as the original recipe. The flaky crust and sweet tanginess of her cream filling allowed her to sell enough pies per week to make the money she needed to buy most of the groceries. Making what she spent on other food items looked like a natural result of her business.

Anton J. Karella—Journal Entry

My Darling Anastasia,

I am so tired of the unnerving things I read. It's not only America facing this economic depression now. America's European allies are feeling the bite of this depression, too, and their borders are being threatened by increased German aggression. I keep hoping, but when will it stop? Recently I read about a man named Adolph Hitler who has risen through the ranks of the German military. He is the leader of a particularly radical group who call themselves Nazis. This faction has become the second largest political party in Germany as of two years ago, and he sounds very dangerous. The whole world is changing and for the worse.

Some of the issues causing these changes are economic, some are resulting from weather like our drought that has been going on for two years, but overseas, the troubles also stem from political and social ambition. Now, all these factors are colliding at the same time. Mama and Papa wanted to protect us by bringing us to a new land. But the life you and I grew up with here in America for over 50 years is gone. I confess in my old age, it scares me. I cannot show this weakness to the family. I must be strong for them. But at least here with you in my journal, I can admit these desperate times scare me. I hope I dream of you tonight, my darling, and may God bring me peace.

As Anton started to put away his writing materials, he suddenly dropped them and grabbed his left arm. Rubbing it to relieve the intense ache there, it took a few minutes for the pain to pass. Confused by this new ailment, he rotated his shoulder and flexed his arm, feeling exhausted.

Picking up the writing materials he had dropped on the floor, he placed them back on his desk, turned down the lamp, and went to bed thinking he had never felt so tired in his life.

News Articles Promote Working Together as a Nation

Rusty and Delora read that Nebraska's bigger cities had problems just like the little farming communities did. Both groups looked to their government for help to solve their problems. The Herbert Hoover Administration was challenged to work in partnership with the whole country to bring it out of its dreadful condition. The ongoing drought in the Midwest was now being called the Dust Bowl because the dry earth was being picked up by the wind sweeping across the plains that became choking dust storms. This widespread economic depression was like none that had ever been experienced or imagined. Though it originated in the United States, the depression spread to include almost every country in the world and was now being called The Great Depression. The combination of the two disasters had disheartened and devastated America's people and destroyed many of their livelihoods.

"Rusty," said Delora as she set down the newspaper she was reading, "we are blessed by God in so many ways through our family and our church community and our town. But I also want to thank you for all the risks you've personally taken to keep us safe."

Rusty's eyes glowed with appreciation for his wife's faith in God, but the smile he bestowed on her was filled with love for her trust and support in him too.

Eight Months Earlier, October 1932

Rusty couldn't sleep once the sun came through the bedroom window. Getting up quietly, he went to the kitchen to make coffee. Sitting down at the table, he picked up yesterday's newspaper and read a presidential campaign article that said, "President Hoover is the first president in our history to offer federal leadership in mobilizing the economic resources of the people." And then Hoover described his own work, saying, "My program is unparalleled in the history of depressions in any country or any time."

As Rusty turned the page, he began to read what the other presidential candidate, Franklin Delano Roosevelt, had to say about the present conditions in America and what he would do about it if he were elected to the presidency of the United States.

Laying down the newspaper, Rusty thought, *I had hoped that the programs Hoover outlined and put into place since the Depression began would be the solutions to our farming problems. He did try to do right by us for the last three years. Yet, none of his programs he set up to help the farmers have worked. What Roosevelt is saying sounds promising. His progressive ideas make him sound like a man of action. Perhaps a change in our government is exactly what we need. This will be a good matter to discuss next week with Uncle Stanislaus and Papa when they come over to help celebrate Delora's 21ˢᵗ birthday.*

Taking a sip of hot coffee, his thoughts were pulled back to what he had read, *The November presidential elections will be next month. The results of this election could have a significant effect on our family's future welfare.*

CHAPTER 18

1933: A New President Brings Unexpected Change

The Choice

The Nebraskan Karellas debated the issues they were dealing with and were trying to decide who to vote for. They had been Republican and voted for Herbert Hoover four years earlier. The man had sounded like a person of the people and one who supported business policies, which the Karellas could believe in at that time.

No one could have predicted what had happened to America in the last four years. Now, as far as the Karellas were concerned, the political party was not as important as the man, what he stood for, and what he proposed to do about the terrible situation their country was in. The Karellas voted Democratic, hoping to help put Franklin Delano Roosevelt into a position to enact his campaign promises.

Inaugural Address of a New President

The newspaper headline read, "32nd President of the United States, Franklin D. Roosevelt, assumes the Presidency and Will Take Office March 4, 1933."

In President Roosevelt's speech, he said, "I promise prompt, vigorous action toward solving the issues we will face together," and he asked the American people to remain strong and to work with him. Then he urged the American people to remember that "the only thing we have to fear is fear itself."

Eight Days Later, the Fireside Chats Begin

The Karellas, just like every American, sat glued to their radios on March 12th, 1933, waiting to hear from their newly elected president. Journalist Robert Trout was fascinated as he listened to President Franklin D. Roosevelt as he broadcasted his first national address directly to the American people through the new medium of radio.

It was such an intimate and inspiring speech that Trout wrote about it, coining a phrase Roosevelt would use from that day on. Trout described his reaction to the President's friendly parental-sounding talk, writing:

> Roosevelt's warmth and understanding for his people was sincerely conveyed in his "Fireside Chat" that rekindled faith and brought hope as he made promises to work at resolving the terrible issues the nation would face together. FDR's voice rode the airwaves and captured every ear and mind as he spoke, saying, "I want to talk for a few minutes with the people of the United States about banking."

Then Harry Butcher of Columbia Broadcasting System (CBS) radio network used those words "Fireside Chat" in his network release before the president made his second Fireside Chat to the American people on May 7th, 1933.

Using his Fireside Chats, Roosevelt went on to explain his recent decisions meant to stop the surge of mass withdrawals led by panicked investors worried about bank closures. He said the banks would be reopening the next day, and he thanked the American people for their "fortitude and good temper during the banking holiday."

The technology of radio allowed FDR, through his Fireside Chats, to enter the home of every citizen and significantly change how

Americans felt about their president and what he was doing to help the United States. Bringing his ideas directly to the people, FDR rebuilt the public's confidence and encouraged them to trust his plans to lead his nation out of the Depression. FDR made each individual American feel involved and engaged in being part of a team effort with him to resolve the country's problems. He said Americans needed a New Deal in the way government was handling the country's problems, and FDR had many ideas on what that New Deal should include.

A Mere Ten Days Later

Rusty, Stanislaus, and Anton felt their hopes begin to sink. The news they had just heard was not welcome nor did it bode well for the stability of the Karella family. On March 22, 1933, FDR authorized the sale of 3.2% beer because it was thought to be too low an alcohol percentage to create intoxication, and he included wine as well. This was the first legal alcohol sales since the beginning of Prohibition on January 16, 1920.

Rusty knew FDR's ruling would cut his jelly enterprise down to grain and apple cider jelly. People would still want their jelly because it was high proof alcohol, but for how long?

One Hoover Idea That Worked

Most of the programs Hoover initiated he hoped would resolve some of America's problems failed. One would be remembered by Nebraskans as a success. A project called the Tri-County Water Project proposed to bring irrigation to Nebraska farmland.

The Karellas had great hopes when they first heard about the water project. As the years passed, those hopes died as the land continued to dry up, and grain prices disintegrated so far below production cost farmers could not afford to plant and harvest. As the spring of 1933 arrived, the Karella's farm produced no grain for sale.

What they did grow on the parched land of the homestead was a small amount of animal feed crops they could use for barter. The farm's deep well provided enough water to grow a garden and water the apple trees.

Anton J. Karella—Journal Entry

Dearest Antonia,

Stanislaus and I have sold off all the equipment at the sawmill, and that business is no more. We sold all but one threshing machine. That way, we can still harvest the feed crops and use some of the oats, barley, and corn for ourselves, besides bartering it for animal feed.

I am ashamed to say the businesses Papa and Mama worked so hard to build for us and left in my care are no more. Stanislaus tells me it is not my fault, but it is hard for me to look at it that way. We are all surviving due to Rusty's ingenuity. Yet, I live in fear we voted a man into the presidency that will change all that and not for the better.

Our love for each other and our faith in God gives us the courage to keep trying and believing that things will work out. We are still so much better off than many people, though the worry still creeps up my spine. I can't help wondering how long we can continue as our neighbors lose their farms and leave town.

Home of Stanislaus Karella

Anna walked into the kitchen and sat down with Stanislaus. "How are you doing, my love?" she asked.

He patted her hand and replied, "I'm fine."

She tipped her head to one side and replied, "That's not how it looks to me. Do you want to talk about it?"

He smiled tiredly. "My dearest, I am worried about Anton. He's getting downright frail. My brother is only a year older than I am, and he is beginning to look ancient. My hair is still dark, and his is completely white now." Looking at her lovely eyes, he went on quietly, "I know it is a disappointment that we never had children." When she started to interrupt, he put his finger to her lips and whispered, "Please let me finish, love." He paused, and she closed her mouth and waited to hear what he wanted to say. "I am so happy to have you for my wife. I do not feel our life has been less because we did not have children. You are what has filled my life with love and support and joy. I don't miss children in this house, but I could not bear to be without you.

"Anton has always had great faith that kept him going. He had a love like ours, and he lost it when Anastasia died. He has had the joy of having six children and lived with their choices in life that at times have caused him pain. He has lived through the anguish of his daughter losing her husband and his son losing a baby. It is exhausting for me, and I am only the uncle.

"What is happening now is different. Seeing the decline of the homestead and the closure of the sawmill, plus the anxiety over what Rusty is doing to keep the family from destitution, is wearing him down. I can see it in his eyes; he thinks this is his failure. I don't know what to do to convince him otherwise, and if he doesn't quit his constant worrying, it will kill him!"

Anna had been quiet and continued to hold his hand while her husband poured out his heart to her. "My dear husband, you have been your brother's rock. You have walked beside him through all his trials and tribulations and his joys. You and I together are strong enough to do this as long as he needs us."

"Thank you, darling. I don't know what would have become of me if you had not agreed to become my wife. You are my rock. You always helped me see what was possible."

An Innocent Escape

Rusty stared at the ceiling, worrying about the fact that the new president had just cut his jelly business in half by legalizing the sale of 3.2 beer and wine.

Delora looked at Rusty as he leaned against the pillows on the bed and said, "You know, I loved the silent movies. Some of my fondest memories of growing up

Ak-Sar-Ben Gate emblem

313

before Mama got sick was seeing silent movies with Mama and Papa in Omaha. That was when Papa would take us on his business trips to see racehorses at the Ak-Sar-Ben Track and Coliseum.

1920s silent movie star Juanita Hansen, Public Domain, Wikipedia

"I have a special memory of my parents taking me and Violet on one of those trips. Papa took us to a fancy restaurant for lunch and then to a movie.

"Mama's favorite movie star in 1920 was Juanita Hansen. The movie we saw on that trip was *The Jungle Princess*. I remember thinking how beautiful she was on that big screen. Mama thought so too. In fact, that is where my baby sister's middle name came from. When she was born in 1922, they named her Marcella Juanita Holt.

"I think I fell in love with music and movies because of those wonderful trips. Both kinds of entertainment help me escape into dreams when I feel sad or worried. Rusty, do you remember the name of the movie you took me to in Sioux City, Iowa, the day after we got married?"

Marcella Juanita Holt Long, 1940s, youngest sister of Delora Lucy Holt Karella

Delora had completely captured Rusty's attention, making him smile as he thought, *I have not heard Delora talk in this fashion since before Ambrose was born. We used to talk for hours just like this.* It warmed his heart listening to her. He could close his eyes and see the girl she had been when he nicknamed her his Bitty girl, back when they first fell in love.

"Rusty, are you listening to me?"

He pulled her into his arms and whispered, "Yes, my dearest Bitty girl. We went to the Orpheum Theatre. Remember how grand it was? All brand new with red velvet seats, the theater had been completed just months before

314

we got there to get married. We saw the movie *Ben-Hur: A Tale of the Christ*. It cost us 50 cents for the two of us to see it, but your happiness was worth it to me."

"It pleases me that you have such a good memory because I was also thinking of when you used to take me to the movies in Norfolk. Do you remember the first talkie we saw there?"

He grinned, saying, "I'm afraid you are going to have to remind me of that one."

"Ok, I'll give you a hint: it was another Bible story."

After a moment, he said, "I've got it! *Noah's Ark*, and as I recall, we both found it very exciting, and I do remember those movie tickets cost us 50 cents too. We saw it at the Grand Theater, built in 1920."

She smiled warmly at him and replied, "How do you know when the theater was built?"

"It is something that my dad and his brother Emil had in common—music, art, the circus—and when movies came along, it was only natural that my dad would want to see the newest form of entertainment. I was already 22 years old when they built it, and my father and I took a trip to Norfolk to one of the first movies they showed in that theater, *The Mark of Zorro*. It was a swashbuckling adventure story that took place in Mexico."

Delora was surprised by what Rusty just told her and replied, "I knew your dad liked music. When we lived with him, he was listening to music on the radio all the time. But I didn't know he liked movies too." She was quiet for a minute, then added, "I miss those trips so much. I know after the banks crashed, gas for the automobile was too expensive, even if the movie ticket had been lowered to 23 cents. I am so happy that you bought us a radio. Have you seen how Ambrose loves to listen to the Lone Ranger and Tonto? I get such a kick out of him when he mimics the Lone Ranger and says, 'Hi-ho, Silver, away!' Now, Charles Dale loves the *Amos 'n' Andy* program. I think it is the laughter that attracts him to it."

"It is money well spent if it makes you and my boys happy," Rusty replied. "Now, wife, do you plan to talk all night?" There it was—her tinkling laugh that he loved so much. Turning out the light, he pulled her into his arms.

January 25, 1934

FDR's announcement in December of 1933 sent a shock wave through Rusty, Stanislaus, and Anton. The jelly business was lost instantly. The president of the United States repealed the Prohibition law, and with strict guidelines, he made the alcoholic beverage industry a legal business throughout the United States.

The blow of what the legalization of alcohol meant staggered Anton. Stanislaus had been trying to calm his brother down for an hour. "What are we going to do?" he raved, pacing back and forth across the floor. "It's over! We've lost everything! There is nothing left we can do. Why has God abandoned us?"

Stanislaus shook his head and replied, "It's not God, Anton. It's the times—it's life. Things happen that are beyond our control. No one is at fault. There is no sense trying to pay the tax on the farm this year. We cannot save it now. We've done all we could. We must move on and decide what is best to do now with the money we have left. We'll sleep on this information and begin a new plan tomorrow. How does that sound?"

Anton sat down and put his head in his hands, then slumped into his chair and was gone. He died instantly without a sound. After sitting by his brother for a bit, with tear-filled eyes, Stanislaus whispered, "Be at peace, Anton. You can rest now that you are with your Anastasia. Rusty and I will take care of business here. Please send us your guidance from heaven. I miss you already, big brother."

Anton Karella, eldest son of Vaclav and Antonia Karella, 1868–1934

Stanislaus stood up slowly and felt something he had never felt before. It was as if Anton had sent him a breath of fresh air that cleared his head, and God replaced his anxiety with peace. *What is done is done,* he thought to himself. *It is time to call the nieces and nephews. I must give them this news, and we must begin to make arrangements . . . for everything to come.*

A Week Later

It was a sad and dreary winter day as Rusty prepared to attend his father's funeral mass. Rusty asked Delora to stay home with their four children particularly, since Florence was only six months old. "It's going to be very cold at the church, Bitty. I don't want you or any of the children to get sick." When it looked like she was going to protest, he said, "Please do this for me and our children. I'll be fine. I won't be alone. When I talked to my brothers on the telephone, they said their wives are staying home as well. Helen will come, but Martha and Mary are going to take care of all the other children. Please rest, and I'll be home by suppertime."

Rusty joined the small gathering at the church to mourn the loss of his father with his siblings. He sat next to Shorty and Uncle Joe Pojar, followed by Frank, Helen, Uncle Stanislaus and Aunt Anna, Uncle Emil, Rudy Pojar, and Stanley Voborny. The rest of the gathering was made up of family members from the Pojars, Vobornys, Holts, Holys, Kuchars, and friends from their church community. Father Brass walked into the sanctuary wearing purple vestments because that color signified Jesus's suffering before his resurrection on Easter Sunday.

He stood at the lectern and began the service, saying, "Anton and Jesus had a lot in common. The times surrounding Jesus's life were turbulent, starting with King Herod trying to kill him as a babe . . . through the joy of being raised by loving parents . . . to his time of wandering the earth as he became a man seeking his Heavenly Father's wisdom regarding what was important in life, facing the challenges of accepting his duty and his purpose for coming into this world.

As human beings are born into a physical life, there must be a physical death—the door the soul takes that leads to eternal life. Jesus, the savior of mankind, walked all the paths of joy and hardship as Anton had to do. They are both in heaven now with God the Father. Knowing them is a blessing.

"Our dear Anton was a son, brother, spouse, father, uncle, and grandfather, and he was my friend. He will be sorely missed. We must give ourselves time to grieve, but we must not linger in sadness. He would not want that for us when he is happy and has been granted the greatest reward for living an impeccable life. He is with God and with his beloved Anastasia again. Let us be happy for him and live with joy, knowing he is beyond pain and suffering now and will always be close to us in spirit."

Heart Attack Is Fatal To A. J. Karella

STRICKEN WHILE RESTING IN A CHAIR AT HIS HOME HERE, TUESDAY.

Star-Mail · Jan. 25 1934

Anton J. Karella, 66, a resident of this community for more than a half century, was stricken with a sudden heart attack Tuesday about 5:00 p. m., while resting in a chair at his home in northwest Madison. Members of his family who were conversing with him when he slumped in his chair, immediately called a doctor but he was dead when the doctor arrived.

Mr. Karella was in apparent good health until a short time before his death. He left some work in his yard and came to the house complaining that he was not feeling well. His son, Ambrose, had just suggested calling a doctor when he was stricken.

About two years ago while ill with influenza he suffered a heart attack but no further complications developed until Tuesday, members of his family said.

Mr. Karella was one of the oldest and most faithful members of the Madison Citizens' band. He seldom missed a rehearsal and never a playing engagement. He joined the organization when a young man living on his homestead northeast of Madison.

Anton Karella was born in Bohemia on May 22, 1868. He came with his parents to Colfax county and for several years lived on a farm near Leigh. Later he moved to Madison county and took up a homestead where he lived until about ten years ago when he moved to Madison. He was married to Miss Anastasia Holy at Battle Creek on April 30, 1895. Mrs. Karella passed away on April 16, 1922.

Funeral services will be held at St. Leonard's Catholic church here Friday morning at 9 o'clock, with Rev. Father A. Brass officiating. Interment will be in St. Leonard's cemetery. Members of the Madison band will act as pallbearers and honorary pallbearers.

He is survived by two brothers, Slanislav of Phillips. S. D., Emil, living northeast of Madison; one sister, Mrs. Anna Kralochvil, of Pierce, Nebr.; three sons, Anastas, Pierce; Frank, Norfolk; Ambrose, Madison. Three daughters, Mrs. Helen Bean, Mrs. Martha Pojar and Mrs. Mary Voborny, all residents of this community. He also leaves thirteen grandchildren.

Newspaper article, January 25, 1934, epitaph for Anton J. Karella, 1868–1934

The actual burial for Anton would have to wait until the ground was not frozen. But since there was no snow on the ground, the family members went to St. Leonard's cemetery and visited the graves of Vaclav, Antonia, and their mother, Anastasia, but chose to say their final prayers standing around their mother's gravestone.

As the eldest child of the family and first-born son of his generation and of Anton Karella, Rusty gave a short eulogy while the family stood among the tombstones. "At the turn of this new century, our grandmother Antonia was the first of us to go to heaven here in America. We will be forever grateful to you, Grandma Antonia, for leading the way to this new land.

"We honor both our departed grandparents and now our parents who will lie beside them. These remarkable people signify the passing of the first and second generation of American Karellas. Without the sacrifice of these courageous men and women, we would not be who we are today. You will all be missed, but we promise none of you will ever be forgotten. Papa, we thank you for all you taught us and gave us. None of it was wasted. We still live in a land of opportunity, and we still have dreams."

Grave plaques for Antonia and Vaclav Karella, Madison, Nebraska—GKM

Then the siblings walked to their mother's graveside and joined hands and prayed the prayer that reminded them the most of their papa, *The Our Father.*

The Karella siblings shared a meal, talking quietly about memories they had made with their father. They told their favorite Anton stories, and eventually, each began to miss their own spouses and children. Frank and Helen, Shorty, and Emil and Raymond went home with Stanislaus and Anna, while the others went home to their separate families.

Grave plaques for Anastasia and Anton Karella, Madison, Nebraska—GKM

Grave markers, St. Leonard's Cemetery, Madison, Nebraska, for Antonia and Vaclav, Anton and Anastasia, signifying the passing of the first two generations of American / Nebraskan Karellas

They would shed many more tears before their hearts found peace in the passing of the old patriarch of the Karella clan in 1934. The new patriarch of the Karella clan, Ambrose Jerome (Rusty) Karella knew the immediate future would not wait. He and his uncle Stanislaus would now guide the decisions and changes that were coming and would require the family's full attention in the following weeks.

Family on the Move

In April, Delora told Rusty she was two months pregnant again. Rusty said they had to plan for their moving, but he would not consider uprooting the family until the weather turned warm.

By June of 1934, the family had divided up what money was left, and the decisions were made regarding each family groups' future and were on the verge of beginning new adventures.

Frank and Helen Craven Karella moved to Pacoima, California, after Helen closed the Music Conservatory in Norfolk. He told everyone he had driven down to see the area and said it was one of the oldest and nicest neighborhoods in the northern San Fernando Valley region of Los Angeles. "You are all invited to come visit. We will miss you all very much," he said as they climbed into the Texas Jackrabbit and waved goodbye as they drove out of Madison for the last time.

Knowing the Federal Government was going to repossess the Karella homestead for unpaid taxes, Uncle Emil didn't want to live in Nebraska anymore. Packing up his and Raymond's belongings, they moved to Rupert, Idaho, in Minidoka County, where Shorty had lived for two years. Shorty wrote to friends he knew in Idaho about his uncle. They wrote back promising to watch for the Karellas and would welcome Emil and Raymond to the community and do what they could to help them settle in their new home.

Uncle Stanislaus and Aunt Anna decided to move closer to her Plouzek family relatives living in Pennington County, South Dakota. They would dispose of the house and move by June.

Helen was invited to live with Rudy and her sister Martha Pojar, who only had two children. Margaret Mary was due to graduate from high school, and Helen did not want to disrupt her daughter's life any more than she needed to. The Pojars remained in Madison and Elgin, Nebraska, near their kin who were cattle ranchers.

Mary and Stanley Voborny said they were moving to Omaha, Nebraska, and with Mary being due in September, they had to get their family moved quickly and left within the month.

Rusty and Delora made plans to use their savings to move to Norfolk, Nebraska. That town would have better opportunities for Rusty to find work, and there were schools for the children. Yet, by the time they had helped Helen go through Anton's home and disperse or sell what they could of those things, it was already September.

Rusty received a call from Stanley and his sister Mary Voborny in Omaha on September 17, 1934. "Rusty," said his ecstatic baby sister, "we had a girl too! That makes three girl cousins now. We named her Marylin Lucille Voborny."

Though Rusty wanted to get moved, Helen begged Delora to stay until her baby was born in December. They had become very close when they lived together at Anton's home. Delora kept changing her mind. One minute, she wanted to go, and then she'd beg Rusty to stay in Madison to have her baby and spend this last Christmas with her parents and Helen. They stayed.

Three months later, Rusty called Delora's parents when she went into labor. They rushed over to help with the four children, and on December 10, 1934, the Karella's second daughter, Marcella Ann, was born. It pleased Delora that Marcella and her cousin Marylin would be the same age and hoped they would become good friends one day.

Up to this point, all Rusty and Delora's children had been born and raised in Madison, Nebraska. They loved their little town and would have continued to live in Madison, except the terrible drought had already been going on four years. If they ran out of money before they made their move to Norfolk, it would be disastrous for his family.

Because of the four-year drought, American farming communities all over the country were broke and desperate, and Madison was no exception. Rusty had heard that President Roosevelt was pushing through Hoover's Tri-County irrigation construction bill for Nebraska. It had taken three years to get the funding, and then the Nebraska Legislature had to create the Central Nebraska Public Power and Irrigation District (CNPPID) to manage the program. Then the CNPPID began construction on the Kingsley Dam and Lake McConaughy to store the needed water for the huge project. It was now 1935, and Roosevelt had proposed many other public work programs around the country as well. If even half of the president's bills passed, there would be job opportunities.

"Delora," Rusty said, "I have high hopes that with all FDR's work programs he has outlined, I will find steady work—if I am in the right place at the right time."

FDR's Second Phase of the New Deal

FDR's second phase of his New Deal proposal called for a Social Security program, better housing laws, equitable taxation, and farm assistance. It all sounded great on the surface, but what all that would mean to the Karella family remained to be seen. Hopefully, Rusty would be able to make more sense of FDR's goals once they got settled in Norfolk, and he found a steady job.

Packing for the Move

While Bitty rested with the baby, Rusty finished packing what they would take with them to Norfolk. Sitting up late, he listened to a news broadcast called *Protecting You from Crime in America*.

Early Spring 1935, Dark Side of Radio News

Glad this program came on after the children had gone to bed, Rusty sat listening to the stories of violence and mayhem the program reported. It made Rusty appreciate choosing to live in a smaller town that felt safer even during hard times than what was happening in the large cities.

Norfolk was only an hour away by car from Madison, and it was still a small community and a good, safe place to raise his family. While it was much bigger than Madison, it was tiny compared to Omaha.

Omaha felt like the cities they described in the program he listened to. Big cities were dangerous. Omaha was even mentioned from time to time in this radio program talking about criminals who robbed banks in that city.

During the past year, the FBI ended the terror and carnage caused by the gangster John Dillinger. Baby Face Nelson was another bank robber who had become friends with Dillinger. Nelson helped Dillinger escape from Crown Point prison in Indiana.

These two had rained terror down on the people of America, robbed money from banks, and murdered anyone who got in their way, and this had been going on for years. Finally, in July of 1934, the FBI shot and killed them.

Part of Rusty was glad these kinds of people had received the harsh punishment they deserved for the crimes committed against good, honest people. Times were bad enough with tens of thousands of Americans looking for work, trying to make an honest living, and these vultures made it even harder for the good people. For similar reasons, Rusty felt just as merciless toward Bonnie and Clyde. They had been nothing more than gangsters, robbing, murdering, cheating honest people, and back in May of 1934, police from Louisiana and Texas and some Texas Rangers had stopped them—dead in their tracks too!

All Rusty could think of was that his children and family were a little safer with these criminals gone from the earth! It felt like justice.

Another program he listened to, *BBC London*, reported international news. For the past year, there had been a lot of talk about the German, Adolf Hitler. The things he said and did made Rusty's skin crawl.

Hitler's Nazi Party promoted German nationalism while advocating anti-Semitism. Nazis stirred up a lot of trouble in Europe. Recently, Hitler had declared himself the ultimate ruler of Germany and was talking about taking back what belonged to Germany.

He had also made statements about being a superior race. It put Rusty in mind of those conversations he had heard between his grandfather Vaclav, his father Anton, Uncle Stanislaus, and Uncle Ed when they were so worried about all the trouble in Europe before World War I broke out. Hitler and his Nazis had Rusty worried too.

A New Town

Delora and Rusty had said goodbye to the Holts the night before and stopped off to see Uncle Stanislaus and Aunt Anna on the way back to Martha's.

It was time to get going, and Rusty made sure Ambrose, Charles, Lloyd, and Florence were securely settled in the back seat of the car. Delora gave baby Marcella to Helen to hold and asked Martha to take a picture of her and Rusty with their Brownie Camera before they left for Norfolk.

Late 1935, Ambrose Jerome (Rusty) Karella and wife Delora Lucy (Bitty) Holt, moving to Norfolk, Nebraska, from Madison, Nebraska

Mary gave Delora a hug, then hugged her brother, and Stanley followed right behind doing the same. Helen hugged them next, then it was Martha and Rudy's turn to say goodbye. "This is silly," Rusty said. "We are only an hour away, and we'll talk to each other often and see each other too. You will come to Norfolk, and we will come here to Madison to see all of you. In fact, at the latest, we will be here to say goodbye to Uncle Stanislaus and Aunt Anna before they leave at the end of the summer for South Dakota." That cheered everyone up considerably, and as Delora took back Marcella, Rusty helped her into the front seat. Then he climbed in behind the wheel, and they were gone.

Helen waved, and thought, *I'm thankful they'll never be that far away.*

Left to right: Ambrose (Rusty) Karella, sisters Martha, Frank, Helen, and Mary. The Children of Anton and Anastasia Karella.

Anastas (Shorty) Karella, youngest son of Anton and Anastasia Karella

Hubands and Wives
First Three Generations of the American Karella Clan

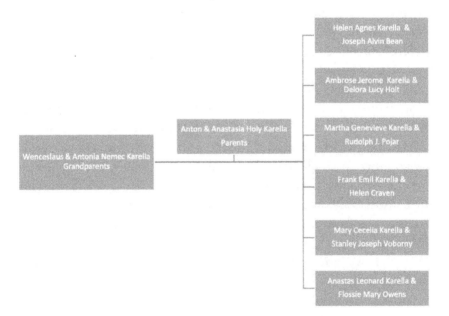

Helen Agnes Karella & Joseph Alvin Bean

Ambrose Jerome Karella & Delora Lucy Holt

Martha Genevieve Karella & Rudolph J. Pojar

Frank Emil Karella & Helen Craven

Mary Cecelia Karella & Stanley Joseph Voborny

Anastas Leonard Karella & Flossie Mary Owens

Anton & Anastasia Holy Karella
Parents

Wenceslaus & Antonia Nemec Karella
Grandparents

CHAPTER 19

1935–1938 Nebraska

Summer 1935, Madison

Having completed high school at St. Leonard's in Madison just as her great-uncle and grandfather did, Margaret Mary Bean was ready to move to Norfolk. She had decided to become a nun and would be entering the convent soon.

Her 66-year-old great-uncle Stanislaus and his wife, Anna, planned to move to South Dakota to be near Anna's family. There was

St. Leonard's Catholic Church in Madison, Nebraska

no telling when they would see each other again, and she wanted to visit with him before either of them left town.

Her uncle and aunt currently lived at her great-great-grandfather Vaclav's old house. Margaret Mary knocked on the door, and her aunt Anna answered it. After a warm greeting, Aunt Anna led Margaret Mary into the living room where her uncle Stanislaus sat by the fire. Then Anna left the room to get tea and coffee for everyone.

"Hello, Uncle Stanislaus. I've come to tell you I am getting ready to go to Norfolk to enter the Benedictine Convent."

Oh yes, he thought, *Helen told me Margaret Mary got accepted as a novitiate to the Benedictines at the Norfolk Priory and would soon start her training to become a nun. I am proud of her, but it was hard for me to grasp that my dear little Margaret Mary Bean has grown up! I have marvelous memories of all my nieces and nephews who have lived in Madison. Now, one of my favorite nieces is a young woman smiling down at me. Where did the time go?* he wondered.

Anton and Stanislaus's high school at St. Leonard's in Madison, Nebraska, 1903

Stanislaus remembered one of the sweeter moments from long ago when he had listened to a five-year-old Margaret Mary tell her stories at the family picnics. "My goodness, Margaret Mary," he said brightly, "do you have any more stories about your aunt Mary Cecilia that you want to share with me?"

Margaret Mary Bean, late teens, before becoming a Benedictine nun

Anna returned with tea for her niece and coffee for her husband, then sat with him by the fire.

Grinning at her great-uncle, Margaret Mary replied, "As it turns out, I do. And I believe it is one you haven't heard." Margaret Mary got comfortable and began. "This story took place one summer a couple of years after Aunt Mary and Uncle Stanley were married. Anyway, it was the hottest summer anyone could remember. The horrible drought hit the fields across Nebraska, though it did not completely kill the crops. If that wasn't bad enough, a plague of grasshoppers swarmed over the meager fields, eating up any plants left standing. While all this stuff was happening, Aunt Mary had a baby, Bernard Charles."

Stanislaus thought, *That would have been the first year of the drought when Bernard was born, back in 1930.*

Margaret Mary continued speaking, "With no crop to sell, there was no money to pay for the doctor who delivered their baby. Being very clever and a quick thinker, Aunt Mary came up with a remarkable solution to the problem. Having raised a large flock of geese, she let half of them lay eggs for hatching new goslings to build up her flock. Then took the other half of the adult geese and plucked them down to the skin. The down and feathers she used to make pillows for her own home. The naked chested geese she used as barter with Dr. Hartner who agreed to accept them as payment for his services for the baby's delivery.

"Aunt Mary told me she thanked God that she and the doctor saw eye to eye on the value of those geese." Margaret Mary finished her story by saying, "Aunt Mary really knew how to barter. It's lucky for her and her family that barter was an everyday part of life back then."

Stanislaus and Anna laughed out loud at the wonderful story. "As your uncle Ed was fond of saying, that was brilliant," her uncle replied with twinkling eyes. "I never doubted little Mary Cecilia for a minute. I was sure she would come away with what she wanted in her bargain with the doctor."

Childhood Memories of the Homestead

Before she finished her visit, Margaret Mary wanted to tell her uncle about a few special memories she had about the old homestead and asked if he was too tired to hear them.

Stanislaus smiled and replied, "I would be delighted to hear these special memories of yours."

Margaret Mary looked around the room and said, "I loved sitting with Grandpa Anton by his fireplace, just like this, when we lived here with him. My favorite place, though, was the homestead, and I loved the family gatherings and picnics that were held there. I remember when we stopped calling it Grandpa Vaclav's homestead and started calling it Uncle Emil's place. Even as a young child, I recall being impressed with the variety of trees that you and Uncle Ed planted out there. I especially loved the catalpa trees lining both sides of the lane."

Plucked geese story by Mary Cecilia Karella Pojar

Her elderly uncle smiled and said, "I loved them too. You know it was your great-grandfather, my papa, who started the tree-planting project. When he and Mama moved to this house, I took over the tree project. That year, we added apple trees."

Smiling at her great-uncle, she replied softly, "I never knew that. What a wonderful idea it was to plant blooming trees right at the highway turnoff from the main road. I can still see them in my mind. How they lined the lane all the way up to the house and how magnificent they were in bloom. They were so tall I believed they touched the blue sky above them. In my memory, the fragrance of those blooms hung in the air for weeks in the springtime."

"Yes, the scent of the blossoms did hang in the air for along time." He added softly, "I remember it well. Please continue with your story."

Nodding, the young woman said, "For some reason, I also vividly remember that large stockyard and the enormous hay pen in the middle of it. As a young child, I seriously considered eating hay because the cattle seemed to enjoy it so much. I also recall the feel of the fence that surrounded the stockyard. I sat on it a lot to watch you and Grandpa with the livestock. It was made of rough-cut cottonwood, wasn't it?"

"Yes, I believe it was," he replied.

Margaret Mary went on softly, "I spent a lot of time sitting on that fence because I loved the animals. Perhaps that is why I am so fond of this memory. And I am very fond of you. Thank you for making the Karella homestead so wonderful that it lives in my mind and in my heart. You and Grandpa made it a grand and beautiful place full of love, purpose, and adventure."

Teary-eyed, she looked at the clock and said, "Oh my goodness, Uncle Stanislaus, it's getting late." Leaning over, she kissed him on the cheek and said, "I must go now."

He squeezed her hand affectionately as he replied, "Thank you, sweet Margaret Mary, for the lovely visit and for sharing your delightful memories with me. I think you will make a wonderful nun."

Just before she walked to the door, she said sweetly, "I love you. Thank you for everything. I hope I get a chance to come and visit you and Aunt Anna in South Dakota."

Stanislaus smiled and took hold of Anna's hand, encouraging Anna to reply with an invitation, and Anna said, "We hope you will come and see us, Margaret Mary. We love you too."

Spring-1935, Norfolk, Nebraska

The last of Rusty and Delora's jelly jar savings was enough to get the family settled in a house in Norfolk and stock the pantry. In this larger town, businesses were still open, and the city government was still running. Rusty told Delora he would take any kind of work he could find.

Rusty also asked Delora not to consider working outside their home until all their children were in school, and she agreed.

Coming to Norfolk was a new start for them. This bigger town felt alive with energy and had lots of people, and those people used tools and equipment that broke. During the Depression, people had to fix cars and household items like clocks, radios, and stoves when they broke down, as they could not afford to buy new to replace the old. Rusty quickly built a reputation for being able to fix or repair anything. He took part-time hours at Roseswalk Blacksmith, Norfolk Farm Equipment, and Turk Plumbing and Heating. Through all the odd jobs, he managed to keep a good roof over his family's heads and food on the table.

Rabbit Hunting Pays a Bounty

Hunting jackrabbits during the Dust Bowl years in Nebraska

Rusty had one other unique way to make extra money while doing something he enjoyed and could share with his son Ambrose on his days off.

Historically speaking, jackrabbits were a menace that overran the countryside in Nebraska during the drought years. Rabbit hunts were organized in counties where farmers reported grain and field devastation by the exploding rabbit population. To keep men and boys hunting the rabbits, the state government paid a bounty of three cents for black-tailed rabbit pelts and five cents for white-tailed rabbit pelts. Eventually, all the government required for proof of a successful hunt was a pair of rabbit ears, which were easily identified as black tails or white tails. These rabbits were used as meat for many families who could not afford anything else to eat. In 1935, one county estimated the rabbit hunts saved enough food to feed 1,450 cows and 7,000 sheep.

When the Karellas moved to Norfolk, jackrabbit hunting still paid five cents per set of ears. Hunting rabbits not only put extra meat on the table, but it also gave Rusty a little more money for extras like going to the movies with Delora and the kids.

When Ambrose turned nine years old, he was very tall and mature for his age group. Rusty took him along on weekend jackrabbit hunts and taught Ambrose to shoot a small .22 caliber rifle and how to prepare the ears to turn in for a bounty. Then Rusty taught his son how to clean the meat so his mama could cook it. Ambrose learned to be an expert shot very quickly. Once Ambrose's cleaning skills improved so his mother no longer complained about the condition of the rabbit meat, Rusty gave his son a folding knife of his own to carry.

One weekend before school began, Rusty and Ambrose were out in a field near some trees. Rusty handed the .22 rifle to Ambrose, put his finger to his lips, and pointed at the bushes ahead.

Ambrose forgot all his dad's instructions in his excitement. As soon as he saw the grass move, he pulled the trigger. When the grass stopped moving, they went to look and found that he had shot a raccoon. From behind the dead animal crawled a baby raccoon. Ambrose started to cry, realizing he had killed the baby's mama. Rusty knelt and picked up the baby raccoon

Jimmy, Ambrose's pet racoon

and brought it to his son, saying, "Ambrose, this little one is going to need a lot of care if he is going to live."

Ambrose instantly wiped off his face and asked, "I can keep it?" His father nodded, and he reached up and took it gently into his hands and cuddled the little furball next to his chest. "I'll call him Jimmy," Ambrose said, petting its tiny head.

"Since you start school on Monday, I expect you to read about raccoons in the library and tell me what they eat. You must learn how to take care of him properly. Can you promise me you will do that?"

"Yes, Dad, I will," Ambrose replied as they walked slowly back to the car. Rusty dropped the rabbits they had shot in a burlap bag and put them in the trunk. Ambrose got into the car, holding Jimmy wrapped in his shirt to keep the baby warm, and then it fell asleep. It was Ambrose's first pet. When they got home, Ambrose told his mother what happened and showed Jimmy to her.

His mother set down a few rules of her own, saying, "Ambrose, you must feed it and keep its box clean. When it is old enough, I will expect that you and your father will build him a cage

Jimmy, Ambrose's pet racoon

333

outside. If it bites anyone, especially your brothers or sisters, it will have to go. Is that understood?"

Ambrose nodded his head and replied, "Yes, Mom, I understand, and I promise I'll take real good care of Jimmy, and he won't be any trouble."

Ambrose went out to the car to get the Brownie camera his dad always carried with him. He wanted to take pictures of Jimmy. He planned to do a report at school on his new pet.

By the time Jimmy was six months old, he was getting into so much mischief in the house that Ambrose knew he'd better ask his father to help him build a pen for Jimmy outside. His timing was very good, because a few days later, he couldn't find Jimmy. The animal wasn't in his box, and Ambrose turned his room upside down looking for his pet. That was when he heard a terrible banging racket in the kitchen followed by his mother's raised voice.

"Jimmy!" he whispered as he ran down the stairs and into the kitchen.

"Ambrose! Get that noisy animal out of my kitchen! You will wash every pot and pan he has been banging on the floor and pulled out of my cupboards. Straighten up this mess immediately!" his mother said with barely controlled anger.

Jimmy, Ambrose's pet racoon

Ambrose and Rusty built Jimmy a very nice pen with a hefty latch. Who knew the raccoon would become a master escape artist? Jimmy could figure out latches and simple locks very quickly. Ambrose kept changing the latches in hopes of keeping Jimmy in his pen when he was gone to school. It never took very long for the raccoon's little hands and fingers to figure out the new lock and let himself out.

Secretly, Ambrose was thrilled every time his pet outsmarted the lock. He did find himself in trouble more than a few times over things Jimmy had gotten into or tore apart after letting himself out of his pen. The worst trouble he got into was when Jimmy would get loose and into the trash and strew it all over the yard.

At the same time, Ambrose was the envy of the neighborhood. He was very proud to say he had a pet raccoon when the other kids had a dog or a cat. He was always the center of attention, too, when he started telling funny stories about Jimmy.

Sacred Heart Catholic School, a combined school system for both primary and secondary education in Norfolk, Nebraska

Enrolled in Catholic School

The Karella's house on Lincoln Street was in a nice neighborhood near the Sacred Heart Catholic Church. Rusty and Delora made an appointment to meet the pastor and introduce themselves.

Delora explained their two oldest boys, Ambrose James and his brother Charles Dale, needed to be enrolled in Sacred Heart's Grade School in September. Their new pastor, Father Hugh Gately, said he would help Delora accomplish that task.

The priest also told Rusty and Delora a little about the history of the school. "In 1926, our Catholic Sacred Heart Parish of Norfolk opened its first school for grades one through eight. At that time, our faculty consisted of four Sisters of Saint Francis who had relocated to Nebraska from Rochester, Minnesota. Our staff has grown a bit since then, and we are proud that the children of our parish have a good grade school and high school to attend right here close to the church."

Delora smiled and replied, "Father, Rusty and I are thrilled that our boys will be attending a good catholic school. We know they will get an excellent education at Sacred Heart. They have three other siblings, so you will be seeing more of our children as the years pass.

Thank you for helping me get them into school. We will see you on Sunday."

End of September, Norfolk

It had been a month since Ambrose and Charles started school. Nicknames quickly found the Karella boys. Everyone at school just called Ambrose James AJ, and they shortened Charles Dale to just Charlie. When they started calling each other AJ and Charlie at home, so did everyone else.

Delora missed her oldest sons when they were gone to school all day, but five-year-old Lloyd, three-year-old Florence, and one-year-old Marcella kept her busy . . . and . . . she suspected she was pregnant again but did not want to mention that yet—not until she was sure.

Kodak Brownie Camera 2, home camera repaired by Rusty and kept in his car— Photo by GKM, 2021

Delora enjoyed life in Norfolk. *Something is always happening here,* she thought as she warmed up a bottle of milk on the stove for baby Marcella. The radio played softly in the background, and Delora hummed along as little Shirley Temple sang "Old Straw Hat" from her latest hit movie, *Rebecca of Sunny Brook Farm.*

Such a beautiful child, she thought. *She has become a huge sensation. Everyone is talking about her movies, and they play her songs on the radio constantly.* Then an idea popped into Delora's head, and she thought, *Tonight, I am going to see if Rusty would mind if I give the kids a treat. The Shirley Temple movie matinee is only 15 cents.*

"Can we afford that?" Delora asked as they were getting ready for bed that evening.

Rusty loved that twinkle she got in her eyes when she asked for something she really wanted. She didn't ask for much, so how could he say no to her beautiful face? Nodding, he replied, "We can make do for such a small treat. I'll come home for lunch early and drop you off at the theater with the kids."

Grand Theater Norfolk—children's matinee costs 15 cents

Delora hugged him with enthusiasm, whispering a delighted, "Thank you, Rusty! I'm just as excited as the kids." He smiled, knowing what she said was very true.

When Rusty pulled up across the street from the theater, there was a crowd of grownups and kids waiting for the ticket office to open. "Don't worry, Rusty. The kids and I are happy to wait."

"Are you sure?" he asked.

"Yes, go back to work. Waiting in this crowd is all part of the fun!"

As Rusty pulled away, he thought, *I'm not surprised that so many people are here to see a movie full of joy and happy endings. It's a needed break from the worry and reality of this danged Depression, though it's not as bad here as it was in Madison.*

The Power of Radio

The Radio provided a constant background sound in the Norfolk Karella's home. It had the power to subliminally change Rusty and Delora's views on many things.

Delora did not know what it was like to be a young girl in high school and experience the fun and freedom of meeting new people or making friends her age each school year. What she did experience was loneliness as she fulfilled the duties of a nursemaid and all the responsibilities of taking care of children and a household from age fourteen to sixteen.

When she did find a friend in the man she loved, she married him at 16, and by 17, she had a husband, a baby, and a household of her own. At 25, Delora had become a responsible wife and mother of five but still was a young girl at heart who just happened to be 25 years old.

Tabletop model 1929 radio

This experience of moving to a new town and the excitement of meeting new people tapped into her undeveloped emotions, and music helped deal with her emerging feelings. It let her cry with a sad song, laugh with a silly song, or feel romance in her heart with a love song. Music filled her day with joy just because of the beautiful sound it added to her life.

Somehow, when she listened to songs like the new Fred Astaire tune, "Cheek to Cheek," playing on the radio, it made Delora imagine herself dressed up and dancing too. Happy thoughts put her in a mood that helped her believe everything would be all right despite their struggles.

Rusty and Delora's life was simple, and money was tighter than ever. Yet, she liked living in their new town where they were free to be who they wanted to be. No aunties, uncles, or in-laws next door wanting to know what they were doing or where they were all the time. Delora loved the family, but for only the second time in her life, she was experiencing an exciting new adventure, and that freedom invigorated her.

Radio news helped Rusty and Delora understand and develop a connection to what was going on around the country as well. The news reports often made them conscious of how fortunate they were to have their own problems compared to people living in Kansas or Oklahoma, where dust storms were literally killing people.

Radio programs served a good purpose too. While the children were down for their naps, Delora would listen to soap operas like *Backstage Wife* and *Death Valley Days*. Those programs were exciting sources of entertainment and information as they described situations in life and gave examples of how to deal with them. The radio made a good babysitter because the children didn't move a muscle when they listened to a favorite serial program. Stories like *Roy Rogers* and *The Green Hornet* allowed her a solid 15 minutes at a time to focus on her infant's needs or get dinner started.

Radio news came from around the world, helping the Karella family develop an understanding of issues affecting America in relation to what was happening in Europe. Living a bit of a distance from the rest of the family, they did not talk to them every day about the news. As a result, Rusty and Delora realized just how much they depended on the radio to know what was going on around them.

Norfolk, Day-to-Day Living Expenses

No one could get more value out of a dollar than Rusty's Bitty. Even so, money was still limited. All items to be purchased were divided into two lists.

One was nice-to-have items, while the other list was comprised of need-to-have items. A priority on the need-to-have list was milk for their toddler and infant daughter. Delora and Rusty gladly did without many things themselves to make up for the cost of buying enough milk for the children.

Years later, Delora and Rusty discovered the milk they had worked so hard to afford was the cause of an infant nutritional health issue. When Rusty's daughter Florence struggled to walk as a young toddler, it was the family doctor who said she suffered from weak bones. Her condition was called rickets, a disease that affected bone development caused by drinking diluted milk as an infant.

Florence Karella, toddler on pony, mid-1930s

Delora did not understand. With alarm, she replied, looking at Rusty and the doctor, "I didn't dilute the milk I fed to my babies!"

The doctor saw the dismay he had caused and told Florence's parents this was not their fault. He recognized the issue right away because it was not the first case like this he had seen. "I hate to be the one to tell you this," the doctor said, "but it was the dairyman who watered down the milk before selling it to markets and, therefore, to you. In fact, the dairyman watered down the milk to such a degree it lacked many of the essential nutrients needed for the formation of infant bones."

When the Karellas discovered the precious milk they had starved themselves for had actually starved their daughter as well, Rusty seethed with fury. They could not afford to give in to the anger they felt over such treachery. What they forced themselves to say publicly was that times had been tough for everyone. What was done was done. They needed to concentrate on finding a solution to Florence's problem.

What Rusty said to his wife privately was a different story. As a father, he really wanted to find that dairyman and beat him until he had problems walking that were worse than his daughter had to live with.

Norfolk, Birth of a Third Daughter

On January 2, 1936, happy calls flew through the telephone lines between Madison and Norfolk as Rusty and Delora celebrated the arrival of their third daughter, Mildred Leona, whom they called Millie. Once Grandma and Grandpa Holt arrived in Norfolk, everyone gathered around the radio. They listened and danced to the lively music of Benny Goodman and Tommy Dorsey as they celebrated. Surrounded by their five older grandchildren, Jim and Margaret Holt watched their daughter Delora glow with happiness. They thanked God both mother and baby were in excellent health.

Spring 1936, Encouraging Information

Breaking news on the radio reported that the government irrigation program would start soon. That news lifted the debilitating anxiety and worry that had been strangling the townspeople of Norfolk.

Shortly after that first announcement, Rusty heard that the Central Nebraska Public Power and Irrigation District (CNPPID) was ready to begin construction on the Kingsley Dam and Lake McConaughey to store the needed water for the huge irrigation project ahead. Within months, Rusty landed a stable full-time job. Based on Rusty's steady paychecks, the Karellas realized Norfolk would be the family's hometown for the foreseeable future.

Across Nebraska, farming and city communities finally felt hope for the first time in years. People were going back to work or knew they would get work soon once Congress finished passing the irrigation support programs for Nebraska.

Soon, construction jobs would open for local hires, and material orders would begin to shore up Norfolk's businesses. Once the pipes began tapping into the Missouri River and water started flowing back into the fields, farmers could start working the land again and put even more people back to work.

For years, Nebraskan farmers and farmers across the breadbasket states of America had been caught between two vicious cycles. The first being the issue of mass surplus products that were warehoused with no market. The second was having no money and no water to produce farm products to sell. As a result of this horrible economic condition, many hardworking citizens lost their farms and were forced to migrate out of the Great Plains. They primarily went west, looking for any kind of work they could find. Many of these people became migrant farm laborers working the planting and harvesting cycles up and down the West Coast of the United States.

November, 1936: America Re-Elects FDR

As the Karellas kept watch on the harsh and frightening changes being reported overseas, the American people re-elected Franklin

Delano Roosevelt to the United States Presidency. He had shown the people of the United States that with hard work and some sacrifice, America could rebound from its state of depression. FDR got re-elected by a landslide for another four years despite the efforts of big business and many political factions trying to undermine what FDR was struggling to accomplish. He campaigned, talking about his "Second New Deal" that highlighted five major goals: improved use of national resources, security against old age, unemployment and illness, slum clearance, and national work relief programs under the Works Progress Administration, which would replace direct relief efforts. FDR believed a man needed to work to bolster his dignity and his self-worth to rebuild his confidence.

FDR also mentioned that in such troubling times, he agreed with 65% of Americans regarding the movies. For 15 cents, they could go to the movies and fill their pockets full of sunshine and joy, helping them escape their worries for an hour, listening to the sweet voice of Shirley Temple singing "On the Good Ship Lollipop." He said, "I certainly enjoyed it too."

FDR had one area of government plagued with considerable division even within the groups of people who voted him into office. Foreign policy was a touchy subject. Any hint the United States might get involved in Europe's struggles, conflicts, and especially war were adamantly rejected.

Summer 1937

Rusty admired his eldest son's hunting skills. The boy had become an excellent shot, and the way he took care of the meat and how he acted when they were afield gave Rusty great confidence in his son's abilities.

For Ambrose's tenth birthday, Rusty gave him his own .22 caliber rifle. There was one stipulation above all the others, and Rusty said, "The most important rule is to always treat your rifle like it is loaded. Now, what do I mean by that, son?" he asked as he handed the rifle to Ambrose.

"Dad, that means it is not a toy. I never point it at another person, even if it is unloaded. I always make sure I have seen and identified what I am shooting at before I pull the trigger. I make a clean, quick, painless one-shot kill if it is possible. And last, I always unload my rifle, clean it, and put it away in a safe place when I come home."

Rusty smiled and replied, "Excellent answer, son. I would only add one thing to that list. Always be careful to carry the muzzle of your rifle pointing at the ground when you are walking with it."

Mildred (Millie) Karella with brother Jerome Ambrose (Pete) Karella

"Yes, Dad," he replied.

With the gift of the gun, Ambrose was also given permission to go rabbit hunting on his own when they needed meat. He could keep the bounty money he made on the rabbits he hunted, and he could invite his friends to go hunting with him.

Rusty turned to his second son, asking, "Charles Dale, do you want to learn how to hunt?"

"Yes, Dad, I do," the boy replied excitedly.

"You and I will start this weekend," Rusty replied.

Birth of the Karellas' Fourth Son

Fortunately, the Karellas were blessed and able to remain in Nebraska. Three years after the beginning of the irrigation project, Rusty and Delora welcomed their seventh child into the world on August 7, 1937. A handsome baby boy christened Jerome Ambrose and whose adoring mother intended to nickname him Jerry. When she mentioned as much to her husband, Rusty startled her with his reaction. He adamantly rejected the idea, saying, "You will not call my son Jerry, and if you do, I'll call him Pete!"

Throughout Rusty's life when he gave a nickname, it generally stuck. His baby son was no exception. The entire Karella clan called this little boy Pete from that day on.

A Madison Cousin Is Born

Twenty days later, the telephone rang, and Delora put baby Pete on one hip and picked up the receiver with her other hand. "Hello?"

—*Madam, one moment please. Go ahead, sir,* the operator said.

"Delora?" came the voice on the other end of the line.

She recognized Stanley Voborny's voice. "Stanley! How is Mary? Did the baby come?"

Switchboard and operators for the telephone systems in the 1930s

"Yes," Stanley replied proudly, "Mary had a little boy, and we have named him Dewayne Richard."

"And Mary?" she asked.

His voice sounded relieved. "Doing very well. Of course, she's tired, but everything is good. Oh, my goodness! The baby just started crying again, and Mary has finally fallen to sleep. I must go and get him before he wakes her. Tell Rusty the news. We will talk later. Love to you both." And the phone went quiet as Stanley hung up the receiver.

Smiling, Delora thought, *Rusty is going to be so pleased to hear the news that his sister is doing well and that our baby Pete now has a cousin the same age.*

1938, a Fourth Daughter Is Born

Fourteen months later, Delora delivered her last baby on October 3, 1938, rounding out the number of children in the Karella household to eight. She chose the name Sharon Barbara and announced her decision to the family. This is when her excited sons, who were home early from school, informed her she could not name their baby sister Barbara. Shaking her head in exasperation, Delora promptly asked, "And why not?" The boys told her that Sharon had been born on the feast day of St. Theresa. That meant the baby should be named after the saint. Delora thought about that fact for a moment and agreed with them.

Being a gracious mother, she let the men in her family sway her decision and named her baby girl Sharon Theresa Karella.

When baby Sharon was old enough to be left with the grandparents, Rusty asked what she would like most just to pamper herself. It didn't take long for Bitty to decide. "I want to go see the new film by Walt Disney. I have been reading the reviews about it in the newspapers, and they are saying that *Snow White and the Seven Dwarves* is the best moving picture they've ever seen!"

Rusty arranged for the children to stay with their Holt grandparents in Madison for a weekend, and he took Bitty to Disney's animated motion picture. The story enchanted them both. It touched Rusty's heart because his father used to read Grimm Brother's fairy tales to him and his brothers and sisters when they were children. Seeing this story come to life was magical for him, and watching Bitty and the emotion it brought out in her and the happiness at the ending was worth every cent of the ticket's price.

Children's Memories

The Sacred Heart school system was teaching grades one through twelve when Delora's last child was born. AJ had turned 12, followed by Charlie at ten, Lloyd at eight, and Florence had turned seven, and all of them went to the same school.

Even with four of her children gone during the day, Delora still had her hands full at home. Marcella had turned four, and toddler Millie was three. Baby Pete was wobbling around on 14-month-old baby legs by the time his newborn sister, Sharon, joined the family in early October.

Karella clan gathering of Pojars, Vobornys, and Beans at the Pojar farm

King of the Castle

In the confined space of one house with two adults and eight children, Rusty and Delora learned ten people could create chaos without strict rules. In the Karella's castle, Rusty was the king, and what he said was law. Delora was the queen, and all the children wanted to stay in her good graces, because if she was on their side, then she could sway their father's decisions.

After the king and queen, the power to give orders came with age. Each child as they got older were given responsibilities and learned to do their part. With responsibility came the right to tell the littler brothers and sisters what to do to keep order in the Karella household.

Delora relied heavily on her oldest son, AJ, to watch out for his younger brothers and sisters. She made it clear they were to listen to AJ and obey his orders. He was the boss when Mommy and Daddy were not with them or away from home.

AJ took his mother's instructions to heart. That meant his guidance and orders began as soon as he and the kids stepped foot out of the house and headed for school. The Karella's home at 504 Lincoln Street was about a mile from the school, and the Karella kids walked to Sacred Heart every day shepherded by AJ, whom they also called *the firstborn.*

School in Norfolk

AJ had begun a growth spurt and already towered over his nearest brother, Charlie, and Charlie had nearly as much trouble as Lloyd and Florence keeping up with AJ on their walks to school. AJ's legs only got longer and faster. But the fuse on his teenage temper grew shorter each time the kids lollygagged, fell behind on their walk, or made them late for school.

As the firstborn, it was part of AJ's job to keep his siblings in line and on time. He took that job seriously because he was the one who got in trouble with his mother if the teachers reported any of the Karella kids for tardiness during the school year.

The Karella children were prone to typical family squabbles between brothers and sisters. When their parents considered the differences in personality, teenage hormones, and the responsibility expected of them, they could see AJ was a bit of a tyrant, but he did keep his siblings in line.

AJ and Charlie, being the two oldest boys, generally teamed up on any important matter, as they were left in charge when their parents were not at home. They were both strong-willed, and Charlie was always trying to impress AJ and his friends and wanted to be part of their group even though he was almost two years younger.

Quite naturally, Lloyd and Florence became the second team. Both had gentler personalities than their older brothers. They also shared a close bond of respect and understanding for one another's feelings. The four littlest kids were ruled almost exclusively by their mother, and that would not change until they started going to school and fell under the command of the firstborn.

Years of Unrest in Europe

Rusty, along with his father, his uncles, and cousins, had been listening to the news and reading about the trouble that had been brewing in Europe for years. Every year, conflicts were escalating. Though these events were perpetrated by different countries, the conflicts felt darkly connected in subtle ways. Back in 1934, Stalin had begun massacring people in Russia. Then, a year later, Nazi Germany repudiated the Versailles Treaty and began rallying its armies. Soon, it was apparent Germany was seeking alliances across Europe.

In 1936 shortly after Japan began a war with China, Japan signed the Anti-Comintern Pact with Germany. And Italy joined the same pact with Germany the same year. Great Britain was destabilized with the death of King George, and the government focus was further preoccupied when the deceased king's eldest son abdicated the throne. While Great Britain's government tried to find balance, Germany was on the move, marching armies into neighboring countries. By the time things settled down in Britain with King George VI on the throne, Italy withdrew from the League of Nations. Then the Japanese sank the United States Gunboat Panay as they invaded China, taking control of most of its coastal areas.

Like his father, AJ and his friends had been listening to both American and international news. Rusty and Delora did not realize AJ was not just getting taller. The boy's sense of right and wrong began to develop through what he heard, and his awareness of the world kept pace with the world as it changed around all of them.

Marine poster on Andy's wall in Norfolk home, 1940

By 1938, Great Britain realized war with Germany was inevitable. The British Empire began talks with their allies, America being one of them. Great Britain's wartime preparations were made public, and this information filtered into the news programs around the world. News of Great Britain's enemies and their aggressive movement in Europe and Asia became flash bulletins over the radio airways and were announced between regularly scheduled programming. As Andy and his friends listened to their favorite radio shows, like *Buck Rogers, Flash Gordon,* and *The Shadow,* they also developed a deep connection with their country, and by association, their patriotism included their country's allies. These boys on the verge of becoming men started to hear the patriotic call. Be on guard. Be ready to defend America against enemy nations. AJ believed Germany was one of those enemy nations, and the name of its leader was Hitler.

Left-to-right back: Delora (Bitty) Holt Karella, Rusty Karella, Andy (AJ), Charles Dale, and Lloyd
Left-to-right front: Millie, Marcella, Florence, Pete, and Sharon

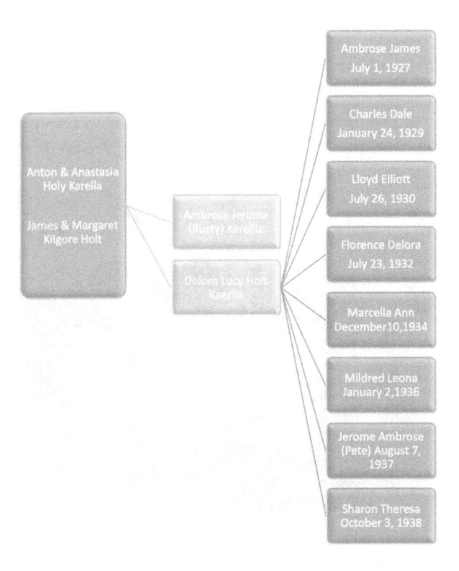

Ambrose Jerome and Delora Lucy Holt Karella Family
Relationship Chart—Norfolk, Nebraska

CHAPTER 20

1939 through Spring of 1941

Norfolk, Nebraska, Home of Rusty Karella

January 1939 began very much like the year before, except Rusty Karella had turned 41. Delora still looked as young as ever at 29, even though she was now a mother of eight children. The children ranged in age from 12 all the way down to the one-year-old baby, which kept Bitty very busy.

Delora Lucy (Bitty) Holt Karella

Moving to Norfolk had been a good choice for them. Rusty thanked the good Lord every day that his employment remained solid. They did not have a lot of extra money, but the bills were paid, they had a well-constructed house, and they lived in a good neighborhood where the church and the children's school were only a mile away.

Housewife and Mother

During the day, Delora liked to listen to the mystery and romance soap operas on the radio when she put the children down for their naps. She loved to hear the music as she did laundry and worked around the house. Delora listened to artists like Perry Como singing his latest hit song, "A Gypsy Told Me," or sang along with Ella Fitzgerald singing "A-Tiskit, A-Tasket." Letting those melodies fill her mind made the hours of housework and chores fly by until her husband and children came home, and she focused on dinner.

Daughter of Rusty and Delora Holt Karella, Mildred Leona Karella, stands in the arms of her grandmother, Margaret Kilgore Holt, 1938

Ambrose James began a growing spurt. At 12, her handsome son already towered over his ten-year-old brother, Charles Dale. It was not just his height that was changing. Ambrose, even as a youngster, wanted to help her around the house. He was always gentle and affectionate with his younger brothers. Ambrose adored having a baby sister and loved to play with Florence when she was born during the tough years in Madison. Her son matured even more as he took on the responsibility of guiding the children as they went off to school after they moved to Norfolk.

These days, Ambrose was doing well at school, excelling in art and writing. He had an ear for music and sang in the chorus at Sacred Heart. The music teacher said Ambrose learned to read music quickly and possessed a strong baritone singing voice with a good sense of pitch. He generally was given a solo to sing in the Christmas pageant at the school each year. During the past year, she thought she had caught glimpses of the man Ambrose would become someday.

She knew Ambrose could be very persuasive when he wanted to be. He could certainly convince his two best friends, Chauncey and George, to go along with just about anything he asked them to do. She was happy to see him revert to just being a boy when the three of them were together. They had been nearly inseparable since they met their first year at Sacred Heart Grade School. Those boys loved to fish, were very good hunters, and several times a week, they brought home fish or rabbits for supper. During hunting season, they even brought home deer.

Her second son, Charles, was very good at bargaining for what he wanted. Charles possessed a wonderful imagination. Warm and spontaneous, the boy admired his older brother and loved his family. A quick study, Charles could do anything in school he put his mind to. Delora could easily guess what Charles Dale wanted most in life at 10 years old. He wanted to be accepted as an equal into the group with Ambrose and his two friends.

Charles and George both had a fascination for airplanes, and Charles was nearly as good a shot with his .22 rifle as Ambrose. He had the skills and the interests to fit in with the older boys and their hobbies. Charles and his older brother generally got along and thought alike too. Delora knew her two oldest sons were strong and brave and extremely protective of their siblings. Those two could talk to anyone for hours and make friends easily. She could always depend on them. The only flaw she saw in her oldest sons was the fact that Ambrose and Charles tended to be a bit bossy at times, and perhaps they enjoyed teasing their sisters a little too much. Florence complained that what her brothers called teasing was more like pestering. The teasing quite often turned into hurt feelings and spurts of temper all around.

Charles and his younger brother Lloyd could not have been more different. Nine-year-old Lloyd was sweet tempered, and he loved school. He treasured books and tended to be a quiet thinker rather than a jabberer. Lloyd had one best friend named Bud Roggenbach. The two of them were very much alike. They would laugh and joke and were sensitive and gentle regarding Lloyd's younger siblings, especially Florence. Florence was a year younger than Lloyd, but she was already as tall as he was at seven years old.

Karella kids:
Millie, Marcella, and Pete

Florence was Delora's eldest daughter. She gave Florence a lot of responsibility because she matured quickly and proved she was dependable at a young age. Delora found Florence to be a great help around the house. Despite her bouts of temper, Florence was a shy girl inside and lacked confidence at times. She and Lloyd had formed a close bond. Lloyd was Florence's staunchest supporter and her protector. That made Lloyd's best friend, Bud, Florence's protector too. The three of them spent a lot of happy times together.

On the other hand, there was considerable friction between Florence and her two oldest brothers. They knew just how to frustrate her. Delora noticed that when Florence looked like a simmering pot of potatoes getting ready to boil over, she generally saw Ambrose or Charles walking away from her. Delora decided it was time to set down some strict rules for the older children's behavior before Ambrose, Charles, and Florence got much older. Teenage hormones on top of Florence's quick temper would not be a good combination. Delora knew she needed to keep the teasing between siblings to a minimum. Too often, a simple thing turned into a squabble, then became an argument, particularly between Ambrose and Florence.

Thankfully, the other four little ones were still just sweet toddlers whose personalities were still forming, and they all got into mischief if she didn't keep her eye on them. Other than that, they took regular naps, and in between the mischief and laughter, they showered her with lots of sweet hugs and wet kisses. What else could a mother ask for?

February 1939

Tuesday, February 7, dawned cold and overcast as 29-year-old Delora Lucy Holt Karella dressed carefully in black. Tears ran down her face as she thought of her

Newspaper article
RE: Holt Daughter
Dies, 1939

beautiful younger sister, Violet, who had just passed away the day before. Deep in thought, Delora did not hear Rusty talking to her.

Violet was only 27, and she spent nearly half of those years stuck at home with Mama and Papa in that wheelchair. That horrible car accident

almost killed her shortly after Rusty and I got married. Everyone rejoiced that she lived even if she was confined to a wheelchair. Over the years when Rusty took me to visit Mama and Papa, I spent most of my time with Violet. She never got to have her own adventures, but she loved to hear about mine. When my children came to visit, she couldn't wait to hold them.

Rusty walked up to her dressed in his best dark suit for the trip to Madison and touched her arm, bringing Delora back to the present. "Bitty, are you ready to go?" She nodded.

Violet Holt, 1913–1939, younger sister to Delora Lucy Holt Karella

Delora had kept her children home from school for the day, and her eldest son was going to watch them. "Ambrose, thank you for taking care of your brothers and sisters so I can spend time with your grandparents and my brothers and sister."

"Mama, I understand. Please tell Grandpa how sad we are that Aunt Violet is gone and that we will miss her. Please tell Grandpa and Grandma how much we love them."

"We will, son," Rusty said as he took Bitty by the arm, and they walked to the car.

The Household Income

In the coming months, Delora felt both sad and restless. She kept thinking of Violet stuck in that wheelchair unable to do so many things. Those thoughts made Delora feel more determined than ever to make every moment count. During the tougher years in Madison, Delora had helped boost their household income by baking and selling pies. Then their family kept growing, and eventually there was little time for anything but trying to keep up with her brood of eight children. Now, half of them spent their days in school.

Things had settled down so much she began thinking about doing something useful with her free time and thought about getting a job. When thoughts like that filled her head, Delora had to remind herself of her promise to Rusty. He made her promise not to even consider working outside their home until all the children were in school. She was determined to keep that promise, but at the same time, she hated being bored. *Maybe*, she thought, *I could start baking again.* The idea kept running through her mind, so she decided to mention it to Rusty at suppertime.

"Rusty, I've been thinking. Now that Marcella is five and the three toddlers have begun taking long naps, I feel ready to start baking and selling pies again." Her husband gave her a sideways glance under a wrinkled brow. Bitty held up her hand, saying, "I am thrilled you have a steady paycheck now, and I know I promised I wouldn't get a job until all the kids were in school. But if I baked and sold pies, I would not be working outside our home, and we could use the extra money."

Rusty looked at her hopeful face, thinking, *Everything Bitty said is true.* After a moment, he nodded and replied, "You are right, and the extra money would help." Bitty gave her husband a radiant smile, happy to find he was in a reasonable mood. She would start three piggy banks. One would be for gas money for taking the kids to Madison to see Grandma and Grandpa Holt and Rusty's family. The second bank would be for going to the movies, and the third would be for Christmas! She couldn't wait to get started selling her pies and putting pennies in her banks.

1940, Norfolk Daily News

The Karellas and the Holts listened to or read the news every day. Sometimes, the things they talked about or wrote about happening in other places did not feel real. Shoot, even the things happening in America's cities didn't feel real compared to her family's life in Norfolk, Nebraska.

Reality for Delora and her family was dealing with the daily limitations of economic depression in their community. They were much better off now that Rusty had a stable job. Yet, even when he was doing part-time work for several companies or taking in extra repair work on his own, they never felt desperate. Not like they had in Madison when they actually broke the law to pay bills and put food on the table. For her, what was happening in big American cities and foreign conflicts between countries in Europe seemed very far away from their families and their life.

For her husband, it was different. When Rusty's people moved to the Madison area back in the late 1800s, there were a lot of old Civil War veterans who lived in the area who had been given government land grants, and they had farms. Rusty's granddad, uncles, and father knew a lot of those elderly men, and they talked a lot about their war days over the years until they all died. The other big difference was that Rusty's family had lived through World War I. Rusty told her his uncle Emil had been within the age group of men who could have been drafted to go to war. Rusty was just a year or so from being old enough to be drafted. That really scared his family. But the war took a turn for the good guys and then ended, and neither Rusty nor Emil went to war. Delora understood all that was in the past, and they were living in the modern age of 1940. But there were a few things that still connected them to the past. War was one of those things. No matter where war took place in the world, that still frightened her now that she had sons of her own.

A Husband and Father

It was part of his job to keep his family calm and thinking clearly. Rusty kept his old memories about World War I in the back of his mind to learn from them. He compared and analyzed what he heard from radio reports and what he read in the newspapers that seemed similar.

He did see some correlation between the rising hostilities in Europe now and the news he read about as a teenaged boy. Back then, those hostilities had eventually turned into World War I. That war had seemed far away, too, until America got involved in it, and American men went off to war. It was now 1940, and they were Americans and belonged to a huge country that was part of one nation. He and his family had a government that protected its people. Rusty also believed in President Roosevelt. He would do what had to be done at the right time. Until then, it did little good to worry about things that were so far away.

Operator's switchboard—for telephone service, photo by GKM 2020

Lately when Delora got worked up over something in the news, he would say calmly, "Look, Delora, I agree we need to keep this information in the back of our minds, but let's not obsess too much over it. We have things to do right here in our town and right now in our home. Let's not turn these reports and bits of information into something that it isn't. I promise we will stay prepared for what comes. Other than that, try not to make a big deal out of what the boys say about becoming soldiers or overreact to things they have heard or the comic books they read. Let them enjoy being young, and we'll handle each situation as it comes, OK? Our boys and their friends remind me of my uncle Emil and my brother Frank.

"When things got too tame for them on the farm, they began looking for excitement elsewhere. Our boys and their friends are 12- and ten-year-olds. They crave a little thrilling adventure right now. I don't believe their daydreams really pose a threat to their future. Let them listen to their radio serials and hunt rabbits. Let's give them as much room as we can to be boys. We must not forget to live the life that is in front of us. Now, tell me what that Shirley Temple movie was about you saw this week."

Karella Home

February 13 brought a late snow, and Delora wanted it to be spring in Norfolk. Waking up to more snow soured her disposition. "Rusty," Delora grumbled, "I hope we get some good news soon. I am sick of winter and hearing about the war in Europe. When did the Vobornys say Mary's baby was due?"

Right then, the telephone rang. Rusty set down his coffee and answered it. *One moment, please. Go ahead sir,* said the operator.

"Stanley, it's good to hear your voice," said Rusty. "Delora was just asking about you and Mary. Congratulations! Yes, that is wonderful news. I'll tell her. Delora will give Mary a call next week." Then he hung up the receiver. "Mary had a little girl. That's their third? Right?"

Delora nodded and asked impatiently, "Well, what did they name her? Is everyone alright?"

Chuckling, Rusty replied, "Sorry. Yes, everyone is fine, and they named their baby girl Blanche Marie."

Three months later, Delora and Rusty received a telephone call from Rudy and Martha Pojar on May 15 with more happy news.

"Yes, Delora," replied Martha Pojar. "He is so handsome," she said proudly. "We named him Leonard Joseph."

Detecting a bit of sadness in Martha's voice, Delora was instantly worried. Martha had been her close friend since the week she and

Rusty got married. That was why she could ask personal questions that might not otherwise have been proper. Delora asked gently, "Are you alright, Martha?"

There was a brief silence, and then Martha spoke again, "Yes, I will be fine. But the doctor said I should not have any more children." She spoke quickly to keep Delora from asking anymore questions saying, "I'm fine with that. I am very blessed with my three sons, and so is Rudy."

Isolated Country Life

When Sacred Heart's elderly pastor Father Huge was ready to retire back in 1936, he introduced his replacement, Father Robert P. Burns, at Mass on Sunday during the first week in March that year. The Karella's invited Father Robert to dinner his second week in town, and over the years, he became a devoted friend of the Karella family. He was often asked to come and bless the house or a baby or play a lively game of pinochle with Rusty and Bitty.

Father Robert admired Rusty and his wife for the way they said their daily prayers. They always gave thanks and gratitude that Rusty had a good, stable job, and their children were healthy and strong. On Sundays, the Karellas took up a whole pew in church. Several of Delora's children had beautiful voices, particularly Ambrose. Her son could also whistle a whole melody perfectly too. When Ambrose sang church hymns, the boy nearly made him cry it was so beautiful. When he ate dinner with them, Dolora would take hold of Rusty's hand and praise God, thankful for the simple, good life they had and for all the blessings God gave them and their children.

Each week, Delora and Rusty banked a few precious pennies until they saved enough money to buy gas for a trip to Madison and back. The Karellas were fortunate to have an automobile and that Rusty knew how to keep the old Model A Ford running. It got him to work, and it gave his family the freedom to get out of town occasionally. When they could afford a visit to Madison, they chose a special occasion like a birthday, Easter, or Christmas. Delora's parents were delighted to have them stay at their home while they were in town, and Rusty's children couldn't wait to go fishing or hunting with their Karella cousins who still lived in the area.

Limited Travel in America

Nebraska had many horse and wagon roads connecting farms to nearby towns in the northeastern part of their state and even had a few roads that went to towns in Iowa. In 1940, there were no roads across the whole country of America. To travel any major distance between the cities across the United States, a person generally had to take a train. Despite it being the modern age of radio, airplanes, and automobiles, farming towns in 1940 remained quite isolated from the rest of the country and from what was happening in the rest of the world.

Even during the hardest years of the Depression, Rusty and Delora's family, their church community, and neighbors in Norfolk all felt fortunate. They were certainly better off than the poor folks in the big cities who lost their jobs, homes, children, and sometimes their lives. Even though they struggled to make ends meet, the Karellas especially felt fortunate compared to those poor farmers in Oklahoma and the Texas panhandle where the drought and Depression hit the hardest and completely obliterated their lives. Delora and Rusty liked living in their little farming town that felt safe and far away from the great big world that surrounded them.

April Radio and Newspapers World News

One evening, Rusty called out to Joe Pojar's place. He needed to talk to his brother about the latest news that was bothering him. Uncle Ed had always kept up with what was happening in Europe when they all lived in Madison, and the Karella men discussed that news monthly. After Ed passed away and Shorty came home, his brother began to watch the international news just as Ed had done.

After traveling extensively across Europe, Shorty's perspective about what was going on over there with the Germans, Poland, and Great Britain was insightful. Rusty and Shorty had grown even closer as men since he went to work on the Pojar ranch out in Elgin, Nebraska. Shorty drove into town quite often to visit him in Norfolk. They had shared many deep conversations about the topics that worried them: things like money, their work, and even love.

Most recently, their discussions were all about issues that could lead to war. Rusty talked about the news reports coming out of Europe, saying, "There are rising tensions in Europe *again* just like the problems prior to World War I caused by the Germans. Now, this new hostility in Europe is being instigated by the Germans *again,* and that is an unsettling trend."

Shorty replied, "I have been following Mr. Churchill's reports on the crisis going on in Europe closely. The man spent a good deal of effort throughout the 1930s warning his government about the dangers of Nazi Germany.

"Finally, the British intelligence advisers are listening to him. They can see Germany's intentions are blatantly clear as they move their armies toward Poland. They had better keep their eye on Stalin too. He and Hitler are two of a kind. On numerous occasions, Hitler has publicly promised to regain lost German territory and reclaim Germany's former glory. I say it's all part of Hitler's plan to rule the neighboring countries to the east and west of him as part of his strategy."

One Year Earlier—International News

As Europe moved steadily toward war again, that same similarity Rusty had noticed fired up a group that called themselves non-interventionists. They could see how dangerous the situation was becoming and quickly reacted by demanding that President Franklin Roosevelt keep America's stand neutral.

To further inhibit the office of the President of the United States, Congress passed the 1939 Neutrality Act in hopes of removing any scenario, action, or type of involvement with a warring nation that had led America to enter the last World War.

In response to Germany's continued aggression and Hitler's alliances with other countries of Europe and Asia, Great Britain was taking defensive action. British Prime Minister Chamberlain launched the Military Training Act in May of 1939 when Winston Churchill was First Lord of the Admiralty. This conscription act made all men between 18 and 40 years of age subject to being called up for military duty.

1939, WWII call to arms,
Great Britain poster

Approximately four months later, on September 1, 1939, German forces under the command of Adolf Hitler bombarded Poland and invaded over land with tanks and armed forces.

The Karella clan along with the rest of America listened to the news. Through the power of radio, people around the world knew what had happened within days of its occurrence and shuddered in dismay as they heard Hitler had invaded and now occupied Poland.

A Year Later—Current Time (1940)

The world-wide population held its breath on June 18, 1940, while listening to the live BBC radio broadcast as the newly appointed British prime minister, Winston Churchill, passionately addressed his nation, saying, "This is a time where every street in every village bristles with resolute armed men ready to defend home and country." Then he went on to say, "Hitler has failed to respond to British demands to leave Poland. "That decision puts this country at war with Germany." In response to Churchill's impassioned speech, a quarter of a million British citizens volunteered for the Home Guard on the first day of recruitment.

The United States Government watched the situation closely and pledged to provide support for its European allies. At the same time, FDR was constrained by the U.S. Senate and Congress from approving any troop involvement in the European conflict itself.

BBC Radio broadcast microphone

As an ally of Great Britain, and at their request for food and supplies, surplus product sitting in American warehouses began to fill orders for wartime essentials. America's existing factories were shoved into high gear, producing food and material being requested by Great Britain to prepare and sustain them during their battles against Germany. The product demand from the allies at war put more Americans to work and brought further stability to the American economy.

Though FDR feared Hitler had his eye on much more than his European conquests, he had to deal with extreme opposition from the American people, even regarding the support role he promised. As president, knowing the countries capabilities and state of preparedness, FDR also knew America was ill-equipped to do any more than was being done at the time. After World War I ended, several things happened that influenced the current situation.

First, after Germany's defeat in World War I, the Treaty of Versailles held Germany responsible for starting the war and was penalized harshly. They paid massive compensation for damages, lost a large portion of land that had been under its control, and was demilitarized. Germany was still angry over that defeat and intended to prove their superiority to the world.

Second, post-World War I, the United States Government mothballed most of the Naval armada and drastically reduced all branches of the American Armed Forces. Only minimal staff were retained in each branch of service. Consequently, America's existing Armed Forces lacked experience in battle, and the soldiers they did have were untrained and unprepared for a military confrontation of any kind.

The condition of America's fighting force was the result of post-World War I sentiments. America's people believed too much had been lost in a war that did not concern America's citizens directly. At that point, Americans were adamantly opposed to any more money being spent on the military or further involvement in any more wars outside their borders. Nothing had happened to change that mood.

Pre-WWII U.S. poster—
America Arise

Now, FDR and his advisors felt an urgent need to start raising awareness of how Europe's war could endanger America, and they wanted to slowly begin rebuilding America's Armed Forces. FDR's administration chose to initiate their plan subtly through a poster awareness campaign. The media messages implied the need to increase United States Military manpower as a precaution in the event of war.

1940 Radio News America

The United States' involvement in the European conflict as reported to the American population was still strictly limited to support. They supplied an array of items like oil, meat, vegetables, grain, clothing, and munitions by ocean-going merchant ships.

FDR had a constant battle on his hands trying to win support for even this much allied assistance. His administration had to fight public opposition to honor the president's word to America's allies. The complaint was that FDR had engaged U.S. Naval ships to escort the merchant supply ships. These ships were grouped together to cross the ocean in convoys. U.S. battleships protected them until the merchant ships could be turned over to the British for protection.

Karella Home and American

Teenagers

1930s–40s radio program

Late in the evenings on many occasions, AJ would hear hushed conversations between his parents. He'd stay out of sight trying to catch what they were talking about just as he did now. He heard his mother's voice say, "I know selling American-made products has put people back to work and is helping bring our country out of this financial depression. I'd rather be struggling as we did during the middle of the Depression than see things getting better because of this war in Europe."

Then his father replied, "You know I feel the same way. These changes worry me too."

Young men like AJ and his friends Chauncey and George felt frustrated with their age because it excluded them from participating in conversations about the war. Instead, they were forced to endure tedious years of high school while adults tried to disregard the threat they all felt. Yet, subjects connected to war tended to creep regularly into conversations around his parent's dinner table. The only way to keep his parents talking was pretending not to understand what he heard.

Every parent in America knew grim and horrific war stories continued to come to light through radio news programs and the newspapers. They could not deny danger was on the rise, and it wasn't only the adults who felt it. Though Europe's war was blamed for causing anxiety and fear in adults, this truth did not dampen interest.

Example of early dime novels. Cover of *Seth Jones* or *The Captives of the Frontier* by Edward S. Ellis (1860)

As far as Delora could tell, it seemed to mesmerize the male population. What she observed was a morbid sort of excitement. It seemed that everywhere she looked, boys like AJ and his friends were keen to hear every scrap of information they could about the war.

Though Delora's children had plenty of chores and other duties to keep them busy in addition to their homework from school, it was still difficult to limit the time her boys spent listening to the radio. But then Rusty and Delora were at a loss to know how to keep a kid's magazine company from promoting national defense through a comic book character that was sold directly to their children.

Inexpensive Entertainment

The harships of the Great Depression created a willing audience who needed an inexpensive escape from their troubles. In the case of the Karella boys, it was more that they were looking for adventure and excitement not found in an abundance in their small farming town of Norfolk. Dime novels were not a new idea. They had been a popular form of fiction issued in inexpensive paperbindings since the mid-1850s. Some dime novels were a single story paper, and others were a series published as weeklies.

Nearly 100 years later, cartoon art had become much more sophisticated and was called a comic. The artists created many crime-fighting heroes with personal lives a readership could identify with. The fans lived vicariously through their comic hero's adventures. It became an immensely popular form of inexpensive entertainment. One superhero inspired readership to such a degree that the character reached right into the homes of every American and captured the hearts of teenage boys and girls across the country.

Marvel Comics (MC): A Teen Hero Emerges

The immense surprise and success of Joe Simon and Jack Kirby's superhero Captain America was completely unpredicted and unprecedented. The duo gave their superhero a tangible human quality through the details of his secret identity under his real-life name Steve Rogers.

Original Captain American Comic cover, March 1941

Captain America's story reflected so much of the typical American immigrant's story that Steve Rogers took on a life of his own. He was no longer a two-dimensional comic strip personality. As Captain America, he transcended into a living, breathing person who had a relationship with his comic book readers. Captain America fans sympathized with his human side, identified with his ideals, and were inspired to support acts of heroism and patriotism based on his actions.

When the artists presented their new hero to the publisher of Marvel Comics, the publisher approved Captain America to have its own comic book series immediately. Plus, he planned to publish the comic book monthly. The publisher and the character's creators could use Captain America as a venue to say much of what they felt as men. At the same time, they could make a statement about the war raging in Europe.

The writers only had to look at the news headlines regarding the war to create the storyline for the monthly issue. This kind of content made the material easy to write and added authenticity to Captain America's stories.

The readership saw their hero dealing with current issues and neutralizing threats. Through Captain America, his creators expressed ideas and suggested actions they felt should be taken concerning the menace threatening all of Europe.

On March 1, 1941, the first Captain America comic book went on sale. On its full-color cover, the superhero was shown knocking out his archenemy, the Nazi leader, Adolph Hitler. The circulation figures quickly showed how undeniable Captain America's success truly was. The superhero's comic book sales remained close to a million copies per month after the character's début. The Captain America comic book count even outstripped retail numbers of leading news periodicals such as *Time Magazine*.

The story, the package, and the image all appealed to Americans young and old. The ideals Captain America represented resonated with girls and boys and made them care about what was happening in the world.

The subsequent emotional camaraderie with Captain America and his examples of patriotism inspired many to take personal action on behalf of their country and the world.

The Karella boys bought one of the first Captain America comic books. All the kids at school were talking about how exciting it was to see Captain America socking Hitler in the jaw and knocking him out cold!

They showed their mother and jabbered on about how Captain America knew what had to be done and did it. Delora didn't quite know what to say to her sons. Nor did she know what she should do to show how she felt about what she was looking at and wondered, *Just how is a mother to protect her sons from that?*

CHAPTER 21

A Divided America—1941

Captain America Infuriates the America First Committee

America First
Committee badge

The sheer sales volume proved a large portion of the American public felt MC's character Captain America's actions were right.

This feeling was far from unanimous. There were factions in the United States who were extremely unhappy with MC's new hero and adamantly opposed to the comic and what it represented. This group called themselves the America First Committee and referred to themselves as Isolationists. The AFC used newspapers, radio, and public protests to let America know what they thought.

Newspapers: America First Committee (AFC) Objects to Captain America

AFC Isolationists believed the war in Europe did not threaten America, and it was none of America's business. American men should not be involved in that conflict in any way. They adamantly opposed any measure President Roosevelt proposed that even hinted at American involvement in the war.

WWII AFC Isolationist protest banner

A year earlier, the AFC had launched a petition to enforce the 1939 Neutrality Act to coerce the president to honor his pledge of keeping the United States out of the conflict in Europe. The AFC distrusted Roosevelt. They were certain he would not keep this pledge. As a group, they made a point of attacking FDR's administration and repeatedly accused him of lying to the American people.

In some ways, the Karellas could sympathize with feelings AFC's members voiced as individual people. But there were many motivations behind AFC's stand on the war. Some members had been immigrants themselves, or their families had been immigrants. Many still had relatives living in Germany or in other European countries involved in the war that could be affected, just as the Karellas did. Others left Europe to find a country where they could be free from war and felt getting involved in this war was a betrayal of their ethics and ideals.

The AFC group didn't mind comic book heroes like Batman or the Green Hornet. But they were united in their rejection of MC's Captain America, who wore the stars and stripes and performed acts of aggression against the antagonist of the European war. The AFC's membership resented any implication that this comic character stood for every American and what they thought or believed. They also made sure newspaper writers and MC's publisher were made aware of how divided Americans were over the war issue.

That division was made perfectly clear when MC started receiving threatening hate mail. The company and its artistic creators were called warmongers. The publisher did not back down and responded with great zeal and wrote, "America is the land of the free. You have a right to your opinions and to demonstrate against participation in the war. We have rights as well and choose to explain how we feel about current events that are affecting the world we live in through this character and we will continue to do so."

Karella Home: Boys and Dreams

1930s radio show, *Tailspin Tommy*

1930s airplane hero movie clip—
T. S. Tommy poster

Though still considered children in the eyes of their parents, AJ at fourteen and his brother Charlie at twelve felt differently. The hardships of the 1930s Great Depression and drought matured many children beyond their physical years.

Delora's children had grown up with chores and responsibilities, and they understood they had to help take care of the family. Her sons had been making money for years hunting jackrabbits after the government issued a bounty on them during the long drought. Since it put meat on the table, which saved grocery money for other things, Delora and Rusty encouraged them to hunt as often as they wanted.

After irrigation brought water back to the fields in Nebraska, jackrabbits were no longer the dire threat they once were. Yet the bounty had not been repealed.

AJ and his friends continued to make easy money while they could.

Hunting jackrabbits was precisely why her boys had coins in their pockets to spend on comic books and Saturday movie matinees.

Delora encouraged her sons to go to the movies featuring fun-loving teenage stars like themselves: just young boys and girls like Mickey Rooney and Judy Garland pursuing their dreams. These young stars acted in films like *Andy Hardy Meets Debutante, Judge Hardy and Son,* and *Strike Up the Band,* which helped balance the comic book superhero stuff with a little romance and comedy.

Her boys wanted to fit in with their friends at school just as all kids wanted to do. When Ambrose started grade school in Norfolk, his friends used his initials and called him AJ instead of Ambrose James, and he had instantly liked that. Years later after watching the Andy Hardy movies, AJ decided he really liked the name Andy. The name felt a little more grown up, and the more Andy Hardy movies he saw, the more he liked the name. It sounded like an all-American name, and he decided that in high school, he would call himself Andy. When he said as much to his childhood friends, Chauncey and George, they thought it was a great name, and they began to call him Andy after that. He even asked his teachers at school to call him Andy when he started tenth grade. Delora became aware of her son's decision about his name from the teachers at his school when she went for parent conferences. She didn't think anything of it. Her son was growing up, and it was a harmless enough change to express a new vision of himself. Unconsciously, she began to think of him as Andy, but generally at home around Rusty, she still called him Ambrose.

The cinema introduced Andy and his friends to more than teen-aged movies stars, though. Before the feature film, the theaters ran what were called movie shorts. The subject matter varied, and a big favorite among the movie shorts were films about a character adapted from a popular radio serial program called *Tailspin Tommy.* Movie shorts were brief, exciting stories. *Tailspin Tommy* was about a young pilot who saved lives and fought for goodness and humanity around the world. Charlie Karella would rave on about each new program on the radio, saying he wanted to fly just like *Tailspin Tommy.* When he got to see a movie short, he changed it up a little, saying he wanted to be a pilot like *Tailspin Tommy* in the Army Air Corps, flying top-secret missions. Each week on the way to the movies, the boys and their friends searched for new military enlistment posters prominently displayed in the downtown store windows. Delora cringed listening to the keen excitement of the boys as they talked about joining up. She always felt like she had a rock in her stomach when Andy would say he was going to join the Marines as soon as he was old enough.

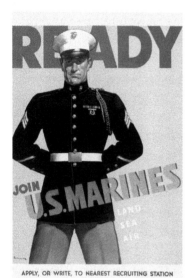

U.S. Marine recruitment poster

Andy's attitude encouraged his younger brother Charlie to daydream out loud about flying in the air command. Times like these were frustrating and more than a little frightening for Delora.

As her sons rapidly matured into young men, she could not shield them from war and worried her boys were foretelling their own futures. Delora considered trying to squash the idea. But at their volatile ages, she feared that kind of negativity might push them toward their attraction to the military rather than discourage it. She took her worries to Rusty instead, knowing he felt the same way. Neither one wanted to give their sons any reason to rush toward what they feared was already destined to be part of their futures.

Roosevelt Says to Treat German U-Boats as Hostiles

Andy and his pals, George and Chauncey, always kept up on the news and gathered regularly to discuss the latest developments. One day in the fall of 1941, Andy waited impatiently for his buddies to show up at his house. He had news, and if they didn't get there soon, he was going to burst.

Finally, a knock sounded on the door, and he ran to yank it open. Motioning the guys in with urgency, he quickly dragged his friends into the farthest corner of the living room. Andy turned on the radio, and the Andrew sisters were singing the snappy tune "Don't Sit Under the Apple Tree." Turning the music up just enough to cover their voices, he turned to his buddies and signaled them to come closer.

"Jeez, Andy! What's up with you?" they whispered as they watched him look around the corner. Andy had to make sure his mom wasn't around where she could hear him.

Turning back to his friends, he motioned for them to pull their chairs into a huddle. Putting his finger to his lips, he whispered, "Did you guys hear the latest news?"

Like conspirators, they hunched even closer, leaning toward Andy's chair, shaking their heads and whispering back, "No, what have you heard?"

"Only that President Roosevelt told our Navy and the Merchant Marines to treat all German U-boats as *hostile*. And . . . they were approved to take *appropriate action*! Do you know what that means?" Andy asked in a rush.

The other two who were usually quick on the uptake merely shook their heads. Andy let his exasperation show and thought, *The guys aren't usually this dense.* Breathing out slowly, he emphatically whispered, "Don't you get it? Our country is really part of this war now!"

Andy Explains Convoys, the Pit, and Wolf Packs

"Ok, boys," said Andy, "let me explain what I've been able to figure out from the news reports. Supply ships leave America filled with provisions the allies need to fight the war in Europe against the enemy Axis armies of Germany and Italy." The guys nodded but did not speak.

"These supply ships are organized into columns as they steam across the Atlantic Ocean. Each column includes up to five supply ships forming a box of up to 60 merchant vessels traveling together in one convoy. The convoy is guarded by our U.S. war ships and water-going aircraft bombers through U.S. waters out into the open Atlantic. That ocean is more than 100 million square kilometers of open water. At the halfway point between America and Great Britain, the deepest part of the Atlantic's open water is called the pit. The pit is too far from land and fuel for aircraft protection. Until a convoy crosses the pit, its only protection is their escort of American combat ships. Once our guys enter British waters, the supply convoy is turned over to British war ships and their aircraft cover.

"The deepest water of the Atlantic pit is the most dangerous part of a convoy's route. This is where enemy German U-boats travel in groups of eight to 20 submarines and call themselves wolf packs. They hunt and sink both merchant and military convoy ships in the pit during night hours when the convoys have no air cover and ships cannot see the submarines or the torpedoes in the water.

"The escorting guard ship's only means of spotting the subs attacking is their military sonar. Last year between June and October, 270 allied ships were sunk in the pit! That's why President Roosevelt said to treat U-boats as hostile, and our guys can take appropriate action to protect themselves when they guard the convoys!"

Andy and his friends were so engrossed in their topic they did not notice Mrs. Karella walk into the room. The boys jumped guiltily, knowing the subject they were discussing was frowned upon by Andy's mother.

"What are you boys doing in the house on a beautiful Saturday like this?" she asked.

"Gosh, Mom. Funny you should ask." While Andy talked, he turned toward his friends, winking and giving them a look. A *look* that told his friends to play along with whatever he said. "We're waiting for Charlie 'cause we promised he could go hunting with us today. Is it OK with you if we go over to the fields south of town to look for game?" Chauncey and George nodded their heads in support of whatever Andy said.

Delora thought it sounded a little too convenient to be true but replied, "That's nice." But to test her theory, she added, "I'll call him for you. I just saw him go upstairs. I'll look forward to making some rabbit fricassee for supper tonight."

Delora saw a brief flash of disappointment rush across her son's face. *Just as I figured*, she thought. *The boy's dreaming if he thinks he will ever be able to pull a quick one over on me.* She didn't smile or chuckle out loud until she left the room.

Breathless and only minutes later, Charlie came running into the living room with his .22 rifle in hand, saying, "Hey, guys, thanks for the invite! I must have forgotten. Mom just reminded me. I'm ready to go. When do we leave?"

Andy believed his mother when she said she expected to make rabbit fricassee for dinner. He and his friends were very accurate with their

Karella boys, back to front: Andy, Charlie, Lloyd, and Pete. Girls, back to front: Florence, Marcella, Millie, and Sharon.

small caliber rifles. That was precisely why Andy had said they were waiting to go hunting. It was a plausible excuse for being in the house. He laughed at being trapped by his own white lie. Seeing the humor in the moment and motioning to his friends, he said, "Well, boys, guess we better get our .22s 'cause it looks like we are going hunting."

Karella Home: Family Matters

October was a busy month for birthdays, and the latest news was that Mary Voborny was due on October 9, and today Delora got the call.

"Gosh, it's good to hear from you, Mary. S-o-o-o-o give me the news!"

"The baby and I are fine, and you have a new niece, and we've named her Jeanette Margaret."

Softly tittering, Delora replied, "What a lovely name and a mouth full too! Jeanette Margaret Voborny . . . wow . . . what is that the whole alphabet?"

Laughing, Mary replied, "N-o-o-o, it is only 23 letters, but I suspect we will just call her Jeanie."

The radio played in the background, and Delora asked, "Have you heard that new song by Billie Holiday? It's called 'God Bless This Child.' Seems like a wonderful affirmation that it is playing today."

Laughing, Mary replied, "I think little Jeanie would like the bouncy 'Boogie Woogie Bugle Boy' by the Andrew Sisters better."

"You are probably right," Delora said. "My kids like those jazzy, poppy tunes too. Well, honey, I've got to run. Talk with you soon! Hugs to your gang from us."

"Same to you," Mary replied.

Thanksgiving Holiday 1941

In the morning on Thursday, November 25, it was 66 degrees and no snow. Delora was delighted because that meant Rusty's sister Martha and her husband, Rudy Pojar, would be coming to Norfolk with their three sons to celebrate Thanksgiving Day with them.

The Pojars brought a huge ham from the ranch, and Delora, Martha, and Florence made creamed green beans and mashed potatoes and gravy to go with the meat. The children were allowed to eat as much as they wanted. By the time they cleared the table, Delora was pleased to see there was plenty of leftover ham to make sandwiches for everyone the next day.

After the kitchen and dishes were cleaned up, Delora set out several of her delicious cream pies on the table with coffee and milk for dessert, and everyone cheered!

Later that evening, the four adults sat around the living room once all the kids had gone to bed. Rusty served homemade cordial in small jelly jars. He smiled at Delora as he handed her one, and her tinkling laughter filled the room at the private joke they shared. Jelly jars remained the best kept secret from the family except for those who had been directly involved.

As the evening went on, the adults talked about FDR's New Deal work programs. The highway project was exciting. Eventually, the system of roads would connect all of America. One day in the future, regular people would be able to drive anywhere in the country in their cars.

FDR's Social Security program sounded promising too. Each person had a chance to talk about people they knew who were now employed, living in good housing, and capable of taking care of their families. They also acknowledged the improvements in their daily lives were not only due to government work programs and jobs.

Everyone in this group admitted the supplies America sold to the Allied Forces played an important role in the economy's improvement. The aid America had provided to support the war in Europe greatly alleviated the financial strain of the past ten years. There was the underlying fear, though: What if this part of America's financial relief came at a terrible price?

The White House

As President Roosevelt's worst fears were realized, he took off his glasses and closed his eyes in pain as he listened to his military commander's report. On December 7, 1941, the American leadership was hit with the answer to all of Hitler's riddles, and the troop movement of the Axis armies were like puzzle pieces falling into place. Now, FDR's military commanders saw how the pieces formed a clear picture of the multi front attack Hitler had planned and executed in Europe, while his Allied Japanese army launched a surprise air attack against all American military bases within the Hawaiian Islands and across the South Pacific.

Karella Home: Norfolk

Sunday, Andy, his friend Chauncey Crocker, and his brother Charlie sat waiting for their favorite serial to start. Suddenly, the radio announcer broke into the broadcast, and in a horrified voice, he said, *"Breaking News! A military bulletin just released! Today, December 7th, the Japanese have bombed Pearl Harbor . . . in Hawaii! The Empire of Japan has destroyed most of the United States Pacific fleet!"* In a nearly hysterical voice, he added, *"There are thousands of wounded soldiers . . . and civilians . . . and many more of our men and women have been killed."*

Karella home radio, 1940s

The radio announcer left the boys both shocked and shaking with anger over this newfound knowledge. Americans had been attacked on American soil! American soldiers had been murdered! "I knew something was about to happen," Andy whispered through clenched teeth.

Chauncey whispered back, "That's what we all believed, but I never imagined this!"

While they talked, Charlie ran from the room, yelling, "Mom! Mom! The Japanese bombed Hawaii!"

Delora nearly dropped the pan she held when she realized what Charlie had said. Fear practically paralyzed her mind, so she clung to the work in front of her. The very normalcy of it helped calm her down. *Finish preparing lunch,* she thought. *Rusty will know what to do. He always knows what to do.* Absentmindedly, Delora asked Florence and Charlie to set the table.

When Rusty walked into the house, his face showed he had heard the news already. He put his arms around Delora and said, "Let's have lunch, and then we will discuss this openly with the whole family."

She nodded and put the hot dishes of food on the table. Charlie poured glasses of water and set them by each plate while Florence rounded up the little ones and got them ready to eat. Delora called into the living room, saying, "Boys! Come and eat!"

The voice of Andy's mother abruptly brought their attention back to the radio still blaring the dreadful news describing the devastation of Pearl Harbor. Andy and Chauncey continued to sit by the radio stunned and whispering to each other. "Can you believe this? Can this really be happening?" Chauncey whispered, still unable to grasp it. He didn't want to consider what he had heard with his own ears was even possible.

Andy looked at his friend and replied in a flat voice, "There is no more wondering what is going on or what will happen. We must help make sure what Hitler and his rats are doing in Europe and Hawaii does not happen here at home, right?"

"How are we going to do anything about that?" Chauncey asked.

Andy was thinking hard and replied, "We've got to join up as soon as we can so we can help. But that is going to take a while. I don't know what we can do right now, but there must be something we can do that will . . . be at least useful. We could—"

"Boys!" came his mother's voice, cutting off his last thought. "Did you hear me? No more talk of war. Come and eat, and we will talk about this with your father after dinner."

Andy responded to the worry in his mother's voice and whispered to his friend, "Come on, Chauncey. Let's go eat and think about what we can do."

Unusually quiet, the family sat around the table not eating much. Each person thought about the scary things they had recently heard. Rusty needed to prepare his family. He was still wrapping his mind around what this would mean to their home, town, country, and the world as they knew it.

"Listen," Rusty said in a grim tone of voice, "we are going to hear additional details about the dreadful attack on Pearl Harbor and much more. It is important to be ready for what else is coming, and it will not be good. We must listen closely to the radio and prepare for what our president says and what our government asks us to do next. There is no doubt in my mind that our country is about to declare war on Japan. Times are going to be difficult. Your mom and I are going to need all of you to help and cooperate with what we ask you to do."

Rusty paused and turned to his wife. "Delora, please gather the family in the living room by the radio after the dishes are done. There will be much more to hear before this night is over."

WWII Japanese newspaper headline after attack on Hawaii

Japanese Navy Mitsubishi A6M2 Zero Fighter, tail code A1-108 Pearl Harbor, Hawaii, 1941 Public Domain—Wikimedia

CHAPTER 22

The United States Enters World War II

December 1941: Karella Home in Norfolk

A s the children's father requested, Sunday evening, December 7, the Karella family gathered around the radio. Information on the Japanese attacks was broadcasted to the American public regularly through government-issued bulletins.

The attack on Pearl Harbor itself was the impetus that united the nation behind President Roosevelt and effectively ended the American Isolationist movement.

President Roosevelt Speaks to the Nation

The following day on December 8, Rusty and his family gathered around the radio

Radio was a main source for news and information during WWII. One of the programs was *This Is America*.

to hear what President Roosevelt would say before Congress. In his speech, the President called the previous day *"A date which will live in infamy."*

Then he went on to say, "The attack yesterday on the Hawaiian Islands has caused severe damage to American Naval and Military forces. I regret to tell you that very many American lives have been lost. In addition American ships have been reported torpedoed on the high seas between San Francisco and Honolulu.

"Yesterday the Japanese Government also launched coordinated attacks against Malaysia.

"Last night Japanese forces attacked Hong Kong.

"Last night Japanese forces attacked Guam.

"Last night Japanese forces attacked the Philippine Islands.

"Last night the Japanese attacked Wake Island.

Roosevelt speech to Congress. Behind him are Vice President Henry A. Wallace (left) and House Speaker Sam Rayburn (right). To the right, in uniform in front of Rayburn, is Roosevelt's son James, who escorted his father to the Capitol, and served as a Marine Corps officer during World War II.

"And this morning the Japanese attacked Midway Island.

"Japan has, therefore, undertaken a surprise offensive extending throughout the Pacific area. The facts of yesterday and today speak for themselves. The people of the United States have already formed their opinions and well understand the implications to the very life and safety of our Nation. . . . I ask that the Congress declare that since the unprovoked and dastardly attack by Japan on Sunday, December 7th, 1941, a state of war has existed between the United States and the Japanese Empire."

Japan made a formal declaration of war against America the same day. Then, on December 11, 1941, Japan's Allies, Germany and Italy, also declared war on the United States of America. In response to the formal declaration by Germany and Italy, the United States Congress immediately reciprocated, making the European and Southeast Asian wars a global conflict.

Standing against Germany, Japan, and Italy were the Allied Powers of America, Britain, France, and Soviet Russia. By the end of 1941, Adolph Hitler's Nazi government had captured the attention of the world. Nations realized they could no longer afford to take a neutral position regarding Hitler's ideology without eventually suffering the consequences for their lack of action.

January 1942

During this frightening time, everything changed so fast Rusty and Delora found it hard to take it all in, let alone keep up with how their lives were affected and how they should be responding. Most households across America, like the Karellas, had at least one family member constantly listening to the radio for updates. Though radio stations continued to air popular daily entertainment programs, they got constantly interrupted to provide updates on battles going on across the South Pacific. Ongoing news releases describing attacks on multiple battlefronts and threatening thousands of American lives created a flood of young volunteers rushing to recruiting offices to join the United States Armed Forces.

The Karellas, along with everyone in America, struggled with the Christmas holidays. There were so many mixed emotions. They thanked God people went back to work, and they had food to eat and money to take care of their families. They thanked God that they lived in a nation that cared about its people and had a president who chatted with them like they were all part of the same team. The price of the comforts they enjoyed was war, and that was hard to accept. So many people had died already in Europe, Asia, and Hawaii, and now American girlfriends, wives, and mothers sent their men off to war. No one knew when and if they would see them again.

There were defined enemies. Americans could see where those enemies were. But with all there was to be done, where did they start, and how could they help? It was too big a notion to take in, so most people just prayed to understand what they should do.

Norfolk: Karella Family

After the holidays, Rusty Karella gathered his family for another serious talk. Looking sternly at his young sons before addressing everyone, he said, "I feel the need to ask you to remember governments and nations are made up of individual lives. I never want you to forget that war ravages land and people alike, not just the brave soldiers who win or lose the battles. War is upon the world, not just America. Time and age have no relevance when it comes to personal ethics; war will always be a complicated issue for everyone. In most cases, people on each side of the dispute believe they are right. But this situation we are in as a nation and a family cannot be ignored or sidestepped, and we will all do what we can to help keep our country safe."

Andy stood up and walked over to his father and said, "Dad, I want to help. What can I do?" Following their brother's lead, all the rest of the children said they wanted to help too.

Rusty and Delora were proud of them, and he replied, "Your mom and I will figure out the best way to help. Then we will discuss it with you and work together. Alright?" They nodded yes in reply.

January War Bulletin: 26 Nations Unite

"Radio News 8 reports . . . conference held in Washington, D.C. . . . British Prime Minister Winston Churchill and President Roosevelt met and held candid conversations with allies that will lead to better cooperation and a united war effort."

President Roosevelt devised the name *United Nation's Declaration* as the title for a document representing the ideals of 26 countries on why they must deal with the aggression of Hitler for their country's defense.

"The declaration affirms 'that complete victory over their enemies is essential to defend life, liberty, independence, and religious freedom, and to preserve human rights and justice in their own lands as well as in other lands, and that they are now engaged in a common struggle against savage and brutal forces seeking to subjugate the world.'

WWII United Nations poster

"This document was presented and ratified at the Arcadia Conference held in Washington, D.C., starting on December 22, 1941, and ending January 14, 1942. The four largest nations forming this coalition against Nazi Germany are the United States, the U.K., the U.S.S.R., and China. A total of twenty-six nations joins this effort, which include nations located in Central America and the Caribbean, British protectorates, British India, and eight Allied governments-in-exile. They have determined the menace and aggression of Hitler's regime is truly a world threat, and the sheer magnitude of worldwide involvement in this war is staggering."

The announcer's voice faded out as the people listening to their radios tried to grasp what it all meant.

Rusty and Delora Listen to Breaking News

After the radio news bulletin, Rusty and Bitty turned out the lights downstairs and went to bed. "What did all that mean, Rusty?" Bitty asked as she snuggled up to her husband to get warm.

Putting his arms around her, he whispered, "My darling Bitty, it means America is not alone in this war. We have 26 nations watching our backs."

Bitty fell asleep feeling comforted by that thought. Rusty lay awake worrying about the future of his 15-year-old son. Eventually, he sighed heavily, not wanting to think about it anymore, and went to sleep.

May 1942

Newspaper Headline: **The United States Office of Price Administration (OPA) Freezes Prices**

WWII OPA reasoning 2

The OPA has begun fixed war pricing starting with sugar and coffee. This is only the first items needed to support the war effort. Watch for the extended rationing list for war items tomorrow. As the list of items in short supply grow, we will print the new postings in the newspapers on a daily basis.

Radio in the Karella Home

Radio broadcasts were the affordable form of daily music and program entertainment, product advertising, and the main outlet for the U.S. Government's information dissemination.

These broadcasts pushed to keep citizens informed about war efforts and encouraged them to help with the causes outlined in the newspapers. The power of radio made the world small. At the same time, they brought the world's huge problems right into the Karella's living room.

The endless amount of information bombarding people intimidated and confused them. It made people wonder what one small person could do to make a difference. Without an answer to this question, it caused a feeling of helplessness that could overwhelm a person with fear.

Rusty could see this in Delora's eyes. He would not allow his wife and children to be frightened by what they needed to hear. He would help them turn the shear mass of information into a smaller more manageable view of the situation. Then he would explain how their family and isolated farming town could help their country. That would build confidence in the belief that they could make a difference by doing their part for the war effort.

The president's radio speeches talked about departments being formed to manage all the work being done on the war front and what needed to be done on the home front.

The newspapers published those lists and the work that each department supervised and managed for the nation. Rusty kept refining his search among those lists and came up with several ways his family could help to support the war effort. He

WWII American Victory Posters 2 & 3

talked with Bitty, and they settled on victory gardens, meticulous food rationing efforts, and scrapping and recycling.

February 1942, Karellas' Victory Gardens

Rusty and Delora gathered their family to share their plan, "Children, your mom and I have decided on the home front efforts that will be our priorities.

"First, your mom has chosen to plant a victory garden. Ambrose, I need you to dig up most of the back yard and start preparing it for your mother's vegetable starters and cooking herbs. If you can get your friends to help, it will make the work go faster.

"I will build a small greenhouse so your mother, Florence, and Marcella can plant starters. That way, the plants will be big enough to move into the ground once the garden plot is ready and the weather warms up. Then it will be the girl's responsibility to water and weed it as it grows until harvest and canning time. That is when we will all help your mama and the girls can and store the food.

"Second, the boys project will begin with Charles, Lloyd, and Pete. They will work with me on collecting scrap metal to recycle. We men will take turns during the week locating and picking up old fencing, tools, toys, and anything that is metal that we see laying around, broken, or has been left to sit. If it is too big to bring home in the wagon, we can go get it in the evenings with the car when I get home from work. Eventually, we may also spend time at the dump going through old trash for the items on the government list that need to be salvaged.

"The third and last project will take all of us. We will focus on ways to use less war-rationed items."

Andy held up his hand and said, "Dad, for the third project, Charlie and I can hunt rabbits several days a week to cut back on store-bought meat."

Rusty nodded and replied, "Good! I'd also like you to catch fish once a week to eat on Fridays when it gets a little warmer out. Do you think you can do that and not have it interfere with school?"

Andy nodded his head and said, "Sure can, Dad."

Rusty handed Delora a paper and said, "Mom will make a list of when berries are ripe, or fruit trees are ready to pick in Madison. Then we will make it a family picnic day so that our food foraging trips will be fun too."

Victory Gardens and Salvage

Delora looked through the paper and found the articles on victory gardens. They were also called *War Gardens for Defense* and were filled with any kind of vegetable, fruit, or herbs people could use in their homes. These gardens were made in yards at private residences. In densely populated high-rise areas of towns and cities with no yards, people were given permission to plant victory gardens for personal use in public parks throughout the United States. All these gardens were planted, tended, and harvested by private citizens to take domestic-use pressure off commercially grown food so more could be sent to feed the soldiers on the front lines. Then she went on to read about "Salvage for Victory." This was a call to private citizens to salvage materials for the American war effort. The list of materials started with items made of paper—like newspaper and magazines— scrap metals, old rags, and rubber. The government continued to ask citizens to comb their homes, neighborhoods, farms, and the municipal dump sites for these items. They were told to make piles of these items in front of their homes and apartment buildings. The department

WWII American Victory poster 1

WWII OPA examples of price freeze and reasoning 1

of sanitation would pick up the salvage piles with dump trucks on specified days on designated time schedules.

When Delora finished reading the news articles, she smiled and thought, *Rusty is so smart! These projects are perfect home-front projects for us.*

War Bulletin—Office of Price Administration (OPA)

WWII poster—
Hitler Wants You to Believe

Radio News 8 reports . . . as of January 1942, a news release from the government states that the OPA has the power to start setting ceilings on all prices except agricultural commodities. They are also in charge of rationing any scarce supply items, which include tires, shoes, nylons, automobiles, fuel oil, meat, and much more. The first list of rationed items was published right after FDR's speech to the nation. Now, the president's administration says newspapers will get new lists of additional rationed items to publish on a weekly basis . . .

Rusty and Delora Support War-Time Efforts

Rusty and Delora had been undecided for a long time about America's involvement in the war. But the attack on Hawaii ended all debate over whether America should or should not get drawn into the war. It was clear the country felt the same as they read the newspapers and listened to the radio. They could see how practically overnight the economy shifted to war production. Consumer goods took a back seat to military production, and within six months after the strike on Pearl Harbor, nearly 90% of retail food prices were frozen. Even restaurant menus had set a price ceiling.

Many people simply called the OPA officers feds. That was natural because they worked for the Federal Government, and it was easier to remember. Like police officers, feds could arrest citizens who broke the guidelines set by the OPA. War-time rationing was a serious business Delora believed in, and she learned to make do for her family within those guidelines, and that made her feel proud.

War-Time Poster Campaigns in 1942

Rusty could easily see how the government used patriotic posters to mobilize the nation and sway public sentiment. It was certainly an inexpensive, accessible, and ever-present way to send a message and explain to the country's citizens how to support the war effort. Government agencies, businesses, and private organizations issued an array of poster themes linking the European military front with the American home front. Every American received the call to boost production at work and at home.

Rusty and Andy had discussed how talented the commercial artists were who had been employed to create poster images. They expressed what Andy had said was multilevel messaging. Just looking at them even without words sometimes inspired and focused a person's attention on the needs and goals of America as a nation. Rusty did notice that some artists were more subtle than others. Most of the war-time posters he had seen displayed underlying messages of patriotism and commitment to personal freedom.

Every day, the radio and newspapers provided Delora and Rusty with more insight into the needs of their towns, cities, and the country in addition to everything else going on with the war. With each new article or report, their vision of their country and the world changed shape.

Newspaper Release: We've Got Jobs

According to the U.S. Government statistics, the unemployment problem caused by the Great Depression has ended with America's mobilization for war. Every man in America that wants a job has a job, and America still faces a huge labor shortage in nearly every existing business around the country. Despite many farmers receiving a draft exemption due to the instant and accelerated demand for food supplies, farms still report labor shortages. School-aged children, retirees and women are encouraged to seek work on local farms and ranches to help.

New factories specializing in production of ships, aircraft, weapons, all-terrain vehicles, tanks, canned and preserved foods, clothing,

cold weather gear, tents, shovels, buckets and other tools and munition assembly plants are reporting a desperate need for labor to fill many positions. They are appealing to high school and college students, retirees and housewives, to apply for full time hours and good compensation packages.

Radio War Bulletin:
Hollywood Helps Fight the War

Radio News 8 reports . . . Hollywood gets behind the war effort. Studios are supporting our government through patriotic messaging, presenting a united view of what is happening in the war. Movie studios send all scripts that are about the war for government review and pre-approval before filming and releasing new movies to the public. It is important that these forms of entertainment give nothing to enemy spies to use against America or our boys on the front lines of the war. Loose lips sink ships. We know enemy spies are trying to infiltrate America. Thank you, Hollywood, for helping to protect our soldiers on the front lines . . .

Three movie cells from
U.S. Military movie shorts
during WWII

Cinematic War Efforts

Andy felt film shorts were an important source of information. They communicated powerful messages. Though radio was affordable to every income bracket, cinema was the most popular form of entertainment if you could afford it. Films could lift the spirit, motivate, and deliver information to the people of the nation. He had heard it said that cinema was deemed to be the most effective medium to help people understand it was their duty to support the war effort

in everyday life. The films also explained why the war was being fought. The cinema news reels gave updates on home-front progress and gave people a view of the battles during the war.

Government films even suggested methods of coping with loss of family members and to caution Americans about the presence of enemy spies. The documentary series released by the US Department of War, *Why We Fight,* was originally written for American recruits and soldiers to help them understand why the United States got involved in the war. But President Roosevelt ordered that the films be distributed to the cinemas and shown to the public. He said, "Everyone needs to understand what America is fighting for." Andy had watched those films and was more determined than ever to be a Marine and help win the war.

Andy Karella and Friends at the Cinema

Andy, Chauncey, George, and Charlie walked out of the cinema deep in thought. The brave young men serving in the Marines and Army Air Forces had captured their teenaged minds and captivated their hearts. They were strong, fit, and smart. Brave honorable young men willing to fight for what they believed in and protect their families from the unspeakable horror of war. Andy and Chauncey walked side by side talking softly about what they had learned and said they wanted to be part of the camaraderie they had seen and help save America. There was a similar conversation going on between Charlie and George, who felt the same way about the Army Air Corps. All four of these boys solidly set their sights on joining these brave groups of fighting men one day when they were old enough.

Private Business Supports the War Effort

Http://comicbookplus. com/?2207 Public Domain Wikimedia Commons

As the Karella boys and their friends bought new comic books each week, the comic creators combined forces with Captain America as other superheroes joined the war effort fighting the bad guys and protecting the innocent. The messages conveyed in the brightly colored action scenes and simple dialogue influenced the minds of their fans. Adolescent boys and girls got excited by the ideas they saw illustrated, and it made an enormous impact on a younger generation. Andy and Charlie as well as the other boys could identify with the superheroes who thought like patriots. The examples they saw helped connect what they felt as patriotism with serving in the military to protect America.

Late Summer in 1942, Andy Karella

George, Chauncey, and Andy had all turned 15 years old and felt as if they could take on the world. Earlier that morning, a very excited George arrived at Andy's house with an invitation. "My folks said that I could take some friends to the cabin. Do you and Chauncey want to come and spend a week with me on the Niobrara River?"

Chauncey could almost always be found at Andy's home and happened to be standing right behind his friend when George offered the invitation.

Andy replied, "Are you serious?"

"We sure would!" added Chauncey with enthusiasm.

George and Chauncey immediately began making plans, but as Andy listened to them, he decided it would be best if he got his mom's permission for the trip before his dad got home.

Turning quickly, he said, "Guys, I'll be right back." He left them deep in their plans as he headed for the kitchen.

Mr. Pierce, George's dad, had purchased the island in the Niobrara River near Butte, Nebraska. The Pierce family named it Coon Island. After his parents refurbished the little cabin on the property, George considered it the perfect hangout place for him and his friends. Ever since his first visit to the island, George had been excited. He bragged about it incessantly, assuring his buddies they would have a great time there and that the hunting and fishing was topnotch.

Andy was already close to six-feet-tall with a lean and wiry build. George was a short, tubby, curly headed blonde. In the woods, he was about as quiet as an old steam engine pulling a steep logging grade. He and Andy constantly argued. George almost always won because the guy knew where to get the proof he needed to win the argument. George could also shout much louder than Andy.

Chauncey was the extreme opposite of George in body structure, being slight to the point of frailty. His slim build coupled with his rather fancy name, Chauncey Cary Crocker, caused his youthful self-esteem to suffer greatly. To dispel that image, he would go to extremes to prove his ability to keep up with anything his more robust buddies decided to undertake.

Generally, when George and Andy resorted to brute strength in one of their endeavors, Chauncey was invariably more successful by applying his gray matter instead. A natural diplomat and amateur psychiatrist, Chauncey was the arbitrator during their many feuds. In any group, Chauncey was the knot who held all the individual personalities to a common purpose. All through high school, the three of them were an inseparable team. Their friendship and common links were based on a boundless love of guns, camping, fishing, and hunting.

Coon Island

As their boat nosed into the shore, Andy easily climbed out of the boat, carrying the anchor rope across wet ground and securing it to the nearest tree. Chauncey hopped out behind him with both their packs. Within minutes, the two of them were ready to follow George to the cabin.

Along the way, the boys found deer signs everywhere, which made them all want to go hunting. George was jittery with excitement and called out a challenge. "Hey, since it's not hunting season yet, let's see which one of us can catch the biggest bass or catfish for dinner."

Andy had to admit—for once, George had not exaggerated. The fishing was great! But something else caught their attention during that afternoon. There were thousands of prairie dogs on the south bank of the river on property owned by another a local rancher.

The following morning, the weather turned, and the next couple of days, it rained too much for fishing. So, the boys used their .22 rifles to hammer away at the prairie dog town with unrelenting intensity. The little animals learned quickly after a few days, becoming so wary of the sharpshooters that the boys couldn't find any more targets.

No one thought badly of this pastime because prairie dogs were a menace to a rancher's cattle. The little rodents ruined acres of grazing land with thousands of burrow holes. Because of these holes, cattle constantly broke their legs, which was why ranchers encouraged people to hunt them at every opportunity.

The boys took a vote and decided to move upstream a couple of miles. There was another dog town a neighboring property owner was anxious to eliminate. As the small group made their way along the dirt riverbank, they came upon a medium-sized stream flowing off the prairie. As it made its way to the Niobrara River, it spread out into a mini delta, which turned the ground on both sides of the water into thick, wet mud that clutched at their feet.

Chauncey noticed a few drier spots. Hopping back and forth, he found his way across the mucky ground as light and swift as a ballet dancer. Once he reached the other side, he taunted his heavier friends about being afraid. George got belligerent and tried to follow the path Chauncey had taken.

He was at least fifty pounds heavier, and by mid-stream, George sank deeper with each step. Suddenly, George yelled, "Hey, I'm stuck! Give me a hand!"

Happy for once to have the upper hand, Chauncey teased George and said, "Stuck like an old cow." Without waiting, Chauncey stretched out his hand as far as he could but was unable to get anywhere near his friend to help. "Oh, come on, George. Dig your own way out! I haven't got a rope or horse with me today."

George shouted, "Hey, no foolin', you guys. I am stuck. And it's getting deeper too."

Andy looked at the muck and suddenly wondered if it could be quicksand. He'd never heard of sinking sand in Nebraska and didn't even know what it looked like. This muck was almost to George's knees, and he was sinking deeper awfully fast. Andy had remained on the other side of the river after seeing George get stuck. Now, he realized he couldn't reach George, either, being farther away from him than Chauncey.

Andy advised George to stand still or lie down so he could roll out. He wasn't sure his advice would work. George looked too scared to get his face any closer to the water than it already was. Andy could see there was no way George was going to lie down in that stuff, so he wouldn't try to roll loose on his own. They couldn't get George to stop struggling, either, which seemed to make him sink deeper. Fear raced through all of them after Chauncey tried to use his rifle to reach George and failed.

Chauncey and Andy started looking for something long enough to reach their friend. They tried breaking off willow saplings, but they were green and wet from the rain. The branches just twisted around and around without coming off. In misery, they chastised themselves, unable to believe they could all have been so stupid. None of them had packed a knife for their hike up the creek.

Andy felt desperate and tried to shoot a thick limb from a tree but failed miserably. Judging the time element in such a hopeless situation was impossible. It seemed like they scrambled for hours trying to find some means to help their buddy.

George was in over waist deep now, and all three boys neared hysteria. "Hurry up, for God's sake," he shrieked. "I can't breathe. I'm going to fall over!" George struggled to stay upright, but regardless of his efforts, he was slowly listing forward and to the left though he fought to remain vertical. Suddenly, he sank much deeper.

Like a horror movie, the muck continued to slowly climb up George's chest. Both Chauncey and Andy could feel his terror, and they saw it in his eyes. Their friend screamed and thrashed wildly with arms fully extended out from his body to each side. George's movements pushed swirls into the sludge, making it flow back and forth like thick pea soup. At that point, the muck oozed with various colors that released a powerful stench.

George was up to his armpits now, and Andy quit trying to break off the branch he'd been struggling with. He clenched his jaw as he slowly and quietly picked up his rifle from where he had dropped it in his panic. *What can I do?* he thought. *Can I let him slowly suffocate in that muck and do nothing? What would I want him to do if that were me?* he asked himself. Clenching his teeth, he stepped quietly and directly behind his weeping friend. George's eyes were rolling frantically, and the sounds he made were beyond description.

Sweating, Andy felt sick to his stomach. *I would not want to feel that stinking ooze fill my mouth and slowly strangle me to death,* he thought. *I would want it over quick and painless. But I don't know if I can do this for him.* Silently, with slightly shaking hands, he pointed the gun at his friend. Andy watched that stinking ooze creep closer to George's face. *No, I can't let it fill his mouth and nose . . . choke out his life.*

Chauncey stared at Andy pale and frozen. He understood immediately what his friend intended to do and why. Chauncey didn't reproach Andy or say a word. George was unaware of what Andy was doing, and in his condition, it was doubtful anything would have registered.

To Andy, it felt as if he'd been standing there for an eternity. His arms ached, legs quivered, and sweat ran into his eyes while he tensed for the shot. All the while, his mind kept chanting, *Maybe he'll touch bottom. Dear God, please let him touch bottom.* Then, ever so quietly, Andy heard one word . . .

"Wait."

That one word was whispered so low Andy felt sure Chauncey had been afraid to startle him. Nervous relief washed over Andy's whole body as he slowly lowered his rifle and stared numbly at Chauncey, who worked desperately to loosen the leather sling from his rifle barrel. Andy suddenly realized what Chauncey had in mind.

Once the end of the strap was free, he held the weapon by the barrel. Then Chauncey waded into the morass slowly until he was close enough to fling the loosened strap to George.

George came out of his frenzy of fear. Hope suddenly blazed in his eyes. But as the sling slid by him on the surface of the muck, Andy heard him whimpering through tightly clenched teeth when he failed to grasp it.

At the next toss, George managed to catch the strap and strained desperately trying to lift himself out of the sucking muck. At the same time, Chauncey heaved backward steadily, fighting to sustain his footing in the slime. Abruptly, the straining young man realized the swivel on the strap was beginning to bend and quietly murmured, "No! Oh, no!" Then, louder, he gasped, "George, you gotta go easy!"

Andy fell to his knees praying as he had never prayed before in his life. "Please, God. Let that swivel hold, *please.*" The minutes seemed to drag dreadfully. Then, ever so slowly, George eased forward. He couldn't be lifted out. The only way was to pull him out. The leather lifeline squeaked, and the swivel stretched completely out of shape, but it held.

Gradually, more and more of his back could be seen until Andy estimated George was leaning forward at about a 50-degree angle. At that point, Chauncey stopped pulling. Perspiration dripped off his nose. Sweat plastered his straight black hair to his head, making it hang down into his eyes. He gulped huge breaths of air and seemed on the point of collapse. Andy had been concentrating so hard on George he did not realize Chauncey was in the muck up to his knees now, and it jolted him back to reality.

Jumping to his feet, Andy ran as fast as he could around the marsh, yelling, "Chauncey! Hold on! Wait for me!" Once he was in position behind Chauncey holding onto his right arm, Chauncey reached out as far as he could, clinging to the rifle barrel with the left, acting as an anchor so George could continue to pull himself out. It was too much weight for one hand to support. Chauncey shook his head at Andy, and he let go of Chauncey's arm. Once again, Chauncey gripped the rifle barrel with both hands heaving so hard he fell backward as the sling swivel pulled out of the rifle stock.

George cried out in dismay as Chauncey lost his balance and dropped into the cloying muck himself. This time, Andy was close enough to grab Chauncey's shirt collar and pull him free. The last big heave Chauncey made helped get George more than halfway out of the quagmire.

Now, George lay on his stomach. His legs were not completely free. But the muck was as thin as water where George lay now mindlessly thrashing about. He used one arm to keep the mud out of his face while his hand clutched the gun strap aloft forgotten.

Andy pried Chauncey's fingers open to get the rifle free and found the barrel slick with his friend's blood. There was no time to see to those wounds. Andy immediately held out the rifle barrel to George now close enough to grab hold. With their combined strength, George made it into the shallows and finally rolled from the water's edge onto solid ground. Crawling on hands and knees, weeping, and still holding the forgotten gun strap, George collapsed face down on the grass.

Andy barely remembered letting the rifle fall to the ground before his legs buckled. He landed heavily on his butt, hanging his head between his knees and immediately threw up. While he retched, all he could think of was that one softly spoken word had saved him from making a horrible mistake.

It was hard to figure how long the three friends lay there, but after a while, Andy glanced up to find Chauncey rolled onto his side. The hand torn by the rifle sight was now covered with congealing blood and cradled against his chest.

George sat with his back against a dirt hump protruding from the riverbank. With his eyes closed, he occasionally released a shuddering sob.

"Hey, are you two OK?" Andy asked through a tight throat.

Slowly, Chauncey sat up, nodding his head, though his eyes were still squeezed shut in pain as he held his throbbing hand by the wrist. Andy was about to repeat his question to George when he heard his friend's hoarse voice whimper in quiet gratitude. "Thanks, fellas."

When Chauncey finally looked over at Andy, he noticed his buddy had heaved his guts. It apparently stirred Chauncey's sense of the ridiculous because a huge grin spread across his face. Then he said, "Gee whiz, big guy! All I need now is a knife and fork!"

Chauncey's sick, humorous comment made Andy smile as he threw a chunk of mud, hitting him on the shoulder and replied, "Shut up! That's just disgusting!" Andy was grateful, though. He thanked God for Chauncey's keen intuition and resourcefulness and now for his warped sense of humor. His friend had prevented a horribly traumatic event from taking place and changed it into a humorous one with one of his bizarre comments. One day at the right time, he would be able to thank Chauncey, but for now, it would remain their secret.

Fall of 1942, Norfolk

After Pearl Harbor, Andy, Chauncey, George, and Charlie all knew they wanted to enlist.

After their trip to Coon Island, Andy and Chauncey were more resolute than ever deciding that they would become Marines. In similar fashion, George and Charlie set their minds on flying for America.

Furthermore, Charlie decided that when Andy and Chauncey became Marines, nothing was going to stop him and George from joining the Army Air Corps.

1930s floor standing radio

WWII Air Force recon photo of Luftwaffe Aircraft

Delora tried not to frown at their enthusiastic talk, which always caused dreadful feelings in the pit of her stomach. She could no more stop her bouts of anxiety than she could stop her sons from listening to intelligence broadcasts regarding the German Luftwaffe.

Charlie whispered to George, "You know, this fleet of aircraft is one of the strongest, scariest, and most battle-experienced air forces in the world. I listened to an interview a while back, and Hitler said he would prove Germany's air superiority across Europe. He bragged endlessly about what he would do with his planes. He said, 'I will keep our opponents off balance by making stealth attacks with my Luftwaffe!'

"Even back in 1935, the whole world admitted the German planes were technically superior. That's why everyone is afraid of the Luftwaffe. The news broadcasters are constantly talking about their Junkers Ju-87s, Stukas, and Messerschmitt Bf-109s. But our guys are making new and better planes too. George, by the time you and I are flying, we will be able to shoot them all down!"

George nodded and replied, "Yep, when we get our chance, we'll knock them all out of the sky."

During all the war talk and the craziness created by three teenaged sons, not to mention Florence's emotional highs and lows, Delora found a little sanity staying in touch with her sisters-in-law.

The women kept up on birthdays, swapped baby clothes, passed around baptismal gowns, and shared news about their children. The babies seemed to be growing so fast. Sometimes that made their mothers laugh, and sometimes they cried, but they were always proud of their children.

School Time Again

September came, and Andy, Chauncey, and George were bored out of their brains with the hum drum textbooks that taught them nothing about what was happening around them or in the world. Eleventh grade seemed to be moving along at a snail's pace. Before long, Andy, Charlie, and his buddies George and Chauncey got into the habit of cutting a class or two to catch the *Armed Forces Radio Service* program.

They always went over to George's house because both his parents worked, and no one was home in the afternoons. Stars from Hollywood and the music industry volunteered their time and talent to entertain the troops. The AFRS put on concerts with Lionel Barrymore, comedy with Bob Hope, music with Frank Sinatra, and interviews with

Lionel Barrymore's Concert Hall Radio Show—AFRS PD—Wikimedia Commons

Bob Hope during Command Performance show for the troops—AFRS Photo PD—Wikimedia commons

the biggest stars on the movie screen like Humphrey Bogart and Lauren Bacall. With all the exciting news about the war as well as a constant stream of big-name entertainment, Andy wanted to listen to Armed Forces Radio all the time.

He disliked being thought of as a child. Even now in the 11th grade, Andy still shepherded his siblings to school. It was a responsibility he had been given by his parents. So, he made the best of it. Being keenly preoccupied with becoming a Marine, Andy decided to treat his siblings like his platoon. He had them marching with him to school. In tenth grade, Andy had included Charles, Lloyd, Florence, and nine-year-old Marcella in his platoon. This year, he had also taken charge of eight-year-old Millie and six-year-old Pete. The youngsters made the marching pretty s-l-o-w.

Walking backward, staring at the three youngest kids, Andy barked like a drill sergeant in one of the movies he had seen. "You young privates back there had best pick up the step—move it, or we are going to be late." Then, talking to Charlie marching beside him, he said, "Charlie, I'm sure glad Sharon is too young to start school this year. Can you imagine trying to march with her? We'd be carrying her all the time just like we do at home." Charlie nodded, and then Andy barked out another order. "Hey, you kids! March faster! We can't be late for school. You know what Dad said about being tardy again!"

Frank Sinatra does an interview with actress Alida Valli for the troops
overseas—AFRS WWII
PD—Wikimedia Commons

AFRS Jack Brown interviews Bogart and Bacall for the troops—AFRS WWII
PD—Wikimedia Commons

CHAPTER 23

The Karellas of Norfolk, 1942

World War II, Home Front

Delora knew many people had difficulty grasping all that had changed in two short years. Some of her neighbors did nothing but talk about the demoralizing days of the Great Depression. "For gracious sakes!" Delora said in exasperation.

"I've found the job where I fit best!"

FIND YOUR WAR JOB
In Industry – Agriculture – Business

WWII patriotic poster calling women into the workforce

"Rusty, you would think those people have their heads stuck in a hole. Don't they listen to the radio? Things have changed. Only a few years ago, there was no money and no jobs. You and I know that, but things are different now. Everyone who wants to work can. You've got a steady job, money for food, and we are even glad to pay higher taxes and spend extra to buy bonds because it helps support the war effort. We even have enough money to spend on something fun occasionally like going to the movies."

"You are right, Bitty. With all those new federally funded factories, they can't find enough men to fill the jobs. I've seen posters around town suggesting women get out of the house and go into the workforce. I suppose if they don't have kids, that's a good idea. As more and more men enlist in the Armed Forces, someone must fill those jobs. You know," said Rusty, "it is a good thing Nebraska got that irrigation program when it did. Our family certainly benefited from it when the construction started. The benefits from regulated water in the farmland is astonishing. Between the health of the land and the escalating demands for farm goods, the farming industry has practically rejuvenated overnight. Sadly, it happened too late to save

WWII newspaper about the home front

the old homestead, but it's been such a blessing for the Vobornys and the Pojars in Madison and Elgin.

"Considering how demoralized everyone was during the drought years, this turnabout has brought hope and pride back to the farming communities here in Nebraska. That is good for all the businesses in town. Everyone I talk to is dedicated to the home-front challenge of feeding our American soldiers and their allies.

"The government has had scientists working on technology that will supply solutions for the labor issue on the farms too. Modernization is transforming the countryside. The farmers coming in with repair items say this new machinery helps them work faster with fewer field hands. Even with a reduced workforce, they are producing more of everything in less time.

"No one is using horse-drawn plows anymore—they've all got steel-wheeled tractors. The men I talk to from Madison are getting rid of their outhouses and installing indoor plumbing. I'm happy about these changes, because when those items break, I'll be there to fix them. It's all work for me and helps me take care of you, my sweet wife," Rusty said as he leaned over to give her a kiss.

Delora blushed and pushed at his shoulder with a tinkling giggle and said, "Oh, go to work. You and Sharon have finished your lunches, and it's time for me to put her down for a nap."

'OF COURSE I CAN!

I'm patriotic as can be —
And ration points won't worry me!"

WWII American patriotic poster

Rusty took hold of her hand a moment and said, "Thank you for making lunch for me . . . and please tell me you are not thinking of taking any of those jobs they talk about on the radio."

Delora shook her head and replied, "I promised you I wouldn't until all our children are in school."

Rusty smiled at her answer and said softly, "Thank you, Bitty."

As Rusty walked out the door and Bitty cleared the table, she thought, *I do have my dreams. But I cannot even think of becoming a nurse and working outside my home until I have everything ready so the girls can take over the household chores once Sharon starts school next year.*

22 USE RABBIT TO SAVE POINTS

The homemaker can stretch her meat ration points, by using rabbit as a meat dish. Young rabbit can be cooked by the broiling or frying methods. Older rabbits need longer, slower cooking. Rabbit can also be served in fricasses, salads, casserole dishes, rabbit pies, croquettes or chop-suey.

MRS. EVELYN SULLIVAN PYSHKA, *Home Service Advisor*
Illinois Northern Utilities Co., Belvidere, Illinois

Page from *Home Service Advisory* to use rabbit to save points on beef needed at the war front

Delora had been reading an article in the newspaper about apprentice programs in the nursing field. Her heart had beaten a little faster as she thought, *I could do that! Become a nurse in a hospital. But if I'm going to even think about starting nursing school, I've got a lot of organizing to do before the kids can take over here at home.*

With that last thought, Delora sat down at her desk and began to make a list of tasks she could begin to delegate. Assigning each child specific chores and making them responsible for managing their time to get it done would be a good beginning. The work would get the children used to handling things at home by the time she was ready to start that nursing program.

Delora had been teaching ten-year-old Florence and eight-year-old Marcella to help her with the baking during the past year. Millie was only six and begged to help too. They had such fun playing with the flour and got really excited about the desserts they were making. No one seemed to mind eating a few burnt cookies when the girls first started baking. However, the three of them were now pretty good at making simple cakes, cookies, and frostings. Delora still made the pies, though little Millie begged to learn how. Florence had begun helping with dinner and could make excellent flour gravy, mashed potatoes, and rabbit fricassee.

Rabbit Fricassee Recipe

Ingredients:

1 medium onion
½ pound mushrooms
2 rabbits cut up in serving pieces
2 tablespoons butter
2 tablespoons flour
1 cup white vinegar
1 cup chicken broth
3 sprigs parsley
3 sprigs thyme
1 bay leaf

Season rabbit pieces with salt, pepper, and onion powder, shake in flour, and brown in bacon grease. (May crumble bacon and add into recipe if desired.)

Cut onion into chunks and slice mushrooms.

In cheese cloth put the parsley, thyme, and bay leaf and tie shut. You will remove this from the fricassee when it is done cooking.

Using two frying pans, place the browned the rabbit in one layer, add onions and mushrooms on top with seasoning bag, pour in liquids over the rabbit, and simmer for 15 minutes on the stove.

Remove rabbit and vegetables—keep warm in serving dish.

Continue simmering sauce, making it into a gravy—may thicken with cornstarch. Once it is as thick as desired, remove spice bag, pour over rabbit and vegetables, and sprinkle with fresh parsley.

Rusty was busy working three jobs when they moved into the Norfolk house and delegated the small outside chores to Ambrose when he was eight. The rest of the outside chores became Andy's responsibility when he had turned nine. Each of his younger brothers joined his team as they turned nine. Now, Charles and Lloyd worked

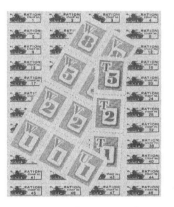

side by side with their big brother, Ambrose. Pete and Sharon were still too young to be anything but a hinderance when any of the kids were doing chores, so Marcella and Millie were generally put in charge of watching the little ones.

More Rationing Rules

Delora did the laundry while she made dinner or worked on her shopping lists.

WWII 1940s newspaper ad explaining rationing shopping with ration stamps

Though, that chore had become much more difficult since the list of rationed items had been growing rapidly and was about to become more complicated than ever based on what she read about in the newspaper.

The first government food restrictions were placed on sugar and coffee. Now, every American housewife including Delora read about the new OPA rationing booklets in the newspapers. The government said this new food and materials program was necessary to ration basic commodities that will be needed as more military bases are built in rural areas across the country. Installations were even being built in the frontier territory of Alaska.

Within weeks of reading about this new measure to create a fair and equal distribution of products, Delora received her war ration books, stamps, and tokens issued to her family name. These credentials dictated quantity allowances for products her family could buy that included gasoline, tires, sugar, meat, milk, eggs, silk, shoes, nylon, and other restricted items. The ration books clearly outlined limits an individual could purchase of each restricted product.

Within a couple of weeks of receiving her ration book, stamps, and tokens, Delora read that the government had set up 8,000 rationing board offices across the country to administer and monitor those restrictions. At dinner that evening, she said, "Rusty, this rationing stuff is getting serious. Did you read that article about it in today's newspaper?"

He replied, "No, but I will after dinner. Is there something specific I should be looking for?"

Delora shook her head and replied, "Just read it, and then we can talk about it. Oh, and look at that wartime edition of the *Victory Cookbook* that came in the mail. They issued it to all housewives. Anyway, I've been experimenting with some of the recipes in it. I don't think those government people who issued it knew how to cook. It con-

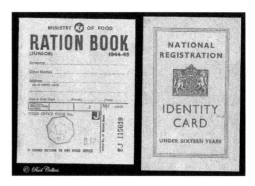

1940s sample of wartime rationing books and ID

tains revised recipes and gives substitution suggestions for rationed food items. Rusty, you are the best cook in the family and taught me everything I know about cooking. Maybe you will have some ideas on how to make those recipes taste better."

Rusty smiled at her compliment and replied, "Thank you, Bitty. I'll look at both."

Thanksgiving at the Karellas in Norfolk

Since Delora's mother had never been much of a cook, Delora and Rusty hosted a traditional Karella family Thanksgiving dinner like his papa used to do. This year, her mother and father drove to Norfolk to join them for the celebration, and dinner would be served around three o'clock. The Holts arrived at 9:00 a.m., wanting to spend more time with their grandchildren. Rusty answered the door because he had just finished his job in the kitchen. At 6:00 a.m., he was preparing rohliky, and dozens of the golden-brown crescent rolls topped with butter and black poppy seeds now sat cooling on trays.

WWII United States official rationing cookbook

Greeting his mother and father-in-law, he took their coats and said, "Everyone is in the kitchen—go take a look." Before they got to the kitchen, they could hear Delora and their grandson Andy singing. As they rounded the corner, they smelled the fresh bread, and they heard Glenn Miller and his orchestra playing "Chattanooga Choo Choo" on the radio. But it wasn't only Delora and Andy singing. All their grandchildren were working at some task and singing along too. What a merry sight to see, and they all had lovely voices.

It lifted James and Margaret's hearts to see their little girl, Delora, so happy as her handsome son washed dishes, and little Millie dried and stacked them. Delora had just put pie crust dough in the two pie tins in front of her, and Florence and Marcella were preparing the filling. Charles and Lloyd were cleaning up the counter space currently covered with flour Delora had used to roll out the dough. Little Pete and Sharon played happily in the flour that had fallen on the floor. *Truly a Thanksgiving sight if ever there was one,* Grandpa Holt thought with a huge smile. "Pete, Sharon, do you have hugs for your grandma and me?" he called out.

The two littlest Karella children squealed in delight when they heard their grandfather's voice, and he knelt on one knee to get on their level. Jumping up, they ran to him, giving him sweet kisses as they held his face, leaving powdery white handprints on his cheeks, making everyone in the room laugh.

Rusty had been taught that when you cook, timing is everything. So, now, it was his turn to get the turkey seasoned and ready in the roasting pan while Bitty made the stuffing. As the pies came out of the oven, the Turkey went in. Anyone not peeling potatoes started clearing away the used cooking utensils and the pots and pans to make room for more pots that would soon hold more food for the feast. Grandpa brought corn on the cob and fresh cranberries to cook to go with the turkey, and they still had to make the mashed potatoes and gravy.

After the turkey went into the oven, Delora felt she could take a break to say hello to her parents. "Delora," her father said, "I know your mother and I did not teach you much about good home cooking. I am certainly happy that you married into a family of excellent cooks. I admire their deeply rooted family traditions. I adore the way everyone helps prepare

Feb. 1, 1944
SPECIAL NOTE:

Token program begins Feb. 27. One-point red tokens will be given in change for Red Stamps and one-point Blue Tokens for Blue Stamps. Stamps will be worth 10 points each. Tear Stamps out across Ration Book instead of up and down. Following Stamps become valid Feb. 27:

MEATS AND FATS

Red Stamps A5, B5 and C5 (Book Four) good for 10 points each, Feb. 27 through Ma. 20.

PROCESSED FOODS

Blue Stamps A8, B8, C8, D8 (Book Four) good for 10 points each, Feb. 27 through May 20. Following Stamps remain at present point values.

PROCESSED FOODS

Green Stamps G, H and J (Book Four) good Jan. 1 through Feb. 20.

Green Stamps K, L and M (Book Four) good Feb. 1 through Mar. 20

MEATS AND FATS

Brown Stamps V (Book Three) good Jan. 23 through Feb. 26.

Brown Stamps W good Jan. 30 through Feb. 26.

Brown Stamps X good Feb. 6 through Feb. 26.

Brown Stamps Y good Feb. 13 through Mar. 20.

Brown Stamps Z good Feb. 20 through Mar 20.

SUGAR

Stamp No. 30 (Book Four) good for five pounds Jan. 16 through Mar. 31.

SHOES

Stamp No. 18 (Book One) good for one pair indefinitely. Airplane Stamp No. 1 (Book Three) good for one pair indefinitely.

FUEL OIL

Period No. 2 coupons good for ten gallons per unit through Feb. 7.

Period No. 3 coupons good for ten gallons per unit through Mar. 13.

Period No. 4 coupons and Period No. 5 coupons good for ten gallons per unit Feb. 8 through Sept. 30.

GASOLINE

No. 10 coupons in A book good for three gallons each Jan. 22 through Mar. 21.

B2 and C2 supplemental ration coupons good for five gallons each. B1 and C1 coupons remain good for two gallons each. All coupons

WWII rationing newspaper clipping

417

the food. These celebrations at Thanksgiving and Christmas here in your home are so magical to us. Your mother and I can feel the love pouring out of this kitchen. Thank you and Rusty for inviting us to share this enchanting time with both of you and our grandchildren."

Sincerely moved by his father-in-law's compliment, holding Bitty's hand, Rusty smiled and replied softly, "And you both will always be welcome to share our celebrations with us."

School Christmas Vacation

During Christmas vacation, Delora and Rusty planned a special surprise for all their children. Delora chose a movie for the four younger children—Marcella, Millie, Pete, and Sharon—and would take them to see Walt Disney's new animated feature film called *Bambi*. Rusty would take Andy, Charles, Lloyd and Florence to a war romance called *Casablanca* starring Humphrey Bogart and Ingrid Bergman.

Each of the children had an envelope under the tree with their name on it. Within the envelope was a handwritten note inviting them to the movie they would see, and it was signed by the parent who would take them. Those special gifts caused a lot of excitement because it was expensive to take so many people to the movie all at once. In fact, this was the only time they had ever done something like this for all the children, and Rusty smiled at Delora and whispered, "My darling Bitty, that was a great idea you had for a special Christmas gift." She smiled back at her husband, thrilled with his compliment.

The children's movie was a matinee. Andy and Charles went to the cellar and brought up ten apples they had picked in the fall. Cutting up the apples, Andy divided them into five kerchiefs, then tied them closed. He gave a bundle to each of the children going to the movie with their mom and said, "Put these in your coat pockets, then you can eat them during the movie."

Marcella and Millie jumped up and down in their excitement, "Mama, Mama, will you buy us some popcorn at the movie to go with the apples?"

Delora smiled as she buttoned Pete's coat and replied, "Yes, I will buy a box of popcorn to share. How does that sound?"

The girls laughed and shouted, "That's wonderful, Mama! We can't wait!"

When the older children got their turn, it was an evening film. They wore big smiles as they climbed into the car with bulging pockets filled with apple slices. When they got to the cinema, they were grinning with anticipation when their dad bought popcorn and sodas for each of them with one strict rule. "You will not tell the little ones you got a whole popcorn and soda for yourself." They all nodded in agreement and laughed happily as they made their way to their seats thrilled about the movie they would see.

When they got home, it was late, and Rusty sent them all off to bed immediately. Andy hung back and said, "Dad, can I talk to you for a bit?"

Rusty nodded as he turned out the kitchen light and replied, "Let's go into the living room, son, where we can sit down and be comfortable." Andy sat down and waited for his father to get in his chair. "Dad, that movie we saw made me think. Well, really, I have been thinking of this all year. I want to join the Marine Corps. The cut off limit is 18 right now. But I started school when I was five, so I'll turn seventeen in July after graduation." His father nodded, agreeing those facts were true but did not say anything.

"Dad, if you signed early enlistment papers for me, I could join when I get out of high school." Rusty looked at the ceiling and expelled a long breath. He had known this was coming, but he still had not been prepared to hear his son put those thoughts into words.

The long silence made him nervous. Then his father said, "Son, I know you have talked about this since the attack on Hawaii. But this is serious and dangerous. This is not like going hunting or fishing, and when you join, you can't quit. I am not sure you truly understand what you are asking permission to do."

"Dad, I listen to the news, both the American and the BBC reports. I've seen the military reels at the matinees. I know I want to be a Marine and fight the Japanese in the Pacific. I'd rather swat mosquitoes in the heat than be fighting winter weather and the enemy in Europe. If I wait until I'm called at 18, I won't have a choice what battle front I serve on. If I volunteer while I'm 17, then I can have my choice. I have been to the recruiter's office and picked up the pamphlets. I do know how serious this is. I know that this will not be easy, yet I feel it is my duty to help keep our country safe. Please, let me do this."

"Son, you must give me time to think about it. Do you remember my old friend Homer Grant, the Marine who served in World War I?" Andy nodded. "I'm going to ask him to come over today so the three of us can talk about what it means to be a Marine. After that, I will consider what you are asking."

That afternoon, Homer came over and brought a bunch of pictures with him. "Ambrose, take a look at these," said his father's friend. One by one, Homer showed Andy pictures of guys in bivouac camps during World War I in Europe. He called each young man by name and recalled where they were when the photograph was taken.

WWII Devil Dog Marines

"There is one story I'd like you to hear about—where the name Devil Dogs came from. Have you heard this name used for Marines?" Andy nodded. "Do you know how our Marines got that name?"

Andy shook his head, replying, "No, but I'd like to hear it if you know the true story."

"My unit along with many other Marine units were deployed to stop the German advance into Paris. This was back in June of 1918. We had marched 50 miles from Paris when we entered a forest called Belleau Wood. The Jerries were already dug in and had secured the high ground. Our Marines were spread out below the rise where the enemy was hiding from us. We stormed them repeatedly. Thousands of us were getting cut down by machine gun fire, and thousands more kept charging, fighting to crawl up that hill. Nothing was going to stop us! Our shear *will* shattered our enemy's morale—because of our men's ferociousness!

"German prisoners that survived that battle said the American Marines fought like possessed Devil Dogs. The Germans feared the Marines, because no matter what they threw at them, those Devil Dogs kept coming for them."

Andy's eyes were intense with determination. It was not the hesitation Homer hoped he would begin to feel about his rash decision to join the Marines at 17. Homer decided to give it one more try and went on to say, "Young man, you might be thinking of our victory in that wood as glorious." Andy nodded slightly without even knowing it. "But the truth is we suffered over 9,000 casualties, and 1,063 of my Marine brothers died in that wood to earn that title. Those numbers are burned into my brain. I don't want anyone I know to forget the dark side of battle and the horror that lies beneath every victory. It is the responsibility of the survivors of war to remind those of these facts while they can still make a difference." Then Homer finished in a whisper, "People must never forget how horrible war is and that war should be the choice of last resort!"

Picking up the stack of pictures he had shown Andy, he finished softly, "Do you know the worst part about the memories of my friends that I have shared with you?" Andy shook his head. "They are all dead. All the friends you saw in my unit in these photographs died over there."

Rusty put his hand on his friend's shoulder and replied, "I'm sorry, Homer. I know you and your unit were close."

After another beer, Homer went home, and Rusty sat across from Andy in the kitchen. "Don't answer me now. Just think about what I'm going to ask. I want you to spend the summer of your senior year here at home with us. Come September, I want you to take one semester of classes at Norfolk Junior College. If by that time you still want to join the Marines, I will sign enlistment papers so that they will activate January 1, 1944, while you are still seventeen."

Andy shot out of his seat, smiling, triumphantly saying, "Thank you, Dad. I will do as you ask." Rusty knew Homer had failed to change the boy's mind. He could see it in his son's eyes: that eagerness and determination to become a Devil Dog helping to defeat the enemies of America. Tired and not wanting to face Bitty just yet, Rusty said, "Let's keep this between us for now, son. I don't think your mother is going to take this well."

A Secret Under Wraps

Andy's alarm rang early. Uncharacteristically, he jumped out of bed and started getting cleaned up. He wanted to be downstairs as soon as Chauncey showed up so they could leave right away for school. Andy and Chauncey had been talking about this for so long he couldn't wait to tell his buddies the great news tonight. Until then, he had to keep it under wraps. Now as he washed his face and combed the jaunty wave into the front of his hair, he thought, *My new goals are to finish my senior year of school with a B average, spend four months at junior college, and then Marines here we come. The war is raging on many Allied fronts, but America's prime concern is in the Pacific, and soon it will also be in North Africa. We've got to keep notes on what we hear from now on and be ready.*

The Promise

Andy forgot his math book and rushed back up the stairs while Chauncy waited in the car. At the last minute, he stopped to talk to his brother. "Charlie! Charlie, are you up yet?" Andy whispered softly, yet urgently, which brought Charlie into Andy's room on the run.

"What's going on?" Charlie asked.

"Last night, Dad agreed. We made a deal, though I only heard the first set of conditions. I'm sure there will be more, but he is going to do it!" replied Andy.

Frowning, Charlie replied, "Do what?"

Andy still had to pinch himself—he could hardly believe it or contain his excitement. "Dad actually promised me he would sign the papers, Charlie . . . my early enlistment papers! Can you believe it?" Charlie's older brother paced back and forth as he spoke.

"Jeez, Andy, that's great," Charlie replied. "Did you ask him about me too?"

Andy stopped pacing and looked at his younger brother when he solemnly replied, "No, I didn't. Not this time." Charlie frowned. "I'm sorry," Andy added.

That whispered apology was not near enough, and the boy resentfully asked, "Why the heck not?"

"Look, Charlie, I've still got to wait until next January." His little brother looked angry, so Andy took a deep breath before he began his explanation. "Charlie, first off, you aren't even fifteen yet." Andy was thinking fast as he looked under his bed for the book. "Secondly, it's going to depend on how good your grades are. I won't be skipping school much anymore either. I've got to hit the books and keep up my grades instead of hanging out with the guys. Dad said I had to prove to him I was responsible and get at least a B average at school this year."

Searching every surface in his room, Andy saw the book he was looking for on his dresser partially covered by a shirt. Through the mirror, Andy saw his brother's glum expression. Picking up the book, he turned to face Charlie with a frown of his own. "Look, Charlie, I don't have time to explain the rest of it to you right now because Chauncey's waiting outside. After school tonight, the guys and I are going over to the back room at the diner to celebrate our future a little early."

As Andy headed out of his bedroom, he said over his shoulder, "Don't worry about it, Charlie. You'll will still get your chance to fly before the war is over. I just know it!"

The boy plunked himself down on Andy's' bed, dejected, as his older brother dashed down the stairs and out the front door.

Mid-Term Parent-Teacher Conference Reveals a Secret

Delora had committed to work on a fundraiser with the Sacred Heart Parish Lady's Guild and was happy to be part of the fundraiser. Only after making the commitment did she realize her Guild event fell on parent-teacher conference night at Sacred Heart High School. These were important meetings where she would get updated on the progress of Andy, Charles, Lloyd, and Florence, who were in secondary grades at Sacred Heart. The rest of their children were still in primary school.

"Rusty, please don't forget the mid-year student reviews tonight at the high school. The note said teachers would be in their home-rooms from 7:30 p.m. to 9:00 p.m. It shouldn't take very long, but the information is important. Particularly for the boys! OK?"

Rusty nodded and replied, "Yes, I'll go." Bitty would need the car to carry baked goods and had to be at church by five o'clock, so Rusty volunteered to walk to school. The mile to Sacred Heart was the same walk his children made every day, so he promised to go after dinner.

Even before dinner was over, two of his younger daughters, Millie and Marcella, began arguing about their kitchen chores. Rusty decided it was a good time to leave for the parent-teacher meetings even if it was a little early. Right as he was sneaking out of the house, he heard his eldest daughter, Florence, quickly lower the boom on the younger kids, instantly settling the dispute. Grinning as he quietly closed the door, he was glad for an excuse not to be drawn into female squabbles.

Rusty stood outside the door of his home and breathed deeply. He noted that for November, the evening had a wintery feel to it. He thought, *A good brisk walk will stretch my legs a bit and keep off the chill.* Rusty arrived at Sacred Heart promptly at 7:30 p.m. and appeared to be one of the first parents to arrive. He decided to visit his eldest son's homeroom teacher first.

Entering the room, Rusty cleared his throat to get the attention of the teacher standing with her back to him. When the nun turned around, he introduced himself. "Good evening, Sister. I am Mr. Karella. I'm here to review the progress of my son, Ambrose Karella."

The sister smiled and shook his extended hand in welcome but looked a little perplexed. "You are talking about Andy, correct?"

Rusty immediately bristled, replying, "My son's name is Ambrose James Karella."

The sister, being the authority in her domain, felt a little miffed by the scolding tone in his reply. In response to the rather belligerent parent, she starchily replied, "Excuse me. Your son requested we call him Andy. Since his request did not fundamentally change his name, the teaching staff here at Sacred Heart saw no reason not to comply with his request.

"Now, if you are ready, we can review your son's progress." Without waiting for Rusty's approval, the teacher pulled Andy's records and discharged her duty.

Rusty didn't give the teacher another thought. He certainly did not pay a lick of attention to the teacher's explanation. Nor did he remember if she reviewed his son's progress. As soon as the educator quit talking, Rusty stormed out of her classroom and out of the building.

Totally consumed and boiling mad over this revelation, he thought, *I can't believe my son . . . my namesake . . . doesn't want his father's name . . . my name!* Rusty continued in this blistering state of mind as he walked home.

Rusty stopped walking for a minute as a dark thought hit him. *Is my firstborn son ashamed of being Bohemian? Is he ashamed of his family? Or . . . could it be . . . that he is ashamed of me?*

I thought after the agreement we made over the weekend that everything was good between us. He will still have to wait another 12 months, but he agreed to that. I guess I will just have to ask him what is going on.

Rusty sat in his living room chair waiting for his son. Delora had been right. The conferences had not taken long. Rusty had been too upset to wait and listen to any of them. He had marched back to the house, entering his home like a cyclone, and sent his mob of younger children to bed.

When Delora returned home, Rusty even asked her to go to bed early. Recognizing her husband was in an extremely agitated mood, Delora asked no questions and went to bed as requested. Now, he sat stewing over his son's offenses, waiting for the boy to come home.

The Celebration

Andy and his friends celebrated with gusto. They were excited to share the fact that within a matter of months, they would be freed from high school. Chauncey boasted that he and Andy had big plans once they graduated from Sacred Heart but would give no details. George became irritated. He was as close of a friend to Andy as Chauncey and kept bugging Andy for more information. Andy finally gave in, and with great pride, he explained, "George, I'm sorry I didn't tell you before, but Chauncey and I are going to take a semester of classes at Norfolk Junior College while we wait to join the Marines in January."

George grinned and replied, "That's killer diller! Honestly, your dad finally agreed?"

"Just this past weekend! That's why I didn't have time to tell you earlier," Andy replied.

"Congratulations! I know how hard it's been waiting for your dad to give his consent. I'm glad I didn't have to work as hard as you did to get my dad to sign the papers. I've already received my information packet from the Army Air Corps."

Andy grimaced. "Congratulations on getting your papers. You are still way ahead of Chauncey and me. Say, I'm sure glad you didn't spill the beans to Charlie. He's a real eager beaver about joining up too. You know there's nothing he wants more than to fly for the Army Air Corps. I hope you'll keep quiet about it around him. Jeez Louise! The kid got really ticked off today when he heard my news."

Those close enough to overhear George and Andy's conversation shot them looks of disbelief. An intense whisper ran through the group. Then a belligerent voice from the back of the pack, shouting, "Andy, snap your cap! You aren't old enough yet! *None* of us here are! And don't think we haven't checked! We've all asked the recruiters about the cut-off age, and none of us qualify to join up for at least two years."

Andy addressed the heckler, saying, "My dad just agreed today to sign a waiver for early enlistment, and Chauncey's dad is going to do the same. George's dad agreed too. "Andy's calm reply was more convincing than if he had shouted down the belligerent kid. George, Chauncey, and Andy celebrated their good fortunes, and as they scanned the room, each distinctly recognized envy in the eyes of several classmates.

Chauncey, lifting his root beer in a toast, said, "To the end of high school and dating college girls before we begin our military lives! Bottoms up, boys!"

The Confrontation

On the way home, Andy was still flying high and in a great mood as he hummed the hit tune "Knock Your Socks Off." He couldn't stop thinking about the great evening he had with George and Chauncey as he walked into his unusually dark and quiet home.

The lack of noise was strange. It wasn't all that late, and he thought, *Now, that's odd. Normally, a few of the kids should still be hanging around downstairs.*

Suddenly, an icy voice made him stop instantly. "What is this I hear about you hating *my name?*"

Andy stood frozen in his tracks as he looked across the room and found his father. He saw the set of his dad's jaw and heard how upset he was by the sting in his words.

Oh good Lord, Andy thought, *how am I going to explain this to him?* Digging deep into his heart, speaking softly and with great respect, he replied, "Dad, I don't hate it. But the whole name is just too old-fashioned."

Not really understanding what he had just been told, his father flung another question at him. "Then what is it? Are you ashamed to be my son?"

Andy stiffened at such an accusation and replied with a little heat of his own. "No! Dad, that's not true!"

It was the young man's immediate and adamant denial of that awful thought that began to calm the situation. Once again, Andy spoke gently, "I am proud to be your son. My first name is just . . . old-fashioned. Honestly, Dad, that's my only reason." Shrugging his shoulders, he went on to say, "I just want to fit in with the guys. Using AJ when I was a kid or Andy when I got to high school is less complicated, and those names can't be shortened to Rose or Rosie. The name AJ or Andy sounds more normal, and that's all there is to it."

It didn't register at first with Rusty that he didn't go by his traditional name either. He had not gone by Ambrose Jerome for many years. When that fact finally entered his conscious thoughts, he brushed it off and justified it. *Sure, I use a nickname. But it was given to me. I didn't plan it. My customers started calling me Rusty, and it just stuck. I was lucky to have it. It helped protect my family during my bootlegging years. But that was different—I didn't ask people to change my name.* But recognizing that fact and out of curiosity, his father asked, "Has anyone called you Rose or Rosie?"

Andy looked at his toes with his hands pushed deep into his pant pockets and answered quietly, "Kids can be awful cruel, Dad, even if you are bigger than they are."

The old Bohemian sat in silence looking at his nearly grown son and replied in a softened, less-injured tone, "I accept your explanation, son. But I may never call you Andy. I will have to think about it. I just don't know."

Andy breathed a little easier now and nodded his head and replied quietly, "I understand your thoughts and feelings, Dad. Thank you for considering mine."

CHAPTER 24

The Gang

Karella Home, School Year of 1943

Charlie sat in his room upstairs on Lincoln Street in Norfolk Nebraska frustrated and wondering, *How did Andy do it? How did my big brother talk Dad into the most important agreement in the world? Andy still thinks I'm a kid. I am not intimidated by what I want. I admit if it was me instead of Andy, I would be on cloud nine too.*

Charlie kept running hot and then cold about his feelings regarding Andy's deal with their dad. *I'm not a hothead like Andy when things get sticky. I'll bide my time, but I won't be left behind.* Then a radical thought popped into his head.

Charles Dale (Charlie) Karella

"I will make my own deal with Dad," he mumbled to himself as he walked into the bathroom preoccupied and not realizing he left the door slightly ajar. Standing defiantly in front of the mirror, he looked at his reflection and said, "You are gonna fly in this war!"

Unbeknownst to Charlie, his sister Florence was walking by the bathroom while he was talking to his reflection. Rolling her eyes at finding her brother talking to himself, she shook her head and then announced her presence by yelling, "Gee whiz, Charlie, so here you are!"

WWII Army Air Corps recruitment poster, Public Domain Military Wiki.

Her voice came from right outside the bathroom door, making Charlie jump. Blushing hot in the face, he hoped his sister had not overheard what he said out loud to himself.

Florence hadn't heard any of the rubbish her brother was saying. She grinned because his face had turned beet red when she caught him play-acting in front of the mirror. Suddenly remembering she had been sent to find him, Florence yelled, "Dinner is ready and on the table. Come downstairs right now! Mom is mad as a hornet's nest because we are all waiting on you to say prayers." After delivering her message at the top of her lungs, Florence turned and rushed down the stairs. Florence decided she had Charlie in a hot spot and decided to use it to her advantage.

It seemed strange she never had problems with anyone accept Andy and sometimes Charlie when he was acting like Andy. Most people found her easy to get along with and liked teamworking with her. *Why can't Andy and Charlie be more like Lloyd and ask for help politely? Perhaps I do like getting payback a little too much. I suppose it's not very Christian of me,* she thought briefly. Shrugging her shoulders to dislodge that conclusion, she reached the table, saying, "Mom, Charlie was goofing around in the bathroom!"

Though Charlie was close on her heels, he was not fast enough to stop her from complaining about him. Right outside the dining room, he yelled at the top of his voice, hoping to drown out Florence's comments, "I'm coming!" In the next instant, he came around the corner and said, "Sorry you had to wait on me." His father abruptly told him to take his seat. Walking past Florence, under his breath, he muttered, "What a pain you can be! You are such a tattletale."

His father's frown turned into a scowl. Charlie quickly apologized again to his mother for making them wait and took the chair next to his youngest brother, Pete.

To pay Florence back for being a pest and to irritate her, Charlie made a point of interrupting anything the little tattletale started to say and kept it up while arrogantly ignoring her glares.

Halfway through dinner, Delora gave Rusty a look, which said she thought he should put a stop to his son's bad behavior.

Rusty prayed for patience. When his children got along, he thought he wouldn't mind having a dozen kids. Now, he missed the days when they were babies and not at each other's throats all the time. Eight of them were more than enough to handle.

Taking a calming breath, Rusty nodded at Delora, then slammed his palm down on the tabletop. With that loud bang, the room went silent. As quiet settled around the Karella supper table, Rusty said evenly, "Charles Dale and Florence Delora! That is enough! I expect better behavior out of an older brother and sister. Act your age, Charles!"

Charlie cringed in reaction to the word age. *Dang,* he thought, *If I don't watch it, that word will be my downfall.*

Blessed silence reigned at the table until supper was over. When the children were excused after dinner, the boys left the room without a word. It was the girls' night to do the dishes, and no one wanted to get their parents riled up again.

WWII Army Air Force recruitment movie Public Domain LOC—Wiki

During the Weeks

Charlie eagerly marched along with the rest of his siblings once Andy started practicing Marine drills on the way to school each morning. Setting a blistering pace with his long legs, sometimes they were all forced to run to keep up with him. No one dared fall behind, and they never had a chance to get cold as they ran the mile to the schoolyard. Because of those forced marches, the Karella kids never got reported for being late to school either.

By the new school year of 1943, Chauncey and Andy both towered over Charlie and Lloyd. At 16, Andy easily stood a head taller than the crowd at school, which made him easy to spot by teachers. There weren't many guys of his stature in school. Charlie was nearly the same height as Lloyd, Bud, and George. Guys his height found it easy to disappear in a crowded hallway to avoid the searching eyes of a teacher or duck out of the building unseen when the gang intended to cut class.

Andy's gang had regularly organized schoolflu skip days during their first several years of high school. They hung out at George's house because his mother was a nurse and worked the swing shift from 3:00 to 9:00 p.m., and his father worked at the courthouse and never got home until after 6:00 p.m. That made George's house a great place to spend the day listening to the radio, catching up on war news or listening to music. Plus, George had a killer diller collection of superhero and caped crusader comic books, including every new edition of Captain America.

Shared Experiences

Andy, Chauncey, and George's senior year was creeping by at a snail's pace. They got sick and tired of the tedious days trapped inside school classrooms. "What a waste of time," Andy whispered to Chauncey during another repetitive lecture on a subject with no apparent relevance to the real world. "I am so tired of listening to boring teachers who never want to talk about anything happening outside of books or this building."

Sister Diphna stopped writing on the chalkboard when she heard whispering but kept talking as she turned to scan the room searching for the ones interrupting her lesson. As she spoke, her eyes settled on three of her troublemakers at the exact time Chauncey and George replied to Andy in hushed voices, "Jeez, you can say that again."

Targets acquired! thought Sister Diphna and barked, "Mr. Crocker! Mr. Pierce! Do you have something of value to share with the class?".

Sitting up straight in their seats, they immediately and respectfully replied in unison, "No, Sister."

As the bell rang, Sister Diphna noticed Mr. Karella and his friends George and Chauncey ran out of her classroom and into the hallway before she could stop them.

In his rush to get out of the classroom, Andy practically ran over his brother Charlie walking by. "Hey, Charlie, how's it going?" Andy asked. Andy, Chauncey, George, and Charlie continued down the hall together, wading through the throng of students headed to their classes.

Thinking fast, Andy tried to justify a skip day or at least skipping a few classes. *I know I wasn't going to do this anymore, but what could a few skip days hurt?* He thought, *It's my last semester of my final year of school. What difference could it make?*

"Boys," said Andy, "I think it's time for a schoolflu day."

"It's way overdue, I'd say, and I think it should be considered an epidemic, don't you, Chauncey?" George asked, giving him the look.

Grinning, Charlie added, "Hey, you guys can count me in on this epidemic. I'll make sure Lloyd catches the same illness as we do."

"Sounds like a plan. We'll talk about it on the way home," Andy announced as he saluted his friends, and they split up to go to their next class.

During Andy's junior year of high school, he and his gang routinely planned and executed skip days. This activity was code-named *schoolflu,* but they quickly realized the importance of having a plausible alibi to go undetected. These clever young men believed the Catholic sisters teaching at their school were somewhat gullible. Or maybe they just lacked imagination as compared to their slightly sneaky male students. Regardless, the boys used the teachers' trusting thought process against them.

Chauncey, being the intellectual of their group who got straight As in all his classes, also received extra credit for working in the front office before school. That put him in a position to ensure forged parental notes that might come in for absentee days or missed classes never got filed into student folders. Being in the office also provided opportunities for Chauncey to overhear conversations between the school's principal and several of the Karella boys' teachers when discussing absenteeism.

They agreed that Lloyd, the youngest of the three Karella boys in high school, liked school. Yet, he seemed to be missing as often as his older brothers. The consensus among the teaching staff was that Lloyd would never skip school, which effectively neutralized their budding suspicions about the other two.

Once Chauncey passed on this conversation, Andy and Charlie insisted on Lloyd's participation in all the gang's clandestine skip days to provide the perfect cover. If Lloyd joined their escapades, he'd keep his mouth shut too. He'd be in as much trouble as them if he divulged the truth, so Lloyd became the insurance. Lloyd also dragged his friend Bud along on these schoolflu days and enjoyed a camaraderie with the gang the younger boys would never have sought out on their own.

A Schoolflu Day

During the chaos caused by the bell and changing classes, the six boys all exited the school building separately. They met down the street around the corner out of sight of school windows, then walked over to the Pierce house.

Being an only child, George was allowed to have the whole basement for his room. Besides his bed, he had an old sofa and two overstuffed chairs. The fantastic floor standing radio was a Christmas gift from his parents some years back. The cabinet filled with George's comic book collection was something the gang found in an abandoned building on one of their weekly hunts for scrap metal. The only decoration on the wall besides George's Army Air Corps posters were his gun and fishing pole rack, a gift that his dad had made for him for his ninth birthday. The Pierces' place made the perfect hideout for schoolflu days, and the boys had free run of the house and the kitchen cupboards packed with great food.

Radio had been changing Charlie and Andy's world since they were toddlers. Unfortunately, at the Karella's home, they were not allowed to reset the radio station without permission, and their mom did not allow them to listen to war news. At George's, they could listen to anything they wanted to hear.

Chauncey, the brainiac of the gang, memorized the stations settings. He could identify what station or network—CBS, ABC, or NBC—played the best music or broadcasted the news they liked to keep up on. The BBC had the most accurate news on the European fronts and air battles. AFRS stayed on top of all American battlefronts and had daily updates on the Navy and Marine movement from the Pacific fleet. That made Chauncey the head of entertainment and programming requests. Since it was George's room, he got first pick of what they listened to, and that was anything to do with aircraft. Chauncey

One of the WWII Luftwaffe Messerschmitt prop fighter aircraft, ME-109
Public Domain Wiki

scanned the regular stations and BBC for news or broadcasts covering air battles. Charlie and Bud were talking about who had the best aircraft when George broke in, saying, "Look, the Wright brothers might have opened the eyes of the world to airflight in 1908. But you've got to admit German aircraft dominated in the 30s. Heck, prior to 1939, jet engines existed only in laboratories. Too bad it was a German physicist that developed a jet-propelled airplane first."

Bud replied, "Come on, George, this is 1943. That old jet-plane rubbish is Nazi propaganda, and that's not the problem. It's the

Luftwaffe's prop-driven Messerschmitt ME-109s. Those are the planes shooting at our boys!"

Then Charlie added, "That may be true, guys, but America has aircraft now that will outperform those old German designs. We've got the big boys like Mitchell B-25s and the Douglass A-26 attack bombers. But the ones that really cut the enemy down to size is our P-51 Mustangs and the Bell P-39 Airacobra fighter planes."

Lionel Barrymore's concert hall radio show—AFRS Public Domain Wiki

All the boys nodded, and then Charlie finished by saying, "Now, you know why George, Bud, and I are going into the Air Corps. We can't wait to fly those fighters and shoot those Zeros and Messerschmitts out of the sky!"

"Hey, Chauncey, would you dial in AFRS? I want to hear what's happening in North Africa and in the Pacific," Andy requested. Then he said, "Did you guys know they call radio the invisible highway? The AFRS uses pre-recorded discs to play music for the troops. They also air programs like Globe Theater and Command performances, *Yarns for Yanks*, and lots of modern American jazz music. In fact, it is the only news service making broadcasts focused on supporting and entertaining all our U.S. troops in the war."

Chauncey replied, "Hold your horses, Andy. I've got George's request first." As he dialed through the crackle and buzzing, he closed in on the signal for the BBC station, and then a voice boomed into the room. "BBC reports . . . Allied forces take back North Africa . . . Italy surrenders to Allied forces . . . U.S. General Dwight D. Eisenhower is now Allied Commander for the United States of America. We'll have more news at 6:00 p.m."

"Wow," the boys murmured.

"Chauncey, will you please dial in the AFRS now? Let's hear what they have to say," Andy asked with concern. When the crackle and buzz of crossing radio signals stopped, a stern voice broke the silence, reporting, ". . . not going well for our American Navy or the Marines in the Pacific . . . the Empire of Japan has control over most of the islands across the South Pacific . . . it is confirmed . . . Japanese have attacked and occupy positions from India to the territory of Alaska. More to come at the top of the hour." A hush fell over the room as the broadcast returned to music programming, and a jazz tune by Tommy Dorsey filled the quiet following that ominous report.

Suddenly, George's stomach let out a loud growl, and the sense of alarm was dispelled by teenaged laughter. "Let's go raid the cupboards for something to eat," George suggested, and they all clamored up the stairs to the kitchen.

Carrying cheese sandwiches back to the basement, Charlie called out, "George, do you have the latest Captain America comic? I haven't read it yet, but I heard he's fighting Hitler again, and I can't wait to read it."

George handed the comic book to Andy to pass over to Charlie. "Guys, get a look at this," Andy said as he pointed to the back of a comic book.

1024px-LibertyBond-WinsorMcCay 2.jpg
Public Domain Wiki

It was Uncle Sam, and beneath the image, the Army recruiting message read: *Boys and girls, if you are not old enough to join the Army, then Uncle Sam wants you to join Captain America's Sentinels of Liberty club and get your own badge that you can wear to prove you are a loyal believer in Americanism.*

Teacher of Sacred Heart School

The Sisters of Sacred Heart School never did figure out what was behind the suspicious plagues that seemed to hit the Karella household in threes.

CHAPTER 25

Delora Lucy Holt Karella

Six Months Earlier, Karella Home, October

While Rusty read the paper, Delora thumbed curiously through the new holiday Sears, Roebuck, and Co. catalog for Christmas present ideas. This catalog also had a spring supplement at the back, and she found a list of rationed farm equipment. She couldn't believe the fencing wire she wanted to order for her victory garden was being rationed. "Rusty, did you know that the chicken wire I wanted to use for my climbing peas this spring is a rationed item?"

Delora (Bitty) Holt Karella

Not looking up, Rusty nodded and replied offhandedly, "Not surprising, considering it's metal, and metal is being salvaged. Makes sense to me that new wire would be a rationed item too."

She frowned at him and replied, "Then what am I going to use for my peas to climb?"

Now, Rusty looked at her as though she had given him a puzzle to figure out. After a few minutes, he said, "Baling twine. I'll make a wooden frame, hang pieces of baling twine, and nail each string at the top and bottom inside the frame. Plant your peas at the base of each string and train them to climb up that."

"Well, I'll be darned," she said softly. Then she added louder, "What a good idea, Rusty. Please make me four of those frames to fit around my Victory Garden, and we'll get a good crop of peas come this next summer."

The Depression years taught most people, including Delora and Rusty, that nearly everything had worth. Junkyards had proven to be a gold mine of opportunity. Repurposing all kinds of materials, Delora and Rusty constantly demonstrated that with a little creativity and resourcefulness, a lot of amazing things could be created from junk, such as the pea frames Rusty made for Delora's garden from repurposed wood, an old ball of baling twine, and salvaged nails.

Early 1900s Singer sewing machine

That kind of mindset helped Delora stretch Rusty's paychecks, but it was still hard to meet the day-to-day pressures of raising eight growing children. Certain situations remained a bit difficult despite the fact that Rusty made steady, decent money.

One of those situations concerned the difference between supplying items that were necessities versus items that were considered extras and cost more. Delora's eight children literally grew out of or wore out all their clothing at least once a year and sometimes twice a year. The fabrics she settled on might not be fancy, but the materials she chose were sturdy and wore-well. Her goal was to see that each of her children had at least three or four changes of clothing per school year. One of the ways she afforded new shoes was with her rabbit fund. Every time her boys brought home rabbit, the pennies she saved from not buying meat at the grocer went toward her account for new school shoes.

January 1943

Now that her kids were back in school after the holidays, Delora could put five-year-old Sharon down for a nap on a regular schedule. The house felt strangely quiet as she sat down with a cup of coffee in her kitchen. Music played softly, and sunshine streamed in the window. *How time has flown,* she thought. *My last baby will be ready to start school in the fall. When I first met Rusty, he was already a man, and I was nothing but a girl.*

He's taught me so much over the 17 years we've been married. It amazes me how good his is at taking care of us. Rusty is much more impartial with the children whether they need praise or punishment. I guess that is because I am with them all the time . . . that they think they can fool me or that I will be softer than their father. Perhaps I do let them get away with too much. She shook her head.

I still can't believe Rusty agreed to let Andy join the Marines. He will only be 17. Maybe his time at college will change his mind. That is what I pray for—that Andy will come to his senses. I guess I will have to wait and see, but as far as I'm concerned, none of my other boys will be joining up early . . . not if I can help it. She hated being at odds with Rusty over anything, and lately, they seemed to be in a constant disagreement over Andy and Charlie's military ambitions.

Closing her eyes and leaning her cheek on her fist, she thought, *We are so blessed to have each other. Rusty and I have made it through the years protecting our children by pulling together. I know him. I just can't figure out what on earth made him*

Left to right—back: Marcella, Lloyd, Florence
Left to right—front: Sharon, Jerome Ambrose (Pete), and Mildred (Millie)— the six youngest of Rusty and Delora Karella's children

promise to sign those papers! Perhaps the reason he gave into Andy's demands is because he is so tired from working all the time.

Rusty does all our household repairs inside and outside, runs a repair shop out of his garage on the weekends, and works weekdays for the local smith and the plumbing and supply store.

He has always been driven to provide for our family, and he has seen this family through some very difficult times. Rusty is such a good man and role model for our children with his kind heart, deep faith, and high moral standards. Those are the strengths I want our children to develop as they grow into their own personalities.

Because of Rusty, I have always felt empowered, strong, and safe. He has willingly shared the responsibilities with me to achieve our goals. Most of all, he has always been honest and straight forward with me. He is my cornerstone, and that holds our family together, but even he gets tired and needs help.

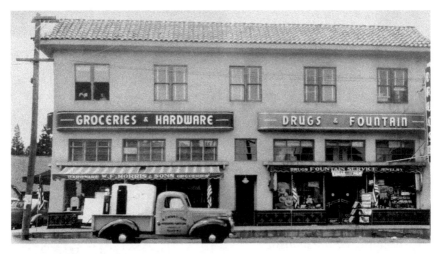

Main street in Norfolk, Nebraska, 1930s, taken at museum—GKM 2020

Delora trusted Rusty with all her heart. He never hid how he felt from her. At the same time, she could tell the long work hours were putting a severe strain on his health. Back in 1938 while she was in labor with Sharon at the hospital, Rusty was so agitated that her doctor had insisted on examining him and discovered he had high blood pressure. Since then, he took medication for that condition. In the last two years, Rusty also started smoking cigarettes, saying that it calmed his mind when he felt stressed about things. He didn't smoke much at home, and she felt that if it helped him feel calmer, perhaps it was helping his blood pressure too.

Suddenly, a conclusion popped into her head: *That must have been why!* She thought, *He was too tired to keep fighting to discourage Andy from joining the Marines early.* Rusty needed her help whether he knew it or not, and he needed all his strength to outwit their strong-minded sons.

A New Career

The idea of getting a job outside their home to bring in extra money had been on Delora's mind a lot during the past year. With Andy away at college, she only had Charlie, Lloyd, and Florence attending high school. Marcella would join them soon. Millie and Pete were doing well in grade school, and next September, Sharon Theresa would start first grade at Sacred Heart as well.

Charlie had been withdrawn and a bit grouchy since his older brother left for college. These days, Charlie kept himself extremely busy doing odd jobs for neighbors. When she asked him why he was gone so much, he replied, "I need to make more of my own money and save up for the future." What that future was Charlie declined to explain. Yet, he had always been goal-oriented, and she knew her second-born son was a good boy, so she let him govern his own time.

Glad these odd jobs helped keep Charlie's mind occupied, his absence improved the general attitude of the other children. Considering what a good team Lloyd and Florence made, she believed those two were mature enough to take over the responsibility of watching the younger sisters and brother.

Thinking hard about what she should do, she arrived at a few conclusions: *Rusty needs my help. Despite what he says, the increased cost of taxes, the added expense of war bonds, and rationing haven't made things easier. On top of increased living costs, the kids are growing like weeds. Every time I turn around, it seems one of them needs new shoes. Lloyd and Pete are growing so fast that there is no more material in the hem of their pants to let down, and they will need new trousers before the next school year starts. Once they are in school, I'm going to get a job and help bring in more money.* Having made her decision, she added a little prayer, *Dear Lord, if it's all the same to you, I'd love to work at Our Lady of Lourdes Hospital.*

That night before she and Rusty fell asleep, Delora snuggled up to his shoulder and whispered, "Please just sleep on what I'm going to say."

With closed eyes, he nodded and rubbed his cheek against her soft hair and squeezed her arm, indicating she should tell him what was on her mind.

"When Sharon starts school, I want to join the nurses training program at Our Lady of Lourdes Hospital and work a few part-time hours during the week. The extra money would help, and I think I could make a good nurse, considering how long I took care of Mama. It will also make it easier to take care of my family's health too."

Rusty softly replied, "'My dear little Bitty, I think you would make a wonderful nurse. You were a blessing to your mother when she was so sick. Look at the marvelous job you've done keeping me and the kids healthy too. I just want you to consider something about the working world before you get your heart too set on a particular job. Sometimes getting the job you want is not what you know but whom you know that becomes a deciding factor." Then he went silent, and she realized Rusty had fallen to sleep.

She lay awake for a while thinking about what he had said. That was when she realized he had not said no. She decided that the very fact he had not said no meant yes!

On Sunday after Mass as Delora and her family walked by Father Robert, Delora said, "Father, your sermon was wonderful." Father Robert thanked her, then introduced them to Father O'Brian, who worked with the sisters at the hospital. The priest smiled and shook hands with the Karellas. Then Delora asked, "We'd love to have you both come over for dinner next Saturday night. Can you come? We could play a little pinochle after dinner, and I make wonderful cream pies."

Smiling broadly, Father Robert replied, "How could we decline such a scrumptious offer?"

Father O'Brian followed that by asking, "What time do you want me to come over?"

After discovering their new friend shared a passion for two of her family's favorite pastimes, Delora began to invite Father O'Brian to dinner and a game of cards at least a couple of times a month. This Saturday evening would give her a chance to find out what Father O'Brian knew about the Our Lady of Lourdes Hospital.

A Week Later, Saturday Night

After enjoying a wonderful dinner with the Karella family, Delora told Father Bob O'Brian she had hopes of joining the nursing program Our Lady of Lourdes offered. "I was wondering if you could tell me anything about the hospital and the staff there?"

Thrilled to share what he knew, the priest said, "I believe a little history on this subject is in order before we talk about the hospital." The priest ate his last piece of pie and pushed the plate away, and Delora refilled his coffee cup. Finally, the priest got comfortable and said, "This story starts back in 1926 . . ."

Delora perked up at hearing that date and whispered to Rusty, "That was our year, Rusty—when we got married." Rusty nodded and put his hand on Delora's and nodded at the priest.

Father O'Brian had not let that whisper interrupt his thoughts, being used to such commotion during his sermons, and just kept talking. "A group of Benedictine sisters came from Germany with a mission to establish Catholic schools and hospitals all over Nebraska. It had been a big deal in the papers when Archbishop Jeremiah Harty of Omaha invited them to come. The Benedictines proceeded to open many schools and hospitals throughout the state, including Our Lady of Lourdes Hospital in Norfolk in 1935. Five years after the

Benedictine's mission began in Nebraska, the main convent for their order was transferred to Norfolk and named Immaculate Convent, so it is quite a coincidence that you and Rusty chose to belong to the Sacred Heart Catholic Church here in Norfolk. I say God works in mysterious ways because I also happen to work closely with the sisters at Our Lady of Lourdes Hospital."

"Father, do you think there is a chance that I could be accepted into their nursing program and work there?" she asked.

He smiled at her and replied, "With God's help, nothing is impossible, Bitty."

Being a close friend of the Karella family, Father Bob O'Brian knew Delora was worried about her husband's health. He also knew she felt she should get a job to help relieve some of the stress her husband was under. Now, he knew she wanted to work at the hospital, and he would see what he could do to help her.

After Mass one Sunday in late August 1943, Father Bob pulled Bitty aside and privately told her the sisters were going to be hiring hospital support staff in the coming month of November.

Thrilled with this news and determined to be one of the people the sisters hired, Delora applied at the hospital for both the nursing program and shift work in September right after school started. She used their family priest as a reference and begged God for help in securing at least a few hours per week at the hospital, sure that even a little additional pay would go a long way to offset grocery and clothing costs.

Thanksgiving

It had been a scrumptious long weekend—one of the best extended celebrations they had ever held in their home. All of Rusty's sisters and their families had come from Madison. The Beans, Pojars, Vobornys, and Karella cousins were thrilled to celebrate Thanksgiving together.

Each family had brought extra food for the whole weekend, and everyone planned to stay Thursday, Friday, and Saturday. Then they would start home after church on Sunday. Delora's kids joined their cousins with stacks of blankets and camped out on the floor so the parents could have the beds and the couch. There was singing and baking going on in the kitchen every day. All the cousins took turns on sink duty keeping dishes washed and put away. The radio constantly played big band jazz music by Glenn Miller and Tommy Dorsey along with great new tunes by up-and-coming young singers like Bing Crosby and Frank Sinatra.

When news bulletins broke into the music program, everyone automatically quieted down to listen. The somber mood the news created dissipated as soon as the music started up again, and slowly, the hum of conversation grew back to its normal pitch.

While the adults played cards and enjoyed homemade cordials, the cousins played jacks and marbles. Some of them read comic books, while others listened to their favorite radio serials like *Captain Silver's Sea Hound Adventures, Bobby Benson and the B-Bar-B Riders, The Lone Ranger, Dick Tracy, Flash Gordon*, and *The Green Hornet*.

Delora kept a list of the programs, the time each one aired, and on what station. This was the list of approved radio shows she and Rusty believed had wholesome and uplifting moral messages. Most of the radio characters made the cut because Rusty and Delora often listened to the programs with their kids. Delora also liked the sponsor's breaks when they introduced new products she could buy in the stores. Each show would last between 15 and 20 minutes, and then the children's noisy activities would resume.

In the evening after the kids fell asleep having collapsed in heaps on the floor, the adults would have some quiet time to visit. They could share their thoughts without little ears listening. They talked about their hopes and dreams for their children. They also said many prayers for family members and friends who were serving in the war and for their safe return.

Sometimes they even asked each other what they thought life was going to be like after America won the war. These clan gatherings made everyone feel deeply connected with each other. The only way Delora could describe the weekend was to say it was heavenly and filled with love, fantastic food, and a tremendous amount of fun.

On Friday during the Thanksgiving weekend, Delora's prayers were answered. When the mail came, she received a postcard with the picture of the hospital on it from Father O'Brian. His note indicated he was sure she would get into the apprentice nursing program. She would have to go for an interview, and then she could talk to them about a paid work shift. The last part of his note said he had been happy to help.

Our Lady of Lourdes Hospital
NORFOLK, NEBRASKA

1940s—Delora Karella's hospital, Our Lady of Lourdes Hospital, Norfolk, Nebraska

Everyone could see she was thrilled about receiving the postcard, and the cryptic message made them curious. Delora didn't know what to say, and Rusty came to her rescue. "Delora promised not to go to work outside of our home until all the children were in school. This past September, she fulfilled that promise, and now she wants to become a nurse. I believe this card is an indication she is one step closer to that goal."

Delora smiled at her wonderful husband as everyone congratulated her and wished her good luck. After the fuss died down, she leaned over and pressed her cheek to Rusty's shoulder and whispered, "Thank you, my dear husband."

The following Monday morning, she called the staffing manager at the hospital, introducing herself as Delora Karella, and the woman confirmed she was scheduled for an interview and orientation meeting in two days at 8:00 a.m.

Though Delora confirmed the appointment with the secretary calmly, as she hung up the telephone receiver, she was nearly dancing with excitement. "Thank you, Lord!" Delora chanted.

If she got the classes and shifts she wanted, she would start at the hospital on December fifth, which gave her five days to get everything prepared and organized for her daughters to take over the chores at home. *The girls are ready,* she thought. *They know how to cook and handle making dinner. But I've always done the shopping. The girls haven't even helped prepare the grocery list with the rationing books. That's alright. I can continue to take care of that.*

Pulling pencil and paper from a drawer, Delora started writing down her to-do list and organizing tasks and thinking, *I need to be sure the pantry is well-stocked.* Her pencil moved rapidly as she listed food items and household cleaning supplies. *Oh yes, I'll need extra laundry detergent, extra clothespins to hang the clothing and bedding to dry on the clothesline. Extra flour and sugar.* Eventually, Delora set down her pencil and reviewed her list. *With all these supplies, the kids will be able to keep up with their chores and make lunches on the weekends and dinners during the week until I can shop again.*

MAKE THIS PLEDGE:
I pay no more than top legal prices
I accept no rationed goods without giving up ration stamps

WWII rationing pledge

Two Days Later, Wednesday Morning

Delora got home from her meeting at the hospital about 10:00 a.m. She pulled the ration books and stamps from the drawer and put them in her purse with her shopping list and set her coat and purse on the couch by the door. She felt good about her interview but wouldn't know anything for certain until after 3:30 that afternoon.

Rusty came home for lunch because Bitty said she needed the car to go shopping once she dropped him back off at work at 1:00 p.m.

During lunch, Delora did not tell Rusty about the hospital appointment. She did not want to disappoint him or herself, knowing there was nothing worse than to count on chickens before the eggs hatched. The best way to handle this was to have her orientation meeting over with and employment papers in hand. More importantly, she wanted to know how much she would be making before she broke the good news to her husband. Delora planned to check in at the hospital after she finished her shopping. Delora couldn't wait. She prayed she would have good news to share when she picked Rusty up after work.

War Rationing Guaranteed a Fair Share

Delora would never delegate the shopping to the girls because rationing during these war years was very serious. They did not understand how the books and stamps worked. She could not afford to have them make mistakes or be misled about how they were to be used. Delora vividly remembered reading the agreement she signed from the OPA before she could use the ration books and stamps assigned to their family.

WWII ration shopping—Safeguard Your Share poster

READ BEFORE SIGNING

In accepting this book, I recognize that it remains the property of the United States Government. I will use it only in the manner and for the purposes authorized by the Office of Price Administration.

War Ration Book Two—January 1943

This book is the property of the United States Government. It is unlawful to sell or give it to any other person or to use it or permit anyone else to use it, except to obtain rationed goods for the person to whom it was issued. Persons who violate Rationing Regulations are subject to a $10,000 fine or imprisonment, or both.

Delora had taken these warnings very seriously, and the penalties were more than sufficient to convince her to comply with all the rules.

Opportunity Knocks

Delora had finished her shopping an hour and 20 minutes earlier. Now, she sat in the parking lot at the hospital with her groceries filling the back seat, yet she just had to sit for a moment trying to absorb the incredible opportunities that lay ahead of her. In six hours, she had gone from no prospects to having more choices than she ever dreamed of having. Biting her lip deep in thought, her mouth began to turn up into a smile.

WWII ration shopping—
Means a Fair Share poster

Sitting in the car, Delora put her face in her hands, thinking, *Dear Lord, thank you, thank you! My dream is coming true—I can hardly believe it. I will go to nursing school and work at the hospital while I study.* She held an OPA agent card in her fingers and could hardly take in the second opportunity that had fallen into her lap. *I believe there might be a way I can take advantage of both opportunities.* "I've got to talk to Rusty!" she whispered aloud.

Waiting at the curb for Rusty, Delora opened the driver's door when she saw him and slid over so he could get behind the wheel. Rusty immediately noticed how her eyes twinkled with happiness, and she wore a beautiful smile. "What has put such a lovely smile on your face, Bitty?" he asked sweetly.

"I've got a lot to tell you," she replied in a tone mixed with laughter and excitement and handed Rusty the postcard with the picture of Our Land of Lourdes Hospital on it. Rusty had seen this postcard before at Thanksgiving, and now he sat looking down at it with excitement growing in his heart, too, thinking he grasped her news. He whispered, "Oh, Bitty! You got the job at the hospital?"

She grinned and nodded her head as the car filled with her tinkling laughter. Then she handed him an OPA agent's card and said, "I have more news too!"

A Second Opportunity

Bitty had finished her interview at the hospital and would not hear anything from the administration until afternoon. She decided to believe and proceed as though she would get the job. That meant she needed to get her shopping done for the week so her girls could take over all the cooking and cleaning duties at home once she started her work shift at the hospital.

Delora Lucy (Bitty) Holt Karella, 1940s

Delora had the list she had prepared and her ration books, stamps, and coupons with her and headed off to the market. The shopping went as planned, but as she headed to her car, she noticed two men in suits and hats watching her. They came to a stop next to her as she finished putting her groceries in the back seat of her car. Delora didn't recognize them, but they looked official as they held out badges for her to look at and said, "Excuse us, please. We are OPA agents on official business and need to have a word with you."

Delora had done nothing wrong, and their credentials looked to be in order, so she politely replied, "Fine, what do you need to talk to me about?"

"We must ask to see your ration books, your ID, your grocery receipt, as well as inspect the grocery items you have in your car, please."

Delora realized she was legally obligated to comply with their request and gave them her documents. Then she opened her car door so they could inspect the grocery items she had purchased.

After a brief search through her bags, they were apparently satisfied and returned her ration books and made sure her groceries were neat and secure in the backseat of her car. Then they asked her a surprising question. "Would you please give us a little more of your time? We have something we would like to discuss with you."

She had given them no reason to make trouble for her, so she nodded.

The tall agent asked if she would sit down with him in the park by the church. Since the bench they indicated was in plain sight, she agreed. After they were all seated, the taller man said, "Mrs. Karella, my name is OPA Agent Oarks, and this is Agent Green. First, we would like to ask you a few questions about your family if you don't mind." Delora nodded, so Agent Oarks asked, "How many children do you have?"

Delora did not know what this had to do with her groceries, but she answered the question, "I have eight children."

"Are they all at home?" he asked.

Delora replied succinctly, "My oldest is attending college and will join the Marines in January. All the rest are in school and still living at home."

Then Mr. Green asked, "Did your husband join up?"

This question immediately irritated her, and she replied crisply, "No. He is past enlistment age to serve. Now, if you are through with your questions, I have things to do." Delora stood up to leave.

Mr. Oarks quickly apologized, saying, "Please excuse us for asking these personal questions, Mrs. Karella. We did not mean to offend you! We were merely trying to ascertain if you had enough income between the adults in your household to take care of your children. Would you sit a moment longer and give us a chance to explain?"

Delora narrowed her eyes, looking at every detail of these men. She had three grown boys and had developed an uncanny way of knowing when one of them were lying or had something fishy up their sleeves. Looking them over carefully, Delora decided they were being sincere and chose to give them a few more minutes. She said, "You have a moment longer to explain."

WWII rationing board office for war for ration Book 1 and 2 OPA office

"Thank you," replied Agent Oarks, and then he said bluntly, "we were trying to determine if you would be interested in a job working for the OPA."

As a 33-year-old wife and mother of eight children, Delora did not think anything could take her by surprise anymore. But this question caught her so off guard she felt dumbfounded as she stood before these two strangers who were waiting for her to answer them. She suddenly found herself more curious than cautious and completely intrigued as she asked, "What kind of job?" Smiling, the two men visibly relaxed, and Delora told herself, *It can't hurt to listen.*

Agent Oarks nodded at Agent Green, and he pulled a folded piece of paper from his pocket. She watched as the man unfolded it carefully, then Agent Green asked, "Have you seen this advertisement?"

Delora nodded and replied, "Yes, of course I have. That is a Sears and Roebucks catalog ad."

Nodding, he affirmed she was correct, then pointed to the fine print on the page and asked her to read it. She took the paper in hand and read the small print he had pointed to and discovered it was the instructions for purchasing shoes from Sears with ration stamps. This 1943 Sears, Roebuck, and Co. catalog ad assured Americans they could buy rationed shoes from their catalog using the following procedure. "Simply detach War Ration Book Stamp

No. 17 from your War Ration Book No. 1 (the sugar and coffee ration book) and pin it to your shoe order."

Suddenly, Deloa's head snapped up, and she looked at Agent Green in the eyes when she said, "But this is not correct. We took an oath not to use the coupons for any purchase except what they are designated for and had to promise this before we received our books. Breaking that oath has serious consequences. We could be punished for this!"

Both agents nodded at her comprehension of the situation. Oarks replied, "You are right, Mrs. Karella. What this ad is telling the buyers to do is illegal. It is our job keep the marketplace fair and honest for everyone. We want you to help us catch grocers that are not living up to the agreements they made regarding the rules governing rationing."

Delora nodded and replied, "Then, in that case, I would be interested in hearing more of what you have to say."

WWII Sears ad instructions on how to buy rationed shoes

Delora Goes Undercover

"Rusty, they want to take me to neighboring towns where I will not be recognized. The OPA agents will provide me with a list of grocery items to buy, but they will let me help select the grocery items on that list. They will also give me the ration stamps to purchase most of the items properly. However, there will be a few items on the list that I will not have the correct stamps for. They want to see if the grocer will suggest I use other stamps like sugar and coffee in exchange for the unauthorized I terms I want on my list. After I purchase the list of items, I will exit the store. They will stop me outside, just as they did today, and inspect the groceries I have in my possession against the list and stamps provided. At that point, my job is finished, and I will be free to go home. They will pay me a salary for this work, and the bonus for us is that I get to keep the groceries I purchased! Rusty, when they said that, they had my undivided attention!"

Rusty nodded in agreement with Delora, amazed at what this job could mean in regards to their food budget plus the extra money from a salary. He asked, "So, Bitty, what did you tell them?"

Holding up her hand, she paused dramatically and replied, "Before I gave them my answer, I did feel obligated to ask what would happen to the grocers who might be discovered doing something illegal. They told me that was federal business but did explain a little, saying one of three things might happen. If it is a first-time offense, they might get a fine or a warning; if they are repeat offenders, they might get fined and get arrested. As I thought about what they told me, I guess I was quiet too long because they asked, 'Well, Mrs. Karella, are you interested in taking the job?'

"I must say their faces looked relieved when I held out my hand to shake on the deal and said, 'Yes, I am. When do we start?'"

"So, which job are you going to take?" Rusty asked.

"Both of them!" replied Delora with enthusiasm.

Rusty frowned and asked, "How will that work with the kids and everything you do at home? Do you think you really have time for all of this?"

"Rusty, I have been thinking about this all afternoon. I know I can do both. I told the OPA I was already committed to nursing school at the hospital and my shift there. I would have Mondays, Tuesdays, and Wednesdays to work with them, and they said that would be fine with them. The girls are old enough to step up with the chores at home, and Charlie and Lloyd can oversee that the chores are done as well. Rusty, will this be ok with you? Did I do the right thing for our family?"

Impressed, Rusty smiled broadly and replied, "Yes, my lovely Bitty girl, you did everything right, and I think you are marvelous! What an amazing story. I am so proud of you! Now, what shall we do to celebrate?"

Delora let out another tinkling laugh and replied, "I know! How about we go on a date to the movies?"

The Karella Children

Delora told Rusty not to worry about the kids. They were going to do fine after school with Lloyd and Florence to handle everything until they both got home from work.

Delora knew each of her children very well. Being a full-time mom at home, she had observed the changes taking place in Andy, then Charlie, and now at fourteen, Lloyd was coming into his personality rather than just being a reflection of his older brothers.

Lloyd had a good relationship with his older brothers, but with Andy gone and Charlie being preoccupied making and saving money, Delora could see Lloyd had begun to flourish in the role of eldest son. As a reward, she was tempted to have Lloyd move into Andy's old room, but she would wait for a while to see how Charlie behaved through the holidays. Delora had noticed her six younger children seemed to get along much better under Lloyd's guidance, and she was especially proud of Florence and how she had taken on her responsibilities as the eldest daughter.

Mildred (Millie) Leona Karella, daughter of Rusty and Delora Karella

Ten-year-old Marcella seemed shy and respectful most of the time. She believed Marcella needed intellectual stimulation like Delora had with her father when she was young. In group discussions, Marcella's maturity and good common sense came to the surface. She was naturally playful rather than competitive and responded to kindness. In most cases, Marcella willingly lent a helping hand without complaint in just about any situation. Delora never saw

pretentiousness in Marcella. She felt her daughter could be trusted and be even-tempered even under pressure and never lacked confidence, though her quiet nature might make people think otherwise. Delora felt she would be a great help to Lloyd and Florence.

This past fall after Andy went off to college, Lloyd volunteered to make sure the younger kids got to school and home on time. Charlie didn't have a problem with that because he said he had more important things to do in the mornings before school. Delora did not let herself become annoyed over Charlie's attitude because the rest of her children were happy to follow Lloyd.

Marcella Ann Karella, 15, second-born daughter of Rusty and Delora Karella

Florence and Marcella would oversee getting homework started and prepared dinner before she and Rusty got home. All the Karella children were well trained in kitchen duties and homemaking chores.

Squabbles were bound to break out between the kids occasionally, but she was confident that between Lloyd and Florence, they would peacefully resolve any issues that came up between their younger siblings.

Millie had turned eight and possessed a brave and vibrant personality. She loved to be busy and never got tired of trying to make a deal for what she wanted or was interested in. Millie liked dressing up and was not afraid to defend herself or her little sister or brother. She was great about sharing what was hers but could be blunt

Sharon Theresa Karella, youngest daughter of Rusty and Delora Karella about someone who was being unfair, and it did not matter if they were younger or older than herself.

When Millie felt strongly about something, she generally did it first, then thought about the consequences later. Delora felt Millie was destined to be independent and would not be afraid to go after what she wanted in life. Her little Millie was devoted to her family even if she did get impatient with them at times.

Between her three older daughters, they would be able to manage all the inside household chores and watch their five-year-old sister, Sharon. Part of their reward for doing a good job would be letting the girls select and make desserts to go with each dinner.

Lloyd would oversee everything, but his main responsibility would be taking care of the outside chores and keeping his seven-year-old brother, Pete, busy and out of trouble.

The night before she was to start at the hospital, Delora snuggled up to Rusty, thinking she was too excited to sleep, and said, "Rusty, this plan of ours will work.

Jerome Ambrose (Pete) Karella, youngest son of Rusty and Delora Karella

Then we can relax a little about our monthly bills and maybe have a little left over for everything extra that costs money. It will be nice to treat the kids once in a while to something special, won't it?"

"Yes," he whispered back and hugged her close. Then he realized she had fallen asleep. "And you thought you were not going to be able to sleep," he whispered and pulled the covers around her shoulders.

Our Lady of Lourdes Hospital

Delora's classes were going well. She had learned the "Nightingale Principles from 1854"and discovered Florence Nightingale had been an upper-class woman with no formal training in nursing. She volunteered to work with and care for British soldiers during the

Crimean War, where she organized the care for wounded military men at Constantinople. This woman's work inspired Delora and made her very excited about beginning a career in nursing.

After reading about this courageous woman, Delora felt she was a kindred spirit. Delora had taken care of her mother for two years with no formal training, and now she was learning how to be a nurse during the war years in America.

As a student nurse, Delora assisted nurses and doctors in the daily care of patients. She took temperatures, learned to take blood pressure readings, kept patients' rooms tidy, changed beds, and emptied bed pans. Because Delora had gained valuable experience as a mother of eight, the nursing staff was thrilled to have Delora's help in the nursery and often had Delora talk with new mothers about breast feeding, caring for their new babies, and caring for themselves.

Delora's classes and part-time shifts took three days: Thursdays, Fridays, and Saturdays and some nighttime study.

The first three days of her work week, Delora set aside for the OPA rationing work. Mondays were spent preparing for two shopping days. Delora would supply two grocery lists for the feds, and they would add their items to her lists.

During the next two days, she would follow them in her car to nearby towns and shop at the store they told her to go to. When she came out of the store, the feds would stop her, check her groceries, and note any discrepancies between the ration coupons and stamps used.

If they found an issue, they took notes. She remained in her parked car, and after the feds finished their work, she was free to go home with her groceries. If there were no discrepancies after they checked her groceries, she was free to drive home immediately with the food. They repeated the same scenario every Tuesday and Wednesday in a new town, and every Friday, Delora received a paycheck in the mail.

Delora was so tickled with how everything was working out she never felt tired during the week and looked forward to Sundays.

The whole family would get up early and go to Mass. Then she and her girls spent the day making special meals. As a family, they listened to the radio, played games, and visited with each other, catching up on the happenings at school and at Rusty's work. It felt good to spend the day with her husband and children.

Rusty could not be more delighted that his Bitty was so happy despite having such a full schedule. He made a point to get home on time so they could spend the evenings together and took time to tell her how much he appreciated her help. Bitty was just as sweet as ever, and he felt so blessed she was his wife.

Sunday evenings after Rusty headed up to their room and the young ones were in bed, Delora spent a little time with Lloyd and Florence. She asked them about their week, and they often related very amusing stories.

After kissing each of them goodnight and sending them off to bed, Delora liked to sit quietly at the kitchen table. It gave her the peace she needed to organize her thoughts so she could thank God for all He had done for her. So many blessings to be thankful for. Then she would pray for Andy, asking God to keep him safe.

Still feeling unusually wide-awake, Delora pulled some paper and a pen from a kitchen cabinet drawer and sat back down at the table to write her father a letter.

Dear Papa,   *December 20, 1934*

I hope this letter finds you and Mama well. I've been thinking a lot about the two of you lately. Everything here could not be better. I've got news to tell you, but first, I wanted to say thank you.

Papa, some of my most precious memories are of you teaching me to read in your study. Those were such happy times! Thank you for loving me. Though I lost several years of my childhood time with my brothers and sisters, I'm happy we are all reunited and share time as a family.

I could not be happier with my life and my choices. Rusty is such a good match for me. I cannot imagine a man more capable of protecting and providing for me and our children through the drought and depression years. I also love being part of this huge Karella clan, and I am so proud of my children. It is hard to believe all eight of them are in school now. It is wonderful they have so many cousins, and the holidays are such fun when we gather, and we sing, play games, and cook together.

The years have been busy and full of happiness as well as sadness, though I would not give up a minute of it. Not even the distress of Ambrose joining the Marines. He is his own man, and though I tried to stop him, Rusty convinced me we had to let our son make his own choices. Ambrose is a good young man, and I pray he has a long future ahead of him.

Now, I can tell you my wonderful news. I have gone back to school. Not high school, but it is an apprentice program. I am studying to become a nurse, and I love it. I also work a paid shift at the hospital where I go to class. It is so exciting! I dream about my future as a nurse and my family's future to come.

But that's not all of it. I also have a part-time job with the OPA. I not only get free groceries, but they pay me too. Can you believe I work for the feds? The idea of it makes me laugh.

Now, between us, Rusty and I make enough money that I can buy each of the girls four pretty outfits, and the boys will get brand-new pants and shirts this Christmas. They will look wonderful when they return to school after the holidays.

Rusty and I are also setting money aside to buy camping and fishing equipment. That way, we can have the kids camp out comfortably in the yard when we come to spend more time in Madison with you and the kids' cousins this coming summer.

For Christmas, Rusty and I are also going to buy each of the children a special present. For Lloyd, we thought we'd give him his own record player. For Pete, we are thinking a new sled and ice skates for the girls.

It will be a fabulous Christmas, Papa. Please come share Christmas Day with us.

We love you and Mama very much,
Your daughter always,
Delora

CHAPTER 26

A Brother and Son Become Soldiers

Reflecting on Life

Rusty finally had a little peace and quiet to reflect. He thanked God regularly for the steady work during the last several years. That work provided money they could count on to pay the bills and buy necessities while Delora took care of their home and children. It was hard for him to realize that after so many years of raising babies, seven of them were in school, and the last one would start school when her eldest brother started college. It boggled his mind that 17 years had gone by so fast.

What had taken place in the last nine months within his family was even harder to grasp as it happened so quickly.

In April, his baby brother broke the news that he was not only getting married but that he was joining the Army. At least Shorty would not fight as an infantry man. He would cook his way through the war. Hopefully, that would keep him out of immediate danger.

Rusty read the letter he received from Shorty that included a picture of him in uniform standing with his new wife, Flossie Mary

Owens Karella. They married three days before he had to report for duty.

Dear Rusty and Delora,   *April 1943*

I hope my letter finds you well and all the kids healthy too. I cannot tell you not to worry about Andy once he heads off to boot camp. Yet, as I get ready for my own report date next week, I thought of something that should give you at least a little peace regarding my joining the Army. I want you to think of it this way: I will not be fighting battles with a rifle but with pots and pans. It makes me happy knowing my part in this war will be to use my cooking skills to keep our American troops strong and healthy. I will write once I get overseas and hope you will write me too. I truly love you both and the kids.

With much thanks and love,

Shorty

P.S. Please keep in touch with my Mary— she's going to need your support as she waits for me.

Setting down the letter, Rusty continued to think about the changes in his family. Yes, he worried about Andy's choices, but then right on schedule, he began attending Norfolk Junior College, and baby Sharon started first grade in the fall of 1943. His kids were growing into their personalities, and he was getting glimpses of changes to come. All he could do was try to accept them one by one.

Ambrose James (Andy, AJ) Karella at NJC

Norfolk, Karella Home on November 24ᵗʰ

When Andy came home for Thanksgiving, it made Rusty feel good that Andy confided in him. It relieved him to know he and his son still had a deep connection. They sat up late talking after everyone else had gone to bed. Andy sounded very serious about a new girl he met at college during orientation and told Rusty about the first time he saw her.

The Story of a Boy and a Girl

"Dad, I caught sight of this striking brunette my first day at college. It took me by surprise how she captured my curiosity, and I almost got up the nerve to talk to her while we were standing in line to sign up for the same writing class. Talking to her then didn't work out because she was surrounded by a group of friends. But then I got a second chance during my first writing class with her.

"I had been excited all day because I knew I would see her in my afternoon class. The angels smiled on me as I walked into Creative Writing 101. I spotted her right off and tried not to stare. She seemed to command everyone's attention giving off pure confidence. She certainly had nothing in common with any of the high school girls I knew here in town. Halfway through the two-hour session, my professor divides up all the students in teams to work on an assignment. I couldn't believe that I got teamed up with her! I looked up at the ceiling and thought, *Now, I know God loves me!*"

Rusty laughed and shook his head, then nodded for Andy to continue.

"I was brought back to earth quickly by a female voice, 'Betty Rossow,' she said, holding out her petite hand and smiling up at me. 'Guess we'll be working together.'

"'Sounds great!' I replied and shook her hand. Then my mind went a bit blank as I stared into her hazel blue eyes. Or were they green?" he wondered out loud.

"But, Dad, it was like I got hit in the stomach. BAM! The hook was set hard and fast. My heart did a flip-flop, and following that crazy feeling, I just knew we were going to make a great team!"

"How does she feel about you enlisting in the Marines?" he asked cautiously.

Andy went on to say they both had dreams, and they were not going to change those plans, but they did agree to stay in touch and write when he left at the end of December. Later that evening as Rusty climbed the stairs to his bedroom, he thought, *I guess that is a good start. I hope Bitty and I get to meet this girl Ambrose is so crazy about.*

Karella's Thanksgiving 1943

Over Thanksgiving weekend, everyone was excited to meet Aunt Mary Karella, Shorty's new wife. Delora's parents arrived, enjoying the house full of happiness, singing, baking, card games, music, and children's laughter. Rusty enjoyed himself immensely. Looking across the living room, Rusty thought, *My brother's wife, Mary, is positively tiny; I don't think she is even five-feet-tall. A good thing, I suppose, since my brother is only slightly taller than that. Maybe five-foot-three. Mary looks so little sitting next to my six-foot-two son. Andy zoomed passed my modest height at fourteen. Not that it was hard to accomplish me being only five-foot-eight. Even in high school, Andy always said he felt like the Flatiron skyscraper in New York City because he towered over everything and everyone around him.*

Mary Karella sat on the couch looking around the room and found herself delighted with Shorty's brother and family. She felt as if she knew them already because her husband had talked about them constantly. Watching Shorty's brother Rusty, she thought she saw several similarities between them. Both lived energetic lives and loved their large, rambunctious family. The difference lay in the fact that Rusty was the head of the Karella clan. He was the authority in family matters and required respect. While her Shorty was just one of the Karella men, and she was very glad of that.

She continued to sit on the edge of the happy commotion made by 13 people thinking about what made the brothers so different. *My Shorty does not want or need the compliance of everyone around him. His opinions do not need to take precedence in a conversation nor did Shorty ever feel he needed permission from anyone to do as his heart dictated. Shorty had always possessed an unlimited capacity for sweetness and endless patience when listening to what others had to say.* He certainly brings out the best in me, she thought. *Gosh, I miss him desperately.*

Mary certainly got a taste of how big the Karella clan was while she and Shorty were dating. She had met Beans, Vobornys, and Pojars who still lived between Madison and her family's place in Elgin, Nebraska. She also met Shorty's uncle Joe Pojar who owned the ranch next to her father's ranch. Then Shorty introduced her to many of the Holy clan members from his mother Anastasia's side of the family at several picnics. At the same time, she also met many of the Kuchar cousins, also from his mother's side of the family from nearby towns.

I sure did like Vlasta Holy Anson and her husband, Lyle, when we met them in Madison at Rudy and Martha Pojar's place. The Ansons said they had land in Casper, Wyoming, and wanted her and Shorty to come and live close by after Shorty finished his tour in the service.

Mary planned to keep in touch with everyone she had met and would write about it in her letters to Shorty. It was wonderful to dream about what they would do and where they would live when Shorty finally came home and the war was over.

Andy sat down next to his aunt Mary and brought her out of her thoughts. "I just wanted to welcome you to the family, Aunt Mary. I'm Andy, Rusty's oldest son and your husband's nephew."

Smiling, she replied. "How nice to have a face to go with a name I have heard so much about."

As Andy talked with Aunt Mary, he found it incredible his Uncle Shorty had fallen in love with a woman who still agreed to marry him even as he was leaving to report for duty overseas.

Andy listened to her talk about her correspondence with his uncle Shorty. Just from the way she said his name, Andy could tell they were happy. Andy told her he had recently written to his uncle Shorty in Belgium, thanking him for helping his dad understand his need to join the Marine Corps.

Rusty sat at the table and looked around the room. The general noise and chaos caused by thirteen people in such a small space could be overwhelming, and he worried a bit about Shorty's quiet wife until he saw her deep in conversation with Andy.

Anastas (Shorty) Karella, military photo taken in Belgium during WWII

Lyle and Vlasta Holy Anson, Casper, Wyoming

"Andy, would you like to see some of the family pictures I brought with me?" Mary asked.

Andy nodded, and Mary pulled out her wedding picture and then several more. They chatted about life as they talked about the people in the photographs.

Holy Clan photograph taken on Grandpa Jacob Holy's 90th birthday—family of Anastasia Holy Karella, who was the wife of Anton Karella. Taken in Newman Grove, Nebraska

Rudy Pojar and Stanley Voborny fishing

Locations of Newman Grove, Madison, Norfolk, and Battle Creek, Nebraska

A Month Earlier: News and Congratulations

On Saturday November 27th, Delora came flying into the room with the mail and caused quite a commotion trying to show him a postcard. After Rusty had a chance to look at it and read the note on it, he smiled.

Simply radiant with the news, Delora whispered breathlessly, "Rusty, it's from Father O'Brian, and from what he's written, I'm going to get into the apprentice nursing program!

By December fifth, his amazing wife was not only studying to become a nurse and working a paid shift as a student nurse at the hospital, but she also found a side job that awarded their family free groceries. Now, between them, they made enough with their stable paychecks to allow him a bit of a rest. Rusty thought he might cut back on the extra hours he spent on side jobs so he could spend more time with Delora and the kids. They even had extra money, which hadn't happened since before Lloyd was born. Now, between his and Delora's wages, they could afford to spend money on a few frivolous items instead of only buying the nessessities. In the last few days, he and Bitty spent a few wonderful hours trying to decide what to buy the children for Christmas.

Christmas Season in Norfolk 1943

Andy and Chauncey spent December 22nd and 23rd with the Karellas of Norfolk. Part of Rusty's joyful holiday anticipation was overshadowed by his promise to Andy about joining the Marines. He and Andy had another one of their long talks, and Rusty found it very enlightening.

"You know, Dad, when I first heard how long I'd have to wait before I could join up, I thought the six months would drag by. To be honest, it had . . . until I met Betty, and college turned out to be more interesting than I thought it would. Gosh, Betty is what every guy on campus refers to as a doll. It surprised me when I discovered she was an upperclassman beginning her sophomore year. I couldn't believe it when I found out she was a Norfolk girl, and then she said her family is Lutheran, so that explains why we never met."

"Have you met her parents?" Rusty asked casually.

"No, not yet. This feeling between us is still pretty new, but I'd like to believe the attraction was instantaneous for both of us. We sure have spent a lot of time together over the last four months. Plus, we've kept up on our schoolwork, and we study together quite often.

"Dad, do you think it should matter that she is two years older than me? I'll admit I felt a little intimidated when I found that out. Yet, the age difference hasn't stopped the way we feel about each other. We have promised to write to each other while I'm away in the Marines."

The morning of December 24th, Rusty signed the early enlistment papers Andy needed to send to the Marine recruitment office.

As his dad handed Andy the signed government waiver, Andy thought, *Isn't that typical? Just when I wish I had more time with Betty and the family, it's gone!* "Dad, I must go and pack. I've got things to finish up at school, and I want to see Betty before I go. I hope you understand."

An hour later, Rusty gave him a hard hug. Then he handed Andy a letter. Andy saw it was from his uncle Shorty, and his father whispered, "Son, please wait to read it. Whatever it says, it will upset your mom. Now, go say goodbye to her."

Andy put the letter in his coat pocket and went to look for his mother and found her in the kitchen and said softly, "Mom, it's time for me to go."

She turned and looked up at her son with teary eyes. He reached for her, and she clung to him, trying not to sob. "Be careful, son. I need you to come home. God bless you wherever you go."

He squeezed his tiny mother one last time and whispered in reply, "I promise." Andy left the kitchen and walked through the living room, hugging everyone as he made his way to his suitcase by the door. Picking it up, he turned and said goodbye and wished them Merry Christmas, then he and Chauncey headed back to college.

No Time for Regrets

Christmas Day after Mass, Rusty and Delora found it exciting to watch the magic created by the special gifts the children found under the tree. The Holts arrived right as the family returned home from church so they could enjoy the ecstatic faces of their grandchildren as they opened the presents.

A Phone Call from College

Rusty heard the excitement in Andy's voice when he called home on December 28th. He and Chauncey were going to catch the morning bus to the Marine Corps recruiter's office in Omaha. Rusty wished Andy and Chauncey safe travels while he thought, *I know Andy is looking at this as a great adventure. Time will tell just how well Andy will adjust to being treated by strangers like a man instead of someone's son or a growing boy.*

What was done was done, and Rusty had no time for regrets or to dwell on what he could not change about his firstborn son. Shaking his head as he hung up the phone, he thought, *I have more immediate issues to deal with. Bitty is really angry at me for letting Andy go into the Marines. Now, I see more drama brewing with Charles Dale. I don't know how I'm going to get Bitty to listen. She is as hardheaded and unbendable as a battleship! I know she is determined to keep her other sons safe at home with her. She has said she will agree to no more early enlistments for her boys, but I don't think she or I will have a choice about that.*

Rusty did his best to explain to Bitty that after Thanksgiving, he had a long talk with Charlie. The boy had agreed to wait as his brother had until he was 17. Rusty had made no promise about letting Charlie join the military. The only

Ambrose James (Andy, AJ, Jr.) Karella, United States Marine, WWII

guarantee he made was to consider Charlie's request when he turned 17. That was why emotions were pretty settled around the house during the Christmas holidays when Andy was home. But when the time came for Rusty to hand over the papers to Andy, all hell broke loose.

Rusty shook his head, remembering how Delora had panicked after Andy left to go back to college. She wouldn't listen to him. Then she cornered Charlie and told him he'd better not have any ideas about enlisting because she would not agree to it.

He remembered watching his wife's face, then saw mutiny on his son's face. All he could do was shake his head, thinking, *Lord love her, she's been such a good strong general with the children for so long that she believes she can stop Charlie from joining the Army Air Corps by refusing to let him go.* He had warned her on more than one occasion that he was sure if Charles Dale hit any resistance to his long-term plans, the boy would take matters into his own hands. Once Andy left for boot camp, Rusty tried to neutralize Charlies growing restlessness by proposing the same bargain to Charles Dale that he'd made with Andy. It seemed to be going well until Delora entered the conversation. At a critical moment, she refused to listen to neither him nor Charlie and made it clear she would not give her consent to enlist early under any circumstances.

Left to right: Rusty Karella, sisters Martha, Mary, and Helen, and Anastas (Shorty) Karella home on leave, during WWII, 1944

As predicted, Charles Dale took matters into his own hands and ran away to join the Army Air Corps two months later. Bitty was panicked, worried, and furious at the same time, and she insisted that Rusty go after Charlie.

Rusty denied that request, replying, "Bitty, it's senseless to drag Charles Dale back here. He'll just run off again. Please let it be. Hopefully, if we don't chase him, he'll contact us when he gets settled like Shorty did."

His wife had already decided Rusty's youngest brother along with all his wild adventures had been a bad influence on their sons. She said as much and often, repeating her observation whenever the deal Rusty had made with Andy was mentioned.

Now, she glared at him, and though she didn't say it out loud, Rusty could tell he should not have mentioned Shorty. "I'm sorry Charlie's gone. But it's a blessing that we at least know where he planned to go," Rusty said softly. When she stormed out of the kitchen without a word, he knew it would be a while before his wife would see reason.

Alone with His Thoughts

Music played quietly in the background. Rusty thought it might be Glenn Miller with his orchestra playing a muted softly swaying arrangement that suited his sad mood. The quiet in the house surrounded Rusty as he bent over, resting his elbows on his knees.

Slowly, he put his face into the palms of his hands and prayed silently. *Dear Lord, I trust in You. You now have my brother Anastas and my two sons, Ambrose and Charles, to watch over. They are in Your hands now. Please bring them home from war safely. I pray this request be in alignment with Your Divine will and may Thy will be done.*

Rusty closed his eyes as tears ran down his face. He hoped with all his heart that none of them would be lost and that the war would end soon.

Shorty Karella and
Stanley Voborny

CHAPTER 27

Boys to Men

Packing Up the Old Room

The day before Christmas, Andy snuck away from the family celebrations of 1943 at his parents' house. He could hear Glenn Miller playing on the radio. The vibrant horns, harmony of the singers, and the sway of the tune had him whistling along. His head bobbed, and his shoulders rocked to the rhythm as he climbed the stairs to his old bedroom.

Andy promised his mom he would box up what he was not going to take with him. He set aside two changes of civilian clothing and his traveling suit. The rest along with his .22 rifle he put in boxes and set them in the hall to be stored in the attic. His parents would decide who got to move into his old room. He supposed it would be Charlie. He was next in line as the oldest and would be at home at least until he was seventeen.

Everything Andy wanted to take fit nicely into one small suitcase. He and Chauncey were headed back to the college campus now. They would only have a couple

Andy Karella,
Norfolk Junior College

of days to finish up a few details at school before they had to report at the recruiting office. Plus, he had a date with Betty to go see the new Bing Crosby movie musical *White Christmas*, and he wasn't going to miss that for any reason.

His college professors had been great. They promised him full credit for the whole semester, though technically he would not be finishing the second quarter. They waived his attendance for the last week because he was joining the Marines. They also told him if he kept taking night classes while he was in the Marine Corps, the half-semester credit he earned at NJC could be applied toward earning a bachelor's degree.

A Dream Girl

Norfolk Junior College turned out to be one of his dad's best ideas. Added to a little divine timing by the Good Lord above, Andy met his dream girl, Betty Le Rossow. That was the only way he could explain how he came to meet such an extraordinary young woman.

Andy found Betty totally unique, self-reliant, and as lovely to look at as she was delightfully spunky! They had never met before because her folks belong to a different church than his family, not to mention her being two years older, and she did not go to a Catholic school.

NJC graduate,
Betty Le Rossow

Yet, she felt so right for him that even from their first meeting, she inspired visions of a future he had never contemplated before. When they talked about what they wanted in life, they had many hopes and dreams in common. Both looked forward to traveling. They wanted to experience life on a grand scale and go on adventures, meet new people, and discover new places together.

When it came time to leave NJC behind for the Corps, Andy could not stop thinking about Betty even if he wanted to. Lucky for him, Betty felt the same way. The instant attraction between them and the time they spent together during the past four months had profoundly affected them both.

Yet, Andy and Betty were committed to the plans they each had for their immediate futures. They would not let the fascination they discovered for each other change their minds. Betty would continue to pursue her degree and finish college. Though Andy suspected he was falling in love with her, he did not let that truth change his plans about becoming a Marine.

Andy and Chauncey assumed when they joined up, they were committing themselves to the Corps for the duration of the war. At the same time, Andy did not want to lose Betty. After telling her it was time for him to go, she seemed almost indifferent. Andy appreciated the fact that Betty was quite different from the other girls he had dated. That didn't mean he wasn't surprised when she didn't cry as he prepared to leave for bootcamp.

Andy's confidence took a shot to his core. His immediate reaction made it clear Betty was a lot more important to him than he had admitted. He desperately needed to know where he stood with her. This was a unique experience; Andy was unfamiliar with feeling insecure when it came to the women in his life.

Betty Le Rossow

Betty could see she had baffled Andy with her reaction to his news. Her cool acceptance of their imminent separation deflated his male confidence. *He's too sweet,* she thought, *to let him leave without a little encouragement.* Standing incredibly close to him as she straightened his tie, Betty whispered, "We should hope it doesn't take you too many years to win this war." Looking up into his eyes, she went on to say, "My immediate plans include finishing college. That will take at least two or three more years. I do plan to travel and see the world but not just yet. So, I figure I'll still be here when you get back."

Wow, Andy thought, *she's as cool as a cucumber. But I like it. I like it a lot!* Andy's confidence was restored a bit by the discovery that Betty's send-off kiss was much warmer than her words. Determined, he thought, *I'll keep her so busy writing to me that between school and answering my letters, she will not have time for anyone else.*

Marine Boot Camp, South Carolina

WWII new military recruits boarding train

Andy read the entire Parris Island bootcamp pamphlet, and it explained that recruits would participate in an intensive program that aspired to develop pride, brotherhood, and a common loyalty within teams made up of virtual strangers. Young men—referred to as boots or recruits—that enlisted to become Marines received technical instruction, used study techniques based on repetition, received fitness training, and participated in hands-on combat and weaponry instruction. It was the goal of every Marine bootcamp to turn raw civilian boys into basically trained soldiers. Managers of the boots' program were drill instructors and were called DIs. These men trained recruits and were the teachers and disciplinarians during this intensive process. Andy set down the pamphlet and decided he knew what to expect.

Parris Island

The destination stamped on Andy and Chauncey's official travel documents read Marine Recruit Training Station, Parris Island, Beaufort, South Carolina. This installation located along an undeveloped stretch of the South Carolina coastline would be their home for the next eight weeks. Excited to get going and keen to travel across the country, they could hardly wait to see the part of America referred to as the South with their own eyes.

The Nebraska boys boarded the train with a slew of other young men. Andy and Chauncey felt like Frank Sinatra and Cary Grant in *The Road to Victory,* a war short they saw at the cinema. It proved to be exciting riding a train, traveling all decked out in their best clothes and new fedora hats. Shortly after stowing the baggage and locating their seats, Chauncey and Andy relaxed as the train pulled out of the station.

While the locomotive headed south, the boys discussed bootcamp as if it were one of their childhood adventures and decided it was going to be a breeze. "How hard could it be? We are both excellent shots, and we've been hunting for most of the last ten years. We are physically fit, and learning to use a new caliber rifle won't take any time at all. What else do you think we have to learn?" Chauncey wondered aloud.

Recruits at Parris Island Marine bootcamp training facility, 1944

Andy shrugged his shoulders and shook his head to indicate he still didn't have an answer to this subject. It had come up before—several times in fact—but based on the number of hair-raising experiences they had survived in their youth, both boys decided they were prepared for just about anything.

When Chauncey dozed off, Andy got up to stretch his legs. Passing through several train cars, he caught snatches from different conversations. The subject matter under discussion was all too familiar. Marine bootcamp was a mystery, and none of the other young guys on the train knew anymore about it than he or Chauncey did. However, on the way back to his seat, Andy noticed a couple of older uniformed Marines. A group of guys his age had gathered around them and were asking all kinds of questions.

Lucky Strike Cigarettes, 1940s—Public Domain Wiki

When the Marines talked, all those boys shut up and listened; and when those experienced soldiers passed around the pack of Lucky Strike Cigarettes, Andy took one just like the other young guys. Then he tried to smoke his first cigarette like he knew what he was doing.

"Chauncey, wake up!" Andy was so excited he shook his buddy rather roughly, wanting to talk about everything he'd heard. "You should have heard these guys and the stories they told. They knew all about the bootcamp we are going to. One of them was a master sergeant and warned us about all kinds of stuff. He told us that as the new recruits in the barracks, we should expect to be put through at least a few harmless tricks."

Chauncey yawned, disgruntled at being shaken so rudely. His fuzzy mind found the voice harassing him irritating rather than informative. Not fully awake and not comprehending anything, all Chauncey wanted to do was go back to sleep. "Jeez, Andy," he said, "don't you remember we don't get to our base until tomorrow afternoon? Isn't that soon enough to talk about all of this? Don't you want to get a little more sleep while we can?"

Men's 1944 fedora hat

Andy shook him again. "I'm too excited to sleep. I can't believe that's all you've wanted to do for two days! Did you hear what I was telling you?" he asked. Andy shook Chauncey a final time, asking insistently, "Chauncey, aren't you at least curious? Don't you want to know what I heard?"

Chauncey remained silent for a moment, then he replied, "No." He was officially irritated now and decided he wanted his friend to shut up and go away. "If you can't sleep, it would be nice if you would let me sleep for you. Why don't you go do something quiet? Like writing a letter to somebody that wants to know what you heard!"

With that last comment, Chauncey changed position, slouching comfortably into the seat. He stretched out his legs and closed his eyes after pulling his fedora over his face. Then he crossed his arms over his chest, which was exactly what he'd seen Humphrey Bogart do in the movies to signal an end to any further discussion. Andy shut up and let his friend sleep.

Chauncey's suggestion made good sense; Andy went in search of paper and a pen to write a letter to his parents. He felt a little guilty as he had only occasionally thought to send a short note to his folks since leaving home for college.

Dear Mom and Dad,   *Train south, January 1944*

Thank you for the pocket money you gave me in that nice card and for all the encouragement you wrote in it. I am keeping it with me in my personal stuff to remind me of you.

Mom, I am sorry that I upset you, but you have always known I planned to do this. So, thank you for not trying to stand in the way and thanks, Dad, for honoring your promise to me.

On the brighter side, the bus ride to Omaha was nice. Chauncey and I slept most of the way. We reported for processing at the Marine recruiting office right after we arrived in Omaha. After passing the physicals, they gave us temporary housing while we waited to get our bootcamp assignments and train and bus schedules.

I'm happy to report our recruiter lived up to his word. Chauncey and I have been assigned to the Marine recruit training station Parris Island in Beaufort, South Carolina.

We boarded the train this morning and will travel the next 1,000 miles to Columbia, South Carolina, in easy comfort.

We have enjoyed the train ride so far. Well, at least I have. All Chauncey has been doing is sleeping. There are lots of guys on this train our age headed for the same training camp. I also met some soldiers who work at our bootcamp, and they provided some good information about what to expect when we get there.

Once we reach Columbia, we will catch a bus. It will take another two and a half to three hours to reach Beaufort on the Carolina coast. I'll write again once I get settled in my barracks. Please tell all the kids their big brother said hello.

Your loving son always,
Ambrose James

Andy's First Letter after Arriving at Parris Island

Dear Betty,   *Parris Island, January 1944*

Marine recruit
Ambrose James (Andy)
Karella 1944

My arrival day in the barracks was rather rocky. I was informed of my duties like this: "Recruit!" I didn't realize I was the one being addressed. When I didn't turn to face the man immediately, the Southerner standing right behind me shouted at the top of his lungs, "I'm addressing you, Yankee!" About that time, another soldier facing me frowned and pointed urgently behind me. Belatedly, I realized it was the drill instructor, and he was yelling at me!

I admit my face must have been sunburn red as I spun around and snapped to attention. My drill instructor was nose-to-nose with me and roared, "You'll be standing guard duty at 02:00, so I suggest you get some rack!"

I am quickly learning that drill instructors (we also call them DIs) have no sense of humor and use two volumes: loud and louder. As far as night guard duty goes, I don't think there's much I can't handle. Well, I had better do as I was told and get some shuteye. It wouldn't do to be caught sleeping on guard duty. Not after such an introduction to the DI. Not my best day for making good impressions! What do you think?

I'll write again soon,
Yours truly, Andy

The new recruits in Andy's unit had three days to get settled in before their real training schedule kicked in. During that time, they got their barracks assignments, their head shaved, two sets of issued clothing, and their watch assignments.

Andy remained unconcerned about the actual training portion of bootcamp. He didn't think of himself as the arrogant sort; he was merely confident in his abilities. He knew that growing up in the farmlands of Nebraska during the Great Depression had prepared him for life.

Dear Betty,   *Second Day, Bootcamp 1944*

I hope your classes are going well. Though I miss seeing you every day, I've got to confess bootcamp gives new meaning to being dead on my feet. I would miss you even more if I weren't so blasted tired.

Remember in my last letter I told you the DI called me a Yankee? I learned something about the true South. What a surprise to discover the Confederacy did not die out after the Civil War as we were taught in American history class. The grey coats are alive and well and still living in what they call the true South. Chauncey and I have been told by the Southern boys working on this base that we will always be damned

Yankees to them. I'm not sure what that really means yet, but I suspect we will find out soon enough.

The land down here is unusual. Unquestionably different from what we grew up with in Nebraska. The swamp water looks black at times. The water's edge is lined with gnarly trees hung with matted light green moss, the kind that floats in the night breeze at the edge of the light.

It feels like the kind of place Alfred Hitchcock would describe in one of his radio show thrillers. I don't know why, but I don't see the stars at night here like at home. By that, I mean the nights are black as pitch. I can deal with the darkness, but the noises that come out of the swamp during that blackness . . . that's what makes you feel like you've stumbled into a horror show.

I want to tell you about my first night on guard duty. By the way, Marines use the 24-hour clock, so I reported for duty at 02:00. Our guard shack has one lamp attached to the outside wall. The thing gives off barely enough light to see a car and the person behind the wheel after we stop them at the gate.

It had been a couple of hours since I came on duty standing my first watch. I hadn't seen a person or a car for an hour, and I could barely see past the length of my rifle. That's when I heard the first blood-chilling scream followed by a hair-curling roar erupting from the darkness. Jeez, Betty! I thought it was a woman being torn to pieces by some kind of monster. To be honest, I reacted on a primal level as the fear rolled over my skin in waves. I had sweat running down my face and chills running down my spine at the same time. Those awful sounds went on and on during the blackest hours of the night!

Good Lord, those nightmare sounds could make the toughest, biggest guys piss their pants. Not me, though, but it was close. The hours dragged by. First would come a scream followed by a roar and then more screams. By dawn, the ghastly sounds finally ceased. When my replacement arrived to relieve me, he started chuckling when he saw my face.

Apparently, I was still white as a ghost.

He clapped me on the back and said, "Don't worry, recruit! You'll get used to it."

I had to ask even if I did sound stupid. "Ok, you've got to tell me what was making those gruesome noises. Jeez! They almost made me piss myself!"

Laughing at my honesty, the soldier replied, "The screams come from the swamp cats, and the roars are made by bull alligators. It's standard procedure to put new recruits out here alone for a night shortly after they arrive just to scare the crap out of them. So, don't spoil the fun and tell anyone in the barracks about last night, OK? Let 'em find out firsthand! Your DI will appreciate you being closemouthed on this, and getting on his good side can only help while you are here at Parris Island. Now, go get some chow and some rack."

South Carolina swamp cat

South Carolina swamp bull alligator

Betty, the only person I warned was Chauncey. The older guys tell me that after a couple of weeks, as we watch all the newer guys go through the same stuff, we will think it's funny too. Especially since we know what's coming and what's going to happen.

Opposite of the pranks, the battle training is dead serious. I can't tell you much about it, either, because of security constraints. What I can say is there is a ton of stuff to learn all the time, and it really keeps me on my toes. Oh hey, the DI just walked into the barracks. I've got to go, but I'll write again soon, and I really look forward to your letters.

I miss you, affectionally,
Andy

P.S. It might be a while before you hear from me again. Our intensive training schedule begins tomorrow.

Definition of Bootcamp

Reporting for orientation in their service khaki uniforms, Andy, Chauncey, and the rest of the new recruits listened to the DI say, "You will learn social military norms and essential tasks of the Armed Forces. This includes foot drills, parade drills, inspections, physical training, weapons training, hand-to-hand combat . . ." On . . . and on . . . in monotone, the DI continued to list duties and responsibilities as Andy and Chauncy stood in line waiting to be issued the rest of their military clothing and personal gear. The men of Andy's unit were given time to stow everything they had been issued and change into training fatigues. The bugle signaled the unit to fall out for the commencement of training drills.

Who Am I?

One week into training, Andy wondered if he had the resolve to make it through bootcamp. What no one mentioned was the gut-wrenching hours of body fatigue and emotional breakdown that took place during the unit's physical and psychological conditioning.

Pounded into his brain repeatedly, this critical conditioning was necessary for every Marine's survival, and it began to reshape Andy's attitudes and behaviors. The harsh techniques used to train the men of Andy's unit often produced brutally unforgiving situations. The goal of every situation was to educate them on how to use skills they developed to stay alive and kill their enemies. The boyish illusions disintegrated as reality began to reveal the true nature of war and how unprepared they were for it.

The mental barrage began precisely the same way with reveille at 04:00 every morning. The unit rolled out of bed to dress in olive green undershirts and shorts for a session of physical training in all-weather conditions. Breakfast followed, and they changed into fatigues for training and drills. Drills could be a long run with fully loaded packs and rifles followed by an obstacle course that had the unit crawling through mud pits and under bobbed wire, running, climbing, or wading through deep water. The day might also include reporting to the gun range to study and practice with combat weapons and additional time firing those weapons on the target range. There were also regular intense sessions of hand-to-hand combat worked into the unit's schedule. During each day's drills, there was a break for lunch and, at the close of the day, dinner and a set barracks curfew with lights out at 22:00.

The DI continually stressed that through their intense conditioning, the unit would build automatic combat and field survival skills. Each day's training constantly pushed the recruits to think and act as a single unit. Each consecutive day accelerated and intensified group pressure within the ranks of the unit and taught Andy and Chauncey to keep up and to win as a unit. Punishment was doled out for failure to conform with unit goals and perform at a proficient level. The bar on a unit's goals was constantly raised, increasing the pace and difficulty of every exercise and field drill while each soldier honed his tactical acuity in weapons training. Every lesson and action was completed with an emphasis on pride and loyalty to the unit, Corps, God, and country.

Andy lost track of time in his exhaustion. He could hardly recall the clueless boy who arrived on a bus with no idea what it meant to be a Marine and not a thing about what it was going to take to earn the title of a Devil Dog.

He desperately missed Betty and her spunky uplifting outlook on life. In hindsight, his time at college was a picnic. With sadness and humility, Andy remembered his father's tone of voice as he tried to help Andy take a second look at the choices he was making. How he missed his dad and asking him for advice. During Andy's training, the DI constantly yelled, "Do that and you're dead, soldier!" Or "Crawl lower, down on your belly, recruit! That sniper just killed you and your unit because you gave your position away." Andy had heard "you are dead" so many times he finally believed the DI when he said, "Keep that up, and you might not come back from this war." The highly controlled days became a blur. Eat, drill, eat, mail call, drill, eat, barracks, bunk, and lights out. Andy would save any letters he received at mail call to read after chow in his bunk.

Dear Andy, *February 14, 1944*

Happy Valentine's Day, Yankee!

I like the sound of that. Maybe that will be my new nickname for you. I am only teasing. It is good to hear the Marines can keep you as busy down there as I am here. I'm not sure I'd respond well to all the yelling you described. It's just not my style. The practical jokes are easier to deal with. Apparently, they are harmless enough if fear doesn't count.

School has been incredibly busy since your departure. My midterms were hard, but I aced them. All those hours of study paid off. Thank you for your encouragement. My little brother, Chuck, is excited about finishing high school and has been looking at colleges. I sent him some brochures from NJC. I hope he chooses this school. I have enjoyed being at NJC myself because I can go home on a regular basis. I fear Mom and Dad will not fare well when both their children leave home for good.

Do you remember my Chinese friend, Mattie Ling? Anyway, she asked me to say hello for her.

She thinks I ought to hold on to you. I told her I have not made up my mind yet and that I like being independent. I did tell her I liked the way you kiss me and that I like the way I feel when I am kissing you. That bit of information should encourage you and keep you on your toes! Between you and me, I am beginning to think Mattie is right. Be strong, smart, and stay safe and write again soon,

Affectionately,
Betty Le

Andy (AJ) Karella, U.S. Marine, 1944–1946

After reading Betty's latest letter, Andy thought, *I hope I get the chance to tell Betty that I am falling in love with her face to face.*

Each day ended with the same body aches and exhaustion. Broken down by hours and hours of being pushed beyond any limit his mind and body had ever known, Andy would find himself laying in his bunk, wondering, *Am I going to be able to make it through another day? I really thought I was tougher than this, but this war could really be the end of me. This is no comic book story I'm in. I guess I am beginning to understand what Dad wanted me to know. I pray I've got the guts to get the job done.* Before falling into a dead man's sleep in the quiet darkness, Andy prayed silently, *Please, God, help me make it through tomorrow* as his mind and body fell into unconsciousness.

The reveille bugle call was the first sound of the day that pierced his brain.

Marine recruit, Chauncey Crocker, 1944

After weeks of repetition, Andy's body automatically responded to the sound. He rolled out of his bunk, scrambled to dress, made up the bunk, and hustled to stand inspection as the DI showed up and called his unit to fall out for calisthenics at 04:00.

Every minute of every day remained highly restrictive in all circumstances from shower and shaving to absolute conformity in uniform, making beds, polishing boots, stacking clothing in foot-lockers, denying privacy, and prohibiting the use of first names to suppress individuality, and any deviations or mistakes were punished. Each day played a part in erasing Andy as an individual while building him into a steel-minded Marine whose every function was motivated by one of four core beliefs: loyalty to unit, Corps, God, and country.

Without realizing it, Andy's exhausted body transformed into fit muscles with an instant and correct response to specific stimuli. His mind began to process things differently as well. Strategy began to play a role in how Andy dealt with the day's challenges. As he grew stronger, he did not fall immediately into a dead man's sleep as soon as he hit the bunk. He had a few minutes to think about what he was doing and why.

WWII rationing poster—Do with Less so the Soldiers Have Enough

During this time of reflection about who they were inside, Andy and Chauncey struck up a friendship with a guy in the bunk next to theirs. Tommy Gervase was a kid their age from New York and told them he had never been out of the city until now. Andy and Chauncey laughed and told Tommy that Parris Island and the surrounding area was not farming country; it was still city.

"OK, let's make a deal. You guys teach me about farming country, and I'll teach you about city life. Is it a deal?"

Andy and Chauncey shook on it, and that gave the three of them something to look forward to in the future.

They helped Tommy during weapons drill. He never fired a gun before, so Andy and Chauncey gave Tommy pointers on how to hold a weapon and how to feel comfortable with his semi-automatic .30 caliber rifle. Tommy watched them on the target range and commented how accurate they were on their bullet patterns.

"Lots of hunting, Tommy," was the answer he got.

Chauncey took aim for another shot, then leaned close to Andy, and whispered, "You know what our first miscalculation was?" Andy just shook his head, keeping his eyes forward. "I was right about our years of hunting teaching us how to shoot and clean our weapons. The problem is we never imagined prairie dogs and rabbits as enemies who shot back at us!"

Battlefield Toughness

Childish misconceptions and softness within Andy were replaced with tenacity, fitness, knowledge, and skill, preparing him and his unit for the reality they were destined to face. The guys in Andy's unit became brothers that fiercely guarded each other's backs. The unit always came first. If one guy underachieved, the whole unit suffered. The men of the unit policed their own, challenging each other to achieve each goal of the drill. When the unit won in a war game, they all owned the victory. The bond between the members of the unit grew tighter because each Marine played an equal role in every win. A camaraderie and unbreakable loyalty between the men of Andy and Chauncey's unit melded them all into a team of determined, disciplined, and confident brothers whose unit found strength in their belief in Corps, God, and country.

By week seven, Andy and Chauncey's unit could perform parade drills with meticulous accuracy, execute precision timing in their march step, and give perfect salutes in unison or give a flawless performance in ceremonial weapon drills. Andy's unit ate, slept, trained, and drilled in perfect team awareness of one another. An unmistakable transformation had taken place in body, mind, and spirit as Andy's unit forged the mentality worthy of a Devil Dog Marine.

When Andy and Chauncey met in grade school, they had instantly bonded and became brothers of the heart. They did everything together. Chauncey spent so much time over the years at Andy's house the Karella family looked at Chauncey as another son. Learning to be Marines in the same unit sealed that bond of brotherhood for life.

Dear Mom and Dad,   *March 1944*

Bootcamp will be over soon, and, Dad, it has been one heck of an education. It's been drilled into me that no job, even the most menial, is without merit. I confess I have learned to wash my own clothing and do a pretty good job of it now.

Don't laugh too hard, Mom! Though, I know you are. I sure do miss Florence! I should have been better at thanking her. At Parris Island, we have had to wash our own clothing in buckets of water and then hang our stuff to dry on clotheslines. It's an important part of battlefield training. I imagine our faces showed our doubts when we first heard that from our DI. We all know differently now.

Andy snapped a picture of Chauncey washing clothing in bucket of water, 1944

I'll say it again. I miss having a little sister around who washes, dries, and folds my laundry and sometimes even puts it away. Florence will probably want to hit me with a broom when she hears what I wrote, being a feisty girl just like her mother. I must say I have gained a new appreciation for what she did for me. Not that a DI gives us much choice in the matter. Nor do the guys in my unit. No one puts up with uncleanliness or a soldier that stinks up the barracks.

By the way, I wanted to let you know Chauncey and I might be going to Nebraska for one day in April. Please don't be mad if we don't stop by. We have a third guy coming with us if we get the chance to go, and we have plans for the day. I wanted you to hear it from me. Just in case someone recognizes me in town and tells you I was in Norfolk.

Mom, I think you would make a trip to Parris Island just to box my ears for not letting you know. And no! Before you wonder or ask, I will not be going to see Betty either. I guess this is a chance for both you and Betty to be mad at me at the same time.

Seriously, though, Chauncey and I are feeling ready and looking forward to graduation. None of my unit have been told where we go from here. As soon as I know, I'll send you word. Must go for now.

My love to you, Mom and Dad, and hug the kids for me,
your son,
Ambrose James

Dreaming of the Future

Andy acquired the mental toughness to consider the dangers and the possible outcomes in the battlefields he would be sent to. At the same time, he refused to let it freeze him in fear. Constructive thinking helped him stay in balance, so he focused on what he would do after the war ended. Andy spent a lot of time during the past weeks imagining the kind of future he wanted for himself. That future he envisioned always included Betty.

Through many long letters and a few precious telephone conversations, Andy and Betty had grown to know each other

Advertising—
WWII war bonds art by
Windsor McCay,
Public Domain Wikimedia

495

better. They shared views on things they saw or heard about in their day-to-day lives. Andy was excited about Roosevelt's Works Project Administration program for the highway system. "Betty, these roads are going to connect America. The road system will allow us to travel affordably using our own automobile!"

Betty talked about the changes in her school curricula and exams at college, how new rationing restrictions affected her family, new war bond drives, and her women friends moving into the mainstream workforce.

Andy's dad wrote about the innovative tractors, roller conveyor automation, and other machinery he saw in his repair shop and how it was increasing farm production as it transformed the Nebraskan economy.

Jeep Willy's Overland ads, 1940s, one for Military, one for civilian sales

As Andy and Chauncey neared the end of field training, they entered the testing week and would undergo written and performance evaluations. Andy, along with many other Marines, attended a series of lectures and viewed military film shorts. These optional lectures and films had several goals. Participation allowed officers to Identify potential candidates to move into Officer's Candidate School (OCS).

OCS programs looked for outstanding trainees who made high marks in the academic portion of basic training. Their performance ratings were taken into consideration as well as how they chose to use their personal time. In Andy's case, attending the lectures and films helped him attain a bigger picture of world events and more about the part the military played in the security of the American nation. The information was designed to help Marines understand why America was fighting the war. Everything Andy learned confirmed he and his unit were protecting the future of America. It was a great comfort to see how the best minds in the country supplied the technology and craftsmanship required to give America's soldiers a battlefield advantage.

The movie shorts Andy watched showed production factories springing up across America practically overnight, supplying anything from electronic field equipment to canned food for field rations. Additional factories produced clothing, tents, and all kinds of bivouac camp equipment. Andy whistled along with every other guy in the room when the films featured facilities filled with women assembling aircraft, bombs, and munitions.

Rosie the Riveter symbolizing American women in the workforce on the home front during WWII

Other military film shorts were shown as a series like the *Road to Victory*. These films focused on the commercial sectors such as large seaports committing huge sections of dock space to ship building, while other companies were dedicated to design, manufacturing, and assembly of specialized war tanks. Smelting factories converted to wartime needs repurposed scrap metals, which became ammunition casings for bullets and bombs. America's home front had undoubtably been mobilized, and its citizens were united in an ongoing battle to supply every item needed to support the war effort and America's soldiers. Andy's supplementary studies were noticed by his DI. It came as a complete surprise when the DI informed Andy he was being considered for OCS training, and he could continue his college night classes after he got assigned to a base where he would wait for further orders.

Growing up in a small down-to-earth farming town in Nebraska gave Andy an insulated, unpretentious, and naïve view of life when compared to the fast-paced lifestyles of big city dwellers. The Marines changed that.

After eight weeks of basic training, Andy believed himself to be a dedicated patriot with a clear understanding of the serious world he lived in and its serious problems. Through his Marine training, Andy achieved a mental confidence about what he did based on facts, not childish assumptions. As a mature-minded Marine, he had attained self-assurance in his physical stamina to execute his duty. Andy accepted the fact that he would meet mortal danger shoulder to shoulder with his unit and prayed that he and Chauncey could fulfill their duty and come home.

Though Andy focused on serving his country for the immediate future, he also planned on coming home after the war. If he did get back, he would have lots of opportunity to create an amazing future for himself. He'd have the personal freedom to follow his dreams. Andy couldn't help feeling it was an exciting time to be alive.

During the last weeks of bootcamp, Andy made a few trips into the city of Beaufort only three miles from Parris Island. On one of these trips, Andy saw a new kind of record player and recording machine. It looked like a phonograph and played music records, but it also allowed a person to record their voice on a blank record, then play it back. He instantly wanted one.

Andy had grown up with a fascination for cameras and music devices. He figured he was almost as captivated by that kind of technology as his father. As a boy, he had been surrounded by all kinds of his father's equipment: items that his dad found in junkyards and repaired or different kinds of electronic equipment people brought to his father's garage shop to be repaired.

Andy remembered getting his first Brownie Camera when he was ten, the same year he found his pet raccoon, Jimmy. He had his own jackrabbit bounty money to use to buy film for his camera and then have it developed into photographs. Andy had a box full of pictures he had taken, along with his phonograph and record collection and the rest of his stuff in storage at his folks' house.

At Parris Island, they listened to the radio when the guys had free time. That made him think of his music collection, and that also reminded him of that machine he'd seen in town. He couldn't stop thinking about being able to record his voice and play it back.

Just a few days before graduation, Andy happened to see a similar machine being used by the captain in the HQ building. When Andy walked up to his desk, the captain was listening to a recording made by the commanding officer and typing the dictated recording into a field report. When Andy asked him about it, the captain called it a transcription machine.

Hearing how that voice sounded made Andy's imagination go wild. He went to town the next day and bought two of the machines and two boxes of blank records from the store where he had seen it demonstrated.

Portable record transcription, recording, and playing machine

To make his idea work, Andy needed two machines: one for Betty and one for him. Then they could send recordings back and forth to each other.

In Andy's initial shipment to Betty was his first recording, and on it, he told her how to use the machine and the records. He decided not to get too personal on that first recording, knowing Betty would be demonstrating it for her friends. He planned to send her love letters in his voice.

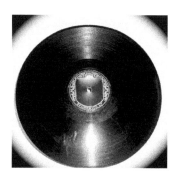

1940s recording and playing Machine, 78 vinyl recording disc

He thought it would be a very romantic way to tell her how he felt and share his dreams with her. Those ideas would mean more coming to her in his voice. He couldn't wait for some quiet time to compose his first message to her.

Andy had been correct; Betty had demonstrated her new machine to her friends at school and took it home over a weekend so her mother, LeOra Rossow, could listen to the record Andy sent.

Placing the needle on the record, Andy's voice filled the room as he said, "Hello, Betty, I sure hope you like the player recording machine I sent to you. I can't wait to hear your voice on a record coming back to me.

"I'd love it if you sang me a song. How about 'As Time Goes By' or 'The Mere Idea of You.' You've got such a great voice! I know you'd sound terrific! Please don't send a record until I get a permanent base assignment. I don't want it being shuffled around in mail call too much. I'd hate to have one get broken.

"You are now hearing the voice of a full-fledged Marine. Chauncey and I graduated with our unit today and will be getting our new base assignments in three days. We are going to use those three days to travel north and stop in Nebraska for one day before we report to our deployment base. As you are in the middle of college exams, I won't bother you on this first return trip to Nebraska.

"Instead, Chauncey and I plan to bring one of our city buddies, Tommy Gervase, to Madison. We'll be staying on a friend's dairy farm for a day. Tommy wants to experience farm life that he's heard us talk about. We'll catch a military air hop to Omaha and take a bus to Norfolk. Once we get to Norfolk, Dad will meet us and drive us to the farm. Then we'll skedaddle off to our new post on the following day."

U.S. Marine symbol and flags

Andy closed his recording by saying, "I promise to tell you all about the trip on another record. I'm putting in for another three-day pass once I get assigned to my deployment base. Just in case they approve it, let's do some planning of what we could do on my visit home, OK? Say hello to your parents for me. Good luck with your exams. I miss you, Betty. I dream of seeing you before I ship out. I'll call you on the telephone when I get to my new base."

After Andy sent his recording off to Betty, he called his dad to confess his dilemma. It was hard for Andy to admit, but even as a tough new Devil Dog Marine, he did not feel up to getting a dose of his mom's temper or her tears. Thankfully, his father answered the telephone, "Dad, I don't want to upset Mom by popping in at the house only to leave in a couple of hours. Would you meet us at the bus station in Norfolk?" he asked.

Rusty looked around the corner to be sure Delora was not within hearing range before he quietly replied, "Son, I agree with you. Your mom would not take that sort of visit very well.

"I will meet you boys at the bus station and take you where you need to go and bring you back. It's a good thing that you told me you might be in Norfolk after graduation. At least I can tell your mom that this trip came up suddenly. She'll probably still be mad as a wet hen, but I can deal with that when the time comes."

Marine recruit, Ambrose James (Andy or AJ) Karella

"Thank you, Dad," Andy replied. "I'm really looking forward to seeing you."

CHAPTER 28

World War II 1944–1945

Flashback—Norfolk Junior College

As Andy and Chauncy prepared their duffels for their three-day pass, he came across the letter from his uncle his dad had given him just before he left home before Christmas. Andy found himself lost in the memory of reading those words for the first time. Back at college, Andy had sat down to read the letter his father had given him from his Uncle Shorty.

Dear Andy   *December 1943*

I hope this letter finds you before you leave Nebraska. I wanted to tell you a few things just between you and me. I deliberately did not write about any of this to your dad because he usually shares everything with Bitty. None of what I'm going to share with you would do anything but worry them.

My unit was stationed for a while in London, picking up provisions, and HQ was having meetings with the Brits about the battles going on across the country between England and Belgium. While we were in London, I was caught in several air raids. I'll be honest with you, Andy. When those sirens start that eerie wail, it sends chills of fear down your spine. But nothing can prepare you for what it's like to be within 100 feet of a bomb blowing up a building. We didn't worry about strafing fire from the enemy planes in the city. They were concentrating on dropping as many bombs as they could and then hightailing it to safety before the RAF could send up fighter planes after them.

The bombs going off at close range are deafening and disorienting. Your head concusses, and you don't think you'll ever hear properly again, and then the next one blows up even closer. Andy, war is brutal and bloody. The most painful part was talking to men I know when an air raid started, then be part of the detail that had to shift through the rubble of blown-up buildings, searching for our missing men, then finding the bloody corpses after the bombing stopped and the air raid siren signaled all is clear. I'll never forget any of that.

My unit made it out of London with only a handful of casualties and two deaths. We are now bivouacked in Belgium. Allied forces took back Belgium in May of 1940, but we still must be careful when we are in the forests. Belgium is a very small country, and it borders both Germany and France, so we have to be on guard against stray French or German troops.

I am in charge of HQ's mess tent. We have a lot of canned vegetables, but our meat is a rationed item and limited in supply. I use ours to make a thick, Bohemian-style stew to stretch the meat we do get. When supply shipments are late and the meat is running low, several of the cooks and I go out early in the mornings hunting wild game. The largest game those woods have is deer. We enjoy shooting Hitler's deer and serving fresh venison steaks to our guys, and our men love it. I'm glad I learned to use a rifle when I was in the French Foreign Legion. Though I never used a rifle in battle, I like being able to take something from Hitler that can do some good and help people.

Andy, I commend you for following the patriotic call. But please keep your eyes and ears open. Be as careful as possible because I dearly want to see you again. God bless you on your journeys and may He protect you in battle.

Love always,
Uncle Shorty

With all those sobering words filling his thoughts, Andy sat down to write his Uncle Shorty. First, he thanked his uncle for the candid message about the reality of war and said he took everything in that letter to heart. Then he told him about meeting Aunt Mary and shared news about family events. Before he closed the letter, Andy wrote down what he had heard his father say, writing that he had taken those words, "He's just like Shorty" as a compliment and hoped he could live up to them.

Andy dropped the letter in the mail as he went to pick up Betty. They planned to go to the cinema to see the last showing of *White Christmas,* and when they left the theater, the two of them sang and hummed the tunes from the show.

"Andy," said Betty as she wrapped her arm through his, "I heard they are making soundtracks of shows like these. I want to collect every record they make of Broadway singing shows and these big screen movie musicals. Wouldn't that be wonderful to listen to? Gosh, think of the memories we would have from when we heard the songs!"

Andy smiled and nodded that he agreed. *Now, I know what I can buy her for gifts,* he thought.

Nine Weeks Later, Three-Day Travel Pass

After graduating bootcamp, three friends traveled in uniform and arrived in Norfolk on a Friday afternoon. Rusty Karella found it hard to believe how changed his son and his friends seemed dressed as they were in their tailored khaki uniforms.

Chauncey felt like one of Rusty's sons, so Rusty greeted both young men by hugging them as he said, "I'm happy to see you boys." Taking a step back, he looked them up and down, then teased them a bit by saying, "You look snappy in those outfits."

Andy started to reply, but Chauncey beat him to the punch, saying, "Uniforms, Dad, not outfits." That correction was accompanied by an audacious grin on Chauncey's face.

"You are getting too smart for your britches, boy," Rusty replied with genuine affection and good humor. Turning toward the young man he did not know, Mr. Karella said, "Hello, I'm Rusty, Andy's father." Then he reached out to shake hands.

"Tommy Gervase. Glad to meet you, sir."

Andy and Chauncey looked at each other startled. Neither one could believe Andy's dad had used that nickname. Though Andy's father had written the nickname in letters to his son, Andy never expected to hear the man say it out loud. That his father would make this effort for him made Andy very proud.

Mr. Karella gave the young marines a ride out to the farm he and Andy had talked about. They would stay overnight, and he would pick them up again the next day after lunch.

It wasn't long before they climbed out of the car to retrieve their duffels from

Andy Karella, 1944, khaki daily work Marine uniform

the trunk and said thank you. Rusty smiled and reminded them to be punctual when he came back for them, saying, "I promise to get you to the bus station in Norfolk in time to catch the evening bus to Omaha on Saturday night." Standing at the end of the short lane up to the farm, the boys waved as Rusty drove away, then they walked up to the large two-story farmhouse.

The Richardsons' Dairy Farm

Their city kid looked a little nervous, and Andy asked him what he was thinking about. Tommy replied, "Well, the only buildings I see are the farmhouse and those buildings over there. Jeez! As far as I can see, it's just fields and a few trees out here. You didn't tell me we'd be going out to the middle of nowhere. Are you sure your dad is going to come back for us? The town back there was small but at least it resembled a city!"

Andy and Chauncey smiled at the slight nervousness they heard in their friend's voice. Evidently, he was a bit jittery about the wide-open spaces. "Don't worry," Andy replied, "my dad will come back for us tomorrow. He is keen on punctuality."

The group walked up onto the porch of the house when Andy remembered something. "Oh! By the way, I forgot to tell you guys. I gave Parris Island HQ my dad's address as an alternate for our notification letters. But don't worry if they haven't arrived at Dad's before we leave. That will mean our papers will be at Marine HQ in Omaha. We can pick them up on Sunday morning when we report in."

Given that news, both Tommy and Chauncey looked relieved. Andy knocked on the door and added, "The duty officer at Parris also told me we'd be catching a military transport out of Omaha to our transitional base. That's where we stay until we get our deployment orders. In the meantime, we have at least two days of fun ahead of us." Chauncey nodded in agreement. Tommy didn't acknowledge anything because a lady opened the door before he had the opportunity to respond.

Smiling broadly, the woman said, "It's good to see you, Andy! We've been as excited as Bristol since he told us you were going to visit. Please come in." Then her son, Bristol, took over the introductions.

Seeing Chauncey remove his cover, Andy and Tommy quickly did the same, holding their hats in their hands. When Bristol got to Tommy, he looked at Andy and didn't say anything.

Andy felt embarrassed, realizing his blunder, and replied, "Sorry, I thought I wrote his name in the letter I sent you, Bristol. Mrs. Richardson, Bristol, this is our friend Tommy Gervase from New York City. Chauncey and I met him in boot camp. Tommy, this is Bristol Richardson. Bristol is a friend we've known all our lives. He went to high school with us in Norfolk."

Mrs. Richardson took over the conversation, saying, "Boys, I think we've spent enough time in the doorway. Please, let's all go into the kitchen for something cold to drink."

An hour later, Bristol showed them to their rooms and asked them to meet him downstairs for dinner.

Before going downstairs to dinner, Tommy asked Andy why Bristol hadn't joined the military. Andy put his finger to his lips indicating Tommy should keep his voice down, then explained. "Bristol was not allowed to join up. His dad died just after the war started. Being the only boy in the family, he had to take over running the family farm. Because Bristol ran a farm supplying food for the military, the government made Bristol exempt from military service. He can't join up. Everyone in control wants him here on the farm. Don't say anything about it, OK?"

"Roger that," Tommy replied.

Farm Life

Tommy believed he was an adventurous sort and was determined to make a good impression by enjoying the farm experience, despite having lived his whole life in the city.

The New Yorker impressed his host and the family with his intelligence and politeness, even more so during dinner when he volunteered to help with chores after supper as did Andy and Chauncey. Mrs. Richardson and her daughters smiled warmly at Tommy and the other boys.

"Isn't that nice, girls? Since you ladies don't have to help your brother tonight, I am happy to let you take over clean-up duties in the kitchen." The girls quit smiling immediately, which made Mrs. Richardson laugh. She walked to the door with the boys, saying, "Thank you for volunteering to help Bristol. Don't stay up too late. Breakfast is at 6:00 a.m. Now, I will say good night."

A big floodlight mounted on a tall pole midway between the house and the barns lit up the yard as dusk set in. Bristol and his three friends fed the chickens first. Then they filled the pig trough and gave grain to the calves last. The work seemed simple enough, and Tommy began to believe there was nothing to this farm stuff.

Bristol motioned for Tommy to join him. At which point, the boy noted that without the floodlight, he would not have been able to see Bristol or the cows standing in the fenced yard near the long squat building. "OK, all we need to do is get behind that last cow over there, and they'll walk into the barn together," Bristol directed. "Oh, and, Tommy, be careful where you step. The cowpies are pretty big, but in this light, you probably won't notice 'em until you step in one."

Tommy wished Bristol had warned him a little sooner, as he tried to rub the muck he'd stepped in off his shoes. *They said I only had to walk behind the herd, and the animals will walk to the building. No one said anything about cowpies!*

Dairy cows

13x18" bale of hay, approximately 50–70 pounds, used for livestock feed

Unexpectedly, a flash of light came from Andy's direction. Andy had been camera crazy all through bootcamp. Apparently, the cows didn't like the light, which spooked them a bit, causing them to speed up to a trot headed for the safety of the milking barn.

Bristol picked up his pace and called out, "C'mon, Tommy, Chauncey! Stay close behind them."

Once the cows were inside the barn, they lined up side by side and put their heads through a line of vertical bars. After Bristol pulled the strings off a fresh bale and tossed sections of the hay in front of each cow, they started eating.

Fascinated at how much the animals looked like they enjoyed the dried grass, Tommy didn't notice anything else until he heard a humming sound. Looking around for the cause of the noise, he noticed Bristol had moved to the back end of a cow and was attaching an apparatus under its belly. Then he noted Andy and Chauncey were attaching more apparatus to other cows. Methodically, the guys moved down the line of cows, hooking them up one by one. "Can I ask what you guys are doing?" Tommy enquired.

His buddies bent down behind their cows and did not answer. Bristol assumed Andy and Chauncey had not heard their friend's question and proudly replied, "This is how we attach cups to the cows. That machine over there," he said, pointing, "is where the milk is stored. Our whole system is automated now."

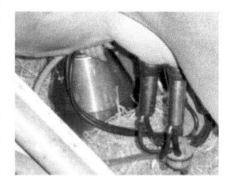

Automated milking device uses suction cups to milk the cows

Waving at Tommy, he added, "Come closer! I'll show you how to hook 'em up. Pull up that short stool—yeah, that one—and sit next to me. Start with the teats furthest away from you, like this—go ahead, just grab it." Bristol chuckled when he heard Tommy gasp as he took hold of the long, thick teat. "It's soft, right? Bet that's the biggest tit you've ever held in your hand."

Considering Tommy's reaction to what he said, Bristol deliberately mispronounced *teat* and kept saying *tit*.

Andy and Chauncey laughed quietly in response to the old joke, remembering the first time they had heard it. Slowly standing up to his full height, Andy then motioned for Chauncey to do the same so they could see over the cow's back and watch Tommy's face as Bristol talked to him.

"Now, with your other hand, take that first cup on the milking head—yeah, that one—and start guiding the cup toward the tit. It has suction, so it'll grab on just like a baby as soon as you put it close enough. There you go! That's right." Bristol was so intent on the process that he didn't notice Tommy's face had changed color.

Andy and Chauncey had been waiting for a reaction and saw that Tommy's face was fire truck red. They held their hands over their mouths, trying not to make a sound as tears of laughter ran down their faces.

Bristol blithely went on talking. "We haven't milked cows the old-fashioned way since I was a kid. Watch this! My dad used to be able to hit a cat's face five feet away." Bristol took hold of the last tit not in a cup and squeezed it; a spurt of white liquid shot straight into his mouth. "You want a squirt?"

Tommy rapidly shook his head right as a sick thought occurred to him. "What is that?" he asked.

"What? This?" Bristol chuckled and replied, "It's the same milk we drank at dinner. It's just warm out of the cow instead of cold out of the refrigerator."

Tommy shoved himself away from the cow so fast he overturned the stool he'd been sitting on. Now sitting on the barn floor, he sat staring at Bristol's back in disbelief.

Oblivious to what was happening to Tommy, Bristol attached the last suction cup and checked the others once more as he kept talking while he worked. "Business has been so good the last few years we've been able to upgrade our equipment. Now, we have the best milking machines on the market."

As Andy and Chauncey watched Tommy sitting on the floor, his face went from confused embarrassment over the tit analogy to mortified at Bristol's little marksmanship demonstration. The progressive changes in his expressions were so comical that Andy and Chauncey couldn't stop the laughter from bubbling over as they watched their friend trying to take it all in.

As observers, they recognized the moment their friend's mind made the connection and the appalling truth hit him square in the belly. Tommy rolled over onto his hands and knees and then got to his feet. Incredulous, he couldn't stop staring at where milk came from. That's when he gagged and ran out of the barn, obviously trying not to throw up on his shoes.

His buddies followed him into the barnyard. They couldn't help but tease him a little more. They playfully asked, "Jeez, Tommy, what's wrong?"

"Didn't you guys see what I saw? The milk was coming out of a cow! Didn't you hear what Bristol said? The milk we *drank* at dinner came out of those cows!"

Still bent over hoping not to throw up the dinner he'd mentioned, Tommy did not see the grin on Andy's face as he feigned innocence and asked, "Where did you think milk came from?"

When the young man could finally speak in between urges to retch, he gritted his teeth and snarled. "From bottles in the corner market!"

Looking at each other with laughter bubbling to the surface, Andy nodded at Chauncey, which was the signal for him to ask the obvious question. "Didn't you ever wonder why cows were always associated with milk?" Chauncey asked.

Hesitating before he replied and glad it was dark in the yard so they could not see his face, he hoped his stomach would not betray him. Then, feeling like a dunce as he thought about the question, he replied softly, "I thought it was just a marketing gimmick to catch attention."

Tommy had been a good sport over the jokes played on him, so his friends quit teasing him. They helped their fellow Marine get to his room and into bed, telling him, "Sleep well, Tommy. We promise tomorrow will be fun."

Mornings on the Farm

It was still dark out when everyone gathered for a hearty breakfast Saturday morning. Mrs. Richardson served homemade toast, scrambled eggs, and thick-cut bacon. When one of Bristol's sisters began filling everyone's glass with fresh milk, Tommy was quick to decline, politely saying he wasn't thirsty.

Everyone smiled but kept quiet. "Would you like more eggs and bacon, Tommy? Maybe a glass of water or juice?" Mrs. Richardson asked.

"Yes, thank you. More eggs and bacon and just water please," Tommy replied quickly, glad to escape the milk pitcher being passed around the table for a second time.

With breakfast over, the guys followed Bristol out to the stockyard. After feeding the pigs the table scraps, they gathered chicken eggs. While Andy delivered the eggs to the kitchen, Chauncey and Tommy hauled bales of hay to the milking barn.

As Tommy worked, his confidence began to return as he thought, *I got some good sleep last night. I avoided that disgusting pitcher of milk at breakfast without insulting Bristol's mom, and the rest of the food was delicious! No one's getting away with any jokes at my expense today. I got the hang of this farm stuff now!*

The New Yorker had his bounce back, and his buddies were happy to see it as Tommy and Bristol herded the cows into the milking barn. Andy could hear Bristol and Tommy talking while he and Chauncey spread hay in the trough for the cows ready to be milked.

Once that chore was done, they looked for Tommy, but he had disappeared. As they helped Bristol hook up the cows to the milking machine, they asked, "Did you see where Tommy went?"

"No, not since he helped me herd the cows in here," Bristol replied as he attached another set of milking cups to the next cow in line.

"Did he say where he was going?" Chauncey asked. "What were you guys talking about?"

"Not much," Bristol replied. "He mentioned he really like the meat we had for breakfast. Said he'd never had that kind of bacon before and that it tasted like a pork chop. I told him it's my own special cut of side pork I make when I butcher the hogs. He sounded a little surprised. I told him the pigs he helped feed this morning are being fattened for slaughter. I mentioned I'd be happy to send him some side pork after I kill the pigs in a couple more weeks. Right after that, he said he had to go to the bathroom. I don't remember seeing him since."

Right before the lunch bell rang, Andy and Chauncey found Tommy sitting in the shade by the house. Tommy turned down the invitation to eat lunch, saying he wasn't hungry.

After a delicious meal of fried chicken, potato salad, and fresh milk, Andy and Chauncey walked into the living room. There Tommy sat dressed in a clean uniform with his duffle bag sitting by his feet. When he saw them, he jumped up and asked with hope in his voice, "Are you guys ready to go?"

"No, we still have to change and pack our duffels," Andy replied with a straight face. "Are you in a hurry? Dad won't be here for another hour. Lunch was great! Are you sure you don't want any of it? Mrs. Richardson would be happy to make you a plate. She makes great fried chicken. I guarantee the meat is fresh. I saw the girls plucking the birds just before lunch."

Tommy swallowed hard and quickly shook his head, replying, "No thanks. It's really nice of her, but I'm really not hungry."

Andy turned to look at Chauncey to hide his smile, replying, "I have to say I'm surprised. Bucking all those bales of hay is hard work. Chauncey and I were starved by the time the lunch bell rang. You sure you're not coming down with something?"

Getting Back to the City

Later while they waited at the end of the lane for Mr. Karella, Tommy confessed he found out the meat he had eaten at breakfast had been a pig in the yard only a week before, and it was too much to contemplate. He wanted no more unpleasant surprises; he preferred foods that came out of nice clean packages or cartons that came from the city grocery store much better.

His last comment caused both Andy and Chauncey to snort with laughter. The two of them cut the jokes when they realized Tommy was getting downright grumpy. "OK, I admit it. You got me. I had no idea what farm life was. Just keep in mind turnabout is fair play. Wait till we are on my turf in the city!" Tommy replied with a grin.

"Your turf, your game. We can take it." They agreed with a smile. Following that statement, another thought occurred to Andy and Chauncey at the same time. They'd better not tell Tommy the eggs he'd eaten that morning came out of a chicken's butt, sure that all hell would break loose. Heck, he might even refuse to eat anything until he was back on a civilized Marine base. As friends, they decided what Tommy didn't know would be much easier on all of them.

All thoughts of teasing Tommy ceased when they heard a car coming down the road and pulled to a stop in front of them.

Rusty was right on time. Though for Tommy, the waiting had seemed like an eternity. Rusty asked, smiling, "Why are you boys standing at the end of the road in the heat? Did Mrs. Richardson kick you out?"

As the boys climbed into the car, Tommy answered before anyone else could. "Not at all, Mr. Karella. We just didn't want to make you come all the way up to the house and agreed to wait for you down here. Right, fellas?"

"Yeah, that's right," Chauncey agreed. Andy nodded his head, going along with Chauncey and Tommy. Rusty heard Tommy muttering about getting out of Nebraska and something about getting back to civilization during the ride back to Norfolk, but he let it slide. He also noticed Tommy didn't seem to relax until he saw the bus station. That seemed odd because it was only 4:00 p.m., which meant the boys still had a two-hour wait ahead of them before the six o'clock bus was ready to leave for Omaha.

Andy wanted to catch up on what was happening at home with his dad and tell him about their weekend. As his friends got out of the car, Andy looked at his watch and then asked, "Dad, do you have time to stay and talk for a while?"

After his dad agreed, Andy excused himself for a moment to have a word with Chauncey and Tommy. His friends were happy to kill some time walking around Norfolk and promised to be back to catch the bus. "See ya later, guys," Andy called out as he walked back to his dad standing by the car.

"Let's go get a burger. I'm starved," Tommy said.

Chauncey laughed and nodded his head, replying, "Good idea! I know just the place too!"

With Andy's friends out of earshot, his dad asked, "How did your friend like farm life?"

Andy tried to keep a straight face while he recounted the whole story but failed miserably. "My guess is that it was a little *too* real for a city boy," Andy replied.

"That would explain what he said about getting out of Nebraska and back to civilization."

"Yes, Dad, I suppose it does."

Rusty just looked at his son and thought fondly, *He might look like a man in his uniform, but he's still only a boy in his heart and still loves to pull pranks on his friends.*

Andy brought his father out of his reflections by asking, "So, Dad, what is going on with Charlie?"

He took a deep breath, and releasing it slowly, he answered, "Charlie ran away right after you left for bootcamp. I knew he was going to join the Army Air Corps. Just not where he was going to join up. He lied about his age, and the Air Corps enlisted him."

Shock struck Andy like a blow to the gut. "How come no one told me? I know he was determined to join up, but I thought I had convinced him to wait until he was at least seventeen."

Rusty shook his head, replying, "What could you have done? You had your own problems to take care of, and you needed a clear head during your Marine training."

Andy could not argue with that logic, nor did he know how to console his father. Abruptly, an idea popped into Andy's head, and he asked, "Dad, you want to have a beer with me?"

Rusty looked sideways at his son and replied, "Last time I checked, you weren't old enough to drink."

Smiling, Andy replied, "In this uniform, they won't ask, and I won't tell if you don't."

As father and son walked side by side to a nearby bar, worry for his younger brother unsettled Andy's thoughts. *Charlie has always been bullheaded but never a hothead. I had no idea Charlie would do something this foolhardy. Dad looks so dejected.*

Andy ordered beers from the bartender, and he was right. The barkeep did not ask about his age. Minutes later, Andy carried two mugs dripping with foam to the corner table and sat down across from his father. Pulling out a pack of cigarettes, he took one and offered the pack to his father, then Andy lit up. Holding it in his fingers, he took a long swallow of cold beer and waited.

After lighting his own cigarette, Rusty took a drink from his mug, and he began to speak. "Just like you, I thought I had convinced Charlie to wait. Predictably, all hell broke loose when your mother adamantly said *no* to early enlistment. I had no doubt about what would happen the minute Charlie's eyes turned hard. He wasn't listening." Andy shook his head and his father held up his hand to stop his son from speaking. "This situation was inevitable. I could have dragged him back home, but we've all seen how headstrong your younger brother can be. He would have disappeared again, and you and I both know it.

Charles Dale (Charlie) Karella, U. S. Air Corps / Air Force WWII

"I finally had to tell your mother that we had to leave it in God's hands. She was furious with me. But I believe letting him go is perhaps why he wrote to us after he got into flight school. Thankfully, he keeps in touch. Charlie even corrected me when I wrote asking how Army flight school was going. In Charlie's letter to us, he said that the guys in the Army Air Corps now call themselves the Air Force. He had the moxie to tell me the Air Corps grew up just like he had."

Agitated, Andy snapped, "Grew up? When? The last time I checked, he was still a kid!" Suddenly, a terrible flash of guilt silenced Andy. He began to think, *Perhaps this was entirely my fault. Did I set a bad example?* "You know," Andy whispered, "maybe if I hadn't let

Charlie hang around with me and my friends, he would not have been so set on enlisting early."

The boy's self-reproach was short-lived as his father shook his head and replied, "I think I know both of you pretty well. I knew we could not stop you from leaving early, and in my heart, I knew the same thing about Charles Dale. I did hope I could get him to agree to the same deal I made with you. But what is done is done. Let's not talk about it anymore and please don't say anything to your mother unless she does. It wouldn't do to get her upset all over again. OK?"

His father's quiet request had a pleading tone in it that made Andy nod his head, then Andy asked what Charlie had written in his letters. Rusty opened his jacket pocket, pulled out two letters, and handed them to his eldest son to read. They were typed, not handwritten.

Dear Mom and Dad,   March 1944

I am excited to tell you I'm training to become an Air Force flight engineer. I must complete basic flight training and graduate from flight engineer school first. Afterwards, I will be stationed at Ladd Army Airfield in Alaska! Can you believe it?

B25 Mitchell Bomber

As flight engineer, I will be working with a team of guys that ferry new aircraft, mostly B25 Mitchell Bombers and Bell P-39 Airacobras from the continental United States to Fairbanks, in the U.S. Territory of Alaska.

Bell P-39 Aircobra

From Fairbanks, we will fly the aircraft north to a village called Nome. That's where we rendezvous with allied pilots at the military airfield. Those pilots will fly the aircraft to the fight in Europe.

By the way, does Andy know about me? Do you have an address for him yet? When you do, would you please send it to me? I will be sure to send my Alaska address to you once I move to my base.

I am sorry to have worried you. I want you to understand I would have gone no matter what. I love you and please don't worry about me. I'm not going to be anywhere near the fighting.

I love you both,
your son,
Charlie

Andy was familiar with the activity Charlie had written about. It was part of an allied support program supplying thousands of aircrafts and munitions, tanks, and trucks to the western front of the European theater of battle. Nome, Alaska—that was where United States aviators handed new aircraft over to Allied pilots who would then fly the aircraft over the Bering Strait and across Siberia. Eventually, they would use them to fly raids against the Axis Powers. These planes were all part of the lend-lease program sponsored by the United States Government. Andy had heard that their Allies didn't have money to

Ladd Airfield, SAC command
Territory of Alaska, Fairbanks

pay for the aircraft upfront, but they had plenty of pilots to send into battle. Putting the first letter away, Andy opened the second one.

Dear Dad and Mom,   April 1944

You'll be happy to hear I'm learning more in the Air Force than I ever did in my geography classes. In my last letter, I mentioned that we turn the aircraft we fly up from the states over to new pilots who fly them to the war front. What I didn't say was that a lot of them are Russian pilots. They fly right over the Bering Strait. There are two facts that make Nome an ideal place to make the crossing between the two continents.

First, our crew can ferry aircraft from any installation within the continental U.S. over land. That includes Canada, the Yukon Territories, and on through the Alaskan Territory with airfield and fueling support all the way to Nome. The second fact concerns the Bering Strait itself.

WWII War Bonds poster—You Buy 'Em We'll Fly 'Em

My instructor said that if you start at the tip of the Siberian Chukotka Peninsula, then cross straight over the two Diomede Islands, and then to Nome, the Bering Strait is only about 50 miles wide. This is important because it keeps our flight path over open water to a minimum. I think that is amazing, don't you?

Before I forget, I asked my captain to explain a normal tour of duty like you asked. This was what he said. If I was in a combat arena, the length of a tour is equal to 30 logged flights, which takes about a year. Don't worry! Right now, they are telling me I am not eligible for a combat zone.

For the foreseeable future, my crew and I will strictly be ferrying aircraft, so I'm going to be OK. Please be sure Mom reads this letter. I hope it will help her feel better about my choices.

I need to get a little shuteye, but I will write again soon. Please give Mom a big hug for me. And, Dad, I hope you know that I love you all.

Your son,
Charlie

Time to Go

Rusty had paid for the beers while Andy read the letters. As he slowly refolded the second letter, he thought, *It is a relief to know he is going to be safe. I couldn't be happier for him. Charlie is experiencing everything he ever dreamed about. Watching all those* Tailspin Tommy *movie clips as a kid, the Army Air Corps was all he ever wanted to talk about. Luckily, unlike his hero* Tailspin Tommy, *Charlie would not be getting shot at by the enemy.*

Despite that small difference from his hero, Charlie's commitment and enthusiasm could easily be felt in the words he had written about flying and going to Alaska. Andy handed the letters back to his father, saying, "He's exhilarated. Charlie has got a passion for this, and I'm proud of him. At least we know he'll be safe and will not be sent into battle to fly in dogfights."

With those words, sadness settled over father and son while something intangible hung in the air between them. Both men keenly felt the realization that Andy's situation had no such guarantee. On the contrary, Andy and Chauncey expected to be sent to the frontlines of battle. There was no surety they would not be injured or killed. With that sobering reality in mind, Andy and Rusty both put out their cigarettes and stood up to leave without saying a word.

As they walked back to the bus station, Andy said, "I almost forgot. I have some exciting news of my own. I received a recommendation for Officer Candidate School. If I get approved, it might mean I won't be deployed to the frontlines as soon as I was expecting. I'll let you know as soon as I hear more about it. Try not to worry too much. I know that sounds like a stupid request, but I promise Chauncey and I will watch each other's backs as we always have. We will be careful."

Though Andy had delivered his news with a calm demeanor, inside, he shook with exhilaration. The reality of the war was still an unknown experience. He couldn't help it. Nothing could dampen the anticipation he felt about getting into the action. Andy and the guys had been on pins and needles for weeks waiting for news about their first official assignments. Now as Andy opened the trunk of his dad's car to retrieve his duffle, his father said, "Son, I almost forgot. I have a letter for you too."

Turning in surprise, thinking it was a letter from Charlie, Andy reached for the packet his father handed him. Then he noticed it was an official envelope from the Marine Corps, and Andy's heart raced. It contained three letters, and he opened his quickly. As he figured, they contained information about the next step toward deployment. Andy looked up at his dad and said, "I'll be leaving from Omaha in the morning. My orders state I am to report to the Brooklyn Naval Base in New York City."

The realization of the moment struck Andy as he thought, *This might be the last time I see my dad before I ship out.* That thought produced a heartfelt demonstration of affection. Andy hugged his father goodbye as he whispered, "I love you, Dad." As defining moments go, this one stunned Andy. His father, who had always seemed larger than life, was actually so small he had to bend over a little to hug him tightly around the shoulders.

The sentimental moment was lost within seconds; Chauncey and Tommy waved their arms and yelled to get his attention. "Hey, Andy, wait for us! We need to get our bags out of your dad's car!"

Andy couldn't wait to tell his friends the news. "Hurry up, guys! I have our base assignment letters!" The other two boys tore open their letters to discover they were all going to New York!

New York, New York, Brooklyn Naval Yard

Being in New York City presented its own kind of thrill. Since discovering the Naval yard would be their permanent station until deployment, the Nebraska boys endeavored to use any free time wisely. They did a lot of sightseeing on weekend passes with Tommy who was an excellent guide.

When Andy and Chauncey were restricted to the base, as the two of them were on this weekend, they amused themselves by initiating new arrivals with some imaginative practical jokes.

Chauncey had always possessed a delightfully mischievous and slightly sick sense of humor. Currently, he did his best to scare the wits out of the new guys in the barracks. Using his hands to emphasize how huge the wharf rats were, he enjoyed watching the guys' eyes bug out when he told them he'd seen these rats while standing graveyard watch.

He visibly shuddered as he explained how spooky it was that these rats weren't afraid of people and what kind of diseases they could give the men if the rats bit them. "I think that is how the Black Death got started in Europe. It was being bitten by wharf rats," he whispered under his breath. Andy listened and grinned as he buffed the toes of his shoes to a mirror shine. He figured Chauncey was trying to get a little payback for some of the Parris Island swamp jokes that had been pulled on him.

Unexpectedly, a challenge came from a few of the toughest-looking recruits who were not sure they should believe Chauncey's stories. That was Andy's cue to back Chauncey up. He didn't need to fake a story because he had a real scary tale to tell about his own rodent encounter.

One Dark Night

Taking time to light up a cigarette, Andy continued to look at the shoe he had just finished when he said, "Guys, I'd say this happened shortly after arriving on base."

Andy walked over and stood up next to Chauncey and gained everyone's attention. "We had to stand late-night guard duty on the big dock. There is no actual guard house down there. You'll see that for yourselves soon enough. Anyway, on the end of the dock we patrol, there is what we call the shack. It's only rafters and a roof, otherwise it's completely open on the sides. But at least we don't have to stand guard duty in the pouring rain.

"Fellas, on this particular night, it wasn't raining. A cold fog began to roll in, making it hard to see more than five feet in front of us. The fog got thicker, and soon, it was impossible to see anything in the dark beyond the lamplight coming from 20 feet above the docks.

"We Marines are only required to patrol the end of the dock cordoned off from the rest of the pier. When you get there, you'll probably think there is nothing out there. But you'd be wrong. You're going to find out that as you walk, the sound of your boots on the boards isn't the only sound you hear.

"On the night I'm talking about, each step we took was accompanied by a constant slap of water on the rocks below. Rotten smells from dead seaweed made it hard to breathe. The wood shifted slightly below our feet as the pier poles groaned, slightly swaying with the tide. Floating junk kept thunking and bumping against the poles and made crashing noised on the rocks below.

"We had just made our turn under the shack and were starting back down the dock when a weird noise gave us the creeps. Looking around, we realized the eerie sounds were coming from the rafters in the blackness above us and sent chills down our backs!

"Abruptly, I heard scuffling noises right over my head. Chauncey and I held our guns at the ready, searching the shadows as we tried to find the culprit making the sounds. Suddenly, something dropped onto my shoulder! I let out a startled curse! Whatever it was leaped to the dock at my feet. I thought it was a cat. But *no,* it was a huge rat the size of a cat screeching and scurrying across the pier. Then out of the shadows leaped a feral cat as big as most dogs, screaming and hissing wildly as it chased the rat. I had to force myself to relax and take my finger off the trigger of my rifle.

"I swear I was shaking like dried leaves in a tree. Then Chauncey and I started laughing at the same time. Personally, I always thought Chauncey was exaggerating when he told his rat stories. But now, I can guarantee you that the incident with my rat made a believer out of me!"

With that last statement, Andy walked back over to his bunk, picked up his polished shoes, and stowed them in his locker, thinking, *Chauncey's nightmare stories of rats terrorizing the docks certainly keep the new guys from even thinking of walking alone on the wharfs at night. We make a great team—he's the opener, and I'm the closer.*

Chauncey lay down on his bunk with his fingers folded behind his head, thinking, *I really admire Andy's ability to make a listener feel like they're right there with him in the moment when his story is happening. By the look of our audience, Andy has succeeded once again, masterfully scaring the bejeezus out of the greenies listening.*

WWII historical photograph, Brooklyn Navy Yard, New York

Seasoned Veterans

The older guys considered Marine Devil Dogs, who had been in the barracks much longer than Chauncey and Andy, smiled as they watched the pups, remembering when they had been both the pups doing the teasing and the greenie who shuffled nervously back to his bunk. They had heard it all before many times and took their turn on both ends of that stick.

These days, the Devil Dogs were more interested in listening to the dame on the radio singing about taking a sentimental journey home. What a voice and what a doll! That beautiful bombshell was Doris Day. She was every guy's idea of a dream girl living next door and much more interesting to listen to. Gee whiz, when she started singing about taking a sentimental journey, it made every guy in the barracks wish he were on that journey with her!

Most of the older guys could care less about the younger guys pulling a few jokes on the greenies unless one of the greenies started a ruckus. Most of the platoon was willing to let them have their fun. The funniest part about the pup's story was that it had happened exactly like the kid said it did. It was true—all of it—and that made it OK in their book. The situation worked out for everyone. The tales were basically harmless and tended to make greenies stick together, being too jumpy to walk around alone. That fact managed to keep most of them out of the barracks. As a result, the older guys had more noiseless free time to listen to beautiful dames on the radio, rather than being forced to listen to mindless puppies yapping.

Duty and Down Time

Andy enjoyed writing letters to his baby brother, Pete, and then Betty about some of the wild things he had seen in the city with Tommy and Chauncey. When he wrote about his bravery with the rat and the cat, the rendition he told his brother Pete was a little more dramatic. But in his letter to Betty, he wrote the story accurately but finished that story quite differently than he had with the guys in the barracks.

"Betty, my heart was in my mouth. I'm amazed I didn't squeeze off a round from my rifle when that huge thing jumped on my shoulder."

Unlike his little brother Pete who idolized his older brother and enjoyed a good scary story, Betty was not impressed, making her sentiments perfectly clear in her return letter. *"Andy, I hate rats and have no desire to meet one of those rats, so you can bet I won't be visiting you in those shipyards!"* Betty seemed fearless to him on so many levels. Her return comments surprised him and gave him insight into her personality that he would not forget.

Brooklyn Navy Yard, Mail Call, Letter from Charlie

Dear Andy,   April 1944

Thanks for your letters. Dad wrote that he saw you and the guys before you shipped out to your base in Brooklyn. Sorry I upset everyone. I had to go, and I hope we can let it go at that. Just like you, I'm doing exactly what I always dreamed of doing.

Talk about dreams. I met some girls that blew my doors off!

Members of the Women's Air Force Service Pilots (WASPs)

Have you heard of the WASPs? They are the Women Air Force Service Pilots. Not only do they ferry the planes to us from the factories across the states. You know the planes I help fly to Alaska. These dolls also do the test flights on nearly every type of new aircraft!

I met some of them in the hanger at Fairchild AFB in Spokane last month. We were picking up a new B25, and that's when I heard Gardner and her team flew in five new B29 long range bombers from Harlingen AAF in Texas. Now, that's a crew I'd like to be assigned to. Captain says the service has more than 1,000 women pilots. Gardner's a real looker, too, even better than the dames I've seen painted on the nose of our fighters.

Yeah, I know. I can hear exactly what you are thinking! Dream on, Charlie! But after seeing her, you'd be dreaming too! OK, that's all for now. Headed off to LADD in the morning.

Women's Air Force Service
Pilots' Badge

Be safe brother.
I miss you.
Charlie

Elizabeth L. Remba Gardner,
Women's Air Force Service
Pilots

New York Naval Base

The Naval Yard in Brooklyn hosted troops from every branch of military service since the war began. For this reason, Andy and Chauncey met guys from all over the country. Andy and Chauncey were fortunate to be serving together. Most guys didn't know anyone in the barracks from their own hometowns.

In high school, Andy and his two buddies, George Pierce and Chauncey Crocker, had been inseparable. It finally took their military choices to split them up. Andy felt bad that he had lost track of George. George got his early enlistment for the Army Air Corps nearly the same time as he got his papers for the Marines. *Maybe*

Mom could call the Crockers and get his address, he thought. *It would be nice to hook up with him again.*

Base Post Office

Nebraska statehood made with a friendship banner, GKM

One early afternoon in April, Andy and Chauncey were just outside the base post office when they found themselves standing toe-to-toe and staring at the chest of a gigantic, trim, curly-headed blonde Airman.

More imposing than the man's height was the insignia he wore on his uniform, indicating he was a United States Air Force officer.

Standing to attention, eyes staring straight ahead, hat brims covering their foreheads and tipped slightly down to shade their eyes, Andy and Chauncey assumed perfect military posture. Then they demonstrated the proper protocol regarding being in the presence of an officer. The young Marines kept a stern countenance in place and held their crisp salute, waiting for the officer to move on. But the shiny shoes on the ground in front of them did not move away. Slowly, the Marines let their eyes travel up to the face.

Feeling confused, they discovered that above the officer's chin was a grin, then their eyes jerked up to take in the whole face. Andy and Chauncey relaxed and broke into laughter.

What a remarkable moment to discover the face belonged to their lifelong friend, George Pierce. Though neither Chauncey nor Andy voiced their thoughts, they were identical—*Jeepers! George has changed!*

This childhood buddy now towered to such a phenomenal height even Andy at six-foot-two had to bend his neck back and look up into George's face. Andy couldn't help but wonder if George might have exceeded some Air Force height restriction. *He's mind-boggling,* Andy thought. *No one will ever describe George as short and tubby again, not like we did the summer when we turned 15!*

Breaking the stunned silence, George said, "Hey, you guys look great!"

"*Us?*" croaked Chauncey, gaping at his giant friend, "Holy cow! What has the Air Force been feeding you? Magic beans?" he quipped. "'Cause if that's the case, sign me up."

The airman smiled and replied, "I believe that would be a Jack that ate magic beans, not a George."

Insignia patch,
U.S. Navy

The guys all laughed at George's jest about the children's fairy tale. Knowing both his friends very well, Andy decided to interrupt their little competition. He didn't want Chauncey trying to best George with some other witticism, so he said, "George, I can't believe it! I was just thinking about you and was going to ask Mom to find out where you were. I can't believe you're stationed here at the same base with us. Do you have time for a couple of cold ones?"

Insignia patch,
U.S. Marines

George smiled at Andy and replied, "Unfortunately, I won't be staying on this base very long. But I'm free this afternoon. Let's go over to the officers' club."

Making a few hoity-toity faces all in good fun, the boys bowed as if to royalty and said, "Please, would the officer lead the way?" George laughed, motioning the guys to follow, then Andy and Chauncey fell in step beside him.

Insignia patch,
U.S. Air Force

Sharing a unique camaraderie, they spent the afternoon catching up on highlights of the last two years, what was going on at home, a bit about bootcamp, and Officer Candidate School. After George filled them in on his OCS training, Andy admitted he was a bit jealous. Then he explained he had been recommended but heard nothing else since.

"There is still plenty of time for that," George replied. "Trust me—you'll hear about OCS soon enough."

Andy took a few minutes to tell George about Charlie. George smiled as he listened, remembering the *Tailspin Tommy* clips had been his favorites too. He said he certainly understood why Charlie was so keen to join up. "He'll be OK, Andy," George assured his friend. "You can tell your folks that being sixteen will restrict Charlie from being sent to the front lines."

"I've got a question for you," Chauncey said. "Exactly when did the Army Air Corps turn into the Air Force?" Andy was curious about the same subject and nodded his head at Chauncey's question.

"Actually, the organizational transition to make the Army Air Corps an independent branch of the United States Military began in 1941. The name unofficially changed from Army Air Corps to the Air Force. However, we are still part of the U.S. Army designation. Technically, we are called the AAF. Our Air Force and our AFHQ are still a subordinate Army combat command."

Andy crossed his eyes at the indecipherable answer, thinking, *No wonder he's an officer.* "Good golly, George! Can you give that to me again in English, please?"

Chuckling, George replied, "OK, our name has unofficially changed. We are recognized as the Air Command, rather than just part of the Army. But we are still part of the Army, and we all work for the same guy who lives in the White House."

Laughing at the short version, Andy replied, "OK, thanks. Now, everything you told us is as clear as mud! I think it's time for more beers. Then maybe it'll all make sense. Say, speaking of mud . . ."

Chauncey had been listening to George and Andy's exchange and piped in, saying, "Did you say muck? We definitely need more beers if we are going to talk about muck!"

Chauncey called it right. After several more beers, the band of friends enjoyed spurts of genuine laughter over a more comical memory of being stuck in the muck.

As the hour grew late, the fading light reminded the young men of their grownup responsibilities and the war. Despite a renewed appreciation of how special their boyhood bond had been, time for reminiscing fled with the setting sun. Their minds had always been in sync as boys, and now the three young military men stood up at the same time. It made them happy to know they had not lost their special connection.

Leaving the officers' club, the three uniformed men stopped and shared warm handshakes of farewell and a heartfelt acknowledgment of a friendship that would never fade with time. *Be safe and Godspeed* was the parting thought they shared, and with a final salute to a friend and officer, the Airman and Marines took separate paths through the darkness.

Waiting for Orders

Andy began taking night classes on base. Two nights a week, he took a writing class where he composed stories and wrote down ideas he could record and send to Betty. She had sent him a few records and sang him a song on one of them. Betty had a beautiful voice, and whenever he got out his record player recorder, all the guys wanted to take a turn recording a record.

On two other nights during the week, Andy studied military history and strategy. He hoped these classes would look good on his record and might help push through his acceptance into OCS.

At the moment, his instructor was going over the progress of the war starting in 1942. That was of particular interest to Andy. The South Pacific battle fronts was where Marines like Andy and Chauncey were being deployed, which was why he was happy to know more details about progress in the Pacific.

As Andy studied, he could see that things continued to go badly in the Pacific even after the battle of Midway. Japanese forces steamed nearly unimpeded south and north along the Asian

The WWII concern over a direct strike on America through Alaska—photo by GKM, WWII exposition

continental coastline and even became a strategic threat to Alaska. If they made landfall, the Japanese could bring in reinforcement troops. Then they could push south through the Yukon Territories, across the Canadian provinces, and down into the continental United States.

Canucks and Yanks Fly Wing Tip to Wing Tip Guarding Alaska's Shores
Canadians Have Already Slapped Down Japs at Continent's Back Door

Taken at a roadside WWII Alaska Highway Museum, Ft. Nelson, Canada, GKM 2018

That very real threat was answered two ways. First, the U.S. Army Corps of Engineers began building a military supply road from the continental United States all the way to Alaska in the winter of 1942, covering 1,600 miles. Meanwhile, the Japanese attacked two of the Alaskan Aleutian Islands in August of 1942 and held ground there for more than a year.

During that time, the Army Corps of Engineers completed the overland support road to Alaska in the spring of 1943. About the same time, America took back those Alaskan islands from the Japanese in May of 1943.

Near the end of the same year, the Allied forces began to make headway in the Pacific.

As Andy and Chauncey went through bootcamp at the beginning of 1944, the Allies took control of the Marshall and Mariana Island chains. At that time, the U.S. Army and Marines began construction on airfields that would be close enough for a direct strike on mainland Japan. Allied forces controlled a large portion of the southwestern Pacific, and by February of 1944, American Allies also made progress in the central Pacific.

After class, Andy met up with Chauncey at the Enlisted Men's Club for a beer. "Chauncey, tonight we were discussing what's been going on in the South Pacific theater. Our guys are building airfields in the Marshal Islands. That might be where the Corps will send us. Maybe we'll be helping build out those airfields for our long-range bombers that Charlie mentioned in his letter."

"I sure wish they'd make up their minds," Chauncey replied. "It's hard just sitting around waiting."

When Andy wasn't in class or standing guard duty or performing other assigned tasks, he wrote letters to his family in Nebraska, to Charlie in Alaska, and most of all to Betty.

Dear Betty,   *End of April 1944*

Gosh, I miss you. I want to know more about you and your family. I'd love to know everything that makes you so unique. Write pages and pages because I am interested in anything you want to tell me. I'm excited about the future. I want you in my future. I hope you want that too.

I've told you a lot about my family already. Well, at least about my brother Charlie, Mom, and Dad. You already know I have seven siblings and that they can be slightly overwhelming to people at first. But they are going to love you!

I cannot wait for you to attend a Karella clan gathering. That kind of gathering is always a HUGE event with at least 70 to 100 people in attendance. My family has scads of cousins, aunts, and uncles, and when we all get together, it's an event not to be missed!

I'm attending two night classes. Hopefully, it will help me get into OCS, and then you'll have an officer for a boyfriend. Pray for me. I hope to hear from you soon.

Yours always and affectionally,
Andy

Brooklyn Navy Yard, Christmas Eve, 1944

"Mail call!" the Marine shouted at the barracks door. "Better get over to the post office quick to pick up your packages. They close at 15:00 today." Andy grabbed his jacket, and Chauncey was right behind him. Standing in line at the post office had been worth it. Andy got a record and a package from Betty and another one from his mother addressed to both him and Chauncey.

He and Chauncey opened the one from Mom Karella first. Peanut butter cookies, homemade taffy, two wool neck scarves, and at the bottom was a second box.

They were amazed to discovered that box contained a beat-up version of one of his mother's amazing lemon pies. She had wrapped it in wax paper, then filled the box with popped corn to cushion the pie in the box. It barely survived. The crust had crumbled, and the pie filling was a little soupy, but they didn't care. Andy and Chauncey ate it with spoons, and the taste filled them with sweet homesickness. Since several guys in the barracks didn't have family to send them packages, Andy and Chauncey passed around the cookies and candy until it was all gone.

Andy took a walk and opened the package from Betty. Smiling, he thought, *Betty has a very practical side for being such a stylish girl.* She sent him a set of knit hunter's gloves. They covered the hand while the tips of each finger on the gloves were cut off. That way, his finger would be unencumbered if he needed to fire his rifle or use his fingertips without the rest of his hand being cold. Under the gloves was a photograph of her. And under the photo was a letter.

My Dear Andy,   *November 1944*

I hope this package gets to you by Christmas and that it helps you feel closer to us at home.

Thank you for the record you recorded for me about your time in Nebraska with Tommy. I know guys have a strange way of showing they like each other, so I hope Tommy forgave you and Chauncey for playing tricks on him. I must admit some of it was quite funny. I'll be looking forward to hearing about the tricks he plays on you when he shows you New York City.

It's been cold here over the holidays, and I am at home with Mom, Dad, and my brother Chuck.

Mom and I were going through some old photo albums. She pulled this picture out and gave it to me. It was taken during my first year in college. There is a special story I want to tell you about this smile you see me wearing. You will have to wait to hear it in person when you come home. But you did ask to hear everything about me, and the story about my smile is something I must share with you.

Betty Le Rossow (Bets),
freshman at NJC

In answer to your question, yes, I am imagining a future. I dream of you being part of that future. There is so much for us to talk about. I hope you and I will be able to see each other before you are deployed. It's good to hear you are taking classes. Congratulations on the OCS recommendation. If you get into OCS, does that mean you plan to stay in the Marines when the war is over? I hope not. I'd rather you came home as soon as you can. Your Christmas present to me was a lovely surprise. The musical Shall We Dance is a favorite of mine, and I will cherish it. You have given me the first album of my collection. Thank you very much for remembering what I said about music records.

I'll close for now, and I hope with all my heart you will be coming home soon.

Love,
Bets

Christmas Day, Norfolk, Nebraska, 1944

Christmas dinner had been wonderful. This year, Rusty cooked a beautiful turkey Delora's parents had brought to Norfolk from the Pojars' place in Madison. Rusty and Delora missed Andy and Charlie. But having Grandma and Grandpa Holt celebrate with them made it easier.

The Holts were never the homecooked holiday dinner type people. They celebrated by going out to eat. So, instead of individual presents, her parents treated the children to a movie. The motion picture they all saw was *Meet Me in St. Louis.* In the movie, Judy Garland sings "Have Yourself a Merry Little Christmas." At first, Delora thought it was going to be a sad story. Then family love and happiness in their old hometown won out over a promotion and making more money in a new town. She clapped when the movie was over just as enthusiastically as her children, especially Florence. The star of the film was a teenaged girl like herself. After the movie, Delora's mom and dad treated everyone to pie and ice cream at a café near the Old Grand Theater.

Rusty held Delora's hand as they walked behind the whole group and whispered, "Being out on Christmas makes me miss the boys less." Putting his arm around his wife, Rusty whispered next to her ear, "Bet the café's pie won't be as good as the ones you make, Bitty."

January 1945

The Karellas always celebrated two birthdays in January. The first was Millie's on January second, which was a Tuesday and a school night. Delora made her a nice birthday cake, Rusty brought home ice cream, and they celebrated Millie's ninth birthday after dinner.

Millie and Pete had been invited to spend the upcoming weekend with their grandpa and grandma Holt in Madison. While they were gone, Delora planned to do some baking. She wanted to send Charlie a box of his favorite cookies for his birthday on January 24th.

Rusty found Delora in the kitchen with her recipe box and baking tins. "Bitty, we got a letter from Charlie. He said he just received his Christmas package you sent."

Delora smiled with relief and replied, "Then I'd better get a move on. I need to ship these cookies tomorrow if I have any hope of getting them to Alaska by Charlie's birthday."

Newspaper Headlines—V-E Day, May 8,1945

"Bitty! Look at this!" cried Rusty as he ran into the room with the newspaper.

"Does this mean Andy and Charlie are coming home?" Delora asked.

Rusty shook his head but replied hopefully. "Not yet. This does not mean America's war with Japan is over. But Germany's surrender is a good sign."

NAZIS QUIT
V-E DAY OFFICIALLY TOMORROW

Victory over Europe—American news headlines

Military Bulletins, Radio and Newspapers

With Nazi Germany's surrender, all American military personnel would remain on standby. All troop movement would hold fast until further notice. Allied and European countries celebrated! Radio and newspapers delivered marvelous reports that America's men stationed in Europe were coming home. Grandparents, fathers, mothers, daughters, little brothers and sisters, and sweethearts all waited eagerly to hear word when their family members would make it home.

Good News

A letter filled with more good news arrived from Nebraska for Andy. His uncle Shorty was home from the war in Europe. Shorty and Mary also announced the arrival of their first child, whom they named Rosemary Lucille, born May 28, 1945.

This was a birthday Andy would never forget. It commemorated both the beginning of a new life and the end of the European war.

It's Not Over Yet

Regardless of the news reports, Andy knew Germany's surrender was only part of the solution. The war could not be considered over until the Japanese were defeated or the emperor of Japan surrendered. Since neither of those events had taken place yet, Andy still hoped he would be approved for OCS. Those hopes were dashed four months later.

Newspaper Headlines, VJ Day September 1945

On September 2, 1945, the Empire of Japan formally signed a declaration of surrender that brought an end to all battles of World War II.

Victory over Japan—American news headlines

VJ Day, Home of Rusty Karella

Rusty hugged Delora, dancing her around the room to the voice of Perry Como singing "'Till the End of Time."

"Now, we can celebrate, Bitty," he whispered in her ear. "Our sons will come home. We are so blessed!" Happy tears ran down both their faces.

That night, Delora snuggled up to Rusty and said, "We have a wonderful future ahead of us! I am so excited about being a nurse and having our family around us. This is going to be the best summer ever."

Delora fell silent and slept on his shoulder. Rusty's head was filled with faith-filled thanks: *Dearest Lord, thank You. You gave me such wonderful parents and grandparents. You helped them achieve their dreams here in Nebraska.*

You gave me Delora and my children. You gave me the talent and the teachers in my life that helped me guard and provide for my family through the bad years of drought and economic depression. Even losing the farm and Papa, You were there to cushion the blows. You help me see new opportunity even in the face of that hardship.

You've helped me, Bitty, and our children to grow strong and prosper here in Norfolk.

Thank you for sparing my sons and my brother from the horror of death in war and keeping them from suffering on the battlefield. I am humbly grateful for Thy endless mercy. We give thanks that these wars have ended, and now I pray You will help heal the world. Amen.

Holding his sleeping wife gently, Rusty sent loving thoughts of thanks to heaven. *Mama and Papa, America was the land of dreams and promise for you and our grandparents. Because of you, we are part of a family born in the land of promise. Thank you for your courage and vision.*

Closing his eyes, Rusty began to dream about a future free of worry. *Bitty is right*, he thought. *We have so much to look forward to. Our country is safe again. After years of worry, our American Dream for our children—of being safe and being free to pursue whatever they want in life—is coming true.*

CHAPTER 29

Everyone Dreams of the Future

Time to Muster Out or Re-Enlist

Dear Betty,   *September 1945*

*How are you? I hope you have got all the classes you wanted for this year.
I wish I were there.*

*At least I know I will be coming back. Now that total victory has been
secured, every branch of the United States Military will initiate a sys-
tematic discharge spanning the next couple of years. The newer soldiers
like Chauncey and me will be discharged after the guys who've seen
active duty, meaning it might take a while for our names to come up
on the roster. Then we have the option of mustering out early, and both
Chauncey and I plan to accept an honorable discharge from the Corps
once we make the list.*

*Considering we signed up to serve for at least five years with the Marines,
we are thrilled with the news that we could be discharged after serving*

*approximately two years at the Brooklyn Navy Yard. My CO believes
we could be home for good by December of 1946.*

I'll keep you posted of any changes I hear.

*You fill my thoughts, Betty, and I can't wait to see you again.
Andy*

Andy wrote his parents telling them he might be home in a year,
possibly even by Christmas of 1946. They wrote back telling
him how happy they were to hear he had decided to come home.
Charlie had been offered an early discharge exactly like Andy's, but
according to his folks, his brother opted to re-enlist.

As Andy read the part in the letter about Charlie, the radio
started playing an Andrews Sisters tune called "Rumors Are Flying."
Well, Charlie's love of flying was never just a rumor, Andy thought.
*It had been pure fact. This news did not come as a surprise. I figured
Charlie would do something like this. Every letter I received from him
had been filled with plans for his future in the Air Corps. It wasn't the
war that made him join up in the first place. He wanted to fly, and
that motivation hasn't changed. I'm sure Charlie has not done enough
flying yet to feel satisfied.*

News from Norfolk, Nebraska

Andy's dad wrote often. In his latest letter, Andy learned that with
the end of the war, the rationing boards were disbanded, and his
mom's job with the OPA ended as well. His dad said the timing
could not have been better. His mom had attained her first nursing
certificate, finishing in the top of her class. The hospital offered her
a full-time position, and she happily accepted. She was also taking
night courses two evenings per week to increase her nursing quali-
fications. Apparently, the additional schooling made her eligible for
increased responsibilities on the wards, in the emergency room, and
in labor and delivery.

Andy could see his mother thrived in her new career and loved learning anything that made her a better nurse. She had always taken great pride in her family and husband's accomplishments. Now, she could feel happy about her own professional accomplishments too. It was easy to tell his dad was delighted for her. His mom had been so strong as a mother and wife over the years. It was amazing that she found a new career that was personally fulfilling and still benefited the family. Andy could see her new accomplishments had made everyone very proud.

Dear Andy,   *October 1945*

I thanked God regularly for giving me such an amazing wife, partner, and mother. Your mom's full-time wage from the hospital more than compensates for the loss of the OPA income and free groceries. I still work at the plumbing company and take in small mechanical repairs on radios, cameras, home appliances, and such to augment our steady income. I'm enjoying tinkering in my shop too. Though money is more plentiful since the war ended, people who lived through the tuff years still preferred to fix and repair what they own. They don't like to buy new unless they are forced to. That attitude is good for my shop. Well, son, that's all for now.

Hope to hear from you soon,
Love,
Dad

Summer of 1945

Andy had a lot of thinking to do now that world events had changed so drastically. In his mind, his military life was over, though technically it looked like it would be at least a year or more before he and Chauncey would be discharged. Andy had been unaware of how the war had created a constant shadow of anxiety and menace in his mind. That apprehension and insecurity kept him from placing too much hope in the future. Until he met Betty, he didn't think very far ahead at all. He let his friends and the Marines fill his entire existence. Andy accepted that dark shadow in his thoughts as part of the reality of becoming a Marine. Betty had been the key who unlocked his ability to dream even a little about the possibilities of a future if he made it through the war.

On V-E Day, a feeling of lightness began to spread through Andy's mind. On V-J Day, his world changed overnight as his mind exploded with a million possibilities. Andy's imagination soared, changing his view of the world from a limited depth of a black-and-white movie to a blazing Technicolor feature event with unlimited prospects. He didn't want to settle down; he wanted to travel and see new places. Andy found himself exhilarated and ready to see the promise of surprise around every corner, and he wanted to see the world and live life as an adventure with Betty.

Trip to Chicago

After receiving letters from Andy talking about the extra time he had while waiting to become eligible for discharge, Rusty thought Andy might like to do a little family research.

Dear Andy   *July 1945*

I thought you might be interested in looking up some of the Chicago Karellas. Your uncle Emil John was married in Cook County in Chicago to a woman whose first name was Bohumila. She was part of the Chicago Bohemian Karella clan. Her family is distantly related to ours, and both families always called her Emily.

Their people came to America about 100 years before ours did. I'm only suggesting that you go to Chicago and see if you can find any of her family that might still be there because you are so close. It would be a short train ride to make on one of those three-day passes you are always talking about.

Thought it might be something interesting for you to do.

I'm proud of you, son,
Love,
Dad

Three-Day Pass to Chicago, Illinois

Dear Dad,   *August 1945*

Chauncey and I took your advice and went to Chicago. We traveled around the city on the elevated train system they call the "L." Our first stop was the oldest graveyard in the area. In St. John's Cemetery, we found a headstone for Private Frank Karella of Company B 5th regiment in World War I. He was born in 1896 and died only a year ago in 1944, according to the headstone.

After finding the grave, we rode the L to the Cook County area and got off on the south side of Chicago. As we walked through a neighborhood, I heard a woman start singing a song from the 1935 musical Porgy and Bess. I looked up, and she was leaning on her open windowsill singing "Summertime and the Living Is Easy." Then another woman in the brownstone across the same alley sang the second line to the song. "Fish are jumping, and the cotton is high." Then people from different windows joined them, so I started singing along too. When it was done, they smiled and waved at us down on the street. It felt just like I walked into a Broadway musical in real life.

As we walked by shops along the street, people said hello to us. A group of old men were sitting on stools outside a barber shop, and we stopped to ask for directions. They complimented me on my voice and then asked what we were doing in their neighborhood. I said looking for some distant relatives that had lived in Cook County and asked for directions to Taylor Street. They pointed us in the right direction and told us to keep walking about eight blocks.

When we got to Taylor Street, we saw a bunch of guys standing on a street corner, and we asked if they knew anyone by the name of Karella. We were shocked when they grabbed Chauncey and I. I thought we were in for it. "What are the Karellas to you?" the leader asked. I told him I was just looking for distant relatives that might have lived in the area. He replied, "Well, forget about it! We are going to take you back to the L, and you'd better get on with no questions. The only reason we don't beat you unconscious is because of those uniforms." Dad . . . we got on the L and didn't look back. Crazy, right?

Elevated Train system in Chicago, Illinois, 1945, also called the "L"

Love always,
Andy

October 1945, Waiting through the Winter

Andy realized he had to think about what he was going to do for money when he mustered out of the Marine Corps. Maybe he could be a freelance writer for a newspaper or magazine. Writing fulfilled Andy, and he decided to continue taking a nighttime writer's class. His college courses would not only look good on an application if a writing job presented itself, but they were making him a better writer too.

When he thought about it, what he really wanted to do was travel and not be tied down to one idea yet. That was why freelance writing felt like it would be a good fit for him. What Andy really wanted to do was talk to Betty. He wondered if she would consider making a trip to New York, or maybe he could get some leave and meet her somewhere. Andy wrote to Betty and asked her about making a trip.

New Year's in Time Square, 1946

New Year's Eve Time Square in New York City, 1945, crowds and lights

New Year's Eve Time Square in New York City, 1945, lights-2

Tommy came running into the barracks and shouted, "Hey, you guys! Let's go to town for New Year's Eve. You've got to bring in the new year in Times Square at least once in your life. It's like nothing you've ever experienced."

Chauncey and Andy were both up for it and nodded with enthusiasm, and Tommy talked about the history of the street party as they were changing their clothes.

"I think my folks attended the first Time Square celebration back in 1904. But the one they really remember was the following year because of Adolph Ochs, the guy who owned *The New York Times* newspaper. He decided to add fireworks to celebrate the opening of his new headquarters at One Times Square and shot them off from the roof of his new building at midnight on New Year's Eve. Boys, we've got to hurry if we are going to get anywhere near the square cause it's going to be jammed!"

Dear Betty,   *January 1946*

Jeez, it's been busy here. I wanted to tell you that Chauncey, Tommy, and I went to Times Square for New Year's Eve. I have never been packed in a mob like that. I saw every branch of military uniform in the crowd, and it looked like the entire base was there. The whole street and square was one huge party. All the hotels had music and dancing going on, and there was even an ice-skating performance on a miniature ice rink. Oh my gosh, you can't believe the lights! You've never seen so many bright lights on one street. I sure wish you had been with us. I didn't have anyone to kiss at midnight. It took us quite a while to work our way out of that crowd, but we got back to base sober and in time to stand night watch at 02:00.

All of us from our barracks still stand watches and take care of our normal tasks. But now in addition, we do temporary jobs all over base each week to fill in for guys that are mustering out and going home.

Chauncey and I generally get weekends free, and occasionally, we can arrange for a three-day pass. Tommy has been a swell tour guide around New York City. Chauncy, Tommy, and I have been to the top of the Empire State Building and looked through the telescopes. We've also walked up the stairs to the head of the Statue of Liberty. This weekend, we are going to Coney Island here in Brooklyn.

I've been thinking, now that we know I won't be shipping out and we have time to kill, do you think there is a possibility you would come to New York for a weekend? Tommy Gervase's folks said you would be welcome to stay with them if you got a chance to come to New York. I thought that since you are on holiday break from school, it might be fun, or maybe you could come this summer when school is out.

If there is a chance you would come, I could get tickets to one of two Broadway musicals playing right now: Annie Get Your Gun or Show Boat, or I could get tickets to both shows. If you said you could come, I could get a three-day pass so we could see those musicals and maybe go to Atlantic City to see that famous boardwalk. Or we could do some sightseeing here in Brooklyn. Please let me know. I hope you will say yes. It would be great fun.

I'd love to see you,
With all my heart,
Andy

Dear Andy,   *February 15, 1946*

I must say your invitation is very tempting. There is a possibility I could come over spring break. I was planning to get a summer job, but maybe I could do that and come out for a couple of days to see you too. Tell you what: see if you can get one of those three-day passes for next month. Maybe I could come out to see you for my birthday on Sunday May fifth. See what you can get around that time, and I'll see what I can do.

If I can arrange to come, I think I would like to see both of those Broadway shows and sightsee around New York with you. I'd love to see Coney Island too. How exciting that would be! But promise we will stay far away from the docks with the rats!

Love,
Betty

Fantasizing about a Journey

The more Betty thought about going to see Andy, the more captivating the idea became. Betty couldn't believe she'd have the chance to see two of the hottest musicals playing on Broadway!

Writing 101 and Music and Choir had been the two classes she and Andy had shared in college. That was when they had discovered their voices matched perfectly in duet. Music was one of the deepest connections they shared. She suddenly shivered with excitement. The thought of sightseeing in New York City with Andy . . . the idea was almost too thrilling to take in.

Betty didn't even wait for Andy's return letter before she started getting her assignments early from her professors. She wanted at least three days off from school plus the weekend for the trip. For her wardrobe, she selected her wool coat, hat, gloves, neck scarves, three outfits she could mix and match for evenings, and two sets of casual clothing for sightseeing. Now, all she needed was to hear from Andy so she could buy her train tickets.

Betty was too excited to sleep and sat up late writing to Andy, telling him she would come. She had two

Andy's map of New York and the Navy Yard and the sights he wanted to show Betty—GKM 2021

days for traveling. It would be a 34-hour train trip, and for her birthday, her parents paid for a sleeping car. She would leave on the noon train on Wednesday out of Omaha and get into New York on Friday in the late afternoon. That would give her three days to spend with him in New York, and she would leave on the late-night train out of New York on Sunday May fifth.

Andy's heart thumped so loudly as he read Betty's letter that he thought Chauncey could hear it laying in the bunk next to his. He put the letter down on his chest, closed his eyes, breathed slowly, and thought, *Betty is really going to come! She'll arrive at Grand Central Station in New York on May second and leave the night of May fifth.*

I'll take her to the Statue of Liberty, the Empire State Building, and Coney Island on Friday and eat out as we make our way around the city. Saturday, we could have an early dinner with Tommy, Chauncey, and the Gervases. Then we could see Annie Get Your Gun. *On her birthday during the day, I could take her for a buggy ride around Central Park, then take her to tea at the Plaza Hotel. Then we could take a walk down 42ⁿᵈ Street and Broadway and find the theaters we'll be going to and see the three o'clock performance of* Show Boat. *Afterward, we could get supper in China Town.* Plans were whizzing around in his head.

My CO already said I could have the three-day pass if my girl came to town, so everything is set. I'll go buy the tickets for the shows as soon as I can and make a tea reservation for Sunday, May fifth. Maybe we will do some kind of cake for her birthday. It can't hurt to ask. It's going to be so hard to wait.

Elegant Train Travel

Betty Le, dressed to go to New York to see Andy in 1946

Betty tried out her sleeping car as soon as the train pulled out of the Omaha station and slept soundly and comfortably. Sitting at breakfast, she couldn't help but think of every movie or song she knew that involved a train ride. She kept seeing flashes from the comedy *Sleeping Car* or *The Palm Beach Express.* Betty spent the rest of her morning trying to study, then gave up, too fascinated with watching the scenery change.

In the dining car, they had the music of Glenn Miller lilting softly in the background while she ate a delightful lunch. The wait staff made her feel like a princess. After lunch, she returned to the day car but never opened her books. Staring out the windows daydreaming, she hummed the peppy tune "Chattanooga Choo-Choo."

Betty pulled Andy's letter out of her handbag, and after rereading it, Betty decided to get to bed early. Apparently, she was going to be a very busy girl for the next few days. She certainly wanted to look her best when Andy picked her up at Grand Central Station in New York.

With that in mind, she made her way to dinner in the dining car early and sat with an elderly couple on their way home to New York. When she mentioned she would be seeing two Broadway musicals, they told her all about the Metropolitan Opera.

By the time Betty made her way to her sleeping compartment, she was so excited about everything she had learned she didn't think she would fall asleep, but she did.

Grand Central Train Station, New York City

Thursday evening, Andy's hopes and dreams were colliding. He could hardly keep his feet on the ground, feeling like a shooting star as he waited at Grand Central Station for Betty's train.

When she stepped onto the platform, the sight of her made his heart pound with excitement. She looked slim, elegant, and sophisticated in her long leather gloves, suit dress, hat, and heels. He thought, *Wow, she looks like a New Yorker!* He waved and caught her eye, then hurried over to help her put on her overcoat. As he turned Betty around, he still had his hands on her arms. When she looked into his eyes and leaned toward him, he kissed her sweetly on the lips and whispered, "Betty, you are a vision from heaven; you took my breath away when you stepped off that train."

Betty's heart started fluttering with his sincere compliment, but she kept her emotions composed and replied, "You look very dashing yourself in that uniform. I am happy to see you."

Andy took hold of her hand, and with the other, he picked up her suitcase, saying, "We'll catch a taxi over to the Gervase's and get you settled. Then I can tell you about all the things I have planned for us to do."

Tommy refused to let Andy use a taxi to go sightseeing. Instead, he borrowed his dad's car, and he and Chauncey played chauffeur. Tommy convinced Andy that it was the best plan, or he would waste most of his three days with Betty being lost and missing out on all the fun. Besides that, Tommy and Chauncey were almost as excited about Betty coming to visit as Andy.

Friday in New York City

Friday, three sharp-looking Marines arrived to have breakfast with Betty and the Gervases. After breakfast, the four of them drove over the Brooklyn Bridge, and their first stop gave them an incredible view of the Statue of Liberty standing on Liberty Island. Betty hopped out of the car to take pictures. Next stop was the Empire State Building where Tommy and Chauncey dropped Andy and Betty off and said they'd meet them in the lobby in an hour.

Coney Island, New York, carousel from 1876—exotic animals, Public Domain

Betty and Andy went straight up to the observation deck to get a bird's-eye view of the city. Their next stop was 42nd Street and Broadway. The four of them walked along the street looking at theater marquees advertising shows playing or coming soon. After finding the two theaters and shows Andy and Betty were going to see, Betty asked if anyone was hungry.

Starving was the way Tommy put it but suggested they wait to eat until they got to Coney Island Amusement Park. There would be a wide variety of food to choose from, and they could spend the rest of the day at the park.

At Coney Island, they found what Tommy called real New York Italian pizza. The pizzas were huge, thick-crusted, and scrumptious. By the time the pizza pans were empty, they felt happily stuffed and ready to split up and wander around the amusement midway. The four of them would meet up at the park entrance at 8:00 p.m.

The first thing Betty wanted to do was ride the Cyclone roller coaster. After getting rattled and windblown on the roller coaster, Betty made Andy laugh when she wanted to ride a camel on the historic carousel. Everything seemed so exciting as they strolled along holding hands and watching smiling people having fun.

It felt natural to talk about how things had changed for them since the war ended. They chatted about things they'd like to do after she finished school and he got out of the Marines.

As the sun began to set in the sky, they chose to ride the Ferris wheel to watch the sun go down and the lights come up on the midway. With all the colorful lights, the park took on a magical atmosphere that made it all the more exciting.

Once the sun set, the sea breeze turned chilly, but the two Nebraska kids were dressed for the cool weather. Walking arm in arm, they enjoyed playing the carnival games.

Coney Island, New York, picture booth—1946; Betty Rossow visits Andy while he was stationed at Brooklyn Navy Yard

Coney Island, New York, picture booth—1946; Andy Karella while he was stationed at Brooklyn Navy Yard

On the way back toward the gate, Andy and Betty found a photobooth. Betty put on Andy's dress Marine Corps hat and stepped into the booth and captured the moment. Andy also carried his soft crusher cap in the epilate of his uniform and put it on to get a picture of himself at the same time. Betty and Andy exchanged photographs, and he said, "Betty, I'll always keep it with me."

At 7:00 p.m., they found a warm eatery where they had tea and coffee before they went to meet up with the guys and head home.

Saturday in New York City

Everyone woke up a little late on Saturday. They all met up at the Gervases' home, where they would have a homemade Italian dinner. Betty told Andy she wanted to go and have a look at the Metropolitan Opera house and Rockefeller Center before lunch. As the couple left, they promised to return by 3:00 p.m. and help prepare dinner.

The Gervases enjoyed Betty's company and told her more than once that they would enjoy hosting an early Saturday dinner for Tommy and his friends. Mrs. Gervase served a delicious dinner at 5:30.

At 6:15, Andy and Betty took a taxi to the Imperial Theatre for the 7:30 performance of *Annie Get Your Gun*. Betty loved Ethel Merman in the role of Annie Oakley and the way she sang "Doin' What Comes Natur'lly" and "You Can't Get a Man with a Gun."

Ray Middleton was cast in the role of Frank Butler. Andy thought the two love song duets between Annie and Frank, "They Say It's Wonderful Falling in Love" and "The Girl That I Marry," were outstanding and made him think of the way he and Betty sounded together singing a duet.

Having thoroughly enjoyed the show, during the curtain call, the two of them jumped to their feet, giving the performers a standing ovation. As Andy and Betty left the theater, they hummed and sang the tune "There's No Business Like Showbusiness" as they walked down 42nd Street. They held hands, feeling giddy under all the bright lights, and were filled with the sensation of being swept away in the moment.

Sunday, Betty's Birthday, New York City

On Sunday morning, Tommy, Chauncey, Andy, and Betty went to St. Patrick's Cathedral for 9:00 a.m. Mass. Afterward, the boys dropped Andy and Betty off in front of Central Park, and Andy took Betty on a long horse and carriage ride through and around the park.

When they finished their buggy tour, they walked to the tearoom at the famous Plaza Hotel located at 5th and Central Park. After drinking tea and eating birthday cupcakes, they finished up in time to catch a taxi to the Ziegfeld Theater for the matinee performance of *Show Boat*. The tune that captured Betty's heart was "Can't Help Lovin' Dat Man of Mine," while Andy's was "Old Man River."

Tommy and Chauncey met them when the show let out. The four of them drove over to the Gervases so Betty could pick up her suitcase and say goodbye to Tommy's folks. Then they all went to China Town to look around and get some dinner together. At 9:00 p.m., they drove Betty back to Grand Central Station. Tommy and Chauncey said goodbye to her at the car and told Andy they'd wait for him.

Andy walked Betty to the platform and waited until the whistle signaled the boarding process. Andy held Betty in his arms and whispered, "I've had a wonderful time with you. I'm going to miss you so much. Thank you for coming."

Betty smiled up at him and whispered in reply, "Thank you. My birthday weekend was spectacularly fun and unforgettable, just like you. I will miss you, too, and will count the days until you can come home and we can spend as much time together as we want to."

They shared a long, sweet kiss that promised warmth and magic in their future together, and then Betty boarded her train, turned to blow him a kiss, and then she was gone.

Brooklyn Naval Base

It had been a fairytale weekend for Andy, and it took him a while to come down to earth. He performed his tasks and duties around the base, stood watches, and took classes automatically, all the while his mind had been set free to dream about the future. He could not wait to get back home to Nebraska and Betty.

Brooklyn Naval Yard, Letter from Charlie

```
Dear Andy                          May 1946

I am loving Alaska! I'm fascinated with the paradox
between our organized military bases, which are islands
of modern conveniences, and the rustic environments
of the communities we visit and fly to.

When we leave LADD, we feel like we've stepped back
in time to the Alaskan gold rush days. I mean all the
way back to the wilderness of the 1800s. Oddly, even
the rustic living conditions don't scare me off. It's
hard to tell which I love most, flying or discovering
all there is up here in Alaska.

Did you know Alaska was purchased from Russia? It
became a United States territory in 1867. Now, it is
totally overseen by the military. We fly patrols along
the whole coastline, and we have air strips in several
villages that we visit regularly.

Have you ever heard of mukluks? The local people wear
them for boots . . .
```

Setting down Charlie's letter, Andy smiled and thought, *If his history teachers in high school could only see Charlie now, they would be amazed. They could hardly get him to open his geography book. Now, it seems even the early history of this arctic paradise has captured Charlie's imagination.* Andy noted that every one of his letters contained a little history, or else they overflowed with information about his job ferrying aircraft, meeting Russian pilots, laying over in Indian and Eskimo villages, or flying missions over the Bering Strait and the Aleutian Chain.

Charlie didn't have to say he planned to go back to Alaska when he mustered out of the service. Andy could read that between the lines easy enough. Charlie's enthusiasm and fascination for the place leaped off the pages. Andy was beginning to think it was a place he and Betty would like too.

Brookland Naval Base: Letter from Charlie

Dear Andy,   Alaska, 8-20-1946

I hear you are about ready to muster out and head home. Dad's letter sounded good, though I think I disappointed him again. I had to do what I felt was right for me, so I re-enlisted. When you get home, please try and help him understand. This is what I want to do!

I do have two things I hope you will help me with. First, I have been granted leave to come home for Christmas. I would like your help to surprise every-one. Will you pick me up at the bus station?

Secondly, I have an import-ant request to make of you, and I really mean this is important! Andy, you can't talk about anything I have written to you about my time here in Alaska.

US B25 Bombers, WWII

I'm going to hold you to that promise because I want to tell you something. I have not only been flying patrols over the Aleutian Chain in Alaska. I have also flown a few top-secret missions over Japan. On one of those flights, I was wounded. I'll have a war souvenir for the rest of my life because I got a little shrap-nel injury to the head . . .

At the words shrapnel injury, Andy sped through the last few lines of the letter and found no further explanation. Charlie didn't say another word about the injury or how he was—nothing! Andy slammed the letter down on the table and shook his head in frustration. He immediately pulled out writing paper and began a letter to his stupid brother!

Letter to Charlie, Ladd Airfield, Alaska

For heaven's sake, Charlie!   *Brooklyn Naval Yard September 1946*

Above: Charlie Karella, 17, Army Air Corps. Ladd Field, Alaska, in front of earth mover tire
Below: Ladd Air Base sign outside Fairbanks, Alaska

What on earth are you doing up there? You can't just drop a bomb on me like that and not explain! News flash: I got shrapnel in my head! You just left me hanging! Good God, brother, explain yourself! I'm worried sick about you! And I'm warning you if I don't get an explanation within the next couple of weeks, I'm going to tell Mom and Dad that you were injured! So, write to me! I need to know you are OK, brother!

P.S. I promise to pick you up at the bus station. Send me your travel plans.

Your very concerned brother,
Love,
Andy

Andy's threat worked! The next letter from Charlie arrived so quickly that his brother must have written his reply and sent it immediately after reading the letter he got from Andy.

In this new letter, Charlie begged Andy not to tell their parents anything. As far as his explanation went, it lacked details, but Charlie confirmed none of his crew had been killed. They had returned to base safely, and he was all healed up and doing fine. No one would ever be able to tell anything had happened to him if Andy kept his mouth shut about what he knew. Then he ended the letter saying he'd arrive in Norfolk December 22nd on the 3:00 p.m. bus.

Brooklyn Navy Yard, November 1946

Dear Betty,   *November 1946*

I am relieved to tell you Chauncey and I made the roster. The final schedule was posted mid-November. HQ stipulates if discharge papers have not arrived to get us home by Christmas, they guarantee we will be home by New Years, January 1947.

I'll send word to you as soon as our discharge papers arrive. Say a little prayer for me that I can make it home to you for Christmas.

Love,
Andy

Betty had been signing her letters with love since she visited him in Brooklyn. Feeling positive that he'd be home for Christmas, he couldn't wait to see her again! The future was so exciting to think about.

Andy needed to get a job right away so he could afford a place of his own. In the meantime, maybe he could bunk at Chauncey's, or maybe his parents would let him stay for a bit. Rent and date money would be his priority once he got back to Norfolk. Excited and unable to sleep, Andy stayed up late scrawling pages full of his thoughts. He closed his latest letter by writing:

Betty,

My days in the Marine Corps are done and unimportant to me now. You are my future, and I am happy that I can finally promise you that I will be at your NJC graduation in the spring of 1948. Once I am home, we can start planning out our dreams together.

Love Always,
Andy

Norfolk, Karella Home Holidays of 1946

Christmas tree at Karella home on Lincoln Street 1946—box of stringed outdoor Christmas lights

Thanksgiving weekend, the family went to Madison to visit. Rusty and the kids and their cousins went scouting for Christmas trees in the old Karella farm forest and marked them with red flags. While they were out tromping around in the cold, Delora visited with her folks and with Rusty's sisters, Helen, Martha, and Mary. After a lovely late lunch, Delora and her family headed back to Norfolk. Rusty and the kids would go back and cut down their tree the second week of December.

This was going to be a very special Christmas, and Delora wanted everything to be as pretty and festive as possible. It would be the first time in two years her son would be home. She talked Rusty into using a little extra money to buy outside Christmas lights. He put them up on the house on Sunday December first after coming home from church. She went out after dark to look at them.

It wasn't a very practical use of their money, but they made her feel wonderful just looking at the merry colors. Delora had to admit she was going a bit overboard planning and preparing for Christmas. She couldn't help it, though. She wanted this to be the biggest, most special Christmas ever.

After that, Delora slowly began decorating the house until all that was left was to put up the tree and the evergreens and holly on the railing of the staircase and on the tables. On Saturday, December 14th, Rusty loaded up the kids, hooked up a small trailer, and drove to Madison to get their Christmas tree. He told the children they would keep it in water. That way, it would stay fresh just like he'd been taught to do by their grandpa Anton who learned to do the same by their great-grandpa Vaclav.

While Delora's family fetched the tree, she made a list of the baking she would do. With no more rationing, she could make anything she wanted. Her baking list was sizable because her Christmas Day guest list was extensive. She would need a lot of snacks, breads, and desserts. Her list included pies, cookies, rohlikys, and kolaches.

Delora's parents and the Beans, Pojars, and Vobornys were coming for dinner Christmas Day. She had invited all of them to come celebrate Andy's homecoming when they had been together for Thanksgiving, and everyone accepted. All her plans were falling into place. Just knowing her eldest son would be home soon filled her with excitement and joy.

Norfolk Bus Station

"Betty!" She turned quickly at the sound of Andy's voice.

There he is, she thought, *so handsome, tall, and lean in his uniform! He takes my breath away.*

Andy dropped his suitcase as she ran to him. He picked her up, wrapping her in a warm hug with her feet dangling in the air. Laughing with the joy of holding each other again, the rest of the world fell away. "I've missed you, Betty," he whispered in her ear.

As Andy set her down, Chauncey swept Betty into another enthusiastic hug, but this time, her feet stayed firmly on the ground.

When Chauncey released her, she shivered and said, "It's cold! Let's get in the car."

The temperature had fallen to -4 degrees. Betty borrowed her father's car, and she kept it running while she waited for the bus. Everyone appreciated the heat in the car as Betty pulled out of the parking lot headed for the Karella's home on Lincoln Street.

As she pulled up in front of the house, Andy said, "Gosh, will you look at those lights on the house? That's new, and it looks so cheery!" Andy leaned over to Betty and asked hopefully, "Are you sure you don't want to come in and be part of my surprise? You could meet my folks."

Betty shook her head and replied, "This is a surprise between you and your parents. After two years of being gone, I think this should be between you and them. I can meet them over New Year's."

Andy kissed her, softly saying, "That is sweet of you. Thank you. I'll call you tomorrow, OK? I want to set a time to meet your folks too." She nodded as they got out of the car. "Goodnight," they called and waved as Betty drove away. Then, laughing, feeling glad to be home, they walked up to the house on Sunday evening on the 15th of December.

Two young men in Marine dress uniforms opened the door without knocking and walked into the house on Lincoln Street at 6:30 p.m. Perry Como sang "Santa Claus Is Coming to Town" on the radio, and the young men caught everyone by complete surprise.

Rusty was up and out of his chair, grabbing his son in a bear hug before Andy could say a word. Then, as he hugged Chauncey, Andy's dad pointed toward the kitchen, knowing Andy was looking for his mom. He quietly made his way around the corner and walked up behind his mother and asked, "Hey, Mom, what's for dinner?"

Delora spun around and threw her arms around Andy, crying and laughing at the same time, saying, "Andy, I am so happy to see you, and I could throttle you two!" She hugged him exuberantly, then went on to say, "You are almost two weeks early, and now you've spoiled my big Christmas decoration surprise I've been planning for you."

Andy hugged her a little tighter, then released her, saying, "Thank you, Mom, for everything you are doing. It all looks wonderful! Tell you what . . . Chauncey and I will go over to his folks' place this week and catch up with them. Then you'll have a week to finish getting everything set, and I promise to act surprised when I see it all again."

With tinkling laughter, she replied, "I know I'm being silly over this." Then, looking around, she asked, "Now, where's my other boy? Chauncey! Where are you?" she called out just as the grinning rascal came into the kitchen and swept her into another warm hug.

Christmas Week at the Karella Home

Andy and Chauncey spent their first week in Norfolk dividing their time between the Crocker and Karella residences, but they bunked at the Crockers' home. Staying with Chauncey's parents made it easier for Andy to spend as much time as possible with Betty.

She happened to be deep into mid-year finals, which meant all Andy could do was meet her for lunch. Betty did allow him to help her study for a few hours in the evenings as well. It felt marvelous just being in each other's company. But they would have to wait until she was out of school for Christmas break to give each other some undivided attention and make any plans.

By December 22nd, Betty's finals were behind her, and the young couple decided it was time to introduce each other to their families. Betty asked Andy to meet her parents on Christmas Eve, then she would come and meet Andy's folks on New Year's Eve.

A Christmas Surprise

The day before Christmas, Chauncey borrowed his father's car, and he and Andy drove to the bus station. Sitting in the parking lot, they lit up cigarettes and waited. "So, how's everything going with Betty?" Chauncey asked.

Andy smiled just hearing her name and replied, "Chauncey, she's the one. I know it."

Chauncey smiled and replied, "You just figured that out? I've known it since she came to see you in New York. Are you going to marry her?"

He nodded his head slowly, then replied, "I am hoping to. But I don't think I can ask her yet. I haven't even met her parents, nor has she met mine. There is still so much to talk about before we can set those kinds of plans." Andy sighed, then added, "Honestly, Chauncey, I can't imagine a future without her."

The bus pulled into the station and distracted them from their conversation as Chauncey pointed and said, "There he is!" They got out of the car and waved.

The trim uniformed Airman waved back. Heaving his duffle to his shoulder, he walked toward Andy and Chauncey. The three men exchanged welcoming hugs, got into the car, and drove off toward Lincoln Street. "Got a smoke on you?" the Airman asked from the backseat. Andy handed him a cigarette and lit it for him. The car was filled with smoke on the short ride to the Karellas' place.

Chauncey parked out front around 4:00 p.m. The house sparkled and twinkled inside and out. The tree and decorations of ever-green bows and holly made a festive scent throughout the house. Bing Crosby's resonating voice was singing "I'm Dreaming of a White Christmas" when Andy walked into his parent's home with an unexpected guest standing between him and Chauncey.

Rusty happened to be sitting in the living room in his chair almost exactly as he had been when Andy arrived a week earlier. When Andy stepped aside, Rusty saw Charlie and was up crossing the room, overwhelmed with emotion. He wrapped his son in a bear hug before Charlie could even say hello. Finally, Rusty backed away from his second-born son with tearing eyes and tight throat and whispered, "Andy, please call your mom! She's in the kitchen."

When Delora entered the room, Charlie could tell his mother had forgiven him for the pain and fear he caused both his parents, as well as the worry they had felt during the war years.

Once again, Delora found herself laughing and crying at the same time as she hugged Charlie, overjoyed to have him back home. "It is so good to see you! How long can you stay? How have you been?" His mother's questions spilled out one after the other so fast Charlie did not have a chance to answer any of them.

Happy and relieved to be forgiven and standing next to his mom, Charlie wrapped his arm around her waist and said, "Mom, Dad, first, I would like to say I am sorry for causing you pain.

"Now, to answer your questions, Mom, I can stay until January first, then I'll have to head back to Ladd Airfield in Alaska. I am doing great, and I'm hoping you have room for me to stay with you. I wanted to surprise you, which is why I did not let you know I was coming."

Chauncey spoke up and said, "You don't have to worry about Andy. My folks said he can stay with us through the holidays."

As the first flurry of hugs from his parents subsided, Charlie received welcome home hugs from Marcella, Florence, Lloyd, Pete, Millie, and Sharon. Everyone tried to talk at once while Pete was trying to tell Charlie he could share his room. Millie was asking about Alaska, and Lloyd was telling Charlie about his friend Bud who also joined the Army Air Corps. Being surrounded by such happy chaos felt so normal it made Charlie smile. He was truly grateful to be home for Christmas.

After dinner, Andy pulled his mom aside for a quiet conversation, "Mom, I hope you won't mind, but Betty asked me to dinner with her folks Christmas Eve."

"Is this the girl your father told me about, the one you met at college?" Andy smiled and nodded. "Christmas Eve is not a problem. But I did plan for you to be here for dinner Christmas Day."

Andy nodded, replying, "I'm all yours Christmas Day."

"Wonderful. The whole family will all go to Mass early. Then I'll need your help to bring up the extra chairs from the basement. Most of the relatives from Madison are coming as well as Father O'Brian, so we'll need chairs for at least 16 adults at the table. The kids will be able to sit on the floor in the living room. We'll have dinner about 3:30, and once everything is cleaned up, we plan to play cards."

"You can count on me, Mom, and I'll volunteer Chauncey and I for kitchen detail. How does that sound?" His mother smiled and accepted his offer.

Boys to Men

Later in the evening, their home hummed with music and chatter. Their children sat in groups listening to the radio or playing marbles or card games. Rusty and Delora noted that Charlie, Andy, and Chauncey sat together sharing stories.

Delora mentioned how proud she was of the men their sons had become. Rusty told her he detected more strength and confidence in the way they talked to each other. Their boys had experienced the world outside their small hometown, yet Rusty still perceived an air of innocence about them.

He thanked God these young men still possessed idealism. He thanked God even more for allowing his sons to remain unbroken and to escape the experiences of losing friends on a battlefield.

Rusty could see his boys believed they had become men, and at the moment, they seemed like it too. Yet despite what the military had trained them to think and do, without experiencing real hardship and loss, they were still only 19- and 17-year-old boys inside.

Christmas Eve, Home of the Rossows

There were only five people at the Rossows' dinner table. Andy's girlfriend came from a small family, especially when compared to his. It felt so peaceful during dinner sitting next to Betty. Andy politely asked questions and listened as each family member talked about what they were interested in.

Her brother, Chuck, told everyone about the play he was rehearsing in drama class and that he was looking forward to their family's annual trip to Wheatland, Wyoming, between Christmas and New Year's to see his grandparents.

Mom Rossow told him about her job at the stationery store in Norfolk and about the new Social Security program she was enrolled in.

Pop Rossow talked to Andy about his custom shoe business and his 100-mile sales route while LeOra and Betty cleared away the dinner dishes.

For dessert, Betty served the pie Andy brought, and LeOra served the coffee. The Rossows commented on how delicious it was. Andy explained, "Mom was taking care of the first six of us at home as she perfected her recipe during the Depression. She made and sold pies to bring in extra money when we lived in Madison. After we moved to Norfolk, my last two siblings were born, and she continued to make and sell pies while she stayed at home with us kids until we were all in school. Two years ago, she became a nurse and now works at Our Lady of Lourdes Hospital."

LeOra smiled and replied, "I am impressed. I look forward to meeting your mother."

Around 10:00 p.m., Andy whis-

Charles (Chuck), Betty Le's only sibling, seven years younger

Fred and LeOra Rossow, Betty Le Rossow's parents

pered to Betty that he should get going. He felt good about his first meeting with Betty's family, and as he put on his coat, he said, "Mr. and Mrs. Rossow, Chuck, it's been a pleasure meeting you. I hope to see you all again soon."

Betty walked Andy out to the car, and as he hugged her, he asked, "So, do you think I passed?"

She smiled up at Andy and kissed him sweetly, replying, "I'll give you an A for effort. Mom and Chuck like you. Dad may take a little convincing. I'm his only daughter, and I don't think he likes the idea of another man in my life, but he'll come around. I'll make sure of that!"

"So, do you think you will be back from your family trip by New Year's Eve?" Andy asked hopefully.

"I'll make sure we are. I am looking forward to meeting your whole family," she replied, then gave Andy a warm kiss goodnight.

LaVere (Bud)
Roggenbach, 1941

Florence Karella, 1941

Painful Misunderstanding

During the week after Christmas, Charlie and Lloyd had been talking about the Army Air Corps. His brother told Charlie that his best friend, Bud Roggenbach, had joined the Air Corps six months ago. Charlie had known Bud in high school and liked him well enough until he heard that Florence and Bud were writing to each other.

Andy and Charlie were outside having a smoke when he brought up the subject with Andy. "Don't you think Florence is too young to be writing to a guy in the Air Corps? You know what guys are thinking at that age. I'm sure the Marines are no different."

"Charlie, we grew up with Bud. He's been Lloyd's best friend all through school. The whole family likes him, and he's not the kind to say anything bad about Florence. Remember, he helped Lloyd look after her. Shoot, we've known Bud as long as we've known Chauncey. I don't see any harm in them writing to each other."

"I guess you are right," he replied as he rubbed the healing scar on his scalp.

Andy noticed a wincing look on Charlie's face and asked, "Is your damaged head bothering you?" Charlie frowned and replied, "Yeah, I get blistering headaches that won't ease up.

The Mail

Thrilled beyond words, Florence received a letter from Bud. Everyone thought he had been writing to her because she talked about writing to him—all the time. The secret only she knew was this was the first letter he had written to her.

Savoring the moment, she carried the unopened letter into the living room. Charlie walked up behind her quietly and saw Bud's name on the envelope and decided to tease her about it and snatched the letter out of her fingers.

On leave—AAC Airman Charlie Karella, 17 years old

Florence responded immediately. Spinning around, she saw the letter in Charlie's hand and demanded that he give it back. Instead of returning it, Charlie said he might read it aloud.

Florence turned bright red. It was half embarrassment—thinking Charlie might actually read her private letter—but the rest of the color was generated by pure Karella temper.

About this time, Andy and the rest of the family arrived in the living room to find out what the ruckus was about. Charlie hadn't noticed Florence had grown. She was now as tall as he was and had developed a temper that could melt bricks. Most of the time, she kept her temper hidden. But this letter was important to her, and she wanted it back.

Charlie held the letter as high as possible over his head, laughing at his sister's attempts to snatch it back. When that didn't work, Florence kicked him hard in the calf muscle, which nearly brought Charlie to his knees. That was when she grabbed her letter back.

"Damn it, Florence! I was only playing with you. That really hurt!" It was Charlie's swearing that brought his mother and father into the room.

Before anyone could say anything, Florence stuffed the letter into her mouth, chewed it up, and swallowed it, then ran from the room crying.

A Knock on the Door

"Hey, sis, please open the door," Charlie said softly. "I'm not going to leave until you talk to me." Charlie had to wait ten minutes, but finally, Florence opened the door. "I'm sorry about teasing you and snatching your letter. I would never have read it out loud. I hope you believe that."

Though she nodded her head to acknowledge his apology, she still acted very upset over it, and that confused him. "Look, Florence," he said sincerely, "it was just one letter. You two have been writing to each other for months now. What could have been in this one that is worth spoiling your holiday over?"

"Tell me why you snatched it away," she said with watery eyes.

"Ok, honestly, I've heard the way guys in the Air Corps talk about the girls they know. When I heard you were writing to someone in the Air Corps, at first, all I could think of was, I didn't want any guy talking about my sister like that."

"Charlie, you know Bud. He would never say anything bad about me. So, are you saying that in your own way, you were trying to protect me?" Charlie nodded in embarrassment. "Charlie, Lloyd and Bud have always watched out for me. They have been as real of a friend to me as Chauncey is with you and Andy, and what you don't realize is this letter was the first one Bud ever sent to me." The last was delivered in a shaky voice. "And now, I'll never know what it said. This was really important to me."

"Oh, Florence, I am so sorry. I didn't know. Can you forgive me? I love you, sis, and in my own misguided way, I was being protective. Tell you what. What do you want me to do to make it up to you? Do you want me to call him and ask him to write you another letter? I could say Andy's raccoon ate it. Or—"

Florence cut him off and said, "I accept your apology, and I'll write him and tell him the letter got ruined before I could read it."

Then Charlie said, "I'll make you a deal. You forgive me and come back and join the holiday fun, and I'll trade you a secret, something to hold over my head. That way, you know I will behave myself and will be proof of how sorry I am to have upset you so much. Do we have a deal?"

Florence was surprised at the secret Charlie told her and forgave him. They went back downstairs and really enjoyed the rest of Charlie's visit before he had to go back to Alaska.

Airman and flight engineer, Army Air Corps, Charlie Karella, 1945

New Year's Eve at the Karella Home

Betty had no idea how fun a big family could be. On New Year's Eve, instead of eating one big dinner, his mom made a serve-yourself buffet. There was thick Bohemian meat stew that she kept warm on the stove. The counter was filled with all kinds of homemade Bohemian rolls and breads with sweet cream butter. The other foods included

LADD Army Air Corps base in the Territory of Alaska where Charlie Karella was stationed in 1945

571

sliced cucumbers in sour cream dill sauce, a tray of sweet pickles, sliced cheese, carrots, celery, and turnips. The desserts were spectacular, starting with more of Delora's delectable pies, cookies, and kolache sweet rolls. Rusty set out his homemade mulberry cordial and hot mulled applejack cider with cinnamon sticks.

For entertainment, there were several tables set up for card games. Delora, Rusty, Father O'Brian, and Grandma and Grandpa Holt played pinochle. Betty challenged Andy, Chauncey, Charlie, Lloyd, Florence, and Marcella to a game of hearts. During their game, Charlie told them all about Alaska and flying coastal watches. The rest of the kids played jacks and marbles, and everyone listened to the radio as it spun out happy tunes until midnight.

Midnight on New Year's

As the radio played "Auld Lang Syne," Rusty asked the adults to join him for mulberry cordial, and Delora brought out a surprise for the kids and poured them each a glass of Coca Cola.

"Hold up your glasses and let's have a toast," Rusty said. "May God bless us with health, happiness, and all we need throughout this new year of 1947. We also thank God that our sons are safe from harm. Happy New Year, everyone!" Rusty motioned for everyone to drink a sip, and then everyone exchanged hugs and kisses to ring in the new year.

Charlie made a point of hugging Florence and asked, "We are good, right?"

She smiled and replied, "Yes, metal head, we're good."

His eyes flashed for a moment, then as she grinned, he kissed her on the cheek, and replied softly, "I love you, sis."

Andy took Betty home and parked in front of her house. "Andy, I loved being with your family. It's big and loud and so fun. I never knew how much I would love big families. Thank you for sharing that with me."

Andy smiled warmly and put his arms around her and whispered, "They loved you too. Betty, I want you to love this family. I dream you will be part of it someday." He put his finger to her lips and went on, "I don't expect you to give me any kind of answer now. I just wanted you to know how important you are to me." She smiled, and they exchanged several long and tender kisses before saying goodnight.

Andy headed back to his parent's house. He'd sleep on the couch tonight so he could be there in the morning. It was time for Charlie to head back to LADD Airfield in Alaska.

What Are Your Plans?

Once Charlie had gone, Delora and Rusty asked Andy to come over and have a talk with them.

The following morning, Andy came over at 6:00 a.m. to have coffee with his parents. Rusty asked, "What are your plans now that you are finished being a Marine?"

Andy blinked in surprise and replied spontaneously, "I've been thinking I need to find a job and save some money."

His parents nodded, and then his mother said, "Son, your dad and I have a proposition for you. You can stay here in your old room as a temporary measure until you have saved enough to get a place of your own. How does that sound to you?" Their son's expression looked relieved, then apprehensive, then relieved again.

After a long moment of hesitation, Andy nodded his head and replied, "Thank you, and I accept. I promise this will only be a temporary arrangement until I find a good job and can afford a place of my own."

His parents nodded solemnly, happy Andy's thoughts mirrored their own.

CHAPTER 30

Andy and Betty's Journey in 1948

Swing Shift, Norfolk

Betty went back to college full time on Monday, January sixth. The weather remained cold, and Andy focused on job hunting around town. Nothing panned out until he applied at the Western Electric Company. He put his military service down as work experience.

The manager, Mr. Pinger, called two weeks later and set up an interview. "I like the fact that you served our country, son. Our company just finished building a new production line for making permalloy power cores. These parts are used primarily in electronic loading devices, electrical filters, and telephone equipment. I have a swing-shift position opening. Are you interested?"

Old Hershey's Cocoa powder tin, GKM photo 2020

Andy nodded and replied, "Yes, Mr. Pinger. I am ready to start right away."

"Alright then, glad to hear it. Take this work order down to personnel, and they'll get you set up with payroll and will give you your training schedule and shift details."

Nearly a month had passed, and now, Andy was relieved to tell his parents he finally got a job. The swing shift allowed him to sleep later in the morning, which he preferred. It would also give him a few free daytime hours to take care of personal business.

Skating Date, Norfolk

After two months of being back in Norfolk and with the money from his paycheck in his pocket, Andy had the funds to buy a pair of ice skates. He wanted to take Betty on an unusual date. March 14th landed on a Friday, and Andy called Betty to see if she could take Saturday the 15th off from school. He intended to take her ice skating on the frozen pond at Ta-Ha-Zouka Park. His dad had said he could use the car, and the weather was clear with the

Betty's ice skates—kept at her parent's home in Norfolk, Nebraska

temperature holding at about -6 degrees below zero. That wouldn't be a problem because they would be dressed for it.

Andy packed matches to build a fire, blankets to sit on, the cocoa and a bottle of milk, plus a camping coffee pot that he could use to make hot chocolate. He also made a couple rohliky cheese rolls for a snack. After putting his skates and supplies in the car, Andy headed over to Betty's.

She watched from the window as he drove up to the house. He no more than knocked on the door when she opened it and handed him a box with her skates in it and called out, "OK, Mom, we are leaving now."

LeOra smiled and replied, "You two have a good time. Keep warm and be careful on the ice, Betty."

Andy had the heat blasting on high. By the time they got to Ta-Ha-Zouka Park on South 13th Street, they felt toasty warm and ready to skate. Originally built in 1936, the pond was a good size for skating and very smooth when it was frozen. Betty had also mentioned she started ice skating at the park right after it was built.

He parked the car close to the pond so he could unload the blankets and food close to a place where he could build a fire. After skating for a bit, he'd get the fire started and make hot chocolate when they needed to warm up.

Betty turned out to be a great ice skater. Andy hadn't done much skating in years and spent a lot of time trying to stay on his feet as Betty skated circles around him, giggling and smiling in pure joy. Andy finally called it quits. "I give up, Betty! My knees and behind need a break. I'm going to put my shoes on and build a fire so I can make us some hot chocolate."

Andy gathered twigs and wood and attempted to build a fire. Betty spent a few more minutes swirling gracefully around the ice. When she saw smoke, she grabbed her snow boots and sat near Andy on the blanket to take off her skates.

No matter how hard he worked with the wood, it was too wet to do more than make a couple of pitiful flames and scads of smoke. Suddenly, Andy started singing, "They asked me when I knew my fire skills were through. I just smile and say you will always know when smoke gets in your eyes." Then he started coughing as the smoke from the fire changed direction blowing straight into his face.

Betty couldn't help but laugh at Andy's rendition of the popular love song, "Smoke Gets in Your Eyes." Then the smoke changed direction and got her as well. By the time their tears cleared from the last gust of smoke and they could see each other again, they broke into a new round of laughter.

Teasing him, she said, "Andy, even if you failed Boy Scout training, I was sure a Marine would know how to build a fire."

"My fire-building skills might be faulty due to wet wood, but how did you like the serenade, my lady?"

Red-cheeked and chuckling, Betty's eyes teared up from another whiff of smoke as she replied, "Your baritone was on pitch until smoke got in your eyes."

Betty was so enchantingly lovely that Andy leaned over and kissed her softly on the lips. Then he broke the mood completely by saying, "Jeez, it's cold. Let's eat our snack in the car where we can get warm."

Andy started the car and turned on the radio, dialing into his favorite station that played lots of love songs. Irene Dunne's sultry voice came over the air waves singing "Smoke Gets in Your Eyes." Andy and Betty busted up into laughter once again. They couldn't believe that song was playing at that very moment.

As the song finished, Betty commented, "Well, Andy, I guess this was meant to be. This has got to be our song from now on." Then she leaned over and kissed him and whispered, "Thank you for that gallant attempt to make me a fire and hot chocolate. I loved the ice skating, and I love you too."

Time flew by between work, hanging out with Chauncey, and seeing Betty whenever Andy could. He still lived in his parents' home, though he generally didn't see anyone. His dad and mom were at work, and all the kids had gone to school by the time he got up in the mornings, and then he worked late. The family tended to be in bed by the time he got home. Of course, several nights a week, he met up with Chauncey, and he kept weekends reserved for seeing Betty.

Summer Job

Once Betty got out of school, she landed a summer job at Larson's Jewelers. Betty turned out to be such an exceptional saleswoman that Larson's asked if she would also do part-time work throughout the year on holidays like Valentine's Day, Mother's Day, Father's Day, and especially the Christmas gift season. Betty was tickled by the offer and accepted. Having the job not only gave her extra money throughout the year, but she got an employee's discount on all her purchases, and she could put things on layaway and pay them off slowly.

On her days off, she hung out with Andy and Chauncey. She even insisted on going rabbit hunting with them once. Andy would never forget finding Betty sitting next to the rabbit she shot and crying. At first, he and Chauncey thought she was hurt. She was sitting on the ground between the corn rows with the rifle on the ground and looking at the rabbit she shot. The only thing that was hurt was her tender heart.

"Betty, I felt the same way at first. Yet, when we eat what we hunt, then we honor the animal as a gift of food from God. That knowledge always made a difference to me when it came to hunting. My mom makes amazing rabbit fricassee. I'm sure she'd make some with these rabbits we shot today. How would you like that?"

Betty nodded her head and wiped away her tears. She smiled as Andy helped her to stand. Then Andy picked up the rifle, handed it to Chauncey, and stuffed the rabbit in the burlap bag he held. After that when they had time, instead of hunting, the three of them chose to go swimming in the Ta-Ha-Zouka Park Pond.

Late Fall, Norfolk, 1947

In September on Betty's first weekend home from college, Andy started seeing advertisements in the newspaper for summer staff at Old Faithful Inn. It was the hotel located in Yellowstone National Park in Wyoming. The hotel would open to visitors on Saturday June fifth for the summer season of 1948.

Andy told Betty about seeing the staff ads in the newspaper. She reacted instantly, saying, "I know! I saw it too! Wouldn't that be fun? I'd love to work at the park for the summer after I graduate. Get away from everything and just relax."

"You too? Say, what's stopping us?" Andy replied. "Let's send in applications and see what happens. Even if we don't get the jobs, we could still plan to travel around and see the parks all summer. I really think we should plan on it, don't you?" Betty nodded enthusiastically.

Newspaper Article, October 1947

Andy had become fascinated with aircraft and Alaska as he read Charlie's letters, and he often talked about both with Betty. That was when she mentioned seeing an advertisement in the paper for an air show being held at the Offutt Air Force Base in Omaha and showed it to him.

He read bits and pieces of the article aloud, "The Air Force will have aerobatics shows along with high-speed demonstrations. It also says the attendees will be able to get close to the aircrafts to take pictures and talk with the flight crews.

"At last year's show, they introduced a brand-new flight squadron called the Blue Angels. This article says they fly Grumman F6F-Hellcats, and that aerobatic team will also be flying at this year's show. The Blue Angels will demonstrate what they call the diamond

The first Blue Angels flight demonstration squadron (l to r): Lieutenant Al Taddeo, Solo; Lieutenant (junior grade) Gale Stouse, Spare; Lieutenant Commander R.M. "Butch" Voris, Flight Leader; Lieutenant Maurice "Wick" Wickendoll, Right Wing; Lieutenant Mel Cassidy, Left Wing. Military photo, Public Domain.

WWII Grumman F6F Hell Cats, aircraft flown by the first Blue Angel Squadron— military photo, Public Domain

formation, will do loops and barrel rolls, along with other high-speed maneuvers.

"Doesn't that sound exciting? How about we call Chauncey and drive over to Omaha? We could stay overnight with your friend Sue Kunagi and take her to the air show with us. Or we could make a weekend trip out of it. There are all kinds of things to see and do. We could catch a Cardinal's baseball game and go to that new movie comedy you were telling me about, *The Egg and I*. What do you say, Betty?"

Betty shook her head and replied, "Not a weekend. I've got to have some time to study, but I'm up for going to Omaha on Friday evening after class. We could stay with the Kunagis and go to the air show in the morning, take in the movie in the afternoon, and then come home. How does that sound?"

Omaha Nebraska, 1947 Air Show

Betty Rossow sitting on an aircraft and Andy Karella standing to her right—Omaha air show, 1947

Andy, Betty, Sue, and Chauncey loved the air show. The flight demonstrations were heart-stopping and incredible! The speed and maneuvering capabilities of the Hellcats were mind boggling. Andy and Betty could see how this type of flying had captured Charlie's heart and imagination. Four hours disappeared rapidly as they walked in and around 20 types of small and large aircrafts, taking pictures and talking to the military crews that flew them and took care of the aircrafts.

After the air show, Sue grabbed some lunch with her Norfolk friends. Then she had to get back, as she was working in her parent's tailor shop and had a special order to finish.

Andy, Betty, and Chauncey went to see a movie described as a situation comedy called *The Egg and I*. As they drove toward home, they talked and laughed about the story. *Bob MacDonald and new wife, Betty, decide to leave their complicated city life behind for the simple country life. Only they end up with a crumbling farmhouse, nosy neighbors, and a misbehaving pig, plus a beautiful and calculating property manager set on making trouble between Fred and his wife.*

"Ha! I'm so glad Old MacDonald's wife, Betty, kicked that woman's behind!" said Chauncey and won a sweet smile from their Betty.

"True love always wins," Betty replied in her own sweet and sassy manner.

Smiling, Andy thought, *Any female dumb enough to tangle with my Betty would lose too!* Thinking about that truth made Andy laugh as they sped toward Norfolk.

A Talk with Father Burns at Sacred Heart

After Mass on Sunday, Father Bob stood at the doors, greeting each person as they left the church. Andy hung back and made sure he was the last person in line. Finally, it was his turn, and Father Bob greeted him, saying, "Andy, it's good to hear your great singing voice again in Mass."

Andy smiled and replied, "It's really nice to be back in Norfolk and coming to this church on Sundays. Father, do you have a minute? I have something really important I'd like to talk with you about."

The priest nodded and said, "Let me change, and then we can sit and have a chat. How does that sound?"

Within ten minutes, Father Bob and Andy were deep in a discussion concerning the churches stand on Catholics marrying Lutherans. "Father, Betty is a deeply spiritual girl, and she has come to Mass with me many times since we've been going together. She will graduate from NJC with the spring class of 1948, and then we plan to get married."

"Andy," Father Bob began, "I've known your family for years. I have nothing but praise for the way your parents have raised all of you kids in faith, and I admire the way all of you have grown into responsible young Christians. Generally, in a case like this, Betty would be required to convert to Catholicism before she could marry you in the church. Do you believe she will embrace your faith and become a Catholic?"

Andy nodded, then added an explanation, "Father, we are in love. We have talked about getting married, and we would raise our children in faith. But Betty has questions about Catholicism. Until she gets the answers to those questions, she will not be pushed into committing to conversion without being sure that decision is right. But when she does, she will be an amazing Catholic!"

"Would you bring her to meet me and allow me to have a discussion with her?" Father Bob asked.

"Yes, Father. Can we meet you next week after Mass?" Father Bob nodded. After their initial meeting the following week, Andy and Betty stopped in regularly to see the priest. Betty's questions were very intelligent, and often, Father Bob had to go hunting for the answers. He grew very fond of Betty and looked forward to their discussions on the Catholic faith.

One Month Later, Norfolk, 1947

It would be Thanksgiving in a week, and Betty would have a long weekend off from school. The timing was good because Andy wanted to set a date to do some early Christmas shopping.

On Wednesday, November 24th, the temperature hovered around -10 degrees. Andy was pleased about that because it gave him an excuse to pull Betty into several shops to warm up while they looked for Christmas gifts. The store he really wanted to get her into was Larson's Jewelers. As they warmed up, he pulled Betty over to the wedding ring case. "If you could have anyone of those rings, which one would you pick?" he asked.

After a moment, she replied, "I think I would go with that simple one on the right. If it was up to me, I'd rather save the extra money to take a trip. I have helped lots of women pick out rings. Most of them like big expensive diamonds. But I say you can't eat or travel if you are wearing all your money in a rock in a ring you wear on your finger."

Suddenly, a lapel pin caught her eye, and she whispered, "Oh, that's new." The clerk on duty was a friend of hers, and she asked, "Linda, could I see that emerald-green bird? Yes, that one. That's really beautiful. I think mom would love it." Betty asked how much it was with her employee discount. She put it on layaway and would pay it off when she started her Christmas holiday shift.

Andy went back to Larson's during the next week while Betty was at school. He bought the engagement ring and wedding band she had liked. Andy's heart was thumping so loud he thought Linda could hear it as he told her which set of rings he wanted. She smiled at him as she put the wedding set in a beautiful ivory box with a red velvet interior. She held it up for him to look at before she closed the box and said softly, "Great choice. Just the kind of ring Betty would like." Then she winked at him and added, "It will be our secret."

Christmas Eve 1947

Betty went to Midnight Mass on Christmas Eve with Andy after having dinner with her family. Her folks were leaving Christmas morning on a road trip to Wheatland, Wyoming. They were taking Chuck and spending Christmas week with relatives. Betty chose to stay home. When her father tried to insist, her mother said Betty was busy studying for school midterms, and that worked.

The last few days had been heavenly. It was so nice having a comfortable place to spend hours talking with Andy alone on their own. Betty still had a gift for Andy under her tree and invited him over for dinner Christmas evening.

Andy happily accepted the invitation because he had two gifts for Betty, and this would be the perfect time to give them to her. He didn't even remember tasting the food while the whole atmosphere seemed magical. The experience of sitting across from Betty, listening to her, looking at her, and talking with her was unforgettable.

He helped her clean up the dishes, and then they went to sit on the floor next to the Christmas tree, and its lights were the only illumination in the room. It was a perfect time to exchange gifts, so Andy handed her a neatly wrapped box with an emerald-green ribbon. He picked that ribbon because it was her favorite color.

He chose a diary she had seen when they were shopping for his mother's Christmas gift. Betty had said her old one was nearly full, and she needed a new one. "This one might go on sale after Christmas because it's so expensive," she had remarked. "I think I'll check back in January and buy it then." Betty's practical side always made him smile. He went back the next day and bought it for her.

Betty held the diary, admiring it, then leaned over and kissed him sweetly on the lips and said, "I love it. It's the one I liked so much in Mom's shop. Andy, thank you for remembering. Now, it's your turn." She handed him a long thin, smartly wrapped box with a beautiful red ribbon.

Andy took it from her and opened it with great relish, though his mind was still half distracted by the question he wanted to ask Betty. Depending on her answer, he hoped he'd be able to give her the second gift still inside his pocket.

Ambrose James (Andy) Karella and Miss Betty Le Rossow, Norfolk, Nebraska, 1947

Removing the tissue paper from the box, he found a rich brown leather item. Picking it up with curiosity, he recognized it as a leather wallet. It was about eight inches long with a slim sturdy chain attached through a grommet that pierced one corner. On the other end of the chain hung a hasp-style latch. This book-style wallet was extremely flat and not designed to go into a back pocket. It was made for an inside coat pocket, and the security chain hooked to a belt loop. "Betty, this is great. Thank you."

"I thought this was a good idea for when we are traveling. It will be a more secure way to keep track of our money, don't you think?" Hearing Betty talk about traveling with him made his heart leap with excitement. He took her in his arms, thinking she was the most splendid thing in his life and whispered softly, "Betty, will you marry me?"

She remained silent for what might have been seconds or minutes, but his heart began to feel crushed and insecure. He didn't know how to respond or proceed in that silence.

The only sound in the room was the radio playing softly with Perry Como's voice singing "Until the End of Time."

"Yes" came a whisper back from Betty.

Andy's arms nearly crushed her in his relief at hearing that splendid word. Then his lips descended on hers in a warm passionate kiss that lasted longer than her silence had.

Suddenly, Andy caught Betty off guard and wrestled her to the floor trying to tickle her, saying, "You little imp! You scared me on purpose! You nearly ripped the heart out of me when you didn't answer my question right away!"

She giggled, pleased she had been able to tease him and admitted it. "Yes, I was teasing you. Will you forgive me?" she asked softly, smiling up into his eyes.

With his hope restored, Andy dredged up the courage to reply, "I'll forgive you only if you tell me how long you want to wait before we can get married."

Betty whispered, "Not until after I graduate."

"I can live with that," he said, then sung the last line of the song with Perry Como. "Take my heart, and I surrender to you and will love you till the end of time." Then he kissed her again, and she willingly kissed him back wholeheartedly.

They had gotten up off the floor and sat on the sofa. Andy leaned back against the couch, and Betty sat beside him. "I have another gift for you." Then he pulled a small ivory-colored box from his pocket and opened it in front of her. In the red velvet lining sat an engagement ring.

Betty looked up at him breathless and whispered, "Andy, it's lovely. It's the one I always thought I would pick!" Then she kissed him sweetly and took the ring from the box, and it fit perfectly. "How did you know?" she asked as she admired the ring. "Linda helped me. I wanted to get you a bigger stone. But then I remembered you told me if you had a choice, you'd save the money for traveling rather than having a big ring on your finger. Remember?"

"Yes, I do remember saying that," replied Betty. "As a matter of fact, I think I also asked you once: what good is a big ring when you don't have money to eat with? I think it's perfect."

As she glanced at her ring again, she whispered, "Andy, please don't be disappointed. I don't want to wear my engagement ring until I graduate. I've got finals coming up, and I'm not ready to talk to my friends at school about us yet."

He nodded, having guessed she would say as much and replied, "This will be our secret until you are ready to announce it."

True Love and Honesty

"Andy, I have a confession to make." At her serious tone, Andy tried to turn her around to look at her face to face, but she resisted. He kept his embrace light yet still encouraged her to talk to him.

Betty began slowly saying, "It's difficult to tell you this. It happened when I was twelve, and there is nothing more to do, except what we've already done."

She was killing him with curiosity. This drawn-out explanation didn't explain anything. He gave her another gentle squeeze of encouragement and said, "Betty, you can tell me anything. Just say it, for goodness sake."

What followed was more silence. Right as he was getting ready to ask her to confide in him once more, she replied in a small voice, "My two front teeth are false."

Andy tried to turn her in his arms to see if she was teasing him again. Betty resisted being turned and would not face him. Speaking softly, he asked, "Betty, are you being serious?" She nodded her head without speaking.

Now, Andy understood, and he needed to defuse her embarrassment. Teasing might work with her as well, so he said, "Can you take them out and show me?"

He asked that question with such boyish enthusiasm Betty immediately turned to face him with a startled look and replied, "No! I won't take them out and show you!"

"Oh, come on!" He teased, "You can't expect me to believe that without seeing it for myself. You're just pulling my leg, hoping I'll fall for it." Andy could see his plan was working. The shy embarrassed Betty of only moments ago had disappeared. That version of Betty was replaced now by the formidable Betty Le with arms folded across her chest and glaring at him with icy blue eyes.

"For your information, Mr. Smarty Pants, I *can* take them out. But I won't!"

"OK, OK," Andy said, holding up his hands in surrender and smiling. "I get the message loud and clear. I believe you." Then he kissed the end of her nose and asked, "Will you at least tell me how it happened?"

Betty had been watching Andy's face closely and realized he had been trying to make her feel better about her honesty concerning something that was hard for her to talk about.

Andy had also been watching Betty closely and was relieved when he could see she began to understand what he had been doing. She started to smile and relaxed as she turned to lean her back on his chest once again while she thought, *He has been sending me an unspoken message that my embarrassing secret doesn't bother him or change the way he feels about me.* That knowledge made her feel she could trust him completely with her heart, and that made her happy. She whispered, "Thank you, Andy."

He dropped a kiss on the top of her head, and with his strong arms, he pulled her a little closer to his body. "Are you going to tell me how you lost them?"

"Ice skating," she replied.

"Really?"

"Sad to say it's true. I fell forward and hit my mouth on the ice and broke out my adult teeth. Mom and Dad had our dentist build a plate for me with new teeth."

"Darling, that must have really hurt. You are the most beautiful girl in the world to me, and I love you just the way you are," he replied sincerely.

She put her hands over his, smiling and thinking, *I've found myself a keeper. I guess I can laugh a little about my teeth now that I know Andy isn't bothered by it. I suppose it is even funnier considering our first date was ice skating.* Betty knew the minute she had fallen hopelessly in love with Andy. It had been when he started singing to her.

Betty remembered those ridiculous smoke tears rolling down his cheeks. She loved his made-up words that fit the verse and thought it was hilarious when his coughs punctuated the words: *When a lovely thing dies, smoke gets in your eyes.*

Andy turned Betty and cradled her in his arms, and with a long and gentle kiss, he proved to her that every word he had said was true. There was something special in the way her heart raced when he was near. She believed their hearts had recognized each other when they met.

End of January 1948

Friday January 30th, Andy and Betty had a terrific reason to celebrate. Both had received letters that confirmed they got their summer jobs at the Old Faithful Inn at Yellowstone National Park. The two of them would have to report for orientation on June 5, 1948.

Andy had a brilliant idea, and in a hopeful voice, he asked, "Betty, what if we made this a honeymoon job for the summer?"

Betty tipped her head to one side and bit her lip as she thought about what Andy had proposed. "You know, I never wanted to be a stereotypical June bride. Since we have to be at work by June 5 and we can't get married until I graduate . . . and that's May 15 . . . Betty put her arms around his waist and asked softly, "How does

May 29th sound to you?" Betty immediately added, "My birthday is May fifth. What if we throw one big party on the 15th? Announce our engagement and our wedding date all at the same time?"

Thrilled with the date she suggested, Andy picked her up in his arms and whispered, "I think it's perfect, just like you."

Betty showed her appreciation for Andy's heartfelt agreement and compliment with a long passionate kiss that sealed their promise. That kiss made both of then wish they didn't have four months to wait for their honeymoon.

Critical Meeting with Father Bob

Andy called the rectory and made a special appointment with Father Bob. During the last few months, he and Betty had met many times with the priest and held lengthy and lively discussions about Catholic Conversion. But now, the situation had changed dramatically, and Andy was really worried, wondering if they would be able to get married in the church.

He explained about the notice they received about their summer jobs. He explained that they wanted to be married honorably in the church before God before they began this new phase of their life.

Father Bob listened to Andy's concerns as he thought about what he had assessed regarding Betty and Andy's characters and their commitment to what marriage meant and their level of commitment to raising their children in faith. He found Betty to be a formidable young woman with a sharp mind. The couple had convinced him they would raise their children to believe in God and to know that His divine protection and help was theirs just by asking for it. They would teach their children how vital faith was and knew it was the key to hope and a fulfilling future.

This young couple's faith and desire to have their union blessed by God was a demonstration of that faith. Betty did not do things halfway. He got the feeling that it was all or nothing with her, and she needed answers to her queries about the philosophies of Catholicism. She was a woman who asked some of the most interesting questions he had heard in his career as a priest. He was sure that with time and Andy's guidance—and the answers she needed—she would convert.

"Andy, stop worrying," Father Bob advised. "We will work this out. I have faith in the two of you, and so I will word the document in such a way that I don't think Betty will mind adhering to the stipulation of the Church about promising to study to become Catholic and committing to raising your children in the Catholic Faith. It will give her the time she needs to choose to become Catholic of her own volition. She is already a strong Christian woman, and she will make an outstanding Catholic. Let me work on it, and I will get back to you."

Early February 1948

Andy and Betty were giddy with happiness and agreed to keep their plans a secret for the time being. Everything they wanted seemed to be falling into place. Yet, while every joyful day with Betty got better, the opposite seemed to be happening as stress built up in him while living in his father's household.

Andy had already been living in his parents' home for a year. Right before he asked Betty to marry him, Andy had decided he had enough savings to move into his own place. Now, all those plans had changed.

He used a good portion of the money he had to buy Betty's ring. Now, he needed to save every penny he could for travel money and their honeymoon. Andy couldn't afford to move out of his parents' house now, and that was frustrating. He discovered firsthand there was nothing simple or easy about moving back home after being out on your own. Andy felt off balance, and it was harder than he could ever have imagined. The only time he felt steady and sure of himself was when he was with Betty.

A Mother's Wisdom

One morning at the end of February after all the kids were gone to school, Andy sat down with his mom before she went to work at the hospital for a talk. "Mom, Betty and I have not told anyone about this yet, so I'd like you to keep my secret for a little while." She nodded, so Andy continued, "I asked Betty to marry me, and she said yes."

Delora nodded her head in understanding, then smiled with twinkling eyes when she replied, "I am so pleased with your choice, son. I'm thrilled for you both. Have you decided when you will get married and where you will live?"

"Not yet. Mom, I know it's been a little inconvenient having me living here like this. I thought I had enough to move out just before I asked Betty to marry me. Then I used quite a bit of my savings to buy her ring. I know we'll need more money for wedding expenses, and I was hoping you wouldn't mind me staying a bit longer so I can save what we are going to need."

Delora patted her son's hand and replied, "Of course, you can stay a bit longer. Now, regarding your continued stay, you know we love you, and so do your brothers and sisters. Families stick together and help each other.

"For the most part, you have been living by your own rules under this roof with no responsibilities except to yourself. Your brothers and sisters live by our rules, and they all have chores. If you continue to live here, don't you think it's a bit unfair that you don't?

"I know you are working, but please pick a chore around the house or do something thoughtful for your brothers and sisters while you are here. I suspect it will make you and them feel better."

Andy nodded, realizing his mother was right. Perhaps he could start doing dishes on the nights he ate dinner at home. They were letting him stay. It would only be for three more months, and if doing a little KP would make his mom happy, that was what he would do.

A Group Outing

The next weekend, Andy invited all the kids to go sledding with him and Betty. Everybody went except Sharon who had a cold. It was a tight squeeze in one car, but no one wanted to be left behind. Andy tied the sleds on the top of the car, and they drove out to Madison.

Andy called ahead to his uncle Rudy Pojar, and Rudy said there was still snow on the side roads. Once they got to the Pojars' place, Rudy and Andy tied several sleds to the back of the car and Rudy's truck. The two men pulled the sleds piled with the kids and their cousins laughing and bouncing, sliding from side to side across the road and at times crashing into each other. Betty took turns riding the sleds with his sisters, too, and laughed when she fell off rolling in the snow.

After several hours of laughing, bumping around, running and falling on icy roads, and rolling in the snow, everyone was cold, tired, and ready to warm up. They crowded into Aunt Martha's kitchen, and she passed out hot chocolate and fresh-baked oatmeal-walnut cookies. Happy and warm, Andy thanked Aunt Martha and Uncle Rudy for the wonderful outing, and then everyone exchanged hugs before heading back to Norfolk. All the kids fell asleep on the way home. Betty's face was still flushed from all the outdoor fun as she cuddled next to him as he drove listening to the melody "Peg of My Heart" on the radio.

When Andy dropped Betty off at her parents' home, she kissed him and said softly, "I had a delightful time with you and your brothers and sisters. I also enjoyed meeting your aunt and uncle and some of your cousins too. I love big families. Thank you for sharing them with me."

His mother had been correct. The restricted feelings he had felt at home was not something his family had done to him. He could see now that it had been him all along. He needed to be free and to be with Betty. Today had been proof, though, that being nice and thoughtful did make a difference. After that enjoyable outing, everything did get easier for a while in his parents' home.

Private News for Parents Only

On Valentine's Day 1948, Andy and Betty announced their engagement to their parents and said they would announce their engagement formally for all their friends and the rest of the family at Betty's graduation party on May 15th. But no other details were forthcoming except that Betty would finish college, and after that, they would consider setting a wedding date. Andy's parents were thrilled about having Betty for a daughter-in-law.

At this time, Betty had a private talk with her mom. There was already a lot to do with her birthday and graduation party that was currently being planned.

That was why it was even more important that she tell her mother about the secret wedding date. There were going to be a lot more things to do that would take a while to prepare. Invitations would have to be sent two weeks before the wedding, then there was the cake, the flowers, her wedding dress, and the attendants' clothing. She and her mom would have to start planning for all this stuff immediately, with only two months to get everything done.

Peacemaker's Perspective

Andy was in a rush. It was a Saturday night, and he had gone to pick up laundry soap and bleach for his mom. He had a date with Betty that evening, so he picked her up on the way home from the grocery store. Now, she waited for him in the living room. All Andy needed was to get into some clean clothing so they could leave. They were going to get a bite to eat before they went dancing.

When he entered the house, Andy saw Florence run into the kitchen. After fetching his clean clothing from his room, he went into the kitchen looking for her. Walking past his sister, he tossed his shirt to her and said, "Hey, Florence, would you iron this? I'm in a hurry."

Florence frowned and replied, "Andy, why can't you ask for my help politely?"

As he began putting on his clean trousers, he looked up and replied, "Come on! It's just a shirt, and Betty is waiting. You know ironing is housework, and that makes it a woman's job."

At that point, a bit of an argument ensued, and Betty could hear it from the living room and decided to see what was going on.

As she walked into the kitchen, she heard Andy say, "Because it is housework, and that makes it women's work."

Andy was standing there in clean trousers and his t-shirt looking at Betty as she walked into the room, and her blue eyes shot fire at him. He knew she had completely misunderstood what she had just heard him say. Trying to explain, he said, "Wait a minute, Betty! I was just repeating what my parents taught us. The girls were responsible for chores inside the house, and the boys were responsible for the chores outside the house. I just wanted Florence to iron my shirt." Florence stood quietly as she looked from Betty to Andy, holding Andy's shirt.

Ambrose James (Andy, AJ) Karella at parents' home in Norfolk, Nebraska

Being a peacemaker by nature, Betty walked over to Florence and took hold of the shirt as she asked a question, taking both brother and sister by complete surprise. "Do you think it is right to punish a girl like my American friend Sue Kunagi because her family lineage is Japanese?" The two listeners shook their heads. "Do you think people in Norfolk should think I am a Nazi because my family lineage is German?" Again, the two listeners shook their heads. "Do you believe that a man should be incapable of taking care of himself or of cooking or cleaning his own clothing?" The shaking heads were now looking at each other, then back at Betty. "Do you think a woman should be incapable of working in the yard or the garden, shoveling snow, or making sure to put fuel in her car?" Silent heads continued to shake from side to side, indicating their answer was no.

"If that is the case, then what I think is going on here is a lack of polite, respectful cooperation. Everyone needs help from time to time, and if the request is made with consideration, generally, cooperation follows. You two don't realize how lucky you are to have each other and this wonderful big family to love and share everything with. I think please and thank you is a small price to pay to gain a happy outcome for everyone."

Both Andy and Florence looked embarrassed by the truth of what Betty had just said.

"Florence, I am sorry I didn't say please or ask for your help nicely. I was in a hurry. I promise to be more polite and more grateful for the things you do for me in the future. Will you forgive me, sis?"

Florence looked at Betty, then Andy, and nodded slowly, saying, "Yes, I will forgive you. I'm sorry I got so mad at you."

Then Betty smiled and walked up to Andy and kissed him sweetly on the lips as she handed him his shirt. "Good!" she replied as she turned to look at Florence. "Because I know just the well-mannered young lady I want to be my bridesmaid when the time comes."

Florence looked at Betty in surprise and asked, "Who?"

Smiling, Betty replied, "Why, you, of course. Now, come talk to me in the living room while Andy finishes getting dressed. Let's you and I go to my house next week to meet with my mom. Would you like that?" Florence nodded happily as they chatted about making a trip to Omaha in the future to have a bridesmaid dress ordered for the wedding, leaving Andy in the kitchen holding his shirt.

Andy grinned, knowing when to surrender to the logic of his stunningly intelligent fiancé and her example of faith and peace in action. He finished dressing as quickly as possible.

Millie Karella and Sharon Karella, Norfolk, Nebraska, youngest sisters of Andy Karella

595

Harmless Way to Make a Point

1940s rotary telephone

As the cold of January faded into February, then March and now April, so did Rusty's patience. His eldest son's temporary housing arrangement with them was passing the 14-month mark. Delora had told Andy it was alright to extend their original temporary agreement, and he approved of her decision when she explained the circumstances.

But that was three months ago, and there was still no hint of a change or additional information that made Rusty believe things would be changing. Rusty loved his son, but there were certain things he found difficult to tolerate.

Betty Le Rossow, Summer 1947, Norfolk, Nebraska

The biggest issue was that Andy didn't get out of bed before noon even on his days off. On workdays, that was understandable since Andy worked a swing shift. Yet, there were things his son could help him with on weekends if Andy would get out of bed early like the rest of his children. At a loss about what to do, Rusty wondered, *How on earth did the Marines do it? My boy is harder to get out of bed now than before he left to join the military. I would pay dearly to know just how the Marines managed to get Andy up and ready to go each day!*

After giving the issue a lot of thought, Rusty decided it was time to address the situation, thinking, *My grandfather Vaclav would have thrown a bucket of cold water on me had he caught me still in bed at lunchtime. That would yield instantaneous results.* Grinning to himself, Rusty decided it might not be the best thing to do no matter how funny the results would be. Yet, addressing the situation was long overdue, and he devised a clever plan to deliver that message.

Rusty chose April Fool's Day. That holiday was celebrated by pulling pranks on people. It also gave Rusty the perfect excuse to play a harmless joke on his boy and teach him a lesson at the same time.

Quietly moving about the house, Rusty tiptoed into Andy's room and tied one end of a long string around the bedpost at the foot of the bed. Then he carefully tied the other end of the string to Andy's big toe. Leaving the room quiet as a mouse, Rusty grinned and thought, *Now, I require a few accomplices.* As he descended the stairs, he motioned for his two youngest daughters, Millie and Sharon, to come to him.

The girls were instantly curious and came immediately to the foot of the stairs. As they neared the bottom step, he held his finger to his lips and issued a soft request. "Don't talk. Just listen. I want you two to run over to Marsh's Market and ask to use the store telephone to call home."

His request surprised Millie and Sharon as they looked at the telephone sitting in front of them on the end table. Being the bolder of the two, Millie asked, "Why, Daddy?"

Rusty's normal reply to that kind of question would be "because I said so, missy," but not today. Instead, he leaned over conspiratorially, crooking his finger at them to come closer as he whispered, "Because I want you to call home from the store and pretend you are Betty. Hurry now! Off you go."

504 Lincoln Street, Karella home, Norfolk, Nebraska

Giggling at the way their daddy acted, the girls nodded. They knew Betty was Andy's fiancé, and even though they did not really understand what their daddy was up to, it sounded fun. Holding hands, they dashed off through the kitchen door.

Rusty watched them until they disappeared around the corner at the end of the street. The Karella home on Lincoln Avenue and 6th Street was one block away from the 4th and Omaha Avenue corner store owned by Rusty's friend Lafe Marsh. Rusty figured his daughters would need about ten minutes to get there, make their request, and then place the call. Rusty was nearly laughing already.

Fifteen minutes later, the telephone rang. Rusty answered it and heard Millie's giggle on the line. He could also hear Sharon in the background complaining. "I wanted to pretend to be Betty." Millie covered the receiver, muffling her voice, when she replied in exasperation, "I'm older, so I get to talk."

Rusty cleared his throat into the receiver to get his daughter's attention. "Hello. This is the Karella residence. Who's calling, please?" he asked.

Millie spoke coyly into the receiver. "Hi, Daddy, it's Betty." Rusty rolled his eyes, thinking, *At least the little hunyuk got the Betty part straight.* Standing at the bottom of the staircase, Rusty shouted with all his lung power, "Andy, get up! Betty's on the telephone for you."

By this time, the rest of Rusty's children were milling about listening and wondering what was going on. No one seemed to know, so Florence whispered into Lloyd's ear, "You should ask Dad what's up." When he did, Rusty put his fingers to his lips and motioned to them to gather close. He whispered a brief explanation of his April Fool's joke.

Bright-eyed with laughter and faces wearing cheeky grins, Pete, Lloyd, Florence, and Marcella waited and watched the stairs. Only seconds passed between their dad's bellow to wake their big brother and his quick explanation of the joke when they heard a big THUD from upstairs.

Amazing, thought Rusty, *out of bed with my first call, and judging by the heavy thud, Andy found the string tied to his toe.* Grinning at the ruckus above their heads, he knew Andy had tripped getting out of bed.

Abruptly, Rusty's oldest son cursing rather loudly hobbled out of his room to stand at the top of the stairs in his underwear and t-shirt. Trying to remove what was left of the string dangling from his big toe, he frowned at all the faces smiling up at him.

Limping down the steps, Andy whispered urgently as he took the receiver from his father, "Has she been waiting long?" Everyone standing around in the living room shook their heads.

His father replied, "Not really." His siblings sputtered and choked about something making a lot of noise. Andy frowned, making a cutting motion at his throat, indicating the kids should be quiet as he put the receiver to his ear.

"I'm sorry for keeping you waiting, Betty. Hello?" Still sleep befuddled, Andy's mind began to clear as he tried to understand what was going on. Giggles erupted on the other end of the line. Then his father and siblings yelled, "April Fool's Day, Andy!"

"Who's on this phone?" Andy asked into the receiver. His father smiled and replied, "Millie and Sharon. My, it is amazing how quickly you got out of bed, son. It's nice to see you up and downstairs before noon."

When Andy told Betty about the April Fool's joke, she laughed,

Karella-Rossow wedding announcement, Norfolk Daily News, May 29, 1947

then kissed him, saying, "Darling, it's almost over, and soon we will be free. You are going to look back on this someday and laugh too. You must admit it was an ingenious prank. Sounds a lot like the ones you like to pull on your friends. How does that old saying go? *Like Father, like son?*"

Andy finally smiled, thinking, *Betty does make sense, and I do love the way she is comforting me over it.* He kissed her again.

Father Bob, Sacred Heart Catholic Church

Father Bob smiled at the lovely young couple. He was so proud of them and their commitment to each other and honoring God with their conduct. They had completed all the necessary forms and paperwork that would allow them to marry with the blessings of the church on May 29th as planned. He gave them each a hug and said he'd see them in church on the 28th at 8:00 p.m. to walk them through the ceremony.

Leaving the rectory office, Andy said, "Talk about cutting it close to the wire, Betty! Gosh, I'm glad Father Bob is in our corner."

Betty nodded and replied, "He is right. I feel good about that document, and now nothing is standing in our way of getting married in the Catholic Church *before* I convert to Catholicism. I know that is a huge deal."

Nodding, Andy replied, "You can say that again." He thought about what the priest had wrote:

Betty Le Rossow Karella has promised to study and take the conversion classes to become a Catholic. She and her husband, Andy Karella, have promised to raise their children in the Catholic faith. As their family priest, I vouch for the truth of the commitments they have both made.

Pastor Robert P. Burns,
of Sacred Heart Catholic Church, Norfolk, Nebraska

Travel Plans, Spring of 1948

Miss Rossow's spring plans were set in motion initiating many changes, and she was at the center of all of them. Betty turned 22 on May fifth, and the combined Rossow and Karella families would attend her college graduation ceremony on May 15th, then help celebrate both events at a big party. At that time, everyone would not only find out she and Andy were engaged, but within two weeks, she would become Andy's wife on May 29th.

The only people who knew all the details were her friend Sue Kunagi, the seamstress making her wedding dress, and her mother who had helped plan everything. Both swore not to tell or spoil the surprise.

But only Betty and Andy knew how the month's events would finish. They would announce their plans for leaving Nebraska on their honeymoon and that they were going to start their jobs at Yellowstone seven days following their wedding. Just thinking about it almost took her breath away.

Leaving Nebraska for their new jobs was only the first step toward their new

Betty Le Rossow graduation at Norfolk Junior College, spring of 1947

adventures. They had a lot to do before the month of May rolled out, yet they were determined not to reveal their secret too soon.

A Mother and Daughter Confidence

On May third, two days before Betty's birthday, both she and Andy had been invited to join the Karella family for dinner.

As they normally did after everyone was finished eating, the girls started clearing the table and taking the dishes to the kitchen. To their complete surprise, their mom shooed them all away, stating she and Betty would finish the clearing and cleanup duties by themselves.

Marcella and Millie looked at one another, thinking their mom was up to something. But they were happy to accept the reprieve from dish duty and made themselves scarce before she changed her mind.

Delora Holt Karella, 1946, in front of 504 Lincoln Street, Karella home, Norfolk, Nebraska

Betty silently watched Delora. It didn't take a genius to figure out she wanted to be alone and purposely banished young ears to keep their conversation private. As Rusty and Andy went into the living room, Betty waited for Delora to tell her what was going on.

The two women walked into the kitchen and stood at the sink side by side. After filling the sink with hot water, Delora started handing soapy dishes to Betty to rinse. That was when Andy's mom quietly began to talk. "I am happy that you have accepted Andy's proposal. Rusty and I are thrilled that you are going to become our daughter-in-law. Knowing that, I hope you will not take offense to my next question.

"Have you two decided on a wedding date and when you'll be moving into your own place?"

Betty had a good idea why Delora asked this question and was not offended. Andy had been right about his guess that he had overstayed his temporary arrangements.

She could not help but smile and admitted Rusty had been very creative with that April Fool's joke he played on Andy. Betty suspected it would be a long time before Andy would appreciate the humor in the joke as much as she and her mother had when Andy told them about it.

This fact also explained the sense of relief Betty had perceived in everyone when Andy announced that after her graduation, they would set a wedding date. It was apparent Rusty and Delora needed assurance she and Andy would be getting a place of their own.

Betty inched a little closer to Delora conspiratorially and whispered, "Listen, I realize that it's been hard on you having Andy move back home, particularly when you still have six kids still living here."

When Delora started to protest, Betty cut her off, saying, "No, Mom, it's OK. I understand your point of view. You may not believe this, but it's been hard on Andy too. Just let me assure you that in a very short while, your current concerns will be happily resolved."

She heard her mother-in-law-to-be let out a long breath of relief and replied, "Thank you. I won't pry for further information. I guess I didn't realize how important it was for me to hear your reassurance. You must know how much we love our son. But there can be only one king in charge of a castle. It's getting very difficult trying to keep the king and his subjects at peace with each other."

Betty nodded with twinkling eyes, and they both laughed. "I come from a small family, and we have the same kind of difficulties too. I can't imagine what that must be like multiplied by nine other people living in the same house."

Delora and Betty chatted effortlessly for the next thirty minutes sharing family stories. After finishing the dinner cleanup, they called everyone to the table for dessert.

The Wedding Conspiracy Continues

The following week, Betty and Florence both got a day off from school. LeOra joined her daughter and Andy's sister on the drive to Omaha to see Sue Kunagi and her family. The primary goal of the

Mrs. Betty Le Rossow Karella, wife of Ambrose James (Andy, AJ, Jr.) Karella, May 29, 1948 trip was the final fitting for Betty's wedding dress and to select fabric and let the Kunagis take Florence's measurements for the bridesmaid dress.

The work Sue had done on Betty's wedding dress was spectacular, and the fitting went off without a hitch. The bridesmaid dress details were quickly finished, which gave the women time for tea and a lovely chat with Sue and her parents. During tea, Betty explained that Sue could now concentrate on making a maid-of-honor dress for herself and Florence's bridesmaid dress. But no mention of the actual wedding date had been made to Florence during that trip.

Privately, Betty and Sue agreed the Kunagis would come to her graduation party. They would bring the dresses and give them to LeOra who would keep them at the Rossow house. Sue would come back to Norfolk on the 28th and stay overnight with Betty's folks. Then she would be part of the wedding as she walked down the aisle as Betty's maid of honor.

As they left the Kunagis' tailor shop, LeOra decided the three of them should have a late lunch. Afterward, they'd fill up the gas tank to avoid another stop on the way home. During the drive back to Norfolk, Betty let Florence in on some of her secret plans. Thrilled to be part of their wedding conspiracy, Florence promised not to tell a soul.

After this outing, Betty also set aside extra girl time with Florence. As they grew closer, she helped the younger girl understand herself and her emotions better, and that made her a little more tolerant with all her brothers.

As Florence and Betty became good friends, Betty confided in her new little sister, asking, "Can you keep a secret?" Florence nodded. "You already know your brother and I are getting married. But now I'm going to tell you when. We are getting married this month on May 29th."

Florence flung herself at Betty, hugging her and whispering, "I am so happy you are going to be my sister. I love you, Betty."

Betty smiled, patted her on the back, and asked, "So, can I count on you to help my mom with the secret wedding preparations?"

Florence nodded eagerly and replied, "Oh, yes!"

Norfolk, May 1948

For the Karella and Rossow clans, the celebrations of May started out rather low key. Betty wanted to combine her birthday party with her graduation celebration, and that made sense to everyone.

Andy and Betty both anticipated the sensational surprise they had in store for the family. Tickled with their timing, everyone attending Betty's huge birthday-graduation bash stood astonished as Andy and Betty formally announced their engagement, then said their wedding plans were set for the 29th of May.

Their news sent shockwaves through family and friends in Madison and Norfolk. Of course, there were rumors and speculation as to why the wedding date was pushed forward so fast. All that was forgotten quickly because of everything that needed to be done in such a short time. Andy and Betty just smiled, knowing some people were betting that Betty was in a family way. The reasons would be revealed soon enough, which would be the biggest surprise of all!

Left to right: Charlie Karella, Chuck Rossow, Chauncey Crocker, Andy and Betty Karella, Sue Kunagi, Florence Karella—wedding party, Rossow-Karella wedding, May 29, 1948

Fourteen Days Later: May 29, 1948

Rusty and Delora sat together in the front pew on the groom's side of the church. Andy and Betty stood facing each other as Father Bob spoke eloquently about the commitment they were about to make to one another.

"Rusty, can you believe how wonderful this moment is?" Delora whispered.

He laced his fingers through hers, kissed the hand he held, and whispered in reply, "My darling Bitty, we are so very blessed. It is hard to credit all that we have been through and seen over the years to get to this moment in our lives.

"I think of what our parents went through and our grandparents before them, and it makes the work we've done seem simple. Both your ancestors and mine left all they knew behind. They crossed the Atlantic Ocean filled with faith in God and armed with hope that they would be able to forge a new life in a new land ripe with opportunity. They took incredible risks to secure a better future for their children.

"Our parents shared their dreams and grew up with the fruits of their labor, and their elders encouraged their children's enterprising spirits. Our grandparents and parents brought their dreams to life. They passed on their ethic of hard work, and we followed in their footsteps, branching out and building dreams of our own.

"We were raised in safety and surrounded with security that was gained through hard work, and they gave us examples of faith to emulate. Our homes were filled with love where we could grow strong and learn how to use our minds and believe in the talents God gave us.

"I know it was divine timing that allowed you and I to meet. If I had not been trained by my grandfather in the leather trade, I would never have met your father, nor would I have found you, my sweet Bitty. I think about that a lot. How God allowed us to grow in love and let us choose our course. You and I both know the choices we made did not make things easy for us." Rusty looked into her lovely blue eyes and added, "But I would not trade one minute of my life with you for anything in the world."

Delora smiled and whispered, "I agree with you. They taught us how to believe in the strength of our faith, and our faith gave us the courage to seek our own dreams."

Rusty nodded and whispered back, "Even when the world changed around us, our faith drew our families closer together. We learned to do that as children in good times and bad. They taught us how to pool our resources and use our wits to survive the droughts, work the land, and develop our personal talents to find different ways to earn or make what we needed. That is the abundance and richness of the legacy we inherited from our parents. The farmland that was the heart of their dream was just a steppingstone to the future. They taught us to persevere in our belief that with God's help, we could achieve anything we set our hearts and minds on.

"I believe the essence of what our parents bequeathed to us is the knowledge that we must make our own choices and be responsible for those choices. We must believe in the life we want for ourselves. In doing so, if we are committed, we can make our dreams come true.

"Bitty, living up to the choices we made prepared us to fight to survive each calamity as it came, from the bank crash and the Depression, to raising our children, even losing the farm, and then losing Papa. It was even part of practicing the fortitude that got us through the war years and fear we had for our sons and my brother.

"Thank you, Bitty, for your strength and perseverance raising our children and all you've invested to make them

Red 1937 Pontiac and best man, Chauncey Carry Crocker, parking Andy and Betty's honeymoon car and the automobile they will drive to the Territory of Alaska in the spring of 1949

wonderful human beings that are unique and talented. Though they have great differences in personality and might even bicker with one another, in their faith and in their hearts, they stand united. They each possess unconditional love for their family and their faith in God. I suppose it is our job now to watch them leave our protection to follow their hearts. We did the best we could to teach them about nurturing faith, hope, and love in their lives. Those strengths will be the foundation for the courage they need to follow the paths they choose.

Left to right: Sue Kunagi, Florence Karella, Millie Karella, Chuck Rossow, Betty and Andy Karella, and on the far right is Marcella Karella—after the ceremony

"We are witnessing our firstborn making one of the most important choices of his life. I thank God for the grown man he has become. One who honors his country, loves his family, and now is building his own American Dream as he takes a wife and starts another generation of this family that will be born in the land of promise."

Bitty wiped away a happy tear and said, "Thank you, my dear husband, for being brave enough to make me your wife, for protecting me, and giving me your love. It amazes me to realize despite the bumps and struggles along the way, we have created a family who has filled my heart with more joy than I could ever have imagined."

Rusty chuckled softly, put his arm around her, and gave her a squeeze, saying, "I was just thinking it won't be long before each of our children follow in Andy's footsteps. Once they are all on their own, my dearest Bitty girl, God willing, you and I will be ready for a new adventure of our own! Isn't that an exciting thought?"

Wedding Announcements

As the reception celebration came to an end, Andy was dancing the last dance with Betty and whispered in her ear, "You make me feel whole and complete. I feel ready to be free and to pursue our dreams. What do you say, my sweet wife? Are you ready to make our announcements?"

Betty grinned, looking up at him, and whispered, "My dearest husband, I could not agree more. I am eager to begin my life with you. It's time to tell our friends and family about our immediate plans and dreams for the future."

Just before the wedding reception concluded, the newlyweds stood up, and the conversation in the room hushed for their announcement. Andy and Betty thanked their guests for attending their wedding celebration and for all their good wishes and gifts. "Now, we have more news for you. Betty and I are excited to tell you we will not only be leaving on our honeymoon. We will be starting our new jobs in Yellowstone National Park. Betty and I must report for our summer jobs on June fifth, and we plan to be gone for a long while. We are thrilled to be embarking on such an exciting future, and you will all be missed."

The entire family was overwhelmed once again—this time by tears. The following day, a crowd of family and friends gathered to see them off. While many hands helped load the car and the baggage into a little trailer, no one wanted to let them leave.

Delora handed Betty a picnic basket filled with fried chicken, her wonderful potato salad, and one of her amazing cream pies. Betty handed it to Andy to put in the backseat of the car, then hugged Delora, whispering in her ear, "Mom, thank you. Now your king has his castle back."

Delora and her new daughter-in-law shared a secret smile, then Betty climbed into the car. She and Andy rolled down their windows, and as Andy yelled his goodbyes, Betty leaned out hers and blew a kiss to everyone as she waved.

Mrs. Delora (Bitty) Karella, May 30, 1948, standing in front of Andy and Betty's 1937 red Pontiac that they would drive to Yellowstone National Park and Sun Valley, Idaho

Towing a small trailer filled with keepsakes, their luggage, and wedding gifts, the newlyweds drove out of Norfolk, Nebraska, headed toward Wyoming and Yellowstone National Park in their red 1937 Pontiac.

Andy took hold of Betty's hand, grinning from ear to ear, embracing the magic of the moment. They could feel excitement running through them, ready for their new adventures to unfold!

This marks the end of *American Dreams*. and Andy and Betty's adventures continue in Book 3, *Alaskan Dreams*.

Alaskan Dreams: Prologue

Newlywed Adventures

After the wedding of Andy and Betty Rossow Karella in Norfolk, Nebraska, on May 29, 1948, they leave Nebraska, not planning to return for quite some time. They had already secured summer jobs at Yellowstone National Park and hoped to land winter jobs at the ski resort in Sun Valley, Idaho. The longest-range plan they had was to return to Yellowstone the following March for another summer season.

Andy and Betty Experience a Change of Heart

The couple's under-wraps honeymoon adventures in Yellowstone National Park were more wonderful than they could have hoped for. In fact, they were so sensational at their jobs both got recommendations to work at their dream ski resort for the coming winter. They saw movie stars and spent exciting evenings listening to the hottest bands in the country that played at the Sun Valley resort. The spring weather came early, ending the ski season in Idaho, so in March of 1949, Andy and Betty are on their way back to Yellowstone for another summer season. Over a conversation about children, Andy and Betty suddenly decide they do not want to settle down yet and choose another course for their immediate future.

April 1, 1949, the dusty 1937 Pontiac is packed and towing a small travel cart. On this journey, Andy, Betty, and best friend Chauncey are making one stop in Omaha to pick up Charlie. Then the band of friends will head north—as far north as the road goes, all the way to the frontier territory of Alaska. They are headed toward 1,600 treacherous miles of frozen, muddy, rocky dirt roads, and river crossings. First will come Canada's rugged wilderness, then the Yukon Territory, before reaching the last United States frontier territory on an adventure they will never forget!

A Family Born in the Land of Promise Trilogy:
Book 3

Alaskan Dreams

A 1949 Journey into the Frontier Territory of Alaska

. . . Flashback—War Department—United States of America

Priority Communication . . . March 1942 . . . contruction approved . . . build land access between the Continental United States across the Canadian provinces, the Yukon Territory, and into the U.S. Territory of Alaska. Over land support for U.S. Military . . . imperative . . . to protect northern most access to U.S. soil against overland invasion by the enemy.

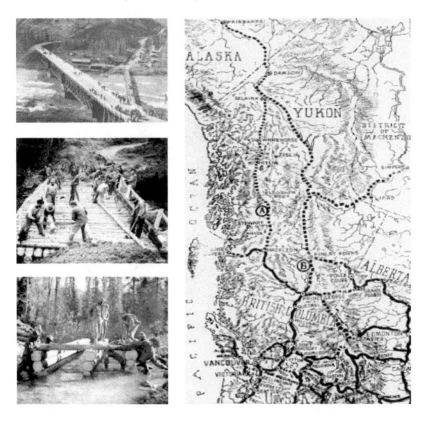

—War Department—United States of America,
June 4, 1942

Urgent! Must complete road to Alaska for military overland support. Japanese have attacked two Alaskan islands: Attu and Kiska.

—War Department—United States of America . . .

Imperative!

Complete route for overland support and defense within Alaska in the most direct manner as quickly as possible: HQ.

US Army operating heavy equipment
on the Alaska Highway

Update to HQ: Trans Alaska-Canada route officially complete . . . open for military transports in November 1942. Overseen by the U.S. Military, the Trans-Alaskan Highway is designated excusively as a military road.

Six Years Later

World War II is over, and the portion of the Trans-Alaskan Highway that traverses Canadian soil is released to the control of the Canadian Government. The Alaskan portion of the new highway is under military jurisdiction. In the fall of 1948, the Trans Canadian-Alaskan route is opened to civilian travel.

The Following Year, 1949; Norfolk, Nebraska

It had been a year since Delora and Rusty Karella's son Andy got married and took off with his wife, Betty, on a working honeymoon. They had summered in Yellowstone National Park and wintered in Sun Valley, Idaho. Though the kids kept in touch and were clearly having the time of their lives, Delora and Rusty missed them and hoped they'd be coming home soon.

When the telephone rang on Saturday morning, Delora answered it, unprepared to hear a long-distance operator ask, "Is this Delora Karella?"

"Yes," she replied.

"One moment please," said the long-distance operator. "Go ahead, sir."

Delora immediately recognized her eldest son as he spoke, saying, "Hi, Mom."

"Andy, how nice to hear your voice. Is everything alright? How is Betty?"

"Mom, we are both great, and it's good to hear you too. Listen, I haven't got much time, but I have some news."

Jumping to conclusions, Delora's heart began to beat faster, and her thoughts went into high gear. *Maybe they want to tell me they are coming home. Or maybe . . . it's about a baby!* Trying to remain calm, she asked, "Are you and Betty already back in Yellowstone? Will you have a break this spring, or will you be able to come home anytime this summer?" The answer that came over the telephone was so unbelievable she shouted at her son. "You and Betty are going to do *what*? You are going *where*? I cannot be hearing this correctly!"

"Mom, please calm down. We don't have much time or money to spend on this call. We are in Montana, getting ready to cross into Canada—that's why I needed to call you and let you know we might be out of touch for a while. We are headed for the Alaskan Territory, and we don't know when we'll be able to send word to you during the trip." Silence reigned on the other end of the telephone.

"Mom, are you still there?"

Mrs. Karella's thoughts buzzed around in her head. *He's going to give me a heart condition! First, it was the scare of him going into the Marines during the war. I finally get him back, and he decides to marry. But does he settle down? No. He runs off with his new wife into the wilds of Timbuktu in Yellowstone National Park immediately after he gets married. Now only a year later, he and his wife are driving to the end of the earth! What is going on in his head? How could he drag his darling, educated wife into the middle of nowhere? How could such a smart, sensible girl like Betty permit this?*

"Mom, if you are worried about us being alone on the road, don't be. Both Charlie and Chauncey are with us. Between the four of us, we'll do just fine. Charlie knows maps and has flown over this route countless times with the Army Air Corps, and we are carrying extra gas and tires with us."

Mrs. Karella's face turned white, and she thought, *Could this get any worse? Now, I am told that after dealing with Charlie running off to the war at 15 and getting him back safe and sound . . . now, I find out he's on this mad escapade too! How on earth did Andy talk Chauncey and Charlie into this? When did they have time to plan it? I talked to Charlie in Omaha last week. He's got that job working at the slaughterhouse. How could he be with Andy?* Then suddenly, the date hit Delora—it was April first. Relief flooded her mind. She smiled, thinking Andy was pulling an April Fool's prank on her. *OK, Andy,* she thought, *I'll play along.*

Andy was getting nervous with the prolonged silences from his mother. There was no way he could leave the country without breaking this news to her before they were completely out of reach. But he had not expected her to go off her rocker either. Chauncey's mom had not reacted as badly as this, and they let him explain what he was doing. Betty had decided to send a postcard to her folks, knowing Andy's folks would talk to hers once they got the call. Still getting the silent treatment, he was just about to break the silence when Delora cleared her throat in the receiver.

Delora actually grinned, expecting the punch line at any moment and thought, *Rusty is going to love Andy's April Fool's joke.* She asked sweetly with a smile in her voice, "Well, son, how long do you expect it will take for you to get to Alaska and back?" She silently remembered an old movie poster for *Nanook of the North* from the 1920s and nearly laughed at her son's sense of humor.

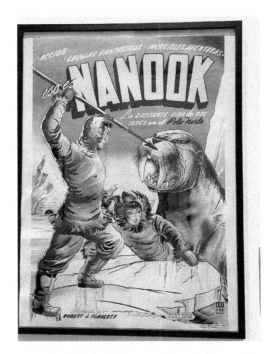

Nanook of the North—1922, debuted in Mexico,
photo taken by GKM 2022 at WS Museum in Arizona

Relieved his mother sounded calm about it, Andy told her he didn't know yet, but as soon as they got to Fairbanks, near Ladd Field, they would send word. "Mom, it's getting late. We need to cross the border and find a good campsite before nightfall. We love you and tell Dad the car is running great." Andy said goodbye, and the line went dead.

Delora stood there with the receiver in her hand, a blank look on her face, and her smile disappeared. It suddenly occurred to her: *Andy's news was not a joke!*

April 2, 1949, original postcard sent to the Rossow family from Andy and Betty Karella before crossing into Canada on the way to the U.S. Territory of Alaska

APPENDIX I

Patriot Pages

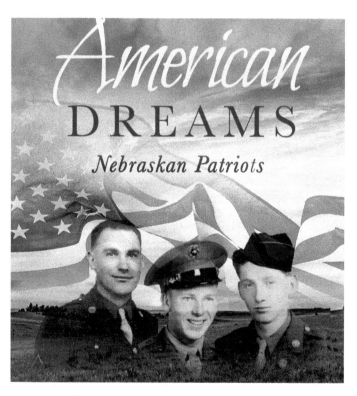

Patriots that served in WWII—Anastas (Shorty) Karella,
Ambrose (Andy) Karella, Charles Dale (Charlie) Karella

Patriot of the United States Cavalry

Wedding picture—Lyle Anson, United States Cavalry; Married Vlasta Holy—sister to Anastasia Holy Karella; and lived in Casper, Wyoming. They were family members and enjoyed a close friendship with Rudy and Martha Karella Pojar and Rusty and Delora Holt Karella and Shorty and Mary Owens Karella.

Dedicated to the Men and Women of the Karella Clan
Who Serve or Served in the Armed Forces

American Military Patriots, Who Are All Related to the Karella Clan

Anastas Leonard Karella, served in the French
Foreign Legion and in WWII

Anastas Leonard
Karella, WWII,
U.S. Army

Ambrose James Karella,
WWII, U.S. Marine

Charles Dale Karella,
WWII, U.S. Army
Air Corps

Uncle Frank Karella when in th
army, Fort Worth, Texas

Frank Emil Karella,
U.S. Army Air Corps, in Biplanes

Francis Bean,
U.S. Army

Dewayne Voborny,
U.S. Navy

Alvin Frauendorfer,
U.S. Army

Lloyd Karella, Korean
War, National Guard

Charles Rossow, U.S. Army, wounded in Korea

Howard Bean, U.S. Navy

Keith Frauendorfer, U. S. Army

Cindy Lee Tyson Allen, U.S. Air Force

Harry Jene Tyson, U.S. Navy

Christine Braun Frauendorfer, U.S. Army

Larry E. Ward, U.S. Army

Timothy Karella Stehwien Seabee, Equipment Ops

Ray Holinrake, U.S. Navy

Joshua Karella,
U.S. Army

Robert Rossow,
U.S. Army

Christopher Karella,
U.S Army

Lyle Ward,
U.S. Army

Tony Bromirski,
U.S. Air Force

Ian Ward,
U.S. Navy

Elias Voborny,
U.S. Marine

Scott Karella Stout,
U.S. Navy

Kendall Frauendorfer,
U.S. 82nd Airborne

Paul Voborny,
U.S. Army

Aaron Stanley Voborny,
U.S. Air Force

Scotty Bartholomew Hoefer
U.S. Navy

Chet Schroeter
U.S. Navy

Kimo Hollinrake
U.S. Army

Olof Sonny Allen Julsen
U.S. Army

Left: Major Lyle Ward,
U.S. Army
Right: Isaac James Ward,
U.S. Army

2nd Lt. Lyle Ward, U.S. Army; SGM Larry Ward, U.S. Army;
WO Kevin Karella, U.S. Army Air Corps

Kevin Karella, US Army Air Corps—
Combat Pilot—Desert Storm

Charles (Chuck) Rossow,
Transferred to Armed Forces
Radio, Korea, after being badly
wounded in battle

Frank A. Karella, U.S. Army WWI of Ward 23, Chicago, Chicago City
1896–1944

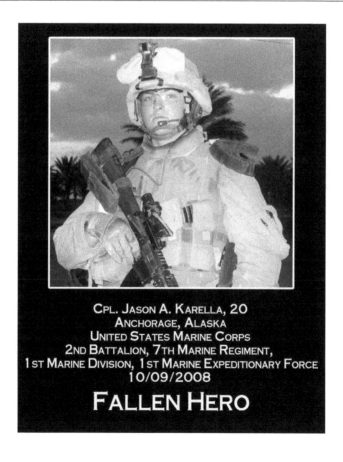

Family Trees

Ambrose J. (Rusty) Karella Family Tree

Delora Lucy (Bitty) Holt-Karella,
1910–2004 and Husband
Ambrose Jerome (Rusty) Karella,
1898–1972, at their 40th wedding
anniversary celebration

Ambrose Jerome
Karella, Born USA
1898

Delora Lucy Holt-
Karella

Born USA 1910

Ambrose James
Born USA 1927

Charles Dale
Born USA 1930

Lloyd Elliott Born
USA 1931

Florence Delora
Born USA 1932

Marcella Ann Born
USA 1934

Mildred Leona Born
USA 1936

Jerome Ambrose
Born USA 1937

Sharon Theresa
Born USA 1938

Left to right, back: Pete, Charles, and Lloyd
Left to right, front: their mother, Delora, and Andy

"...Mr and Mrs. Karella resided in Madison after their marriage until 1936 when they moved to Norfolk. Mr Karella was employed by the Rosewalk Blacksmith, Norfolk Farm Equipment and Turk Plumbing and Heating. In 1956 they moved to Fairbanks where Mr. Karella was employed by his eldest son, Ambrose, carrying U.S. mail until his retirement in 1965.

Excerpt from obituary of Ambrose Karella found in the Norfolk Daily News

Left to right, back: Sharon, Florence, Millie
Left to right, front: their mother, Delora and Marcella

Rusty and Delora's daughters grew up and married, adding new connections to the Karella clan. Florence Delora married LaVere (Bud) Roggenbach; Marcella Ann married Alvin (Al) Frauendorfer; Mildred Leona married Fred Ridder and Sharon Theresa married William (Bill) Frost.

Anton Jerome and Anastasia Holy-Karella

1868–1934

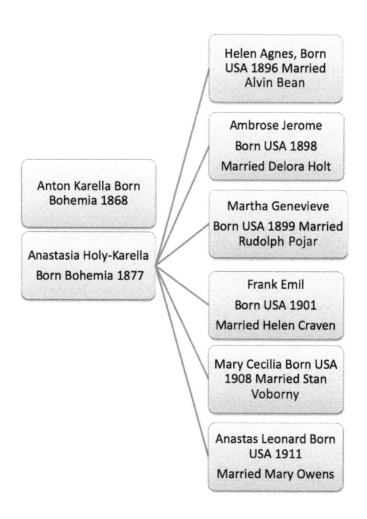

James and Margaret Kilgore-Holt

1884–1978

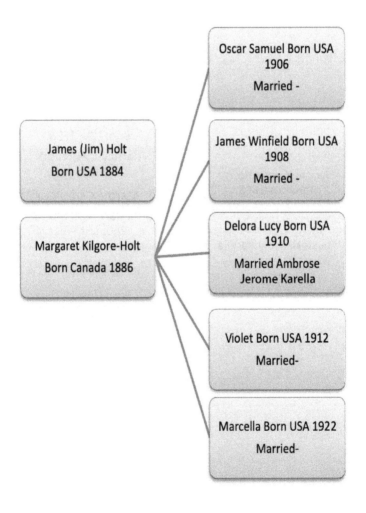

James (Jim) Holt
Born USA 1884

Margaret Kilgore-Holt
Born Canada 1886

Oscar Samuel Born USA
1906
Married -

James Winfield Born USA
1908
Married -

Delora Lucy Born USA
1910
Married Ambrose
Jerome Karella

Violet Born USA 1912
Married-

Marcella Born USA 1922
Married-

Anastas and Mary Owens-Karella

1911–1994

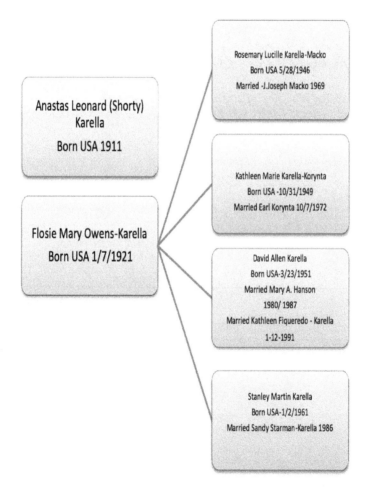

Karella & Clan Family Relationship Charts

Karella and Bean

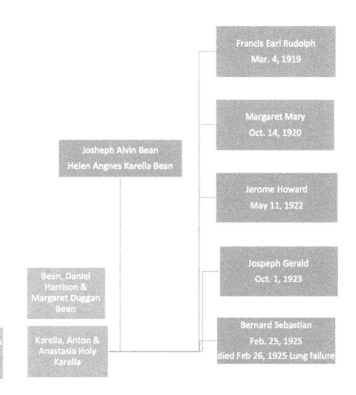

Karella-Craven

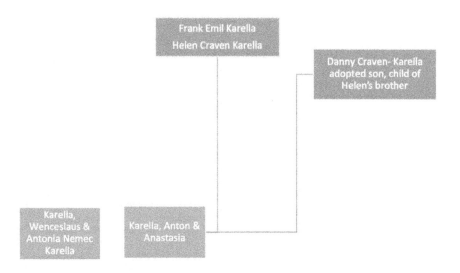

Karella and Pojar

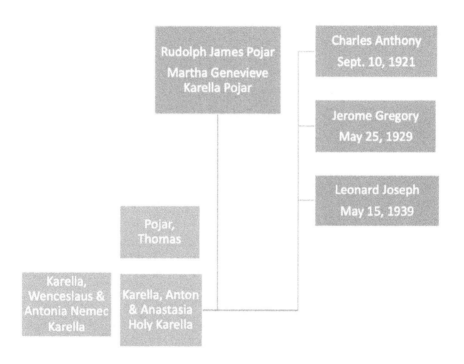

Karella and Voborny

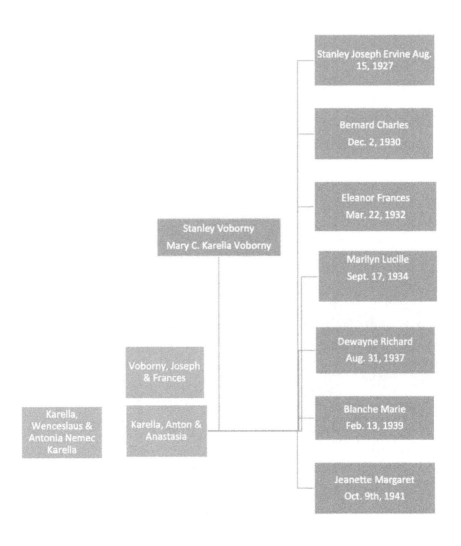

Stanley Joseph Ervine Aug. 15, 1927

Bernard Charles Dec. 2, 1930

Eleanor Frances Mar. 22, 1932

Marilyn Lucille Sept. 17, 1934

Dewayne Richard Aug. 31, 1937

Blanche Marie Feb. 13, 1939

Jeanette Margaret Oct. 9th, 1941

Stanley Voborny Mary C. Karella Voborny

Voborny, Joseph & Frances

Karella, Wenceslaus & Antonia Nemec Karella

Karella, Anton & Anastasia

The picture above shows Mary holding baby Jeannette, others included are Eleanor, Ervin, Bernard, Marilyn, Stanley, Dewayne, and Blanche. This photo was taken in May of 1942, at Dist.74 during a school picnic. Stanley died the following year on February 4, 1943, at the age of 40, of blood poisoning as a result of Vincent's Disease.

Mary Cecilia Karella-Voborny holding baby Jeanette Margaret
and husband Stanley Voborny with their children:
Stanley Joseph Ervin, Bernard, Eleanor, Marylin, Dewayne, Blanche

James Madison Holt Sr. Ancestor Family Tree
James (Jim) William Holt Parents of

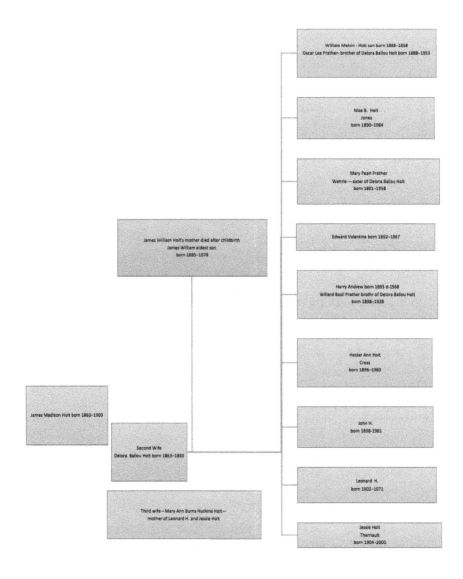

James William Holt's Ancestry

James Madison Holt was twice widowed and married three different women. His eldest son, Jim (James William Holt Junior), grew up with siblings and also several cousins who came to live with them when their own parents died. Jim was the firstborn child of the Holt family who lived most of their lives in Madison, Nebraska. Jim Holt met his future wife at the Madison Downs' stables. Her father, Samuel Kilgore, came to see Jim's spring foals. Samuel's daughter, Margaret Kilgore, had a natural way with horses that caught Jim Holt's eye immediately.

About Holt Family Details

Jim Holt (James William Holt Junior) was born October 15, 1885, in Jackson County, Iowa. Jim's mother died shortly after he was born. His father, widower James Madison Holt, remarried two years later to a woman named Delora Ballou of Springfield, Missouri. William and Delora moved their budding family to Madison, Nebraska, when their oldest son, James, whom they called Jim, was a young boy. At this time, James Madison Holt started his horse breeding business. Young Jim Holt grew up in a household with eight siblings and three cousins. When Jim grew up, he took over the family business and horse breeding operation, and at that time, he added racehorses to his breeding stock.

Margaret Kilgore Holt Family Ancestor Tree

Margaret was born on April 14, 1886, and raised in Manitoba, Canada. She had three older siblings. Her eldest brother, Joseph, was born in 1877; her eldest sister, Elizabeth, was born in 1879; and her brother George was born in 1882. Margaret was born in 1886, followed by a brother, James, born in 1892, and the last child—her sister, Lena—was born in 1897.

Margaret's parents, Samuel and Mary Anne Schmidt Kilgore, moved their family from Canada to Newman Grove in 1894. Margaret and her six siblings grew up and lived in Newman Grove, Nebraska, a town close to Madison, Nebraska.

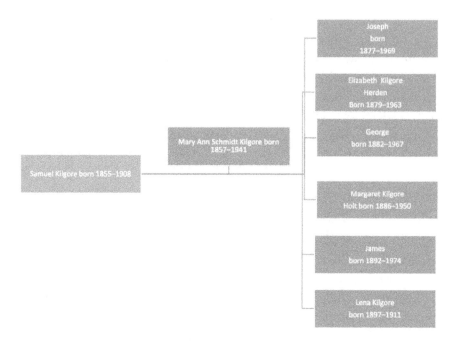

James (Jim) William Holt-Kilgore Wedding

Jim Holt and Margaret Kilgore married on January 2, 1905, in Madison, Nebraska. Together, they had five children during their marriage. Jim's first-born child and son was named Oscar Samuel and was born on August 24, 1906. The couple had a second son two years later, whom they named James Winfield (JW) on August 24, 1908.

When Margaret announced she was going to have another baby, her husband, Jim, tried to explain the concept to their four- and two-year-old sons. The boys did not have much of a reaction to that news until they were allowed to hold their baby sister, Delora Lucy, born on October 29, 1910. The Holt's daughter was named after Jim's beloved stepmother who had raised him.

The Holt's eldest son, Oscar, loved his baby sister nearly as much as his parents did and would seize any opportunity to hold her the moment his mother or father set her down.

Two years later, Margaret had another baby girl on February 12, 1912. They named her Violet Leona. Baby Violet and her brother JW became inseparable. When Margaret had other things to attend to, JW was always nearby begging to take care of the baby for her. The family of six seemed to naturally divide into two groups. Papa and Oscar took charge of two-year-old Delora, while Mama and JW were preoccupied with Violet. With JW's dedication to his baby sister, Margaret had no problem keeping up with her other family duties and housework while Jim managed his thriving horse business.

Jim observed his children were maturing and developing unique personalities. Six-year-old Oscar was bright but a bit flighty. The boy resisted being forced to do one thing too long or to be stuck in a small space. Oscar loved to see new things. He would beg Jim to let him go on road trips that he took for the racing stables. Since Jim and Oscar were especially fond of two-year-old Delora, the three of them spend a lot of time together at home or at the Madison Downs' Stables and took a few short road trips together.

JW's personality differed greatly from his older brother, Oscar. He could calmly concentrate and stay on track until the task he set for himself was completed. JW loved to help his mother and baby sister, Violet, and showed great loyalty to his family, and also made long-lasting friendships.

By the time Jim's sons spent all day at school, Violet, who was nearly three, continued to prefer her mother's company and would follow Margaret happily around the house, while little Delora favored her papa's company. Jim loved babysitting his little girl and found delight in Delora's bright mind. She soaked up his answers to her very intelligent questions, like the dry toast he liked to dip in his morning coffee.

Everyone knew little Delora was his pride and joy. He loved all his children dearly, but Delora adored him as much as he adored her. Jim had been free to build an amazing relationship with his spunky little Delora, who liked to trot around the stables with him to see the horses as soon as she could walk. She could also sit quietly for hours with him in his study, keeping herself busy looking through his bookshelves. He read aloud to her at a very early age, and she learned to read quickly. When she was in his study, she rarely disturbed him when he was doing his book work, though she could capture his complete attention with a quiet request. Even at five, his daughter asked very mature and clever questions. Out of respect for Delora's intelligence, he would generally stop what he was doing and give her a precise answer.

He vividly recalled a day when Oscar was about 11 years old. His son had come to him in his study to ask if he could go to a girlfriend's birthday party. Delora sat on the sofa in his study while they talked about the girl and her party. She listened politely and kept respectfully silent.

When Oscar left, she asked, "Papa, when do I get to go to a boyfriend's birthday party?"

Her papa had replied, "Delora, you are too young to have boyfriends. But you are my girl, aren't you?"

Delora sweetly replied, "Yes, Papa. But when will I be old enough to have a boyfriend?"

Knowing she would not stop until he answered her questions, Jim replied, "Not until you are at least sixteen, and that's eleven whole years away. So, until then, your papa and your brothers will be your friends who are boys, and we will all celebrate our birthdays together, right?"

Jim remembered Delora thought about what he said for a moment, then nodded happily and replied, "That's right, Papa!" and he had replied, "That's my girl!"

Summer of 1920

During the summer of 1920, Jim began taking Margaret, ten-year-old Delora, and eight-year-old Violet with him on his monthly business trips to Omaha. During his meetings with the racing association at

The Knights of Ak-Sar-Ben livestock and race grounds, Margaret would take the girls for a walk around the stables. When his meetings were finished, he and his ladies would have lunch at a nice restaurant. To treat his daughters for being good girls, they were allowed to order anything they wanted to eat off the menu. To treat his wife, they would take in a movie at the Lothrop Theatre on North 24th Street. On this trip, his girls wanted to see *The Jungle Princess,* starring Juanita Hansen. Margaret became an instant fan of the beautiful silent movie star.

The Knights of Ak-Sar-Ben Association Emblem

It had been ten years since Violet was born, and the Holts' life had settled into a nice predictable rhythm. They went on short summer trips, then the children would spend all day in school during the winter, which gave Jim and Margaret time to have quiet breakfasts and lunches together alone and take afternoon naps together.

During the early part of the winter of 1920, Margaret seemed to catch every cold and flu that hit the schools or could be caught in Madison. Her continued illnesses made her sink into a mental depression.

Delora stepped up to help take care of the house and learned to cook and took over making school lunches for her brothers and sister. If her mother went to bed early, sometimes Jim took his children out for dinner.

After many visits to the family doctor, the doctor told Margaret she wasn't getting well because she wasn't getting any sleep. At that time, the doctor gave Margaret a sleeping potion and a tonic to help her rest better. That way, she could get rid of the illnesses she was suffering from.

Margaret used the tonic and sleeping potion for the rest of the winter. With the warmer weather in the spring of 1921, Jim decided

Margaret needed to get out of the house. He took all his children to stay with their grandmother Kilgore in Newman Grove for the

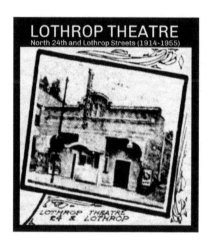

Lothrop Theatre, Omaha, built in 1914

weekend, and Jim took Margaret on a trip to Omaha in late August, just the two of them. While in Omaha, they saw another Juanita Hansen film. This one was called *The Yellow Arm*. It had been a wonderful weekend. Margaret's health seemed to be improving throughout that summer. They took trips together alone to Omaha as often as one of the aunts, uncles, or grandparents were willing to watch their four children. Not so much on those trips, but on their return home, Jim noticed that his wife was still using the tonic given to her by the doctor. When he asked her about it, she said she used it just to take naps and at night to calm her nerves and to relax so she could sleep.

When Thanksgiving and Christmas arrived, Jim took Margaret and the children out for their holiday dinner because Margaret did not feel up to cooking. By February 1922, Margaret was feeling even more tired every day. This continued to occur even after sleeping late into the morning. Between Oscar and Delora, they had gotten pretty good at making the breakfast and getting everyone off to school on time, and Jim was usually at the house when his children got home. But he was really worried about what was happening to his wife.

The Doctor's Surprise

Jim waited in the lobby until the doctor's nurse asked him to join the doctor in his office. As Jim entered, the doctor was grinning, and Margaret looked ready to faint. "Please sit down, Jim. You can stop worrying. There is a good reason Margaret has been so tired. She has something she would like to tell you."

Margaret smiled shyly, not expecting to tell her husband her news in front of their doctor, but he insisted. "Jim, I'm pregnant."

That night, the children had been told there would be a new baby in the house. Margaret went up to bed, and Jim made sure all his children did the same, then joined his wife in bed. "Well, my darling, I guess this baby will always make us think of those long weekends we spent in Omaha," he whispered as he settled Margaret's head on is shoulder.

Silent movie star,
Juanita Hansen, 1920

She smiled and snuggled closer to him and whispered back, "Especially the movies, Jim. I loved going with you to those Juanita Hansen movies."

"I can't say I was completely surprised by what the doctor told us today," he whispered back with a soft chuckle. Those long weekends in Omaha were wonderful." When his wife didn't react to what he said, he realized by her soft breathing, Margaret had fallen asleep.

Margaret and Jim's last child was born on September 25, 1922, and it did not surprise him when Margaret decided to name their beautiful baby girl Marcella Juanita Holt.

Final Note Concerning Canadian-Indian Connection with the Holt-Karella Families

Cathy Le Karella was looking through a box of old photographs at Grandma Delora's house when she came across a picture of two remarkable-looking people and asked Delora who they were. Delora said her great-grandmother on her mother's side of the family was a Canadian Indian from the Chippewa Nation. Delora's sister Marcella Holt Long verified that story when she showed that same photograph to Kevin Karella.

Delora told Cathy, "In my mother Margaret's family, there is a legend that we had a Canadian-Indian great-grandmother." That information stunned Cathy, but at the same time, she found her grandmother Delora's secret very exciting. Then Delora interrupted her thoughts, saying, "That is the woman in this picture with the striking Indian features. The red-haired Scotsman wearing the stove-pipe top hat who is standing next to his Canadian First Nation wife is my great-grandfather Kilgore."

Both Cathy and Kevin felt this was an important and fascinating memory to share with the Karella family.

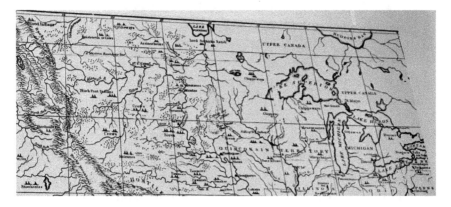

1800s Indian Nations of Canada above the Great Lakes—
Photo taken at the WS Museum by GKM 2022

APPENDIX IV

Final Notes Regarding Stanislaus and Anna Karella

After the death of Stanislaus's older brother, Anton, in 1934, his wife, Anna, said she would like to move closer to her people in South Dakota. With the hard times of the Great Depression, after the farm was repossessed by the government, Stanislaus supervised selling off what was left of the family property. It didn't add up to much. What money they had was divided up among the family members. In 1936, Stanislaus and Anna moved to South Dakota to be near the Plouzek relatives where they resided until their deaths.

Shown here are examples of how Stanislaus's name was recorded as it sounded—Stanislov—and it had been shortened to Stanley as he got older.

The records here also show an incorrect birthplace for Stanislaus—in New York. This is an understandable error because he came to America through Castle Garden Gate in New York City, New York. Those were the oldest American records of this man, and they did not have any documentation on his birth in Bohemia when he was buried. All the other family member data points match: his wife, Anna Plouzek-Karella, his parents, and his siblings.

Stanislov "Stanley" Karella	
BIRTH	Dec 1870 New York, USA
DEATH	11 Sep 1942 (aged 71) Pennington County, South Dakota, USA
BURIAL	Masonic Cemetery Philip, Haakon County, South Dakota, USA
PLOT	D-8

Photo added by Brent Richardson

Family Members

Parents

 Vaclav Karella
1839–1922

 Antonia *Nemec* Karella
1839–1900

Spouse

 Anna M. *Plouzek* Karella
1878–1979

Siblings

 Anton J. Karella
1868–1934 (m. 1895)

 Anna *Karella* Kratochvil
1873–1966

 Emil John Karella
1878–1941

Final Notes on Emil John Karella

Emil John Karella married Bohumila Karella. However, everyone called Bohumila Emily. She descended from the Chicago Karellas. Emily came from a distantly related line of Karellas who settled in Chicago, Illinois, 100 years before Antonia and Wenceslaus Karella settled in Nebraska. Emil John and Emily were married in Cook County, Illinois, and they had one son they named Raymond.

In December of 1928, Emily Karella died suddenly of pneumonia on a trip to see her family in Chicago. Seven years later due to the Great Depression, Emil John couldn't pay the taxes on his inherited land-grant homestead bequeathed to him by his father, Wenceslaus Vaclav Karella. The U.S. Government foreclosed on that land. At that time, Emil and his son moved to Rupert, Minidoka County, Idaho.

Emil John Karella

BIRTH	1 May 1878
	Leigh, Colfax County, Nebraska, USA
DEATH	19 Feb 1941 (aged 62)
	Rupert, Minidoka County, Idaho, USA
BURIAL	Minidoka Acequia Rupert Cemetery
	Rupert, Minidoka County, Idaho, USA
PLOT	G5

Final Notes on Little Anna Karella Kratochvil

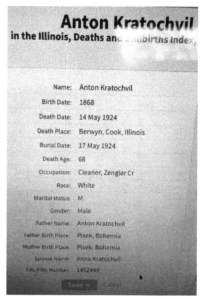

Kratochvil family, back row: Anton Jr., Rose, Louis, Katherine, and Emil
front row: Ed, their father, Anton Sr., Ray, Mary, their mother,
(Little) Anna Karella Kratochvil

Little Anna Karella Kratochvil and Her Husband, Anton Kratochvil

Final Notes on Joseph and Helen Karella Bean

Final Notes on Martha Karella Pojar and Husband,
Rudolph J. Pojar

Final Notes on Frank Emil Karella, Husband of Helen Craven Karella and Brother to Ambrose Jerome Karella-

Final Notes on Stanley and Mary Cecilia Karella Voborny

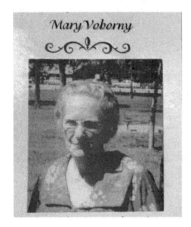

Karella/Voborny family picture and comments by David Voborny

The picture above was taken in 1975, of Mary and all her children.
Back row: Bernard, Ervin, Dewayne, Jeannette, Marilyn
Front row: Sr. Marie, Mary, and Eleanor
Mary died at the age of 75, at an Omaha Hospital from a stroke.

Final Notes on Anastas Leonard (Shorty) Karella

Anastas Leonard (Shorty) Karella and wife, Flossie Mary Owens Karella, met in Nebraska, lived in Nebraska until after they were married, and had their first child, Rosemary Lucille, born May 28th, 1945. After World War II, Shorty and his small family moved to Wyoming and tried homesteading for three years. Then Shorty moved his family to Rupert, Idaho, in 1948. While in Idaho, Mary bore another daughter, Kathleen Marie, on October 31st, 1949. The following year, she bore a son they named David Allen on March 3rd, 1951. Ten years later, Mary bore her last child, Stanley Martin, on January 2nd, 1961. In 1962, Shorty packed up his family and moved to Fairbanks, Alaska, to help his nephew Andy Karella with their business, Flying Saucer Delivery.

After the death of Andy's wife, Betty, in 1963, the following summer, Shorty moved his family to Soldotna, Alaska.

Left to right: eldest daughter of Great-Uncle Shorty and Aunt Mary Karella, Rosemary Lucille. Behind her is Cousin Andy Karella, then husband Shorty with youngest son Stanley on his lap, Shorty's wife, Mary, next to their son David, and daughter Kathy

KARELLA	ANASTAS L KARELLA	22-Sep-1911	10-Dec-1994	99669 Soldotna, AK	(none specified)	Wyoming
KARELLA	FLOSSIE KARELLA	7-Jan-1921	1-Dec-1973	99669 Soldotna, AK	(none specified)	Michigan

Photo from the Cover of American Dreams

A portion of the Karella clan born in the land of promise. Front to back, left to right—find the names of each person below:

Sitting in Front

Blanche Voborny, Leonard Pojar, Dick Voborny, Millie Karella, Marcella Karella, Sharon Karella, Pete Karella

Standing Middle

Bernard Voborny, Marilyn Voborny, Florence Karella, Elinor holding Jeanette Voborny, Leonard Pojar, Lloyd Karella, Helen Bean, Martha Pojar, Dale Karella, Ervin Voborny

Standing in Back

Shorty Karella, Andy Karella, Mary Voborny, Mary Owens Karella, Delora Holt Karella, Stanley Voborny, Howard Bean, Francis Bean, Charles Pojar, Rudy Pojar

The Notables Missing:
Gerald Bean, Frank Emil, and his wife, Helen Craven Karella

APPENDIX V

Final Note on Sister Margaret Mary's Childhood: Memories and Research Documents

Memories about Margaret Mary's Uncle Ambrose, Uncle Frank, and Aunt Mary

"Uncle Ambrose came back to Grandpa Anton's house when he wasn't working, and he would tell us wonderful stories. He would sit with us kids at night for hours drawing pictures just to amuse us. The people in town had given him the name Rusty, but he liked it, and the rest of the family began to call him Rusty too.

"I remember when Uncle Frank joined the Army. After he enlisted, he was stationed at Fort Worth, Texas. My fondest memory of him back then was that burlap bag of pecans he used to send home at Christmas time.

"I remember when Aunt Mary didn't want to finish high school, and Mama and Aunt Martha were fighting with her. Aunt Mary said she didn't need any more schooling because she was going to be a housewife like her mama had been. Her two older sisters threatened that if she didn't promise to finish high school, they would turn their father against the union. So, Aunt Mary agreed to finish high school. But she did marry Stanley Voborny when she was 17, right after graduating from high school on May 7, 1902.

Sister Margaret Mary Bean, daughter of Alvin and Helen Karella Bean; cousin Rosemary Lucille Karella Macko, daughter of Shorty and Mary Owens Karella

"Now, I do recollect one other story about Aunt Mary and her Stanley. This story took place one summer many years after they were married. It was during a horrible drought, and then a plague of grasshoppers swarmed over the pitiful plants left standing and left nothing in the fields. Mary had just given birth to a new baby. They had no crop and no money to pay for the doctor who delivered their baby.

Mary came up with an innovative idea on how to pay her doctor bill. She plucked half her flock of adult geese down to the skin. She used the down and feathers to make pillows for her home. Then she traded the geese to Dr. Hartner, who agreed to accept them as payment for his services," Sister Margaret Mary finished.

Childhood Memories of Sister Margaret Mary Regarding the Karella Homestead

"Even after we no longer lived with Grandpa Anton, we loved to go back to visit Grandpa's place, meaning the homestead farm. Yet, I remember, as we grew into our later teen years, we began calling the homestead Uncle Emil's place.

"I recall, even as a young child, being impressed with the variety of trees that had been planted on the homestead. I especially loved the catalpa trees lining both sides of the lane. They started right off the highway turn-off from the main road and were planted at regular intervals along the lane all the way up to the house. I can still see them in my mind and how magnificent they were in bloom, standing tall and reaching up into the blue sky above. That wonderful fragrance produced by the blooms hung in the air for nearly two weeks. I also vividly remember Grandpa's house. It had two stories but was quite square in design, and he had painted it a pale yellow with white trimming.

"For some odd reason I cannot fathom, I also vividly remember the large feedlot. Now, within the larger main lot, there was a good-sized hay pen, and as a young child, I remember seriously considering eating hay because Grandpa's cattle seemed to enjoy it so much. I also recall the feel of the fence that surrounded the stockyard when I sat on it to watch Grandpa's livestock; it was made of hefty cottonwood boards. I spent a lot of time sitting on that fence because I loved the animals, so perhaps that is why I am so fond of this memory.

"Yet, regardless of the idiosyncrasies of my eccentric memories, the ancestral Karella homestead lives in my mind, and in my heart, as a grand and beautiful place full of love, purpose, and adventures," Sister Margaret Mary concluded.

Handwritten Notes by Sister Margaret Mary, about Frank Emil Karella and His Travel though South America

Final Notes on the Old Karella Homestead

Copy of U.S. Land Deed for the original 160-Land Grant Homestead

Madison Plat Map Showing the Karella and Pojar Lands

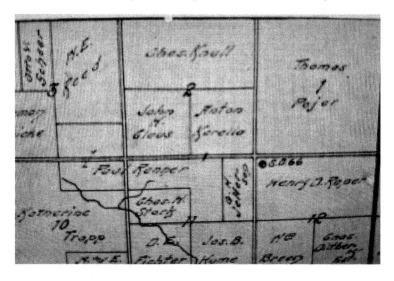

Area Map—Madison, Elgin, Battle Creek, and Newman Grove—all historical Karella Clan Sites

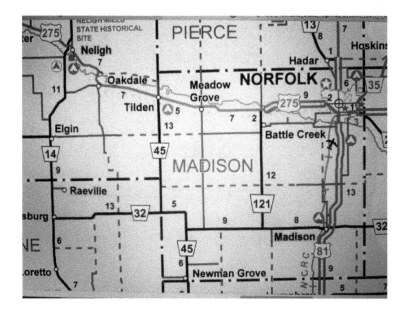

Final Notes for Anton Jerome Karella and the Rest of His Children's Families

Wenceslaus's first-born son was named Anton Jerome. Then Anton named his own first-born son Ambrose Jerome. Ambrose Jerome named his first-born son Ambrose James, making three generations of Karella men who used the initials A.J. Karella.

Heart Attack Is Fatal To A. J. Karella

STRICKEN WHILE RESTING IN

A CHAIR AT HIS HOME

HERE, TUESDAY.

Star-Mail · Jan. 25 - 1934

Anton J. Karella, 66, a resident of this community for more than a half century, was stricken with a sudden heart attack Tuesday about 5:00 p. m., while resting in a chair at his home in northwest Madison. Members of his family who were conversing with him when he slumped in his chair, immediately called a doctor but he was dead when the doctor arrived.

Mr. Karella was in apparent good health until a short time before his death. He left some work in his yard and came to the house complaining that he was not feeling well. His son, Ambrose, had just suggested calling a doctor when he was stricken.

About two years ago while ill with influenza he suffered a heart attack but no further complications developed until Tuesday, members of his family said.

Mr. Karella was one of the oldest and most faithful members of the Madison Citizens' band. He seldom missed a rehearsal and never a playing engagement. He joined the organization when a young man living on his homestead northeast of Madison.

Anton Karella was born in Bohemia on May 22, 1868. He came with his parents to Colfax county and for several years lived on a farm near Leigh. Later he moved to Madison county and took up a homestead where he lived until about ten years ago when he moved to Madison. He was married to Miss Anastasia Holy at Battle Creek on April 30, 1895. Mrs. Karella passed away on April 16, 1922.

Funeral services will be held at St. Leonard's Catholic church here Friday morning at 9 o'clock, with Rev. Father A. Brass officiating. Interment will be in St. Leonard's cemetery. Members of the Madison band will act as pallbearers and honorary pallbearers.

He is survived by two brothers, Slanislav of Phillips, S. D., Emil, living northeast of Madison; one sister, Mrs. Anna Kralochvil, of Pierce, Nebr.; three sons, Anastas, Pierce; Frank, Norfolk; Ambrose, Madison. Three daughters, Mrs. Helen Bean, Mrs. Martha Pojar and Mrs. Mary Voborny, all residents of this community. He also leaves thirteen grandchildren.

Final Important History for Nebraska and the Midwest States of America

Farming in the 1930s on the Great Plains was perhaps one of the most difficult occupations in the world. Facing global economic failure of historic proportions, the crash of the banks caused a tremendous glut of agricultural product sitting in storage. Those products range from wheat to wool, which people around the world had no money to purchase. The summer of 1930 brought on more disaster with the onset of the worst, longest, and most devastating drought in American history. This drought dried up most of Nebraska's farmland and made growing crops nearly impossible. Between the huge surplus of stored merchandise, and the dried-up fields, even the small amount of harvestable goods that were produced did not sell.

Calamity Compounded by a Lack of Knowledge

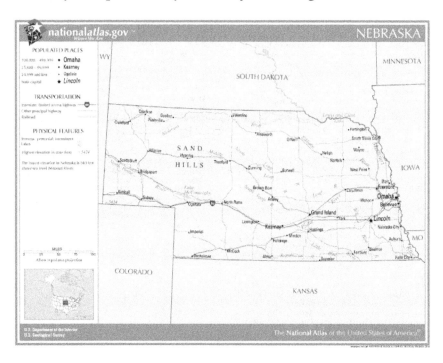

Only much later would prairie communities in the Midwest of America learn how vital indigenous prairie grasses were to the overall health of the land, particularly during periods of drought. However, throughout the huge 1920s farming expansion into the Midwest, farmers erroneously believed that if you tilled the ground and planted seed, crops would grow. With thousands of acres put under the plow and no rain, not only did crops fail, but winds whipped across the prairie states, carrying the dried earth away in dense clouds, like a sandstorm in the great Sahara Desert. The Midwest became so parched it spawned nothing but dust storms, and this terrible period in American history was nicknamed The Great Dust Bowl.

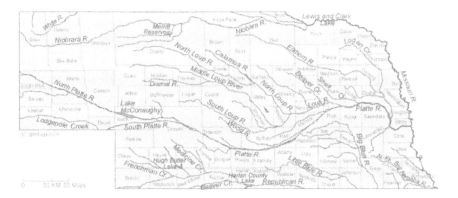

Descriptions of Nebraska's Land

Fortunately, the Karella clan chose to settle in the northeastern region of Nebraska in a triangle between the Elkhorn and Platte Rivers. These rivers flow into the great Missouri River just a little southwest of the towns of Madison and Norfolk. This location turned out to be the primary reason for the family's survival during the Great Depression while the horrendous drought devastated land and destroyed many farming communities.

The eastern part of Nebraska, along the Missouri, is usually moist, prone to flooding, and has rich soil. West of the lowlands is the south-central region of Nebraska called Loess Hills. It has many rivers that have carved the land into hills and valleys; however, this region is prone to drought, and the rivers even go dry at times. The Sand Hills are in the western part of Nebraska. In fact, during the early settlement of the state, they were often mistaken as being part of the high plains farther to the west.

This misconception was due to the areas vast region of sand dunes, which is the third largest expanse of sand dunes in the world behind the Sahara and Arabian Deserts. Much of this land is also covered in a tough indigenous sod made up of drought resistant grasses and plants, which keeps the hills intact like a net. Then there are the hidden lakes and streams of Sand Hills, which enabled those who knew about them to farm and survive during droughts. The other reason Nebraska did better than most farming states during the ten-year drought is due to the Ogallala Aquifer that lies under 80% of the state of Nebraska and stretches in varying degrees beneath the high plains and includes portions of Dakota, Wyoming, Colorado, Oklahoma, New Mexico, and Texas. However, the deepest part of this natural water source is found directly below Nebraska land and renews itself slowly naturally.

HIGH PLAINS AQUIFER
Saturated Thickness in 1997

meters		feet
0-15		0-50
15-30		50-100
30-61		100-200
61-122		200-400
122-183		400-600
183-244		600-800
244-305		800-1000
305-366		1000-1200
		Island

Source: USGS OFR 00-300

https://commons.wikimedia.org/wiki/
Commons:GNU_Free_Documentation_License,_version_1.2

Original Saint Leonard's Church and School in Madison, Nebraska, 1903–1904

675

Historic Photographs of the St. Leonard School, classes, and teachers in
Madison from the years 1903 and 1904

Joseph & Katherina Koryta Kuchar   Jacob & Mary Koryta Holy

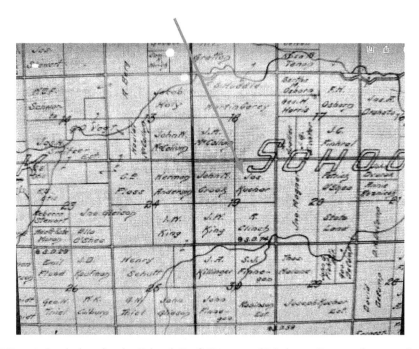

Historic land plats for the School Craft District of Madison County showing the location of Joseph and Katherina Kuchar's land. Katherina and Mary were sisters. Katherina and Joseph invited Mary and Jacob Holy and their children to come and live with them. Mary and Jacob were Anastasia Holy karella's parents.

Image supplied by R. Pfeifer 12-2020

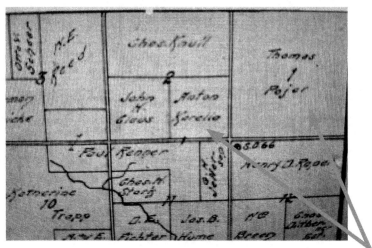

Historic land plats for Madison County, showing the location of the property of Anton Karella, and right next to it was the ranchland of Thomas Pojar, grandfather to Rudolph J. Pojar, who married Martha Genevieve Karella in 1919.

Image supplied by R. Pfeifer 12-202

Appendix Recipies

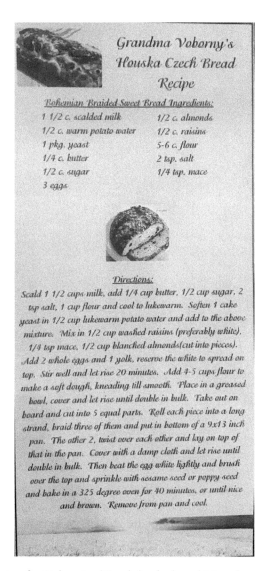

Grandma Voborny's Houska Czech Bread Recipe

Bohemian Braided Sweet Bread Ingredients:

1 1/2 c. scalded milk	1/2 c. almonds
1/2 c. warm potato water	1/2 c. raisins
1 pkg. yeast	5-6 c. flour
1/4 c. butter	2 tsp. salt
1/2 c. sugar	1/4 tsp. mace
3 eggs	

Directions:

Scald 1 1/2 cups milk, add 1/4 cup butter, 1/2 cup sugar, 2 tsp salt, 1 cup flour and cool to lukewarm. Soften 1 cake yeast in 1/2 cup lukewarm potato water and add to the above mixture. Mix in 1/2 cup washed raisins (preferably white), 1/4 tsp mace, 1/2 cup blanched almonds (cut into pieces). Add 2 whole eggs and 1 yolk, reserve the white to spread on top. Stir well and let rise 20 minutes. Add 4-5 cups flour to make a soft dough, kneading till smooth. Place in a greased bowl, cover and let rise until double in bulk. Take out on board and cut into 5 equal parts. Roll each piece into a long strand, braid three of them and put in bottom of a 9x13 inch pan. The other 2, twist over each other and lay on top of that in the pan. Cover with a damp cloth and let rise until double in bulk. Then beat the egg white lightly and brush over the top and sprinkle with sesame seed or poppy seed and bake in a 325 degree oven for 40 minutes, or until nice and brown. Remove from pan and cool.

The recipe for Bohemian/Ceczh huska bread Mary learned from her mother and grandmother Karella and supplied by David Voborny

December 2020, Uncle Dewayne (Dickie) Voborny and his little great-granddaughters, Jessa and Joslynn Kraft, came over to see their great-granddad and bake 7x Great-Grandmother Antonia's recipe for Bohemian kolache sweet bread with berry filling.

(The recipe can be found in the appendix section of *A Bohemian Dream*.)

Bohemian Braided Houska Bread

Ingredients

- 2 cups warm milk
- 1 cup granulated sugar
- 3 1⁄2 tsp. active dry yeast (2 packages)
- 3 large eggs
- 1 cup unsalted butter
- 1⁄2 cup heavy cream
- 1 Tbsp. plus 1⁄8 tsp. kosher salt, divided
- 1 tsp. ground nutmeg
- 1 cup chopped toasted almonds
- 3 Tbsp. grated lemon zest
- 7 cups bread flour
- 1 Tbsp. unsalted butter, melted
- 1 egg yolk
- 1 Tbsp. water
- 2 cups warm milk
- 1 cup granulated sugar
- 3 1⁄2 tsp. active dry yeast (2 packages)
- 3 large eggs
- 1 cup unsalted butter
- 1⁄2 cup heavy cream
- 1 Tbsp. plus 1⁄8 tsp. kosher salt, divided
- 1 tsp. ground nutmeg

- 1 cup chopped toasted almonds
- 3 Tbsp. grated lemon zest
- 7 cups bread flour
- 1 Tbsp. unsalted butter, melted
- 1 egg yolk
- 1 Tbsp. water

Directions

- **Step 1**

  In a large bowl, combine milk, 1 tablespoon granulated sugar, and yeast. Stir to dissolve and let stand until foamy—about 10 minutes.

- **Step 2**

  Stir in remaining sugar, eggs, butter, cream, 1 tablespoon salt, nutmeg, almonds, lemon zest, and raisins (drained). Add enough bread flour to create a firm dough. Add flour only to reduce stickiness. Turn out onto a floured surface and knead 8 to 10 minutes. Return to bowl, dust the top with flour, and cover with a damp cloth or plastic wrap. Rise at room temperature until doubled in volume—about 2 1/2 hours.

- **Step 3**

  Line a baking sheet with parchment. Turn risen dough onto a floured surface and divide into 3 portions: one large, one medium, and one small. Divide each into 3 equal sections and roll into tight ropes about 18 inches long.

- **Step 4**

  Starting with the largest ropes, make a 3-strand braid. Place onto prepared pan, press a slight indentation down the center of the braid, and brush with melted butter. Repeat with the medium braid and place it in on top of the large braid. Brush with melted butter. Finish by braiding the small section and place it on top of the medium braid. Cover loosely with plastic wrap and proof for 30 minutes. Preheat oven to 375°F.

- **Step 5**

Whisk the egg yolk with a tablespoon of water and remaining salt and brush onto the top of the risen loaf. Bake 30 minutes. Reduce heat to 250°F and continue baking until golden brown and hollow sounding—about 30 to 40 minutes. Cool completely on a rack.

22 USE RABBIT TO SAVE POINTS

The homemaker can stretch her meat ration points, by using rabbit as a meat dish. Young rabbit can be cooked by the broiling or frying methods. Older rabbits need longer, slower cooking. Rabbit can also be served in fricassees, salads, casserole dishes, rabbit pies, croquettes or chop-suey.

Mrs. Evelyn Sullivan Pyszka, *Home Service Advisor*
Illinois Northern Utilities Co., Belvidere, Illinois

Page from Home Service Advisory to use rabbit to save points on beef needed at the war front

Rabbit Fricassee Recipe

Ingredients:

1 medium onion
1/2-pound mushrooms
2 rabbits—cut up in serving pieces
2 tablespoons butter
2 tablespoons flour
1 cup white vinegar
1 cup chicken broth
3 sprigs parsley
3 sprigs thyme
1 bay leaf

Season jackrabbit pieces with salt, pepper, and onion powder, shake in flour, and brown in bacon grease. (May crumble bacon and add into recipe if desired.)

Cut onion into chunks and slice mushrooms.

In cheese cloth put the parsley, thyme, and bay leaf and tie shut. (You will remove this from the fricassee when it is done cooking.)

Using 2 frying pans place the browned the rabbit in one layer, add onions and mushrooms on top with seasoning bag pour in liquids over the rabbit and simmer for 15 minutes on the stove.

Remove rabbit and vegetables—keep warm in serving dish.

Continue simmering sauce, making it into a gravy—may thicken with cornstarch. Once it is as thick as desired, remove spice bag, pour over rabbit and vegetables, and sprinkle with fresh parsley.

Bibliography

Chapter 17

Editors of Encyclopaedia Britannica, The. "Golden Age of American Radio." *Britannica*. Accessed December 15, 2021. https://www.britannica.com/topic/Golden-Age-of-American-radio/.

Hamilton, David E. "Herbert Hoover: Domestic Affairs." Miller Center. Accessed December 15, 2021. https://millercenter.org/president/hoover/domestic-affairs/.

Hoover, Herbert. "Herbert Hoover Papers." Herbert Hoover Presidential Library and Museum. Accessed December 15, 2021. https://hoover.archives.gov/research/collections/hooverpapers/descriphooverpapers/.

Hoover, Herbert. *The Memoirs of Herbert Hoover: The Great Depression, 1929–1941*. Whitefish, Montana: Kessinger Publishing, LLC, 2010.

Morehead State Public Radio. "Golden Age of Radio." WMKY. Accessed December 15, 2021. https://www.wmky.org/programs/golden-age-radio/.

Rothbard, Murray N. *America's Great Depression*. New York City: BN Publishing, 2009.

Wikipedia, the Free Encyclopedia. "Calvin Coolidge." Accessed December 15, 2021. https://en.wikipedia.org/wiki/Calvin_Coolidge/.

Wikipedia, the Free Encyclopedia. "History of Radio." Accessed December 15, 2021. https://en.wikipedia.org/wiki/History_of_radio/.

Chapter 18

Kuehl, Rebecca A. "Fireside Chats." *Britannica*. Accessed December 15, 2021. https://www.britannica.com/topic/Anglo-American-Chain-of-Command-in-Western-Europe-June-1944-1673115/.

Roosevelt, Franklin D. "Address to Congress—Declaring War on Japan." Transcript of speech delivered at the Capitol in Washington, D.C., December 8, 1941. http://www.fdrlibrary.marist.edu/_resources/images/msf/msfb0002/.

Roosevelt, Franklin D. "Fireside Chats." Franklin D. Roosevelt Presidential Library and Museum. Accessed December 15, 2021. http://docs.fdrlibrary.marist.edu/firesi90.html/.

Roosevelt, Franklin D. "First Inaugural Address of Franklin D. Roosevelt." Transcript of speech delivered at the Capitol in Washington, D.C., March 4, 1933. https://avalon.law.yale.edu/20th_century/froos1.asp/.

Chapter 21

Sanderson, Peter. "Captain America." *Britannica.* Accessed December 15, 2021. https://www.britannica.com/topic/Captain-America/.

Wikipedia, the Free Encyclopedia. "Captain America." Accessed December 15, 2021. https://en.wikipedia.org/wiki/Captain_America/.

Chapter 22

Barber, James. "How Hollywood Supported the War Effort During WWII." Military.com. November 18, 2021. https://www.military.com/off-duty/movies/2021/11/18/how-hollywood-supported-war-effort-during-wwii.html/.

Encyclopedia.com. "World War II And The Ending Of The Depression." Accessed December 15, 2021. https://www.encyclopedia.com/economics/encyclopedias-almanacs-transcripts-and-maps/world-war-ii-and-ending-depression/.

Ferrara, Peter. "The Great Depression Was Ended by the End of World War II, Not the Start of It." *Forbes.* November 30, 2013. https://www.forbes.com/sites/peterferrara/2013/11/30/the-great-depression-was-ended-by-the-end-of-world-war-ii-not-the-start-of-it/?sh=342edf8b57d3/.

Margasak, Larry. "Hollywood went to war in 1941—and it wasn't easy." National Museum of American History. May 3, 2016. https://americanhistory.si.edu/blog/hollywood-went-war-1941/.

Stewart, Phillip W. "The Reel Story of World War II." *Prologue Magazine.* Accessed December 15, 2021. https://www.archives.gov/publications/prologue/2015/fall/united-newsreels.html/.

Wikipedia, the Free Encyclopedia. "*Why We Fight.*" Accessed December 15, 2021. https://en.wikipedia.org/wiki/Why_We_Fight/.

Lightning Source UK Ltd.
Milton Keynes UK
UKHW020649040722
405345UK00008B/265